Brethren in Scotland 1838-2000

A Social Study of an Evangelical Movement

STUDIES IN EVANGELICAL HISTORY AND THOUGHT

A full listing of all titles in this series
appears at the close of this book

STUDIES IN EVANGELICAL HISTORY AND THOUGHT

Brethren in Scotland 1838-2000

A Social Study of an Evangelical Movement

Neil T. R. Dickson

Foreword by D. W. Bebbington

PATERNOSTER PRESS

First published 2002 by Paternoster Press

Paternoster Press is an imprint of Authentic Media
P.O. Box 300, Carlisle, Cumbria, CA3 0QS, U.K.
and P.O. Box 1047, Waynesboro, GA 30830–2047, U.S.A

08 07 06 05 04 03 02   7 6 5 4 3 2 1

British Library Cataloguing in Publication Data
A catalogue record for this book is available from the British Library

ISBN 1–84227–113–X

Typeset by A.R. Cross
and Profile
Printed and bound in Great Britain
for Paternoster Press
by Nottingham Alpha Graphics

Series Preface

The Evangelical movement has been marked by its union of four emphases: on the Bible, on the cross of Christ, on conversion as the entry to the Christian life and on the responsibility of the believer to be active. The present series is designed to publish scholarly studies of any aspect of this movement in Britain or overseas. Its volumes include social analysis as well as exploration of Evangelical ideas. The coverage extends backwards to the Reformation, when the term 'Evangelical' was first used in roughly (though not exactly) its modern sense, and forwards to the present day, when the movement is one of the most prominent features in the religious landscape. Most books in the series, however, consider aspects of the movement shaped by the Evangelical Revival of the eighteenth century, when the impetus to mission began to turn the popular Protestantism of the British Isles and North America into a global phenomenon. The series aims to reap some of the rich harvest of academic research about those who, over the centuries, have believed that they had a gospel to tell to the nations.

To my parents
Tom and Jessie Dickson

Contents

List of Tables

List of Figures
in Appendix 1

List of Maps
in Appendix 2

Foreword

'To all who desire to be loyal to God and faithful to men', declared a contributor to the main Brethren periodical in 1920, 'I would say, "Beloved, let us beware of a *spurious* separation."'[1] The magazine, *The Witness*, was published in Glasgow; the writer, W. J. Grant, wrote from Kilmarnock. The subject of discussion was also distinctly Scottish. It was whether or not it was legitimate for the believer to cast a vote in the forthcoming polls that would decide if particular towns in Scotland should prohibit the sale of strong drink. Was this issue of the local veto a political question so tainted by the world as to be anathema to the true follower of Christ? Or was it a moral question on which, for the sake of the welfare of the weak, a vote should be recorded in the cause of righteousness? Several contributors to the periodical's question and answer section supposed the proper response was clear: all those who had been called out of the world into an assembly of God had no part to play in any social or political matters. Grant thought otherwise. According to the apostle Paul, he pointed out, it was right to do good to all men, and so it was imperative in such cases as this to take action on behalf of others. The editor, Henry Pickering, though showing greater sympathy for Grant's point of view, commented that the two sides were divided roughly equally. The movement was split between those who wanted to withdraw entirely from public affairs and those who wanted, like Grant, to avoid 'spurious separation'.

The division of opinion reflected two tendencies that ran through the life of the Brethren. On the one hand, they formed a small body observing strange practices such as weekly communion services run by ordinary laymen. On the other, they claimed kinship with all who wanted to spread the gospel to those who did not yet believe. They were subject to the rival claims of a sectarian impulse and of broader influences. The sectarian side is fascinating in its own right. Brethren had a doughty capacity for rejection. As Neil Dickson shows in this study, they tended to make blanket condemnations of novels, films and (sometimes at great cost) war. Football was a special *bête noire*, so that in the pages of *The Witness* in the same year, a former footballer who had dropped the game on his conversion warned that it inevitably encouraged 'exhibitions of passion on the field'.[2] The characteristic preoccupation of the Brethren with biblical prophecy led them to anticipate the imminence of the second advent, implying that human efforts for the world's improvement were futile. Other branches of the Evangelical movement, on this reading

---

1   *The Witness*, 50 (September 1920), p. 323.
2   *Ibid.* (July 1920), p. 304.

of world history, might be expected to fall into laxity and error. It is not surprising that there was an early welcome in *The Witness* for the opening salvoes in the Fundamentalist campaign in America.[3] There were also tendencies within the movement to insist on restricting fellowship to those who upheld specific details of belief and practice. Tighter Brethren were inclined to engage in rigorous monitoring of developments elsewhere lest there should be lapses from fidelity and purity. So there were many signs that, often out of the highest motives of loyalty to the truth once delivered to the saints, Brethren could adopt highly sectarian attitudes.

There was, however, a countervailing tendency towards breadth. The very title informally used by the movement, *Open* Brethren, points to a contrast with the more sectarian group the Exclusive Brethren. The two had common origins in Dublin, Plymouth and elsewhere around 1830, but the Exclusives soon took a separate path under the leadership of J. N. Darby and remained much smaller, especially in Scotland. *The Witness* called itself 'An Unfettered Monthly Journal' to mark its temper of spiritual independence. At some stages in their history Open Brethren believed in close co-operation with Evangelicals of other persuasions, especially in the work closest to their heart, the communication of the faith. They played a particularly prominent part in the revivals that swept parts of Scotland in the late 1850s and 1860s, showing some surprising traits. In the north-east, for example, many of their assemblies allowed women to preach. The desire to spread the gospel by any available means could be a powerful solvent of inherited assumptions. So could assimilation to the everyday opinions of neighbours and the practical needs of the assemblies. Legal requirements, for instance, meant that Brethren officiating at weddings had to describe themselves as pastors, a term they would normally have eschewed. In the late twentieth century the impulse towards social assimilation and the dropping of distinctives led to something approaching schism, with traditional Brethren distancing themselves from the more progressive party. The polarisation is another indication of the enduring tension between the desire for principled separatism and the fear of a spurious variety.

Neil Dickson has painted a remarkably vivid portrait of this movement in all its diversity. In an unusually comprehensive book, he discusses the evolution of the Open Brethren over the whole period of their existence in Scotland. He discusses their background and origins, dissects the growing movement into its component parts and shows its impact on such groups as the miners of Lanarkshire and north Ayrshire. A sensitivity to locality is, in fact, one of the great qualities of the book. It is also noteworthy for paying close attention to individuals, since undergirding it is a database consisting of obituaries from *The Witness* that includes

---

3   *The Witness*, 49 (November 1919), p. 170.

information on over 8,000 people. Some of the figures, such as the poet Robert Rendall, an archetypal Orcadian, have as much significance outside as within the religious group to which they belonged. Places and people are the stuff of this history, but their spirituality and theology are not forgotten either. The Brethren were always a small group within Scotland, but their ideas and methods sometimes influenced other Christians and many of their number travelled elsewhere as emigrants and missionaries. Hence historians of Evangelical religion in other denominations and other lands will find material in Neil Dickson's masterly account that illuminates the stories they have to tell. They will discover that the tensions felt so acutely among the Scottish Brethren were reproduced in large measure elsewhere. They will be alerted to the twin impulses within Evangelicalism to turn away from the world and to penetrate it for the sake of the gospel.

David Bebbington
University of Stirling
February 2002

Acknowledgements

Permission to quote from the following copyrighted material is gratefully acknowledged: *The Cradle of the King: the story of the birth and early days of Jesus, retold for young people* ([1929]) by Andrew Borland, published by John Ritchie and copyright held by Mrs Mary Thomas; 'The Offering' in *Dreaming Frankenstein and Collected Poems* (1984) by Liz Lochhead, published by Polygon Press; *Highland Journey: a sketching tour of Scotland retracing the footsteps of Victorian artist John T. Reid* (1992) by Mairi Hedderwick, published by Canongate Press. Permission to quote from Crown copyright material held by the National Archives of Scotland, IRS21/1811, is likewise gratefully acknowledged. Every effort has been made to contact the holders of copyright, and gratitude is also extended to those whom it was not possible to contact. Material incorporated in this book has appeared in the following articles by the present writer: 'Scottish Brethren: division and wholeness 1838-1916', *Christian Brethren Review*, 41 (1990), pp.5-41; 'Brethren and Baptists in Scotland', *Baptist Quarterly*, 33 (1990), pp.372-87; 'Modern prophetesses: women preachers in the nineteenth-century Scottish Brethren', *Records of the Scottish Church History Society*, 25 (1993), pp.89-117; '"Shut in with Thee": the morning meeting among Scottish Open Brethren, 1830s-1960s', in R.N. Swanson (ed.), *Studies in Church History*, 35 (Woodbridge, 1999), pp.276-89; 'Open and closed: Brethren and their origins in the North East', in James Porter (ed.), *After Columba —After Calvin: religious community in North-East Scotland* (Aberdeen, 1999), pp.151-170. The permission of the editors of the above to use material from these papers is also gratefully acknowledged.

The generous financial support of the Aitchison Trust has enabled publication of this present work. Many people helped in its making, by giving or lending me books, papers or records in their keeping, supplying me with a reference or with translation: Dr Edward Adams; Dr Eddie Adams; Mr Ian Adams; the late Mr John Adams; Mr Joe Adrain; the late Mrs Eva Aitken; Mr James Aitken; Mr Alex Allan; Mr John Allan; the late Mr James Anderson; the late Mr William Barclay; the late Prof. F. F. Bruce; Dr Ivy Barclay; Mr James Burton-Smith; Mrs Sarah Campbell; Mr James Capie; Mr David Clarkson; Mr Roy Coad; Miss Maggie Cochrane; the late Mr William Cochrane; Dr David Cook; Mr Robert Craig; Mr William Cuthbertson; Dr John Dempster; Mr Gordon Farquhar; Mr Ian Ford; Mr Campbell Fullarton; Mr Tom Glidden; Mrs Helen Gordon; Mrs Katherine Gordon; Dr John Hannah; Dr Marjory Harper; Mr Robert Hawthorn; the late Mr James Hislop; Prof. Neil Hood; Mr Bert Innes; Miss Anna Irvine; Mr John and Mrs Ella Jack; the late Mr Stephen Johns; Miss Catherine Johnston; the late Mr William Landles; the late Mrs Margaret Lightbody; Dr Peter Lineham; Mr Ian McDowell; Mr Norman Macdonald; Mr James S. McFarlane; Mr Gordon McGibbon; Mrs Margaret McGuinness; Mr William McKee; Mrs Elizabeth McKinnon; Prof. Sam McKinstry; the late Mrs Martin; Mr and Mrs Stewart Moar; the late Dr William and the late Mrs Nora Montgomerie; Mr James and Mrs Cynthia Naismith; Dr W. E. F. Naismith; the late Mr Jimmy Paton; the late Mr Robbie W. Orr; Mr Don Palmer; Mr Alex and Mrs Morag Paterson; Mr George Peterson; Miss Nancy Reid; Mr Geoffrey Robson; Dr Elizabeth Sanderson; Dr Margaret Sanderson; Mr Alex Stewart; Revd Harry Sprague; the late Mr Fred Stallan; Dr Timothy Stunt; Mr Allan Taylor; Dr James Thomson; the Trustees of Auchlochan; the former Trustees of Netherhall Conference Centre; Mr John Watson; Mrs Val Wells; Mr John Wright; Dr Max Wright; and the late Mr John and Mrs Amy Wylie. I am aware that so many people have assisted me that I may have inadvertently omitted some. To any such, I apologise. In addition, a number of people (some now deceased) replied to my letters or granted me interviews. They are either listed in the Bibliography or, to protect their confidentiality, not thanked by name. Nevertheless my gratitude to those not listed above is real. Needless to say, none of the above bears any responsibility for what I did with the help with which they so freely gave me, and occasionally individuals made their disagreement with my own views plain. Responsibility rests entirely with myself.

Works such as this would not be possible without the help of those most helpful of people, librarians. Among those which assisted me thanks must go to those in: the British Library; the Dick Institute, Kilmarnock; Dundee City Library; the Mitchell Library, Glasgow; the National Library of Scotland; Stirling University Library; Special Collections, University of Aberdeen Library; and to three archivists in particular: Miss Alison Fraser of the Orkney Archive; Mr John McLeish of East Kilbride Public Library; and above all Dr David Brady of the Christian Brethren Archive, John Rylands University Library of Manchester. Not only has his help been constant, but so too has his friendship.

A number of friends generously gave me hospitality (sometimes *en famille*) when I have been using libraries in various parts of Britain: Andy and Alyson Bathgate; David and Hilary Brady; Graham and Mary Brown; the late John Boyes and Louise Boyes; Elizabeth Candlish; Ian Gall; Ken and Donna Mackintosh; the late John Oddie and Daisy Oddie; and Neil and Pauline Summerton. I am extremely grateful to them, not least because they helped lessen the costs of the research.

The research may be said to have begun through a comment to me during the course of a doubtless long-forgotten conversation on the Aberdeen to Stirling train with Prof. Andrew Walls. About ten years later I did some basic digging for a talk to my Friday night youth fellowship which made me ask some questions that coincided with ones being asked by Alastair Noble and Alex McIntosh. The questions led (another fifteen years later) to this as an answer. Several people have given me encouragement in beginning the research and during it: Dr Valerie Conway; Dr Alisdair Durie; Prof. Donald Meek; Dr Alastair Noble; Dr Harold Rowdon; and Dr Margaret Sanderson. Mr Keith Ferguson has helped me with my mathematical worries and Dr Roddy Gooding with my statistical ones. Individual chapters have been commented on by: Mr David Clarkson, Mr William Gilmour, Prof. Neil Hood, Mr W. K. Morrison and Mr Geoffrey Robson. Prof. Stewart J. Brown and Dr Ian Hutchinson made several invaluable suggestions for improvement. In both encouraging me to commence and in commenting on progress, Dr Alex McIntosh has been unsurpassed. Although the comments of these last eight individuals have been invaluable, again responsibility for the interpretation advanced herein rests with myself. I have been greatly assisted in turning the manuscript into a book by Mrs Ella Jack and, at Paternoster Press, Dr Anthony R. Cross, and Mr John Longridge of Profile. Thanks must also go to my father who trawled through the various volumes of the Glasgow Post Office Directory to help trace assemblies in the city and my mother who aided the work's progress by generously (and frequently) looking after her grandchildren.

Special thanks must be made to Beth, Katie and Mary who have long lived with this research and will be glad to see it contained within covers and not spilling over into their lives. Prof. David Bebbington supervised the thesis on which this book is based. He has been a continual source of attention, encouragement, learning and correction and I am grateful to him for writing the Foreword to the present work. His generous and stimulating friendship is enriching.

Neil T. R. Dickson

Abbreviations

A	*Aware*
AT	*Assembly Testimony*
BAHNR	*Brethren Archivists and Historians Network Review*
BDEB	*The Blackwell Dictionary of Evangelical Biography 1730-1860* (ed.) Donald M. Lewis (Oxford, 1995)
BJS	*British Journal of Sociology*
BM	*The Believer's Magazine*
BP	*The Believers' Pathway*
BQ	*The Baptist Quarterly*
'BQB'	'The believer's question box'
CBA	Christian Brethren Archive, University of Manchester
CBR	*Christian Brethren Review*
CBRJ	*Christian Brethren Review Journal*
CMHU	*The Christian Magazine and Herald of Union*
CW	*The Christian Worker*
DNB	*Dictionary of National Biography*
DSCHT	*Dictionary of Scottish Church History and Theology* (eds) Nigel M. deS. Cameron *et al.* ((Edinburgh, 1993)
H	*The Harvester*
HA	*Hamilton Advertiser*
HS	*Herald of Salvation*
JEH	*Journal of Ecclesiastical History*
JCBRF	*Journal of the Christian Brethren Research Fellowship*
KS	*Kilmarnock Standard*
LR	*The Latter Rain*
MÉ	*Le Messager Évangelique*
NA	*The Northern Assemblies*
NEI	*The Northern Evangelistic Intelligencer*
NI	*The Northern Intelligencer*
NT	*Needed Truth*
NW	*The Northern Witness*
OA	Orkney Archive, Kirkwall
OLOT	*Our Little One's Treasury*
PT	*The Present Testimony*
PWHS	*Proceedings of the Wesley Historical Society*
'QA'	'Questions and answers'
R	*The Revival*
RSCHS	*Records of the Scottish Church History Society*
S	*The Scotsman*
SCH	*Studies in Church History*

SHR	*The Scottish Historical Review*
SSW	*The Sunday School Worker*
TSA	*The Third Statistical Account*
TP	*The Truth Promoter*
W	*The Witness*
'WW'	'Witness watchtower'
'YBQB'	'The young believer's question box'

CHAPTER ONE

A Great Recovery: Introduction

Brethren: the story of a great recovery
—book title by David J. Beattie (1939).

In 1927 Thomas Caldwell disarmingly explained to the Inland Revenue the lack of accounts for the new building planned for the Brethren assembly to which he belonged, then meeting in the Co-operative Hall, Kilmarnock:

> I may say we don't keep a note of what goes on in our meeting and it was arranged that all should do their best to give and raise a good sum so that we should start and build and the only way we get money is the one gives say £5 another say £10 and so on we have no sale of work or anything like that. One brother may hand me some money and he gets a receipt from me and when I have £40 or £50 I take it to D.&D. Carruthers [Kilmarnock solicitors] and what they do with it I can't tell but they give me 5% less tax. So I trust this will explain matters.[1]

Perhaps the picture of financial naiveté in writing to a tax officer is intentional, as unusually for a Brethren member Caldwell, who was a small businessman, had some financial investments.[2] However his attitude towards record keeping was entirely typical of them. Accounts, minutes of elders' meetings and roll books were rarely kept or even needed because of the absence of central institutions which required returns to be made and the informal way in which affairs were transacted. The standard history of the Scottish church in the nineteenth century noted that 'The Brethren have been reserved on their Scottish history'.[3] Access to their past has been a problem, not only for historians in general, but also for Scottish Brethren themselves.

---

1. Edinburgh, Scottish Record Office, IRS 21/1811, Thomas Caldwell to the Inland Revenue; I am indebted to Dr Elizabeth C. Sanderson for this reference.
2. Oral information, 10 August 1997, from a Kilmarnock assembly member.
3. Andrew L. Drummond and James Bulloch, *The Church in Victorian Scotland 1843-1874* (Edinburgh, 1975), p.57.

Perspectives

The Brethren movement grew out of Protestant Evangelicalism and shares
its religious characteristics. In a definition which has won wide acceptance
the features of the latter have been formulated by D. W. Bebbington as
being: conversionism, the call for a change of life; activism, an energetic
expression of the individual's faith; biblicism, a high regard for scripture;
and crucicentricism, belief in the cardinal importance of Christ's atoning
death.[4] These attributes were conspicuous in the Brethren movement
which first emerged in Dublin during the late 1820s. The impulse soon
spread to England with early influential churches (or 'assemblies' or
'meetings') existing at Plymouth and Bristol. In 1848 the movement split
into 'Exclusive Brethren' (also known as 'Close Brethren'), who
followed the former Anglican priest, John Nelson Darby, and 'Open
Brethren'.[5]

In the popular mind the Exclusives form the group which is most often
associated with the name of the movement. In Scotland they grew at
fairly much the same time and in the same kind of places as their Open
counterparts.[6] By 1860 they had only two or three assemblies, which met
in private houses,[7] but the 1859 Revival and the movements of religious
fervour which followed it proved a turning point for them. By the years
around 1870 their presence was being noted from Shetland to the
Borders,[8] leading one United Presbyterian minister to complain that they
were 'found in the wake of religious awakenings as constantly as sharks
follow ships.'[9] By about 1878 they had seventy-five meetings and their

---

4. D. W. Bebbington, *Evangelicalism in Modern Britain: a history from the 1730s to
the 1980s* (London, 1989), pp.2-17.

5. For this division, see below, pp.47-8; the standard histories of the movement are:
W. Blair Neatby, *A History of the Plymouth Brethren*, 1st edn (London [1901]); H. H.
Rowdon, *The Origins of the Brethren* (London, 1967); F. Roy Coad, *A History of the
Brethren Movement: its origins, its worldwide development and its significance for the
present day*, 2nd edn (Exeter, 1976).

6. For an example, see Neil Dickson, 'Open and closed: Brethren and their origins in
the North East', in James Porter (ed.), *After Columba—After Calvin: religious
community in North-East Scotland* (Aberdeen, 1999), pp.151-170.

7. Andrew Miller, *The Brethren: a brief sketch of their origin, progress and testimony*
(London [1880]), p.83.

8. J. N. Darby to a 'Beloved Brother', 20 November 1868 in [J. N. Darby], *Letters of
J. N. D.*, 1 (Kingston-on-Thames, n.d.), p.536; Peter Mearns, *Christian Truth Viewed in
Relation to Plymouthism* (Edinburgh, 1874), p.v; *NA*, No.15 (March 1874), p.12;
Andrew L. Drummond and James Bulloch, *The Church in Late Victorian Scotland 1874-
1900* (Edinburgh, 1978), p.161.

9. Mearns, *Christian Truth*, p.40; this work is principally a critique of the Exclusive
Brethren, but the comment may also include some Open Brethren activity.

1885 address list recorded 115 assemblies, three more than the previous year.[10] In this period they probably attained their maximum number of congregations, for many of their meetings remained small and only survived for their founders' generation. The Exclusives adopted a relatively centralised control and the principle of assemblies being united in their judgement of disputes. As a result, they splintered into several bodies. The largest group throughout Britain was sometimes called the London Exclusives because of the importance of the decisions made by meetings at the assembly in the capital. In Scotland, the Stuart Party, which seceded in 1882 as a result of its leader, C. E. Stuart, being accused of Christological heresy, was eventually largely absorbed into the Open Brethren.[11] Better represented in the country was the Glanton Party, a 1908 secession which placed greater emphasis on evangelism.[12] Scottish Exclusives probably shared in the post-World War I growth enjoyed by their assemblies in Britain as whole, and possibly continued increasing in membership until the 1950s.[13] The estimate made in 1960 that in Scotland the London Exclusives had 3 to 5,000 members and the Glantons about 1,000 was probably made close to the period when they had achieved their maximum strength.[14] Their numbers in the north-east fishing communities have been greatly exaggerated; however, with the exceptions of Aberdeen and Peterhead, their meetings there have always been small.[15] The London Exclusives are intensely secretive. 'We shun everything that would draw attention to ourselves in an outward way... The path of obscurity, unknown to the world, is ours', one researcher was told in the 1950s.[16] There has been a sharp decline in their numbers, especially after 1970 when one of their leaders, James Taylor Jnr, attained some notoriety due to an alleged sexual scandal. They have subsequently

---

10. Andrew Miller, *Short Papers on Church History*, 3 (London, 1878), p.660; *References [January 1884]* (n.p., 1884); *References [January 1885]* (n.p., 1885).

11. See below, pp.157, 241, 288-90.

12. For Exclusive divisions see Napoleon Noel, *The History of the Brethren*, 2 vols (Denver, CO; 1936); Coad, *A History of the Brethren Movement*, pp.209-22; B. R. Wilson, 'The Exclusive Brethren: a case study in the evolution of a sectarian ideology', in *idem* (ed.), *Patterns of Sectarianism: organisation and ideology in social and religious movements* (London, 1967), pp.287-342; Roger Shuff, 'Open to closed: the growth of exclusivism among Brethren in Britain 1848-1953', *BAHNR*, 1 (1997-8), pp.10-23.

13. Shuff, 'Open to closed', pp.17-23.

14. John Highet, *The Scottish Churches: a review of their state 400 years after the Reformation* (London, 1960), p.37.

15. Dickson, 'Open and closed', in Porter (ed.), *After Columba*, p.160.

16. Anonymous Kilmarnock Exclusive assembly member quoted in John Strawhorn and William Boyd, *TSA Ayrshire* (Edinburgh & London, 1957), p.256.

fragmented into five small bodies, with perhaps just under 1,000 members,[17] and they are increasingly withdrawn from society.[18]

It was the Open Brethren which eventually became the larger section in Britain. They are a looser grouping of independent churches, and the lack of a credal statement has led them to debate their own distinctive practices. Writing in 1913 Arthur Rendle Short, a Bristol surgeon, felt there were four which distinguished them: believer's baptism, weekly communion at which open ministry was allowed, no ordained ministry and reception to the Lord's table of all believers.[19] In 1961 F. F. Bruce, a native of Scotland who held a chair in biblical criticism, reduced Short's list to three by combining the second and last items.[20] A different list was produced in 1990 by the Australian evangelist Kevin Dyer. His Brethren distinctives were multiple eldership, the autonomy of the local church and open communion. By this last Dyer meant freedom for the members to participate in worship, and he relegated association with other Evangelicals to a 'secondary issue'.[21] Recently two historians have tried to isolate the controlling principle of the movement from which all else flows: Harold Rowdon has maintained that this is its determination to derive its practices from scripture; a view criticised by James Patrick Callahan who has substituted primitivism, the ecclesial veneration of the earliest model.[22]

However, the section of the movement analysed in the present work, the Scottish Open Brethren, does not quite fit any of these offered definitions. As will become clear, from the 1860s onwards (the seminal period for the movement in Scotland) there were assemblies which did

17. Dickson, 'Open and closed', in Porter (ed.), *After Columba*, pp.151, 157, 162; Peter Brierley (ed.), *UK Christian Handbook Religious Trends No. 1—1998/99* (London and Carlisle, 1997), p.9.4; in this last source, the Glantons are estimated as having some 500 members (this estimate and the one in the text above were supplied by the present writer).

18. Bryan R. Wilson, 'A sect at law: the case of the Exclusive Brethren', in *The Social Dimensions of Sectarianism: sects and new religious movements in contemporary society* (Oxford, 1992), pp.87-102.

19. A Younger Brother [i.e. Arthur Rendle Short], *The Principles of Open Brethren* (Glasgow, [1913]), p.77.

20. F. F. Bruce, 'Who are the Brethren?', *W*, 91 (1961), pp.406-7; later printed as a pamphlet of the same title and as Appendix 1 in *idem, In Retrospect: remembrance of things past* (London and Glasgow, 1980), pp.313-17.

21. Kevin G. Dyer, *Must Brethren Churches Die?* (1990) UK edn (Exeter, 1991), pp.28-30.

22. Harold H. Rowdon, 'The problem of Brethren identity in historical perspective', *Biblioteca Storica Toscana*, 11 (Firenze, 1988), pp. 159-174; James Patrick Callahan, *Primitivist Piety: the ecclesiology of the early Plymouth Brethren* (Lanham, MD; 1996), pp.ix, xiv, 21, 32.

not receive all Christians to the Lord's table.[23] Even among those who did, 'Christians' is too broad a term: it is unlikely, for example, that a Roman Catholic would have been accepted. More properly it was pan-evangelical ecumenism which a section of Scottish Brethren maintained, and by the mid-twentieth century this view was not conspicuous in many places.[24] The movement itself refused to use a name.[25] However, although the vocabulary of the movement is often used in the present work,[26] the customary title 'Open Brethren' has been retained and, unless obvious from the context, it is to their Scottish section that 'Brethren' will refer.[27] But it should be noted that the former title was often a misnomer in Scotland.[28] The practices which are taken to distinguish the Brethren are

23. See below, p.87.

24. See below, pp.231-43.

25. John Bowes, *The Autobiography: or the history of the life of John Bowes* (Glasgow, 1872), p.361, quoted below, p.65; cf. 'QA', *NW*, 12 (1882), p.32; R. T. H[opkins]., 'Thoughts on Deuteronomy', *ibid.*, p.131; W. B. C. Beggs, 'The teaching of church principles', *BM*, 53 (1943), pp.7-8.

26. The exceptions are the occasional use of non-Brethren synonyms in the interests of stylistic variety and more economical expressions for 'coming into fellowship' or 'those in fellowship' such as 'to recruit', 'to join' or 'member'. Strictly speaking, the Brethren as a *Gemeinschaft* had no concept of institutional membership but the periphrastic Brethren phrase has not generally been preferred; likewise the use of their own vocabulary of 'believers', 'brethren' or 'saints' does not (as was intended) distinguish between Brethren and Christians in general.

27. The need to refer to the movement as a whole gave rise to various solutions among the Brethren: sometimes 'the meetings' (e.g. L. W. G. Alexander, 'Decadence or revival, *W*, 46 [1916], p.136) but more usually, with or without a capital, 'Assemblies' (e.g. Tom Wilson, 'Conservation, *BM*, 85 [1975], pp.316-7, quoted below, p.440). Some used 'Brethren' in inverted commas, and David Beattie adopted this last for his *The Believer's Magazine* series on which his book, *Brethren: the story of a great recovery* (Kilmarnock, [1939]), was based (the inadvertent dropping of the inverted commas led to complaints, 'Editorial note', *BM*, 45 [1935], p.77). However, there were those willing to use 'Brethren *simpliciter*, and this was the solution adopted by Thomas Stewart Veitch, *The Brethren Movement: a simple and straightforward account of the features and failures of a sincere attempt to carry out the principles of Scripture during the last 100 years* (London and Glasgow, [1933]). 'Plymouth Brethren' is widely used to refer to the movement, but this term was regarded unfavourably by Scottish Brethren at least: see Veitch, *The Brethren Movement*, p.33; A. Borland, 'Things most surely believed among us', *BM*, 72 (1962), pp.106-9.

28. In a forthcoming University of Wales thesis on the Brethren in England in the twentieth century Roger Shuff prefers the term 'independent Brethren' for the Open Brethren. This distinguishes them by their organisation from the other sections of the movement, which have degrees of federation, and not by their attitude to reception at the Lord's table, which as Shuff points out, could vary; in an earlier paper he has also shown that the exclusivism of the Exclusives was initially directed against the Open section only: Shuff, 'Open to closed', pp.10-23.

those in the Short-Bruce list modified in the light of Dyer. They are: the autonomy of the individual assembly; believer's baptism; a weekly Lord's supper at which the worship was from among the members; and no ordained ministry.[29] The Brethren have remained a movement consisting of independent congregations which have no controlling central institutions; believer's baptism was the practice which ensured the assembly would be a gathered church; the weekly Lord's supper ('the morning meeting' or 'breaking of bread') with its spontaneous worship was the most distinctive service; and although itinerant evangelists, Bible teachers and more recently resident full-time workers have been used, no distinction exists between clergy and laity. The present work does not attempt to isolate one guiding principle. For the Scottish movement, as will become clear, the appeal to the Bible and its description of the practices of the primitive church were certainly important. But there were other historical and cultural factors which shaped the movement in Scotland. One of these has again been identified by D. W. Bebbington— the influence of nineteenth-century Romanticism in a heightened sense of the supernatural.[30] But among other components to which attention will be paid are the revivalism of the movement and the cerebralism of its members.[31] Different elements within Brethrenism created stresses which had profound implications for its development.

The Open Brethren were always aware of the wider Christian Church.

---

29. The definition adopted is phenomenological rather than prescriptive: it describes what has been encountered historically rather than enjoining an ideal. Dyers redefinition of the commemoration of Lord's supper is accepted as is his addition of congregational autonomy, but as not all Scottish assemblies had identified elders (see below, p.150), Dyers' first characteristic of a multiple eldership is rejected. The definition adopted above would also fit the Scotch Baptists and some independent mission halls (sometimes called 'breaking of bread' missions). The former are difficult to distinguish from the Brethren on the basis of practices (see below n.43 for an example of the two bodies being confused); they were, however, different in terms of mindset—the former being influenced by eighteenth-century values and the latter by nineteenth-century Romanticism. Mission halls were the product of the same spirituality as the Brethren, but they often appointed formal office bearers; as will become apparent in the present work, they readily transferred to the movement.

30. Bebbington, *Evangelicalism*, pp.74-104; see below, pp.89-90, and Chpt 8 *passim*.

31. For the former, see below, pp.36, 48-9, Chpts 3 & 4 *passim*, and pp.185-199; and for the latter, Chpt. 8 *passim*.

Table 1.1 Analysis of Jimmy Paton's library, *c*.1950

	Open Brethren	Exclusive Brethren	Other Christian	Unidentified
Books	70	102	32	6
Bible translations	2	2	9	-
Multiple author commentaries	-	-	3	1

Source: writer's collection, II., Jas. Paton, 'Where Is It?', MS notebook, *c*.1950.

Table 1.1 analyses a handlist from the early 1950s for the library of Jimmy Paton, then a plasterer and slater from Stevenston, Ayrshire, and a leading preacher in the movement.[32] Only five Brethren works—by J. R. Caldwell, John Ritchie and the Exclusive Andrew Miller—in the collection were by Scots. Although the movement in Scotland gave Brethren theology a distinctive cast, it inherited its doctrines ready made and there were few Scottish authors. The largest group of writers included in the library were moderate Exclusives, a fact which is due to Paton's predilection for William Kelly, Darby's leading disciple who in 1879-81 had separated from him. With thirty-five works Kelly was the best represented writer.[33] However, some 19.4 per cent, about a fifth of the books, was by Christian writers from outside the movement. The most collected writer here was the Baptist F. B. Meyer with seven items, but also included were Presbyterian James Moffat, the Anglican Archbishop of Dublin, R. C. Trench, and a New Testament commentary issued by the Methodists. In addition the three best represented Open Brethren writers, Sir Robert Anderson (ten works), H. A. Ironside (six works) and Andrew Jukes (three works), all left the movement.[34] As Paton belonged to the school of west of Scotland preachers who emphasised assembly

---

32. Writer's collection, II., Jas. Paton, 'Where Is It?', MS notebook, *c*.1950; the writer is indebted to the late Mr Paton for the gift of this item; for Jimmy Paton, see Alex Aikman *et al.*, 'James Paton 1914-1999', in Robert Plant (compiler), *They Finished Their Course in the 90s* (Kilmarnock, 2000), pp. 229-36.

33. By 'moderate Exclusive Brethren' is meant pre-Stoneyite London Exclusives, the Kelly-Lowe and Glanton Parties and the North American Grant division. In addition to Kelly, J. G. Bellett with 14 works and J. N. Darby with 12 works are well represented; if the books in multi-volume works are counted singly, then Darby has 17 items and C. H. Mackintosh has 12.

34. Ironside's pastorate of the Moody Memorial Church, Chicago from 1929-48 is felt by the present writer to have effectively taken him outside the movement, although in his *A Historical Sketch of the Brethren Movement* (1945) he continued in dialogue with it.

distinctives in the mid-twentieth century, this collection of Christian writers from outside the Brethren might be taken as a fairly minimal one.[35] The proportion in some other libraries would be higher.

The Brethren also saw themselves as but the latest in a long line of Christian bodies who had upheld primitive Christian practices.[36] Anti-Catholicism led the Exclusive Andrew Miller, a Scottish merchant based in London, to include the Albigensians among them in his three-volume *Short Papers on Church History* which appeared in 1873-8.[37] Miller's work, until the second half of the twentieth century the only history of the Christian Church read among Brethren, chronicled '*the silver line of God's grace in true Christians*'.[38] In Scottish ecclesiastical history he was positively disposed to St Columba and the Culdees, because of what he perceived as the anti-Romanising influence of the Celtic church, and in later centuries he favourably noticed John Knox, the Covenanters, Ebenezer Erskine, the Cambuslang Revival, and the Disruption.[39] The Celtic church was also the subject of an anonymous children's book issued by Open Brethren publisher John Ritchie, and in addition he reprinted a number of works relating to the Covenanters who were especially revered in the movement's account of Church history.[40] Others also saw Brethren predecessors in John Glas, the Relief Church, the

---

35. Jimmy Paton's library continued to grow considerably and the present writer is indebted to him for the gift of a number of items used in this research; for the school of preachers to which he belonged, see below, pp.234-7.

36. The most complete historical account of this view is by the English missionary to Europe, E. H. Broadbent, *The Pilgrim Church: being some account of the continuance through succeeding centuries of churches practising the principles taught in the New Testament* (London & Glasgow, 1931).

37. Miller, *Church History*, 2 (1876), pp.246-7; in a note Miller stated he had changed his view that they were Paulicians and he now held they were orthodox; cf. [John Ritchie], 'Answers to correspondents, *BM*, 16 (1906), p.71.

38. Miller, *Church History*, 1 (1873), p.4; in 1928 Open Brethren publishers Pickering & Inglis reprinted Miller's history in an edition revised and incorporating additional material by William Hoste; in 1964 they published it as a one-volume edition with additional material by Kingsley G. Rendell which was in print until the late-1970s.

39. Miller, *Church History*, 1, pp.495-6, 499-501, 506-7; 3 (1878) pp.563-6, 616-17, 619-21, 624-6, 661-5.

40. Anon., *In Scotia's Wilds: the story of how the gospel entered the land of the thistle and wrought its wonders among the ancient dwellers there* (Kilmarnock, [1927]); cf. [Neil Dickson], 'Editorial, *BAHNR*, 2 (2000), pp.1-2; among the works on the Covenanters Ritchie published were Anon., *Tales and Sketches of the Covenanters* (1880), John Ritchie edn (Kilmarnock, n.d.); Robert Pollok, *Tales of the Covenanters* (1833), John Ritchie edn (Kilmarnock [1928]); and J. H. Thomson, *The Martyr Graves of Scotland*, (ed.) Matthew Hutchison, 2nd series (1877), John Ritchie edn (Kilmarnock, n.d.); for other non-Brethren material issued by Brethren publishers see the appropriate section in the Bibliography below, pp.455-7.

Paisley Pen' Folk (independents who met in a Paisley pend),[41] the Northern Separatists (Evangelical secessionists in the Highlands),[42] and the Scotch Baptists—the last even being mistaken for early assemblies.[43] Evangelical missionaries were also admired. For children, Ritchie wrote a book on pioneers to the Pacific islands and published a series of brief missionary biographies by Brethren schoolmaster Andrew Borland.[44] In 1926 when Henry Pickering, another Open Brethren publisher, wanted to print works bolstering Fundamentalism he began with two nineteenth-century books, one by the Evangelical Anglican T. D. Barnard and the other by High Churchman H. P. Liddon.[45] The Brethren did not see themselves as being isolated in the history of the Church.

Nevertheless they gave themselves a unique position. They took as their due the compliment, made most recently by Gordon Donaldson, that they 'presented the most clearly recognisable re-creation...of the primitive church of the days of the apostles'.[46] Thomas Veitch, a solicitor from Linlithgow, was stating a truism of their historiography when he asserted in *The Brethren Movement* ([1933]) that Martin Luther had restored 'the forgotten truth of justification by faith alone' and the Brethren had restored 'forgotten truths concerning His Church and its

---

41. For this group see, Anon., *Reminiscences of the "Pen" Folk, by one who knew them* (Paisley, 1871).

42. For these groups, see John McLeod, *By-Paths of Highland Church History*, (ed.) G. N. M. Collins (Edinburgh, 1965), pp.78-135 .

43. For this list, see respectively: T. Wilson, 'A little light recovered', *BM*, 108 (1998), pp.358-60; Veitch, *The Brethren Movement*, pp.104-5; anon [title missing in extant copy], *NI*, 3 (1873), pp.109-110, and anon., 'Fragments from the "Northern Radicals"', *NI*, 4 (1874), p,151; C. J. Pickering *et al.*, *1865-1965: the Half-Yearly Meetings of Christians in Glasgow* (n.pl. [1965]); the mistaking in this last work of the Glasgow Scotch Baptist congregation for an early nineteenth-century pre-Brethren assembly is due to the reprinting among Open Brethren of anon. (ed.), *Letters Concerning their Principles and Order from Assemblies of Believers in 1818-1820* (1820) rpt (London, 1889), which is a correspondence among Glasite churches that included several letters from Baptist churches in Scotland.

44. John Ritchie, *Among the Cannibals: peeps at the South Sea Islands and their savage inhabitants with life stories of their missionary heroes*, revised edn (Kilmarnock [1930]); Andrew Borland's biographies were of: Mary Slessor, James Hannington, Hudson Taylor, Adoniram Judson, John G. Paton and Alexander Mackay; they were later collected in Andrew Borland, *Crusaders for Christ in Heathen Lands: short biographies of six noble men and women who went forth into the dark places of the earth with the light of the gospel (with original poems)* (Kilmarnock, 1928).

45. T. D. Barnard, *The Progress of Doctrine in the New Testament* (1866), Pickering & Inglis edn (Glasgow [1926]); H. P. Liddon, *The Divinity of Our Lord and Saviour Jesus Christ* (1866), Pickering & Inglis edn (Glasgow [1926]).

46. Gordon Donaldson, *The Faith of the Scots* (London, 1990), p.134; cf. James Anderson, *Our Heritage* (Kilmarnock, 1973), p.13.

Scriptural fellowship and worship.'[47] James Patrick Callahan has argued that Brethren were primitivist but were anti-restorationist, wanting to follow the original ecclesiology but believing it was impossible to establish that pattern in its entirety in contemporary conditions.[48] Pessimism over restoring the Church marked Exclusive thought, given expression in the phrase of J. N. Darby 'the Church is in ruins'.[49] Miller commented that in the Brethren there was no thought of 'reconstituting' or 'restoring' the Church 'to its Pentecostal glory', the snare into which he felt Satan had trapped Edward Irving. He ended his *Church History* gloomily, observing that corporate Christianity had been penetrated by evil and counselling an 'intensely individual' faith with Christians breaking bread among those gathered to Christ's name.[50]

Darby's language was occasionally echoed in Open Brethren writings.[51] But one group which emerged within the latter that decisively rejected his phrase were those who absorbed the teaching of the magazine *Needed Truth*.[52] In 1892-4 they seceded to form the Churches of God, perceiving themselves as a remnant rebuilding the House of God on earth.[53] J. R. Caldwell, the influential editor of the Brethren magazine *The Witness*, was scornful of this notion, maintaining that although some have thought that 'there may be a reconstruction of the Church such as will surpass in character and permanence even the apostolic Churches', such '"High Church" claims' were misplaced.[54] However, Caldwell clearly believed there was a congregational ideal which could be reclaimed in the present, a pattern he sought to elucidate in *The Charter of the Church*

---

47. Veitch, *The Brethren Movement*, p.12; cf. Callahan, *Primitivist Piety*, p.113.

48. Callahan, *Primitivist Piety*, pp.183-208, 216-42; in a review of Callahan, T. C. F. Stunt has criticised this distinction as hard to identify, *BAHNR*, 1 (1997-8), pp.119-20.

49. Shih-An Deng, 'Ideas of the Church in an age of reform: the ecclesiological thoughts of John Nelson Darby and John Henry Newman, 1824-1850' (University of Minnesota Ph.D. thesis, 1994), pp.42-8.

50. Miller, *Church History*, 3, pp.655, 669, 670.

51. T. C[ochrane]., 'The One Body', *NA*, 10 (1873), pp.37-40; [A. J. Holiday], 'The Church in ruins', *BP*, 8 (1887), pp.104-6.

52. C. M. Luxmoore, 'Department of question and answer', *NT*, 5 (1892-3), p.161.

53. Charles Morton, 'The House of God forsaken', *NT*, 3 (1890-1), pp.82-8; David Smith, '"Remnant Days"', *NT*, 6 (1894), pp.225-30; for an account of this secession in Scotland, see below, pp.158-169.

54. J. R. Caldwell, *A Revision of Certain Teachings Regarding the Gathering and Receiving of Children of God* (Glasgow, [1906]), p.9; Caldwell's views were criticised by W. H. Hunter, *The Gathering and Receiving of Children of God: a review of a recent booklet* (Kilmarnock [c.1906]), pp. 17-18, as being '"the-Church-is-in-ruins do-what-you-like" theory'.

(1910), his exposition of 1 Corinthians.[55] John Ritchie did not accept that the Church was in ruins, but, he noted, its original 'unity and power' had gone, 'never to be restored'.[56] Awareness of other Evangelicals tempered Open Brethren claims, but nevertheless in their own eyes the movement was—declared the title of a history by David Beattie published in 1939—*Brethren: the story of a great recovery*.[57] In a more modest assessment F. F. Bruce saw it as an example of 'Reformation according to the Word of God'.[58]

Another commonplace of Brethren historiography was that the movement was a work of the Holy Spirit, and support for this was found in the seemingly spontaneous generation of the movement in several places.[59] When writing on Scottish Brethren, Beattie—a native of Langholm, Dumfriesshire, who owned a monumental sculptor's business in Carlisle—was able to cite several examples of independent growth.[60] His original contribution to British Brethren historiography was in moving away from the Dublin-Plymouth-Bristol axis to study the growth of the movement elsewhere. As well as using printed sources, he wrote to individual assemblies asking them what they knew of their origins. From the replies he received he was able to chart the spread of the movement throughout Britain.[61] A perhaps unintentional effect of this methodology was to demonstrate how much of the movement's history has been devolved, residing in the affairs of individual congregations. It is, in effect, an exposition of the autonomy of Brethren assemblies. In-

---

55. John R. Caldwell, *The Charter of the Church: revised notes of an exposition of the First Epistle to the Corinthians*, 2 vols (Glasgow [1910]).

56. [John Ritchie], 'Answers to correspondents', *BM*, 16 (1906), pp.142-3; *idem*, 'The Way, Which They Call Heresy: remarks on Mr. W. Blair Neatby's book, "A History of the Plymouth Brethren'* (Kilmarnock [c.1901]), pp.22-3; cf. *idem*, 'Revival times and work in Aberdeenshire', in C. W. R[oss]. (ed.), *Donald Ross: pioneer evangelist of the North of Scotland and United States of America* (Kilmarnock [1903]), p.169; and below, p.180.

57. The second printing of this book states it first appeared in 1940; but the writer has seen a copy which was given as a present on Christmas 1939; it originally appeared as a series which commenced in 1934 in *The Believer's Magazine* (see above n.27).

58. F. F. Bruce, 'Church history and its lessons', in J. B. Watson (ed.), *The Church: a symposium* (London, 1949), p.179.

59. Miller, *Church History*, 3, p.645; Veitch, *Brethren Movement*, p.30; Beattie, *Brethren*, p.viii; Hy Pickering (ed.), *Chief Men Among the Brethren*, 2nd edn (London, 1931), p.iv: the favourite example of spontaneous generation was that of Leonard Strong of Georgetown, British Guiana; however T. C. F. Stunt, 'Leonard Strong: the motives and experiences of early missionary work in British Guiana', *CBRJ*, 34 (1983), pp.95-105, has shown this example originates in a misdating.

60. Beattie, *Brethren*, pp. 202, 211, 266, 265.

61. Unfortunately Beattie's correspondence was destroyed shortly before the present research was undertaken.

dependent growth was used by John Ritchie to distance himself from the movement's earlier history. In a review pamphlet of W. Blair Neatby's *A History of the Plymouth Brethren* (n.d. [1901]), for long the standard account, Ritchie sought to inform Neatby that thousands in the movement in Scotland had no knowledge of earlier events but were merely being obedient to the word of God.[62] Ritchie, who joined the movement through the independent accession of the north-east assemblies, was insulating himself from what he felt were previous mistakes, but in this contention he was echoing Brethren in his native region who did not take as a guide the movement in England and their original principles of open communion.[63] When in the aftermath of the Churches of God division some argued for association with other Christians, Ritchie was able to present their views as a departure.[64] Quite different was Veitch's *The Brethren Movement* which concentrated on origins in Dublin and the south of England and the subsequent arguments over a restricted communion. It was essentially a plea for returning to what he termed '*the scriptural principles and Catholic fellowship of believers*'.[65] Veitch, in common with others of a more open persuasion, was ready to admit to Brethren failings in the past.[66] But doctrinal and ecclesiastical purists showed a marked coolness to their history, especially when it involved inconvenient facts. For example, the eschatological opinions of Bristol pioneer George Müller, which differed from the majority view, were deemed to be irrelevant by Andrew Borland for 'Our chief concern should be to discover...what the scriptures teach.'[67] Tradition was a poor second-best to the Bible.[68]

These attitudes to history display some of the tensions which have marked the movement. After the Second World War it became increasingly polarised between those who wished to continue in isolation and those who wanted varying degrees of contact with other Christians. History continued to be contested. The appearance in 1968 of *A History of the Brethren Movement* by the English Brethren member Roy Coad brought criticisms from Scotland that there was a bias in it towards the 'more open-minded' brethren.[69] The Glasgow-based Gospel Tract

---

62. Ritchie, '*The Way...*', pp.19-20.

63. J. A. Boswell, 'The Open position', *NT*, 12 (1900), pp.74-5; Bruce, *In Retrospect*, p.2.

64. See below, p.226.

65. Veitch, *Brethren Movement*, p.104.

66. *Ibid.*, p.102; cf. Alexander Marshall, '*Holding Fast the Faithful Word': or whither are we drifting?* (Glasgow [1908]), pp.38-9.

67. [Andrew Borland], 'George Müller's second advent teaching', *BM*, 64 (1954), p.95.

68. See below, p.220.

69. A. B[orland]., 'Review', *BM*, 78 (1968), p.283.

Publications began in 1981 a series of reprints of early Brethren writers and from 1987 reprints of the biographies of earlier Brethren leaders. These publications were entirely cynical in their attempt to manipulate history, deliberately excising any reference to an open communion.[70] James Anderson, a lecturer at Ayr College, endeavoured to find a middle way, compiling two volumes of profiles of leading Brethren who had died during the 1970s and 1980s which included individuals of both tendencies.[71] But a mediating position was increasingly difficult to hold, as his booklet *Our Heritage* (1973) showed. It gave an account of traditional features of Brethren life illustrated from history and called on the young to cherish them.[72] But he was writing in the context of radical change which many of those whom he addressed would embrace. The ecumenical strain that was present in the Brethren and which became more pronounced in the post-war era was represented by two works of popular history. F. F. Bruce wrote in 1950-2 a non-partisan history of Christianity until the seventh century, entitled in its one-volume edition *The Spreading Flame*, which was informed by his considerable scholarship.[73] The other popular work was *The Evangelicals* (1989) by John Allan, an Anglo-Scottish church youth worker, which traced the roots and worldwide growth of Protestant Evangelicalism.[74] Neither book mentioned the Brethren and Scottish Brethren members who wrote academic history in this period also did not discuss the movement. The sole exception was an article by J. A. H. Dempster on Scottish Brethren publishers which appeared in 1986. The study took a critical look at their

70. This censorship includes a paragraph from HyP[ickering]., 'John R. Caldwell, in *idem* (ed.), *Chief Men*, pp.150-4; a paragraph from Tom Rea (compiler), *The Life and Labours of David Rea, Evangelist: largely written from his own MSS* (Belfast, 1917), p.210; and all but a page and a half of a chapter from John Hawthorn, *Alexander Marshall: evangelist, author and pioneer* (Glasgow [1929]), pp.127-141.

71. James Anderson (ed.), *They Finished Their Course* (Kilmarnock, 1980); *idem*, (ed.), *They Finished their Course in the Eighties* (Kilmarnock, 1990); for Anderson see Alan Gamble *et al.*, 'James Anderson 1925-1992', in Plant (compiler), *They Finished Their Course in the 90s* , pp.9-17. This last book continues Anderson's project.

72. Anderson, *Our Heritage*; the material in this booklet first appeared as articles in *The Believer's Magazine* during 1971.

73. F. F. Bruce, *The Spreading Flame: the rise and progress of Christianity from its first beginnings to the conversion of the English* (Exeter, 1958): this is a revised one-volume edition of three works published from 1950 until 1952; in addition Bruce published the following significant historical works: *History of the Bible in English*, 3rd edn (Guildford and London, 1979); *Israel and the Nations: from the Exodus to the fall of the Second Temple* (Exeter, 1963); *New Testament History*, 3rd edn (London & Glasgow, 1980); for Bruce, see below, pp.247-8.

74. John Allan, *The Evangelicals: an illustrated history* (Exeter, 1989).

productions but utilised an insider's understanding.[75] Other writings contributed to Scottish history on the Reformation, architecture, business, religious publishing and women.[76] Most notable here was Margaret H. B. Sanderson whose insight into Ayrshire Lollardy as being a 'lay-orientated "do-it-yourself" element' was clearly influenced by her Brethren background, and she has written sympathetically of both sides in the Reformation struggle—something almost impossible for earlier generations of Brethren.[77] There always had been Scottish Brethren interested in secular history: David Anderson-Berry, a Scottish physician practising in London, instituted a gold medal for an essay on an aspect of Scottish history which from 1930 was awarded by the Royal Historical Society;[78] David Beattie, the historian of the Brethren, was also a Fellow of the Society of Antiquaries (Scotland) who wrote two works on Border history;[79] and Robert Rendall, a Kirkwall draper, made significant archaeological discoveries in the 1920s and 30s.[80] But the post-war involvement was more marked. The later writers were typical of a broadening which had affected a section of the movement.[81] This further

---

75. J. A. H. Dempster, 'Aspects of Brethren publishing enterprise in late nineteenth century Scotland', *Publishing History*, 20 (1986), pp.61-101.

76. See, John A. H. Dempster, *The T. & T. Clark Story: a Victorian publisher and the New Theology with an epilogue covering the twentieth-century history of the firm* (Durham, 1992); *inter alia*, Sam McKinstry, *Rowand Anderson: 'Scotland's premier architect'* (Edinburgh, 1991); *idem*, *Sure as the Sunrise: a history of Albion Motors* (Edinburgh, 1997); *idem* and Gavin Stamp (eds), *'Greek' Thomson* (Edinburgh, 1994); Elizabeth C. Sanderson, *Women and Work in Eighteenth Century Edinburgh* (London, 1996); *inter alia*, Margaret H. B. Sanderson, *Scottish Rural Society in the Sixteenth Century* (Edinburgh, 1982); *idem*, *Cardinal of Scotland: David Beaton c.1494-1546* (Edinburgh, 1986); *idem*, *Mary Stewart's People* (Edinburgh, 1987); *idem*, *Robert Adam and Scotland: portrait of an architect* (Edinburgh, 1992); *idem*, *Ayrshire and the Reformation: people and change, 1490-1600* (East Linton, 1997); in addition the economic historian Alasdair J. Durie had a Glanton Exclusive upbringing and was in the Open Brethren for a time; for the Highland historian Donald E. Meek, see below, p.360, n.161.

77. Sanderson, *Ayrshire and the Reformation*, p.41.

78. The competition, known as the David Berry Essay, was instituted in memory of Anderson-Berry's minister father and was originally for an essay on James Hepburn Earl of Bothwell to be awarded by The Society of Antiquaries (Scotland), but an alteration to the terms of the will were sanctioned in 1930 to permit the Royal Historical Society to offer it for an essay on the reigns of James I to VI and then varied in 1978 to include any period of Scottish history with the prize being a sum of money.

79. David J. Beattie, *Prince Charlie and the Borderland* (Carlisle, 1925); *Langsyne in Eskdale* (Carlisle, 1950); for Beattie's other work, see below pp.248-9, 324.

80. Neil Dickson, 'Robert Rendall: a life', in *idem* (ed.), *An Island Shore: the life and work of Robert Rendall* (Kirkwall, 1990), pp.17-49. On Rendall, see pp.249, 324-5.

81. See below, pp.341-3.

phase of Brethren historiography demonstrated the tensions current within the movement.

Sources

The problem of sources alluded to in the first paragraph of the present chapter is an immediate one in researching Brethren history. A range of printed and oral sources has been drawn upon. Brethrenism valued literacy and had several publishers who serviced the movement in Scotland.[82] The production of these firms has been researched, especially three magazines issued by them which are the principal primary sources for Scottish Brethren history: *The Truth Promoter, The Witness* and *The Believer's Magazine*.[83] Among much else, these journals carried news of evangelists and assemblies which are invaluable in tracing the growth of the movement.[84] Brethren congregations could be commenced on the initiative of one or two individuals and were as easily discontinued; in addition schisms were frequent. It is not always easy to determine if meetings had a continuous history and even the assembly address lists which are extant from 1895 onwards were not always accurate.[85] It is most usually the magazines which provide notice of a congregation's founding or discontinuation or even evidence of its continued existence in, for example, news of an itinerant evangelist's movements.[86] *The Witness* and *The Believer's Magazine* also carried brief obituaries that preserve much valuable material which would otherwise have been lost. These notices are an additional source for the commencement of assemblies as the circumstances and date would often be recorded in a founder's obituary. And they often listed the significant spiritual events

82. See below, pp.39, 146-8, 278.

83. However, not all copies of these magazines are extant: the final years of *The Truth Promoter* (1870-5) are missing from Dundee City Library which holds the only run of the magazine known to the writer; and the first volume of *The Witness* (1870/1) is missing with 1872-6 contained in a single mutilated volume in the writer's possession; also there are gaps in the preservation of parts of this magazine: the British Library run of the magazine preserves the news sections for 1879-89 (with some gaps) and 1907-80; the Mitchell Library, Glasgow, has these sections for 1902-20; see also below, n.89.

84. If a reference in the present work is only to a magazine page number, then it is to such an item.

85. The earliest known lists for 1886 and 1887 are not extant.

86. By the application of Occam's razor, assemblies have not been unnecessarily multiplied: unless evidence exists to the contrary, it is assumed they have had a continuous history; the exception to this are assemblies which existed before 1859 where the contrary rule is applied: because of the differences which there were between many pre- and post-1859 assemblies, it is assumed that the former were discontinued unless there is evidence demonstrating a continuous existence.

in an individual's life—in Brethren eyes the year or age when its subject
was converted (or 'saved') and joined a meeting (or 'came into
fellowship'). Although such a source has considerable limitations, a
computer data base of all members of Scottish assemblies who received
an obituary in *The Witness* (the principal Brethren review) was
compiled.[87] From this data base it has been possible to abstract numerical
series which, in the absence of total membership numbers that many
counted sinful to collect,[88] allow the growth of the movement to be
estimated.[89] A separate computer data base was also constructed for

---

87. This was done on an Apple Macintosh Performa 475 using Claris Works 2.1.

88. On the basis of 2 Sam. 24: 10.

89. The obituaries in *The Witness* were used from 1903 until 1978. This feature started
in April 1903 and after 1978 Scottish deaths were rarely reported. The data base of
Scottish Brethren members compiled from the obituaries contains information on 8,381
individuals. However, their accuracy is severely limited, not least because being
obituaries they either do not have data for those still living in 1978 or, when the series
starts, those already dead. In addition some obituaries are exceptionally brief—women
especially might not have much more recorded than their date of death. Furthermore,
whether an individual had an obituary recorded was dependent on such factors as their
status within the movement (thus men were more likely to have one than women) or
where they lived (larger congregations tended to be more punctilious in submitting an
obituary than smaller, remote ones). Also years or ages were sometimes prefaced by such
formulae as 'more than', 'about' or 'almost', and a year of birth had most frequently to be
calculated from age at death. Not all conversions, particularly earlier ones, recorded in
obituaries were as a result of Brethren evangelism but this fact was not always stated. In
294 cases the date of conversion and the date of joining differ and in many of these cases
the conversion is probably a non-Brethren one for usually these dates, except in the case
of children, tended to be close to each other. In addition, the average age of conversion is
falsely raised as a childhood conversion, an exceptionally common phenomenon in the
Brethren, was either noted as being such with no precise details given or was not recorded
at all.

Growth series abstracted from the obituaries are probably at their most accurate for the
period 1869-1923 for conversions and 1879-1928 for Brethren membership. These dates
were arrived at by calculating the average ages of death, conversion and joining for those
receiving an obituary in the decades 1903-13 and 1969-78: these were respectively 60.6,
26.7 and 36.7 for the former period and 75.4, 25.1 and 25.5 for the latter; however the
lack of recording of childhood conversions probably means an extra five years should be
subtracted from the latter conversion date: the years between which the data achieved
maximum accuracy were then calculated from 1903 and 1978. The years of conversion and
of joining are available for 4,645 individuals (55.4% of the data base) of which the year
of conversion is available for 2,688 individuals, of which 23.3% (627 individuals) are
indicated as being approximate; and the year of joining is available for 2,449
individuals, of which 32.6% (798 individuals) are indicated as being approximate. It is
clear that the data must be used with caution, but correlated with other sources, give a
suggestive picture of Brethren growth. In stacked graphs estimating growth (i.e. Figures
3.1, 4.2, 4.3, and 6.1) the following data is not included: non-Brethren conversions and

emigrants where a year of emigration could be established, using, in addition to *The Witness* obituaries, those of *The Believer's Magazine* and other sources such as the few congregational roll books which were available to the writer.[90]

History has traditionally privileged the written over the spoken, for most often a document or printed matter is what remains. The Brethren, however, had a vibrant unwritten culture, much of their thinking being transmitted in sermons, conversational Bible readings and informal house discussions. Oral history has formed another source. Interviews were undertaken with several individuals, most of them elderly, and valuable information and a sense of the movement's ethos was acquired through these.[91] In addition many Brethren churches were contacted to establish how much had been preserved of their history.[92] As a result, a substantial collection of manuscripts was built up.[93] Although gaps remain in knowledge, an eclectic approach to sources allows a reasonably comprehensive picture of Scottish Brethren history to emerge.

Prospective

The present writer is a participant observer who through one branch of the family is fifth-generation Brethren. The advantages of this in writing on a movement which has been neglected or often seemed obscure to historians are obvious. The search for sources is made a little easier and a feeling for the subject already exists. The present work is in its own way an attempt to rescue the movement from what E. P. Thompson in a different context famously called 'the enormous condescension of posterity'.[94] However, it might be felt, both by external and internal readers, that impartiality will be sacrificed. The bane of older denomi-

the year of conversion if the year of joining an assembly is also known. However, in Table 3.1 (average ages of conversion and joining) coincident dates of conversion and joining are admitted to the calculations, but to eliminate potential non-Brethren conversions, not adult conversions (i.e. age 21 and above) which differ by more than a year from that of joining, or childhood ones when the year of joining is in adulthood.

90. See below, pp.306-7.

91. As most of my interviewees are Brethren members who may not wish to be identified it has seemed best to extend confidentiality to all of them; however, the provenance of an oral source is indicated. Tapes and notes of interviews will be lodged in the Christian Brethren Archive, John Rylands University Library of Manchester.

92. It was not thought necessary for the purposes of the present work to write to every assembly; those which initially seemed to have the most obscure history were targeted.

93. These are listed below in the Bibliography, pp.434-9; they will be lodged in the Christian Brethren Archive, John Rylands University Library, Manchester.

94. E. P. Thompson, *The Making of the English Working Class* (1963), Penguin edn (Harmondsworth, 1968), p.14.

national histories was their propensity to become polemics which could alienate outsiders. In addition the conflicting currents within Brethrenism mean that increasingly individuals within the movement have *ipso facto* to decide within which stream they are going to move. The present writer grew up within one tendency and has since his undergraduate days belonged to another. Brethren readers might feel that one inclination rather than another is favoured. It has been a cliché, persuasively stated by E. H. Carr's *What is History?*, that historians bring their own values and presuppositions to their writing and historical interpretation is the result of an interaction between author and topic.[95] This does not mean, however, that objectivity is a chimera. As Richard Evans has recently stressed, the past is a reality to be encountered and 'the historian has to develop a detached mode of cognition, a faculty of self-criticism and an ability to understand another person's point of view.'[96] The present work is a necessarily provisional attempt to find, not invent, patterns within history.

The aim is to analyse the development of the movement incorporating its social history. This objective is not an exercise in reductionism, as if the Brethren could not be explained in any other way, but it is an attempt to use the categories of historical analysis to understand them. Three polarities of the movement in relation to society are of thematic importance to the investigation. These are: integration and withdrawal; continuity and change; and growth and decline. Attention will be paid to how they embedded themselves in concrete features of the movement, such as church-planting, cultural activity, doctrine and practice, social class and women's roles. Each of the above three themes relates to significant areas of historiographical interest. The motif of continuity and change, for example, is one of the central concerns of historical (and perhaps any) investigation. In the present work the interest will be in the relationship of the Brethren to their religious and social origins; the innovations of their beginnings when they saw themselves as a renewal movement; what possibilities there were for alteration once the movement reached its mature phase; and the changes of the contemporary movement. The other two themes have over recent years produced a large secondary literature and the interpretation of the Brethren offered will be related to this discourse.

In analysing degrees of integration and withdrawal within the movement the sociological typification of sect and denomination will be drawn upon. The Brethren were a protest movement against sectarianism. One of the objections to independent mission halls was that they associated too readily with the institutional church—theirs was 'a

---

95. E. H. Carr, *What is History?* (1961), Penguin edn (Harmondsworth, 1964).
96. Richard J. Evans, *In Defence of History* (London, 1997), p.252.

"halfway" theory of separation'.[97] The Brethren prided themselves on their stand which they felt was common to all Christians. It was for this reason they refused a denominational title and used only such names which were common to all believers.[98] But it is not the common pejorative usage of 'sect' for ecclesiastical divisions displaying mutual animosity, against which the Brethren protested, that is intended by sociologists.[99] Troeltsch used the term of small, lower-class perfectionist groups in the Middle Ages which placed great stress on the original ideas of Christianity. They were indifferent or hostile to the state and their opposite type was the church.[100] Attention focused on the ways in which they became a denomination, a category between the restricted membership of the sect and the universal church.[101] But J. Milton Yinger noted how sectarian characteristics might persist over several generations and posited the established sect, a more structured body.[102] The definitions which form the starting-point in the present work are those of Bryan Wilson. According to Wilson, the sect demands total commitment, and is a voluntary society entered by proof of some personal merit such as a conversion experience; it emphasises exclusiveness, being willing to expel those who infringe its rules; it claims the possession of some special enlightenment; there is a high degree of lay participation; and it is hostile or indifferent to the wider society. The denomination, on the other hand, is also a voluntary society but with a more relaxed commitment and more formalised membership procedures; it emphasises tolerance, accepting it is one movement among many and not commonly expelling those who lapse; it has a professional ministry while allowing for lay participation; and it accepts the values of its society with membership tending to be

97. [John Ritchie], 'Separation in worship, but not in service', *BM*, 29 (Feb 1919), pp.22-3.

98. A[lexander]. M[arshall]., *Wandering Lights: a stricture on the doctrines and methods of Brethrenism. A review by A. M.*, 3rd edn (Glasgow, n.d.), pp.28-9.

99. This definition is sometimes used by historians, see Paul T. Phillips, *The Sectarian Spirit: sectarianism, society and politics in Victorian cotton towns* (Toronto, 1982); Tom Gallagher, *Edinburgh Divided: John Cormack and no popery in the 1930s* (Edinburgh, 1987); idem, *Glasgow: The Uneasy Peace: religious tension in modern Scotland* (Manchester, 1987); T. M. Devine (ed.), *Scotland's Shame: bigotry and sectarianism in modern Scotland* (Edinburgh, 2000).

100. Ernest Troeltsch, *The Social Teachings of the Christian Churches*, 1 (1911), Eng. trans., (New York, 1931), pp.331-43.

101. H. Richard Niebuhr, *The Social Sources of Denominationalism* (1929) New American Library edn (New York, 1975); Liston Pope, *Millhands and Preachers: a study of Gastonia* (New Haven, CT, 1942), pp.117-24; John H. Chamberlayne, 'From *sect* to *church*', in British Methodism, *BJS*, 15 (1964), pp.139-49.

102. J. Milton Yinger, *The Scientific Study of Religion* (New York, 1970), pp.266-73: this is an adaptation of an earlier work by Yinger, *Religion, Society, and the Individual: an introduction to the sociology of religion* (New York, 1957).

socially compatible.[103] The use of church-sect typology has been criticised recently by the New Testament scholar David Horrell, who sees it as potentially concealing why, for example, particular sects are hostile to secular society by appeals to it being 'typical' behaviour for this form of community. However, as Horrell recognises, Wilson's work is based on empirical studies and Wilson is alive to the danger of typologies obscuring the variety of phenomena.[104] In addition, Wilson has developed a varied typology of sects which can fit different groups, and these sect sub-types are, he has argued, of greater predictive use than the larger category of sect.[105] His theory is not a procrustean bed into which disparate groups are made to fit.

In a study of the Quakers, Elizabeth Isichei has pointed out how both sectarian attitudes and denominational attitudes may co-exist in a single group making generalisations about typical sect development difficult.[106] Scottish Brethren of different emphases have accepted that in the sociological sense, the Brethren are a sect.[107] Although the term is not entirely satisfactory because of the derogatory overtones it has in common parlance, in the present work 'sect' will be used in its neutral sociological sense for the movement; 'sectarian tendency' for, among other features, a persistent bias towards increased withdrawal from society and institutional Christianity; and 'denominationalising tendency' for those who permitted a more tolerant attitude to integration with church and society. A useful test of the presence of the last is a pragmatic approach to issues which according to David Martin is an implicit tendency of the denomination.[108] However, it should be noted that none of these terms will be applied with a predetermined meaning as if those who represented one inclination or the other were pressing for all the characteristics present in some ideal type. It is assumed that the Open Brethren are a conversionist sect marked by a literalist orthodox biblicism

103. B. R. Wilson, 'An analysis of sect development', in *idem* (ed.), *Patterns of Sectarianism*, pp.23-5.

104. David G. Horrell, *The Social Ethos of the Corinthian Correspondence: interests and ideology from 1 Corinthians to 1 Clement* (Edinburgh, 1996), pp.14-16, 287-8.

105. Wilson, 'Sect development', in *idem* (ed.) *Patterns of Sectarianism*, pp.1-2; see also *idem*, *Sects and Society: a sociological study of three religious groups in Britain* (London, 1961); *idem*, *Religion in Secular Society* (Harmondsworth, 1966); *idem*, *Religious Sects* (London, 1970); *idem*, *Religion in Sociological Perspective* (Oxford, 1982); *idem*, *The Social Dimensions of Sectarianism*.

106. Elizabeth A. Isichei, 'From sect to denomination among English Quakers', in Wilson (ed.), *Patterns of Sectarianism*, pp. 161-181.

107. Anderson, *Our Heritage*, p.47, quoted below, p.354; John Boyes, cited in Andrew Walker, *Restoring the Kingdom: the radical Christianity of the House Church Movement* (London, 1985), p.216 n.7.

108. David Martin, 'The denomination', *BJS*, 13 (1962), pp.1-14.

and a primary concentration on evangelism.[109] What precisely is meant by 'sect' and 'denomination' in discussing them will emerge from historical analysis.

Growth and decline, another of the central themes of the present work, will engage with the ever increasing literature on patterns of church growth in the nineteenth and twentieth centuries and on religion in industrial society. Until the 1970s historical orthodoxy was that the Church lost membership and influence throughout the nineteenth century and that among the working classes with increasing urbanisation this process was even more marked.[110] Wales, where working-class adherence was high, was seen as being atypical.[111] However, this view has been challenged more recently by a number of historians who have seen the churches' influence in the nineteenth century as widely diffused with continuing high levels of working-class adherence.[112] Revisionist

---

109. Wilson, 'Sect Development', in *Patterns of Sectarianism*, p.27; however, Wilson avoids categorising the Open Brethren (he rarely mentions them in his writings on sects) and he placed Peter L. Embley, 'The early development of the Plymouth Brethren', in *Patterns of Sectarianism*, pp.213-43, under introversionist sects in the contents page; this led one Open Brethren reviewer to express the hope that they were conversionist rather than introversionist: T. C. F. Stunt, 'Article review: Patterns of Sectarianism', *JCBRF*, 19 (March 1969), pp.35-9.

110. E. R. Wickham, *Church and People in an Industrial City* (London, 1957); K. S. Inglis, *Churches and the Working Classes in Victorian England* (London, 1963); Robert Currie, Alan D. Gilbert and Lee Horsley, *Churches and Churchgoers: patterns of religious growth in the British isles since 1700* (Oxford, 1977); Alan D. Gilbert, *Religion and Society in Industrial England: church, chapel and social change, 1740-1915* (London, 1976); Geoffrey Robson, 'The failure of success: working class evangelists in early Victorian Birmingham', in Derek Baker (ed.), *SCH*, 15 (Oxford, 1978), pp.381-91; David Englander, 'The Word and the world: Evangelicalism in the Victorian city', in Gerald Parsons (ed.), *Religion in Victorian Britain Volume II: controversies* (Manchester, 1988), pp.15-38; for this view among Scottish historians see, Donald J. Withrington, 'Non-church going, c.1750-c.1850: a preliminary study', *RSCHS*, 17 (1970), pp.99-113; A. Allan MacLaren, *Religion and Social Class: the Disruption years in Aberdeen* (London, 1974); Olive Checkland, *Industry and Ethos Scotland 1832-1914* (London, 1984), pp. 123-5; T. C. Smout, *A Century of the Scottish People 1830-1950* (London, 1986), pp.181-208.

111. W. R. Lambert, 'Some working-class attitudes towards organised religion in nineteenth-century Wales', in Gerald Parsons (ed.), *Religion in Victorian Britain Volume IV: interpretations* (Manchester, 1988), pp.96-114; cf. E. T. Davies, *Religion in the Industrial Revolution in South Wales* (Cardiff, 1965).

112. C. D. Field, 'The social structure of English Methodism: eighteenth - twentieth centuries', *BJS*, 28 (1977), pp.199-225; Jeffrey Cox, *English Churches in a Secular Society: Lambeth 1870-1930* (Oxford, 1982); Hugh McLeod, *Religion and the Working Classes in Nineteenth-Century Britain* (London, 1984); *idem*, 'New perspectives on Victorian working-class religion: the oral evidence', *Oral History Journal*, 14 (1986), pp.31-49; Donald M. Lewis, *Lighten Their Darkness: the evangelical mission to*

historians have also examined Scottish churches and found the same pattern.[113] Particularly significant is the work of Callum Brown who has argued that urbanisation did not lead inevitably to decline in membership and that serious reduction did not come until the 1960s.[114] The argument

working-class London (Westport, CT, 1986); Gerald Parsons, 'A question of meaning: religion and working-class life', in *idem* (ed.), *Religion in Victorian Britain Volume II: controversies* (Manchester, 1988), pp.64-87; Jeremy N. Morris, 'Church and people thirty-three years on: a historical critique', *Theology*, 94 (1991), pp.92-101; *idem*, *Religion and Urban Change: Croyden 1840-1914* (Woodbridge, 1992); Hugh McLeod, *Religion and Irreligion in Victorian England: how secular was the working class?* (Bangor, 1993); Mark Smith, *Religion in Industrial Society: Oldham and Saddleworth 1740-1865* (Oxford, 1994); Michael R. Watts, *The Dissenters. Volume II: the expansion of Evangelical Nonconformity* (Oxford, 1995); Hugh McLeod, *Religion and Society in England, 1850-1914* (Basingstoke, 1996); Gerald T. Rimmington, 'Methodism and society in Leicester, 1881-1914', *The Local Historian*, 30 (2000), pp.74-87.

113. Peter L. M. Hillis, 'Presbyterianism and social class in mid-nineteenth century Glasgow: a study of nine churches', *JEH*, 32 (1981), pp. 47-64; Callum G. Brown, *The Social History of Religion in Scotland Since 1730* (London, 1987); *idem*, 'Religion and social change', in T. M. Devine and Rosalind Mitchison (eds), *People and Society in Scotland: I 1760-1830* (Edinburgh, 1988), pp.143-62; Peter L. M. Hillis, 'Education and evangelisation: Presbyterian missions in mid-nineteenth century Glasgow', *SHR*, 66 (1989), pp.46-62; Callum G. Brown, "Each take off their several way? The Protestant churches and the working classes in Scotland', in Graham Walker and Tom Gallagher (eds), *Sermons and Battle Hymns: Protestant popular culture in modern Scotland* (Edinburgh, 1990), pp.69-85; *idem*, 'Religion, class and church growth', in W. Hamish Fraser and R. J. Morris (eds), *People and Society in Scotland: II 1830-1914* (Edinburgh, 1990), pp.310-335; *idem*, *The People in the Pews: religion and society in Scotland since 1780* (Dundee, 1993); Peter L. M. Hillis, 'The sociology of the Disruption', in Michael Fry and Stewart J. Brown (eds), *Scotland in the Age of the Disruption* (Edinburgh, 1993), pp.44-62; Callum G. Brown, *Religion and Society in Scotland since 1707* (Edinburgh, 1997); Peter Hillis, 'The 1891 membership roll of Hillhead Baptist Church', *RSCHS*, 30 (2000), pp.170-92; positive assessments of religion and the Scottish working classes can also be found in Barbara Thatcher, 'The Episcopal Church in Helensburgh in the mid-nineteenth century', in John Butt and J. T. Ward (eds), *Scottish Themes* (Edinburgh, 1976), pp.98-123; James Hutchinson, *Weavers, Miners and the Open Book: a history of Kilsyth* (Cumbernauld, 1986); and T. M. Devine, *The Scottish Nation 1700-2000* (Harmondsworth, 1999).

114. Callum G. Brown, 'Did urbanization secularize Britain?', in R. Rodger (ed.), *Urban History Yearbook 1988* (Leicester, 1988), pp.1-14; *idem*, 'Faith in the city', *History Today*, 40 (1990), pp.41-7; *idem*, 'A revisionist approach to religious change', in Steve Bruce (ed.), *Religion and Modernization: sociologists and historians debate the secularization thesis* (Oxford, 1992), pp.31-58; *idem*, 'Religion and secularisation', in Tony Dickson and James H. Treble (eds), *People and Society in Scotland: III 1914-1990* (Edinburgh, 1992), pp.48-79; *idem*, 'The mechanism of religious growth in urban societies: British cities since the eighteenth century', in Hugh McLeod (ed.), *European Religion in the Age of the Great Cities 1830-1930* (London, 1995), pp.239-62; *idem*,

looks set to continue for some time especially as it is related to a further contentious issue—the theory of secularisation.[115] The present work will seek to examine the Brethren in relation to this debate by analysing their patterns of growth and their social class. It will attempt to establish how far the movement, the largest sect in Scotland for the first half of the twentieth century, was typical of ecclesiastical bodies. In the contemporary period several studies of Scottish churches, among them the Brethren, will provide material from independent sociological perspectives.[116] There is another sense of 'growth' which is less accessible to the historian: the self-development of the individual (and here its opposite is constriction). Corporate growth can be measured through statistics but the existential dimension of people achieving their potential has no ready measure. Nevertheless, as a frequent criticism of sects is that they stifle personal fulfilment, some tentative judgements in relation to the Brethren will be attempted. The discussion here will be related to the literature on the social role of religion.[117]

The Death of Christian Britain: understanding secularisation 1800-2000 (London & New York, 2001).

115.   Owen Chadwick, *The Secularization of the European Mind in the Nineteenth Century* (Cambridge, 1975); Alan D. Gilbert, *The Making of Post-Christian Britain: a history of secularization of modern society* (London, 1980); Bruce (ed.), *Religion and Modernization*; Robin Gill, *The Myth of the Empty Church* (London, 1993); Grace Davie, *Religion in Britain since 1945: believing without belonging* (Oxford, 1994).

116.   D. R. Robertson, 'The relationship of Church and class in Scotland', in D. Martin (ed.), *A Sociological Yearbook of Religion in Britain*, 1 (London, 1968), pp.9-31; Kenneth J. Panton, 'The Church in the community: a study of patterns of religious adherence in a Scottish burgh', in Michael Hill (ed.), *A Sociological Yearbook of Religion in Britain*, 6 (1973), pp.183-206; Peter L. Sissons, *The Social Significance of Church Membership in the Burgh of Falkirk* (Edinburgh, 1973).

117.   Max Weber, *The Protestant Ethic and the Spirit of Capitalism* (1904-5), Eng. trans. 1930; rprt (London, 1992); R. H. Tawney, *Religion and the Rise of Capitalism* (1922), Penguin edn (Harmondsworth, 1975); Thompson, *English Working Class*, pp. 385-440; Robert Moore, *Pit-Men, Preachers and Politics: the effects of Methodism in a Durham mining community* (Cambridge, 1974); T. W. Laqueur, *Religion and Respectability: Sunday schools and working-class culture, 1780-1850* (New Haven, CT; 1976); R. Q. Gray, 'Religion, culture and social class in late nineteenth and early twentieth century Edinburgh', G. Crossick (ed.), *The Lower Middle Class in Britain 1870-1914* (London, 1977), pp.134-58; Gilbert, *Religion and Society*, p.87-93; Hugh McLeod, *Class and Religion in the Late Victorian City* (London, 1974); Steve Bruce, 'Social change and collective behaviour: the revival in eighteenth-century Ross-shire', *BJS*, 34 (1983), pp.554-72; J. L. Duthie, 'Philanthropy and evangelism among Aberdeen seamen, 1814-1924', *SHR*, 63 (1984), pp.155-73; Robert Colls, 'Primitive Methodists in the northern coalfields', in Jim Obelkevich et al. (eds), *Disciplines of faith: studies in religion, politics and patriarchy* (London, 1987), pp.323-34; Wayne J. Johnson, 'Piety among "The Society of People": the witness of Primitive Methodist local preachers in the North Midlands, 1812-1862', in W. J. Sheils and Diana Wood (eds), *SCH*, 26

The main principle of organisation which has been adopted is chronological. A sequence of chapters will trace the expansion and contraction of the movement and its internal development from 1838, when the first known assembly came into existence, until 2000. Chapter 2 will examine the largely Bowesite movement of the 1840s and 1850s and Chapter 3 will analyse the crucial decade which followed the 1859 Revival.[118] In these chapters growth and development will be studied in conjunction with each other. The period of greatest increase for the movement was the late Victorian period, and Chapter 4 will analyse contraction and expansion until the outbreak of World War I. The Brethren were in their most developed form in the inter-war period and this phase had an after-life until the mid-1960s. Chapter 6 will examine patterns of growth and decline from 1914 until 1965 with, in addition, an investigation of the ethos of the movement when it was in its mature form. Complementary to Chapters 4 and 6 are Chapters 5 and 7 in which the internal development of the movement will be examined for the respective periods. The classic era of the Brethren might be said to have ceased in the mid-1960s. Chapter 8 will be devoted to an investigation of the spirituality of the movement from the 1830s until that decade and Chapter 9 to the relationship of the Brethren to culture and society for the same period. Chapter 10 is a coda which will recapitulate the topics of the previous chapters through exploring the movement from the mid-1960s until the end of the twentieth century, examining internal development and changes in membership size, spirituality, and attitudes to culture and society. The conclusion, Chapter 11, will attempt to draw together the central themes—integration and withdrawal, continuity and change, growth and decline—and arrive at some assessment.

(Oxford, 1989), pp.323-34; John Coffey, 'Democracy and popular religion: Moody and Sankey's mission to Britain, 1873-1875', in Eugenio F. Biagini (ed.), *Citizenship and Democracy: Liberals, radicals and collective identities in the British Isles, 1865-1931* (Cambridge, 1996), pp.93-119.

118. It should be noted that, as will become apparent in Chapter 2, John Bowes would have been appalled by the name 'Bowesite', but it is used in the present work as a convenient way of distinguishing churches in which his influence was stronger from those more clearly in the Bristol tradition.

CHAPTER TWO

The Name of Christ Alone: Growth and Development 1838-1858

'At Dundee, Liverpool, Arbroath, Aberdeen and many other places in England, Ireland and Scotland, Switzerland, and the East and West Indies, believers may be found who meet, not in the name of man or sect, but in the name of Christ alone.'
John Bowes, *The Christian Magazine and Herald of Union*, 1 (1842), p.11.

In 1828 Benjamin Wills Newton, having attained earlier in the year a first in classics from the University of Oxford, toured Scotland, casting a rigorous eye on its churches.[1] At Oxford Newton was one of a number of individuals who had adopted Calvinism, among them his friend Henry Bulteel, an Anglican curate,[2] and Newton had come to favour a message of individual salvation.[3] He claimed that after visiting about a hundred Scottish churches he had found only two individuals with 'the sort of Gospel that Bulteel delivered'. This state of affairs he blamed on the absorption of the Church in social and political matters, a fault that he felt had persisted since the Reformation. The prominent Congregationalist Ralph Wardlaw, Newton alleged, 'I found not to have the Gospel', while even Thomas Chalmers was accused of being 'more interested in parish matters and poor law'. Newton felt the Scots 'despised England while',

---

1. For Newton see *BDEB*, 2, pp.822-3; Jonathan David Burnham, 'The Controversial Relationship between Benjamin Wills Newton and John Nelson Darby' (University of Oxford D.Phil. thesis, 1999): due to university regulations Newton did not graduate until 1829.

2. T. C. F. Stunt, *From Awakening to Secession: radical evangelicals in Switzerland and Britain 1815-35* (Edinburgh, 2000), pp.194-200.

3. Cf. CBA 7049, Fry MS, Benjamin Newton to Joseph Treffry, 15 August 1828, pp.148-151: this letter, written to an uncle, shows what Newton considered 'the Gospel' during this period; he gave a 'statement of my religious sentiments—at least those which are considered peculiar and these are the total depravity of mankind and the necessity of regeneration by the sovereign influence of the Holy Spirit.'

he asserted, 'there is more Gospel in Oxford and Cambridge'.[4] Newton was representative of the new forces, adumbrated in many respects by the Haldanes, which in the 1820s had begun to make themselves felt in Evangelicalism.[5] Shortly after his Scottish tour Newton was to become a seminal figure in the English Brethren movement, but he had clearly found the Scottish Church out of sympathy with his developing ideas. Another later Brethren leader, Henry Craik, a native of Prestonpans who left Scotland in 1826 upon graduation from St Andrews University, was also to claim that it was not until he went to Exeter and met Anthony Norris Groves, who was then developing ideas which would lead to the forming of the Brethren in Dublin, 'that the Lord taught me those lessons of dependence on Himself and of catholic fellowship, which I have sought to carry out.'[6]

However despite the experience of Newton and Craik, the religious life of Scotland was changing in a manner which would favour the growth of the Brethren. Developments, especially among non-Presbyterian dissenting bodies, were conducive to the formation of assemblies. Presbyterianism itself was also touched by change, as will become apparent through the discussion of James Morison in the present chapter, and many of those influenced by the new currents found the older church life wanting.[7] The discussion below will trace the movements in

---

4. *Ibid.*, p.145, 'B. W. N. in Scotland'. The Fry MS contains a transcript of Newton's journals and the account of the visit to Scotland was left undated by him. The editor, however, dated it as 1828 because of the existence of a letter from Scotland in that year. Elsewhere in his journal (pp.146-8) Newton states he was in Scotland in 1828. The two individuals who met Newton's approval were 'Hamilton of Strathcarn' (probably William Hamilton of Strathblane was intended) and an anonymous preacher near John o' Groats House.

5. D. W. Bebbington, *Evangelicalism in Modern Britain* (London 1989), pp.75-86.

6. Quoted in G. H. Lang, *Anthony Norris Groves: saint and pioneer* (London, 1939), p.20; for Craik's Scottish background, see, W. Elfe Tayler, *Passages from the Diary and Letters of Henry Craik of Bristol* (London, 1866), pp.6-10; Stuart Piggin and John Roxborogh, *The St Andrews Seven* (Edinburgh, 1985); *DSCHT*, p.222; *BDEB*, 1, p.266, i.

7. Among the leaders of new theological thought, John McLeod Campbell and Thomas Erskine of Linlathen were in touch with G. V. Wigram, one of the leaders among English Brethren (F. Roy Coad, *A History of the Brethren Movement: its origins, its worldwide development and its significance for the present day*, 2nd edn [Exeter, 1976], p.60). Erskine was critical of the Brethren (*Letters of Thomas Erskine of Linlathen* (Edinburgh, 1878), William Hanna (ed.), pp.382-6), but more sympathetic for a while was A. J. Scott, the theologian and educationalist, who edited Groves' journal (*Journal of a Residence at Bagdad, during the Years 1830 and 1831 by Mr. Anthony N. Groves, Missionary* (London, 1832), A. J. Scott (ed.); Scott may also have edited Groves's earlier journal for 1829-30). Also Horatius Bonar noted that he was 'on most brotherly terms'

the Scottish churches and factors within society which were of
significance for the emergence of the Brethren. Two are of particular
importance. One was what Nathan Hatch has called in an American
context the democratisation of Christianity. Hatch saw this process as
being marked by the rejection of traditional orthodoxies and of the
clergy as a separate caste; the empowering of ordinary people by taking
their spiritual experiences seriously without subjecting them to
theological scrutiny; and dreams of power to change things for the
better.[8] The second process which is of significance was a new phase of
revivalism that was urban, anti-institutional and nondenominational and
which mobilised the laity, softening, as it progressed, the scholastic
Calvinism of Scotland.[9] Hatch depicted the conjunction of 'evangelical
fervour and popular sovereignty' as having a deep impact on American
society.[10] He saw English Christianity as being handicapped by gentility
and compromised by the establishment, but *pace* Hatch, the trends he was
examining also had considerable effect on nineteenth-century Britain,
one of their consequences being the spread of Brethrenism.[11] After
examining the emergence of the Brethren within Scotland, the present
chapter will trace their growth and the cohesion of the still precarious
movement in the decades before the revivals of 1859-60.

Edinburgh Beginnings

Ten years after Newton, John Nelson Darby had quite a different
experience of Scotland. Darby, who had become the Brethren leader with
the greatest influence due to his itinerancy in the United Kingdom and in
continental Europe,[12] reported in 1838 that 'I am invited this week to

with several Exclusive Brethren, evidently partly because of a shared interest in
millennialism, Horatius Bonar to B. W. Newton, 24 December 1859, Fry MS, pp.17-18.

8. Nathan O. Hatch, *The Democratization of American Christianity* (New Haven, CT, 1989), pp.9-11.

9. For this revivalism see: Richard Carwardine, *Transatlantic Revivalism: popular Evangelicalism in Britain and America, 1790-1865* (Westport, CT, 1978); John Kent, *Holding the Fort: studies in Victorian revivalism* (London, 1978); *DSCHT*, p.715, i; Janice Holmes, *Religious Revivals in Britain and Ireland 1859-1905* (Dublin, 2000).

10. Hatch, *Democratization*, p.9.

11. *Ibid.*, pp.5, 8; however, this is to ignore churches such as the Primitive Methodists, the spread across the Atlantic of some of the groups discussed by Hatch, and some of the movements surveyed in the present chapter.

12. On Darby see, W. G. Turner, *John Nelson Darby: a biography* (London, 1926); Max S. Weremchuk, *John Nelson Darby* (1988) Eng. edn (Neptune, NJ, 1992); *BDEB*, 1, pp.290-1; *NDNB*.

Edinburgh, where thirty-six are gathered together.'[13] This church, Darby discovered, had been in existence for some years and it had evidently seceded from a larger body for he referred to it in a letter to Swiss correspondents as being 'a small fragment of a flock'.[14] There had been a second, more recent split because the majority of the church had wanted to receive only those baptised as believers and also, according to Darby, they had denied the influence of the Holy Spirit in conversion. The rationalism evident in its pneumatology and the arguments over the relationship of believer's baptism to membership, suggest that the congregation might have originated among the Scotch Baptists. In the 1830s this body was divided over the issue of admission to communion, and certainly their practice of exhortation from among the members would have made absorption into the Brethren easier.[15] However, the controversy over the Holy Spirit suggests that there may have been an infusion of ideas emanating from Alexander Campbell, the founder of the Churches of Christ, then new to Britain and which were attracting Scotch Baptists.[16]

The small group of seceders which invited Darby to Edinburgh had held the minority view in the recent troubles. He taught them his eschatology, which demanded that true believers should separate from the professing Church to await the imminent return of Christ, and he emphasised the need for an entire dependence on the Holy Spirit which would, he felt, lead to unity among Christians. There was in Scotland, Darby stated:

> an ardent desire on the part of several to find something more spiritual, more devoted and a complete denial of the world, 'this evil generation', an idea of denial too little known in Scotland, despite the great profession of religion.[17]

---

13. J. N. Darby to Genevan Christians, in [*idem*], *Letters of J. N. D.*, 3 (London, n.d.), p.234; the letter is in an appendix to the collected letters with a note at the end: 'Hereford (not before 1837)'. The letter is given in its original French in *MÉ* (1971), pp. 122-9, where it has an introductory note stating: '*addressée de Hereford aux frères de Géneré, vraisemblablement en 1838.*' However, a letter dated 1838 is extant which was written from Edinburgh immediately after Darby first made contact with the church (see below n. 14). I am grateful to Dr T. C. F. Stunt for the references to *MÉ*.

14. J. N. Darby to A. M. Foluquier, 6 Octobre 1838 (Commencée en septembre), 'Lettres de J. N. D.', *MÉ* (1897), p.294: '*un petit fragment d'un tropeau*'; I am indebted to Mr Joe Adrain for the translations from Darby's French.

15. D. B. Murray, 'The Scotch Baptist tradition in Great Britain', *BQ*, 33 (1989), pp.186-98.

16. David Thompson, *Let Sects and Parties Fall: a short history of the Association of Churches of Christ in Great Britain and Ireland* (Birmingham, 1980), pp.13-32.

17. Darby, '*Lettres*', p.294: '*un désir ardent de la part de plusieurs de trouver quelque chose de plus spirituel, de plus dévoué, et un renoncement plus complet au monde, <<ce*

It is likely, given the enthusiasm with which Darby wrote of the encounter, that he was successful in winning the Edinburgh church to his views. Two women with Scottish aristocratic connections were also attracted to the Brethren in this period. Caroline Margaret Douglas, the Marchioness of Queensberry, wife of the 7th Marquis, became a member of the movement. Like many contemporary women of her class, she engaged in philanthropic work, helping in missions among prostitutes.[18] In addition, Mrs Isabella Hutchinson, the daughter of Lord Cunningham and wife of an army colonel, also joined the movement. Both women were certainly active in Edinburgh,[19] and an assembly seemingly existed there for a while at least.[20] But it is unlikely that the majority of the new assembly came from the same social strata as these two women, for part of the attraction of the Brethren for the upper classes was their classless simplicity. Much to the annoyance of the Marquis of Queensberry, his wife withdrew from court where he held an important position, and was known in the Brethren as plain 'sister'. In Edinburgh, in all probability, most of the members were of classes lower than hers.

Methodist Developments

Trends in Scottish Methodism had greater significance for Brethren growth. From its inception Methodism had encouraged the use of local lay preachers and appealed to and produced self-directed individuals who desired autonomy. A reaction in the nineteenth century against a more rigid connexionalism and a corresponding move towards independency made several Methodists open to accepting Brethren ecclesiology. The principal individual for Brethren growth in Scotland in this period was John Bowes and as his career typifies the contemporary democratisation of Christianity, it is worth tracing in some detail. Born in 1802, a farmer's son from Swineside, a remote upland hamlet in Coverdale on the north Yorkshire moors, some of the robust individualism of the area was apparent in him. His father had embraced Wesleyan Methodism, but Bowes, one of whose heroes was the revivalist William Bramwell, was attracted to Primitive Methodism because it was winning larger numbers

---

siècle mauvais,>> idée trop peu connue en Écosse, quoi-qu'il ait grande profession de religion.'

18. CBA 7049, Fry MS, pp.152-3; *BDEB*, 2, p. 909, i.

19. CBA 7049, Fry MS, p.153; Thomas Croskery, 'The Plymouth Brethren', *The Presbyterian Quarterly and the Princeton Review* (New Series), 1 (1872), p.48; W. G. Gorman (ed.), *Converts to Rome* (London 1910), p.227: I am indebted to Dr T. C. F. Stunt for these references.

20. See below, p.48.

of converts than the older, parent body.[21] Primitive Methodism was strongly revivalist in character, believing that ecstatic awakenings were the essence of original Methodism and in addition it appealed to those looking for greater democracy in church affairs.[22] Bowes became a circuit preacher with them and was involved in their revivals and camp meetings in Yorkshire in which there was participation from among those attending.[23] A Primitive Methodist mission had been established in Edinburgh by the Sunderland circuit in 1826, and it achieved early success.[24] It was soon in trouble, however, when Nathaniel West, one of the missionaries, seceded, taking most of the members with him. Bowes was sent north in 1827 in an attempt to reclaim West. But once in Edinburgh, Bowes sided with him, and he also found himself in disagreement with the formally recognised missionary, Thomas Oliver, with the result that Bowes too was taken off his circuit. He quickly decided, however, that West was a tyrant and parted company with him.[25]

Scottish Methodism was in disarray. The problems that were troubling the Edinburgh mission were found throughout the denomination during this period. Senior figures in Wesleyan Methodism had doubts about the validity of the Scottish enterprise, believing that it was too costly for the limited success which it had achieved.[26] Strong-minded preachers, remote from central control, were often inclined to adopt the Scottish preference for a settled ministry called by a congregation rather than having preachers imposed and withdrawn at will by their circuits. This was coupled with a move towards a form of Congregationalist independency, an issue that was agitating the whole Methodist body. Jabez Bunting, the

21. John Bowes, *The Autobiography: or the history of the life of John Bowes* (Glasgow, 1872), pp.1-12; *DNB*, 2, pp.966-7.

22. Wayne J. Johnson, 'Piety among "The Society of People": the witness of Primitive Methodist local preachers in the North Midlands, 1812-1862', in W. J. Sheils and Diana Wood (eds), *SCH*, 26 (Oxford, 1989), p.344; Robert Colls, 'Primitive Methodists in the northern coalfields', in Jim Obelkevich *et al.*, *Disciplines of Faith: studies in religion, politics and paternity* (London, 1987), pp.323-34.

23. J. Bowes, 'On the work of God in Keighley Circuit, Yorkshire', *Primitive Methodist Magazine*, July 1826, pp.242-9.

24. H. Bickerstaffe Kendall, *The Origin and History of the Primitive Methodist Church*, 2 (London, 1906), pp.206-8; A. Skevington Wood, 'Methodism in Scotland', in Rupert Davies, A. Raymond George and Gordon Rupp (eds.), *A History of the Methodist Church in Great Britain*, 3 (London, 1983), pp.272-3.

25. Bowes, *Autobiography*, p.55; cf. the account of this incident in George Herod, *Biographical Sketches of some of those Preachers whose Labours Contributed to the Origination and Early Extension of the Primitive Methodist Connexion* (London, n.d.), pp.326-8 n., and Bowes's response, 'The attack of Geo. Herod (Primitive Methodist preacher) on J. Bowes, and his reply', *TP*, 6 (1858-9), pp.89-92.

26. Wesley F. Swift, *Methodism in Scotland: the First Hundred Years* (London, 1947), p.70.

most influential figure in Wesleyan Methodism in the first half of the
nineteenth century, wanted to centralise authority in the London-based
Conference. He had a more exalted conception of the role of the pastor,
wishing to concentrate the government of the congregation in his hands.
Methodism was being institutionalised, and Bunting and his supporters
were turning it from being a loose aggregation of societies into a tightly
disciplined denomination.[27] The price it had to pay was a number of
secessions by the supporters of what came to be known as Free
Methodism. Its exponents had what has been described as 'an essentially
local, lay perspective', wanting a weaker central authority and the
government of the church to reside in the entire congregation.[28] The
collapse of the work, the arguments over Methodist polity and many local
disagreements produced a number of dissidents throughout the country.
It was a period of contraction for Methodists in Scotland.[29]

Bowes, as a supporter of a more democratic church order, was among
the dissidents. In a letter to the anti-Bunting *Christian Advocate* in 1836
he deplored 'the usurping domination' of the conferences in the three
main Methodist bodies—Wesleyan, New Connexion and Primitive
Methodism. The decisions of their conferences, he felt, were promulgated
as laws which were replacing scripture.[30] The schisms in Edinburgh had
left Bowes in charge of two congregations in Edinburgh and Leith. He
was deeply impressed by his reading of Peter King's *An Enquiry into the
Constitution Discipline Unity and Worship of the Primitive Church* (2nd
edn 1713). King, an early eighteenth-century Lord Chancellor, had
intended it to promote understanding of dissenters.[31] He had been
accused of supporting Presbyterianism when the work was published, and
it is likely that what attracted Bowes was his appeal for the unity of all
Christians based on an acceptance of the diversity of rites. Bowes assisted
in the formation of a new body entitled the Christian Mission and in

---

27. John H. Chamberlayne, 'From *sect* to *church* in British Methodism', *BJS*, 15
(1964), pp.139-49.

28. A. J. Hayes and D. A. Gowland (eds), *Scottish Methodism in the Early Victorian
Period: the Scottish Correspondence of the Rev. Jabez Bunting* (Edinburgh, 1981), pp.9-
14; W. R. Ward, 'Scottish Methodism in the age of Jabez Bunting', *RSCHS*, 20 (1979)
pp.17-63; D. A. Gowland, *Methodist Secessions* (Manchester, 1979).

29. Oliver A. Beckerlegge, 'In search of forgotten Methodism', *PWHS*, 29 (1954),
pp.160-1.

30. John Bowes to the *Christian Advocate*, 7 November 1836, quoted in *idem*,
Autobiography, pp.162-3.

31. [Peter King], *An Enquiry into the Constitution, Discipline, Unity and Worship of
the Primitive Church, That Flourish'd within the first Three Hundred years after Christ.
Faithfully Collected out of the Extant Writings of these Ages. By an Impartial Hand*, 2nd
edn (London, 1713); the work was published anonymously in 1691 being subsequently
revised by Lord King in 1712 and 1713: *DNB*, 11, pp.144-7.

1830 he went to Dundee to be pastor of its congregation there. At his
induction there were ministers present from Aberdeen, Perth, Kirkcaldy,
and Newburgh, Fife.[32] The Christian Mission leaders were independents
in ecclesiology, accepted a charismatic rather than a trained ministry, held
that congregations should call their own pastor, and professed anti-
sectarianism. The Methodist historian Oliver Beckerlegge has linked the
rise of Free Methodism to contemporary voluntaryism, the movement
taking root among several Scottish dissenting bodies, which was opposed
to state religion and held that churches should be supported by voluntary
contributions only.[33] Both Congregationalism and voluntaryism appealed
to individuals with desires for self-determination and those who were
economically independent.[34] They were part of wider social and political
longings for greater autonomy among the working and middle classes.[35]
The emergence of the Christian Mission, largely in weaving and textile
communities, was one more group which expressed this spirit.

Hugh Hart, the Aberdeen minister present at Bowes's induction to the
Dundee church, typified the advancement of working-class interests in
the Christian Mission. Hart shared the anti-sectarian emphasis of Bowes
and his writings were undertaken to promote Christian unity.[36] He had
been a Wesleyan Methodist in Paisley, but had turned to Congregationalism before becoming minister in 1825 of a church in
Aberdeen which had seceded from the Relief Church.[37] A flamboyant
individualist, whose speculations on the Trinity led to accusations of

---

32. *Ibid.*, p.91.

33. Oliver A. Beckerlegge, 'Early Methodism in Paisley', *PWHS*, 29 (1953), pp.76-
83.

34. Callum G. Brown, *The Social History of Religion in Scotland* (London, 1987),
pp.41,43.

35. Cf., Harry Escott, *A History of Scottish Congregationalism* (Glasgow, 1960),
pp.105-6; Hayes and Gowland (eds.), *Scottish Methodism*, pp.11-13.

36. Hugh Hart, *A Diversity of Theological Subjects scripturally stated, illustrated, and
defended; calculated under the benediction of the Great Head of the Church amicably to
compose the religious differences existing among biblical Christians, and respectfully
designed not only as a Compendium of Faith to assist in repairing the breaches
occasioned by schism, in the organic walls of the Militant Jerusalem, but also as an
assistant to ministers and students in their theological pursuits* (Aberdeen, 1833); *idem,
An Outline and a Defence of Consultative Presbyterian Government designed to assist in
repairing the disciplinary breaches, and building up the organic walls of the militant
Jerusalem to which is subjoined, an epitome of the faith of the members constituting the
churches in fellowship with the Original United Relief Association* (Aberdeen, 1833).

37. 'The Late Rev. Hugh Hart, minister of Zion Chapel, Aberdeen', in John Hunter,
*Funeral Sermon for the late Rev. Hugh Hart pastor of Zion Chapel, Aberdeen, preached on
Lord's Day May 4, 1862* (Aberdeen, 1862), pp.14-6; Alexander Gammie, *The Churches of
Aberdeen* (Aberdeen, 1909), gives 1823 as the date of Hart's induction to Aberdeen.

heterodoxy,[38] his congregation was composed of sailors, weavers and factory girls. Although he was spurned by most of the city's ministers, he was popular among the working classes,[39] and John Bowes claimed that when he preached for Hart it was to 'vast congregations'.[40] Part of Hart's attraction was his enfranchisement of these classes, for he practised what he called 'Consultative Presbyterianism', a mixture of Congregationalist and Presbyterian ecclesiology. He habitually prayed that the labouring classes might have 'adequate renumeration for their labour'.[41]

Bowes dreamt of a new age in which the world would be transformed. A magazine had been founded in 1831 and shortly after this the title United Christian Churches, suggested by Bowes's reading of the Puritan John Howe, had been adopted.[42] In 1834 he broke with Hart because Bowes alleged that Hart practised an impure communion by receiving those who were not true believers to the Lord's table, probably because in that year Hart had apparently accepted Swedenborgians.[43] Nevertheless, the problems of Christian unity were uppermost in Bowes's mind. He wrote his first book, *Christian Union* (1835), lamenting the evils of division, and arguing for a unity of Christians based on essential matters of faith and practice and against tests of membership based on non-essentials. Bowes had great expectations of such a union and in its *Epitome of Faith* (1835) the United Christian Churches gave it an eschatological dimension, asserting that the unity of all true Christians in

38. Aliquis [i.e. William Henderson], *Letters Philological, Theological and Harmonological addressed to Hugh Hart, minister of Shiprow Chapel on his embracing and Preaching the Sabellian Heresy* (Aberdeen, 1838); cf. Hugh Hart, *idem, A Dissertation Theological and Philological in which the doctrine of the Holy Trinity is scripturally stated, illustrated, and defended* (Aberdeen, 1834); *idem, William Henderson, A. M. Rebuked for the ignorance, impudence, misrepresentation, and falsehood, contained in a pamphlet entitled 'Letters to Hugh Hart', and published under his authority* (Aberdeen, 1840).
39. Gammie, *Churches of Aberdeen*, pp.376-8.
40. Bowes, *Autobiography*, p.134.
41. James Riddell, *Aberdeen and its Folk* (Aberdeen, 1868), p.76; cf., the discussion of Hart in A. Allan McLaren, *Religion and Social Class: the Disruption years in Aberdeen* (London, 1974), pp.195-6.
42. John Bowes, *Christian Union: showing the importance of unity among real Christians of all denominations, and the means by which it may be effected* (Edinburgh, 1835), p.171.
43. Bowes, *Autobiography*, p.134; Archibald MacWhirter, 'The Church of the New Jerusalem in Scotland', *RSCHS*, 12 (1956), pp.202-19; for Bowes's attitude to Swedenborgianism, see Woodville Woodman and John Bowes, *Report of a Public Discussion between the Rev. Woodville Woodman and Mr John Bowes on the Doctrines of the New Jerusalem Church concerning Heaven and Hell, the Trinity, Justification, and the Resurrection* (Bolton, 1858). After the split with Bowes, Hart retained the name United Christian Church.

both love and name would lead to the conversion of the world.[44] They had congregations in Dundee, Edinburgh, Newburgh, Dalbeattie and Castle Douglas.[45] Rapprochement was attempted with two Free Methodist bodies, first in 1835 with the Protestant Methodists and then the following year with the United Methodist Churches of Scotland.[46] These overtures came to nothing: in the former case because the English body was unwilling to relinquish the title 'Methodist' and in the latter because Bowes and his churches insisted that Calvinist ministers should be admitted to communion and be allowed to preach.[47] But the difficulty for Bowes was finding a church which would include true believers only, yet which would not exclude any. He next turned his attention back to England to attempt uniting all Christian churches throughout Britain. Although his congregation in Dundee was growing rapidly and had begun an expensive building project, he moved south to Liverpool in 1837 where he joined Robert Aitken, a former Epsicopalian curate, but then an immensely popular freelance revivalist who had his own two chapels in the city. The move was a disaster, for Aitken was a domineering individualist, an eccentric who later returned to Anglicanism, combining High Church views with a revivalist Evangelicalism.[48] The two men became embroiled in a lengthy power struggle and after an unseemly and litigious dispute, Bowes found himself alone, in charge of a chapel in Liverpool with all his schemes for union having failed.

Finally in 1839 Bowes found a church order which gave expression to many of his concerns yet which left him as a free agent. Bowes was also part of the contemporary search for Christian primitivism—a primary concern of the early Brethren—which challenged established structures.[49] He underwent believer's baptism in 1839 after being challenged to read

44. 'An Epitome of the Faith, and an Outline of the Essential Principles of the United Christian Churches' (1835), in Bowes, *Christian Union*, Appendix C, pp.307-10.

45. Bowes, *Autobiography*, pp.156-7.

46. For these bodies see: A. N. Cass, 'Developments in Dundee Methodism, 1830-1870', *Journal of the Scottish Branch of the Wesley Historical Society*, 2 (1973), pp.3-7; A. J. Hayes, 'A Warrenite Secession in Edinburgh', *ibid.*, 10 (1977), pp.3-18, and, 11 (1978), pp.3-6; Beckerlegge, 'Methodism in Paisley', pp.98-100; *idem, The United Methodist Free Churches* (London, 1957), pp.72-3, 77.

47. Bowes, *Autobiography*, pp.125-7, 157.

48. Charlotte E. Woods (ed.), *Memoirs and Letters of Canon Hay Aitken with an introductory memoir of his father by the Rev. Robert Aitken of Pendeen* (London, 1928), pp.15-46; *BDEB*, 1, p.6; Malcolm R. Thorp, 'Popular preaching and millennial expectations: the Reverend Robert Aitken and the Christian Society, 1836-40', in Malcolm Chase and Ian Dyck (eds), *Living and Learning: essays in honour of J. F. C Harrison* (Aldershot, 1996), pp.103-117.

49. James Patrick Callahan, *Primitivist Piety: the ecclesiology of the early Plymouth Brethren* (Lanham, MD, 1996).

the Bible on the subject. Although he was invited to join a Baptist church, his unsectarian principles would not allow him to become a member. Bowes heard in 1839 of Henry Craik, by now established as a Brethren leader in Bristol, whose principles seemed to agree with his.[50] He wrote to Craik, and among the books Craik sent Bowes with his reply was the autobiography of his associate, George Müller. Bowes proceeded to give up his salary and to adopt the 'living by faith' advocated by Müller: that Christian workers should not make their needs known but rely on freewill giving to supply finance.[51] Bowes journeyed south in September 1839 to investigate the new movement. He was impressed with what he saw, and he found that Craik agreed with him about Christian unity.[52] On his return to Liverpool Bowes instituted a weekly breaking of bread, and early next year he toured the assemblies in Exeter, Plymouth, Barnstaple, and London, meeting most of the early leaders including Newton and J. L. Harris in Plymouth and R. C. Chapman at Barnstaple. Relationships with the exacting Newton were strained. He was unhappy with Bowes's postmillennial eschatology, his Wesleyan Arminianism, and the freedom with which he associated with other churches. Bowes for his part came away with the feeling that 'the brethren in Exeter and Plymouth are Sectarian in withdrawing from all intercourse with the Saints in the Sects.'[53] Despite the reservations, however, his ecclesiastical pilgrimage was at an end.

Although Bowes enjoyed good relations with Craik and Müller, there had been frictions at Bristol as well as at Exeter and Plymouth. Partly this was due to Bowes's personality. He possessed an unfailing sense of the rightness of his own principles which was at once his greatest strength and his greatest weakness. Lacking a sense of humour, he was frequently obstinate and vain.[54] He was a tireless and often tactless controversialist.

---

50. This was possibly through Peter G. Anderson, who had pastored the United Christian Church in Newburgh, Fife, and who had moved to Liverpool and then Birmingham where he became the founder of a Brethren assembly: Bowes, *Autobiography*, pp.218, 228-9; 'P. G. Anderson', *W*, 37 (1907), p.123; W. A., 'P. G. Anderson', in Hy Pickering (ed.), *Chief Men Among the Brethren*, 2nd edn (London, 1931), pp.35-6; however, as Anderson did not commence the Birmingham assembly until 14 December 1839 (*The Witness* obituary mistakenly gives 1838), more probably it was Bowes who influenced Anderson.

51. For this practice, see: Harold H. Rowdon, 'The concept of "living by faith"', in Antony Billington, Tony Lane, Max Turner (eds), *Mission and Meaning: essays presented to Peter Cotterell* (Carlisle, 1995), pp.339-56; Timothy Larsen, '"Living by faith": a short history of Brethren practice', *BAHNR*, 1 (1997-8), pp.67-102.

52. Bowes, *Autobiography*, pp.211-232.

53. *Ibid.*, pp.233-6.

54. For critics of Bowes see: Dundee City Library, Lamb Collection, Box 398, 'Newspaper Cuttings, Biographical Notices of Dundee Men', pp.51-8; G. Joseph Holyoake, *The History of Co-operation in England: its literature and its advocates*, 1,

He wrote letters to the youthful C. H. Spurgeon (suggesting how he could improve his preaching), to the Prime Minister, Lord John Russell (asking for an end to paper tax), Her Majesty's ministers (accusing them of 'murder and treason' in licensing alcohol), and, in 1853, the Czar of Russia ('wishing you a better state of mind and heart, for the sake of suffering humanity').[55] He even managed to offend the eirenic George Müller. He had found superior intellects and strong personalities in the Brethren leaders whom he had met, and he subsequently visited Bristol only once. Bowes's robust individualism made it difficult for him to coexist in any body alongside other leaders. The Brethren, however, gave him the perfect structure. The rock his earlier attempts at unity had foundered on was the need to form a Methodist-style connexion. The complete autonomy of Brethren congregations now meant that he could be an independent force among a loosely connected circle of churches.

Bowes commenced spreading his new principles. He revisited the Dundee chapel and began a weekly breaking of bread.[56] Apart from this congregation, it would appear that the United Christian Churches had dissolved after Bowes moved to Liverpool, at the mercy of divisive forces.[57] He was still in contact with the United Methodist Churches of Scotland and various individuals in Edinburgh, Glasgow and elsewhere who were discontented with the state of their churches. In Arbroath (see Map 6) there were three main causes of discontent: the ministers encouraged the consumption of alcohol, the gifts of the Spirit were 'shut up to the one-man ministry', and the divisions of Christianity were unscriptural. In 1841, at the instigation of Bowes, thirteen individuals began breaking bread independently.[58] That same year he accepted an invitation to go to Aberdeen where he addressed large crowds. In July Bowes and ten others began breaking bread, although some of those who had initially intended joining wished to retain their church membership. A period of ecstatic revivalism followed with outbursts of weeping and conversions. The new congregation grew rapidly and Bowes settled in the

---

2nd edn (London, 1875-77), pp.326-7; and [Joseph Barker], 'Note', *The Christian*, 1 (1844), pp.165-6.

55. 'Letter to Mr. Spurgeon', *TP*, 4 (1855-7), pp.257-9; 'To Lord John Russell', *TP*, 1 (1849-51), p.209; 'The murder and treason of Her Majesty's ministers', *TP*, 5 (1856-8), pp.281-3; John Bowes to the Czar or Emperor of Russia, 6 December 1853, quoted in Bowes, *Autobiography*, pp.516-18.

56. *Ibid.*, p.274.

57. *Ibid.*, Appendix A, p.209 reported a schism in the United Christian Church in Edinburgh in 1838.

58. *Ibid.*, p.274.

city to teach the young church which met in Loch Street (see Map 5 inset).[59]

He was aware that the movement he was now part of was growing. A passionate believer in the power of print,[60] in November 1842 he marked the new phase by founding the *Christian Magazine and Herald of Union*, 'to oppose corrupt denominations', to teach his ecclesiology, and to promote his views on war and temperance.[61] He also wrote a tract, *A Hired Ministry Unscriptural* (c.1843), holding up as an example to the Christian world those Brethren leaders who were former clergymen, and also the Quakers and the Scotch Baptists who, through having no 'hired ministry', were able to provide for the poor.[62] Bowes claimed that those ministers he had worked with—Nathaniel West, Hugh Hart, Robert Aitken—had 'caused him intense mental agony',[63] but the strain of anti-clericalism present in his background was probably a more significant factor in the formation of his views. He now argued that not only was a salaried minister a burden to the people, but the minister himself was fettered by the doctrines of his church.[64] Part of the attraction of the Brethren for Bowes was that, bound only by scripture, he could pursue his own course.

The democratisation of Christianity detected by Hatch was strong in Bowes's thought. He looked for a transfigured social order and adopted several causes which had radical political implications. He became a pacifist, was an opponent of slavery, and took an active part in the movement to shorten factory hours.[65] He had a concern for the welfare of the working classes and the poor, among whom he was genuinely popular, maintaining in 1850 that the 'first duty of the church was to provide for the poor and then preach the gospel.'[66] He proposed redistributing land so that every family had fourteen acres, a response to poverty which had been part of radical politics since the Spencean Thomas Evans wrote his *Christian Policy* (2nd edn 1816).[67] Evans had

---

59. *Ibid.*, pp.282-300; Bowes used the word 'church' initially, but he later adopted 'assembly', cf. John Bowes, 'Preface', in *The New Testament translated from the purest Greek* (Dundee, 1870), [p.ii]; the vocabulary in the present chapter reflects this more flexible terminology.

60. Cf. Hatch, *Democratization*, p.11.

61. [John Bowes], 'Prospectus', *CMHU*, 1 (1842), pp.1-3.

62. John Bowes, *A Hired Ministry Unscriptural* (Manchester [c.1843]), pp.17, 23.

63. Bowes, *Autobiography*, p.299.

64. Bowes, *A Hired Ministry*, pp.22-3.

65. 'Dundee Men', p.52.

66. [John Bowes], 'The hired ministry. Public meeting at Preston', *TP*, 1 (1849-51), p.26.

67. Thomas Evans, *Christian Policy, the Salvation of Empire: being a clear and concise examination into the causes that have produced the impending, unavoidable*

supported these ideas from the Old Testament laws of jubilee and Bowes appealed to the same source—as did others such as Feargus O'Connor. Restitution for the large landowners scarcely troubled Bowes because he felt they were beneficiaries from centuries of injustice. Instead he saw his scheme as abolishing poverty and its effects, while relieving the unhygienic squalor of the urban poor.[68] In the manner of Evans, he calculated the huge cost of maintaining an army and clergymen and urged government retrenchment.[69]

Primitive Methodism gave the Chartist movement a number of its leaders, and although Bowes disapproved of the methods of Chartism, he shared a set of social attitudes and assumptions with its adherents.[70] His location of the production of wealth in the labourer and his demand for a more equitable distribution of the nation's resources owe much to widespread artisan aspirations. His proposals for the redistribution of land were made after O'Connor's landplan had collapsed in 1847,[71] and they were evidently meant to supplant the latter's scheme. Likewise the establishment of both a day and night school attached to the church in Aberdeen rivalled Chartist institutions.[72] Not only did he have his search for primitive Christianity in common with the Scottish Chartist Churches, but his attack on the socially divisive effects of pew rents and his complaint against ministers consuming the wealth of the labouring poor without contributing in return, also had similarities with the critique of the institutional church which they offered.[73] Bowes appealed to the con-

---

National Bankruptcy, and the effects that must ensue, unless averted by the Adoption of this only real and Desirable remedy, which would elevate these realms to a pitch of greatness hitherto unattained by any nation that ever existed, 2nd edn (London, 1816), pp.8-9; on Evans see, Iain McCalman, *Radical Underworld; prophets, revolutionaries and pornographers in London, 1795-1840* (Cambridge, 1988), pp.7-49.

68. [John Bowes], 'The land: a lecture by J. Bowes, delivered in Bell Street Hall, Dundee, 7 mo. 28th, 1851, showing how every family of five persons may have fourteen acres of land', *TP*, 1 (1849-51), pp.233-6.

69. [John Bowes], 'A lecture on the evils of the nation and their cure: delivered at Preston by J. Bowes 11th mo. 2d., 1849', *TP*, 1 (1849-51), pp.12-15; Evans, *Christian Polity*, pp.26-7.

70. Dorothy Thompson, *The Chartists: popular politics in the Industrial Revolution* (Aldershot, 1984), pp.113-15; Brian Harrison and Patricia Hollis (eds), *Robert Lowery: Radical and Chartist* (London, 1979); for Bowes's views on Chartism see his critical comments on the dispute he witnessed in Aberdeen between O'Connor and Patrick Brewster, *Autobiography*, p.297.

71. Thompson, *The Chartists,*, pp.299-306.

72. Bowes, *Autobiography*, p.297.

73. *The Chartist Circular*, 28 September, 1839, p.1; *ibid.*, 29 August, 1840, p.197, quoted in Donald C. Smith, *Passive Obedience and Prophetic Protest: social criticism in the Scottish Church 1830-1945* (New York, 1987), pp.163, 171; cf. [Bowes], 'The hired ministry', pp. 25-7.

stituency among which these ideas had currency and he attacked those who attracted popular support and whom he perceived as threats to true religion: Thomas Paine and Robert Owen; freethinkers such as Charles Bradlaugh; and Mormons and Swedenborgians.[74] His tactics were those of early nineteenth-century popular lecturers, and in preaching he proposed abandoning textual exposition. Questions should be asked by the preacher and invited from the audience, he held, for this was the way Christ taught.[75] His Christianity empowered the laity.

Bowes also eagerly challenged accepted orthodoxies. He was a man dominated by the demands of his own, often curious, reason. 'The only arms we can use', he wrote in his proposals for land distribution, 'must be reason, truth, prayer, activity, and such constitutional measures as Divine providence has placed within our reach'.[76] The items in his list are significant: he saw the need for peaceful politics as well as piety. But the order in which they occur is also important. For Bowes, idiosyncratic though he could be, reason was always the first weapon in his armoury. The emphasis on human liberty found in radical politics, a legacy of the Enlightenment, was one he shared. In 1849 he was to found a second journal entitled *The Truth, the only Way to the Freedom, Elevation and Happiness of Man* (later shortened to *The Truth Promoter*). In the prospectus he declared, 'Our confidence is entirely in *enlightenment*, and therefore our greatest endeavours shall be put forth to make men free, just, honest, pious, and, above all, loving, even to their enemies.'[77] At times this programme could look eccentric. He renounced the conventional names of days and months because of their pagan origins and adopted the Quaker custom of using numbers instead.[78] He was attracted to practices which could claim to be health-giving on a rational basis: he advocated vegetarianism, cold-water baths and uncut beards, and, because of their deleterious effects, denounced tea, coffee, alcohol,

---

74. 'The life and death of Thomas Paine', *TP*, 1 (1849-51), p.78; 'Public discussion at Northampton between C. Bradlaugh and J. Bowes', *TP*, 6 (1858-9), pp.192, 205-8, 257-63, 289-293, 297-300; John Bowes, *Mormonism Exposed in its Swindling, Polygamy, & Licentious Abominations, Refuted in its Principles, and in the Claims of its Head, the Modern Mohammed, Joseph Smith, who is proved to have been a Deceiver and no Prophet of God. Addressed to the serious Consideration of the 'Latter-Day Saints', and also to the friends of Mankind*, 2nd edn (Cheltenham, 1854); Woodman and Bowes, *Report of a Public Discussion*.

75. [John Bowes], 'Modern preaching wrong', *TP*, 1 (1849-51), pp.7-8.

76. [Bowes], 'The land', pp.236-7.

77. [John Bowes], 'Prospectus', *TP*, 1 (1849-51), p.1.

78. [*idem*], 'Origin of the present names of our months and days' *CMHU*, 1 (September 1843), pp.131-2.

tobacco, and tight-lacing.[79] Alternative medicine was one further way of rejecting the professional.[80] Bowes was to remain in many respects a figure of early nineteenth-century radical Christianity. He was led in part towards his ecclesiology by the upsurge of interest in democracy which came in the wake of the American and French Revolutions. 'All Christians', he proclaimed, 'should be reformers'.[81]

Yet he was a pivotal figure in the transition from the Evangelicalism of the early nineteenth century to that of the Victorian period and he displayed significant discontinuities with the past. He tended to define faith in terms of knowledge, and this meant that he never fully shared the mystical immediacy of popular Victorian piety.[82] However, the dispute in Edinburgh with Thomas Oliver had been over the place of faith and reason and Bowes gave the former priority, an order which made him open to the heightened supernaturalism of contemporary Evangelicalism.[83] He shared its interest in eschatology and he adopted 'living by faith' for Christian workers. As he was caught up in revivalism in the 1850s he came to emphasise that the church's task was to seek the salvation of sinners, an alteration in his order of priorities.[84] His challenge to established interests in church and state made him open to innovation and changes of mind. Bowes's eclectic beliefs were a 'blurring of worlds'.[85]

Bowes was also a lay activist. He was a capable preacher with a powerful voice and he possessed a strong constitution. If he lacked self-doubt, then his self-belief made him indefatigable in spreading his principles. From 1844 until 1859 he was resident in England again, first in Manchester and then in Cheltenham, but as will become apparent, his influence in Scotland remained strong. Eminently suited to the railway age, he spent the rest of his life forming assemblies and itinerating in the North of England and in Scotland, preaching wherever he could gain a hearing.[86] In his portmanteau, which he carried on a staff across his

---

79. [*idem*], 'Bad customs', *TP*, 1 (1849-51), pp.173-4; [*idem*], 'Hydropathy or the cold water cure', *ibid.*, pp.217-9; [*idem*], 'The moustache movement' *TP*, 3 (1854-5), pp.157-8; [*idem*], 'The beard', *ibid.*, pp.267-8; *TP*, 7 (1860-1), p.64; Bowes, *Autobiography*, p.185.

80. Hatch, *Democratization*, pp.28-9.

81. [Bowes], 'Bad customs', p.174.

82. [John Bowes], 'Men are saved by knowledge', *TP*, 2 (1852-3), pp.10-2; cf. [*idem*], 'Supernatural agency', *TP*, 1 (1849-51), p.5.

83. Bebbington, *Evangelicalism*, pp.78-94.

84. *TP*, 6 (1858-9), pp.13-14.

85. Hatch, *Democratization*, p.34.

86. The evidence for this comes from Bowes's reports of his activities in his *Autobiography* and *The Truth Promoter*. The growth of the the Brethren movement in the North of England has been poorly covered in the standard histories and Bowes's writings

shoulder, he had a waterproof baptising suit ready for use in the nearest stream when the occasion demanded.[87] After one of his annual tours of Britain, he calculated that he had travelled 1,800 miles and preached to 10,000 people in two months.[88] As well as in Liverpool, he helped to establish assemblies in Manchester, Carlisle and several other places in the North of England.[89]

A number of those who formed the nucleus of these assemblies were, it would appear, like Bowes himself, discontented Methodists. The freedom given by Methodism to lay preachers and the movement to congregationalism in reaction to the centripetal force of the conferences, had led many within it to a position where the Brethren appeared attractive. These factors were prominent, for example, in the secession from the Methodist New Connexion in 1841 of William Trotter, who joined the Brethren movement, and Joseph Barker, who founded the similarly named Unitarian Christian Brethren.[90] Methodism was one of several streams which fed into the growing Brethren movement throughout the United Kingdom.[91] In the new movements with which Bowes was in contact, a professional clergy was rejected, conventions were overturned and the laity were empowered. Christianity was being democratised.

Evangelical Union Secessions

Revivalism as well as a more egalitarian Christianity was present in Bowes's activities, and the latter was also present in other contemporary movements such as the Mormons, the Swedenborgians and the Churches

---

are an untapped source for the area: one exception is David Brady and Fred J. Evans, *Christian Brethren in Manchester and District: a history* (London, 1997).

87. 'John Bowes', *CW*, 36 (1921), pp.50-1.

88. *TP*, 3 (1854-5), p.240.

89. Brady and Evans, *Manchester*, pp.20-35; the Carlisle assembly Bowes was in contact with later died out.

90. J. Barker and W. Trotter, *A Brief report of the Proceedings of the Conference of the Methodist New Connexion in the case of Joseph Barker and Wm. Trotter* (Newcastle, [1841]); W. Trotter, *The Justice and Forbearance of the Methodist New Connexion Conference, as they were illustrated in the case of W. Trotter* (London, 1841); on Trotter, see Harold H. Rowdon, *The Origins of the Brethren 1825-1850* (London, 1967), p.175; Peter L. Embley, 'The early development of the Plymouth Brethren', in *Patterns of Sectarianism: organisation and ideology in social and religious movements* (London, 1967), p.241; on Barker's Christian Brethren see H. McLachlan, *The Story of a Nonconformist Library* (Manchester 1923), pp.152-183.

91. Bowes, *Autobiography*, p.241.

of Christ which appeared in Scotland in this period.[92] In the mainstream denominations, too, Evangelicalism was giving an increased role to the laity through, for example, the work of Thomas Chalmers,[93] and in the 1840s the popular form of this piety which favoured Brethren growth was further diffused throughout Scotland. The decade commenced with the revivals associated with William Burns and in 1843 the Disruption released Evangelical activity into many parishes throughout Scotland in the newly formed Free Church.[94] The increased concern for home evangelism, which was accompanied by an interest in foreign missions, indicated that a significant shift in Scottish church life had taken place. Transatlantic revivalist influences led to the formation of a further denomination, the Evangelical Union (EU), and the new body was to have significance for Brethren growth.

James Morison, the eventual founder of the EU, was a zealous young evangelist with the United Secession Church, the denomination formed in 1820 out of the union of the New Licht branches of the Burgher and Anti-Burgher Secession bodies. Morison's evangelism was considerably influenced by his reading of Charles Finney's *Revivals in Religion* (1839).[95] In 1840 Morison was called to Clerk's Lane Secession Church, Kilmarnock, and the membership of the church soon swelled as new converts were made and members from the other Kilmarnock churches joined.[96] Morison had begun to modify his church's Calvinism as part of his evangelistic and pastoral concern. He had departed from the teaching of the Westminster Confession, which held that Christ died for the elect only, and he had begun to preach a universal atonement, stressing the love of God.[97] Clerk's Lane had the reputation of being a difficult church, and there had been an attempt by some of the membership to

92. Bernard Aspinwall, 'A fertile field: Scotland in the days of the early missions', in R. I. Jenson and M. R. Thorp (eds.), *Mormons in Early Victorian Britain* (Salt Lake City, 1989), pp. 104-117; MacWhirter, 'The Church of the New Jerusalem in Scotland', pp.202-219; Thompson, *Let Sects and Parties Fall*, pp.13-32.

93. Stewart J. Brown, 'The Disruption and urban poverty: Thomas Chalmers and the West Port operation in Edinburgh, 1844-47', *RSCHS*, 20 (1978), pp.65-89; *idem*, *Thomas Chalmers and the Godly Commonwealth in Scotland* (Oxford, 1982).

94. Cf. the account of the West Port Free Church missionary and later Brethren member Donald Ross, quoted in C. W. R[oss]. (ed.), *Donald Ross: pioneer evangelist of the North of Scotland and United States of America* (Kilmarnock, [1903]), pp.30-2.

95. Garth M. Rosell and Richard A. G. Dupuis (eds), *The Memoirs of Charles G. Finney: the complete restored text* (Grand Rapids, Michigan, 1989), pp.590-1, see especially n.6.

96. Congregational Church, Kilmarnock, 'Communicants' Roll Book; or Names, Designations, etc., of Members belonging to Clerk's Lane Congregation, Kilmarnock 1840-1950', shows that 589 new members joined the church in the first two years of Morison's ministry.

97. Escott, *Scottish Congregationalism*, p.116.

stop him accepting the call.[98] He was not long there before it found itself embroiled in the dispute over his new teaching, and in the spring of 1841, amid scenes of near riot in Kilmarnock, Morison was suspended from the ministry of the Secession Church. Part of the dispute was about Presbyterian subordinate standards, and in their memorial to the Secession Synod Morison's supporters wanted 'a direct appeal to the word of God'.[99] When Morison was subsequently deposed from the ministry of the denomination, the majority of his congregation seceded with him.

One of Morison's closest friends in Clerk's Lane during the troubles of 1840-41 was John Stewart, a prominent member of the kirk session. It was partly due to a letter which Stewart had written to Morison that the attempt to stop him accepting the call had been frustrated.[100] Stewart, whose father had also been a leading member of the church, was a wealthy Kilmarnock clothier, highly praised by his contemporaries for his Christian character. A lay activist and a devoted Evangelical, who had reflected deeply on his attitude to wealth, Stewart was an enthusiast for home and foreign missions.[101] He was closely involved in inter-denominational ventures in Kilmarnock and was a director of the Bible Society for twenty years, donating a Bible carriage for the society's work in Spain.[102] He ran a Sunday school, at one point holding a visitation programme to extend its membership, and for some forty years was secretary of the Kilmarnock Sabbath School Society. He also engaged in philanthropic work. He founded two orphanages for boys in Ayrshire, at Pitcon House, Dalry, and at Shawhill House, Hurlford, where the orphans were taught a trade and given religious instruction.[103] He built a schoolroom in Kilmarnock where he maintained both an industry school for the daughters of poor families, in which they could have an education and learn Ayrshire needlework, and also an elementary school to give an

---

98. Oliphant Smeaton, *Principal James Morison: the man and his work* (Edinburgh, 1902), pp.71-76; Smeaton's book was dedicated to Morison's sister and John Stewart's sister-in-law, Mrs Andrew Stewart: she is also one of his principal sources.

99. William Adamson, *The Life of the Rev. James Morison, D.D., Principal of the Evangelical Union Theological Hall, Glasgow* (London, 1898), pp.118-119.

100. Smeaton, *Principal James Morison*, p.75; probably it is this letter by an anonymous elder 'who espoused the cause of Mr. Morison from the first' which is quoted in Adamson, *James Morison*, p.86.

101. 'Mr John Stewart', in Anon. (ed.), *Jubilee of the Rev. Wm. Orr* (Kilmarnock, 1880), p.80.

102. 'The late Mr J. Stewart and the Bible Society', *KS*, 10 December 1887, p.2.

103. 'The Late Mr J. Stewart of Shawhill', *KS*, 10 December 1887, p.3; 'Reminiscences of the Stewart Brothers', *KS*, 17 December 1887.

affordable education to the children of poor people with large families.[104]

Stewart's activities were typical of many wealthy Evangelicals of the period, and his evangelistic zeal made him a natural supporter of Morison. It is probable that he was untroubled over the disagreements about the extent of the atonement for there already had been rumours in Kilmarnock that Stewart's theology leaned towards that of the Methodists.[105] In addition, he was one of the memorialists to the synod who had wanted appeal made to the word of God only.[106] But while in England, he had made contact with the Brethren movement there[107] and after being refused the pulpit for a Brethren preacher he resigned his membership claiming, according to an eyewitness, that he 'called no one master' and that he could not remain 'where the one-man system prevailed'.[108] Only six months had passed since Morison's trial. The communicants' roll noted against Stewart's name 'left on account of peculiar views of the Spirit'.[109] He evidently found attraction in the Brethren charismatic concept of the church. Some family members and one of his servants seceded with him to form the nucleus of the new meeting, as did a woman who had recently joined Clerk's Lane from the Scotch Baptist church in Kilmarnock.[110]

Morison's breach with the Secession church caused a stir throughout Scotland. He launched on an evangelistic career, preaching in the villages around Kilmarnock and further afield in Ayrshire and Lanarkshire. Some of the churches which were founded as a result of these evangelistic campaigns, joined by four Secession and nine Congregational churches, banded together in 1843 to form the EU, initially intended as an unsectarian, nondenominational association to spread revivals, but which soon became a separate body.[111] Among the churches founded by Morison was one in 1844 in Darvel, eleven miles to the east of

---

104. Archibald McKay, *The History of Kilmarnock* (Kilmarnock, 1864), p.148.

105. However, this may not have been because of Arminianism, but may have been a reference to some other feature of his outlook, such as his style of evangelism.

106. Adamson, *James Morison*, p.119.

107. It is possible that, like Bowes, Stewart's initial contact with the Brethren was through George Müller's growing reputation. Stewart's concerns paralleled Müller's in several respects, and later he was certainly a friend and supporter of Müller, the latter visiting him in Kilmarnock on one occasion, cf. David J. Beattie, *Brethren: the story of a great recovery* (Kilmarnock, 1939), pp.223-4; 'Mrs Jas. B. Hunter' *BM*, 46 (1937), p.252.

108. Quoted in Adamson, *James Morison*, p.219 (cf. quotation from Bowes below p.46); cf. Smeaton, *Morison*, pp.132-3, 242: neither Adamson nor Smeaton names Stewart, but it is clearly he who is intended.

109. 'Communicants' Roll Book', p.6.

110. Neil Dickson, 'Brethren and Baptists in Scotland', *BQ*, 33 (1990), p.372.

111. Escott, *Scottish Congregationalism*, pp.121-6.

Kilmarnock (see Map 13). William Landels, one of the first graduates of the theological academy which Morison had founded in Kilmarnock, was appointed as minister. Two years after his induction, however, Landels underwent believer's baptism and left the church in 1846 to become a Baptist minister in Cupar.[112] The now pastorless congregation in Darvel was expelled from the EU because it had continued to accept Landels as a preacher after he had been immersed and also because it had intimated its intention of having John Bowes to preach.

Bowes, always eager to influence those who had similarities to himself, had been following Morison's development: the latter's temperance views would be one further attraction for him. He sent Morison an outline of his principles as early as March 1841, and he had probably made contact with several of the other new EU churches. His action, typically, alienated Morison, and when Bowes sent him a letter inquiring about the truth of a report that Morison had travelled first class, Morison's reply was positively frosty.[113] There were, however, others willing to listen. As William Adamson admits in his biography of Morison, the appeal to the Bible alone made by Morison and his supporters predisposed them to giving Bowes a hearing.[114] A pamphlet in favour of unsalaried ministers was published in Kilmarnock and Morison responded with *Should There Be a Paid Minister?*[115] From 1844 until 1847 five members of Morison's Kilmarnock congregation left to join a Bowesite church that had been formed in Kilmarnock which was independent, it would appear, of Stewart's assembly.[116] In addition, about fifty-five members of the

---

112. *Ibid.*, p.329; D. W. Bebbington (ed.), *A History of the Baptists in Scotland* (Glasgow, 1983), pp.39-40.

113. Bowes, *Autobiography*, pp.273, 426-7. That Bowes had contacted a number of Evangelical Union congregations might be deduced from his own report that the denomination thought he '"was on a mission to Scotland to break up the Union!"', a charge which Bowes naturally denied, Bowes, *Autobiography*, pp.427-8.

114. Adamson, *James Morison*, p.262.

115. *Ibid.*, pp.262-3; James Morison, *Should There Be a Paid Minister?: an examination of the text Acts xx. 33-35 in three letters* (1846), cited in Adamson, *James Morison*, p.437; I have been unable to trace this work.

116. 'Communicants' Roll Book', pp.8, 40, 44. It is possible that these seceders did join Stewart, but the evidence appears to tell against this. Bowes nowhere mentions Stewart (a curious omission if he knew him), and more significantly Adamson discusses both men separately and does not connect them. He refers to Stewart becoming a 'Plymouth Brother' (Adamson, *James Morison*, p.219), but to Bowes as an 'advocate of the non-paid ministry' (*ibid.*, p.262). This last description fits the comment in Clerk's Lane roll book where the seceders have against their names the comment: 'Gone to the non-paid pastor party.' But that they did not join Stewart is almost certainly established by Bowes's report that when he was in Kilmarnock in 1847 he attended the breaking of bread in Clark Street, apparently in the same schoolroom in which he preached in the evening (*Autobiography*, p.440). *The Kilmarnock and Riccarton Post-Office Directory*

expelled Darvel church, Bowes proudly reported, began 'to meet in the Lord's name alone, being under no obligation to have any master but Christ'.[117]

The ferment created by Morison's 'New Views' and the revivalism associated with the rise of the EU had begun a process of exploration for those affected by them which brought some to a Brethren ecclesiology. This development can be seen most clearly in Wishaw, the third EU congregation where a secession is known to have produced an assembly. John Kirk, the Congregational minister of Hamilton, was one of the ministers who founded the EU. In 1843, the same year as the new denomination was born, Kirk held a series of evangelistic meetings in Wishaw, and as a result of this effort some sixty converts were made and a church was established.[118] A weekly fellowship meeting was held in nearby Newmains (see Map 10) for Bible reading and mutual edification. The group which met there began to be dissatisfied with the government of the Wishaw church, feeling that a plurality of elders was the scriptural pattern. When the congregation's student preacher, John Hamilton, decided that he should be ordained, one member suggested that he should be sent out to evangelise the surrounding villages one Sunday a month and in his absence they should provide ministry from among themselves. Hamilton began preaching against those who supported this scheme, advising them to leave the church. After a final, difficult meeting with him, a group of sixteen began breaking bread on 11 April 1847 in a workshop in Newmains belonging to one of them, a few weeks later transferring to rented accommodation in Wishaw.[119] In their 'Church Record' for that month they determined 'to acknowledge no other name but Christ' and 'to make our only tests of membership, union with Christ'.[120] When one member began teaching believer's baptism, one of the leaders withdrew because he felt that the issue was divisive. By August

---

for 1855-56 (Kilmarnock, 1855), p.72, in addition to Stewart's congregation (designated 'Plymouth Brethren'), noted that 'Meetings are also held for Public Worship in Clark's street school.' These were most probably the services of the Bowesite church.

117. Bowes, *Autobiography*, pp.427-8. Escott is apparently unaware of the expulsion of the Darvel congregation from the Evangelical Union and of its continued existence; in *Scottish Congregationalism*, p.329, he states that the Darvel members travelled to the Evangelical Union church in Galston: it is probable that some continued to meet in Darvel while those who remained loyal to Morison travelled to Galston.

118. Helen Kirk, *Memoirs of Rev. John Kirk D.D.* (Edinburgh, 1888), pp.180-206; Beattie, *Brethren*, pp.201-3.

119. James Smith, 'The rise of the meeting at Wishaw', 12 October 1848, quoted in Bowes, *Autobiography*, pp.455-7.

120. 'Church Record', April 1847, quoted in Beattie, *Brethren*, pp.202-3: this document has apparently been lost since Beattie made use of it in the 1930s.

they had made contact with John Bowes who visited them.[121] In May, after a subsequent visit from Bowes, four of the members were baptised in the River Calder.[122]

It would appear that this evolution was initially conducted independently of Brethren influence. There was, perhaps, an infusion of Glasite ideas. The phrase used for ministry from among the members— 'the church should edify itself'—was a Glasite one and at the first communion one of the members presided, a Glasite practice. If there were such an influence, then it was possibly indirect, derived from the general familiarity with such ideas through such bodies as the Scotch Baptists.[123] In the account of their development given by James Smith, one of the leaders, there is no mention of contact with any other churches or individuals until Bowes appeared, and David Beattie in his history explicitly states that their development was spontaneous.[124] However arrived at, the significant features in the new Wishaw assembly were the exploration of Scripture to recover the pattern of the primitive church; the use of lay members; its vision of the unity of all true believers; and the desire to transform its environment through evangelism. These were a nexus of practices and attitudes which connected the Wishaw church with the democratised Christian bodies with which Bowes was in contact and made it part of the Brethren movement. Its EU background had given the new assembly a taste for revival, and this—the first meeting in Lanarkshire—made it an important influence in the development of the Brethren in the county.

Further Growth

There were strains at Plymouth between Darby and Newton which became an open breach when Darby accused the latter of undue domination of the assembly at Plymouth in 1845 and then of Christological heresy in 1847. The split became irremediable when Darby widened it in 1848 to include Craik and Müller. Despite their condemnation of Newton's heterodoxy, Darby refused to have any further communion with them because they had received someone at

---

121. Bowes, *Autobiography*, p.441.

122. Beattie, *Brethren*, p.203; Bowes, *Autobiography*, p.448.

123. *Ibid.*, p.456. The Wishaw group was doubtless aware of churches, such as the Scotch Baptists, who had a Glasite ecclesiology. However, the use of the phrase 'edify itself' by Smith does not conclusively point to a Glasite influence, for his document was written after the Wishaw church had made contact with Bowes, and it may have been he who led to its adoption.

124. This evidence needs to be treated with caution given Beattie's tendency to stress the spontaneity of the Brethren movement (see above, pp.11-12).

Bethesda Chapel, Bristol, from Newton's assembly in Plymouth. 'The Bethesda Question' became a test for Darby and his followers of the acceptability of an assembly, and those which refused to denounce Müller and Craik were cut off by them.[125] Although the then majority of English assemblies went with the Exclusive Brethren, in Scotland, of the meetings that are known to have existed, possibly there was a group which followed him in Edinburgh.[126] However, there was apparent resistance to him even there, if the Mr Nelson of Edinburgh who in 1848 at a meeting in Bath supported Lord Congleton in his criticisms of Darby's actions can be taken as evidence of an anti-Darby faction in the capital.[127] Darby had little influence north of the border.

***Table 2.1.* Aberdeen Bowesite church: additions and withdrawals 1841-42**

56 from 'the world'	5 from the Baptists
16 from the Church of Scotland	2 from the Episcopalians
7 from Zion Chapel[1]	1 from a Secession church
7 from the Methodists	1 from the Roman Catholic Church
5 from the Congregationalists	2 from a 'sister church'

Total additions = = 102

　　　　　　　　　　3 withdrew
　　　　　　　　　　1 moved
　　　　　　　　　　1 excommunicated

Total left = 5
Total membership = 97

Note:

1. Hugh Hart's congregation.

Source: John Bowes, *The Christian Magazine and Herald of Union*, 1 (1842-3), p.21.

The division into Exclusive Brethren associated with Darby and Open Brethren outwith his control was antecedent to any significant Brethren presence in Scotland, and the two sections of the movement grew

125. Rowdon, *Origins*, pp.236-66.

126. That some of the Edinburgh assembly followed Darby is an inference from Fry MS, pp.152-3, which states that the Marchioness of Queensberry followed Darby; however, this assumes that the Marchioness was associated with this assembly. The Marchioness and Mrs Hutchinson eventually became Roman Catholics: Gorman, (ed.), *Converts to Rome*, p.227.

127. W. Trotter to Thomas Grundy, 15 July 1849, in *The Origin of the (So Called) 'Open Brethren:' a letter by W. Trotter giving the whole case of Plymouth & Bethesda* (London, n.d.), p.27.

independently of each other.[128] Revivalism ensured that the growth of the independent wing of the movement in this period could, in its initial phase be considerable, as John Bowes's list of additions and withdrawals for 1841-42 of the Aberdeen church demonstrates (Table 2.1).[129] Much of the growth had come from denominations which had similarities with Bowes's congregation, but in the revivalist conditions, which held for the first year of the church's existence, those who had no significant church attachment had comprised more than half of the additions.[130] Where these conditions were absent, however, it is likely that most of those joining the new assemblies were transferring from dissenting churches. They were small tenant farmers, artisans, or middle-class businessmen. In Aberdeen, a former Chartist preacher joined, while in Kilmarnock the members of Clerk's Lane who became Bowesite Brethren included a blacksmith, a joiner, two miners and a servant girl.[131] The number of assemblies continued to increase. In 1848 the Wishaw meeting entered into a correspondence (a Scotch Baptist custom) with seven other churches. Not only were the Kilmarnock and Darvel congregations included, but so too were ones in Cumnock, Paisley, Helensburgh, Motherwell and Rutherglen.[132]

Apart from Helensburgh, the precise origins of the congregations in these last mentioned places are not known. It is possible that the Paisley assembly (see Map 12) was a splinter from the Methodists, for after Bowes came back from England in 1841 on more than one occasion he was in contact with John Kennedy, minister of the Paisley congregation of the United Methodist Churches of Scotland. However, Kennedy apparently left Paisley in 1847 (before the correspondence commenced),[133] and it is more likely that the communication was with

---

128. For Exclusive Brethren growth in Scotland, see above, pp.2-4.

129. *CMHU*, 1 (1842-3), p.21.

130. The sixteen from the Church of Scotland possibly obscures this point, it being probable they came from congregations which later helped form the Free Church, and therefore shared Bowes's Evangelicalism. The 'world' probably includes both those who had no church attachment at all and those whom Bowes regarded as having merely a nominal church connection.

131. Bowes, *Autobiography*, p.393; 'Communicants' Roll Book', pp.8, 40, 44.

132. Smith, 'the Meeting at Wishaw', in Bowes, *Autobiography*, p.457.

133. Bowes, *Autobiography*, pp.274, 282. The date of Kennedy (1784-1851) leaving Paisley is given in Robert Brown, *Paisley Poets with brief memoirs of them and selections from their works*, 2 (Paisley, 1890), p.66 n. When Bowes met Kennedy in March 1841 the latter was speaking on unity, and when he met him in Glasgow later that year, Bowes was hopeful that an assembly would be established in the city. *The Paisley Directory, 1836-7*, p.108, lists C[itizen]. John Kennedy (not John C. Kennedy as Bowes refers to him) as minister of the Dissenting Wesleyan Methodists, and the 1841-2 *Directory*, p.118, lists him as minister of the United Methodists, but the 1848-9

another of the town's numerous dissenting bodies. The Cumnock
assembly was in existence by 1847 and initially it appears to have
consisted of the family of one man, Ivie Campbell of Dalgig, whose farm,
where the breaking of bread was held, was about six miles outside the
town. Bowes had initially heard that Campbell would receive the baptised
only (a rumour which proved false) and it is possible that he had a Scotch
Baptist background.[134] More probably, the black servant whom Campbell
had points to a West Indies connection, where Campbell might have come
in contact with the Brethren, something which seems plausible given the
geographical remoteness of the assembly from other Scottish ones (see
Map 13).[135] What is clear is that the movement was tending to grow in
weaving and textile communities, or, in the case of Newmains, places
where the new iron and coal industries were appearing.[136]

Helensburgh (see Map 12), a residential town from its inception in the
late eighteenth century, is again an exception to this pattern. The church
there which was corresponding with the others was that of Robert Dickie,
the Scotch Baptist pastor. Dickie had lived in Dublin for a while where he
attended the church of Thomas Kelly, the proto-Brethren hymn-writer
who had gathered a number of independent congregations around
him.[137] Dickie and his wife were both convicted of the worldliness of
their enjoyment of singing and dancing and love of good clothing. Back
in Glasgow, they underwent an Evangelical conversion through a Baptist
minister, and in 1826 Dickie gave up his lucrative clothier's business to
become a preacher. He settled in Helensburgh where he founded a
Baptist church.[138] He was interested in Irving's Catholic Apostolic
Church, having heard Mary Campbell using *glossolalia*, and his wife was
particularly inclined to join it, but they were dissuaded by criticisms of
the phenomenon. Dickie and his wife were open to the new currents in
Evangelicalism, and he was evidently in contact with the Brethren by the

Directory, p.8, as minister for the Congregationalist Methodists; this last body
Beckerlegge, 'Methodism in Paisley', pp.98-101, identifies with the other two.

134. Bowes, *Autobiography*, pp.437, 494.

135. However, Bowes mentions that there were 'a few brethren' in Mauchline,
probably pointing to the existence of a congregation there, and he then proceeded to
visit Kilmarnock, indicative of a network of contacts in Ayrshire, see Bowes,
Autobiography, p.440. T. C. F. Stunt, 'Leonard Strong: the motives and experiences of
early missionary work in British Guiana', *CBRJ*, 34 (1983), pp.93-105; and the epigraph
to the present chpt.

136. Cf., below, p.304.

137. H. H. Rowdon, 'Secession from the Established Church in the early Nineteenth
Century', *Vox Evangelica*, 3 (1964), pp.76-88; Grayson Carter, *Anglican Evangelicals:
Protestant secessions from the via media, c.1800-1850* (Oxford, 2000), pp.69-77.

138. John Bowes, 'Memoir of Mrs Jessie Dickie', *TP*, 7 (1860-1), pp. 111-7, 121-5;
this memoir was later published separately but the present writer has not been able to
locate an extant copy.

1840s. In 1847 Dickie opened the Lord's table to all true believers, and in May of the following year Bowes met him in Wishaw.[139] Thereafter the latter was a regular visitor to Helensburgh while Dickie's involvement with the Brethren increased.

Dalgig and Helensburgh were not the only exceptions to the appearance of the Brethren in industrialised communities. Aberdeenshire was another one. Bowes, who had itinerated in the county when he stayed in Aberdeen, continued to visit individuals who sympathised with his principles, such as George Smith, the Free Church doctor in New Deer who later joined Bowes's Dundee congregation.[140] Bowes made contact mainly among dissenters, preaching in their churches or debating with them, and he met Aberdeenshire preachers who were holding revival services. In 1844 he briefly accompanied Alexander Burnet, the laird of Kemnay who was a local preacher among the Baptists, on a preaching tour. After leaving him, Bowes went to Duncanstone where he stayed with Peter Ferres, a local revivalist, and he talked with the Congregational minister and some members of his church. Everywhere he went Bowes left copies of *The Christian Magazine* and he recorded that it was making a considerable impression in the area.[141] It was shortly after the visit to Duncanstone that James Shearer reported that ten individuals had begun to break bread at his farm, Croft End of Auchlyne, Clatt parish, to exhort each other and to be free from a hired ministry.[142] The members of the new meeting evidently lived some distance apart and they met on alternate Sundays in Clatt parish and in New Leslie parish. By 1845 a second assembly had been formed at Insch, the largest town of the area.[143] A farmer in the Glens of Foudland had fitted up one of his barns as a preaching place for ministers of various denominations, and the Brethren associated with these services, John Bowes preaching there on a number of occasions.[144] These new meetings were geographically isolated (see Map 5), but favourable conditions for Brethren recruitment had been provided by the few local revivalists and small groups of dissenters which Aberdeenshire contained.

Throughout the 1850s, however, it was mainly in the cities and industrialised towns and villages that the Brethren continued to grow. Since his return to Scotland in 1841, Bowes had tried to establish an assembly in Glasgow, talking mainly with Congregationalists and Scotch Baptists. In 1844 he recorded that there were two groups 'meeting in the

---

139. Bowes, *Autobiography*, p.447-8.
140. *Ibid.*, p.363.
141. *Ibid.*, p.376.
142. *Ibid.*, p.398.
143. *Ibid.*, p.406.
144. *Ibid.*, p.409; *TP*, 5 (1856-8), pp.143-4; *TP*, 6 (1858-9), pp.47-8.

Lord's name alone', and that he hoped to unite them.[145] Possibly one of these groups was associated with James Begg with whom Bowes was largely in agreement. Begg, formerly a Reformed Presbyterian, was a Glasgow bookseller who favoured a return to 'primitive Christianity'.[146] His congregation designated itself 'a Christian church' only, favoured a Glasite order, practised believer's baptism, and taught universal atonement, premillennialism and that tongues and healing would be restored to the Church.[147] This eclectic mixture shows that Begg had been shaped by the same forces which produced the Brethren. Bowes evidently had support among some of the Glasgow individuals with whom he was in contact, for among those who in 1846 preached in Kilmarnock in support of unsalaried ministers and against Morison were two preachers from the city.[148] But Bowes's associates seemed to disappear. When he next visited Glasgow, those he met, while meeting weekly, were afraid of founding a church.[149] Eventually, in 1850 he met with a group of individuals to discuss breaking bread regularly, and that afternoon fifty of them commenced to do so.[150] Events in Edinburgh followed much the same pattern, with visits from Bowes to interested individuals and groups. In 1851 he met with a group who, it appears, were already breaking bread in a hall at 84 High Street and succeeded in uniting them with another body who met separately.[151] This union marked the formation of the

---

145. Bowes, *Autobiography*, p.367

146. William Fulton, 'In Memory of James A. Begg, Bookseller, Argyll Arcade, Glasgow', in James A. Begg, *Summary of Doctrines Taught in the Christian Meeting House, 90 Norfolk Street, Laurieston, Glasgow* (Glasgow 1869), pp.iv-xxxvii.

147. James A. Begg, *A Connected View of Some Scriptural Evidence of the Redeemer's Speedy Personal Return, and Reign on Earth with His Glorified Saints, during the Millennium; Israel's Restoration to Palestine, and the Destruction of Antichristian Nations with Remarks on Various Authors who oppose these Doctrines* (1829), 3rd edn (Paisley, 1831); idem, *The Condition in Which All Men Are Placed: being an examination of the sentiments of Dr. Wardlaw of Glasgow and Mr. Russell of Dundee, regarding the atonement, forgiveness, and justification of faith* (Glasgow, 1834); idem, *Summary of Doctrines*. Begg also practised a Saturday sabbath: idem, *An Examination of the Authority for a Change of the Weekly Sabbath at the Resurrection of Christ: proving that the Practice of the Church in Substituting the First day of the Week, for the Appointed Seventh day is Unsanctioned by the New Testament Scriptures* (Glasgow, 1850).

148. Adamson, *James Morison*, p.262.

149. Bowes, *Autobiography*, p.408.

150. *Ibid.*, p.481.

151. Perhaps one these groups had been the possible anti-Darby faction of 1848. However, Bowes's contacts tended to be in the lower social classes and the Mr Nelson who in association with Lord Congleton opposed Darby in Bath was probably from a higher social class. The balance of probabilities is that Nelson's putative group and the Bowesite ones were separate.

assembly which eventually met in Adam's Square (see Map 8, inset).[152] In the weaving village of Neilston, Renfrewshire (see Map 12), by 1854 Bowes was in contact with a group, possibly from the EU church which had been formed there by John Kirk.[153] They were in contact with Robert Dickie and the assemblies in Glasgow and nearby Kilmarnock. Due to the visits of Bowes and Dickie, a number of them were baptised by immersion and a church was formed.[154]

It was in Lanarkshire, the county which was becoming the most industrialised in Scotland, where the greatest number of assemblies were established. Apart from the ones in Wishaw, Motherwell and Rutherglen which existed in 1847, several others were formed. A meeting was planted in Douglas towards the end of 1847, and by 1849 one had been formed in Hamilton (see Map 10). Relations between the EU church in Hamilton and the assembly were strained for a long time, and this may have been because the meeting had drawn members—perhaps even the founding ones—from it.[155] Certainly individuals were attracted from other churches and among those baptised was an elder from a United Presbyterian Church.[156] When Bowes toured Lanarkshire in 1850 he reported small groups breaking bread in Carluke and Airdrie. In Lanark he met some individuals who had a weekly meeting and they agreed to break bread also.[157] The following year Bowes found twenty-eight individuals in an assembly in Newarthill, and in 1854 after his visit to Strathaven, the breaking of bread was commenced there.[158] The origins of these widely dispersed Lanarkshire assemblies (see Map 10) have not been recorded, but the general pattern of individuals dissatisfied with their churches being attracted to the small fellowship groups of the Brethren and their administration of the Christian ordinances by lay members is clear enough.

---

152. *TP*, 1 (1849-51), pp.247-8; John Robertson to John Bowes, 5 September 1851, *TP*, p.279.

153. *Ibid.*, 3 (1854), pp.143-4; Kirk, *John Kirk*, p.207. When Bowes first mentions the Neilston group, he states that there is a 'New View Church' (i.e. EU) in the village. It is not entirely clear from Bowes, however, if the group he met in Neilston already constituted a church. It is possible that the group there had no connection with the EU and that it was a congregation belonging to some other dissenting denomination which Bowes and Dickie influenced in a Brethren direction.

154. *TP*, 3 (1854-5), p.159.

155. Bowes, *Autobiography*, pp.457; *TP*, 1 (1849-51), pp. 189-91.

156. Bowes, *Autobiography*, p.462-3.

157. *TP*, 1 (1849-50), pp.102, 107.

158. *TP*, 1 (1849-51), pp.254-6; *ibid.*, 2 (1852-3), pp.141-2; *ibid.*, 3 (1854-5) pp.143-4.

The Making of a Movement

The new assemblies displayed some diversity and their sense of identity was not entirely clear. Bowes always denied he belonged to the Brethren. When challenged in Old Meldrum, Aberdeenshire, to declare if he were Plymouth Brethren, he tacitly admitted affiliation before proclaiming, 'We do not wish any party name. We have no law-book but the Scriptures'.[159] He still wished a wider union, and he proposed a merger of the Open Brethren, the Churches of Christ, the Scotch Baptists and the Exclusive Brethren because of their similar practices.[160] However, the Dundee church always stood aloof from the Scottish Open Brethren while John Stewart, on the other hand, was happy to identify himself in 1855 as 'Plymouth Brethren'.[161] Although he used the name which Bowes disavowed, it was Stewart who had the more catholic spirit. Robert Dickie in Helensburgh presented a greater anomaly. Despite his increasingly open identification with the Brethren, he continued to associate with Baptists, and Baptist history was to claim him as one *simpliciter*.[162] The actual situation was more complex. The nondenominationalism of the Brethren and their similarities with the Scotch Baptists enabled Dickie to keep a foot in both worlds.

Among assemblies, practices also varied. It has been already noted above how the first breaking of bread at Newmains tended to follow a Scotch Baptist pattern. The new Edinburgh assembly gave a description of its morning service:

> One brother gives out a song of praise; another reads a portion of God's word; another engages in prayer; another gives an exhortation; after which we all join in conversing upon a chapter in Isaiah...[163]

This, however, was not entirely to Bowes's satisfaction and he rather condescendingly remarked that 'many have progressed further than this meeting'. However, Bowes own commemoration of the Lord's supper probably followed a Glasite plan, for in one church formed in the following decade his account of the worship was that 'three or four generally speak.'[164] This pattern allowed scope for contributions from the members, but at Neilston the difficulty was in getting the members to adopt unstructured, open participation and to cease relying on one

159. Bowes, *Autobiography*, p.361.

160. [John Bowes], 'A step in advance—who will take it?', *TP*, 9 (1863-6), pp.18-19.

161. *Kilmarnock...Directory for 1855-56*, p.72.

162. George Yuille (ed.), *History of the Baptists in Scotland* (Glasgow, 1926), p.192.

163. John Robertson to John Bowes, 5 September 1851, *TP*, 1 (1849-51), p.279.

164. John Bowes, 'The work of God at Dundee and Lochee', *TP*, 7 (1859-61), p.11.

person fulfilling a ministerial office.[165] Across the movement, however, there was a sense of identity being formed. Bowes's visits probably tended to smooth out the differences. Even more influential were his magazines, especially, after its founding in 1849, *The Truth Promoter* (the *Christian Magazine* was merged with it a few months later). The growing movement was linked by its reports and by its articles expounding Brethren ecclesiology.

Mutual consultation among congregations also forged links, and the need to extend the movement in Scotland was a central preoccupation of the new assemblies. When the eight churches first entered into a correspondence with each other in 1847, it was to consider the best means of obtaining and supporting evangelists. As a result of the contact they met to confer on the subject in Paisley, and a second conference was held by the Lanarkshire churches in 1851.[166] There were others concerned with the problem, and shortly after the 1847 meeting, Frederick Daniel from Carlisle, whom Bowes had first met at Bethesda Chapel, Bristol, and James Wisely from the Clatt assembly embarked on an evangelistic tour during which the meeting in Douglas had been formed.[167] Others who had joined the Brethren also undertook evangelistic and pastoral tours, such as Robert Dickie and his wife who in 1850 visited many of the new assemblies in England, and Dickie subsequently itinerated among the Scottish meetings until his health broke down about 1855.[168] But despite this activity the evangelists remained few and the meetings remained small. 'The churches in Scotland', John Bowes lamented in 1854, 'much need an Evangelist at least among them.'[169] The assembly at Wishaw had grown from its original sixteen to thirty within a matter of months, but twenty years later in 1857 it still had the same number of members.[170] At Hamilton the assembly went from having fifty members in 1850 to twelve six years later, and it was probably discontinued about then.[171] A number of others also ceased: Arbroath, Paisley, Motherwell, Airdrie, Newarthill, Carluke, Lanark, and Strathaven all apparently ceased soon after their inception, and Aberdeen, the Kilmarnock Bowesite church, Darvel, Glasgow, and Edinburgh died out after an existence of a few years, as probably also did Cumnock. Although Clatt, Insch and Douglas continued into the 1860s, they were not in a healthy condition. By the end of the 1850s (if Bowes's Dundee congregation and Dickie's Helensburgh one are excluded) there were probably only six Open

165. *TP*, 3 (1854-5), pp.238-40; *TP*, 6 (1858-9), pp.127-8.
166. *TP*, 1 (1849-51), pp. 254-6.
167. Smith, 'the meeting at Wishaw', p.457.
168. 'Mrs Jessie Dickie', p.115.
169. *TP*, 3 (1854-5), p.144.
170. Smith, 'the meeting in Wishaw', p.457; *TP*, 5 (1856-8), pp.143-4.
171. *TP*, 1 (1849-51), pp.254-6; *TP*, 4 (1855-7), pp.221-2.

Brethren assemblies in Scotland.[172] The movement was having difficulty in establishing itself.

The lack of evangelists was one reason why assemblies were failing to grow or were declining. Not only did evangelists aid recruitment, they also linked congregations together. Certainly Bowes felt that isolation had been a cause in the collapse of the meeting at Lanark.[173] There were a number of other reasons why so many of the new churches were soon discontinued. James Smith of Wishaw felt that potential evangelists were reluctant to adopt living by faith and assemblies were slow to support those subsisting in this manner.[174] This resistance to new ideas, such as the use of lay members, was undoubtedly another reason why the Brethren failed to attract people from other churches. The antagonism with which the new meetings were viewed also made the addition of new members difficult. The resultant paucity of numbers created difficulties for many assemblies in having a viable church life. Overseas emigration was high in Scotland around 1850, and it had a decided effect on the decline of the meetings at Darvel, Hamilton, Douglas and Clatt, and probably this was the case elsewhere.[175] It was also the more active members who tended to emigrate. James Wisely, who had promised well as an evangelist, was lost to the Scottish movement in this way,[176] and losses like this drained the pool of potential leaders. One major cause of decline was the unstable nature of many of the new churches. Aberdeen suffered a schism in 1845 when two individuals (the former Chartist preacher one of them) led a secession to the Churches of Christ and the meeting never recovered from this division.[177] In Edinburgh, shortly after Bowes reported dissension over reception to the breaking of bread, there was a schism, and in Wishaw splits led to the existence of two or three assemblies in the early 1850s.[178] Sometimes, as at Hamilton, more than one factor was at work.[179] Lack of vision, declining numbers, and frequent dissensions led to a steady attrition.

By 1855 the divisions of Wishaw had been healed and the assembly had united at Newmains. In the later 1850s the worst of the difficulties were over in a number of congregations. Bowes reported in 1857, 'Upon

---

172. These were: Kilmarnock, Neilston, Newmains, Douglas, Insch, and Clatt. Unfortunately the 1851 Religious Census has no data on Brethren numbers as they are not distinguished by name in it; for Exclusive Brethren in this period, see above, p.2.

173. *TP*, 1 (1849-51), p.255.

174. James Smith to John Bowes, *TP*, 1 (1849-51), p.144.

175. See below, Figure 9.1, p.392.

176. *TP*, 1 (1849-51), pp.238-9; Frederick Daniel also emigrated: Bowes, *Autobiography*, p.226.

177. *Ibid.*, pp.393-4.

178. *TP*, 4 (1855-6), pp.53-4, 119-20; *TP*, 4 (1855-6), pp.53-4.

179. *TP*, 4 (1855-6), pp.221-2.

the whole the churches have rest, and are in several cases adding to their number.'[180] Good leadership was important. Newmains had forward-thinking individuals and John Wardrop, a Wishaw businessman and town bailie, was coming to prominence in the assembly. T. J. Hitchcock, an English evangelist, had settled at Neilston, and, although he still itinerated, he provided leadership for the meeting there.[181] In Kilmarnock, John Stewart also saw a resident evangelist as a solution. In 1858 he brought to the town John Dickie, a candidate for the ministry who had withdrawn due to ill health, to teach in the assembly and evangelise in the community.[182] Dickie undertook a scheme of regular visitation, and, although the congregation remained small, his tact and patience were successful in achieving some notable converts.[183] Growth was also experienced at Newmains, Helensburgh and Neilston, and there were reports of revivals in all three places.[184] The settled leadership of these churches had made it possible for them to consolidate. In addition, the increasing permeation of Scotland by the new forces in transatlantic revivalism meant that by 1858 the Brethren movement in Scotland was on the eve of a major period of expansion.

The movements examined in this chapter, a number of which coalesced in the Brethren, had been to a greater or lesser extent democratised. They challenged established traditions, empowered the laity, and had visions of a transformed society. The upsurge of interest in self-determination among the working classes and its connection with the origins of the lay-directed Brethren movement can be seen most clearly in John Bowes. The religious and social flux of the times provided a favourable climate for the creation of new Christian bodies, and in these conditions, the Brethren grew. The emergence of Victorian revivalism, with its transatlantic influences, had also led to the rise of assemblies and their growth closely mirrored the advance of the piety associated with it. As it appeared in Scotland it eroded the older patterns and formularies of the churches. Yet there were continuities with the past. Bowes was also a link with radical early nineteenth-century Christianity, and figures such as John Stewart, Robert Dickie, and James Smith connected the new movement with older

---

180. *TP*, 5 (1856-8), p.144.

181. *TP*, 4 (1855-6), pp.221-4.

182. James Todd, 'Preface; with sketch of the life and work Mr. John Dickie', in John Dickie, *Words of Life Hope and Love* (London, 1900) pp.v-xxvi; J. T[odd]., 'John Dickie', in Pickering (ed.), *Chief Men*, pp.157-160.

183. John Dickie, *The Story of Philip Sharkey, the Kilmarnock Blacksmith* (Kilmarnock, n.d.); *idem, The Story of William Cochrane: or knowing about it, and yet not saved* (Kilmarnock, n.d.).

184. T. J. Hitchcock to John Bowes, 4 July 1855, *TP*, 4 (1855-7), pp.94-5; *idem*, to John Bowes, 6 December 1856, *TP*, 5 (1856-8), pp.62-3; *TP*, 6 (1858-9), pp. 13-4, 57-8, 111-12.

Scottish dissent in both its Presbyterian and non-Presbyterian forms. Brethren concern for a primitivist ecclesiology gave them one further appeal to those within the latter tradition where such thinking had a long influence.[185]

These origins blended a variety of traditions. The mixture created difficulties in forging an identity in a body which refused to develop central structures and which did not see itself as establishing a separate denomination but as 'gathering to the name of Christ alone'. Although Stewart and Bowes both claimed no master but Christ and criticised the clergy, influences from the English movement and Bowesite ones could not always co-exist, as was almost certainly the case in Kilmarnock. Anti-clericalism showed there was some animus against aspects of other churches, but the first period in the existence of the Scottish Brethren movement was essentially a pre-sectarian phase when the boundaries of identity were still loosely defined.[186] While there had been withdrawal from the institutional church, isolation from society was not marked, and engagement with its problems was a feature of the activities of individuals such as Bowes, Stewart and Wardrop. But the future of the movement was still precarious, for Bowes was over the period the sole itinerant charismatic leader, and temperamentally he was not given to consolidation. Growth had led quickly to decline. With the expansion of the next decade would come increased problems of definition.

185. Derek B. Murray, 'The influence of John Glas', *RSCHS*, 22 (1984), pp.45-56.
186. Bryan Wilson, *Religious Sects* (London, 1970), pp.28-9.

CHAPTER THREE

Days of Power:
Growth and Development 1859-1870

'Long ago we made no bones about it when I preached in Baptist
Churches, and when Hopkins and Boswell went into all the churches in
Orkney and Shetland. But these were days of power...'
J. R. Caldwell to Alex Marshall, 30 August 1909, quoted in John
Hawthorn, *Alexander Marshall: evangelist, author and pioneer*
(Glasgow [1929]), pp.137-8.

'When we were queans,' one eighty-year old woman in a north-east
fishing village wept to a visiting missionary, 'there was no word about
conversion or revival, and naething said about gueed ava. We gaed to kirk
noo's and than's and when we cam hame and got our denner we just
gaed to the Heughs and played the rest o' the day.'[1] But by the early
1860s, when this particular woman was speaking, her community had
been transformed. J. Edwin Orr calculated that some 300,000 individuals,
or one tenth of the Scottish population, were converted during the 1859
Revival.[2] There are difficulties in such estimates as most of those affected
by the revivalism in Scotland were already associated with the institutional
church and did not show up as new members. More recently historians
have criticised the notion of a British revival in 1859, although Janice
Holmes has accepted it affected districts in the western Lowlands of
Scotland to which may be added the north-east Lowlands.[3] However, even
if the larger numbers that have been offered for the scale of conversions
are treated with some scepticism, it is clear that there were traditional

---

1. *Fourth Annual Report of the North-East Coast Mission 1862-3* (Aberdeen,1863),
p.10: 'When we were girls there was no word about conversion or revival, and nothing
said about good at all. We went to church now and then and when we came home and got
our dinner we just went to the Cliffs/Banks and played the rest of the day.'

2. J. Edwin Orr, *The Second Evangelical Awakening* (London, 1949), p.201.

3. John Kent, *Holding the Fort: studies in Victorian revivalism* (London, 1978),
pp.71-131; Janice Holmes, *Religious Revivals in Britain and Ireland 1859-1905*
(Dublin, 2000), p.19; for north-east Scotland, see Kenneth S. Jeffrey, *When the Lord
Walked the Land: the 1858-1862 Revival in the north east of Scotland* (Carlisle, 2002).

spontaneous revivals in some areas of Scotland. There were communities which were changed as a result, and the ubiquity of more orchestrated revivalism ensured it too had considerable impact on Scottish society in the second half of the nineteenth century.[4] Commentators at the time and later detected various social causes behind the awakenings: trade depressions; the insanitary conditions which were endemic to early Victorian towns and cities; and more general social change which continued unabated throughout Scotland in rural and urban communities.[5] The flux provided a favourable context for the activities of Evangelicals.[6] But longer-term trends in contemporary religion also lay behind the revivalist explosion. The building of new churches, the mobilisation of the laity, and the founding of agencies to evangelise hitherto unreached sections of the population extended modern Evangelicalism in Scotland[7] and were among the causes of the awakenings when they came.

Mid-Victorian revivalism was increasingly urban in character and came through means developed to reach such populations: special mission halls, evangelistic meetings, street preaching and services in buildings hired for the occasion.[8] It sought to achieve Christian unity on the basis of the minimalist message of individual salvation which it disseminated. It encouraged lay activity and had an impatience with institutions, a pronounced supernaturalism and a strong eschatological emphasis. Within it there was a shift to a more pietistic faith. Peter Drummond, for example, had commenced publishing tracts at Stirling on social issues such as Sabbatarianism and temperance, but as he was caught up in revivalism from 1854 onwards he began disseminating news of the awakenings and issuing tracts pressing salvation on the reader.[9] However,

---

4. For definitions of 'revival' and 'revivalism', see Holmes, *Religious Revivals*, pp.xix-xx, 52-3.

5. Richard Carwardine, *Transatlantic Revivalism: popular Evangelicalism in Britain and America, 1790-1865* (Westport, CT, 1978), pp.159-7; Callum G. Brown, *The Social History of Religion in Scotland Since 1730* (London, 1987), p.14; Andrew D. Buchanan, 'Brethren Revivals 1859-70' (MA thesis, University of Stirling, 1991), pp.24-5; Geoffrey Robson, 'Between town and countryside: contrasting patterns of churchgoing in the early Victorian Black Country', in Derek Baker (ed.), *SCH*, 16 (Oxford, 1979), pp.401-414; Christopher B. Turner, 'Revivalism and Welsh society in the nineteenth century', in Jim Obelkevich *et al.* (eds), *Disciplines of Faith: studies in religion, politics and patriarchy* (London, 1987), pp.311-22.

6. D. W. Bebbington, *Evangelicalism in Modern Britain: a history from the 1730s to the 1980s* (London, 1989), p.115.

7. Brown, *Social History*, pp.158-9.

8. *DSCHT*, p.715.

9. Stirling University Library, MS50, Peter Drummond, 'The Stirling Tract Enterprise: its rise and progress', MS, Stirling 1860; cf. Michael J. Cormack, *The Stirling Tract Enterprise and the Drummonds* (Stirling, 1984).

despite the claims that Orr made for it, the revivals were not a unitary phenomenon,[10] nor were they necessarily a unifying force within church and society. Just as social change was favourable for its growth, so the religious change that revivalism itself brought aided the growth of new ecclesiastical bodies, the Brethren movement among them.[11] The present chapter will analyse assembly growth during this period, dividing it into two phases of 1859-66, when the initial wave of revivals was having effect, and 1866-70, when more routinised procedures were appearing. The emergence of assemblies will also be related to features of contemporary Evangelicalism.

Brethren Growth 1859-66

The general pattern in the formation of Brethren assemblies during the 1860s was for some members of churches affected by revivalism to form one with further growth following. It can be seen in the earliest Glasgow meeting of the period. In the wake of the 1859 Revival a group of Scotch Baptists who had a hall in West Campbell Street had been feeling their way towards a Brethren form of ecclesiology, a process completed by 1860 (see Map 11 no.17).[12] The most significant accession to the new assembly was some members of Ewing Place Congregational Church where the revivalist Gordon Forlong had held a series of meetings earlier that same year. Forlong had encouraged Bible reading and lay-witness among the converts, but the minister had been unhappy with meetings outwith church control. Some had been gathering for discussions in a house, and eventually a group left Ewing Place—among them silk manufacturer William Caldwell and his son John—to join the former Scotch Baptists' assembly, in the process undergoing believer's baptism. Later an outreach was begun in Dumbarton Road, and in 1866 twenty individuals, including John R. Caldwell, formed a new congregation in the Marble Hall (see Map 11, no.15) as most of their recent converts lived near it.[13] Other assemblies were formed in the working-class areas near Glasgow Cross and in the east of the city. During the summer of 1863 John Bowes, who had moved north to Dundee, attracted by the news of

10. Orr, *Second Evangelical Awakening*, p.201; cf. Bebbington, *Evangelicalism*, pp.116-17.

11. Orr, *Second Evangelical Awakening*, pp.201-3; F. Roy Coad, *A History of the Brethren Movement*, 2nd edn (Exeter, 1972), p.169; Bebbington, *Evangelicalism*, p.203; Orr, *Second Evangelical Awakening*,, pp.201-3; Buchanan, 'Brethren Revivals', pp.47-8.

12. Hy Pickering, 'Home-call of John R. Caldwell', *W*, 47 (1917), p.17.

13. J. G[ray]., 'John R. Caldwell, Christian teacher and writer', *BP*, 38 (1917), pp.22-4; Pickering, 'Caldwell', p.18.

the revivals and resuming the pastorship of the Christian Church there towards the end of 1859, had a mission with a church which met in the City Hall, Candleriggs. This congregation appears to have been in a transitional stage, for James Ritchie, who was described as its pastor, was baptised during the mission.[14] In October Bowes was again in Glasgow, this time at an assembly in Hutcheson Street, off the Trongate (see Map 11, no.18), which was evidently growing.[15] During the previous month there had been sixty baptisms and when Bowes first visited it, there were fifty-seven in fellowship. By the end of the year its membership had reached about seventy.[16] In 1864, when Bowes held a conference in Glasgow for the assemblies with which he was in contact, both these meetings were represented as well as another small one in Parkhead, where he had occasionally preached, on the east side.[17]

The factors which were operative in Glasgow held elsewhere. To the west of Glasgow, Greenock, on the south bank of the Clyde (see Map 12), had been among the first places to have a revival in 1859[18] and in 1862 a group began breaking bread in a house in the town.[19] Greenock was a centre for revivalism and it was visited by several English evangelists associated with the Brethren.[20] Undoubtedly such visits, while largely interdenominational in character, helped strengthen the meeting. In Dumbarton, on the other side of the Clyde, another assembly was commenced, probably in the mid-1860s, when four individuals who had moved to the town for work began to break bread. They met in the home

---

14. *TP*, 9 (1863-6), p.55.

15. *Ibid.*, pp.71-2.

16. *Ibid.*, pp.79-80, 88.

17. 'The Glasgow Conference', *Ibid.*, pp.118-20.

18. K. Moody-Stuart, *Brownlow North, B.A., Oxon: Records and Recollections* (London, 1878), pp.219-80.

19. 'Thomas Black', *W*, 35 (December 1905), endpp. is quite precise that the assembly began '43 years ago' (cf. 'Thomas Black', *BM*, 15 (December 1905), p.i). However, 'David W. Greenlaw', *W*, 48 (1918), p. 62, gives the founding date as 1866 and when Bowes visited Greenock in July 1864 he met a Helensburgh convert who had moved there and who told him that there were some in the town wanting 'to meet in the Lord's name alone', *TP*, 9 (1863-6), p.144. Either: (i) the date in Black's obituary is wrong and the meeting was not formed until later or (ii) Bowes's evidence further shows the separateness of his movement from the emerging Scottish Open Brethren and (iii) the date in Greenlaw's obituary is wrong and the explanation preferred in the text above is correct.

20. J[?ohn]. B[?rown]., 'Some of God's doings in Greenock', *R*, 14 (1866), p.175; *idem* to the editor, *R*, 15 (1866), p.231; J[ohn]. Rae, 'Joy in Greenock', *LR*, 1 (1867), p.61. If the attribution of the first two reports to John Brown is correct, then, in view of his later opinions (see below, pp.203-10), there is a nice irony in the approval of the evangelism being conducted in 'a truly catholic spirit'.

of John Millar, formerly from Randalstown, County Antrim.[21] Further
south in Ayrshire (see Map 13) five assemblies apparently were formed
during the early 1860s. One town on the Ayrshire coast which had been
affected by the 1859 Revival was Irvine, and one of its converts, James
Holmes, along with four others founded the meeting which was
established in the town, possibly in 1862.[22] The county town of Ayr also
had a revival in 1859, and William Brown, the leading individual in the
Wooden Church, a mission in the crowded working-class area of
Wallacetown, was among those influenced by it. One of the first converts
of the revival in the town had been the sixteen-year-old John Justice. A
precocious individual, Justice began evangelising his friends and became
uneasy that his denomination, the Free Church, admitted those he deemed
unconverted to communion. He eventually left it in 1862. Justice was
among those deeply impressed by Gordon Forlong's emphasis on
studying the Bible daily and witnessing to others. He began organising
weekend outreaches to the villages around Ayr,[23] and in August 1863
Brown, Justice and sixteen others were baptised in the sea at Newton
beach.[24] This was possibly a transitional phase for the group, for later

21. David J. Beattie, *Brethren: the story of a great recovery* (Kilmarnock [1939]),
p.257, states 'about seventy years ago' (i.e. *c*.1866, dated from when the articles
appeared in *The Believer's Magazine*); 'John Millar', *W*, 58 (1928), p.279, states that
the assembly began in Millar's house 'over sixty years ago' (i.e. before 1868). However,
writer's collection, I.G.2, photocopy of holograph letter, Robert Boyd to Alex
McIntosh, 21 April 1987, reports oral traditions that the assembly was founded in 1861,
and in the home of Mr Galloway. John Bowes had visited Dumbarton in 1864 where he
had found a group which he encouraged to begin breaking bread (*TP*, 9 [1863-6], p.232)
and several individuals did so immediately after his visit. That it was separate from the
Open Brethren assembly seems certain as none of the individuals credited with founding
the meeting in Millar's house were those of Bowes's contacts. But it is unlikely that the
Brethren assembly existed before the (probably short lived) Bowesite congregation for
the members of the latter claimed that no-one in Dumbarton 'attends to the primitive
practice', Allan Munro to the editor, 13 August, *ibid*, pp.239-40.
22. Beattie, *Brethren*, p.228; however there is considerable variation in the dating of
Irvine assembly's commencement: 'James Holmes', *BM*, (March 1922), p.iii, gives the
date 1870; D. T. H., 'James Holmes, of Irvine, Ayrshire', *BP*, 43 (1922), pp.54-5 gives
the date 1872; but a date in the early 1860s has been preferred here as 'David Gibson',
BM, 16 (November 1906), p.i, states that its subject was a member for over forty years
(i.e. before 1866); if it is assumed that the obituaries of Holmes are ten years out, then
possibly 1862 is the correct date (1860 being a rounding down) and this would
correspond closely with the date of 1860 given in Beattie. The former Labour Cabinet
minister Tony Benn is a great-grandson of James Holmes (oral information, 22 April
1990, from another of Holmes's descendants).
23. M[ark]. K[err]., *Memoir of John Justice* (Ayr, 1875), pp.20-1.
24. 'Unseemly conduct', *The Glasgow Daily Herald*, 2 September 1863, p.5, quoted in
K[err]., *Justice*; p.30-1 (which wrongly gives the date as 3 September 1863); against the
quotation of this article in a copy of the latter work which belonged to William Martin,

tradition held that the assembly was not formed until the following year.[25] The Free Church missionary in Dalry, Samuel Dodds, was another individual troubled by the mixed communion of his denomination.[26] While visiting potential communicants, Dodds became alarmed when he discovered that he could not consider them converted. He began a Bible study in his home, and this led to a small group forming an assembly in 1864.[27] Also in north Ayrshire, an assembly was formed in Largs towards the end of the following year. A popular Clyde holiday resort, two Brethren from Glasgow had seen conversions during their holiday there in 1864.[28] When a newly-married Brethren couple moved to the town, eight individuals began breaking bread supported by the visit of a Glasgow assembly member.[29] In Dalmellington, in the south of the county, two evangelists, both with later associations with the Brethren, had seen conversions in the early 1860s and a group began breaking bread some time after their visit.[30] When the town was visited in 1865 by the evangelist Arthur Massie, a native of the place who had been baptised by Bowes during his mission of 1863 in Glasgow,[31] he reported that the 'brethren' held the breaking of bread monthly and apparently none of them had been baptised as believers.[32] This uncertain start led to the gathering being discontinued some time later.

The county which saw most assemblies planted during this period, however, was Lanarkshire. The Brethren movement in Lanarkshire, aided by the existing assembly at Newmains, emerged out of a group of lay preachers active in the west of the county (see Map 10). The 1859 Revival had made a considerable impact on a number of Lanarkshire towns, and many of the converts continued revivalist activities. Strathaven had been 'one of the most favoured in Scotland' during 1861.[33] The following year Bowes baptised seven individuals in the river there, five of them active in lay preaching, and after the baptisms nine local men observed the Lord's supper, including one individual who had been in

---

Ayr (in the possession of the Martin family), there is a marginal annotation which identifies Brown and Justice as part of the group which was described. There was a family connecton between the founding of the meetings in Ayr and Greenock, for William Brown of Ayr was brother to John Brown of Greenock (see n.20 above).

25. Beattie, *Brethren*, p.233.

26. Anon., 'Samuel Dodds', in J. G. Hutchinson (ed.), *Sowers, Reapers, Builders: a record of over ninety Irish evangelists* (Glasgow, 1984), p.92.

27. Beattie, *Brethren*, pp.218-19.

28. 'Mrs Jessie Flarty', *W*, 57 (1927), p.119.

29. R. Patterson [*sic*] to the editor, 17 January 1866, *TP*, 9 (1863-6), p.288.

30. 'Robert Brackenridge', *BM*, 35 (December 1926), p.iii.

31. *TP*, 9 (1863-6), p.77.

32. Arthur Massie to the editor, 16 January 1866, *TP*, 10 (1866-9), p.288.

33. *R*, 12 (1865), p.268; 'The Revival in Scotland', *R*,16 (1867), p.81.

the discontinued assembly of the 1850s.[34] A year later James Stone, a tenant farmer and one of the lay preachers who had been baptised,[35] wrote to Bowes reporting that an assembly had been formed in nearby Chapelton with about twenty members.[36] Individuals such as Stone had been moving towards Brethren practices when Bowes came in contact with them. This was also the case in Lesmahagow, a town deeply affected by the 1859 Revival, where the assembly apparently evolved independently of the knowledge of Brethren practices elsewhere.[37] Bible reading had continued among the Revival converts, and late in 1864 four of them commenced breaking bread in the joiner's shop of Charles Miller, one of the group.[38] By October 1865 they had made contact with other Lanarkshire Brethren, and Miller was the first of them to be baptised by John Wardrop, watched by almost half the town.[39] The movement in the county was growing. In 1863 an assembly had been founded in Hamilton, probably with some continuity of membership from the Bowesite congregation of the previous decade.[40] At the Hutcheson Street conference of 1864, in addition to representatives from the Lanarkshire meetings in Newmains, Chapelton, and Hamilton, there were ones from an assembly which had been formed at Rutherglen by a Brethren member from Ayr who had moved there.[41] Chapelton and Hamilton both had memberships of twenty, Rutherglen had one of thirty, and Newmains was the largest with sixty.[42]

Revivalist activities continued as the pattern for the Lanarkshire assemblies. In 1864 the Chapelton assembly transferred to nearby East Kilbride, as most of the recent converts were from neighbouring Maxwelltown, and from there the members continued to evangelise the surrounding villages.[43] Assisted by the removal of a Glasgow Brethren

34. *TP*, 8 (1861-2), p.176; writer's collection, I.M.26, 'List of the Members of the Strathaven Brethren' (1862-75), inside cover page; Bowes, evidently including visitors such as himself, noted that 14 broke bread.

35. Strathaven Evangelical Church, Strathaven, 'Roll of Members of Strathaven Assembly 1876-1897', p.3.

36. James Stone to the editor, 23 April 1863, *TP*, 9 (1863-6), p.24.

37. Hope Hall, Lesmahagow, James Anderson, 'A Brief Record Concerning the Early Days of the Assembly in Lesmahagow', MS, 1960, pp.15-16.

38. *Ibid.*, p.17.

39. *TP*, 9 (1863-6), pp.263-4.

40. Oral information, 29 July 1997, based on a note copied from an early roll book (now lost) which gave the founding date as 1863; it appears from *The Truth Promoter* that Bowes continued to be in touch with individuals in Hamilton after the apparent discontinuation of the meeting c.1856 and with the new one from its formation: this suggests some continuity between the two.

41. 'William Wason', *W*, 59 (1909), p.119.

42. 'The Glasgow Conference', pp.118-20.

43. *TP*, 9 (1863-6), p.168.

member to Cambuslang, revivalist services were held by them there, a meeting being formed in 1866.[44] This last year saw a fresh wave of awakenings throughout Scotland[45] and impetus was given to them in Lanarkshire by the visit of Thomas Holt and George Geddes, two young English Brethren evangelists.[46] Their tour of Scotland was largely under the aegis of the Scottish Evangelistic Association (SEA), an inter-denominational organisation founded in 1862 to hold informal meetings and obtain suitable evangelists for them.[47] Holt and Geddes saw their most impressive results in Lanarkshire, claiming, for instance, some 200 converts in Stonehouse.[48] In nearby Larkhall there had been a number of individuals meeting for some time in each others' homes and in the open country for 'Bible searchings'.[49] Several of them had been converted in 1859 or subsequently, and they held gospel services in the district. Larkhall was a centre for revivalism, and it was against this background that the Bible searchings were being conducted. The first baptism among the Larkhall group had taken place in October 1865 when John Wardrop, witnessed by a crowd of several hundreds, immersed one individual.[50] Some time after the visit of Holt and Geddes, and probably later in that same year, nine individuals—all men—commenced breaking bread.[51] About the same time an assembly was also founded in the neighbouring village of Netherburn.[52]

Newmains assembly had succeeded in forming another meeting in the nearby ironstone mining village of Crofthead, West Lothian (see Map 9), in 1861.[53] Other assemblies were formed in the east and north. In Tillicoultry, Clackmannanshire (see Map 7), Robert Archibald, one of the local mill owners who engaged in Evangelical activities, was won over to Brethren principles it would appear some time about 1859. He founded a

---

44. *TP*, 10 (1866-9), pp.12-13; 'George MacLachlan', *W*, 37 (1907), p.155.

45. *LR*, 1 (1866-7), p.53; John Macpherson, *Life and Labours of Duncan Matheson* (London, n.d.), p.167.

46. W. H. Clare, *Pioneer Preaching: or work well done* (Glasgow [1923]), pp.25-30.

47. Gordon Forlong, 'Scotland', *R*, 7 (December, 1862), p.178.

48. Alexander Taylor, 'Showers of blessing in Scotland', *R*, 15 (1866), p.229; 'Times of refreshing in Scotland', *R*, 16 (1867), pp.31-2.

49. Robert Chapman, *The Story of Hebron Hall Assembly, Larkhall, 1866-1928: a short history of the inception, progress and personalities of the assembly* (Kilmarnock, 1929), p.10.

50. Massie to the editor, p.288.

51. Chapman, *Hebron Hall Assembly*, p.11.

52. 'Finlay McDonald', *W*, 46 (1916), p.157; writer's collection, I.M.20, James McAulay, 'A Minor Survey of "The Assembly"', n.d., typescript copy, 1964, gives the date of founding as 1862; but as Finlay McDonald, who is named as a founder member, was not converted until 1866, then it must have been on or after this last date.

53. T. J. Hitchcock to the editor, 27 March 1862, *TP*, 8 (1861-2), p.144.

meeting, building a hall for it in 1864.[54] Further east, in Grangemouth (see Map 9), an assembly was formed in 1866 by a group of individuals who had been converted in the immediately preceding years.[55] The earliest evidence of renewed Brethren activity in Edinburgh also comes from this period. It is probable that the member of the 'Plymouth Brethren' from Edinburgh who preached at a chapel in North Yell, Shetland, in 1863 was Open Brethren.[56] By 1866 a 'brother' was requesting prayer through the pages of *The Revival* for visits to Edinburgh, Glasgow, Tillicoultry and Ayr, an itinerary which suggests visits to assemblies,[57] and certainly one was in existence in the capital by the following year with forty to fifty members.[58] A few assemblies came into existence further north. Dundee had one formed during this period. The city was deeply affected by revivalism and among those influenced was William Scott, a partner in James Scott & Sons, who in 1861 opened a mission schoolroom in the Mid Wynd for the firm's employees.[59] Day-school teachers were appointed to teach and in the evenings Scott and his brother James conducted evangelistic services.[60] Scott was an elder in the Established Church, but he left when he accepted believer's baptism, apparently in 1866, and he began breaking bread with a number of others in his Mid Wynd hall (see Map 6, inset).[61] This was separate from Bowes's congregation, although he occasionally preached for Scott.[62] At Fettercairn, Kincardineshire (see Map 6), in 1862 Bowes made contact

---

54. *TP*, 9 (1863-6), p.128; *The Alloa Advertiser*, 10 November 1864 quoted in Stephen Lennox Johns, *The Gospel Hall Tillicoultry: A Short History* (n.p., 1990), Appendix 3. Johns places the founding of the assembly some twenty years earlier (p.1): the reason for doing so was the recollection that one deceased member of the meeting had stated she was carried to the services as a baby in the early 1850s. However as the individual in question died in 1950 aged 92 ('Mrs Margaret Snadden', *W*, 80 (1950), p.187), this would place this event about 1859.

55. Anon, 'How it began: in Grangemouth', *BM*, 90 (1980), p.66.

56. W. G. Sloan's diary, quoted in Fred Kelling, *Fisherman of Faroe: William Gibson Sloan* (Göta, Faroe Islands, 1993), p.78; this individual was a believer's baptist. The evidence, however, is not conclusive: some Exclusive Brethren were believer's baptists and they were much more likely to call themselves 'Plymouth Brethren'. However, the designation is that of Sloan in his pre-Brethren days (all Brethren tended to be grouped together), and the individual was preaching at a denominational chapel: it seems reasonable, then, to assume he was Open Brethren.

57. *R*, 15 (1866), p.269; this request was possibly from Shadrach Leadbetter.

58. *TP*, 10 (1866-9), p.168.

59. Raymond J. Scott, *History of Mid Wynd International Investment Trust PLC* (Dundee, 1987), p.7; 'Mrs Scott', *W*, 51 (1921), p.96.

60. *TP*, 8 (1861-3), pp.60, 280.

61. Don Palmer's collection, York, interview with Mr Alex Webb, December 1988.

62. *TP*, 8 (1861-3), pp.60, 280.

with one meeting which had fourteen members,[63] and in January 1864 he was present at the second breaking of bread held at Erigmore, Birnam (see Map 3), the home of Mrs Napier Campbell, a lady who preached to her servants and who had come across *The Truth Promoter* in India.[64] An assembly was also founded during this period in Lerwick, Shetland (see Map 1). There had been a revival in the town during the winter of 1862 which had affected all its denominations.[65] Among the visiting revivalists drawn to the islands by the news was J. Albert Boswell, a member of the same family which had produced Dr Johnson's biographer.[66] He made contact with William Sloan, a colporteur with the Edinburgh Tract and Book Society, who had already left the Church of Scotland because he wished to be free of denominational ties.[67] During the following winter the two men evangelised together and in 1864 they began breaking bread in an attic, joined by three women.[68]

Some assemblies whose origins are now lost were possibly formed during this period.[69] One anonymous individual wrote of the development of a meeting in a town designated only as 'B'—possibly Bellshill, Lanarkshire, where an assembly was meeting by 1866.[70] It had been established by converts of the 1859 Revival in the town who had been disturbed by the mixed communion of their former Free Church congregation and its lack of enthusiasm for awakenings. The formation of the assembly was accomplished independently of direct contact with the Brethren movement.[71] But once more it was those affected by revivalism who had created it.

---

63. *Ibid.*, p.240.

64. *TP*, 9 (1863-6), pp.95-6.

65. 'Shetland Isles', *R*, 7 (1862-3), pp.248-9; (1862), pp.262-3; *R*, 8 (1863), pp.18-19.

66. For J. A. Boswell, see J. J. Park, *The Churches of God: their origin and development in the 20th Century* (Leicester, 1987), pp.86-7.

67. Kelling, *Fisherman of Faroe*, pp.60-79.

68. [George Peterson], *A Century of Witness in Ebenezer Hall, Lerwick 1885-1985* (Lerwick, 1985), p.1.

69. Possible candidates for being founded in the 1860s are those designated as existing by a certain date (i.e. the first known reference to the assembly which may, of course, have been founded earlier) in the lists below, Chpt. 4, ns 137, 146, 159, 160, 161, and 293.

70. *TP*, 10 (1866-9), p.72; however, the designation was changed to 'K' in a later publication (see n.71 below) which only came to light when the present work was in an advanced state of preparation.

71. Anon., 'Assembly-life experiences. Letters of an octogenarian', *BM*, 29 (1919), pp.8-9, 21, 33, 117; this was later published as a booklet entitled *Assembly-Life Experiences* (1932) by an Old Disciple.

Brethren and Revivalism

The Brethren movement had had a significant role in the shaping of mid-Victorian revivalism,[72] and it is hardly surprising that revivalism in turn played an important part in spreading assemblies within Scotland. Itinerant evangelists were prominent in bringing the movement north, but apparently in at least two cases—at Lesmahagow and the town of 'B'—assemblies were formed independently of contact with Brethren elsewhere. There are a number of features within the revivals which help to explain this spontaneous process and also the attraction assemblies held for those influenced by revivalism. One explanation might be the eccentric behaviour manifested during awakenings. James Gilchrist, a master baker and a founder member of Strathaven and Chapelton assemblies, created a considerable stir when, dressed in black and mounted on a black horse, he rode from Chapelton to Larkhall carrying a banner inscribed with 'Prepare to meet thy God'.[73] It is possible to see the radical step of severing a church connection and commemorating the Lord's supper with a few others in a house as one more unusual occurrence of the revivals.

An important catalyst in the formation of assemblies was dissatisfaction with the impurities which were perceived in the established churches. Revival preaching stressed the necessity of regeneration and gave an impetus towards the concept of the gathered church, one consisting of true believers only. The newly regenerate individual looked with dismay at those who had not been similarly awakened yet who were still partaking of communion alongside him. 'Why should believers', John Justice wrote to one convert who had joined the Free Church in Ayr, 'be connected with those that don't bear testimony to the truth that God's church is composed of believers alone?'[74] This feeling that the unconverted should be excluded from church fellowship also lay behind the practice of believer's baptism, which stresses that the only fit candidates for the ordinance are those who have made a profession of faith. The only true baptism was that subsequent to conversion, and as with communion, the unconverted could not know its reality. The opposition of many ministers to revivalism was also of significance. At Auchinheath, Lanarkshire, in 1869 one convert was advised by his minister to 'read Burns and Shakespeare, and take care of quacks'.[75] He later became Brethren. Dissatisfaction with the state of the professing

---

72. Kent, *Holding the Fort*, p.116; Bebbington, *Evangelicalism*, p.117; Holmes, *Religious Revivals*, pp.142-4.

73. Chapman, *Hebron Hall Assembly*, p.17; Amos 4:12.

74. K[err]., *Justice*, p.24.

75. *TP*, 10 (1866-9), p.300.

church among the newly awakened made the gathered communities of the movement attractive.

There were, however, several features germane to the Evangelicalism of the period which help explain why revivalist fervour and dissatisfaction with a denomination should lead to the adoption of the Brethren form of the gathered church. The message the revival evangelist had to convey was strongly future-directed and emphasised the brevity of life and the certainty of death. This emphasis on the end of human life made future judgement a reality of consciousness which impinged on daily life. As Robert Miller trimmed a gooseberry bush at Millheugh near Larkhall in 1866, he weighed 'the momentous matters of eternity'. He was converted, pruning knife in hand.[76] An emphasis on hell continued in many Victorian churches.[77] The only solution was redemption through the blood of Jesus and so evangelists laboured tirelessly to save souls.[78] The sense of urgency which the revivals engendered was a powerful influence on those affected by them. When Alexander Taylor, a master baker and Free Church elder in Strathaven, was converted, he commenced two weekly evangelistic meetings and wrote and distributed a tract throughout the town.[79] He later joined the Strathaven assembly, and for individuals such as him the Brethren represented a movement which was continuing the pattern of intense activity that was a marked feature of revivalism. The imperative which the fate of the unconverted created was reinforced by the adventism of contemporary Evangelicalism (to be discussed more fully in Chapter 8).[80] Both factors made the business of propagating the faith the main concern of life for those affected by the awakenings. It was also the central purpose in the existence of assemblies during this period which made them attractive to the zealous convert.[81]

The unsophisticated theology which the revivalists shared made it possible for evangelists of different persuasions to work together. One commentator, writing in 1862, felt of the revival that 'Its glory is that it has no set system of theology, and no stringent creed, beyond those fundamental elements of the faith without which there is no salvation.'[82] Union prayer meetings and unsectarian open-air services were, like the simple message of the evangelists, directing those affected away from the traditional concerns of Scottish church life. A new mood of unity was abroad which anticipated that the Evangelical message and the Bible

---

76. Chapman, *Hebron Hall Assembly*, p.22.

77. Geoffrey Rowell, *Hell and the Victorians* (Oxford, 1974), pp.1-3.

78. Cf. MacPherson, *Matheson*, p.144.

79. Massie to the editor, p.288; the firm Taylor founded still trades under his name.

80. See below, pp.259-66.

81. Cf. the opinion of Hay Macdowell Grant cited in M. M. Gordon, *Hay Macdowall Grant of Arndilly: his life, labours, and teaching* (London, 1876), pp.211-12.

82. M., 'Revival truths', *R*, 7 (1862), p.41.

would provide the basis for union, free from the traditional theological formularies that divided churches. In 1866 a number of leading Scottish churchmen issued a pamphlet calling for unity of creed among the churches based on the Bible. They proposed a series of inter-church meetings which would eliminate conflicting biblical interpretations, for only then 'the fellowship of the Christian Church can be expected to reach its proper development, and her evangelistic work to be blessed with full success'.[83] The project of establishing a universally acceptable interpretation of the Bible was impractical, but it was part of the new spirit of unity for the sake of evangelism and increasing unease with denominational divisions. At a popular level such desires for unity could become frustrated by the continuing divisions.[84] Part of the appeal of the Brethren lay in their claim that they were, in the words of Arthur Massie, 'meeting in the Lord's name' free from 'the evils of denominational-ism'.[85] Assemblies were perceived as expressions of unity having a simple faith based on the Bible and centred on Jesus.

An impatience with institutionalism was apparent in the desires for unity. It is also evident in the way Evangelicalism was being spread by lay preachers and undenominational agencies—the 1859 Revival was known as 'the Layman's Revival'.[86] There had been lay preaching within Scotland, but it had frequently met with disapproval and its most acceptable representatives, such as the Haldanes or Brownlow North, had been from the upper classes.[87] During the 1859 Revival, however, working-class preachers were widely used in Lowland Scotland. In the north east, for example, the cooper James Turner was joined by others such as Duncan Matheson, a former stone mason. These individuals attained a popularity because of their unclerical nature: one of Matheson's converts commented, 'Never till then had I seen a man in the pulpit—only a minister.'[88] Widespread strains began to emerge between the advocates of lay preaching and the clergy.[89] Many lay preachers

---

83. Anon., 'Unity of creed the union of the Christian Church', *R*, 15 (1866), pp.71-3.

84. Cf. K[err]., *Justice*, p.24.

85. Massie to the editor, p.288.

86. Anon. (ed.), *Reminiscences of the Revival of Fifty-Nine and the Sixties* (Aberdeen, 1910), p.xiii.

87. Cf. Arthur Fawcett, 'Scottish lay preachers in the eighteenth century', *RSCHS*, 12 (1955), pp.97-119; D. E. Meek, 'Evangelical missionaries in the early nineteenth-century Highlands', *Scottish Studies*, 28 (1987), pp.1-34.

88. MacPherson, *Matheson*, p.212.

89. Cf., 'The Coasts of Moray and Banff', *R*, 8 (1862), pp.110-11; J. Mackay to the editor, *R*, 7 (1862), pp.79-80; James Stewart, 'The religious quickening in the parish', *R*, 17 (1868), pp.210-12; anon. (ed.), *Reminiscences*, pp.xviii, 46; Orr, *Second Evangelical Awakening*, p.200; MacPherson, *Matheson*, pp.168, 172.

became impatient with clerical domination and the way in which it could render converts inactive. 'The work has for too long a time been thrown over on "ministers",' complained Captain Mackenzie, the secretary of the SEA, 'and their being "specially set apart" has become a shield under which sleepy and self-indulgent Christians have slept on.'[90] The perception of some clergy as being unconverted[91] and the discouragement of converts in witnessing were additional discontents with institutional religion. Much of the work of the revivals was done outside church buildings, in the open air or in halls hired for the occasion, and lay agencies provided independence from unsympathetic ministerial control. The institutional power of the established churches was being circumvented. The link between itinerant revivalists and the Brethren was marked, and a number either belonged to the movement or, like Gordon Forlong,[92] were closely associated with it. The unsophisticated, non-institutional nature of assemblies, maintained entirely by lay people for the spread of the Evangelical message, was a congenial environment for them. It was natural this should also be true for some of those influenced by the evangelists.[93]

For those involved in the 1859 Revival its single most important cause was prayer.[94] It had began in the groups which met for prayer in 1858, and after the first wave of revivals passed one individual believed that 'Scotland would be found covered as with a network of praying people'.[95] These prayer societies are further evidence of the way contemporary religious life was not contained by institutions. They are also an example of an intensified sense of the supernatural which was due to the influence of Romanticism on Evangelicalism.[96] Heightened supernaturalism can be detected in a number of other features present in contemporary piety: in the eschatological note present in revivalist preaching; in the popularity of adventism; in the determination by evangelists such as Arthur Massie to live by faith;[97] in the valuing of the

---

90. Captain Mackenzie, quoted in 'Scottish Evangelistic Association', *R*, 17 (1868), p.168.

91. E. McHardie, *James Turner: or how to reach the masses* (London, 1889), p.154.

92. *The Dictionary of New Zealand Biography. Volume Two, 1870-1900* (Wellington, NZ, 1993), pp. 148-9; despite never associating himself fully with the movement, he was included in Hy Pickering (ed.), *Chief Men Among the Brethren*, 2nd edn (London, 1931), pp.67-9.

93. Cf. anon., 'Assembly-life experiences', p.9.

94. G. F. Barbour, *The Life of Alexander Whyte* (London, 1923), p.101; anon. (ed.), *Reminiscences*, pp.xii-xv; *BM*, 5 (1895), p.3.

95. G. R., 'Scotland', *R*, 7 (1862), p.272.

96. Bebbington, *Evangelicalism*, pp.80-1.

97. Massie to the editor, p.288.

spontaneous above the prepared in preaching;[98] and in attitudes to the Bible. Gordon Forlong was preeminently the evangelist who encouraged new converts to read the Bible,[99] but other evangelists did so too.[100] Contemporary views of scriptural inspiration contributed a powerful effect to revival meetings.[101] It was with an increased sense of awe at God speaking through the very words of the Bible that people listened to the evangelists' preaching and the new converts read it. In the groups which met for 'Bible searchings' after the revivals, a number of features within contemporary Evangelicalism coalesced: the attempt to recreate the fellowship of the primitive church, the Spirit speaking directly to the individual, a unity based on the Bible, and hearing the voice of God in the scriptures. Robert McKilliam, an Aberdeenshire physician, recalled the homely Bible readings, 'when a Bible hunger was strong within us' which were held in Old Meldrum after revivalist Reginald Radcliffe's visit in 1859. 'We used to meet night after night', he wrote, 'in each other's houses, sit around the table with a Book in our hands, with our eyes up to Jesus, our Lord, and talk out to each other our thoughts as He gave them.'[102] The ethos is that of a Brethren meeting. McKilliam later left the Free Church to found an undenominational congregation in Huntly which eventually united with the town's assembly[103] and when he moved to London in 1880 McKilliam himself became Brethren.[104] The spontaneity of the awakenings and the impetus they had given to lay activity, coupled with the increased supernaturalism of contemporary Evangelicalism, were all factors in making the unsophisticated, revivalist, gathered churches of the Brethren movement, with their charismatic, lay-led ministry, attractive to those touched by the awakenings.

New Communities

Apparent in McKilliam's description is one additional appeal the Brethren had. They exemplified the contemporary 'ethical, utopian vision'.[105] The attempt to recover the life of the primitive church was one

98. Chapman, *Hebron Hall Assembly*, pp.18-19; McHardie, *Turner*, p.165.

99. Gordon Forlong to the editor, *R*, 7 (1862), p.296; *R*, 5 (1861), p.92; K[err]., *Justice*, p.21; 'Thomas Cochrane', *BM*, 21 (May 1911), p.iv.

100. Cf. McHardie, *Turner*, p.150; Moody-Stuart, *North*, pp.240-1.

101. Cf. below, pp.176-7.

102. [Jane Radcliffe], *Recollections of Reginald Radcliffe by his wife* (London [1896]), pp.71-4.

103. 'Dr Robert M'Killiam, London', *BP*, 36 (1915), pp.54-6; *W*, 40 (1910), p.55.

104. Pickering (ed.), *Chief Men*, p.176.

105. Bernard Aspinwall, *Portable Utopia: Glasgow and the United States 1820-1920* (Aberdeen, 1984), pp.16-17; cf. *idem*, 'A fertile field: Scotland in the days of the early

such project. It can also be seen in the way the commonplace was felt to be transformed. The descent of Christ was hourly expected, and for those touched by the revivals, daily life was metamorphosised. A camp meeting was begun at Lesmahagow and fellowship meetings were held, cementing the warm association into which members were introduced.[106] The weekly Lord's supper was often an emotional occasion.[107] In Lanarkshire and Glasgow, where Bowes's influence was strongest, individuals such as James Stone, James Ritchie and the evangelist Arthur Massie adopted Wesleyan perfectionism.[108] It was perceived as the issue which had led to the secession of those members of East Kilbride Free Church who had founded the meeting in Chapelton.[109] At Lesmahagow, too, one minister preached against separatists who were 'ignorantly and unblushingly affirming that they are in a state of absolute perfection'.[110] Evidently the assembly members were his target. The entrance into perfect holiness displayed the zeal for building renewed communities in which the quotidian was transfigured.

The passion for the renovated society can also be seen in the acceptance of female preaching among assemblies and the arguments which were used to justify it. Long disapproved of in Scotland, female preaching was regarded by many as one of the excesses of the 1859 Revival in Ireland, but which during the awakenings had spread to mainland Britain.[111] There was a strong antipathy to the practice in Scotland and when women preachers emerged they were regarded unfavourably even by those who were closely involved in the revivals.[112] The liberty allowed to lay people and freedom from the controls of

---

missions', in R. L. Jensen and M. R. Thorp (eds), *Mormons in Early Victorian Britain*, (Salt Lake City, Utah, 1989), pp.104-117.

106. *TP*, 10 (1866-9); C. J. [*sic*] Miller to the editor, 24 September 1868, *ibid.*, p.240.

107. See below, p.259.

108. Stone to the editor, p.24; *TP*, 9 (1863-6), p.88; 'Glasgow Conference', p.120.

109. Moncrieff Parish Church, East Kilbride, 'Minutes of Kirk Session [East Kilbride Free Church]', 2 (1848-83), 25 June 1863.

110. *HA*, 22 June 1867, p.2.

111. Olive Anderson, 'Women preachers in mid-Victorian Britain: some reflexions on feminism, popular religion and social change', *The Historical Journal*, 12 (1969), pp.467-84; Jocelyn Murray, 'Gender attitudes and the contribution of women to evangelism in the nineteenth century', in John Wolffe (ed.), *Evangelical Faith and Public Zeal: Evangelicals and society in Britain 1780-1980* (London, 1995), pp.97-116; Lesley Orr Macdonald, *A Unique and Glorious Mission: women and Presbyterianism in Scotland 1830-1930* (Edinburgh, 2000), pp.182-7; Holmes, *Religious Revivals*, pp.101-33.

112. James Gall to a 'brother', *R*, 10 (1864), p.412; 'Female preaching and preaching in general', *R*, 13 (1865), pp.129-30, 412; I. T. Armstrong, *Plea for Modern Prophetesses* (Glasgow, 1866), p.3; H. I. G., *In Memoriam: Jessie McFarlane a tribute of affection* (London, 1872), p.23.

institutional religion gave the Brethren a predisposition to accepting the practice. Bowes, as a former Primitive Methodist, had always accepted women preaching,[113] and by early in the 1860s assemblies in Lanarkshire also accepted female preaching to mixed-sex audiences.[114] Four women in particular with Presbyterian backgrounds were prominent, two of whom became well known throughout Britain. One of these was Jessie Macfarlane of Edinburgh who came to accept Brethren ecclesiology and adventism and was credited with introducing these ideas into the north east.[115] The other was Isabella Armstrong, an Irish immigrant who had begun preaching during the 1859 Revival in County Tyrone. When she resided in Wishaw, she spoke at the outreach held in the town by the Newmains assembly with which she possibly broke bread.[116] The other two women, Mary Hamilton and Mary Paterson, were converts of the 1859 Revival whose renown tended to be confined to Lanarkshire, possibly because their working-class origins made their wider promotion less acceptable.[117] They were among the group of lay preachers out of which the Brethren in the county emerged in this period, preaching at the Larkhall gospel meetings held prior to the commencement of the assembly there, and active elsewhere in the revivals of the 1860s. Mary Hamilton associated with the Larkhall meeting and Mary Paterson was a founder member of the one in Chapelton.[118] They attained prominence when the second wave of revivalism swept much of Scotland and Lanarkshire in particular.[119]

The novelty of the women preachers drew large crowds and this was obviously one way of justifying their use.[120] There were other ways to sanction the practice, and John Wardrop of Wishaw appealed to two of them. One was the pragmatic argument that their evangelism was effective.[121] To Wardrop's mind the necessary implication of the women's success was that they had been divinely gifted. Given the

113. Mrs Stevens to a friend, 27 August, 1828, published as 'Should women preach and teach?' *TP*, 2 (1852-3), pp.225-8.

114. Neil Dickson, 'Modern prophetesses: women preachers in the nineteenth-century Scottish Brethren', *RSCHS*, 25 (1993), pp.89-117.

115. H. I. G., *In Memoriam*, pp.28-9 .

116. *HA*, 13 June 1863, p.2; *HA*, 27 June 1863, p.2; *TP*, 9 (1863-6), p.46.

117. Mary Paterson, however, preached for the Brethren in Ayrshire and later (as Mrs Gilchrist), for D. J. Findlay in his Glasgow independent mission hall: K[err]., *Justice*, p.78; below, p.94; Alexander Gammie, *Pastor D. J. Findlay: a unique personality* (London, 1949), p.121.

118. Chapman, *Hebron Hall Assembly*, p.13; Moncrieff Parish Church, 'Minutes', 25 June 1863.

119. 'Death of Mrs Fischer', *HA*, 16 May 1925, p.8; 'The late Miss Mary Hamilton', *HA*, 25 October, 1925, p.9.

120. *HA*, 6 October 1866, p.2; Chapman, *Hebron Hall Assembly*, p.18.

121. John Wardrop, 'Revival work in Wishaw', *TP*, 10 (1866-9), p.62.

Brethren acceptance of a charismatic ministry, proven ability was a persuasive argument. The movement also took the Bible seriously and literally, and arguments drawn from expediency could never be enough for individuals in it. One biblical justification which was offered was the interpretation that was adopted of Joel 2:28-9, 'And it shall come to pass afterward, that I will pour out my spirit upon all flesh; and your sons and your daughters shall prophesy'. The Apostle Peter assigned the fulfilment of this prediction to 'the last day', and the appearance of women preachers was seen as indication of the end times.[122] Wardrop also accepted the eschatological significance of female preaching. Quoting the relevant text from Joel, he commented that, 'Truly in these last days he has been making good his word spoken of old'.[123] The prevailing premillennial expectation found among the Brethren made them almost alone in Scotland in espousing this justification for women preaching.[124]

The exegetical key to understanding the scriptural teaching on women preachers was perceived as being the existence of Old Testament prophetesses. Isabella Armstrong entitled the lengthy pamphlet she wrote in 1866 on female preaching *Plea for Modern Prophetesses*. It was an attempt to provide a reasoned case from the Bible to support women preaching. She adduced the eschatological argument to support her case, and she also attempted to harmonise scripture claiming that Paul had been mistranslated.[125] But her central argument was the existence of Old Testament prophetesses and their continuance in the early church. Biblical prophecy, she contended, included teaching as well as foretelling the future, and the prophetess Anna she saw as being a particularly significant example, arguing that Anna was preaching to the crowd when she was presented with the Christ child.[126] Armstrong was expanding arguments which can be paralleled in contemporary writing. They can be found, for example, in the pamphlet which Jessie Macfarlane had written in 1864, *Scriptural Warrant for Women to Preach the Gospel*. They were also used by James Stone in a lengthy letter he wrote defending the practice of women preaching. Stone was prepared to go further in his case, maintaining that women could teach Christians, for Anna addressed the believing remnant and therefore 'she also taught the saints'.[127]

---

122. Anderson, 'Women preachers', pp.470, 480.

123. Wardrop, 'Revival work', p.62.

124. Anderson, 'Women preachers', p.479.

125. Armstrong, *Plea*, pp.52, 17-27; that Paul had been misinterpreted was apparently not accepted by Bowes, as can been seen from his translation of the relevant texts in John Bowes, *The New Testament translated from the purest Greek* (Dundee, 1870), pp.277, 327.

126. Armstrong, *Plea*, pp.46-52.

127. James Stone to Br[other Robert]. Martin, 22 December 1874, transcript in Anderson, 'Lesmahagow', pp.94-103.

Stone's letter is evidence that some Brethren individuals had accepted the biblical case for female evangelists and were willing to enlarge the roles available to women. In other assemblies women were encouraged to participate in meetings for prayer or conversational Bible reading.[128]

Stone also used an additional argument for women preaching. In the conclusion to his letter he found support for his case in the nature of the Church as he understood it. The new birth took precedence over earthly and physical states, and in the Church the born-again have already embarked on the life of heaven:

> As in heaven there is neither marrying, or giving in marriage so let us, who worship God in the spirit consider that here as well, we are all one having been Baptised into one body by one Spirit and all may prophesy, one by one that all may learn and that all may be comforted.

> For there is neither Jew nor Greek there is neither bond nor free there is neither male nor female for ye are all one in Christ Jesus.[129]

The acceptance of women preachers demonstrated the dissolving of society's mores and the creation of a community of equality. Brethren reasoning was that of a movement which, amid adventist expectations, existed for the conversion of others, and which was non-institutional, provided freedom for lay people, and attempted to achieve a primitive, united Christian community based on the experience of the new birth and the Bible. All of these features assemblies had continued from the Evangelicalism out of which they had emerged,[130] and they demonstrated the conjunction of revivalism and the democratisation of Christianity examined in the previous chapter.[131] The arguments for women preachers also exhibit Brethren zeal, which they shared with others among their contemporaries, for establishing renewed communities.

---

128. [John Ritchie], '"A Plea for Sisters": remarks on a recent pamphlet', *BM*, 33 (1923), p.33; Ritchie dated this to 'the early days of assemblies'. However, he did not join the Brethren until 1871 and may be referring to this later period.

129. Stone to Br. Martin., p. 103; the second paragraph is a quotation of Gal. 3: 28.

130. Kent, *Holding the Fort*, p.101.

131. See above, p.27, cf. Nathan O. Hatch, *The Democratization of American Christianity* (New Haven, CT, 1989), p.9.

Table 3.1. **Average ages of converts, 1860-1923, and individuals being received into fellowship, 1860-1928**

	conversion age	reception age
1860-9	19.7	27
1870-9	20.9	26.9
1880-9	22.6	26.4
1890-9	21.9	26.7
1900-9	22.2	26.5
1910-9	20.7	29.3
1920-3	24.1	-
1920-8	-	30.8

Source: 'With Christ', *The Witness*, 33-108 (1903-78).

Continued Growth 1866-70

During the second half of the 1860s the Brethren enjoyed vigorous growth, seen in Figure 3.1. Particularly striking are the peaks in the additions data created by the formation of new assemblies which attracted revival converts from other churches. The percentage increase suggested by the figure is undoubtedly inaccurate as the data on which it is based is less reliable for this period,[132] but the general pattern of greater growth in the later part of the decade accords with that of individual congregations (Figure 3.2).[133] Assemblies appealed mainly to those in early adult life. William Scott at 40 was one of the older individuals involved in the formation of one; more typical were William Sloan, who was 25 in the summer of 1864, and Albert Boswell, who was 24. The average age of sixteen individuals who were founder members of meetings in the early 1860s was 28.5 and all but three of these individuals were born after 1830.[134] This corresponds closely with the age of 27 given for those joining an assembly during the 1860s by *The Witness* obituaries (Table 3.1).[135] This last evidence gives the average age of conversion through Brethren evangelism for the decade as 19.7, and if those converted through other evangelistic agencies from 1859 until 1869 are counted, then this rises to 20.5. These age groups were more responsive to new

132. For the use of this evidence see above, p.16 n.89.

133. Cf. below, pp.80-1.

134. The date of birth may be a year out in some instances as in most cases it has been calculated from ages in obituaries and census returns.

135. For the use of this evidence see above, p.19 n.89.

trends and they had come to maturity in a modernising economy. An analysis of the socioeconomic background of the Brethren in Scotland will be undertaken in Chapter 9,[136] but here it should be noted that those places where assemblies were formed had undergone social change (most usually taking the form of industrialisation) but they retained elements which gave them communal stability, and assembly members tended to belong to the more independent and articulate sections of their society. The energy these middle- and working-class individuals possessed, and the youthfulness of the members, account for much of the vigour of the movement.

The Brethren also continued the theology and practices of contemporary revivalism. Not only the milieu of adventism, but also the revivalist gospel, with its offer of 'instant salvation' and assurance based on scriptural propositions,[137] were continued. Novel techniques to procure conversions, such as several converts giving their testimony at revival services or holding inquirers' meetings, were adopted. It was after the 1859 Revival that hymns, which until then had hardly been used in Scotland, began to be acceptable in religious services and assemblies continued to sing them.[138] In many areas the Brethren also became the pioneers of street preaching and services in specially erected marquees.[139] There were limits, however, to the acceptability of revival phenomena. An individual such as Wardrop had reservations about their more ecstatic manifestations.[140] Novelty *per se* did not meet with approval. It seemed characteristic of the restless *zeitgeist*.[141] The search for a warm, intensely personal faith and the emotional temper of revivalist practices, nevertheless, signalled a shift in the religious life of Scotland. The continued growth of the Brethren was one further indicator of this change and revivalism continued as the principal factor in their increase.

In Glasgow Gordon Forlong's preaching led to the formation of another meeting. He hired a large circus tent at the foot of the Saltmarket for services. After the mission some of his converts continued to gather, eventually forming an assembly, probably in 1866, which later

---

136. See below, pp.289-97.
137. See below, pp.268-9.
138. For examples, cf., Anderson, 'Lesmahagow', p.7; anon. (ed.), *Reminiscences*, pp.14, 112; Barbour, *Whyte*, p.95; K[err]., *Justice*, p.20; McHardie, *Turner*, p.75; James Paterson, *Richard Weaver's Life Story* (London [1897]), pp.131-2; *R*, 8 (1863), p.51; cf. below, pp.174, 314, 346-9.
139. For examples, cf., Carnegie Library, Ayr, ACL 671 BL, H. L. Allan, 'Ayr Half a Century Ago and Since' (series from *Ayr Advertiser*, 1889), XXIX, 'Ministers, &c.'; Samuel Blow, *Reminiscences of Thirty Years' Gospel Work* ([c.1890]) rpt (Glasgow, 1988), p.89; David Pride, *A History of the Parish of Neilston* (Paisley, 1910), p.150.
140. Wardrop, 'Revival work', p.62.
141. Murray McNeil Caird, 'Communion and apostasy', *LR*, 3 (1870), pp.60-4.

met in the Tontine Hall in the Trongate (see Map 11, no.21).[142] The Brethren often attracted the converts of missions held by those revivalists who continued to visit Glasgow. Prominent evangelists associated with the movement also preached at campaigns held by assemblies and individual members hired halls in various parts of the city to conduct gospel meetings.[143] This activity maintained the continued expansion of its assemblies. In 1867 Shadrach Leadbetter, an English Brethren evangelist, reported there had been 105 baptisms during a sixteen-week mission he had held in the city and many more conversions,[144] while by that same year the Marble Hall had grown from its original twenty members to about seventy members and Tontine Hall, which held 700, was filled on Sundays and had 130 members.[145] At least one additional assembly was also established in the east end in Camlachie, where by 1866 a meeting had been formed,[146] possibly the one that was reported the following year in Nelson Street, off the Gallowgate (see Map 11, no.23) with fifty-five members.[147] The emergence of new assemblies near Glasgow Cross and in the east end were signs that growth was taking place and that, as before, it was mainly among working-class individuals.[148]

But the process of planting new churches was again most marked in Lanarkshire where the existence of a strong group of assemblies helped spread the movement until there were some twenty by the end of the 1860s. The growth that three congregations in the county achieved during the decade is shown in Figure 3.2. Revivalism remained strong in the later 1860s in both Newmains and Lesmahagow, and the effect of this can be seen in numerical growth in those places.[149] Brethren evangelistic activities in both communities attracted large crowds. During one period of revivalist fervour in Lesmahagow, the assembly had to abandon its hall and take to preaching in the street to accommodate the hundreds of hearers who had congregated.[150] Additional members were probably recruited from the successful outreaches held in the nearby villages of

142. Beattie, *Brethren*, pp.238-9 (mistakenly referred to as 'Quontine Halls'); 'Mrs Thomas Walker', *W*, 40 (1910), p.151.

143. *LR*, 1 (1867), p.127; 'John P. Sinclair', *W*, (1923), p.26.

144. S. Leadbetter to the editor, 28 November 1867, *TP*, 10 (1866-9), p.180.

145. *TP*, 10 (1866-9), pp. 87-8; Leadbetter to the editor, p.180; *LR*, 1 (1867), pp.68-9.

146. *Ibid.*, p.68: the assembly had a mission in January 1867, and it must have come into existence during the preceding year at least.

147. Leadbetter to the editor, p.180.

148. In addition, there was possibly an assembly in existence in Norfolk Street, Gorbals, by 1867. 'The Glasgow conference on church government, &c', *TP*, 10 (1866-9), pp.97-9.

149. Figures for Newmains 1866, and Lesmahagow 1868, are approximate.

150. Miller to the editor, 24 September 1868, p.240.

Auchinheath and Kirkmuirhill, with Mary Paterson and Mary Hamilton having fervid revivalist missions in both places during 1868.[151] At the beginning of 1866 the Newmains meeting could attract an audience of 4 or 500 to its services held in a schoolroom in Wishaw,[152] and in the last four months of the year there were 150 conversions due to the visits of various evangelists to the outreach there.[153] An increasing number of the converts were from the latter place. In 1869 Wardrop built a hall in Wishaw with greater accommodation and the congregation was transferred there from Newmains.[154] After it was opened Samuel Blow, a Brethren evangelist from London, held a mission during which 'a marvellous wave of blessing rolled over the town' and as a result a further 150 individuals were converted,[155] bringing the total for the period to some 300.[156] However, the kind of steady growth seen in Strathaven was possibly more typical as most assemblies were still small at the end of the decade.

In 1867 assemblies were formed in Rosebank and Holytown (see Map 10), and in the latter place Jessie Macfarlane taught the new members.[157] The following year ones were formed in Kirkfieldbank and in Lanark.[158] Both of these last two meetings were supported by the Lesmahagow assembly which was engaged in outreach to the surrounding towns and villages. Early in 1867 Charles Miller and Miss McCallum of Glasgow were preaching in Carluke and, a little later, Mary Hamilton.[159] By the end of the year several individuals, assisted by Miller on Sundays, had begun to break bread.[160] The following year Mary Paterson held a thirteen-week mission in Motherwell during which there were a number of conversions. As a result of her preaching it was predicted that a church would soon be formed at Watson's Vale near Motherwell[161]— probably a mistake for Watsonsville where Hope Anderson, a former Lesmahagow assembly member, lived and in whose home the meeting began about this time.[162] The advance of the Brethren into those places

---

151. *Ibid.*; Charles T. Miller to the editor, 20 December 1868, *TP*, 10 (1866-9), p.264.

152. *TP*, 9 (1863-6), p.296.

153. Wardrop, 'Revival work', p.62.

154. *TP*, 10 (1866-9), p.299.

155. Blow, *Gospel Work*, pp.87-8; *LR*, 3 (1870), p.22.

156. 'G. F. Jackson', *W*, 65 (1935), p.48.

157. *TP*, 10 (1866-9), pp.144, 180.

158. Miller to the editor, 24 September 1868, p.240.

159. *HA*, p.2; *HA*, 2 March 1867, p.2; *HA*, 4 May 1867, p.2; *R*, 16 (1867), p.133.

160. *TP*, 10 (1866-9), pp.180, 184.

161. *TP*, 10 (1866-9), p.232.

162. Beattie, *Brethren*, pp.215-6; [John Waddell], *Roman Road Hall Motherwell: Centenary 1875-1975* (Lanark, 1975), p.3.

undergoing the latest phase of industrialisation, such as Wishaw, Carluke and Motherwell, was accomplished by the church-planting activities of assemblies in the older industrial communities. There were visitors among the 200 who broke bread in Hamilton at the opening of Baillies Causeway Gospel Hall in 1871,[163] but the size of the gathering demonstrates the expansion which had taken place in Lanarkshire since 1864 when Hamilton had twenty members and the total membership of assemblies in the county had been some 131.[164]

The south and west also had additional assemblies formed. The Helensburgh congregation planted a new assembly at Renton, Dunbartonshire (see Map 12), in 1868.[165] In Ayrshire four new ones were formed (see Map 13). About 1867 a meeting was founded by a group which had been meeting for Bible study in Stevenston, an industrial community which had been the subject of revivalist activities,[166] and it was certainly in that same year that the removal of a Newmains assembly member to Kilbirnie, a growing steel town, led to the formation of one there.[167] In the coastal resort of Troon the assembly was begun by Glasgow Brethren holidaymakers who commemorated the Lord's supper,[168] first meeting in an empty stable in 1868.[169] The visit of Robert Paterson, accompanied by his evangelist sister Mary, to Dalmellington in 1870 saw the re-formation of the assembly there.[170] After they had left, four individuals began breaking bread in a house.[171] Further south in Wigtownshire Murray McNeil Caird had seen an awakening in Stranraer (see Map 14) in 1866.[172] McNeil Caird, the son of the county procurator fiscal, was a former law student who had become an itinerant evangelist and joined the Brethren in Glasgow.[173] Most likely as a consequence of his mission he helped found the meeting in Stranraer which certainly

163. Anderson, 'Lesmahagow', p.59.

164. 'The Glasgow conference', p.118.

165. *TP*, 10 (1866-9), pp.215-16, 279.

166. Beattie, *Brethren*, p.223; 'Mrs Ferguson', *W*, 48 (1914), p.14; 'Rebecca Figgins', *BM*, 32 (1922), p.11; McPherson, *Matheson*, pp.170-1.

167. *TP*, 10 (1866-9), p.96.

168. [Robert Fulton], *Bethany Hall Troon: a Hundred Years of Christian Witness* (n.p. [1970]), pp.1-2.

169. 'C. W. Goodson', *BM*, 29 (July 1919), p.iv, however, the assembly was possibly not consolidated until the arrival of Peter Hynd in 1870, 'Mrs Peter Hynd', *BM*, 17 (November 1917), p.i.

170. 'Robert Brackenridge', *BM*, 35 (December 1926), p.iii.

171. 'Mrs Geo. Wilson', *BM*, 19 (March 1909), p.iv; *BM*, 30 (June 1920), p.i; 'James M'Culloch', *CW*, 42 (1925), pp.82-4; 'James McCulloch', *W*, 55 (1925), p.79; anon., 'The Kindness of God', *Green Pastures* (1908), reprinted as 'How it began: Dalmellington, Ayrshire', *BM*, 97 (1987), pp.232-4.

172. J. G[ray]., 'Murray M'Neil Caird', *BP*, 39 (October 1918), p.102.

173. J. G[ray]., 'Alexander Stewart, Christian solicitor', *BP*, 44 (1923), pp.70-2.

existed by 1868.[174] Revivalism was a persistent feature in Brethren evangelism in western Wigtownshire and in 1869 a further awakening spread from Stranraer to the Rhinns of Galloway and led to several assemblies being founded there in subsequent decades.[175]

The later 1860s also saw the formation of additional assemblies in the east and north. After a mission in 1867 one was formed in Falkirk (see Map 9).[176] By 1868 at Mayfield near Edinburgh (see Map 8) seventeen individuals were in fellowship while in Armadale, West Lothian (see Map 9), there was a small assembly in existence.[177] Boswell and his friends, the English evangelists Rice T. Hopkins and Samuel Blow, were involved in the planting of other assemblies in the east.[178] During 1867 Hopkins and Blow met the converts of recent missions in Aberdeen,[179] and it was probably during this visit when they encouraged a 'little company' to form an assembly in the city[180] which apparently began breaking bread the following year in the Castlegate (see Map 5, inset).[181] When Blow went on to visit Peterhead (see Map 5) he met William McLean, a Scotch Baptist who had been an associate of James Turner, and they held evangelistic services together.[182] McLean had already left his church in 1866 when, after a being involved in a fresh awakening, a female visitor (possibly Jessie Macfarlane) had criticized denominational titles. It was against this background of continued evangelisation and a desire for an undenominational unity that McLean put an advert into the local newspaper in 1868 announcing that 'the Church of Christ' would meet above his ironmongery shop. Among those who responded to the advert was an English visitor who was a Mildmay deaconess, an Evangelical Anglican order of female helpers. Her advice helped McLean establish the assembly.[183]

Boswell and Hopkins also assisted in the formation in assemblies in Orkney (see Map 2). While he was still a nondenominational evangelist,

174. 'Mr John Craig', *Wigtown Free Press*, 27 March 1913, p.5; 'James D. Kennedy', *W*, 46 (1916), p.50.

175. *W*, 32 (March 1902) endpp.; see below, p.129.

176. *TP*, 10 (1866-9), p.96; John Sommerville to the editor, 4 December 1867, *ibid.*, p.168; John Robertson to the editor, 22 April 1868, *ibid.*, pp.199-200.

177. *TP*, 10 (1866-9), pp.207-8, 255.

178. For Hopkins see, Ian McDowell, 'Rice Thomas Hopkins 1842-1916: an open brother', *BAHNR*, 1 (1997-8), pp.24-30; and for Blow, his autobiography, *Gospel Work*.

179. *R*, 16 (1867), pp. 279, 413, 591.

180. Donald Munro, in C. W. R[oss]. (ed.), *Donald Ross: pioneer evangelist of the North of Scotland and United States of America* (Kilmarnock [1903]), p.105.

181. 'John Bendelow', *BM* ,18 (February 1908), p.iv; 'Mrs Peter Tait', *W*, 40 (Apr. 1910), p.71; however, 'David Fowler', *W*, 36 (May 1906) end pp. gives the founding date as 1869.

182. *LR*, 1 (1866-7), p.149.

183. Beattie, *Brethren*, pp.274-6.

Hopkins had been involved in a mission in the islands during the winter of 1866-7, being particularly successful on Westray and in the Scotch Baptist-type congregation there.[184] In 1868 he returned to Orkney for a longer visit accompanied by Boswell. During the intervening year Hopkins had become more fully convinced of Brethren practices. The opposition he had encountered earlier was prepared for him, and Hopkins in return was deeply critical of many of the churches.[185] In private meetings and discussions with converts and supporters the two men taught believer's baptism and Brethren ecclesiology.[186] On Westray Hopkins and Boswell discovered that there was dissatisfaction among the Baptists at the erosion of mutual exhortation from among the members.[187] Hopkins and Boswell visited many of the congregation in their homes, and after the evangelists left the private meetings continued. When a sermon was preached denouncing the new views, some two-thirds of the congregation—about 150 individuals—left to form a Brethren assembly.[188] Meetings also came into existence on the Orcadian Mainland at Stromness and the parishes of Harray and Evie, and on the island of South Ronaldsay.[189] Further south Hopkins and Boswell were among the evangelists in 1869 who had a mission in Dunfermline (see Map 7) which led to the formation of an assembly there. When Samuel Blow visited it the following year there were some forty to fifty members,[190] and Fife had a second assembly founded at Buckhaven in 1870.[191] The Brethren were still growing through attracting others from their churches but increasingly meetings were being formed as a result of their own evangelism.

Yet the 1860s were not a period of unalloyed success for the movement. Despite the impressive growth in Wishaw assembly, the membership lagged behind the number of listeners and conversions, and this was true of elsewhere. There were several factors which hindered growth. Assemblies were still a novelty and were not regarded with universal approval. It was often only the strong minded who joined, for within their communities assembly members were frequently subjected to

---

184. Henry Harcus, *The History of the Orkney Baptist Churches* (Ayr, 1898), p.92.

185. R. Hopkins to the editor, *LR*, 1 (1868), p.199; reprinted as 'Shocking account of the religious state of Orkney', *Orkney Herald*, 14 April 1868.

186. [John Ritchie], *Donald Munro*, ([1909]), rpt (Glasgow, 1987), pp.40-1; Donald Munro, in R[oss]. (ed.), *Ross*, p.117.

187. J. A. Boswell to the editor, *LR*, 2 (September 1869), p.323.

188. *Ibid.*; Harcus, *Orkney Baptists*, p.94.

189. Alex. Goodfellow, 'Death of the founder of the "Hopkinites" in Orkney', *The Orcadian*, 29 April 1916, p.3; Munro, in R[oss]. (ed.), *Ross*, p.117.

190. *LR*, 3 (October, 1870), p.231.

191. 'David Cowan', *W*, 63 (1933), p.71.

obloquy, derision and other forms of persecution.[192] The first baptisms at Ayr were interrupted by a gang of youths who threw wet sand and shouted abuse.[193] Some difficulties were self-inflicted. Soon after the meeting in Ayr was formed it had a division[194] and the Clatt one was discontinued in 1862 due to personal animosities.[195] Revival passed by some existing congregations. The Insch meeting was discontinued some time after 1863,[196] while the same appears to have happened to the Douglas one in the later 1860s. Mrs Napier Campbell's assembly and those in Crofthead, East Kilbride, Falkirk, Fettercairn, Kilbirnie, Mayfield and the Glasgow Bowesite ones, all had an ephemeral existence. The connection between revivals and the formation of assemblies was strong but not ineluctable. Broader support for revivalism in the churches of the north east may help explain why the movement was slower in emerging there, and evidence elsewhere suggests that the presence of a congregation which conducted revivals could inhibit Brethren growth. Contentment with the condition of their church made individuals unlikely to seek change.

Possible Futures

Despite these caveats, however, the 1860s firmly established the Brethren within Scotland, and 1870 brought the promise of further growth (Figs 3.1, 3.2). The revivalist piety of the period left an indelible mark on the movement, contributing a salvationist message and a zeal for spreading it which would be a hallmark of assemblies.[197] John Bowes was no longer the sole Brethren itinerant in Scotland, for in addition to the women evangelists he had been joined by several others. However, the period marked the apogee of his influence. In the heightened enthusiasm of the revivals Bowes's peculiar blend of Methodist and Brethren spirituality found acceptance with many and he still tirelessly itinerated. Yet the future did not belong to him. The meetings in Glasgow with which Bowes

---

192. For examples, cf., Anderson, 'Lesmahagow', pp.38-9, 59-60; anon., 'Assembly-life experiences', p.55; Beattie, *Brethren*, p.241; Chapman, *Hebron Hall Assembly*, p.13; K[err]., *Justice*, p.22; Blow, *Gospel Work*, p.88; John Graham, to the editor, 22 January 1866, *TP*, 9 (1863-6), p.288; Kelling, *Fisherman of Faroe*, pp. 79-80; Miller to the editor, 24 September 1868, p.240.

193. 'Unseemly conduct', *The Glasgow Daily Herald*, p.5.

194. K[err]., *Justice*, p.44.

195. *TP*, 8 (1862-3), p.240.

196. *Ibid*, p.62.

197. Thomas Stewart Veitch, *The Brethren Movement a simple and straightforward account of the features and failures of a sincere attempt to carry out the principles of Scripture during the last 100 years* (London & Glasgow [1930]), p.66.

had been in contact had their own conferences in 1864. But it was the series of believers' meetings begun the following year by Marble Hall members during the twice-yearly Fast Days which became the sole gatherings for Glasgow Brethren and one of the movement's focal points.[198] In Dundee it was William Scott's assembly and not the Bowesite congregations to which subsequent Brethren meetings would trace their lineage. Later one individual was to honour Bowes as a pioneer of anti-sectarianism but as someone also teaching 'things which I have not yet found in the Word.'[199] To those in what was becoming the mainstream, Bowesite assemblies were marked with peculiarities.[200] Although a number of these churches were absorbed into that mainstream, it would become clear that the 1860s led to the eclipse of Bowes's influence and ensured the triumph of traditions associated with individuals such as Darby and Müller—a process hastened by Bowes's death in 1874.

Contemporary Brethren were probably not entirely aware of the latent tensions within the movement. It is possible that there were Brethren who completely rejected female preaching, as some other supporters of revivalism did. More probably, given the absence of a record of dissent from this period, any who were uncomfortable with the practice took the same attitude as two English Brethren critics, Samuel Blow and Russell Hurditch, who did not openly oppose the women but admired their success.[201] Certainly among those who later criticised female preaching some were happy enough to report their activities in religious journals alongside the female preachers and John R. Caldwell, a later critic, preached at the same Wishaw outreach as the women.[202] More certain evidence of potential development in different directions can be found in relationships to other churches. Despite the inevitable breach establishing a separate congregation would cause, many Brethren still perceived themselves as being engaged in a wider movement of revival which was finding expression in various denominations. Much evangelism by them in this period was, in the words of Wardrop, 'free from anything that would lead any one to think it was sectarian in its aims'.[203] Brethren preachers, such as Holt and Geddes in 1866, attempted to make converts, not to procure Brethren proselytes.[204] It was Charles Miller who reported

---

198. C. J. Pickering *et al.*, *1865-1965: The Half-Yearly Meetings of Christians in Glasgow* (n.p., [1965]).

199. 'John Bowes', *CW*, 28 (1913), pp.162-3.

200. J. A. Boswell, 'The Open position', *NT*, 12 (1900), p.74.

201. Blow, *Gospel Work*, pp.86-7; [C. R. Hurditch], 'Female preaching', *LR*, 1 (1867-8), pp.235-6.

202. *HA*, 16 February 1867, p.2; *HA*, 13 April 1867, p.2; for Caldwell's views see below, p.152.

203. Wardrop, 'Revival work', p.62.

204. *HA*, 26 January 1867, p.2.

in the nondenominational paper, *The Revival*, a week of special meetings held in 1867 by the Lesmahagow churches, and the assembly joined in by inviting the SEA to its Gospel Hall.[205] When William Arnot, the Hamilton agent of SEA, joined the Brethren about 1868 he continued an outreach he held under its auspices assisted by the town's assembly members.[206] Glasgow Brethren also engaged in interdenominational cooperation. At a meeting in Hamilton chaired by Arnot, held to report on the 1866 Lanarkshire revivals, Caldwell preached on the second advent.[207] Brethren preachers also helped in the revival services held in the Circus in Ingram Street and assisted in teaching young converts there.[208] Nor were assemblies consistently baptistic in their practice. The Strathaven membership rolls had a separate column for those in fellowship who were baptised as believers. The issue led the Scotch Baptist element to secede from the Helensburgh congregation in 1869 for a closed communion in contrast to those members who identified with the Brethren and who held that the Lord's table should be open.[209] For many individuals in this period, the Brethren were an instinctive extension of their piety and they had no wish to establish a rival grouping. For them, assemblies were a natural emanation from contemporary Evangelicalism.

But a negative response to the mixed communion of the existing churches was there from the beginning. Strains between revivalists and the institutional church have already been noticed and these continued to sour relations between assemblies and other Christian bodies. For McNeil Caird all denominations were wrong: 'men are wrong, systems wrong, creeds wrong, principles wrong, the church wrong, everybody and everything wrong'.[210] At 'B' the Lord's table was closed to those still in a church.[211] In addition a number of the visiting English revivalists advocated isolation. 'God seems to be showing his own children separation', Shadrach Leadbeatter noted contentedly during his tour of

205. C[harles].T. M[iller]. to the editor, *R*, 16 (1867), p.204.

206. Ernest Baker, *The Life and Explorations of Frederick Stanley Arnot* (London, 1921), p.18.

207. 'Christian Conference at Hamilton', *R*, 16 (1867), pp.31-2.

208. *LR*, 1 (1866), pp.12, 37, 126.

209. *TP*, 10 (1866-9), p.299; cf. Anderson, 'Lesmahagow', p.41; John Bowes, 'Christian communion and sectism', *TP*, 9 (1863-6), pp. 9-11; J. R. Caldwell to Alex Marshall, 30 August 1909, quoted in John Hawthorn, *Alexander Marshall: evangelist, author, pioneer* (London and Glasgow [1929]), p.138; Chapman, *Hebron Hall Assembly*, pp.61-2.

210. McNeil Caird, 'Communion and apostasy', p.62.

211. Cf., anon., 'Assembly-life experiences', p.69.

Scotland in 1867.[212] In the second year of the Glasgow Fast Day meetings one visiting preacher urged his hearers to go *far* outside the camp, an image for joining an assembly.[213] As the experience of Hopkins and Boswell in Orkney demonstrated, some found cooperation with other Evangelicals increasingly difficult.[214] They had arrived at the point which those engaged in transdenominational revivals characteristically reach between giving the higher value to evangelistic or ecclesiological factors.[215] And even the attitude of those who seemed open to co-operation was ambivalent. It was reported that the Lesmahagow Brethren would not enter a church, holding that those who did not agree with them were in 'utter darkness'—undoubtedly a calumny which nevertheless probably had some substance in acerbic criticisms of the institutional church by the meeting members.[216] It was his contacts with individuals such as Caldwell which won William Arnot for the Brethren.[217] As Orkney had shown, cooperation could become a cover for proselytism.[218]

Mid-Victorian revivalism established the Brethren within Lowland Scotland. The planting of new assemblies was initially dependent on awakenings in established churches, but increasingly meetings became capable of sustaining their own recruitment. The Brethren were themselves an innovative renewal movement, embracing and promoting the new features of contemporary popular Evangelicalism, such as women preachers or its gospel of instant salvation and propositional assurance. They balanced between withdrawal and integration. For some this was a pre-sectarian phase, when interdenominational revivalism was the most salient feature of their religious experience. An individual such as John Wardrop even continued to share the mainstream Evangelical attitude of involvement in the affairs of society. As a bailie he helped in burgeoning Wishaw being founded as a Police Burgh and at the height of the awakenings of the early 1860s he was its provost. He was part of the

---

212. Leadbetter to the editor, p.180; cf. [John Bowes], 'The Perth Conference', *TP*, 9 (1963-6), p.59.

213. C. S. Blackwell to ——, 4 November 1866, in *A Living Epistle: or Gathered Fragments from the Correspondence of the Late Caroline S. Blackwell* (1873) John Ritchie edn (Kilmarnock, n.d.), p.79.

214. Anon., 'Assembly-life experiences', p.55.

215. Klaus Fiedler, *The Story of Faith Missions: from Hudson Taylor to Present Day Africa* (Oxford, 1994), pp.169-77; cf. K. B. E. Roxburgh, 'George Whitefield and the Secession Church in Scotland: an unpublished letter from Ralph Erskine', *Journal of the United Reformed Church History Society*, 5 (1995), pp.375-382; D. W. Lovegrove, 'Unity and separation: contrasting elements in the thought and practice of Robert and James Alexander Haldane', *SCH: Subsidia*, 7 (Oxford, 1990), pp.153-77.

216. *HA*, 22 June 1867, p.2.

217. J. G[ray]., 'Mrs William Arnot', *BP*, 46 (1925), pp.82-4.

218. For this point, see below, p.175.

base on which Gladstonian Liberalism was being built.[219] The intensely personal piety revivalism fostered, however, led most Brethren to withdraw into a private spiritual world.[220] The pull of separatism could be seen most clearly in relations with other Christian bodies. Brethren itinerant preachers had found undenominational revivalism congenial because of their lack of a developed institutional sense, their concept of an unsophisticated unity based on a minimalist Evangelical message, and the urgent priority which they gave to evangelism. Assemblies formalised these features, along with several other emphases of contemporary popular piety, into an ecclesiology. From the inception of their meetings, there were those who made both its acceptance and the separation from a mixed communion a condition of fellowship. The strains which this engendered became more pronounced towards the end of the 1860s. The obverse of the zeal with which the renewed communities of the Brethren were entered was the horror with which the impure bodies that had been left behind were regarded. Outward expansion and the dynamic impulse of sectarian separation were to be the main concerns of Scottish Brethren for the rest of the century.

219. 'Death of Mr John Wardrop', *HA*, 3 September 1892, p.6.
220. J. R. Caldwell, 'Earthly things and things above', *LR*, 3 (1870), pp.206-8.

CHAPTER FOUR

A Grand Missionary Institution:
Growth 1871-1914

'Let each teacher with his assistants have two meetings every week for preaching the Gospel to the ungodly, and all this quite independent of your church meetings. In this manner you become a *grand missionary institution.*'
Donald Ross to 'one who had begun a meeting in the name of the Lord Jesus', 1 September 1871, quoted in C. W. R[oss]. (ed.), *Donald Ross: pioneer evangelist of the North of Scotland and United States of America* ([1903]), p.97.

When Rice Hopkins and Albert Boswell first came north it was to meet Duncan Matheson at the Perth Religious Conference.[1] This annual conference had been founded in 1860 by John Milne, a Perth Free Church minister, in imitation of the Barnet (later Mildmay) conferences.[2] It became the centre of the Scottish revivalist network and was important for diffusing nineteenth-century transatlantic revivalism within the country. Matheson was one of the acknowledged leaders among the Scottish lay evangelists. In 1868 in his final address to the conference before his death he described the new breed of itinerant revivalists: 'I call the majority of them irregulars, free lances, knowing no church, understanding nothing of parochial divisions, subject to no master but Christ...'.[3] He was aware of the tensions between them and the clergy: he was critical of the officiousness of some ministers and their lack of sympathy for revivalism.[4] His answer to the problem was to concentrate

---

1. Ian McDowell's collection, Chadstone, Australia, W. H. Hopkins, untitled typescript on the early life of R. T. Hopkins, n.d., Chpt. IV; J. A. Boswell, 'The Open position', *NT*, 12 (1900), p.74.

2. Horatius Bonar, *Life of the Rev. John Milne of Perth*, 5th edn (London [1868]), pp.337-40.

3. John Macpherson, *Life and Labours of Duncan Matheson: the Scottish evangelist* (London, n.d.), p.234.

on the task of evangelism and he went on to plead with his audience to avoid controversy and to 'pray, labour and live for the lost'.[5] 'We have nothing to do with the bagging of the game,' he reputedly said to Boswell.[6]

But it was to the problem of what to do with the converts that some of his associates began to turn. Matheson's closest friend among the itinerant evangelists was Donald Ross, the superintendent of the undenominational North-East Coast Mission (NECM) which had helped spread revivalism to the fishing communities of the north east since its founding in 1858.[7] It was due to Ross's influence that the Brethren movement was established in the region. The present chapter will examine the process by which Ross came to join the Brethren along with many of his adherents and followers during 1871 until 1873. The discussion will then turn to analysing the growth of the movement in the rest of Scotland before World War I. The period will be divided into two, the secession of the Churches of God during 'the Separation' of 1892-4 forming the dividing line.[8] The first twenty years will be analysed by regional growth, as this allows separate discussion of growth in rural and industrialised contexts to illuminate the similarities and contrasts between them. However, the industrialised communities themselves will be analysed by causes of formation, the procedure which will also be followed for the second two decades. The former two decades demonstrated more vigorous growth than the latter and some of the underlying causes of this increase and its slackening will be noted throughout the chapter with a final section which will seek to isolate the factors behind the growth in more detail. There is, however, a difficulty with sources for this period. The final extant volume of *The Truth Promoter* is 1869,[9] and although the predecessor of *The Witness* magazine, which carried news of assemblies and itinerant evangelists, was founded in 1870,[10] there are large gaps in the preservation of the news

4. C. W. R[oss]. (ed.), *Donald Ross: pioneer evangelist of the North of Scotland and United States of America* (Kilmarnock [1903]), p. 41; W. H. Clare, *Pioneer Preaching: or work well done* (Glasgow [1923]), p.64.

5. Macpherson, *Matheson* , p. 236.

6. Duncan Matheson quoted in [Alexander Marshall], *Wandering Lights: a stricture on the doctrines and methods of Brethrenism. A review by A. M.*, 3rd edn (Glasgow, n.d.), p.17; Matheson is quoted as speaking to 'Mr. B.' who later became Brethren, evidently Boswell: for the association between the two men see, Macpherson, *Matheson* , pp. 177-9; and Boswell, 'Open position', p.74.

7. *DSCHT*, pp.324, i.

8. For discussion of this schism, see below, pp.158-69.

9. See above, p.15 n.83.

10. For the history of this magazine, see below, p.146 n.33.

sections in extant copies.[11] With the founding of *The Believer's Magazine* in 1891 and the conservation of *The Witness* news sections after 1902, contemporary sources improve, but much of the history of the earlier part of this period has been reconstructed from obituaries. Nevertheless, it is clear from the existing evidence that the four decades discussed here saw the greatest increase in both the number of assemblies and Brethren membership in the history of the Scottish movement.

The Northern Evangelistic Society

Matheson had acted as a brake on Donald Ross, but after Matheson's death in 1869 Ross's discontent with the institutional church increased.[12] His dissatisfaction had several sources. The acceptance by his denomination, the Free Church, of those whom he felt were unconverted was one cause of his disaffection, a feeling which existed before he had any solution for it. At Aberlour on Speyside he preached on the text 'Come out from among them, and be ye separate'.[13] After the service an elder in the Established Church put his hand on Ross's shoulder and said, 'All true, dear brother Ross; but where are we to go?' Ross answered, 'That is what is troubling me.'[14] One communion Sunday (probably in 1869) he noticed two sellers of alcoholic spirits present. 'By my very presence with them', he thought 'I am encouraging them to think they are Christians, and thus helping the devil to lead them down to hell. I shall certainly never be found here again.'[15] For the next two years, he took communion only at the Perth Conference with his fellow Evangelicals because it was a *'select company'*.[16] The direction in which his mind was moving was shown by his acceptance in 1870 of believer's baptism. All thirteen of his children had been baptised as infants, but his growing doubts were confirmed by an elderly Baptist woman who explained the bad behaviour of some young people by noting that they were unconcerned because they believed christening made them Christians. A farmer friend, John Davidson of Gowanwell, New Deer, had already been baptised by John Rae, who apparently had earlier considered joining the Brethren and was in this period the Baptist pastor in Aberchirder, Banffshire.[17] Davidson baptised Ross in the River Dee at

---

11. See above, p.18 n.83.
12. R[oss]. (ed.), *Ross*, p.41.
13. 2 Cor. 6:17.
14. R[oss]. (ed.), *Ross* , pp.45-6.
15. Donald Munro, in *ibid.*, p.110.
16. *Ibid.*, pp.110-11.
17. Wm M. Rae, 'John Rae, pioneer evangelist, western Canada', *BP*, 41 (1920), pp.70-4; H. A. Ironside, *A Historical Sketch of the Brethren Movement* (1942), rpt

Aberdeen several days after the comment from the Baptist woman.[18] Revivalism had directed him towards the gathered church.

Another principal source of Ross's dissatisfaction was the faults he saw in the ministers themselves. He blamed them for the lack of conversions and the spoiling of those which were made. The only role churches provided for new converts was a very circumscribed one instead of further involvement in the aggressive evangelism he favoured. Ross complained of the ministers to a friend:

> the *real* converts trained under them, instead of being *reproductive* in saving others, are, with few exceptions, withered and wasted...they waste the little fragrance they have on seat-letting, standing by the plate on a Sunday morning, or giving a few coppers to make up the minister's salary.[19]

Given to strong utterance, he published a tract suggesting that if the majority of church ministers were removed for ten years or more and nine pairs of evangelists were let loose in Scotland, then greater changes would be effected than were achieved at present through all the clergy.[20] Ministers, he felt, 'in the name of God, were doing the devil's work.'[21] The 1859 Revival had made a deep impression on the north east but a decade later not all clergy favoured the lay revivalism fostered by the NECM. A number of individuals in places such as Speyside had joined

---

(Grand Rapids, MI, 1985), pp.71-2; 'John Davidson', *W*, 35 (July, 1905), end pp.; George Yuille (ed.), *History of the Baptists in Scotland* (Glasgow, 1926), p.275. There is some difficulty in dating Rae's first association with the Brethren. His final break from the Baptists undoubtedly took place in Elgin in 1872 as his letter to *The Latter Rain* of 1873 shows (see below, n.49); but W. M. Rae (probably a son) appears to place Rae's first contact with the Brethren during his spell as a Baptist evangelist in Greenock, where Rae had initially been a Presbyterian missionary, prior to Rae's time in Elgin. He wrote that Rae found 'a little company of simple believers in the community' and the context suggests that the last word quoted here refers to Greenock. Certainly while there Rae corresponded with *The Latter Rain*, edited by Brethren member C. Russell Hurditch (see above, p.62 n.20), and associated with Brethren evangelists who worked interdenominationally. W. M. Rae also portrays Rae's decision to sever his connection with the Baptists as being taken over a period and made after that of his wife. However, he compresses his account of Rae's final years among Baptists, omitting Rae's pastorates in the north east. At least two of Rae's associates there became founders of the New Deer assembly: John Davidson and Rae's brother-in-law, William Ironside in whose house the meeting first gathered. Unless the elisions in W. M. Rae's narrative are held to undermine its trustworthiness, some initial contact with the Brethren assembly in Greenock is therefore probable with deeper contact following in Rae's native north east.

18. Munro, in R[oss]. (ed.), *Ross*, pp.107-8, 112-13.

19. Quoted in R[oss]. (ed.), *Ross*, pp.45-6

20. Quoted in Hugh McIntosh, *The New Prophets: being an account of the operations of the Northern Evangelists* (Aberdeen, 1871), p.20.

21. Donald Ross, *Our Record*, quoted in R[oss]. (ed.), *Ross*, p.46.

Baptist churches or, as had happened in the coastal village of Newburgh, had severed all church associations because they felt the ministers were unsympathetic to their piety.[22] In addition, Ross felt that ministerial control of the NECM was growing excessive. Early in 1870, he resigned from it and established the Northern Evangelistic Society (NES) to evangelise the inland parishes of the north east.[23] Ross began living by faith and his new venture was financed by relying on 'God for Supplies' and with 'no committee of directors but the Father, Son and Holy Ghost'.[24]

Theological factors were also of significance in creating tension between the NES and Presbyterian churches. The society maintained in an extreme form that assurance was of the essence of salvation and therefore individuals who, in the older Scottish manner, expressed uncertainty about their final salvation were deemed not to be regenerate.[25] The evangelists assumed that most ministers and church members were not Christians at all and as a result they tended to exaggerate greatly the decline of Evangelicalism in the churches. Ross strongly denied that he was a Morisonian in theology and he remained a life-long Calvinist.[26] But undoubtedly a modified version of Finney's ideas concerning revivals was present in the NES. It was accepted that prayer led to revival, it was hindered by Christians not being in a proper condition, and God made promises to his servants concerning specific communities which could be claimed by faith.[27] Practices were also used such as praying by name for individuals who were present and bluntly informing people in conversation that they were going to hell.[28] Because

22. Mrs Innes in R[oss]. (ed.), *Ross*, pp.203-4; Donald Ross to a Newburgh clergyman, 12 April 1867, in *ibid.*, p.88.

23. The NES was possibly founded in May 1870; J. A. H. Dempster calculated that Ross commenced publishing *The Northern Evangelistic Intelligencer* in June 1870 (see below, p.146 n.33), and probably the new publishing venture coincided with the formation of the new institution.

24. R[oss]. (ed.), *Ross*, pp.46-7.

25. The NES motto was: 'Eternal salvation is a free, present, attainable, inalienable, imperishable gift; i.e., any man or woman in this world, be he or she the blackest sinner in it, may, in one moment, be justified for ever, from every charge of sin; and may beyond all doubt, that he is justified; and may rest as sure of Eternal Glory as he is certain in himself he never has deserved and never will deserve, anything but eternal damnation,' *NEI*, 2 (1872), p.6.

26. Ross to a Newburgh clergyman, in R[oss]. (ed.), *Ross*, pp.86-9.

27. Donald Ross to a NECM candidate, 16 December 1862 in *ibid.*, pp.78-9; *idem* to a missionary, 11 July 1863, in *ibid.*, p.80; *idem* to anonymous correspondent, 5 February 1867 in *ibid.*, p.83; *idem* to two missionaries, 17 March 1868 in *ibid.*, p.90; *idem* to a missionary, 22 January 1870 in *ibid.*, p.92; McIntosh, *New Prophets*, pp.14-17.

28. G. R. Masson, *et al.*, 'Footdee Recollections', in Ross (ed.), *Ross.*, p.144; McIntosh, *New Prophets*, pp.26-7.

of the importance assigned to the agents of revival, a heightened state of holiness was eagerly sought. Some evangelists in the NES had adopted the ideas of 'the higher Christian life', a phrase given currency in the title of a book by William Boardman, the American holiness teacher.[29] The links between the Mildmay and Perth conferences probably were an influence here. Boardman had spoken at Mildmay in 1869 where he expounded his concept, derived from Methodist perfectionism, that the individual could know victory over sin through consecrated faith.[30] This teaching was certainly promulgated by Donald Munro,[31] one of the most prominent evangelists in the NES, and by Ross himself, who thought that by walking in the Spirit the believer might 'live in perpetual victory',[32] and who in his magazine, *The Northern Evangelistic Intelligencer*, published articles expounding the higher life.[33] 'Baptism by the Holy Ghost', it was claimed, was the beginning of revival.[34] The mixture of revivalism, absolute assurance, the experience of the higher life, and claims to discern the will of God was a heady one. The NES evangelists were moving towards a less institutional, more charismatic Christianity. It was a further upsurge of a democratised religion, and it drove an additional wedge between them and the churches.[35]

Matters came to a head early in 1871. The NES came to the Garioch district of Aberdeenshire (see Map 5) in the spring of that year to hold a series of missions. Feelings were running high. When Donald Munro and Alex Carnie began their mission in Inverurie, the second evening meeting was disrupted by about thirty individuals who shouted continuously and at the end of the service attempted to attack the preachers. Converts were made, but because of the prevailing hostile atmosphere they underwent a fair degree of persecution. The society and the churches were now competing: after Munro and Carnie left Inverurie the ministers held their own special services,[36] and the same happened later in Huntly.[37] When

---

29. W. E. Boardman, *The Higher Christian Life* (Edinburgh, 1859).

30. *BDEB*, 1, p.113, i.

31. [John Ritchie], *Donald Munro 1839-1908: a servant of Jesus Christ* (Kilmarnock [1909]), rpt (Glasgow, 1987), p.72.

32. Donald Ross, 'A clear statement', *W*, 69 (1939), p.5; this article was written about 1870.

33. Anon., 'Loose him, and let him go', *NEI*, 2 (1872), pp.13-4; W. H. W., *NI*, 3 (1873), pp.7-10; W. E. Boardman, 'Faith and Consecration', *NI*, 3 (1873), pp.44-7; H. V[arley]., 'Trust in the living Father', *NEI*, 4 (1874), pp.37-41; *NI*, 4 (1874), pp.137-41; Anon., 'Power from above', *NW*, 5 (1875), pp.73-6.

34. *NEI*, 2 (1872), p.59.

35. Nathan O. Hatch, *The Democratization of American Christianity* (New Haven, CT, 1989); cf. above pp.27, 29-41, 77.

36. *The North Star*, 11 April 1871.

37. *NA*, no. 2 (February 1873), p.8; *NA*, no. 4 (April 1873), p.16.

Munro moved on to Kemnay the local laird Alexander Burnet, John Bowes's erstwhile companion,[38] attempted to stop those in his employment from attending the meetings.[39] A Free Church licentiate in Inverurie, Hugh McIntosh, wrote a series of letters to the *Aberdeen Free Press,* criticising the NES, dubbing it 'the New Prophets' because of the similarity he saw between it and movements such as Montanism.[40] His sources were a mixture of personal observation, NES publications and hearsay (his least dependable one).[41] McIntosh was an Evangelical and was not opposed to revivals, but he objected strenuously to some of the more extreme anti-clerical NES statements, and he claimed that various expressions of the evangelists about forgiveness and sanctification, which obviously arose out of their doctrine of assurance and from higher-life teaching, were heretical.[42] He regarded the type of revivalism fostered by the NES as being extremist, and significantly he quoted extensively from Asahel Nettleton's strictures on Finney's 'new measures'.[43] McIntosh's letters were soon published in expanded form as a pamphlet which received a considerable circulation.

Ross had reached the point where to follow Matheson's advice of 1868—'pray, labour and live for the lost'—was no longer a solution to disagreement with ministers but had become the cause of the disagreement.[44] The churches he regarded as being peopled mainly by the unconverted, and the ministers were either passively acquiescing in something hopelessly corrupt or giving positive encouragement to it. Ross felt that most of his converts must come from among the respectably religious. He left the Free Church determining to have nothing more to do with denominations. He seemed to have few options open to him, and in August 1871 he disbanded the NES so that its members would be alone responsible for their actions. Though not without grave doubts initially, he began breaking bread with the small assembly in Aberdeen, where he lived, eventually merging forces with it in his chapel in the Castlegate (see Map 5, inset).[45] In a favourite phrase, he had been 'squeezed out' of the existing denominations.[46]

---

38. See above, p.51.
39. [Ritchie], *Munro,* p.57-8; Burnet is not mentioned by name but is evidently intended.
40. Hugh McIntosh, 'The New Prophets', *Aberdeen Free Press,* 7, 14, and 21 April, and 12 May 1871.
41. Cf. McIntosh, *The New Prophets,* p. 20, and John Ritchie, 'Revival times and work in Aberdeenshire', in R[oss]. (ed.), *Ross,* pp.161-2.
42. McIntosh, *New Prophets,* pp.5-12.
43. *Ibid.,* pp.18, 21, 27, 36.
44. Cf. Ross, *Our Record,* quoted in R[oss]. (ed.), *Ross.,* p.44-5.
45. R[oss]. (ed.), *Ross,* pp.54-5.
46. *Ibid.,* p.61.

In the Garioch the converts from the society's campaigns also puzzled over their relationship to their churches. They were finding it increasingly difficult to stay within them, as sermons and conversations were against their continued activities in evangelisation. In their zeal, it was later admitted, not all their actions were wise. When the church choir in Inverurie performed at a concert in the town hall, some of the NES converts gave out tracts at the door.[47] Various groups throughout the north east were gathering for prayer and Bible readings, looking for a way forward. The group at Old Rayne acted first (probably in advance of Ross), meeting to break bread in a joiner's shop in April 1871, and they were apparently followed by the Inverurie one in the autumn.[48] Others who were searching took similar action, including most of the society's ten evangelists, and during 1871-3 some twenty-eight meetings were formed in the region[49] and two further south in Perth and Kirriemuir, Angus (see Map 6).[50] All churches suffered in the secession, but particularly affected were the region's small Baptist churches: Elgin, Grantown, New Deer, Kemnay, Inverurie and Banchory-Ternan, all lost

---

47. Ritchie, 'Revival times', in *ibid.*, p.167.

48. *Ibid.*, p.174.

49. These were in: Moray and Nairn (see Map 4): Aberlour (*NA*, no. 13 (May 1873), p.14); Boharm (R[oss]. (ed.), *Ross*, p.174); Dufftown ('Mrs Farquharson', *W*, 51 (1921), p.12); Elgin (John Rae to the editor, *LR*, 5 (1873), p. 83); Findhorn (*NA*, no. 15 (March 1872); p.12); Keith (R[oss]. (ed.), *Ross*, p.115); Forres (*ibid.*); Nairn (*NA*, no. 3 (March 1873), p.12); Rothes (*NA*, no. 2 (February 1873, p.8); Aberdeenshire (see Map 5): Auchterless ('William Cowie', *BM*, 16 (November 1906), end pp.); Braco (R[oss]. (ed.), *Ross*, p.174); Old Flinder (*ibid.*, p.197); Fraserburgh (*NA*, no. 15 (March 1874), p.12); Huntly (*NEI*, 2 (1872), p.48); Insch (Fordyce Hall, Insch, Minute and account book of Insch assembly, 1873-1891, p.1); Inverurie (R[oss]. (ed.), *Ross*, p.174); Kemnay (*ibid.*, p.114); Kennethmont ('Mrs Adam', *W*, 52 (1922), p.264); Newburgh (Mr Alex. Stewart's collection, Hopeman, F. F. Bruce to Alex. Stewart, 15 July 1974, in [Alex. Stewart (compiler)], 'A Record of Gospel Work. Christian Brethren. Moray & Nairn', MS, n.d.); New Deer (R[oss]. (ed.), *Ross*, p.186); Old Meldrum (*ibid.*, p.114); Old Rayne (*ibid.*, p.193); Oyne (*ibid.*, p.114); Premnay ('James Thomson', *BM*, 39 (September 1919, p.v); Rhynie (*NA*, no. 2 (February 1873), p.8); Tarland ('John Glass', *W*, 41 (1911), p.87); Turriff (*W*; 54 (1924), p.247); Kincardineshire (see Map 5): Banchory (*NA*, no. 2 (February 1873), p.8.

50. *NA*, no. 10 (October 1873), p.44; [John Ritchie], 'Mrs Jeanie Liveson Ritchie', *BM*, 34 (1924), pp.53-4.

substantially to the new movement.[51] Alexander Burnet responded in a
tract entitled *Plymouth Brethren is Antichrist* (1873).[52]

The movement in the north east was produced independently of
contact with Brethren elsewhere.[53] 'We had heard of "Brethren"', wrote
Ross himself, 'but only as bad, bad people, and we resolved to have
nothing to do with them'.[54] Knowledge of the earlier Bowesite movement
had been lost, possibly because it had eventually been absorbed into the
Scotch Baptists, and the assemblies in Peterhead and Aberdeen apparently
had no formative influence on Ross's thinking.[55] But many Brethren
ideas were probably familiar to him. At least one member of Newmains
assembly had assisted him during the 1850s when he was an industrial
missionary there.[56] His friend, John Davidson, in addition to being
baptised by someone who had apparently already made contact with the
Brethren, had been influenced by C. J. Davis, the Afro-Caribbean doctor
who founded the Exclusive assembly in New Deer,[57] and Hopkins had
associated with both Ross and Munro.[58] The new churches, however, soon
made contact with assemblies in Glasgow and identified with them. The
accession of the north-east movement greatly strengthened the Brethren

---

51. Rae to the editor, p. 83; writer's collection, II, John S. Fisher to the writer, 3
September 1990; Alexander Burnet, *Plymouth Brethren is Antichrist* (Aberdeen, 1873),
pp.12-13, quoted in William Reid, *Plymouth Brethrenism Unveiled and Refuted*
(Edinburgh, 1875), p.31; cf. Neil Dickson, 'Brethren and Baptists in Scotland', *BQ*, 33
(1990), pp.372-87.

52. Special Collections, University of Aberdeen, holds a copy of this pamphlet, but
along with another anti-Brethren tract—the anonymous *Prevalent Errors: a reply to a
lecture by Mr C. J. Davis regarding the opinions of the party known as 'Brethren' by an
elder* (Aberdeen, 1871)—it cannot be located despite repeated searches by the librarians.

53. Evidence to the contrary is apparently supplied by the date '1 January 1871' on
the title page of *The Northern Intelligencer* that is shown as a facsimile in *W*, 100
(1970), p.8, and which also has an address by the Glasgow Brethren preacher Alexander
Stewart. However, the date is evidently a printing error in the original. Stewart's address
is dated 1873 on the same page and in 1871 the magazine was still entitled *The Northern
Evangelistic Intelligencer*, 'Evangelistic' only being dropped in January 1873.
Unfortunately the extant copy of the magazine for January 1873, which would confirm
this supposition, has had the title page removed.

54. Ross, *Our Record*, quoted in R[oss]. (ed.), *Ross*, p.48.

55. Munro, R[oss]. (ed.), *Ross*, p.116.

56. 'John Smith', *BM*, 21 (March 1911), p.iv; in addition John Wardrop supported
the NECM financially.

57. 'John Davidson', *W*, 35 (July 1905), end pp.; for C. J. Davis, see Neil Dickson,
'Open and closed: Brethren and their origins in the North East', in James Porter (ed.),
After Columba—After Calvin: religious community in North-East Scotland (Aberdeen,
1999), p.154; see also p.75 above for the influence of Jessie Macfarlane in introducing
Brethrenism to the north east.

58. *R*, (1867), p.408; [Ritchie], *Munro*, pp.40-1 (Munro's first name is misprinted as
'David').

in Scotland. As well as the increase in membership, it gave them several more evangelists. Both Ross and Munro were native Gaelic speakers and this gave the Brethren a means of entry to the northern Highlands, where some four assemblies had been formed by the later nineteenth century.[59] Also of great importance to the future development of the Scottish movement was Ross's interest in publishing. Pickering & Inglis, eventually the major British Brethren publisher, grew out of his work, and John Ritchie, the founder of the other important Scottish Brethren publishing house, had been among the Inverurie converts.[60] The interest in cheap, special-interest publishing was something which Ross carried over from his revivalist background, it bearing strong resemblances to the programme of Richard Morgan in which Duncan Matheson had been involved.[61] The formation of the Brethren movement in the north east is a particularly clear example of how assemblies grew out of mid-Victorian revivalism.

Rural Growth 1871-91

One of Hugh McIntosh's criticisms of the NES was that it tended to 'disturb the peace of society'.[62] To join the new meetings was to make a decisive break with the local community. At Huntly the demonstrations against the evangelists had been so violent that the worst troublemakers were prosecuted.[63] Until 1843 religious dissent had been weak in the north east but the Disruption had coincided with a time of agricultural improvements and the Free Church, though still relatively weak, was supported by many who had suffered under the changes.[64] In the early 1870s the region was still relatively prosperous, but social change had continued and the successive waves of emigration from the area suggest

---

59. In this period assemblies existed in (see Map 3): <u>Conon</u>: *NA*, no.11 (November 1873), p.47; <u>Inverness</u>: see below p.109; <u>Thurso</u>: J. W. Jordan, *List of Some Meetings in the British Isles and Regions Beyond* (London, 1904) p.164; and <u>Wick</u>: *idem*, *List of Some Meetings in the British Isles and Regions Beyond* (Greenwich, 1897), p.136. Although Inverness owes its origins to separate and later influences, the first of these meetings was founded by Ross and the others were all areas in which both he and Donald Munro were active; in addition Ross may have succeeded in forming one briefly in Halkirk, Caithness (*NA*, no. 21 (September 1874), p.34).

60. For a discussion of these publishers, see below, pp.146-8, 275-8.

61. P. G. Scott, 'Richard Cope Morgan, religious periodicals, and the Pontifex factor', *Victorian Periodicals*, 5, no. 16 (June 1972), pp.1-14.

62. McIntosh, *New Prophets*, p.21.

63. *NA*, no. 2 (February 1873), p.8; *NA*, no. 4 (April 1873), p.16.

64. Ian Carter, *Farmlife in Northeast Scotland 1840-1914: the poor man's country* (Edinburgh, 1979), pp.163-5.

that people were aware of the new opportunities to improve their economic status.[65] The emergence of the Brethren in the region was one indication that the traditional bonds of society were being further loosened.

Brethren churches continued to be formed within the rural north east and its fishing communities after the initial surge of the early 1870s. Over the succeeding two decades perhaps some twelve further assemblies were established there.[66] The precise origins of all these additional meetings are not known, but the migration of Brethren individuals importing new thinking probably had some influence. The meeting in Aboyne was founded by two brothers and their families from Kenmare, County Kerry, who had been assembly members in Ireland. At Montrose the residence after 1875/6 of A. O. Molesworth, an English lieutenant colonel of aristocratic descent and a Brethren preacher, had an influence, if not in the formation of the assembly, then in its consolidation.[67] Revivalism continued to be influential. During the 1880s an awakening again swept through the Buchan district,[68] and revivalist converts were also attracted to the Brethren. The Inverbervie assembly was formed by a group of women who began to break bread without knowledge of the movement elsewhere and who were drawn into it through contact with Donald Ross.[69] A Christian Union (CU) was one solution to the problem, which had so troubled Ross, of how to keep revivalist converts contained within the institutional church and active in evangelism. Individuals

---

65. Marjory Harper, *Emigration from the North East* , 1 (Aberdeen, 1988), pp.167-9.

66. Assemblies came into existence in Moray (see Map 4) at: Buckie (1879): *W*, 19 (1889), p.vi; Craigellachie (by 1889): 'James Smith', *BM*, 22 (September 1912), p.iv; in Banffshire at: Forres (*c*.1883): 'Alexander Taylor', *BM*, 23 (July 1913), p.iv; and Bridge of Marnock (*c*.1890): 'Mrs Duncan', *W*, 40 (1910), p.103; in the Buchan district, Aberdeenshire (see Map 5), at: Millbrex, Fyvie (1880); 'William Ingram', *W* 40 (1910), p.71; and Boddam (by 1881): 'John Bruce', *W*, 58 (1919), p.148; on Deeside, Aberdeenshire (see Map 5) at: Aboyne (1872): 'Robert Milne', *W*, 80 (1950), p.168; in Kincardineshire (see Map 5) at: Rickarton (*c*.1884): 'Mrs Rankine', *W*, 75 (October 1945), p.iv and 'Mrs Allan' *W*, 81 (1951), p.147; Cove (1888): James Cordiner, *Fragments from the Past: an account of people and events in the assemblies of northern Scotland* (London, 1961), p.19; and Inverbervie (1873): 'Ann Duncan', *BM*, (July 1917), p.iv, 'Mrs T. Anderson', *W*, 51 (1921), p.26, 'Mrs Hill', *W*, 61 (1921), p.192, 'Mrs John Allan, *W*, 64 (1934), p.120, and 'Mrs H. Clark', *W*, 71 (1951), p.55; and in Angus (see Map 6) at: Brechin (1891): David J. Beattie, *Brethren: the story of a great recovery* (Kilmarnock [1939]), p.271; and Montrose (*c*.1872): 'Jessie Robbie', *W*, 62 (1932), p.168.

67. 'Colonel A. O. Molesworth', *W*, 47 (Apr. 1917), p.52; Jessie Robbie (see n.66 above) was a convert of Molesworth in 1872, suggesting he was evangelising in Montrose before removing there.

68. 'James Taylor', *W*, 79 (1949), p.86.

69. 'Mrs M. Grindlay', *W* 82 (1952), p.107.

would band together and hold informal evangelistic services in mission halls procured for these purposes. They sprang up in many places during this period, organising themselves into county associations which remained nondenominational.[70] Their lay ethos was close to that of the Brethren. In Brechin it was some of the town's CU members who were won over to Brethren principles,[71] and as will become apparent, it was not there only that their members were attracted to assemblies.

The Brethren made advances in other rural areas during the 1870s and 1880s. Further north in Shetland (see Map 1), which was in this period experiencing a decline in subsistence agriculture and a corresponding rise in the importance of fishing,[72] revivalism was strong in the country areas, and two additional assemblies were formed, apparently in the 1870s. On the west side of Mainland during 1874-5, William Sloan, assisted by several visiting Brethren evangelists, saw a number of conversions and 'the Lord...reviving some of his people'. In 1875 Sloan's diary first mentioned the breaking of bread at Selivoe, and at Sandwick on south-eastern Mainland, intensive evangelism led to the formation of an assembly in 1878.[73] In 1879 there were further awakenings near Selivoe and at Sandness, with the converts in the latter place being threatened with eviction.[74] On at least one island it was found that crowds could be drawn quickly and easily to hear preaching even during the harvest season.[75] This was possibly Papa Stour which, despite having only two houses, had twelve members in the assembly which existed by 1884.[76] That same year one Glasgow visitor was reporting that in the Shetland assemblies there were 'several hundreds' with the summer Half-Yearly Conference in Lerwick having two to three hundred people in attendance.[77] In 1887 the assembly at Selivoe was re-formed when, amid scenes of revivalist fervour, Sloan assisted by his fellow-evangelist Colin Campbell saw some forty converts, and an assembly appears to

70. N. W. Bryson (compiler), *History of the Lanarkshire Christian Union: instituted 1882* (Strathaven, 1937); anon., *Ayrshire Christian Union: a century of witness 1878-1978* (Beith [1978]).

71. Beattie, *Brethren*, p.271.

72. Hance D. Smith, *Shetland Life and Trade 1550-1914* (Edinburgh, 1984), pp.155-206.

73. Diary of W. G. Sloan, quoted in Fred Kelling, *Fisherman of Faroe: William Gibson Sloan* (Göta, Faroe Isles, 1993), p.93; *W*, 67 (1937), p.95; Alex S. Rigg to the editor, 11 August 1878, *NW*, 8 (1878), p.127.

74. 'Shetland', *NW*, 9 (1879), p.47.

75. R. T. Hopkins quoted in 'Glasgow Fast-Day believers' meetings', *NW*, 6 (1876), p.189.

76. Thomas McLaren, 'Visit to the Shetland Isles', *NW*, 14 (1884), p.140.

77. *Ibid.*, p.140.

have been formed in Whiteness about the same time.[78] In Orkney (see Map 2) the removal of some Westray assembly members to Kirkwall accompanied by vigorous evangelism led to an assembly being formed there about 1873.[79] Itinerancy produced additional smaller meetings on the islands of Eday about 1876 and Sanday about 1887.[80]

In southern Scotland a significant presence was also established in rural areas. The growth of assemblies in the Borders is poorly documented, but by 1891 several towns in the region had one (see Map 14). Beyond their existence, little is known of the origins of the assemblies in Galashiels (founded *c*.1870),[81] Moffat (*c*.1877),[82] Selkirk (1878),[83] Kelso (*c*.1881),[84] and Dalbeattie (by 1887).[85] However, it would appear that similar factors were operative in the Borders as were in northern Scotland. The assembly in Langholm was probably founded in 1884 when two Brethren itinerants, Thomas Elliott and James Brown, had a mission.[86] In 1887 revivalism affected Walkerburn (a village which had recently undergone rapid expansion) and neighbouring Peebles,[87] and possibly it had been influential in the formation of the assemblies which existed in both places by 1886 and 1889 respectively.[88] At Chirnside a group of converts (some recent) were baptised as believers and in 1875 began breaking bread, practices arrived at independently through Bible reading, before Colonel Molesworth drew them into the Brethren movement.[89] At Hawick, two undenominational evangelists, James Scroggie and W. D. Dunn, held revival services, the converts forming a CU. Scroggie, a former NECM evangelist, was sympathetic to Brethren concepts and was sponsored by a Carlisle manufacturer and assembly member.[90] He gave teaching on worship which in 1877 led some of the converts to begin

---

78.   James Moar, 'How it began—Selivoe, Shetland', *BM*, 90 (1980), pp.2-4; Kelling, *Sloan*, p.161.

79. *NA*, no. 9 (September 1873), p.36; 'William Reid', *W*, 58 (1928), p.288.

80. 'William Peace', *W*, 56 (1926), p.279; *W*, 17 (January 1887), end pp.

81. 'James Robertson', *W*, 52 (1922), p.204.

82. 'W. Stewart Henderson', *W*, 36 (October 1927), p.iv.

83. 'Mrs Smith', *BM*, 21 (March 1911), p.iv.

84. 'Alex. Carson', *BM*, 46 (1936), p.281.

85. *W*, 17 (October 1887), end pp.

86. 'William Beattie', *W*, 34 (April 1904), end pp.

87.   I. R. Govan, *Spirit of Revival: the story of J. G. Govan and the Faith Mission*, 3rd edn (Edinburgh, 1960), pp.44-7.

88. *NW*, 16 (August 1886), end pp.; *W*, 19 (September 1889), p.v.

89. Beattie, *Brethren*, p.265.

90.   W. Graham Scroggie (ed.), *The Story of a Life in the Love of God: incidents collected from the diaries of Mrs James J. Scroggie* (London [1938]), pp.77, 88.

breaking bread in the Brethren manner.[91] In the Borders, as elsewhere in Scotland, assemblies proved attractive to those influenced by contemporary revivalism.

The later nineteenth century was a time of agricultural depression. Throughout Scotland there was a thirty-three per cent reduction in farm servants and labourers between 1861 and 1891, and the worst affected regions were the north east and Wigtownshire.[92] Both were the rural areas in which the Brethren had the greatest effect during this period. Although most of the Border assemblies remained small (possibly one reason for the lack of sources), in the south west the movement made greater impact (see Map 14). Migration was one important way in which Brethren thinking found its way into the region. One Brethren individual moved for employment in the granite quarry near Creetown on the Solway Firth. Due to his witnessing, he saw some individuals converted and an assembly established about 1874.[93] Also on the Solway, a meeting was formed in Glenluce in 1887/8 through the return to his native district of William Henry, a convert of Murray McNeil Caird who had joined the Brethren while learning his trade as a grocer in Kilmarnock.[94] The assembly in Aird, which commenced about 1881, was founded by William Erskine who had been converted in 1866 while a soldier in India.[95] Similar factors were at work in Leswalt in the Rhinns of Galloway where the meeting was founded in 1888.[96] William Clannahan, a joiner and a local farmer's son, had emigrated to Chicago four years earlier where he was converted through a Brethren preacher. He wrote to his family urging the same experience on them, and when they stopped answering his letters he crossed the Atlantic again. He held kitchen meetings in the locality, and eventually succeeded in winning his family to his new views.[97] It was the converts of Clannahan's evangelism who formed the assembly in Leswalt.[98]

---

91. Writer's collection, I.S.1., [autograph page missing] to William Landles, 29 July 1955, photocopy of holograph letter; the date is given in 'Mrs John Elliott', *W*, 39 (1909), p.87.

92. T. M. Devine, 'Scottish farm labour in the era of agricultural depression, 1875-1900', in *idem*, (ed.), *Farm Servants and Labour in Lowland Scotland 1770-1914* (Edinburgh, 1984), pp.243-55.

93. Oral information, 16 May 1988, from a south-west evangelist.

94. A. M[arshall]., 'A Scotsman's conversion', *HS*, no. 579 (March 1927), [pp.12-13]; 'William Henry', *W*, 58 (1927), p.278; writer's collection, I.V.1., William Henry, untitled history of Glenluce assembly, MS [1989].

95. 'William Erskine', *W*, 47 (Apr. 1917), p.54.

96. *W*, 18 (February 1888), p.v.

97. A. M[arshall]., 'The Scotsman's discovery in Chicago', *HS*, no. 339 (March 1907).

98. Oral information, 16 May 1988, from a south-west evangelist.

Also of significance for the establishment of the movement in the area was evangelistic itinerancy. It was through this means that members of both the Free Church and Congregational Church in Lowthertown were won over to Brethren ecclesiology in 1873 and an assembly established.[99] In Newton Stewart four women converts who met in a store for prayer and Bible study were drawn into the movement about 1880,[100] apparently through contact with the evangelist James McAlonan,[101] a former Presbyterian missioner who, after a spell among the Baptists in Peterhead, had in the later 1870s joined the Brethren.[102] An assembly had existed in Dumfries from at least 1889,[103] and after an evangelistic campaign in 1892 one flourished briefly in nearby Thornhill.[104] In Castle Douglas a meeting had been founded the previous year through the work of the evangelist Arthur Hodgkinson.[105] Brethren missions in the coastal communities of the Rhinns of Galloway led to the formation of additional assemblies there. Due to the labours of John Walbran, a former master mariner from Liverpool,[106] evangelistic campaigns had been conducted on the peninsula since the late 1860s,[107] and among the fishermen of Port Logan, Walbran experienced revival.[108] Meetings were formed at Port Logan (*c*.1870), Drummore (*c*.1883),[109] and Sandhead (1887).[110] Factors similar to elsewhere in the south west were probably at work in the assemblies which were also formed in the county town of Wigtown (*c*.1882)[111] and Gatehouse-of-Fleet (by 1889).[112]

The establishment of the movement in the region was not without its opposition. In Creetown youths threw clods of earth at the Brethren

99. *NA*, no. 4 (April 1873), p.15; this assembly later transferred to Annan and then Eastriggs.

100. 'Mrs R. S. McLaren', *W*, 60 (1920), p.216; 'Miss Moorhead', *W*, 62 (1932), p.71.

101. Oral information, 16 May 1988, from a south-west evangelist.

102. 'Mr. James McAlonan 1843-1906', in J. G. Hutchinson (ed.), *Sowers, Reapers, Builders: a record of over ninety Irish evangelists* (Glasgow, 1984), pp. 263-6; W. Baird Ferguson to the writer [6 April 1999].

103. 'Hugh Reid', *W*, 36 (1906), end pp.

104. *BM*, 2 (1892), p.11.

105. *BM*, 1 (1891), p.11.

106. 'John Walbran', *BAHNR*, 1 (1987-8), pp.103-4.

107. 'Mrs Thomas Henry', *W*, 65 (1935), p.264; see above, p.103.

108. *W*, 35 (1905), p.103.

109. 'Robert McGaw', *W*, 63 (1933), p.215.

110. *W*, 17 (August 1887), end pp.

111. 'Mrs Clachrie',*W*, 52 (1922), p.180.

112. *W*, 19 (December 1889), p.v; however the evangelist Robert Kennedy stated in the 1920s that Gatehouse-of-Fleet assembly was one of the oldest in Scotland and was about 100 years old (oral information, 4 March 1990, from a former assembly member); a date in the 1820s appears unlikely, but the statement may point to an earlier foundation.

founder and at Sandhead one young farm labourer kicked a burning ball of straw into the gospel tent, and only the alertness of the evangelist David Robertson averted disaster.[113] Intriguingly, the persecutors in both places were among the first converts. Some of the communities surveyed above, such as Walkerburn and Hawick, were industrialised ones. Most of them, however, were fishing communities, market towns, and predominantly rural settlements. The advance of the Brethren into these last two types of place, is a mark of the agricultural and economic change which was affecting the Scottish countryside during these decades.

Industrialised Communities 1871-91

Once more, however, it was mainly industrialised communities in which the Brethren grew during this period. Here, too, the movement gained transfers from other Christian groups. This appears to have been the origins of the parent meeting of Paisley Brethren which had contacts with the movement as early as 1867 when the English evangelist Howard Johnston had held a mission with some members of the future assembly.[114] After this group came together with some others, they began breaking bread in a house about 1870.[115] They probably existed for a while as a nondenominational body, but gradually the company identified with the Brethren, a process which appears to have been completed some time after 1873.[116] Also in Renfrewshire (see Map 12), the assembly in Kilbarchan was formed out of a gospel mission hall begun by a brother and sister in 1884,[117] and in Kilmacolm another such mission hall and its converts were drawn into the movement in 1887 through contact with a Brethren family who had moved to the village.[118]

The same process was at work elsewhere. In Ayrshire (see Map 13) William Lindsay, an itinerant Baptist preacher, made contact in Galston with some individuals who had seceded from the town's Methodists upon their congregation accepting Christadelphianism. Lindsay and the former Methodists formed themselves into an assembly in 1871.[119] In the south

---

113. Oral information, 16 May 1988; my interviewee, a south-west evangelist, was told this by the individual who kicked the ball of straw.

114. *LR*, 1 (1867), p.69.

115. 'William Scott', *CW*, 38 (November 1923), pp.162-3; 'William Scott', *BM*, 33 (1923), p.113.

116. 'William Reid', *CW*, 37 (October 1922), pp.146-7; [William Geddes], *Link: Jubilee/Centenary Edition* (n.p., 1978), p.1.

117. 'Miss Williamson', *W*, 71 (1941), p.225.

118. Beattie, *Brethren*, p.258.

119. J. S. Borland, *History of the Brethren Movement in Galston* (Kilmarnock [1948]), pp.2-4.

of the county, 'the Maybole Revival' of the 1870s affected all the town's churches,[120] and in 1877 some of its converts formed a meeting.[121] Further north in Ayrshire, some members of Kilbirnie CU—formed in 1882 after a mission by the female temperance preachers of the Blue Ribbon Gospel Army—were won for the Brethren in 1889 through contact with Peter Hynd, a Brethren businessman from Troon.[122] The following year a meeting was commenced in the mining village of Annbank by a group of Established Church members who were involved in the lay evangelism of their district.[123] In Glasgow, John McLachlan had begun a gospel mission in Duke Street in the early 1870s. McLachlan, his co-workers and their converts formed themselves into an independent fellowship. They were drawn into the Brethren movement in 1887 through contact with the evangelist William Montgomery, eventually forming Porch Hall in Dennistoun (see Map 11).[124] As had happened in the 1860s, those engaged in revivalism continued to be attracted by the lay ethos of the Brethren and their appeal to Christian primitivism.[125]

Existing assemblies also planted further ones. Members of the Greenock meeting succeeded in forming one in neighbouring Gourock (see Map 12) in 1887.[126] In Lanarkshire (see Map 10), Lesmahagow assisted in the formation of assemblies at Leadhills (1879), Ponfeigh (1883), Kirkmuirhill (1884), and over the Ayrshire border in Glenbuck (1887);[127] and in Plains a meeting was formed in 1882 as a result of evangelism by Longriggend assembly.[128] In Ayrshire (see Map 13) the new congregation in Galston helped spread the movement within the Irvine Valley to Hurlford in 1877 and Newmilns in 1878,[129] and in the

---

120. Hugh Douglas, 'Roderick Lawson of Maybole', *Ayrshire Collections*, 12 (1978), p. 80.

121. 'Alex. Brackenridge' *CW*, 34 (1920), pp.1-2; for further discussion of the founding of Maybole assembly, see below, p.142.

122. 'John Mackenzie Barclay', *W*, 60 (1930), p.168; 'John Peebles', *W*, 64 (1934), p.216; Beattie, *Brethren*, pp.235-6.

123. Dr M. H. B. Sanderson's collection, Linlithgow, Robert McPike, 'Annbank Assembly 1883-1875 [*sic*]', MS, 1975; cf. Sam Hay, 'How it began: in Annbank Ayrshire', *BM*, 89 (1979), pp.290-1.

124. Beattie, *Brethren*, pp.253-5.

125. See above, p.77.

126. G. E. Tilsley, *Dan Crawford: Missionary and Pioneer in Central Africa* (London [1929]), pp.8-24.

127. Hope Hall, Lesmahagow, James Anderson, 'A Brief Record Concerning the Early Days of the Assembly in Lesmahagow', MS, 1960, pp.44, and Beattie, *Brethren*, pp.214-15; 'Hugh Reid', *W*, 60 (1930), p.96; *W*, 53 (1933), p.237.

128. 'James Wardrope', *BM*, 59 (1929), p.170; anon., 'How it began—in Plains, Lanarkshire', *BM*, 90 (1980), p.226.

129. Borland, *Galston*, p.13.

centre of the county the removal of a Brethren family from Auchinleck led to the formation of an assembly in nearby Catrine about 1885.[130] At Busby, Renfrewshire (see Map 12), members of the Newton Mearns assembly formed a meeting in the village in 1891.[131] The congregation in Cockenzie (see Map 8) was a distant planting: some local fishermen were converted in a revival in Peterhead and baptised in Lerwick Sound; on their return home they formed a meeting in 1882.[132] The process of church planting by existing assemblies was most marked in the cities. In Aberdeen (see Map 5 inset) in 1879 a second meeting was formed in Footdee, the fishing community at the river mouth where Donald Ross had seen three successive revivals,[133] and in 1881 one was formed in the developing area of Woodside.[134] In Dundee (see Map 4 inset) a second assembly was founded in 1878 in the Wellgate.[135] Brethren history in Edinburgh is difficult to trace in this period, but by the early 1890s it would appear there were two meetings in the city centre with a third being formed in Jamaica Street in 1891.[136] Among the cities, it was Glasgow assemblies which saw the most vigorous growth (see Map 11) where some eighteen new meetings were formed in this period.[137] Not all these

130. Beattie, *Brethren*, p.232; *W*, 66 (1936), p.69.

131. Alex. McAllister and Jack Vernal (compilers), *Busby Gospel Hall: a short history of early days 1891-1964* (Glasgow, 1964), pp.2-3.

132. 'William Brown', *W*, 62 (1932), p.72; 'Robert Hunman', *W*, 67 (1937), p.18; J. 3. Blackie, 'How it began: Port Seaton [*sic*]', *BM*, 97 (1987), pp.342-3: in 1922 Cockenzie assembly transferred to Port Seton.

133. [Matthew S. R. Brown], *Aberdeen Christian Conference Centenary 1874-1973* (Aberdeen, 1972), p.34.

134. 'Mrs Cooper' *W*, 71 (1941), p.283; *NEI*, 10 (1882), p.88.

135. *NW*, 8 (1878), p.175.

136. *BM*, 1 (1891), p.95.

137. These were: Hope Hall, Renfrew St (1872) (see Map 11, no.13): J. R. C[aldwell]., 'Glasgow', *LR*, 5 (1872), p.182; Abingdon Hall, Partick (1874) (see Map 11): *NA*, no. 20 (October 1874), p.40; Eglinton Hall, Eglinton Street (1874) (see Map 11, no.40): *NA*, no. 16 (April, 1874), p.16; Beattie, *Brethren*, pp.242-3; Greenview Hall, Pollokshaws (1874) (see Map 11; originally Gospel Hall, Green Street): *NA*, no. 18 (May 1874), p.24; and *NW*, (1875), p.111; [Joseph L. G. Walker], *Centenary of the Pollokshaws Assembly 1873-1973* (n.p. [1973]); anon., 'How it began—in Pollockshaws [*sic*], Glasgow', *BM*, 90 (1980), pp.98-9; Gospel Hall, Townhead (1875) (see Map 11, no.20): *NW*, 5 (1875), pp.95, 111, 159; Ebenezer Hall, Bridgeton (by 1876) (see Map 11, no.32): the earliest extant reference to this assembly is in Kelling, *Sloan*, p.96; however, it is probable that it was the later meeting place of one of the assemblies founded in the east end in the 1860s; Gospel Hall, Cathcart Road (c.1877) (see Map 11, no.47): the date is an inference from the conversion of one the members of Cathcart Road in a tent mission at Queen's Park Gate in 1877; it seems likely that this was close to the assembly's founding, 'William Paterson', *BM*, 15 (January 1905), end pp.; however, the first extant reference to the assembly is in *W*, 18 (May 1888), p.v; Elim Hall, Crosshill (1882) (see Map 11, no.46): *Elim Hall, 5 Prince Edward Street,*

congregations existed co-extensively, but by 1897 the assembly address list contained twenty-five Glasgow congregations.[138] These meetings were either founded in the older districts (such as Townhead) by evangelism, or in the newer districts which were being developed or incorporated in the city's late nineteenth-century expansion (such as Maryhill and Pollokshaws) by a mixture of recruitment and the immigration of Brethren members.

Among the lacunae of this period is the history of Brethren itinerancy—undoubtedly a significant cause in the formation of new assemblies—and the effects of Brethren individuals migrating in search of employment. When John Ritchie, having become an evangelist, moved from Inverurie to Dalmellington in 1874, he found three itinerants devoting their time to evangelising Ayrshire,[139] and Ritchie himself became an advocate for 'pioneering the villages'.[140] The 1870s and the 1880s were fruitful decades for the formation of meetings in Ayrshire (see Map 13). It is known that the evangelists Colin Campbell and William Hamilton were respectively responsible for the formation of the assemblies in Auchinleck about 1874[141] and Skelmorlie in 1887.[142] The meeting in Dailly was founded about 1881 through an estate worker in the area coming in contact with the Brethren in Maybole[143] and in 1886 an assembly was planted in Girvan due to the removal of a Brethren

Crosshill, Glasgow: 60th annual report 1st January to 31st December, 1949 (n.p. [1949]), pp.3-9; there had been an earlier, abortive attempt to plant an assembly in Crosshill in 1876 in the Queen's Park Rooms: *NW*, 6 (1876), p.159 (see Map 11, no.45); Bethesda Hall, Govan (1874) (see Map 11, originally Gospel Hall, Graham Street, Govan): *NA*, no. 20 (October 1874), p.40; Parkholm Hall, Paisley Rd (1876) (see Map 11, no.37): 'Ebenezer Ross', *W*, 51 (1951), p.36; Eastpark Hall, Maryhill (by 1879) (see Map 11): *NW*, 9 (1879), p.47; Gospel Hall, Springburn (1881) (see Map 5): [Sam Thomson], *The Springburn Assembly 1881-1981* (n.p. [1981]), pp.1-2; Wolsley Hall, Oatlands (1882) (see Map 11, no.48): Beattie, *Brethren*, pp.245-6; Hebron Hall, Kelvinside North (by 1886) (see Map 11, no.4): *NW*, 16 (October 1886), end pp.; Hope Hall, Parkhead (1886) (see Map 11, no.32): *NW*, 16 (October 1886), end pp.; Shiloh Hall, Shettleston (1884) (see Map 11): 'Robert Gilmour', *BM*, 36 (September 1920), p.iv; Harmony Hall, Govan (by 1889) (see Map 11 no.24): *W*, 19 (1889), p.v; and Round Toll Hall, Possilpark (1889) (see Map 11, no.5): Beattie, *Brethren*, pp.255-6.

All the assemblies in the above list are given the name of the building with which they had the longest association and by which they were generally known in the movement; these often differed from that which they had when they were founded.

138. Jordan, *List*, p.124.
139. *NA*, no. 17 (May 1874), p.20.
140. John Ritchie to the editor, 13 May 1883, *NW*, 13 (1883), pp.93-4.
141. *NA*, no. 24 (December 1874), p.48; writer's collection, I.C.1., James McCombe, 'A History of Auchinleck Assembly', typescript, 1981, p.1.
142. *W*, 17 (March 1887), end pp.;*W*, 19 (August 1889), p.vi.
143. 'James Happell', *CW*, 56 (1939), p.49.

individual to the town.[144] It is, however, no more than a likely supposition that the revival which affected the mining village of New Cumnock about 1882 was a factor in the formation of the meeting there.[145] The other sixteen assemblies which were commenced in Ayrshire at this time must have been formed due to some combination of the effects of population migration, Brethren evangelism, and attracting members from other churches.[146]

The same is true of other areas. In Inverness a group, led by an individual who had previously been in an assembly elsewhere, began breaking bread in 1884 after the evangelist Thomas Holt had visited the town.[147] To the west of Glasgow (see Map 12) the growing middle-class

---

144. 'James Barron', *BM*, 42 (May 1932), p.iv.

145. *W*, 52 (1922), p.146.

146. By 1891 there were also assemblies in Ayrshire in: <u>Ardrossan</u> (1888): 'Mrs John Cairns', *W*, 56 (1926), p.358; <u>Ballochmyle</u> (1891): *BM*, 1 (1891), p.59; <u>Beith</u> (*c*.1890): 'Mrs David Bell', *BM*, 62 (1952), p.80; <u>Burnfoothill</u> (by 1874): 'John Stewart', *W*, 54 (1924), p.329; <u>Darvel</u> (1880): Beattie, *Brethren*, p.234; <u>Dreghorn</u> (by 1887): *W*, 17 (January 1887),end pp.; <u>Drongan</u> (by 1885): 'Mrs William Hamilton', *W*, 67 (1937), p.191; <u>Kilwinning</u> (1874): anon., 'How it began: Kilwinning, Ayrshire', *BM*, 98 (1988), pp.307-8; <u>Lugar</u> (1875): 'James Welsh', *W* 60 (1930), p.240; <u>Mauchline</u> (*c*.1877): 'James Vallance', *W*, 37 (1907), p.155; <u>Muirkirk</u> (*c*. 1878): 'Andrew Adams', *W*, 58 (1928), p.318; <u>Plann</u> (1882): *BM*, 41 (November 1932), p.41; <u>Prestwick</u> (1877): Beattie, *Brethren*, p.234; <u>Rankinston</u> (by 1879): 'Thomas Menzies', *W*, 60 (1930), p.24; <u>Saltcoats</u> (by 1888): *W*, 18 (October 1888), p.v; <u>Springside</u> (*c*. 1886): 'Mrs Thomas Gaw', *BM*, 60 (1950), p.71.

147. Beattie, *Brethren*, pp.269-70; Clare, *Pioneer Preaching*, pp.80-2, 89; Frank Edgar *et al.*, 'To Beloved Brethren in Christ', April 1894, in Arthur Chamings (compiler), 'Some Papers and Letters in Connection with the Separation of the 1880's and 1890's', p.57. Beattie states that the Inverness group were unaware of the Brethren movement, but Clare states that a number of the founder members had previously been members of assemblies elsewhere. In addition Beattie does not mention John Bright who, according to Clare, was a key individual in the formation of the assembly. It is possible that the writers are discussing two separate formations, but it is more likely that Beattie's claim is explained by the facts that Holt did 'not teach separatist doctrine' and the formation of the assembly was due to Bible studies. The same address is given by Beattie and Clare for the meeting (Beattie, *Brethren*, p.269; Clare, *Pioneer Preaching* , p.89). The absence of Bright's name in Beattie might be explained by the subsequent history of Inverness assembly which largely seceded in the Churches of God schism (see below, pp.158-169). If Bright left in this division, then the expunging of his name would be comprehensible. Alternatively the memory of his role may have been lost when Beattie collected his information some ten years after Clare had his from Holt himself. Earlier in 1867, John Bowes had broken bread in Inverness at Dr Mackay's house while Bowes and Mrs Bell were together preaching in the town (*TP*, 10 (1867), pp.135-6). This breaking of bread was possibly a unique occasion or the residence in Inverness of a Helensburgh 1859 convert may indicate the existence of a Bowesite church in this

dormitory town of Bearsden gained an assembly in 1880 when John R. Caldwell's brother-in-law moved there and Caldwell himself held public meetings attracting the converts of an earlier evangelistic campaign of W. D. Dunn, by then pastor of Anniesland Hall, an independent Glasgow mission hall.[148] The migration of Brethren members was also a factor at Clydebank where Nellie Wood, formerly of Inverbervie assembly, was a founding member during this period,[149] and evangelism was probably a component in the formation about 1876 of Port Glasgow meeting on the other side of the Clyde.[150] But the origins of the other Dunbartonshire and Renfrewshire assemblies (see Maps 9 and 12) which were formed at Alexandria (*c*.1875),[151] Kirkintilloch (by 1876),[152] Barrhead (1884),[153] Renfrew (by 1886),[154] and Newton Mearns (1886)[155] are obscure. At Falkirk (see Map 9) the assembly was re-founded after the evangelist Alex Livingstone had a mission in 1889.[156] In the Lothians (see Map 8) one was formed at Rosewell in 1875 after a campaign by Donald Ross who had moved to Edinburgh in that same year[157] and another at West Calder about 1879 after a mission by the Irish evangelist John Knox McEwan.[158] The removal of its members and further evangelism led to meetings also being formed in Bonnyrigg and Penicuik in 1875,[159] but

period, but on either interpretation it is unlikely that it influenced the foundation of the meeting in 1884.

148. 'William McCrone', *W*, 54 (1924), p.349; 'Thomas Daisley', *W*, 81 (1951), p.35; Margaret Sanderson's collection, Linlithgow, 'Milngavie per Mr Daisley, Eastbourne', holograph MS [1974]; writer's collection, I.G.4., [Clem Round], 'Milngavie Assembly', typescript [1988]. In 1892/3 the Bearsden assembly transferred to more working-class Milngavie.

149. 'Mrs T. Anderson', *BM*, 31 (August 1921), p.iii; 'Mrs William Ingram', *W*, 61 (1931), p.71: the former obituary states the founding date was 'some fifty years ago' (i.e. *c*. 1871), and the latter 'nearly fifty years ago' (i.e. after 1881).

150. 'James McKechnie', *BM*, 17 (March 1907), p.iv.

151. 'Samuel Kennedy', *W*, 46 (1916), p.50.

152. Kelling, *Sloan*, p.106.

153 J. J. Park, *The Churches of God: their origin and development in the 20th century* (Leicester, 1986), p.101.

154. *NW*, 16 (October 1886), end pp.

155. *NW*, 16 (July 1886), end pp.

156. *W*, 18 (February 1888), p.v; *ibid.*, (August), p.v; *ibid.*, 19 (June 1889), p.i.

157. *NW*, 5 (July 1875), p.iii; *ibid.*, (August) 127; *NA*, no. 20 (September 1874), p.30; Beattie, *Brethren*, p.263: Beattie mistakenly gives the date as 1876.

158. R. Miller, 'John Knox McEwan (1853-1944)', *BM*, 110 (2001), p.116; however, 'Mrs Thomas McQueen', *W*, 70 (1940), p.140, suggests a founding date nearer to 1890.

159. *NW*, 5 (July 1875), p.iii; *ibid.*, (June), p.95; Beattie, *Brethren*, p.264; Bonnyrigg assembly moved to Loanhead in 1889.

how the other three assemblies in Stirlingshire[160] and three in the Lothians were formed during this period is unknown.[161]

It is a similar picture in Fife and Lanarkshire. Of the nine assemblies formed in Fife (see Map 7) the precise origin of only three is known: Tayport received an assembly in 1873 when William Arnot of Hamilton and his family moved there;[162] similarly the removal of a Brethren farmer from Leven led to the formation of an assembly in Lochgelly, west Fife, some time in the 1880s;[163] and, after an earlier abortive attempt to begin a meeting, one was founded in Kirkcaldy about 1890 when a Brethren couple moved there from Bo'ness.[164] In Lanarkshire the opening of a new coal seam at Haywood led to the formation of a meeting there in 1883,[165] and a mission in 1889 by William Blane, a South African emigrant from Galston who had briefly returned to Scotland, saw the replanting of the one in East Kilbride which had been discontinued. Airdrie also had its assembly formed in 1883 through Brethren individuals removing to the town.[166] About 1872 a meeting had been formed in Stonehouse, but it remained small and was apparently discontinued. It was re-formed, probably in the later 1880s, by John Curr, a member of Larkhall assembly.[167] There were, however a further ten assemblies formed in the county during the period whose cause of origin has been lost.[168]

---

160. These were: Limerigg (by 1888): *W*, 18 (May 188), p.v; Stenhousemuir (1885): 'John Anderson', *W*, 58 (1928), p.279; Stirling (by 1882): Clare, *Pioneer Preaching*, p.71.

161. These were in West Lothian (see Map 9): Bo'ness (*c*.1883): 'Peter Ritchie', *W*, 63 (1933), p.168; and Broxburn (*c*.1880): *NW*, 10 (1880), p.188; and in Mid-Lothian (see Map 8 inset): Newhaven (1887): *W*, 17 (March 1887), end pp.

162. *NA*, no. 4 (April 1873), p.16; Ernest Baker, *The Life and Explorations of Frederick Stanley Arnot* (London, 1921), p.18. The other Fife assemblies were: Burntisland (by 1887): *W*, 17 (May 1887), end pp.; Kelty (*c*. 1880): writer's collection, I.I.7. (ii), Helen B. Gallacher to the writer, 30 June 1987; Upper Largo (by 1880): *NW*, 10 (1880), p.188; Newport (*c*.1888): *W*, 18 (July 1888), vi, and 'John Mackaskill', *W*, 67 (1937), p.48; Pitlessie (1888): 'David Scott', *W*, 58 (1928), p.478; St Andrews (1888): *W*, 18 (June 1888), p.v.

163. [Kenneth A. Munro], 'How it began: Ballingry', *BM*, 98 (1989), pp.300-1.

164. 'Mrs Peter Chalmers', *W*, 68 (1938), p.192; *NW*, 16 (September 1886), end pp.

165. 'Isaiah Stewart', *W*, 64 (1934), p.167; writer's collection, I.M.10.(i) Tom Aitken to the writer, 8 April 1989.

166. Anon., 'How it began: Airdrie, Lanarkshire' *BM*, 98 (198), pp.53-5.

167. Report dated 6 October 1872, *TP*, (1872), quoted in Anderson 'Lesmahagow', p. 64; 'John Curr', *W*, 78 (May 1945), p.iii. The date of the re-founding is calculated from (i) John Curr (b.1864) being a member of Larkhall assembly when it met in Frame's Hall, *c*.1872-1891, and (ii) he was an adult after the mid-1880s.

168. These were: Auchentibber (1885): 'Joseph McFarlane', *W*, 50 (1920), p.304; a second assembly in Bellshill (1887): writer's collection, I.M.3., Jim Lewis, 'Some

Unparalleled Growth

The twenty years from 1871 until 1891 were ones of unparalleled growth in the Scottish Brethren movement. Some of the twenty-five meetings which are known only from their inclusion in the 1897 and 1904 assembly address lists were almost undoubtedly formed during this period.[169] There were most likely others which were formed through schisms, such as was probably the case about 1873 in Kilmarnock,[170] and certainly was in 1887 with Bethany Hall, Dundee, which reunited with its parent assembly two years later.[171] That the Brethren founded assemblies wherever they went during these years can be seen from the number of holiday locations which had meetings formed in them. Not only were ones founded in the Ayrshire coastal resorts of Ardrossan and

Notes re. History of Bellshill Assembly', MS 1989; Bothwell (1884): 'Joseph McKechnie', *W*, 67 (1937), p.48; Coatbridge (*c*.1874): 'James Halyburton', *BM*, 30 (January 1920), p.vi; Dykehead, Shotts (by 1889): 'Mrs Logan', *W*, 69 (1939), p.168; Douglas (1883): *W*, 63 (1933), p.237; Longriggend (*c*.1873): 'John McPherson', *W*, 66 (1936), p.23; Newarthill (by 1878): 'John Thompson', *W*, 53 (1923), p.26; Roughrigg (1873): *NA*, no. 7 (July 1873), p.28; and West Benhar (1888): *W*, 18 (October 1888), p.v.

169. These are: in Jordan, *List* (1897): Baillieston, Lanarkshire; Gospel Hall, Dundee; Durris, Kincardineshire; Gospel Hall, Dalmarnock, Glasgow; Loan, Stirlingshire; New Lanark, Lanarkshire; Northaven, Aberdeenshire; St John's Town of Dalry, Dumfriesshire; and Sinclairton, Fife; in Jordan, *List* (1904): Campbeltown, Argyll; Kirkerton, Aberdeenshire; Crossford, Lanarkshire; Garelochead, Dunbartonshire; Garscube Hall, Garscube, Glasgow; Hamnavoe, West Burra, Shetland Isles; Lumphinnans, Fife; Methil, Fife; Mintlaw, Aberdeenshire; Patna, Ayrshire; Sanquhar, Dumfriesshire; and Thurso, Caithness; and in both 1897 and 1904: Arbroath, Angus; Clackmannan, Clackmannanshire; Dyce, Aberdeenshire and Whinnyfold, Aberdeenshire.

170. *LR*, 6 (1873), p.118; this notice evidently refers to an assembly distinct from the one John Stewart founded: it met in the Corn Exchange, Kilmarnock, while the existence of Stewart's assembly in his Nelson Street school continued to be reported in the *Post Office Directory* until 1879. It is probable that the notice was placed close to the Corn Exchange assembly's foundation for it is described as consisting of 'a few believers', and it is probable that it was a schism from Nelson Street as differences existed between Stewart and the later practices of Kilmarnock Brethren (see below, p.199). Beattie, *Brethren*, p.233, dates the founding of Kilmarnock to '1870 or earlier'. His account makes plain that there were tensions among Kilmarnock Brethren during this period but he does not refer to a split. However he treats Kilmarnock Brethren as having a continuous history (evidently reflecting his local correspondent's account), but his characteristic practice throughout his history is to avoid mentioning divisions. If 1873 is indeed the year of the Corn Exchange assembly's commencement, then Beattie's dating may indicate that it was known Nelson Street predated it but that it was not known by how many years.

171. *W*, 17 (November 1887), end pp.; *ibid.*, (December 1887), end pp.; *W*, 19 (October 1889), p.v.

Saltcoats,[172] but assemblies were also founded in Rothesay (by 1879),[173] Dunoon (1882),[174] Millport (1887),[175] Sandbank (by 1887)[176] and in the Highlands at Oban (by 1884).[177] Millport was begun after a mission by the evangelists Alex Livingstone and Alex Anderson and one of the founder members of Dunoon was a Brethren individual formerly of Kilmarnock. Probably Rothesay was founded by Colin Campbell when he moved there in 1879 to open his 'House of Rest' and Oban by A. M. Riddle when he established himself as a photographer in the town—the dates of both men's removals are the earliest references for Brethren in each place. Although these origins are now uncertain, what is incontrovertible is that both itinerants and those in secular vocations were labouring continually to found further assemblies in conditions which were propitious for their growth.

But the growth was not unalloyed. In 1888, when herring fishing was in a difficult period,[178] it was reported that one-third of the assembly in Lerwick had emigrated overseas or to the Scottish mainland because of economic conditions. Among those who went were the most gifted members, and the three Shetland country assemblies had no gospel meetings or anyone able to supply Bible teaching to Christians.[179] North-east Scotland was equally affected. Out-migration from the region was high during this period, although its precise effect on individual assemblies is not known. Certainly the pioneer assembly at Old Rayne ceased in 1890, and possibly the removal of members to Aberdeen was a factor in this.[180] Probably the new meeting at Kemnay, where most of the converts had been among the quarrymen, was short-lived because the members were caught up in the emigration of that occupational group there to North America.[181] Amongst those who left the north east were most of the NES evangelists who had seceded to the Brethren, including

172. See above, n.146.

173. 'Colin Campbell', *CW*, 45 (1928), pp.146-7.

174. 'James Petrie', *W*, 42 (1912), p.255.

175. *W*, 17 (October 1887) end pp.; *The Eleventh Hour* (1887), p.4; however, Millport's early existence was evidently fitful, for in the early years of the twentieth century the breaking of bread was held during the summer season only, *W*, 32 (August 1902), end pp.

176. *W*, 17 (June 1887), end pp.

177. 'A. M. Riddle', *W*, 46 (1916), p.50.

178. Smith, *Shetland*, p.158, and figs 26 and 40.

179. *NW*, 18 (1888), p.iv.

180. Mrs Gordon's collection, Kennethmont, MS notebook on history of Insch assembly by Mrs Helen Gordon; George Taylor, for example, a founding member of Old Rayne moved to Aberdeen; also short-lived among the north-east assemblies appear to have been Findhorn, Forres, Fraserburgh, Kennethmont and Nairn.

181. Harper, *Emigration*, 1, p.257.

Donald Ross in 1876.[182] Forty per cent of all Brethren emigrants from the region whose date of emigration can be established left between 1871 and 1891.[183] However, this is twelve individuals out of only thirty and is too small a sample to be reliable, but it does suggest that this period was the peak one for the emigration of Brethren members from the region.[184] In the process north-east emigrants founded the Open Brethren movement in North America.[185] As was maintained above, the Brethren had profited from social and demographic changes in the countryside, and their continuing effects had consequences for the movement. Although rural Scotland was especially affected,[186] the period also saw emigration touching industrial areas of the country and Brethren members there also left for a new life overseas.[187] After an initial surge in growth, it would appear that some assemblies experienced decline.

There was, in addition, some loss of membership to the Exclusive Brethren.[188] At Larkhall a schism in 1874 led to the establishment of an Exclusive assembly[189] and, as certainly happened at Strathaven in 1876 and 1877, small numbers elsewhere probably seceded.[190] One other loss of membership which is difficult to chart is that which inevitably follows a revival as ardour cools. Figure 4.1 shows the membership of the assembly in Lesmahagow from 1876 until 1891.[191] Until 1882 the gross membership increased from ninety-two to 105, having an annual average of 94.4. In 1884 twenty-seven individuals left to establish the meeting in Kirkmuirhill and the membership remained lower until 1891, having an annual average of 59.7 in this period. The figures for net gains and losses through lapses in membership (arrived at by subtracting the figure for the latter from that for the former) show how fruitful 1881 had been

---

182. Ross, however, had already moved to Edinburgh in 1874.

183. Emigration data base; for the use of this material, see below, p.386 n.80.

184. The same might be argued Orkney, where five out of the seven Brethren individuals from Orkney whose year of emigration is known left in the 1880s, again a decade of high emigration there, cf. William Thomson, *A History of Orkney* (Edinburgh, 1987), p.253.

185. Ross H. McLaren, 'The Triple Tradition: the Origin and Development of the Open Brethren in North America' (M.A. thesis, Vanderbilt University, USA; 1982); Robert Baylis, *My People: the story of those Christians sometimes called Plymouth Brethren* (Wheaton, Ill, 1995), pp.83-99.

186. Malcolm Gray, *Scots on the Move: Scots migrants 1750-1914* (Edinburgh, 1990), pp.33-7.

187. See below, Figure 9.1.

188. For the Exclusives in Scotland, see above, pp.2-4.

189. Robert Chapman, *A Short History of the Inception, Progress and Personalities of Hebron Hall Assembly, Larkhall: 1866-1928* (Kilmarnock, 1929), pp.25-6.

190. Strathaven Evangelical Church, Strathaven, 'Roll of Members of Strathaven Assembly', 1876-1897, [pp. 5, 6]

191. Hope Hall, Lesmahagow, Gospel Hall roll book, 1876-1907.

when there was a net gain of thirty-one members. However, subsequent years, when the gross membership was lower, also saw marked gains in membership, with 1885 seeing a net increase of nineteen members and 1887 a net increase of twenty-three. There were two years, 1886 and 1890 (both closely following years of large net increases), when there was a net decrease. The data, however, must be treated with caution. While they separate out reasons for leaving the assembly (so that deaths and removals can be excluded), they do not similarly treat reasons for joining. Some of the increases in membership might be due to individuals removing to the area for employment. This possible difficulty, however, should not be exaggerated. Because national Brethren membership was still small in this period, there were few individuals available to transfer in. It is more likely that most of the increase in membership was due to non-Brethren individuals joining, such as happened in 1881 when there were twenty-eight baptisms.[192] In all but two years there was some growth, and decline in gross membership at Lesmahagow—largely caused by members leaving the district—was gain for the movement elsewhere. This evidence suggests that while some were lost to the movement after a period of greater increase, the growth of the period more than compensated for those who lapsed.

Figure 4.2 also suggests that overall losses were more than offset by gains.[193] According to these data, derived from *The Witness* obituaries, 1890 was the year in which the largest number of individuals joined the movement during this period. But it would appear that throughout the 1880s there was a substantial increase. The date of conversion was the most frequent one cited in an obituary of individuals who entered the movement in this period, but it can be seen from the graph that peaks in the number of conversions tended to coincide with high points for those joining an assembly (shown by the thickness of the top band). The exceptions to this correlation are 1871-2 and 1877 where the year of membership of a greater number of individuals can be established. In the case of the former dates this is because of the accession of the north-east movement which comprised 48.8 per cent of all reported additions in these two years. Brethren numbers were also boosted by gains from the Scottish missions of the American evangelist D. L. Moody in 1873-4 and 1881-2, as many who had been converted in his campaigns found their way into an assembly. One worker in Moody's first mission who, probably in 1874, joined the Marble Hall, Glasgow, was Alexander Marshall, a potential candidate for the EU ministry and a member of the city congregation of which James Morison had become minster. Marshall

---

192. *Ibid.*, p.52.
193. For the explanation of *The Witness* obituaries, see above, p.19 n.89.

became the evangelist of the Scottish movement *par excellence*.[194] A number of other individuals who transferred to assemblies in this period also went on to become influential. Two Baptist leaders who joined the movement were John Rae, who, with the majority of his flock, founded a meeting in Elgin, where at the time he had been the evangelist *cum* pastor, in 1872,[195] and William J. Grant who, along with a number of others, left his congregation in 1880 to join the Kilmarnock Brethren.[196] The scale of conversions and additions and the number of assemblies which were formed in 1871-91, both suggest that during these two decades the Brethren in Scotland enjoyed their most vigorous growth.

Along with this numerical increase, the movement in this period continued to be widely touched with a desire for the transformation of the commonplace.[197] The higher life was not only accepted in the north east but elsewhere too. About the time when Alex Marshall joined the Brethren in Glasgow he was reading *Trust in the Living Father* (1873), a booklet by the undenominational preacher, Henry Varley, who had been influenced by Pearsall Smith.[198] The Keswick Convention, founded in 1875, had an influence too:[199] W. J. Grant became an exponent of its spirituality among Scottish Brethren,[200] and, along with a number of others from the Greenock assembly, the newly converted Dan Crawford visited the Convention itself.[201] In 1888 Crawford went on to become a missionary, one of the movement's most famous overseas activists.[202] Grant's brother Alexander, a missionary with the English Presbyterian

---

194. John Hawthorn, *Alexander Marshall: evangelist, author, pioneer* (London [1929]), pp.27-31.

195. Rae to the editor, p. 83; Ironside, *Brethren Movement*, pp.71-2; F. F. Bruce, *In Retrospect: remembrance of things past* (London & Glasgow, 1980), p.6.

196. J. G[ray]., 'William J. Grant, Kilmarnock', *BP*, 51 (1930), pp.98-101; G. G[ray]., 'W. J. Grant, M.A., Kilmarnock', *CW*, 45, no. 536 (July 1930), [pp.2-3]; *CW*, 45, no. 535, (July 1930), [pp.98-9]; HyP[ickering]., 'Home-call of W. J. Grant, M.A., Kilmarnock', *W*, 60 (1930), pp.187-8; Yuille, *Baptists in Scotland*, p.284; but cf. below, p.163.

197. Cf. above, pp.73-4.

198. D. J. Findlay quoted in Hawthorn, *Marshall*, p.38; Henry Varley, *Henry Varley: the powerful evangelist of the Victorian era* (London [c.1913]), pp.103-6.

199. For Keswick and the Brethren, see below, pp.269-71.

200. G[ray]., 'Grant', pp.98-101; P[ickering]., 'Grant', pp.187-8; for further discussion of Grant on this point, see below p.269 n.104.

201. Tilsley, *Dan Crawford*, pp.26-9.

202. *DSCHT*, p.574, i; Stephen Neill, *A History of Christian Missions* (Harmondsworth, 1964), pp.380-2; Robert I. Rotberg, 'Plymouth Brethren and the occupation of Katanga, 1886-1907', *The Journal of African History*, 5 (1964), pp.285-97; Paul Hyland, *The Black Heart: a voyage into Central Africa* (London, 1988).

Church in China, had already been won for the Brethren,[203] but during the wave of enthusiasm for foreign missions which followed the death of David Livingstone in 1874,[204] Scottish assemblies had begun to send out their own foreign missionaries, the first ones being in 1876 the Shetland evangelist William Sloan to the Faroe Isles and Norman Macrae to India.[205] Others were to follow quickly, with two of the most noted Scottish Brethren missionaries, John S. Anderson and Frederick Stanley Arnot, respectively leaving for Italy in 1880 and Central Africa in 1881.[206] Before going to Africa, Arnot had evangelised in the south west along with John Ritchie. It was to help teach the converts of a revival in the Dalmellington assembly in 1874 that Ritchie had moved to Ayrshire,[207] and he transferred to Kilmarnock in 1879 when there was a large number of conversions there under Rice Hopkins and Alex Marshall.[208] Local awakenings were continuing as a significant factor in Brethren growth. The marked peaks and troughs in the net gains and losses in the membership of Lesmahagow assembly (Figure 4.1) suggest a revivalist pattern there. These several elements—higher life, missionary enthusiasm, and continuing revivalism—kept the temperature of the movement high.

Growth 1892-1914

The first statistics which are available from an address list of Open Brethren assemblies shows that in 1886 there were 184 meetings in Scotland.[209] In the address list for 1897 this had risen to 236, and in that of 1904 to 285.[210] Assemblies continued being formed into the twentieth century, but the rate of increase slowed and there was, perhaps, a net loss of membership in the years before World War I. The period 1892 until 1914 also began with the Scottish Open Brethren suffering their greatest

---

203. J. W. J., 'Alexander Grant', *BP*, 35 (1914), pp.70-1; 'Alexander Grant', *W*, 44 (1914), p.12: it would appear that this was before W. J. Grant joined the Brethren.

204. Andrew C. Ross, 'Scottish missionary concern 1874-1914: a golden era?', *SHR*, 51 (1972), pp.52-72.

205. W. T. Stunt *et al.*, *Turning the World Upside down: a century of missionary endeavour*, 2nd edn (Bath, 1973), pp.562-7.

206. *Ibid.*, p.562; Baker, *Frederick Stanley Arnot*, pp.20-1; for Arnot, see also Robert I. Rotberg, *Christian Missionaries and the Creation of Northern Rhodesia 1880-1924* (Princeton, NJ, 1965).

207. R[itchie]., 'John Ritchie', [pp.1-4].

208. Beattie, *Brethren*, p.224.

209. Sprague's *List of Assemblies* quoted in *The Eleventh Hour* (January 1887), p.4; cf. above p.15 n.85.

210. Jordan, *List* (1897), pp.116-44; *List* (1904), pp.128-64.

single loss of members with the secession of the Churches of God in
1892-4. This separation will be discussed more fully in the following
chapter,[211] but here it should be noted that it had consequences for the
continued growth of the movement. There were a few assemblies, it would
appear, which seceded in their entirety with the new body, such as appears
to have happened at Orton, Moray, and in Lanarkshire at Dykehead,
Shotts.[212] Other meetings such as the ones in Inverness, and Buchanan
Court Hall, Glasgow, apparently never recovered from the loss of
members.[213] Those which suffered a schism found it drained the morale
of the company,[214] and it was evidently due to the secession that
Edinburgh Open Brethren were in a state of disarray in the 1890s.[215] In
all some seventy Scottish Churches of God came into existence by
secession,[216] and one commentator has speculated that perhaps a tenth of
the Scottish Open Brethren membership seceded.[217] There were, in
addition, at least thirteen further schisms in assemblies which remained
with the Open Brethren, and it is likely that a number of other meetings
came into existence in a similar manner during this period. Controversial
issues, which shall be more fully dissected in the following chapter,
agitated the movement throughout these years and deflected energy and
attention away from recruitment.

---

211.   See below pp.158-69.

212.   There were, in addition, Churches of God in the north east in Macduff,
Bannshire (see Map 4); and Cuminestown, Aberdeenshire (midway between New Deer and
Turriff). Macduff was also probably an entire assembly which had seceded, but
Cuminstown was possibly a new meeting place for secessions from nearby assemblies;
because of the proximity of Orton, in the parish of Rothes, to Boharm (see Map 4), it is
assumed that this is the assembly which originally met there.

213.   Beattie, *Brethren*, pp.243, 270.

214.   [John Waddell], *Roman Road Hall Motherwell Centenary 1875-1975* (Lanark
[1975]), pp.5-6.

215.   Beattie, *Brethren*, p.262.

216.   Norman Macdonald, 'One Hundred Years of Needed Truth Brethren 1892 to 1992:
a historical analysis', typescript [1992], p.23.

217.   Macdonald, 'Needed Truth Brethren', p.23; it is not clear, however, what the
basis of this calculation is.

Table 4.1. **Attendance at Brethren morning meetings in Dundee (1881, 1891 and 1901) and Gospel Hall, St Paul St., Aberdeen (1891 and 1901) compared with attendance at morning service in other churches in both cities**

Dundee

	1881	1891	% growth	1901	% growth
Brethren					
No. of congregations	2	2	0	2	0
No. in attendance (adults & children)	146	128	-12.3	138	7.8
Other churches					
No. of congregations	83	91	9.6	99	8.8
No. in attendance (adults & children)	30,512	24 ,227	-20.6	26,000	7.3
Total population	142,000	168,000	18.3	167,000	-0.6

Aberdeen

	1891	1901	% growth
St Paul St			
No. of congregations	1	2	50
No. in attendance (adults & children)	190	219	15
Other churches			
No. of congregations	87	-	
No. in attendance (adults & children)	26,785	26,144	-2.4
Total population	110,541	153,503	39

Sources: *The Dundee Advertiser*, 1 April 1901, p.5 ; *The Aberdeen Journal*, 15 April 1901, p.5.

Yet the 1890s was a decade of growth, and even the Churches of God schism can be seen as an indication of vigour, for ecclesiastical divisions

often occur in periods of expansion.[218] As Table 4.1 shows, in both St
Paul Street, Aberdeen, and the two assemblies in Dundee, attendance at
the morning meeting had increased in the decennial survey of attendance
carried out by local newspapers, despite there having been a Church of
God schism in both cities.[219] The morning meeting is attended by
members rather than adherents,[220] and enumeration of those at this
service therefore provides a reliable guide to fluctuations in membership.
In Dundee attendance at the morning meeting had been lower on the
census Sunday in 1891 than it had been in 1881. The poor weather
conditions on the later occasion had been blamed for the markedly lower
attendance figure in all churches, but it would seem that Dundee had
been one of the places in which the Brethren declined during the 1880s.
By 1901, however, although attendance had not recovered to its 1881
level, there had been a 7.8 per cent increase in attendance. But although
this rise was a greater percentage increase than that of other churches, it
was a lower aggregate increase in attendance from 1881 than theirs. In
other congregations it had risen from a 20.6 per cent decline between
1881 and 1891 to a 7.3 per cent increase between 1891 and 1901.
Probably, however, the more committed Brethren would not have been so
adversely affected by the inclement weather of 1891, and the percentage
increase in 1901 would more accurately reflect active membership levels.
In Aberdeen, Brethren growth in the 1890s is more apparent. In 1900 St
Paul Street Gospel Hall had planted an additional assembly in the new
suburb of Torry (see Map 5 inset), and the attendance at these two
meetings in 1901 has been aggregated in Table 4.1 to provide a
comparison with the 1891 figure. Although the percentage increase in
attendance on the second census Sunday was not as large as the thirty-
nine per cent growth in the city's population, at fifteen per cent it was
considerably better than that of the other churches whose attendance was
lower by 2.4 per cent.[221] Aberdeen's three other Open Brethren
assemblies were not counted in 1891 which does not allow any
comparison with the 260 adults and children in attendance at their
morning meetings in 1901. The evidence of these census suggests that,
despite the Churches of God separation, assemblies in both cities had
enjoyed growth throughout the 1890s.

---

218. John Wilson, 'The sociology of schism', in Michael Hill (ed.), *A Sociological
Yearbook of Religion in Britain*, 4 (London, 1971), pp.1-20.

219. *The Dundee Advertiser*, 1 April 1901, p.5 ; *The Aberdeen Journal*, 15 April
1901, p.5.

220. See below, p.258.

221 One of the United Free churches was omitted on census Sunday and the estimated
figure of its attendance has been included in Table 4.2, 'The Aberdeen church census', *The
Aberdeen Journal*, 16 April 1901, p.5.

Figure 4.3, extrapolated from *The Witness* obituaries, also points to the decade as being one of growth.[222] According to these data, 1893 (when the Churches of God secession was at its height) was the year in which the largest number of individuals joined the movement in any one year. There were also peaks of substantial increase in 1894-5, 1900 and 1904-5. Revivalism continued as a factor in growth. It was in 1895, for example, that the evangelist W. S. King saw a further awakening on Westray,[223] and that same year James Anderson had a 'remarkable time of revival' in Troon,[224] while the Irish evangelist David Rea accompanied by Alexander Marshall baptised sixty-two individuals after a mission in Glasgow.[225] Revivalism also continued in south Ayrshire in the mining hamlets around New Cumnock where John Harper and J. M. Hamilton both saw conversions which led to the establishment of meetings in Burnfoot (*c*.1893)[226] and Bank Glen (1897).[227] The activities of the undenominational revivalist James McKendrick in the fishing communities of the north east during this period also increased Brethren numbers. The most successful of his missions was the one in Findochty, Banffshire, in 1893. During its five weeks the whole community was moved and fishing was abandoned. It was the only occasion McKendrick witnessed the 'the Gospel dance', when the converts, sometimes in groups of several hundred, would join hands and keep time with their feet to the rhythmical singing of a hymn.[228] He was invited to Sandend (see Map 4, Portsoy) next,[229] and not long after his mission, a group of his converts, after making contact with Aberdeen Brethren, began breaking bread, probably in 1894 after the evangelist Duncan McNab had been there.[230] When McKendrick held a mission in Portessie at the end of 1896 he met an air of 'hardness and indifference', but he persevered until he saw revival there too.[231] Methodism was strong in the village due to the earlier work of James Turner,[232] and it was mainly from this denomination, but

---

222. For the explanation of *The Witness* obituaries, see above, p.16 n.89.

223. *BM*, 5 (1895), p.24.

224. *W*, 52 (1922), p.216.

225. Tom Rea (compiler), *The Life and Labours of David Rea, Evangelist: largely written from his own MSS.* (Belfast, 1917), pp.138-9.

226. 'Andrew Barbour', *BM*, 53 (1943), p.80.

227. 'James R. Hood', *W*, 62 (1932), p.72; 'Mrs James Stewart', *W*, 67 (1937), p.143; 'Robert Geddes', *W*, 83 (1953), p.50.

228. James McKendrick, *Seen and Heard During Forty-Six Years' Evangelistic Work* (London [*c*.1927]), pp.88-99.

229. *Ibid.*, pp.100-3.

230. Writer's collection, I.D.2., James Merson to the writer, 28 November 1988; *W*, 4 (1894), p.71. The latter source states that the assembly had commenced in 'Southend', evidently a misprint for Sandend.

231. McKendrick, *Seen and Heard*, pp.139-42.

joined by some others from Findochty, that a group of sixty to seventy individuals, most of them converts of McKendrick's revival, met to break bread in 1901.[233] The formation of an assembly some time after nondenominational revivalism had been a recurring pattern in the nineteenth century.

In the early twentieth century the years around 1905 also saw revivalism widespread when the awakening in Wales of 1904-5 aroused interest among Scottish Brethren.[234] An increased number of conversions is particularly noticeable at Lesmahagow (Figure 4.4) where a sustained period of revivalism in 1904 during a campaign by the former missionary James Anderson in the town (see Map 10) led to the addition of fifty-two new members to the meeting in 1904.[235] After another mission by the evangelist Thomas Sinclair an assembly was formed in neighbouring Coalburn by forty-seven members of Lesmahagow the following year,[236] but the addition of the same number of new members at Lesmahagow in 1905 meant that the gross membership figure of the assembly scarcely dropped (Figure 4.4.). The effects of revivalism in these years can also be seen in Elim Hall in the Crosshill district of Glasgow where only an annual gross membership figure is available (Figure 4.5). In 1905 the membership increased by thirty-nine individuals and continued to increase annually until 1907 when it reached its prewar peak of 317.[237] Many other assemblies had substantial increases in these years.[238] In places with traditions of revivalism such as Stranraer, Portessie and Westray there were emotional scenes in advance of the Welsh revival[239] and coinciding with the awakening in Wales multiple conversions were reported elsewhere. In 1904 the Strathaven assembly, after five weeks of nightly prayer meetings, had a sustained

232. E. McHardie, *James Turner: or how to reach the masses* (London, 1889), pp.168-85.

233. D.1., Tom Morrow to the writer, 8 December 1988.

234. *SSW*, 20 (1905), p.34; William Shaw, 'The Revival in Wales: has it a voice for us?', *W*, 35 (1905), pp.27-8; Alex Marshall to the editor [1905], *ibid.*, pp.64-66; cf. *BM*, 15 (May 1905), end pp.; on the Welsh Revival see C. R. Williams, 'The Welsh religious revival, 1904-5', *BJS*, 3 (1962), pp.242-59.

235. Gospel Hall, Lesmahagow, roll books, 1876-1907 and 1980-29, in the possession of Hope Hall, Lesmahagow; Anderson, 'Lesmahagow', pp.44-5; *W*, 34 (December 1904), end pp.

236. *W*, 35 (May 1905), end pp.

237. *Elim Hall, 98th Annual Report, 1st January to 31st December, 1981* (n.p. [1981]).

238. See 'Signs of revival', *W*, 35 (March, April, May, June 1905), end pp.; *BM*, 15 (March 1905), end pp.; [Waddell], *Roman Road Hall*, p.7.

239. See respectively, *W*, 32 (March 1902) end pp.; *W*, 33 (May 1903), end pp.; *W*, 34 (February 1904), end pp.; cf. Stephen Lennox Johns, *The Gospel Hall, Tillicoultry: a short history* (Tillicoultry, 1990), pp.6-7.

period of conversions which, the following year, spilled over into the neighbouring villages of Chapelton and Glassford with sixty conversions in the latter place.[240] At Kinning Park, Glasgow, the evangelist John McDonald reported some 200 conversions in 1905 and John Ferguson saw a similar number in Cambuslang.[241] That same year in Coatbridge the assembly had to build a new hall to accommodate the increased numbers, and in Govanhill, Glasgow, and Kilbirnie football teams were disbanded due to the players being converted.[242] Shetland Brethren also saw some seventy to eighty conversions in 1905 and a new meeting was formed at Northmavine (see Map 1, Brae) the following year.[243] Revivalism was a continued factor in Brethren growth.

Yet in the early twentieth century the community-based phenomenon of revivals decreased as a significant component in Brethren growth. It was the more routine operations of the movement and its members which led to greater recruitment. In their activities the spontaneous folk movement had been formalised into techniques for producing conversions, which could at times, as appears to have been the case in some of the examples surveyed in the previous paragraph, touch the wider community. The process had been at work since the 1840s.[244] Revival was replaced by revivalism, and even the latter had less effect.[245] Perhaps the principal means of spreading it was itinerant evangelists, a number of whom dedicated themselves to one district remote from areas of Brethren strength. John Stout, a member of Lerwick assembly, had been working as an evangelist in Shetland since about 1898, and it was he who planted the meeting in Northmavine.[246] In the Hebrides, Lewis (see Map 3) received an assembly at Port of Ness when John M. Nicholson, a native of the island who had been converted in America, returned in 1894 to work as an evangelist.[247] In the Highlands and north-east Lowlands in the early years of the twentieth century there were several evangelists itinerating: the brothers Francis and Matthew Logg, Gaelic-speaking William Mackenzie and Peter Bruce. Among them, they were responsible

---

240. *BM*, 15 (January 1905), p.i; *W*, 43 (1913), p.139.

241. 'Signs of revival', *W*, 35 (March, April 1905), end pp.

242. 'Signs of revival', *W*, 35 (March, June 1905), end pp; *W*, 36 (January 1906), end pp.

243. A. M[arshall]., 'Shetland', *W*, 37 (1907), p.134; *BM* 16 (October 1906), p.i; the assembly transferred to Brae in 1976.

244. John Kent, *Holding the Fort: studies in Victorian revivalism* (London, 1978).

245. For this distinction, see Janice Holmes, *Religious Revivals in Britain and Ireland 1859-1905* (Dublin, 2000), pp.xix-xx, 52-3.

246. 'John Stout', *W*, 82 (1952), p.28.

247. *H*, 4 (1926), pp.90-1; 'John M. Nicholson', *W*, 63 (1937), p.71; however, it was not until 1905 that he acquired a hall, *W*, 35 (April 1905), end pp.

for the founding of some six assemblies.[248] Further south existing
congregations could cooperate in the outreach and at least twenty-two
meetings were formed in this way during this period.[249] The most

---

248. These were (the evangelist's name is given with the founding date): Highlands:
(see Map 3): Dingwall (1907, Francis and Matthew Logg): Beattie, *Brethren*, p.273; *BM*,
17 (August 1907), p.i; Inverness (re-formed 1911, William Mackenzie): *BM*, 22 (January
1912), p.i; 'William Mackenzie', *CW*, 42 (1925), pp.129-130; Beattie, *Brethren*, p.270;
Kiltarlity (1911, Peter Bruce): *BM*, 21 (September 1911), p.i; Moray (see Map 4):
Lossiemouth (1902, Francis Logg, and Peter Bruce): 'Mrs Edwards', *W*, 77 (August
1947), p.96; Banffshire (see Map 4): Macduff (1904, Francis and Matthew Logg): *BM*,
14 (December 1904), p.i; *W*, 58 (1928), p.256; Aberdeenshire (see Map 5): Collieston
(*c*.1892, Francis Logg): J. Hay Ritchie, 'Brethren—let us pray', *BM*, 80 (1970), pp.116-
17.

249. These were (the evangelist's name, where known, is given with the founding
date): Dundee (see Map 6 inset): Lochee (1907, William Hill): *W*, 37 (1907), p.152; Fife
(see Map 7): Saline (1904, evangelist unknown): *W*, 34 (April 1904), end pp.; *W*, 35
(May 1905), end pp.; Clackmannanshire (see Map 7): Alloa (1904, John Ferguson): *W*,
34 (June, September, October, December 1904), end pp.; *W*, 35 (January 1905), end pp.;
Alva (1905, John Ferguson): *W*, 35 (October 1905), end pp; Stirlingshire (see Map 9):
Kilsyth (1903, John Ferguson): *W*, 33 (July 1903), end pp; *ibid*, (September), end pp;
ibid, (October), end pp.; Bannockburn (1905, Malcolm McKinnon): *W*, 34 (April 1904),
end pp; *W*, 35 (February 1905), end pp.; Airth (1906, Richard Loydale): *W*, 36 (April
1906), end pp.; *BM*, 16 (April 1906), p.i; Laurieston (1909, John McDonald): *W*, 39
(October 1909), end pp.; East Dunbartonshire (see Map 9): Cumbernauld, (1913, Arthur
Gilmour): *BM*, 23 (August 1913), p.i; *W*, 43 (1913), p.332; Lanarkshire (see Map 10):
Low Waters, Hamilton (1899, Alex Lamb): *BM*, 9 (1899), pp.84, 96, 132; Overtown
(1905, W. J. Meneely): *BM*, 15 (September 1905), pi; writer's collection, I.M.23.,
[James Hislop], '"Seventy Years On" or "These Seventy Years": the story of Overtown
Assembly of Christian Brethren', photocopy of MS [1971], p.1; Halfway, Cambuslang
(1906, John Ferguson): *BM*, 16 (September 1906), p.i; Annathill (1910, John Carrick):
W, 68 (February 1911), end pp.; 'John Ireland', *W*, 63 (1933), p.96: this assembly was
also known as Glenboig; Glasgow (See Map 11 no.3) Balmore Hall, Possilpark: (1910
evangelist unknown): *W*, 40 (June 1910), end pp. (there had been an earlier, apparently
abortive attempt to found an assembly in Possilpark at Mosshouse Gospel Hall, 8
Saracen St., in 1902, *W*, 32 (October, 1902), end pp.); Renfrewshire (see Map 12):
Thornliebank (1902, John Ferguson): 'William Wilson', *W*, 57 (1927), p.138; 'John
Cameron', *W* 59 (May 1929), p.122; Ayrshire (see Map 13): Stewarton (1898, John
Ferguson): *BM*, 5 (1898), p.84; *W*, 33 (March 1903), end pp.; Crosshill (1902, Thomas
Sinclair): *W*, 32 (April 1902), end pp.; 'Thomas Steed', *W*, 95 (1965), p.436; Crosshill,
Gospel Hall, H. Wright, 'Crosshill's Diamond Jubilee', typescript poem dated 21
February 1962; West Kilbride (1914, William Taylor): *W*, 44 (1914), p.36, end pp.;
Wigtownshire (see Map 14): Kirkcowan (1892, Arthur Hodgkinson): Beattie, *Brethren*,
p.205; Whauphill (*c*.1895, evangelist unknown): *BM*, 5 (1895), p.108 (this is the first
extant reference to Brethren activity there and is probably close to the assembly's
founding); Portpatrick (1909, Duncan McNab, Caledonian Bible Carriage): *W*, 39
(1909), p.87;*W*, 41 (June 1911), end pp.; Selkirkshire (See Map 14): Selkirk (1911,
Arthur Gilmour): *BM*, 22 (May 1912), p.i.

successful evangelist in this respect was John Ferguson but he was far from being alone and the substantial number of itinerants the Brethren now possessed meant that the movement could recruit both from areas in which they were already strong and in more remote ones.

Existing assemblies also continued to plant additional ones. The meeting in Windygates, Fife (see Map 7), was founded early in 1914 by members of Innerleven assembly.[250] In Edinburgh, matters had stabilised with two assemblies on the north and south sides of the city centre (see Map 8, inset) which began to enjoy some growth.[251] It was from these centres that the Leith assembly was formed around 1900,[252] as were those at Portobello in 1905,[253] and Davidson's Mains in 1911.[254] Also in the Lothians the meeting in Newtongrange was formed in 1913 through members of Dalkeith,[255] which had itself been formed in 1902 by Brethren members removing there.[256] In Lanarkshire (see Map 10) mention has already been made of Coalburn,[257] and additional meetings were planted in the county by Blantyre assembly in 1895 at Burnbank,[258] and Motherwell in 1908 in the Flemington district of the town.[259] Once again, however, this process was marked in Glasgow where at least seven assemblies were formed by existing ones, the most active congregation in this regard being Elim Hall, Crosshill.[260] An outreach over several years

---

250. Alexander Rollo, *The Story of Innerleven Assembly* (n.p., n.d.), p.11.

251. Beattie, *Brethren*, p.262.

252. *Ibid.*; 'James P. Taylor' *W*, 83 (1953), p.129; Mrs Effie McGregor', *BM*, 87 (1977), p.233.

253. Beattie, *Brethren*, p.262; *BM*, 15 (July 1905), p.i: this assembly moved to Musselburgh in 1908 (*BM*, 18 (August 1908), p.i), where it was apparently discontinued, and the meeting in Portobello was re-founded in 1910 (*BM*, 21 (January 1911), p.i).

254. *W*, 41 (June 1911), end pp.; 'Robert Ainslie', *W*, 81 (1951), p.56.

255. *W*, 43 (1913), p.306; oral information, July 1988, from a founding member of Dalkeith; Newtongrange assembly moved to Mayfield in 1970.

256. *W*, 32 (October 1902), end pp; 'John Fraser', *W*, 96 (1966), p.236.

257. See above, p.152.

258. Ransome W. Cooper, *James Lees: shepherd of lonely sheep in Europe* (London, 1959), p.18.

259. *BM*, 18 (May 1908), p.i; *BM*, 19 (April 1909), p.i; [Waddell], *Roman Road Hall*, pp.7-8.

260. These were (parent assembly given with the founding date): <u>Eglinton Hall</u> (See Map 11 no. 40) (1892, from Buchanan Court Hall): Beattie, *Brethren*, p.243; <u>Summerfield Hall</u>, <u>Whiteinch</u> (Map 11 no. 8) (1902, from Abingdon Hall): *W*, 33 (January 1903), end pp. <u>Salem Hall</u>, <u>Ibrox</u> (Map 11, no. 26) (1903, from Elim Hall): anon., 'Those sixty years 1890-1950', in *Elim Hall*, pp.5-6; <u>Hermon Hall</u>, <u>Govanhill</u> (Map 11, no. 50) (1904, from Elim Hall): *ibid.*; *W*, 34 (March 1904), end pp; <u>Albert Hall</u>, <u>Shawlands</u>, (1909, from Elim Hall): anon., 'Those sixty years', in *Elim Hall*, pp.5-6; <u>Holmlea Hall</u>, <u>Cathcart Road</u> (Map 11, no. 52) (1911, from Elim Hall): anon., 'Those

in the Radnor Park area of Clydebank, Dunbartonshire (see Map 12) resulted in an assembly being formed in 1913.[261] In north Ayrshire (see Map 13), as the majority of the members of Beith assembly lived in or near Barrmill, a meeting was formed in the village in 1902;[262] and in 1906 Kilbirnie member Robert White founded one in the hamlet of Barkip where he lived.[263] Assemblies were concerned to create new ones around them.

The planting of assemblies by existing ones surveyed in the previous paragraph is hard to disentangle from the migration of Brethren members. New industrialised communities attracted Brethren in search of employment and they would often travel to a nearby meeting, but their ambition would be to establish one in their place of residence. Sometimes this would be achieved through evangelism and sometimes through a mixture of evangelism and further Brethren members moving to the new area. The effects of the immigration of labour can be seen at its simplest in places such as that of Cowie, Stirlingshire (see Map 9), when the opening of a new coal mine brought Brethren miners to the village where they began an assembly in 1895,[264] or in the expansion of the west Fife coalfield (see Map 7) where in the newly founded burgh of Cowdenbeath the meeting went from its original four members in 1898 to forty in two years,[265] and additional meetings were formed in Cardenden in 1905,[266] and Low Valleyfield in 1910.[267] There were at least another twelve places in this period where the migration of Brethren led to assemblies being formed,[268] but in some cases it seems to be a mixture of causes. Some

sixty years', in *Elim Hall*, pp.5-6; W, 41 (June 1911), end pp.; Baltic Hall, Dalmarnock (Map 11, no. 44) (1912, from Rutherglen assembly): *BM*, 22 (August 1912), p.i.

261. *BM*, 43 (December 1913), p.ii.

262. Writer's collection, I.C.2., David Bell, 'A Short History of the Christian Brethren Movement with Special Reference to the Origin of the Barrmill Assembly', typescript June 1986, p.4; Beith assembly was discontinued shortly after the Barrmill assembly was formed.

263. 'Robert White', *W*, 68 (1938), p.72.

264. Dr M. H. B. Sanderson's collection, Linlithgow, Joseph Waugh, 'Cowie Assembly', holograph MS, 26 November 1974; writer's collection, I.U.1., Danny Sharp to the writer, 13 August 1988.

265. *BM*, 10 (February 1900), p.i.

266. *BM*, 15 (September 1905), p.i; this is undoubtedly the assembly which is referred to as being in the adjacent village of Auchterderran in *W*, 35 (September 1905), end pp.

267. *BM*, 20 (December 1910), p.i.

268. These were: Moray & Nairn (See Map 4): Inchberry (1909): 'George Mouat Johnson', *BM*, 84 (1974), p.127; Nairn (1894, re-formed 1899): Beattie, *Brethren*, p.272 and William Wright to Alex Stewart, 27 November 1974, in Mr Alex. Stewart's collection, Hopeman, [Alex. Stewart (compiler)], 'A Record of Gospel Work. Christian Brethren. Moray & Nairn', MS, n.d.; Aberdeenshire (see Map 5): Ballater (1906): *BM*, 17

Brethren members of nearby meetings lived in these places and evangelism gathered more together until it became possible to form a separate congregation, and this was the case especially in the cities and larger conurbations.

The Brethren in this period continued to attract individuals from other churches. The Exclusive Stuart Party meeting in Hamilton, Olive Hall, associated with the Open Brethren about this time, appearing in the 1904 assembly address list.[269] Baptist church members were particularly likely to be gained in this way.[270] In Fife (see Map 7) members of the Inverkeithing Christian Endeavour, an activity of the Baptist Church, who met by candlelight to study the Bible in a barber's back shop, formed an assembly in 1910.[271] At Lochore, one of the new mining communities of west Fife, a Baptist mission had been commenced about 1910.[272] It met in premises known locally as 'the Glory Shop' due to its shop-window front and the revivalist activities of the members. The services were conducted by the lay members themselves and only occasionally was a Baptist pastor present to help. Among the immigrant miners who associated with the mission were ones who had previously been in assemblies. They talked of Brethren practices with the result that most of the mission seceded and it erected its own building in 1913.[273] The attempt to found a Baptist cause in Plean, Stirlingshire (see Map 9), foundered, it appears, when the group merged about 1910 with a Brethren assembly, probably the one in neighbouring Cowie.[274] At Ratho in West Lothian (see Map 9), the Baptist church was so reduced in numbers owing to individuals leaving for the Brethren that in 1912 the pastor had to resign and the church failed to

---

(February 1907), pi; Perthshire (see Map 6): <u>Doune</u> (1903): *W*, 33 (April, 1903), end pp.; 'Willie Rew', in James Anderson (ed.), *They Finished their Course in the Eighties* (Kilmarnock, 1990), p.163; <u>Perth</u> (1902): *W*, 32 (July 1902), end pp.; writer's collection, I.Q.2., Wm Walker to the writer, 13 April 1989; East Lothian (see Map 8) <u>Dunbar</u> (1895): 'Mrs Charles Spence', *W*, 75 (May 1945), p.iv; West Lothian (see Map 9): <u>Bathgate</u> (*c.*1906): 'A. Mabon', *BM*, 27 (March 1917), p.iv; <u>Philpstoun</u> (1895): 'Joseph Lindsay', *W*, 61 (1931), p.72; Stirlingshire (see Map 9): <u>Shieldhill</u> (1895): 'Alex. Ferrie', *BM*, 46 (1936), p.56; Lanarkshire (see Map 10): <u>Douglas Water</u> (c.1909): *W*, 39 (1909), p.167; <u>Muirhead</u> (1892): 'John Pirie', *W*, 74 (March 1944), p.iv and oral information, 27 February 1991, from an assembly member; Dumfriesshire (see Map 14): <u>Kirkconnel</u> (1910): *W*, 40 (October 1910), end pp.

269. Jordan, *List* (1904), p.150; for the Stuart Party, see above, p.2.

270. Dickson, 'Brethren and Baptists', pp.372-87.

271. *W*, 40 (March 1910), p.iv; Kilmarnock, writer's collection, I.I.6.(i), Archie Carmichael, MS history of Inverkeithing assembly ([1988]); *ibid.*, I.I.6.(ii), Harry Edwards to the writer, 1 September 1988.

272. Yuille (ed.), *Baptists in Scotland*, p.286.

273. Oral information, 19 November 1988, from a woman who was a teenager at the time.

274. D. W. Bebbington (ed.), *The Baptists in Scotland* (Glasgow, 1988), p.206.

recover from the loss.[275] Two secessions in 1907 which are known from single mentions in *The Witness* were the groups which left the Churches of God in Musselburgh and the Baptists in Springburn, but whether they were absorbed into other assemblies or failed to remain with the movement is not known.[276]

It was in 1910 when the mission hall founded in Huntly by Robert McKilliam united with the town's meeting.[277] Earlier in Kilwinning, Ayrshire, a group of recently converted lay activists, who had gradually adopted Brethren practices, had begun breaking bread in 1892. Shortly afterwards, they had united with the assembly there.[278] Transfers from such bodies provided the greatest number of accessions of Evangelical Christians in this period. The removal of a couple, who were members of the Kilbarchan meeting, to Bridge of Weir led to a mission hall there being formed into an assembly in 1903.[279] Also in Renfrewshire (see Map 12) some members of the Linwood Gospel Mission who had been in contact with the Brethren in Paisley turned the Mission into an assembly in 1904.[280] In Glasgow two men, both named James Wilson, had begun evangelistic work in the Garngad district of the city (see Map 11, no.12) in 1888 and through Bible study they and their converts had begun to observe the Lord's supper together. In 1892 James McAlonan drew them into the Brethren movement.[281] Elsewhere in Glasgow's east end, the Camlachie Carters' Mission (see Map 11, no.31)—founded in 1873 after Moody's evangelistic campaign—formed itself into an assembly in the early 1890s.[282] Bethesda Hall in Govan also became Brethren in 1909.[283] In Lanarkshire (see Map 10) members of Wrangham Free Church mission hall, New Stevenston, felt their independent Bible studies were disapproved of by the congregation. They seceded in 1897 to form a meeting in the village.[284] In the same county, when the Exclusive assembly in the mining hamlet of Wattstown was discontinued, some

275. Yuille (ed.), *History of the Baptists*, pp.127-8; Bebbington (ed.), *Baptists in Scotland*, p.101.

276. *W*, 37 (1907), pp.58, 184.

277. See above, p.73; 'Dr Robert M'Killiam, London', *BP*, 36 (1915), pp.54-6; *W*, 40 (1910), p.55.

278. Anon., 'Kilwinning', pp.307-8.

279. Beattie, *Brethren*, p.259; 'David Wight', *BM*, 64 (1954), p.20.

280. Anon., *These Are My Brethern [sic]: Linwood Gospel Hall 1953* (n.p. [1953]).

281. Beattie, *Brethren*, pp.246-9.

282. 'J. A. Garriock', *W*, 78 (1948), p.iii; 'James Moffat', *W*, 92 (1962), p.236.

283. *W*, 39 (June 1909), end pp.; this mission met in premises formerly occupied by the assembly which by then met in Bethesda Hall, Linthouse.

284. Writer's collection, I.M.21., David Wilson, 'A Brief History of the Assembly of Christian Brethren Meeting in Gospel Hall, Hall St., New Stevenston, Motherwell', MS [1989].

members joined the Evangelistic Gospel Band in Greengairs and in 1908 it formed itself into a Open Brethren assembly.[285] So too in 1913 did the mission hall in Coatdyke, Airdrie.[286] At Shotts, however, the mission divided about 1902 when some members wanted to begin breaking bread,[287] and in Motherwell, when some individuals from Hallelujah Hall seceded in 1911, they were acknowledged as an assembly.[288] At Haggs in Stirlingshire (see Map 9) a meeting was formed in 1902 out of the Faith Mission in nearby Banknock,[289] and the new assembly in turn led the mission in Bonnybridge to become an assembly in that same year.[290] Camelon assembly was formed when a group of twelve individuals, led by Robert Easson who had been a member of the Brethren in his native Cowdenbeath, left the Miller Hall in Falkirk in 1913.[291]

Most of these transferences were apparently amicable, particularly in places such as Coatdyke where only one member was lost as a result of the mission becoming an assembly. There could be a grey area between Brethren and mission hall identities. On the island of Flotta, Orkney, a meeting was formed in 1910 probably through the evangelist James Stephen, but it failed to be included in any assembly address list and it was not entirely clear whether it was a mission hall or an assembly.[292] But other transfers were more troubled. In Falkirk, for example, the soured relations between the mission and the assembly lasted for a long time. Here the familiar accusation was raised that the Brethren were 'sheep-stealers'.[293]

There were in addition at least a further fifty-three assemblies which probably came into existence between 1892 and 1914 but whose causes

---

285. Writer's collection, I.M.13. (i), 'Assembly of God, Greengairs', anonymous MS [1989]; *ibid.*, I.M.13. (ii). untitled history of Greengairs assembly, anonymous typescript, n.d. It would appear that in 1904 there had been an earlier attempt to form an assembly in Greengairs, *W*, 34 (March 1904), end pp.

286. James McLachlan, *Ebenezer Hall, Coatdyke* (n.p. [1946]), pp.8-9.

287. Oral information, 18 April 1987, from a former assembly member; 'John Smith' *W*, 79 (1949), p.151.

288. Oral information 18 November 1986, from a Motherwell assembly member; 'Malcolm Sinclair', *W*, 91 (1961), p.356.

289. Writer's collection, I.U.3., Russell Turnbull to the writer, 30 October 1988.

290. Oral information 24 December 1988, from a Haggs assembly member; *W*, 32 (March, 1902), end pp.

291. Anon., 'How it began: Camelon', *BM*, 98 (1988), pp.261-2.

292. *W*, 40 (August 1910), end pp.; *BM*, 21 (November 1911), p.i; Stephen was active in holding services for Christians on Flotta in November 1910, see writer's collection, II, Charles Smith's papers, James Stephen to Charles Smith, 30 November 1910.

293. Sally Herring, 'Dissent in Scotland', in Peter L. Sissons, *The Social Significance of Church Membership in the Burgh of Falkirk* (Edinburgh, 1973), p.343.

of founding have not been recorded.[294] Undoubtedly the factors
discussed above would be involved in their formation. But despite the

---

294. These are: Banffshire (see Map 4): <u>Cullen</u> (by 1904): Jordan, *List* (1904), p.142
(however one its members had been converted in 1889, 'George Gardiner', *BM*, 59
(1949), p.72); Aberdeenshire (see Map 5): <u>Cruden Bay</u> (by 1897): Jordan, *List* (1897),
p.120; <u>Fraserburgh</u> (re-founded *c*.1890): James Cordiner, *Fragments from the Past: an
account of people and events in the assemblies of northern Scotland* (London, 1961),
p.78 ([William Noble], 'How it began: Fraserburgh', *BM*, 99 (1989), p.182, places the
founding in the early twentieth century, a dating which is too late as the assembly
appears in Jordan, *List* (1897), p.122; <u>Haugh of Glass</u> (by 1897), Jordan, *List* (1897),
p.124; <u>Logierieve</u> (1901): *BM*, 11 (February 1901) p.i; *ibid* (June), p.i; Kincardineshire
(see Map 5): <u>Auchenblae</u> (*c*.1911): 'William Douglas', *W*, 61 (1931), p.192; <u>Gourdon</u>
(1904): *W*, 34 (May 1904), end pp. (but see *BM*, 16 (August 1906), end pp., which
suggests this might have been a schism); <u>Stonehaven</u> (1914): *W*, 44 (1914), p.29;
Perthshire (see Map 6): <u>Abernethy</u> (1901): writer's collection, I.Q.1., [J. A. Wilkie],
'Abernethy Gospel Hall', typescript, 1990; <u>Crieff</u> (by 1897): Jordan, *List* (1897), p.120;
<u>Pitlochry</u> (1907): *W*, 37 (1907), p.71; <u>Arbroath</u> (1911); [John Beattie], 'How it began:
Arbroath', *BM*, 99 (1990), pp.133-4; Angus (see Map 6): <u>Carnoustie</u> (1910): *W*, 40
(December 1910), end pp.; <u>Forfar</u> (1901): 'Peter Wilkie', *W*, 81 (1951), p.15; Fife (see
Map 7): <u>Oakley</u> (*fl.* 1905): *W*, 35 (November 1905), end pp.; <u>Upper Largo</u> (1909): *BM*,
19 (May 1909), p.i; Lothians (see Maps 8 and 9): <u>Edgehead</u> (1908): *W*, 38 (1908),
p.167; <u>Fauldhouse</u> (1913): *W*, 43 (1913), p.279; <u>Linlithgow</u> (by 1897): Jordan, *List*
(1897), p.130; <u>North Berwick</u> (1907): *W*, 37 (1907), p.71; <u>Uphall</u> (1905): 'Henry
Forsyth', *W*, 62 (1932), p.119; <u>Stoneyburn</u> (*c.* 1905): *BM*, 38 (March 1918), p.i;
<u>Whitburn</u>, (*c*.1901): 'Neil Menzies', *W*, 72 (1942), p.iv; Lanarkshire (see Map 10):
<u>Caldercruix</u> (1893): 'Andrew Wilson', *W*, 58 (1928), p.299; <u>Douglas Water</u> (*c*.1909): *W*,
39 (1909), p.167; <u>Harthill</u> (by 1904): *W*, 35 (1905), p.1; <u>High Blantyre</u> (by 1893): *W*,
65 (1935), p.191; <u>Glengowan</u> (by 1904): Jordan, *List* (1904), p.148; <u>Kirkwood</u> (by
1897): Jordan, *List* (1897), p.128; <u>Morningside</u> (*c*.1893): 'William Brown', *BM*, 45
(1935), p.307; <u>Tarbrax</u> (1908): *W*, 38 (March 1908), end pp.; <u>Uddingston</u> (*c*.1895):
'William Stewart', *W*, 60 (1930), p.168; writer's collection I.M.27., Andrew McNeish to
the writer May 1988; Glasgow (see Map 11): <u>Cumberland Hall, Eglinton</u> (no.41) (disc.
1905): *BM*, 15 (March 1905), end pp.; <u>Tylefield Hall, Gallowgate</u> (no.27) (by 1897):
Jordan, *List* (1897), p.124; ; <u>Gospel Hall, Keppochhill</u> (no.6) (*c*.1908): *BM*, 18 (May
1908), p.i; <u>Wyndford Hall, Maryhill</u> (no.2) (by 1897): Jordan, *List* (1897), p.124;
<u>Mathieson St. Hall, Oatlands</u> (disc. 1907): *W*, 37 (1907), p.87; <u>Gospel Hall, Parkhead</u>
(no. 33) (1896): *BM*, 6 (1896), p.132; Dunbartonshire (see Map 12): <u>Hope Hall,</u>
<u>Clydebank</u> (1900): *BM*, 11 (January 1901), p.i; Renfrewshire (see Map 12): <u>Elderslie</u>
(1908): *BM*, 19 (March 1909), p.ii; <u>Howwood</u> (by 1897): Jordan, *List*, p.126; <u>Johnstone</u>
(by 1892): 'Robert Stewart', *W*, 62 (1932), p.216; <u>Lochwinnoch</u> (*c*.1886): 'William
Brown', *W*, 67 (1937), p.48; <u>Bethany Hall, Paisley</u> (by 1897): Jordan, *List* (1897),
p.132; <u>Moorpark, Renfrew</u> (by 1914): *BM*, 24 (July 1914), p.i; Ayrshire (see Map 13):
<u>Glengarnock</u> (by 1891): *BM*, 1 (1891), p.142; <u>Ochiltree</u> (by 1904): Jordan, *List* (1904),
p.158; <u>Old Cumnock</u> (by 1892): *BM*, 3 (1892), p.11; <u>Trabboch</u> (1900): *BM*, 10
(November 1900), p.i; <u>Waterside</u> (1895): *BM*, 5 (1895), p.24; Wigtownshire (see Map
14): <u>Port William</u> (by 1897): Jordan, *List* (1897), p.132; <u>Stoneykirk</u> (by 1902): *W*, 32

increases of the two decades before World War I, it appears that growth was slowing as the movement entered the twentieth century. There were occasional local outbreaks of revivalism after 1905, such as the one W. J. Gerrie experienced on Westray in 1913 or which Percy Beard witnessed that same year in Galston when about sixty individuals—half of them young female textile workers from the same factory—were converted.[295] But awakenings became a decreasing factor in Brethren growth. Although the data extracted from *The Witness* obituaries suggest that the opening years of the twentieth century had been favourable ones for the movement, since about 1895 the underlying trend had been for the growth rate to decrease (Figure 4.3). If the number of additions and conversions in these data are aggregated, then the percentage increase for the decade 1882-91 is 100 per cent, but the equivalent figure for 1905-14 is 25.9. These data, of course, only register those joining and do not take account of losses which were higher in the later period. But they suggest that net increase had slowed considerably, and probably Brethren growth was behind that of the population in the years before the World War I, something that was certainly the case in other churches.[296] It is likely that it slowed sufficiently for the Brethren to suffer some slight overall decline in the pre-World War I period: this is suggested by the membership of both Lesmahagow and Elim Hall, Glasgow (Figures 4.4 and 4.5).

Assemblies in many rural areas were struggling. While conducting services in St Margaret's Hope, South Ronaldsay, James Stephen lamented that 'the situation in the assemblies in Orkney is not too bright as we contemplate the future. Surely there is room for a nightly revival...'.[297] The assembly address list which was published in 1921

(August, 1902), end pp.; Dumfriesshire: Lockerbie (1897): writer's collection I.F.2. [Alex Traill], 'Lockerbie Assembly' typescript 1987.

There were also apparently abortive attempts to found assemblies in Monifieth, Angus (*W*, 40 (December 1910), end pp.), and Bishopbriggs, Lanarkshire (*W*, 43 (1913), p.139). In addition it is likely that six meetings whose existence was first recorded in the assembly address list published in 1921 were formed before World War I; these were: Portmahomack, Easter Ross (*fl.* 1921-2); Fallin, Stirlingshire (*fl.* 1921-2); California, Stirlingshire (*fl.* 1921-2); Tranent, East Lothian (by 1921-59); Cobbinshaw, Lanarkshire (fl. 1921-2); and Mossend, Lanarkshire (*fl.* 1921-2). Excluding Tranent assembly, the only other reference to them was in the 1922 address list.

295. *W*, 44 (January 1914), p.1.

296. Callum G. Brown, 'Religion, class and church growth', in W. Hamish Fraser and R. J. Morris (eds), *People and Society in Scotland: II 1830-1914* (Edinburgh, 1990), Figure 1, p.314; and *idem*, 'Religion and secularisation', in Tony Dickson and James H. Treble (eds), *People and Society in Scotland: III 1914-1990* (Edinburgh, 1992), pp.48-55.

297. Writer's collection, II, Charles Smith's papers, James Stephen to Charles Smith, 19 December 1910.

revealed that the number of assemblies in Aberdeenshire (excluding Aberdeen city) had been virtually halved since the previous list of 1904, dropping from twenty-three to twelve, and most of these had probably been discontinued before World War I.[298] But even in Glasgow elders met in 1910 to discuss 'The Decline in the Spiritual Birth Rate: Its Cause and Remedy'.[299] Competition was growing from new secular forms of leisure.[300] 'Now-a-days some effort has to be made to get people to hear the Gospel,' John Ritchie noted in 1899.[301] As factors in spiritual decline Henry Pickering, recently appointed as editor of *The Witness*, could point at the war's commencement to 'the enormous increase in football thousands, picture palace queues (even on Lord's days), professional sports, resorts of pleasure and sin, and such-like'.[302] Recruitment was proving more difficult. But probably the biggest single factor in net decline in this period was overseas emigration which reached its Scottish peak in 1911.[303] As will be seen in Chapter 9, Brethren members were more likely to emigrate than the general population,[304] and it would appear that Brethren emigration had peaked the previous year when 'Large Numbers [*sic*] of Christians' had left.[305] Glasgow assemblies were particularly affected during the depression in shipbuilding of 1910:[306] by the spring of 1913 it was being noted that the attendance at the Half-Yearly Conferences was reduced due to emigration.[307] Meetings elsewhere were depleted. When gold mining was being developed in South Africa after the Boer War, many Brethren miners and their families from Auchinleck emigrated to work there, and others in the assembly went to the United States to work in the American coalfield. Altogether some seventy individuals were lost to a meeting of about 100 members,[308] and some eighty to ninety people—just under a third of the

---

298. Jordan, *List* (1904), p.128; *List of Some Assemblies in the British Isles: where believers professedly gather in the name of the Lord Jesus for worship and breaking of bread in remembrance of him upon the first day of the week* (London & Glasgow [1921]), pp.38-49; Dickson, 'Open and closed', p.159, Table 3.

299. *BM*, 21 (January 1911), p.i.

300. Brian Harrison, *Peaceable Kingdom: stablity and change in modern Britain* (Oxford, 1982), pp.123-56; Callum G. Brown, *The Social History of Religion in Scotland Since 1730* (London, 1987), pp.182-3.

301. *BM*, 9 (1899), p.94.

302. HyP[ickering]., 'The world at war', *W*, 44 (1914), p.166.

303. Michael Flinn (ed.), *Scottish Population History from the 17th Century to the 1930s* (Cambridge, 1977), pp.441-55; M. Anderson and D. J. Morse, 'The People', in Fraser and Morris (eds), *People and Society*, p.15.

304. For Brethren emigration, see pp.380-82.

305. *BM*, 20 (October 1910), p.i; cf. below, Fig. 9.1.

306. Writer's collection, II, Malcolm Leslie to George Budge, tape cassette, 1979.

307. *W*, 43 (May 1913), p.139.

308. McCombe, 'Auchinleck Assembly', pp.5-6.

membership—of Roman Road Hall, Motherwell, also left for America.[309]
A number of assemblies never recovered their pre-World War I numbers:
emigration probably explains, for example, why those in the shipbuilding
district of Govan were discontinued before the mid-twentieth century.

Elements in Growth

The apparent downturn before 1914 should not obscure the fact that in
the forty years after 1870 the Brethren movement in Scotland enjoyed its
greatest single expansion. By the late nineteenth century, reckoned Jamie
Clifford, a missionary from Kilbirnie, south-west Scotland had the highest
concentration of Brethren assemblies in the world.[310] The first Ayrshire
conference of 1872 had 200 present at it, but by 1903 there were some
1,000 in attendance, an increase of 400 per cent.[311] Throughout the
period the data in *The Witness* obituaries show the average age of
conversion to be between 20 and 22 and that of reception into fellowship
as being 26 until just before World War I when it rose to 30.8 (Table
3.1).[312] The movement continued to appeal to young adults and not
merely the children of members. A causal nexus is impossible to prove,
but it seems likely that the constant social and demographic change of
the era was a critical element in growth. As was seen above, it not only
affected industrialised communities but rural ones also. Change made
people open to new influences, and both conversion and the stability
assembly membership offered lessened anomie. However, this last point
should not be exaggerated,[313] for too much social unrest hindered
evangelism, as was found during a miners' strike of 1912.[314] Much of
Brethren success rested in their ability, often after a period of persecution,
to penetrate communities.

There were other factors. There was a shared ethos among mission
halls, certain types of Baptist churches, and the Brethren which allowed
individuals to exchange easily from one to the other, such as philosopher

---

309. Beattie, *Brethren*, p.216.

310. A. C. T[homson]., *Un Hombre Bueno: vida de Jaimie Clifford* (n.p., Argentina,
1957), p.24.

311. John Ritchie Jnr, *'Feed My Sheep': memorials of Peter Hynd of Troon*
(Kilmarnock, 1904), p.16.

312. This last figure is for 1910-13, remarkably similar to the 29.3 given in Table
3.1 for 1910-19. However, this figure may reflect the inaccuarcy of the data for later
periods.

313. Mark Smith, *Religion in Industrial Society: Oldham and Saddleworth 1740-1865*
(Oxford, 1994), pp.32-3, found evidence for anomie lacking in his study of religion in
Lancashire industrial communities; cf. below, pp.303-4.

314. 'Notes', *BM*, 22 (April 1912), p.i.

John Macmurray's father, a Glasgow mission hall member who joined a Baptist church on moving to Aberdeen, then switched to the Brethren, and on returning to Glasgow went back to a mission.[315] However, most individuals who transferred remained Brethren. Another reason for the growth of the movement was dissatisfaction with existing churches. The Free Church of Scotland father of Brethren surgeon, William Strain, was influenced by a mid-nineteenth century revival while living in Wales and on returning to Scotland joined an assembly.[316] He was typical of many who found that the Brethren movement was the body which most closely continued aspects of the awakenings. Features of the new industrialised hamlets and villages were also significant. The gospel hall provided a religious alternative to the public house which was often their only recreational facility. Benquhat, a mining hamlet near Dalmellington in Ayrshire where the Brethren gained converts, was described as being without 'kirk, public house or prison'.[317] Traditional ties had also been loosened in the industrial village. *The Believer's Magazine* noted of Glenbuck that 'the Kirk has little hold on the villagers, which is a mercy, and leaves them free to go and hear the Gospel'.[318] The coming of an evangelist—often during a long winter or afterwards in the spring—was a break in an uneventful routine,[319] and crowds gathered at open-air preaching. There was the 'poor mother, with half-a-dozen children around her' whom John Ritchie encountered in an Ayrshire village in the summer of 1880:

> living away near a colliery, far from 'church', 'chapel' or 'meeting house'. She has been 'thinking of these things for a long while now,' and says sometimes she is 'like to lose her reason,' but she has no one to speak the word that will set her troubled soul at peace. Sitting with her babe on her knee she passes from death to life....[320]

The lack of social and religious competition favoured Brethren evangelism.

But it is also apparent from Ritchie's description that the appeal of his message was grounded on the woman's prior assent to the Christian

315. John Macmurray, *Search for Reality in Religion* (London, 1965), pp.7-8; I am indebted to Prof. Sam McKinstry for this reference.

316. Anne Arnott, *Wife to the Archbishop* (London & Oxford, 1976), pp.6-7; W. L. Strain was father of Jean Coggan, wife of Donald Coggan, Archbishop of Canterbury.

317. *BM*, 14 (September 1904), p.i; for the similar example of Drongan, Ayrshire, see below, p.205.

318. *BM*, 5 (1895), p.24; however, it is significant that by 1904 Glenbuck was being described as '"A truly Gospel-hardened place"', *W*, 34 (April 1904), end pp.

319. Cf. the experience of the future Mrs James Scroggie in Newburgh, Aberdeenshire, Scroggie, *Life in the Love of God*, p.11.

320. John Ritchie, 'Evangelistic tour among the villages', *NW*, 20 (1880), p.77.

worldview. The future missionary James Lees was converted in 1895 when someone in Hamilton handed him a tract which merely left the reader to complete the phrase 'If I die to-night, I will be in H—.'[321] Certainly Victorian religious doubt had penetrated working-class culture: in 1900 the evangelist John Ferguson felt it necessary to give one convert in the mining hamlet of Fergushill near Kilwinning, a booklet defending the integrity of the gospels, evidently because the man was troubled by critical theories.[322] Nevertheless the Christian world-picture was still popularly accepted, and possibly this was a decisive factor in explaining the appeal of the evangelist's warnings of future damnation and offer of present salvation. From this perspective it might be argued that all churches profited from religious teaching in elementary schools provided for by the 1872 Education (Scotland) Act and each other's work in disseminating a common Christian message. Religious competition was healthy.

The techniques which were deployed in evangelism were also a powerful factor in Brethren growth. The plentiful use of itinerant evangelists has already been discussed, but there were a number of other methods which the movement took over from popular nineteenth-century Evangelicalism. Sunday schools and children's meetings were almost universally used means in the Brethren. The assembly at Coalburn had grown out of a Sunday school commenced by George and Catherine McGowan, natives of the village, which went from six attenders to 100 in its first year, and by the time of the meeting's founding in 1905 had some 300 children with a further ninety young people attending a Bible class.[323] At Larkhall by the turn of the century five Sunday schools were maintained, and when they were at their peak in 1905 a special train had to be hired to take 1,100 scholars on the annual excursion to Strathaven.[324] Perhaps the numbers involved at Larkhall, doubtless inflated by irregular attenders attracted by the outing, were exceptional, but it was by no means uncommon for substantial proportions of village children to attend such excursions. Brethren Sunday schools offered Bible lessons and appeals to be saved, but their jaunty choruses and Evangelical enthusiasm could make them lively affairs. *The Witness* editor, Henry Pickering, was an advocate of 'eyegate lessons', simple

---

321. Cooper, *James Lees*, p.17; cf. Hy Pickering, *One Thousand Tales Worth Telling: mostly new/strictly true/suitable for you* (London & Glasgow [1918]), p.44.

322. Mrs Elizabeth McKinnon's collection, Crosshouse, John Ferguson, holograph flyleaf inscription to Robert Morrison dated July 1900 on copy of anon., *The Gospels: why are there four, why do they differ and are they fully inspired?* (London, n.d.); cf. *BM*, 10 (July 1900), end pp.

323. 'George McGowan', *BP*, 47 (1926), p.24; 'Mrs Catherine McGowan', *W*, 82 (1953), p.12; the latter source gives four initial attenders.

324. Chapman, *Hebron Hall Assembly*, p.49.

object lessons which usually demanded some ability in handicrafts to construct. In one such lesson, a joiner had to be enlisted to build a model of an asymmetrical, double gateway, with one door painted black and the other red, respectively symbolising the wide and strait gates of Christ's saying.[325] Pickering wrote a book containing examples of his lessons which had a wide influence, and there were many other Brethren publications available for children and workers among them.[326] One of John Ritchie's first publications was a monthly paper for the former begun in 1883, and there were two other such magazines commenced in the 1880s. Nor were the teachers left out, and in the same decade two monthly magazines were initiated which gave lesson plans and other aids for them.[327] Although numbers were to remain high, Brethren Sunday schools appear to have reached their zenith in the Edwardian era, by which period the movement had been accepted as a familiar feature in many communities. Undoubtedly many of the children were multiple attenders of Sunday schools, such as one woman from Stirling who went to those of the Brethren and Church of Scotland.[328] The vast majority of scholars would not go on to join an assembly. But the large numbers which often were found at the work among children gave the movement an important role in the diffusion of Evangelical Christianity in late Victorian and early twentieth-century industrial Scotland.[329]

The locations in which Brethren evangelism took place were also important. The simplicity of the structures which were used brought recruitment near to the people. Kitchen meetings, held in the larger room of a two-roomed house, were widely used. Through using her home in this way Essy Rabey, a single woman from Glengarnock who was converted in 1892, saw ten of her family saved.[330] In 1904 at least forty-six assemblies were meeting in rented accommodation and the address of a further ten was a private house, together comprising 19.6 per cent of all

---

325. Hy Pickering, *How to Make and Show 100 Object Lessons: suitable for Sunday schools, annual treats, seaside services, open-air gatherings, happy evenings, at home, Bible classes and all work among young or old* (Glasgow, 1922), p.11; cf. Matt. 7:13.

326. Cf. John Ritchie, *500 Children's Subjects: with outlines of blackboard and emblematic gospel address for workers amongst the young*, 2nd edn (Kilmarnock, 1911); idem, *How to Teach and Win the Young: a practical handbook for Sunday school teachers and all evangelistic workers amongst young folks* (Kilmarnock [1924]).

327. See below, p.267; Brethren publications for children and Christian workers are surveyed in J. A. H. Dempster, 'Aspects of Brethren publishing enterprise in late nineteenth century Scotland', *Publishing History*, 20 (1986), pp.61-101.

328. Callum G. Brown and Jane D. Stephenson, '"Sprouting Wings?": women and religion in Scotland c.1890-1950', in Esther Breitenbach and Eleanor Gordon (eds), *Out of Bounds: women in Scottish society 1800-1945* (Edinburgh, 1992), p.103.

329. For the latent functions of Brethren Sunday schools, see below, p.301.

330. 'Essy Rabey', *W*, 70 (1940), p.90.

assemblies.[331] These meeting places were a measure of how small many congregations were. But even the halls which were acquired were simple. A few in this period erected larger buildings, such as the new Hebron Hall, Airdrie, which was acclaimed as being 'one of the finest in the country' when it opened in 1905.[332] More typical of Brethren halls, however, was the small, box-like structure of Gospel Hall, Kirkintilloch, with its rooflights over the blind wall and solid-fuel stove standing against it (Figure 4.6). It was squeezed into a site between the River Luggie and a commercial property, and the equally inauspicious location of many others was described in a rhyming couplet:

> Through a close and up a stair
> You're sure to find the Brethren there.[333]

It was in such places that the evangelistic Sunday evening gospel meeting was held, and although Alexander Marshall warned that ill-ventilated buildings in similar locations would discourage the respectable,[334] the features of even the better halls made them less imposing than a church. The preaching in outlying areas was conducted in large marquees. In the firm founded by Thomas Black of Greenock Scottish Brethren possessed their own tent maker,[335] and such marquees were felt to be an advantage because of 'coolness, novelty, and noiselessness...and there are no stairs to ascend'.[336] Glasgow Brethren had one since 1864,[337] and ten years later it had been joined by another two as well as ones in Greenock, mid-Scotland and the Highlands.[338] By the early twentieth century many counties possessed one, assemblies in a shire associating for united missions during the summer. The novelty of tents was especially singled out as an attraction,[339] but it proved to be a short-lived one for by 1894 it was reported they no longer had the drawing power they once had.[340]

---

331. Figure abstracted from Jordan, *List* (1904); there undoubtedly were a number of others in rented accommodation, but only those halls with names which clearly show they were rented have been counted.

332. *W*, 35 (1905), p.1.

333. Quoted in Neil Dickson, 'Brethren and their buildings', *H*, 68, no. 5 (October 1989), p.13.

334. Alexander Marshall, 'Hindrances to progress in the Gospel: paper III', *W*, 35 (1905), p.184.

335. *W*, 38 (February 1908), end pp; the firm still trades at present as Black's of Greenock.

336. *NA*, no. 7 (July 1874), p.28.

337. *W*, 57 (1927), p.116.

338. *NA*, no. 18 (May 1874), p.24; *NW*, 5 (1875), p.95.

339. Samuel Blow, *Reminiscences of Thirty Years' Gospel Work and Revival Times* [*c*.1890] rpt (Glasgow, 1988), p.89; *NA*, 7 (July 1873), p.28; *NA*, 57 (1875), p.127.

340. *BM*, 4 (1894), p.95.

Bible carriages were another innovation which the Brethren used. The earliest one, the Caledonian Gospel Carriage, a gift in 1886 of Colonel Molesworth, was horse drawn, heavily decorated with Bible texts and with sleeping quarters for the evangelists who staffed it.[341] It was originally manned by John Ritchie, and at the end of its first season of operation 100,000 tracts had been distributed and 10,000 scriptures had been sold.[342]

This profligacy with which tracts—short leaflets containing a summary of the gospel—had been distributed was typical. The Glasgow Postal Workers' tract band, founded in 1897, specialised in sending them through the mail, and in 1911 alone they distributed 14,664 tracts through this means.[343] In the space of thirty minutes 16,000 leaflets were distributed by eighty Brethren members in a Glasgow street in 1913. The publishers supplied a steady flow. In 1878 the Glasgow Publishing Office began publishing a monthly magazine for gratuitous circulation, *The Herald of Salvation*, imitated by John Ritchie's *The Gospel Messenger*, commenced about 1887. These magazines were little more than a series of tracts, but the rubric enabled them to be given to the same people and households repeatedly.[344] Evangelistic tracts were also designed for special interest groups—such as seamen, emigrants or Gaelic speakers—and evangelism was also targeted at these groups, or places where it was felt people might be receptive—such as esplanades, fairs, racecourses, hospitals and prisons.[345] J. A. H. Dempster is critical of the indiscriminate nature of tract distribution, but the occasional conversion achieved through its profligacy probably justified it in Brethren eyes.[346]

One ethnic minority which received some attention from the Brethren was the Jewish community. Dispensationalism, the prophetic scheme espoused by the Brethren, is markedly philo-semitic.[347] The postal workers mailed tracts to Jews, and in 1905 Dr J. Muir Kelly founded the Glasgow Jewish Medical Mission in Cumberland Hall, Eglinton (see Map

341. *NW*, 16 (April 1886), end pp.; *NW*, 16 (July 1886), end pp.; T. Baird, 'Duncan M'Nab, Caledonian Bible Carriage', *BP*, 48 (1927), pp.114-17.

342. *NW*, 16 (November 1886), end pp.

343. *W*, 41 (May 1911), end pp.; *W* 45 (April 1915), p.52, end pp.

344. Patrick Scott, 'The business of belief: the emergence of 'Religious' publishing', in Derek Baker (ed.) *SCH*, 10 (Oxford, 1973), p.218 n.23; for a full discussion of the series of tracts offered by these two publishers, see Dempster, 'Brethren publishing', *passim*.

345. For evangelism at fairs see: *NEI*, 2 (1872), pp.11-12; at racecourses: *BM*, 3 (1893), p.120; and in hospitals: *W*, 39 (March 1909), end pp.

346. Dempster, 'Brethren publishing', pp.85-6; for an example of a conversion through a tract, see above, p.135.

347. David S. Katz, 'The phenomenon of philo-semitism', in Diana Wood (ed.), *SCH*, 29 (Oxford, 1992), pp.353-9; for dispensationalism, see below, pp.260-6.

11 no.41).[348] He offered medical treatment and held evangelistic services among the impoverished East-European immigrant community.[349] However, it is doubtful how successful the latter were. Despite the opening in 1910 of another hall in Clyde Terrace for outreach and open-air services among Jews, until the Mission ceased its operation in 1916 due to the war, it did not report any converts.[350] The other major immigrant group, the Catholic Irish, were largely ignored by the movement, and possibly anti-Catholicism was a factor here.[351] The four Roman Catholics baptised after David Rea's Glasgow mission of 1895 were rare recruits.[352] The lack of success in dealing with ethnic minorities, where Brethren were outsiders, contrasts with the conspicuous achievement of the movement among the population at large. The face-to-face nature of the industrial village or the communities of work and neighbourhood favoured personal testimony to the efficacy of salvation and was a potent cause of evangelistic effectiveness.

It was a commercial age and the Brethren had to persuade. Undoubtedly the means used could be tasteless.[353] But readiness to embrace novel means raised the problem for the Brethren themselves of how far an evangelistic method was permissible. Sandwich boards were employed, and in Glasgow a Text-carrier Band was formed.[354] To facilitate village visitation Ritchie offered a discount from a Christian bicycle manufacturer, a bicycle combining 'needed exercise with real service in the Gospel',[355] and his eldest son, also John Ritchie, sold acetylene lamps for open-air services in ill-lit streets. 'No danger, no dirt, no difficulty, no darkness', he promised.[356] The techniques of the Victorian entrepreneur were not very far away here. Other approaches could appear eccentric. Donald Ross forced a fellow evangelist to witness by shouting across a crowded Union Street, Aberdeen, 'Well Masson, how's your soul?'[357] An additional pressure to use any method which

---

348. *BM*, 15 (March 1905), end pp.; *W*, 35 (February 1905), end pp.; it later transferred to Eglinton Hall, Eglinton Street (see Map 11 no.40).

349. *BM*, 15 (September 1905), end pp; *BM*, 16 (February 1906), end pp.; *BM*, 16 (January 1906), end pp.

350. *BM*, 25 (August 1910), p.i; *BM*, 26 (August 1916), p.i: the argument from silence is, of course, perilous, but given the strong philo-semitism of the movement it seems likely that if there had been converts then their existence would have been trumpeted.

351. See below, p.312.

352. Rea (compiler), *David Rea*, p.139.

353. Dempster, 'Brethren publishing', pp.85-6.

354. 'James Imrie', *W*, 64 (1934), p.264.

355. *BM*, 1 (1891), p.94.

356. Ritchie Jnr, *'Feed my Sheep'*, end pp.

357. F. F. Bruce, 'The origins of "The Witness"', *W*, 100 (1970), p.7.

presented itself was the zeal with which Brethren pursued evangelism. Witnessing was the duty of every Christian,[358] and the need to warn individuals of hell was widely used as an incentive.[359] It could justify preaching which roused emotion or breaking the rules of etiquette,[360] and the innovation of after meetings was accepted by many.[361] But generally methods which were felt to be too much like entertainment or were too emotional were avoided. Bible women who did house-to-house visitation were used in some assemblies, especially in Glasgow, but increasingly, as will be seen in the next chapter, women preachers were condemned.[362] In 1905 John Ritchie felt he had to warn against ephemeral revivals which were 'got up'.[363] The evangelistic styles which had gained popularity through Moody and his associate Ira D. Sankey were also viewed with suspicion by some. Excessive use of 'anecdotes, pathetic and sentimental, which work on the natural emotions' and the use of solo singing and 'an American organ' were criticised.[364] However, some Brethren adopted solo singing, most notably Robert F. Beveridge who was known as 'Scotland's Sankey'. He received the urge to use his singing voice after hearing the American singer in Glasgow, and he also wrote his own evangelistic hymns.[365] But most Brethren felt that the unadulterated use of the word of God was the principal, if not the sole, means of evangelism.[366]

By 1914 the Brethren were widely dispersed throughout the Lowlands, especially in industrial central and south-west Scotland. Not all the assemblies formed in this period managed to establish themselves for more than a short time and others remained small, but the demographic and social changes of the late Victorian and Edwardian eras had proved favourable for the new religious movement to grow. Although there were limits to what proved acceptable, innovative evangelistic techniques were embraced. Its lay ethos, furtherance of aggressive evangelism, and appeal

---

358. Anon., 'What is to be done?', *NW*, (1875), p.100; A. M[arshall]., 'Full Gospel', *W*, 41 (1911), pp.127-8.

359. A Lover of Souls, 'Letter to a young preacher on closet prayer', *NEI*, 2 (1872), pp.2-3; anon., 'Christian consistency', *NEI* , 3 (1873), pp.135-7; Alexander Marshall, 'Hindrances to progress', p.149.

360. Anon., 'Sensational preaching the only effectual sort', *NEI*, (1872), p.18; Ritchie, 'Evangelistic tour', pp.77-8

361. *NA*, no. 21 (September 1874), p.34; A. J. H[oliday]., 'After meetings', *BP*, 7 (1886), pp.102-4.

362. See below, pp.151-2.

363. *BM*, (May 1905), end pp.

364. R[?ice]. H[?opkins]., 'Instrumental music', *NW*, 6 (1876), p.185.

365. 'Robert F. Beveridge', *W*, 82 (1952), p.91; R. F. Beveridge (compiler), *Celestial Songs: a collection of 900 choice hymns and choruses* (London [1921]); for discussion of one of Beveridge's hymns, see below, pp.279-80.

366. For views of the Bible, see below, pp.176-80.

to the primitivism of the early Church made it well-placed to attract from existing Christian bodies those who had been influenced by contemporary revivalism. As one critic caustically noted in 1875, 'the Brethren live upon revivals.'[367] Not that the movement was dependent on the activities of other denominations, as it had often been in the 1860s. During this period it became self-sufficient in its ability to propagate itself through its capacity to sustain its own revivals, its increasing number of itinerant evangelists, the migration of members, and the outreach of assemblies. Recruitment techniques were populist and suited to an age of mass democracy.[368] Both external and internal factors were responsible for Brethren growth.[369] The advance eventually slowed as the movement found itself in competition with new leisure pursuits and as religious concerns began retreating to the periphery of society. Emigration may have caused a drop in the gross membership, but secularisation slowed Brethren growth. In addition the increase of the movement was self-limiting. To join an assembly was to retreat in some degree from the norms of society. The high level of zeal for evangelism and the behaviour expected during it—such as standing in open-air services, distributing tracts or witnessing to neighbours and workmates—would frighten off all but the most committed of Evangelicals. The movement was also becoming more institutionalised as awakenings became a less significant element in growth and as the routine work of assemblies and evangelists became more so. Even acquiring its own building tied an assembly more firmly to a structure—John Ritchie advised shutting them up for several months to force the members to go to the people, and Alexander Marshall recommended renting secular buildings for evangelistic purposes.[370] But less formal revivalist procedures were being eclipsed. In the history of the movement during this period there is a parallel process to its growth. It concerns how the Brethren developed into an established sect, and it is the subject of the next chapter.

---

367. Reid, *Plymouth Brethrenism*, p.25; cf. anon., 'The Lord's work', *NEI*, 2 (1872), p.57.

368. Cf. John Coffey, 'Democracy and popular religion: Moody and Sankey's mission to Britain, 1873-1875', in Eugenio F. Biagini (ed.), *Citizenship and Democracy: Liberals, radicals and collective identities in the British Isles, 1865-1931* (Cambridge, 1996), pp.93-119.

369. Cf. David Luker, 'Revivalism in theory and practice: the case of Cornish Methodism', *JEH*, 37 (1986), pp.603-19.

370. *BM*, 9 (1899), p.94; Marshall 'Hindrances to progress', pp.184-5.

CHAPTER FIVE

A Steady Tightening Process: Development 1870-1916

'While professing to be as "open" as ever, we cannot disguise the fact that in the course of the last twenty years a steady *tightening* process has been at work.'
William Shaw, 'Fellowship among saints', *The Believer's Treasury*, 10 (February 1895), p.19.

William Shaw, a banker and committed church member, experienced an Evangelical conversion through a series of meetings held in Maybole, south Ayrshire, by two itinerant preachers.[1] Shaw became a central figure in the Maybole Revival of the 1870s, founding the *Maybole Evangelist* in 1874, a periodical tract which was issued round the houses of the town,[2] and three years later, when he was 27/8, he and some others commenced an assembly.[3] He went on to become a prominent Brethren member, founding and editing a further two magazines. In 1895 Shaw described the thinking of many like himself when they had formed an assembly:

We had no call to 'found a church'. We were in the Church—we realised that we were bound up, with every believer, in the bundle of life with the Lord our God; and we found it blessed to be in the bundle. Neither had we any call to invent a form of Church-government. The Lord Himself, who has given us all things pertaining to life and godliness, has already furnished us with the New Testament pattern. All, therefore, that we had to do was to sit down with the open Bible before us, and seek to carry out, in the fear of God, what we found written there.[4]

But as Shaw fondly recalled the nondenominational *mentalité* of the mid-Victorian revivals, he was doing so in the shadow of events which

---

1. A. M[arshall]., 'William Shaw's conversion', *HS*, No.599 (January 1928), [pp.9-12].

2. 'William Shaw', *W*, 57 (1927), p.238; cf. Hugh Douglas, 'Roderick Lawson of Maybole', *Ayrshire Collections*, 12 (1978), p.80.

3. 'Alex. Brackenridge' *CW*, 35 (1920), pp.1-2.

4. William Shaw, 'Fellowship among saints', *The Believer's Treasury*, 10 (1895), pp.17-18; this article was later widely circulated as a tract of the same title.

demonstrated that the presectarian phase of the Brethren in Scotland was irrevocably over.

He dated the period during which a sharper ecclesiastical definition emerged to the twenty years after the mid-1870s, almost exactly the time of his association with the Brethren.[5] As the excitements of the revivals died down, there was a move towards greater uniformity and regulation of church order within Scottish assemblies. It was, Shaw stated in the colloquial jargon of the time, a process of 'tightening'. Those who effected it were concerned with its opposite, 'looseness', a range of practices that they maintained fell short of biblical standards and whch they wished to eliminate. In the typology of a church life cycle developed by David Moberg the movement was moving from the phase in the 1860s of incipient organisation, characterised by unrest and dissatisfaction with existing churches, to that of formal organisation when cohesion is achieved and orthodoxy is established.[6] For Moberg this is a process of institutionalisation, characterised by Peter Berger and Thomas Luckmann as one in which a social order emerges through a shared history, is transmitted through the construction of roles, and community control is established.[7] The development of the Brethren movement in the period discussed in the present chapter demonstrates an interesting series of choices about how far standardisation should extend in the definition of the sect. Some of these choices will be examined first before turning to study the Churches of God secession. Those involved in it proposed the establishment of controlling institutions as part of a programme of sectarian intensification. Scottish Brethren were ineradicably altered by the schism, and the chapter will also examine its aftermath and causes.

The Due Order

Given the unorchestrated emergence of the movement in the previous decades out of nondenominational revivalism, a certain amount of regulation was inevitable, but it was never absolute. There was a simultaneous move towards more settled patterns of church life. One sign of this emerging order was the disappearance of the 'open platform', preaching meetings open to any participant. These charismatic occasions,

---

5. *Ibid.*, p.19.

6. David O. Moberg, *The Church as a Social Institution: the sociology of American religion* (1962) 2nd edn (Grand Rapids, MI, 1984), pp.118-124.

7. Peter L. Berger and Thomas Luckmann, *The Social Construction of Reality: a treatise in the sociology of knowledge* (1966), Penguin edn (Harmondsworth, 1967), pp.65-109.

it would appear, had initially been the norm in many places.[8] At Larkhall the practice was discontinued in the 1870s because of ungifted preachers, some individuals preaching too often, or long pauses. Speakers were thereafter booked, although the opening of a new factory in 1879 which brought Brethren members from Glasgow reopened the debate for a while. But, noted Robert Chapman, the historian of the assembly, the prearrangement of speakers allowed 'all things be done decently and in order'.[9] Because of the need for having someone gifted addressing the unconverted, appointed speakers were accepted at gospel meetings even by many supporters of open meetings for Christians.[10] However, the open platform at the former was still being criticised in 1905, evidence of its continued use,[11] and it never entirely disappeared at the latter, the system lingering longest at conferences.[12] But although the morning meeting would remain open for participation from among the men in fellowship,[13] by 1904 it was noted that the booking of preachers at conferences had been 'generally adopted'.[14]

A number of institutions which evolved at regional and national levels standardised practices and reinforced group identity. When meetings in a county or district procured a tent for evangelistic purposes (discussed in the previous chapter)[15] a committee was formed to discuss its use and assemblies would send delegates to such bodies. They could often establish what was considered acceptable within a region.[16] The one formal national institution which evolved was concerned with missionaries. The Home and Foreign Mission Funds (HFMF) was established soon after the first Scottish missionaries were commissioned in 1876. Based in Glasgow, it was administered by Thomas McLaren, a city assembly member, until his death in 1908.[17] By then the number of

---

8. Robert Kerr in 'Friday's conference', *NEI*, 2 (1872), pp.74-5; [?J. A.] B[?oswell]., undated letter, *NA*, No. 13 (January 1874), pp.2-4 ; HyP[ickering]., 'WW', *W*, 65 (1935), p.66.

9. Robert Chapman, *The Story of Hebron Hall Assembly, Larkhall, 1866-1928: a short history of the inception, progress and personalities of the assembly* (Kilmarnock, 1929), pp.24, 30; this is a quotation of 1 Cor. 14:40.

10. [John Ritchie], 'Answers to correspondents', *BM*, 10 (1900), pp.59-60; 'Answer to special questions', *BM*, 15 (1905), pp.59-60, 75.

11. Alexander Marshall, 'Hindrances to progress in the Gospel', *W*, 35 (1905), p.183.

12. 'Answers to special questions', *BM*, 12 (1902), pp.107-8.

13. For open participation at the morning meeting, see below, p.256.

14. Editor's note [i.e. John Ritchie], 'Answers to special questions', *BM*, 14 (1904), p.84.

15. See above, p.137.

16. For an example, see below, p.240.

17. M., 'Thomas McLaren', Henry Pickering (ed.), *Chief Men Among the Brethren*, 1st edn (London, 1918), pp.156-9.

Scottish missionaries had increased considerably and in that year a Missionary Council was formed consisting of various leading Brethren individuals.[18] This committee interviewed prospective missionaries, and while it claimed not to be a selection board—the sending bodies remaining individual assemblies—most considered its approval vital. Also in 1908 a meeting of 'elder brethren' appointed treasurers to administer the HFMF.[19] The money handled by them rose from £2,106 annually at the death of McLaren to £6,515 in 1917.[20]

The other institutions which ensured cohesion were informal ones. Large conferences were held in central locations on the Scottish holidays during Fast Days and on New Year's Day, the pioneer from 1865 having been the Glasgow Half-Yearly Meetings, but joined throughout the 1870s by several others.[21] These regional conferences aided the cohesion of the movement: at the first Aberdeen one in 1873 there were people present from Orkney, Nairn, Moray, Banffshire, Kincardineshire, Angus, and Lanarkshire; Dundee, Glasgow, and Dumbarton; Ireland and England; and 'almost all the towns and parishes of Aberdeenshire'.[22] Over the first three days of 1910 Brethren conferences drew audiences of 500 in Glasgow, 700 to 1,000 in Ayr, 400 in Dundee, 150 in Bathgate, and 800 in Larkhall, some 2,550 to 2,850 individuals.[23] By the 1890s many smaller local conferences had been commenced, with September particularly favoured.[24] 'In districts where the working classes have the half-holiday on Saturday,' it was noted, 'these gatherings afford opportunities for many of the Lord's people coming together.'[25] Conferences, it was stated in 1908, 'are becoming quite an institution in Scotch assemblies. As a rule they are homely and helpful, affording meditation to believers who are unable to reach the larger centres.'[26] The social function of these occasions was so evident that it was feared that

18. W. T. Stunt *et al.*, *Turning the World Upside down: a century of missionary endeavour*, 2nd edn (Bath, 1973), pp.562-3; for further discussion of the Council see below, p.300.

19. 'John M. Scott', *W*, 90 (1960), p.157.

20. HyP[ickering]., 'Home-call of Mr C. P. Watson', *W*, 48 (1918), p.46; cf. Stunt *et al.*, *Turning the World*, p.564.

21. For Glasgow see above, p.86; other important regional conferences were established in: Ayrshire in 1872 (John Ritchie Jnr, *'Feed My Sheep': memorials of Peter Hynd of Troon* (Kilmarnock, 1904), p.16); Hamilton in *c*.1875 (transferred to Motherwell in 1901: *BM*, 10 (January 1900), end pp.); Aberdeen in 1873 (see below, n.22); and Shetland in 1878 (Alex S. Rigg to the editor, *NW* 8 (1878), p.127).

22. *NEI*, 3 (1873), p.20; cf. [Matthew S. R. Brown], *Aberdeen Christian Conference Centenary 1874-1973* (Aberdeen, 1972), p.16.

23. *W*, 40 (February 1910), end pp.

24. *BM*, 20 (September 1910), p.i.

25. *BM*, 3 (1893), p.47.

26. *W*, 35 (November 1908), end pp.

many in the audience were there only 'for a day's outing and pleasure, to meet with friends, &c.'.[27] But despite these apprehensions, the manifest function of conferences to inculcate doctrine remained prominent and this helped establish sufficient uniformity of teaching which, as well as the social aspects of the gatherings, aided Brethren cohesion.[28]

The two unofficial institutions which probably had most influence were the publishers Pickering & Inglis of Glasgow and John Ritchie of Kilmarnock.[29] In 1876 Donald Ross opened the Publishing Office in Sauchiehall Street, Glasgow,[30] and when Henry Pickering (its manager from 1886) formed a partnership in 1893 with printer William Inglis, it combined both men's names in its title.[31] The other leading Scottish Brethren publisher John Ritchie began his business in Kilmarnock in 1880, commencing his first magazine, *The Young Watchman*, in 1883.[32] Through their bookshops and their printing both these publishers made available the work of Brethren authors and were therefore a principal means of disseminating the teaching of the movement and in ensuring uniform doctrine. Particularly important were two magazines, *The Witness* (founded in 1870 by Donald Ross)[33] and *The Believer's Magazine*

---

27. *BM*, 7 (1897), p.60.

28. For a fuller discussion of the function of conferences see below, pp.209-13.

29. For a discussion of the output of these publishers see below, pp.275-8; and J. A. H. Dempster, 'Aspects of Brethren publishing enterprise in late nineteenth century Scotland', *Publishing History*, 20 (1986), pp.61-101.

30. *NW*, 6 (1876), p.64; earlier Ross had bookshops in Aberdeen (opened 1872, *NEI*, 6 (1872), p.48) and Edinburgh (opened 1875, *NW*, 5 (1875), p.80), each of which closed on the later shop opening.

31. HyP[ickering]., 'William Inglis', *BP*, 29 (1908), pp.22-5; In 1919 Pickering & Inglis absorbed Brethren publishers R. L. Allan of Glasgow, Alfred Holness of London, and Yapp and Hawkins of London: 'James Hawkins', *W*, 49 (1919), p.35; HyP[ickering]., 'Home-call of a colleague', *W*, 56 (1926), p.453. It became a limited company in 1937: 'John Hawthorn', *W*, 67 (1937), p.47.

32. J. R[itchie]. Jnr, 'The Editor goes "Home"', *BM*, 40 (1930), p.74 ; D. R[itchie]., 'John Ritchie of Kilmarnock', *CW*, 45, No.532, (April 1930), [pp.50-2] (reprinted in *KS*, 22 March 1930, p.5); *BM*, 90 (1980), p.1.

33. C. J. Pickering, 'The history of The Witness', *W*, 90 (1960), pp.106-8; and F. F. Bruce, 'The origins of "The Witness"', *W*, 100 (190), pp.7-9, state that the magazine was founded in 1871, and certainly volume numbers were calculated from that year; but a note from the publishers entitled '"These forty years"', *W*, 39, (December 1909), end pp., states it was founded in January 1870; The Publishers, 'Concerning "The Witness"', *W*, 34 (1914), p.109, also states that it was founded in that year. However, the former article wrongly gives the year of Caldwell's appointment as editor as 1874 (it was 1876). Dempster, 'Brethren publishing', p.64, basing his claim on the publication of 18 issues before December 1871 (for which he gives no source), states that the magazine was founded in mid-1870. It began as *The Northern Evangelistic Intelligencer*, became *The Northern Intelligencer* in 1873, *The Northern Witness* in 1875, and *The Witness* in 1887.

(commenced in 1891), issued respectively by Pickering & Inglis and John Ritchie. The former of these journals became the principal Brethren review worldwide, having an initial monthly circulation of 1,500 to 2,000, rising to 12,000 in 1886 and to 16,000 by 1914.[34] Its editor from 1876 until 1914 (appointed by Donald Ross when he left for America) was Glasgow businessman John R. Caldwell.[35] Caldwell was also responsible for the production by the Publishing Office of *The Believers Hymn Book* in 1885, the collection which came to be most widely used in meetings for Christians among Scottish Brethren.[36] A somewhat stolid individual, well suited to the phase of consolidation, he had a strategic role in the formation of the movement. Circulation figures were not released by *The Believer's Magazine* but it too had considerable popularity in Scotland,[37] helped by the pungent prose of the dogmatic John Ritchie who edited it until 1930.

In his study of the Scottish publishing enterprises J. A. H. Dempster has argued that both journals aided the cohesion of the Brethren through publishing news of evangelists and assemblies, and that the editors found that their writings allowed them authoritatively to formulate and spread its doctrines.[38] This last feature was reinforced by the suppression of debate except within narrowly defined limits by the editors. From the beginning Ritchie did not carry dissenting viewpoints,[39] and even before 1876 Ross had begun to move away from a degree of diversity of opinion initially allowed in the magazine to a much more uniform body of teaching, a process furthered by Caldwell.[40] Both journals also had question-and-answer features which established acceptable beliefs and practices, and in addition the editors were consulted privately by individuals on difficult

---

34. HyP[ickering]., 'About "The Witness"', *W*, 57 (1927), p.213; the figure for 1886 is based on Pickering's statement that the magazine sold 6,000 per week that year.

35. In addition Caldwell may have had a crucial role in the development of Pickering & Inglis for in 1886 The Publishing Office shared premises with Caldwell's firm (Dempster, 'Brethren publishing', p.70) and J. B. Watson stated that it was Caldwell who invited Pickering to take up the appointment of bookshop manager (Watson, 'Pickering'; however, see below p.203). These evidences of control suggest that Caldwell may have also supported the publishers financially during this period.

36. J. R. C[aldwell]., 'Praise', *NW*, 15 (1885), p.48; the title of the hymnbook had no apostrophe 's'.

37. A partial exception is *BM*, 19 (January 1909), ii, where it was noted that 600 new subscribers were taking the magazine in 1909; however, this exception is understandable in the light of Marshall's attack on Ritchie during the previous year (see below, pp.173-4).

38. Dempster, 'Brethren publishing', pp.80-1, 83.

39. *BM*, 1 (1891), p.1, cited in Dempster, 'Brethren publishing', p.83.

40. 'To our contributors', *NW*, 6 (1876), p.191; cf. Caldwell's successors: HyP[ickering]., 'Policy of "The Witness"', *W*, 66 (1936), p.206; and J. B. Watson quoted in F. F. Bruce, 'His writings', *W*, 85 (1955), p.199.

points.[41] Their pronouncements were widely accepted as authoritative and aided the establishment of normative thinking. As shall emerge, the editors' powers led to accusations that they were abusing their position.[42]

Other roles were defined more formally. The office of evangelist was one which had been inherited from revivalism. Within a locality the movement possessed influential individuals—such as Peter Hynd in Ayrshire[43]—who were consulted on troubling issues, and others—such as James Wilson 'the Bishop of Garngad'[44]—were dominant in particular assemblies. Organisational demands made some allocation of roles necessary. At Kilwinning, Ayrshire, soon after the assembly was founded in 1874, for example, a simple division of duties was made.[45] But more formal recognition of local leadership was established and most assemblies began to adopt elders. As the Scottish movement emerged out of revivalism, Rice Hopkins claimed, 'there seemed little need for rule', and many assemblies had a 'church meeting' at which all the brethren in fellowship would discuss matters of consequence.[46] One potential check on the appointment of elders was Exclusive Brethren writings. J. N. Darby had rejected the use of elders because their adoption would have been restoring the apostolic church and displacing the rule of the Holy Spirit.[47] Alexander Stewart, who had joined the Open Brethren in

---

41. HyP[ickering]., 'Brief life of the author', in John R. Caldwell, *Epitome of Christian Experience in Psalm XXXII with the development of the Christian life* (Glasgow [1917]), p.xvii. Examples of such correspondence to W. H. Bennet and W. E. Vine, editors of journals in England, exist in writer's collection II, Charles Smith, Kirkwall, papers; and in addition two examples to J. R. Caldwell are extant: Newmilns, Ayrshire, Gospel Hall: J. R. Caldwell to a 'Brother', 14 September 1892; and Charles Smith papers: J. R. Caldwell to Charles Smith, 18 March 1909. It is probably not a coincidence that Caldwell, who was in poor health from 1905, is terse in both and irascible in the former (it was written as the Churches of God division was beginning when according to Pickering, 'Brief life', pp.xx-xxi, he was under 'great stress'); such demands upon his time were considerable.
42. See below, pp.173, 174.
43. Ritchie Jnr., *Peter Hynd*, p.16.
44. Writer's collection, II, Malcolm Leslie to George Budge, tape cassette, 1979; cf. David J. Beattie, *Brethren: the story of a great recovery* (Kilmarnock [1939]), pp.246-7.
45. Anon., 'How it began: Kilwinning, Ayrshire', *BM*, 98 (1988), p.307.
46. R. T. H[opkins]., 'Suggestions as to rule', *NW*, 10 (1880), pp.57-60.
47. J. N. Darby, 'Scriptural views upon the subject of elders in answer to a tract entitled, 'Are Elders to be Established?', in [*idem*], *Collected Writings of J. N. Darby*, 4, (ed.) William Kelly (Kingston-on-Thames, n.d.), pp.280-348; cf. three Exclusive writers popular among Scottish Open Brethren: C. J. Davis, 'Christian ministry; its source, object, relationship &c.', in [*idem*] *Aids to Believers: being all the writings for the Lord's people of the late Dr. C. J. Davis* (Glasgow [1912]), pp.120-4; W. Kelly, *Lectures on the Church of God* (London, n.d.), pp.190-217; C. H. Mackintosh, 'The discipline of the assembly; its ground nature and object', in [*idem*], *Miscellaneous Writings of C. H.*

Glasgow from an Exclusive assembly, appears to have come nearest to this position, although he did not condemn their use.[48] But increasing size, a growing need for congregational discipline and the unmanageable nature of church meetings meant most assemblies began to appoint them.[49] In Glasgow there had been some agitation over the use of elders, and in 1867 a conversational conference on the issue had been held at which it would appear widely varying views were expressed.[50] Larkhall assembly, where elders became more prominent in the 1870s, was probably typical of many existing meetings,[51] but as late as 1882 it was noted that the question was 'exercising many'.[52]

Initially there were some differences in opinion about how elders might be appointed. At the Glasgow conference of 1867 one individual had suggested a form of Presbyterianism, with someone being elected and appointed as a teacher. John Bowes, however, felt that the 'church might be governed too much' and love was more important, but he was not averse to the appointment of a plurality of elders which he felt should be done by evangelists.[53] This was also the opinion of at least one other individual (possibly Bowes's friend, William Scott of Dundee) who argued that evangelists were the equivalent of scriptural apostles,[54] a view which probably indicates the status itinerant revivalists had. At the first conference in the north east, held at Inverurie in 1872, Rice Hopkins, who had possibly been influenced by the Exclusive writers, maintained that the New Testament distinguished between 'elders' and 'them that have the rule over'. In the contemporary Church, he argued, there were 'no officially appointed elders' but there were those to whom the Holy Spirit had given 'the gift of rule'.[55] This was an attempt to balance his desire for strong congregational government and the need to avoid reconstructing an apostolic succession. But the doctrine which eventually won acceptance was a development of the system formulated at Plymouth

M. (London, n.d.), pp.26-33: C. J. Davis's writings were published by Pickering & Inglis.

48. 'Alexander Stewart', *CW*, 38 (1923), pp.82-3; A. S[tewart]., [title page missing], *NI*, 3 (1873), p.4 .

49. H[opkins]., 'Suggestions as to rule', pp.57-60.

50. 'Alexander Stewart', pp.82-3; 'Glasgow conference on church government', *TP*, 10 (1866-9), pp.97-8; only the views of those who approved of elders is given, but see the comment by James Stone which suggests considerable disunity. The subject of elders had also been debated earlier in 1864, 'The Glasgow conference', *TP*, 9 (1863-6), p.119.

51. Robert Chapman, *Hebron Hall Assembly*, p.25.

52. R. S., 'Weakness and encouragement. A letter', *NW*, 12 (1882), pp.93-4.

53. John Bowes quoted in 'Glasgow conference on church government', pp.97-8; this also seemed to be the majority consensus at the earlier conference of 1864, 'The Glasgow conference', p.119.

54. W. S[?cott]., 'III.—For the consideration of believers', *NI*, 3 (1873), pp.36-9.

55. R. T. Hopkins, quoted in ' Friday's conference', *NEI*, 2 (1872), p.74.

under B. W. Newton and adopted in 1839 by Henry Craik and George Müller: in post-apostolic times it was the Holy Spirit who appointed elders and it was the place of the assembly to 'receive' them by acknowledging those who clearly had the gift of eldership.[56] This theory combined a charismatic ministry with church government, and it was championed in Scotland by a number of influential individuals, most notably J. R. Caldwell.[57] By 1880 Hopkins, who had evidently been won over to this last view, was suggesting how elders might act as a corporate oversight.[58] However, many assemblies, especially smaller ones, did not need such arrangements as formally recognising elders or organising regular oversight meetings, and the important decisions tended to be taken by the older members or jointly by all the brethren in fellowship.[59] Nevertheless the role of elder had been established and by the later 1880s it would appear that elders from the assemblies in a district were occasionally gathering to discuss matters of mutual interest,[60] continuing to do so in places such as Glasgow and Ayrshire into the early twentieth century.[61]

---

56. [B. W. Newton], '"Letter by John William Peter, late incumbent of Langford, Berks, on his resignation from his living and secession from the Established Church"', *The Christian Witness*, 1 (July 1834), rpt as *Scripture Subjects: Truths for the Church of God* (London & Glasgow, 1882), p.333; [George Müller], *A Narrative of Some of the Lord's Dealings with George Müller: written by himself*, 1, 9th edn (London, 1895), pp.276-80; Jonathan David Burnham, 'The Controversial Relationship between Benjamin Wills Newton and John Nelson Darby (University of Oxford D.Phil. thesis, 1999), pp.168-9.

57. Mr [J. R.] Caldwell quoted in 'conference on church government', pp.97-8; J. R. C[aldwell]., 'To the editor of the "Northern Intelligencer"', *NI*, 3 (1873), pp.58-9; *idem*, 'On ordination and acknowledgement of overseers', *W*, 26 (1896), pp.136-8; for similar views cf. John Wardrop of Wishaw (the minority voice at the 1864 Glasgow conference), quoted in 'The Glasgow conference', p.119; and John C. Ritchie of Aberdeen and Inverurie in J. C. R[itchie]., 'Gifts, and our recognition of them', *NA*, No.13 (1874), pp.1-2.

58. H[opkins]., 'Suggestions as to rule', pp.57-60.

59. C. M. L[uxmoore]., 'The fellowship of assemblies', *NT*, 2 (1889-90), pp.71-2. It is impossible to determine how widespread this practice was. Several assemblies in the north east never formally recognised elders, something which Norman S. Macdonald, 'One Hundred Years of Needed Truth Brethren 1892 to 1992: a historical analysis', typescript [1992], p.6, thinks was due to the influence of neighbouring Exclusive assemblies; however, it is more likely to be the lack of necessity for formal arrangements. Albert Hall, Glasgow, was governed by a 'brothers' meeting' until 1991 when elders were appointed (oral information, February 1992, from assembly member).

60. The earliest example of elders from different assemblies consulting is in 1876: editor's note [John Ritchie], 'Answers to special questions', *BM*, 16 (1906), p.84; cf. G. A[dam]., 'Thoughts on church government—IV', *W*, 21 (1891), p.103; Peter Hynd to the editor, 1 September 1891, *ibid.*, p.159.

61. *W*, 35 (1905), p.149; *W*, 42 (1912), pp.279, 331.

One other role which received attention was that of women. In the early 1870s preaching by women was being questioned even among those who supported it.[62] Writing of this process, Robert Chapman gave the impression that the questioning was gradual, accompanied by no great struggle.[63] On the other hand, according to John Anderson, a doctor from Rhynie, Strathbogie, who became a missionary in China, the issue 'caused a great deal of disturbance in Aberdeenshire' where there was some resistance to the practice being abandoned in the 1880s. The Rhynie meeting, despite pressing requests from several prominent individuals in Scotland and England, decided that it would not prohibit the public participation of women in worship and preaching.[64] As a result, it was ostracised by other assemblies, and, although it was never published, Anderson claimed that Pickering & Inglis held the manuscript of a pamphlet arguing against Rhynie's practice.[65] It is not only the evidence from the north east which suggests that the suppression of women preachers might have been less free from controversy than Chapman implied. James Stone's letter defending the practice (quoted above in Chapter 3) was written in 1874, evidently to vindicate a custom that was being called into doubt.[66] In 1882 women were still permitted to take part at conversational Bible readings in Galston, Ayrshire,[67] and as late as 1889 when *The Witness* invited opinions on whether women might participate publicly, two of the three replies received were in the affirmative. But the practice was eventually eroded, and it would appear that Rhynie, remote even from other north-east assemblies, was left as the sole supporter of female preaching.

Perhaps the acquisition by assemblies of their own halls told against the practice. It disappeared in both Larkhall and Wishaw about the same time as the meetings moved into larger and more permanent accommodation.[68] Possibly, as the Methodists had already found, the more formal setting was less favourable to unconventional activities.[69] But more crucially, the supporters of female preaching lost the biblical argument.

---

62. Neil Dickson, 'Modern prophetesses: women preachers in the nineteenth-century Scottish Brethren', *RSCHS*, 25, pp.110-15.

63. Chapman, *Hebron Hall Assembly*, p.24.

64. John A. Anderson, *Autobiography of John A. Anderson* (Aberdeen, 1948), pp.21-2; writer's collection, II, F. F. Bruce to the writer, 26 April 1987.

65. John A. Anderson, *The Authority for the Public Ministry of Women* (Braemar, n.d.), p.4.

66. See above, p.77.

67. John S. Borland, *History of the Brethren Movement in Galston* (Kilmarnock [1948]), p.14.

68. Chapman, *Hebron Hall Assembly*, pp.23-4.

69. Dorothy M. Valenze, *Prophetic Sons and Daughters: female preaching and popular religion in industrial England* (New Haven, CT, 1985), pp.274-5.

By 1882 one writer was using Darbyite dispensationalism to reject the interpretation of Joel which had prevailed among supporters of female preaching.[70] Dispensationalism located the crucial era, 'the day of the Lord' or 'the last days', in the millennium and after the rapture of the Church. The place of women, this writer concluded, 'in presence [*sic*] of men in a public assembly is to be "in silence", "in subjection" (1 Tim. ii.11,12).'[71] In areas congenial to popular revivalism female preaching adapted and continued to exist in the later nineteenth century,[72] but its cessation in the Brethren is an unambiguous marker of the shift which was taking place within the movement in this period. The role of women was redefined and most accepted the contemporary notion that a woman's sphere was primarily the home. For one individual, a more advanced education for a woman might have its place but it would 'prove little use in household duties'.[73] Her dress should be inexpensive and unobtrusive, without jewellery, her long hair a sign of subjection.[74]

But Brethren activism, which was primarily expressed in the urgent imperative to evangelise, meant that many would not totally confine women to their houses. The dual role for women allowed by some was given its fullest expression by J. R. Caldwell in a series of articles in *The Witness* in 1895, later published as *The Ministry of Women*. The articles were mainly an exegesis of the relevant biblical passages in which Caldwell argued that the texts could not sustain the interpretations of the supporters of female preaching. Yet at the outset he maintained that the question for a woman was 'not as to gift, or ability, or responsibility, but simply and only as to the sphere in which gifts and abilities she undoubtedly possesses are to be exercised'.[75] And he closed the series with an appeal for women workers in tending the sick, visiting, teaching children and other women, and as missionaries. Caldwell's writings elsewhere allow us to deconstruct these views of a woman's status. Although in principle any individual could dispense the elements at the breaking of bread, Caldwell felt 'it would not be fitting that a woman should do it, or a very young believer'.[76] She had the same standing as an immature Christian. The status of women could fluctuate between one

---

70. See above, p.96; for dispensationalism, see below, pp.260-6.

71. W. F. H. N., '"Forbid him not"', *NW*, 12 (1882), p.116.

72. Janice Holmes, *Religious Revivals in Britain and Ireland 1859-1905* (Dublin, 2000), pp.108, 115-133.

73. W, 'Women's rights', *W*, 20 (1890), p.29.

74. 'The dress of Christian women', *NEI*, 3 (1873), p.183; J. A. B[oswell]., 'Department of question and answer', *NT*, 4 (1891-2), pp.139-40; [John Ritchie], 'Dress at the Lord's table', *BM*, 12 (1902), p.140.

75. J. R. Caldwell, 'The ministry of women', *W*, 25 (1895), p.141.

76. *Idem*, 'The breaking of bread', *W*, 39 (1909), p.77; cf. J. A. B[oswell]., 'Department of question and answer', *NT*, 4 (1891-2), p.45.

which accorded them an active role and one which regarded them as being not entirely responsible members of the assembly, certainly ones that lacked authority. But even in the readjustment of their roles there was room for disagreement. In some assemblies the sisters might be solo singers or Bible women and Mrs Lundin Brown (née Christie), an evangelist's widow, continued to pray publicly at prayer meetings until her death in 1924.[77] But in the stricter meetings even the limited public roles Caldwell had allowed them were not permitted.[78] Misogyny could take root here. For J. Albert Boswell 'much of the evil that arises in assemblies today may be justly described as women's work...[for] her worldliness of heart gradually tells upon her husband'.[79] Woman's work had been redefined.

It was not just in the role of women that some diversity of practice was allowed. Another example can be seen in the morning meeting. In the nascent Inverurie assembly Scotch Baptist ideas had been considered,[80] and at Insch the order of service from the first breaking of bread in 1873 had also appeared to be close to the Glasite pattern of mutual exhortation. It had consisted of a series of scripture readings with a prayer of thanksgiving at the dispensing of each element and followed by a hymn and an exhortation.[81] But by the following year the service had been assimilated to the pattern of alternating prayers and hymns which J. R. Caldwell stated was the normal pattern of a morning meeting.[82] The same process was evidently at work elsewhere in the north east, for John Ritchie confessed of his first morning meeting at Old Rayne that by later standards not everything was done '"after the due order"'.[83] Some assemblies in the early 1870s, it would appear, did not have a spontaneous form. One writer claimed he had found some meetings

---

77. F. F. Bruce, 'Women in the Church: a biblical survey', *CBRJ*, 33 (1982), p.14; cf. 'Mrs Lundin Brown', *W*, 54 (1924), p.299; the Lundin Browns lived in Fife in the late nineteenth century, but Mrs Lundin Brown died in Craigellachie, Banffshire. For further examples, see Dickson, 'Modern prophetesses', p.115.

78. John Brown, *'Spoken Words' on Profitable Themes* (1886), rpt (Dundee & Edinburgh, 1938), pp.19-20; C. Morton, 'Christendom brought to the test', *NT*, 1 (1888), pp.142-4; B[oswell]., 'question and answer', pp. 139-40.

79. J. A. Boswell, 'The revelation of the Lord: "whom Jezebel his wife stirred up"', *NT*, 4 (1891-2), p.23.

80. John Ritchie, 'Revival times and work in Aberdeenshire', in C. W. R[oss]. (ed.), *Donald Ross: pioneer evangelist* (Kilmarnock [1904]), p.173.

81. Insch, Fordyce Hall, Minute and account book of Insch assembly, 1873-91, p.1.

82. J. R. Caldwell, 'Object of the Lord's Supper', *W*, 22 (1892), pp.126-7: as the evidence from Insch demonstrates, the pattern described by Caldwell was evidently widely accepted much earlier but this is the first extant explicit descripton of it of which the present writer is aware.

83. Ritchie, 'Revival times', in R[oss]., *Ross*, p.171: the phrase is from 1 Chron. 15:13. For Ritchie's account of the Old Rayne service, see below, p.255.

which were 'nothing else than baptist meetings, where a studied address is given, then the bread and wine distributed by the "ministering brother"'.[84] But such an order of service, with its similarity to the English Baptist practice, was eventually replaced by a charismatic meeting. Some Glasgow assemblies had what Henry Pickering called 'The Twofold Meeting' with the first hour having spontaneous worship and after an interval a further hour at which a prearranged preacher would speak.[85] However, 'ministry' (the word preferred by the Brethren for addresses to Christians) continued to be under pressure at the morning meeting, not because it was Glasite, but because of the definition of worship which was adopted. Ministry was seen as being received passively while worship was thought to be offered actively[86] and therefore even devotional homilies could be perceived as a distraction at the breaking of bread, the only service acknowledged for worship. Those who wished stricter practices disapproved of even short addresses or Bible reading at the morning meeting and their use was constantly questioned. But the consistent advice from *The Witness* was that ministry should be permitted since the scriptural evidence did not allow one 'to lay down rules'.[87] Throughout the period under discussion there was a tension between desiring order and eschewing over-regulation.

Music was another area in which there was diversity of practice. All assemblies had accepted the revivalists' new practice of hymn-singing. At Larkhall singing classes were held, and some assemblies went further and had choirs which were used in 'deputation work', singing at Saturday night tea meetings and the like.[88] Others encouraged solo singing, the proper use of which, J. R. Caldwell claimed, was exemplified by Ira Sankey who had shown it was not just a 'mere 'American innovation' but a divinely appointed means of blessing'.[89] But typical of many others was John Ritchie's criticism of '"lady soloists" and other such

84. B[?oswell]., undated letter, p.3.

85. HyP[ickering]., 'The order of the morning meeting', *W*, 54 (1934), p.85.

86. G. A[dam]., 'QA', *W*, 30 (1900), p.132; cf. Caldwell, *Christian Experience*, p.111; Ritchie, 'Revival times', in R[oss]., *Ross*, p.171.

87. G. A[dam]., 'QA', *W*, 29 (1899), p.83; see also 'QA' in: *NW*, 8 (1878), pp.17-18; *W*, 29 (1899), pp.83-4; *W*, 30 (1900), pp.131-2; *W*, 33 (1903), pp.34-6; *W*, 41 (1911), pp.33-4; *W*, 44 (1914), pp.177; *W*, 45 (1915), pp.176-7; cf. 'Answers to correspondents', *BM*, 14 (1904), pp.143-4. The issue continued to agitate the movement outside the period discussed in the present chapter; see 'QA' in: *W*, 48 (1918), pp.18-19, 26-8, 43-4, 60, 90-1; *W*, 55 (1925), pp.112-13; *W*, 56 (1926), pp.208-9, 384-5; *W*, 57 (1927), pp.153, 159; *W*, 59 (1929), pp.280-1; *W*, 60 (1930), p.66; *W*, 74 (1944), pp.95-6; *W*, 75 (1945), pp.15-16, 21-2; *W*, 77 (1947), p.141; 'BQB', *BM*, 31 (1921), pp.55-6; for examples of meditations at the morning meeting see Dan Crawford, *Thirsting After God* (London [1927]), pp.3-69.

88. Chapman, *Hebron Hall Assembly*, p.35.

89. Caldwell, *Christian Experience*, p.43.

"crutches"' as signs of 'fake revival'.[90] Similarly, when Sankey's use of a harmonium led some to introduce musical accompaniment at evangelistic meetings, others kept to the older practice of unaccompanied singing.[91] This, however, remained the universal practice at the breaking of bread because praise was spiritual.[92] The use of fiddles or silver bands, features of working-class culture that had been adapted by some Evangelicals, were stopped in missions which became assemblies.[93] In the Baptist mission at Lochore the musically talented Halliday family had a small band which included several fiddles, a mouth organ, a piano harp, a cornet and a trumpet. About 1913 disapproval of this ensemble culminated one Sunday when two women, whom Mr Halliday had invited from Dundee to sing and preach, participated at the morning meeting. One individual in favour of adopting Brethren principles stopped the proceedings and declared that, 'Women should keep silence in the church...there should be no singing like this, we'll have none of this music.' Some members left for other churches and although the Hallidays made the transition to the assembly, eventually the family moved away.[94] Other mission halls which became meetings also discontinued their bands. In New Stevenston the proceeds from its sale were given to missionaries and at Greengairs they were used to buy a fence for the building.[95] Musically, despite some innovation, Brethren worship remained true to its Calvinist inheritance.

The area in which uniformity was most complete was that of doctrine. It was as advocates of the tenets of Evangelicalism that the Brethren had left their former churches and they were deeply committed to them. Until the mid-1870s there was a period of some theological exploration, but after that date it was suppressed. In the early 1870s conditionalism—the doctrine that the soul is not immortal but eternal existence is granted to the saved alone with the damned ceasing to exist—made some impact in

90. *BM*, 15 (August 1905), p.i.

91. R[?ice]. H[?opkins]., 'Instrumental music', *NW*, 6 (1876), pp.185-6; J. R[itchie]., 'From Egypt to Canaan. Chap. XV.—The song of Redemption', *NW*, 10 (1880), p.105; [*idem*], 'Answers to correspondents', *BM*, 12 (1902), p.59.

92. A. A. R., 'Worship', *NW*, 10 (1880), p.162; cf. C. Morton, 'Christendom brought to the test', *NT*, 1 (1888-9), pp.140-1.

93. See above, pp.106, 128-9.

94. Oral information, 19 November 1988, from a woman who was teenager at the time.

95. Writer's collection, I.M.22., David Wilson, 'A Brief History of the Assembly of Christian Brethren Meeting in Gospel Hall, Hall St., New Stevenston, Motherwell', MS [1989]; *ibid.*, I.M.13., (ii). untitled history of Greengairs assembly, anonymous typescript, n.d., p.1.

Britain.[96] In Scotland it found little acceptance,[97] but within the Brethren it would appear there were those who found it attractive, evidently because they felt the force of the dilemma posed by Alexander Marshall in a tract entitled *Will a God of Love Punish Any of His Creatures for Ever?*[98] John Ritchie was deeply troubled over the issue, a phase which he dated to 1876.[99] But it had been three years earlier that the controversy had been at its height. It was claimed then that a number of individuals and some assemblies had come to accept conditionalism, something which Donald Ross blamed on the influence of Dr John Thomas, the founder of Christadelphianism.[100] Ritchie was typical of the majority in eventually rejecting it, and the assembly in Edinburgh divided over the issue, the section accused of holding conditionalism being shunned by other meetings.[101] In 1873 a number of 'leading and ministering brethren' were able to sign a statement denying that any assembly condoned the non-eternity of punishment.[102] Although complaints that it was being tolerated continued until 1900,[103] it is more likely that those making the claims had a vested interest in proving the existence of heresy.[104] Even the large assembly in Edinburgh which tolerated the doctrine had, it appears, soon dwindled away.[105] Orthodoxy was represented by Marshall who answered his own question in the

---

96. Geoffrey Rowell, *Hell and the Victorians: a study of the nineteenth-century theological controversies concerning eternal punishment and the future life* (Oxford, 1974), pp.180-207.

97. *Ibid.*, pp.189-90; but cf. *W*, 18 (December 1888), p.vi, which claimed that belief in the non-eternity of hell was 'making rapid headway' in Aberdeenshire.

98. Alexander Marshall, *Will a God of Love Punish Any of His Creatures for Ever?: a plain answer* (Glasgow, n.d.). For the influence of conditionalism on the Brethren, see Le Roy Edwin Froom, *The Conditionalist Faith of Our Fathers*, 2 (Washington DC, 1965), pp.397-9; and of universalism on the English Brethren writer Andrew Jukes, see Rowell, *Hell and the Victorians*, pp.129-31.

99. John Ritchie, *Man's Future State: an examination of Scripture testimony on this great subject* (Kilmarnock, 1912), [p.3].

100. [Donald Ross], 'A word to assemblies', *NA*, No.4 (April, 1873), p.14; [*idem*], 'The breakers a-head', *NA*, No.9 (September 1873), pp.35-6.

101. *NEI*, 2 (1872), p.88; however, only the word of their accusers exists that they actually held this doctrine.

102. E. S., 'Answers to special questions', *BM*, 16 (1906), p.12.

103. J. A. Boswell, 'The Open position', *NT*, 12 (1900), p.76; in this article Boswell claimed that an assembly had recently been formed in Aberdeen in which the non-eternity of hell was tolerated.

104. G. R. Geddes, 'Fellowship or independency?', *NT*, 2 (1889-90), pp.180-6; W. Paterson *et al.*, 1 December 1892, in Arthur Chamings (compiler), 'Some Papers and Letters in Connection with the Separation of the 1880's and 1890's', unpublished typescript, 1987, p.13; cf. 'Answers to special questions', *BM*, 16 (1906), pp.11-12.

105. Boswell, 'Open position', p.74.

affirmative,[106] and belief in the non-eternity of punishment was regarded as a doctrine worthy of excommunication.[107] The need to exclude the holders of heresy led Ross to propose a 'note of introduction' for Brethren when visiting another meeting. Later called 'letters of commendation', these were increasingly demanded and, although they never became the universal custom, they became a powerful tool for regulating the inter-communion of assemblies.[108]

Theological innovation was also eliminated in other areas. It was probably the death of John Bowes in 1874 which led to the disappearance of Wesleyan perfectionism among its Brethren adherents.[109] An article critical of Wesley's views of sanctification which appeared in 1875 in Ross's *The Northern Witness* also signalled the disappearance of higher-life teaching from his journals,[110] a move undoubtedly finalised by J. R. Caldwell who was the leading Scottish exponent of the distinctive Brethren thinking on sanctification. However, although not promoted widely, holiness teaching survived in its more acceptable Keswick form, or as modified by individuals such as John Ritchie.[111] Even in doctrine, given the nature of the Open Brethren, it was impossible to have absolute uniformity. Although it would appear everyone accepted premillennial dispensationalism, there were differences over whether the ascension of the Church to Heaven ('the rapture') would take place before or after a period of intense trouble ('the great tribulation') which the scheme predicted.[112] The stricter individuals were certain it was before,[113] but as late as 1904 it was stated that it was difficult to discuss the issue without causing 'hurtful controversy'.[114] Perhaps the

---

106. Cf. 'Conference at Sheffield', *NEI*, 3 (1873), pp.189-90; [Donald Ross], 'A word to assemblies', *NA*, No.4 (April, 1873), p.14; [*idem*], 'Charity! Charity!', *NA*, No.5 (May 1873), p.18; 'Sectarian exclusiveness', *NA*, No.7 (July 1873), p.27; 'QA', *NW*, 10 (1880), pp.173-4; [Henry Pickering,], 'What are we coming to?', *W*, 18 (February 1888), p.v.

107. [John Ritchie], 'Answers to correspondents', *BM*, 15 (1905), p.59.

108. [Ross], 'A word', p.14; cf. T. C[ochrane]., 'Are assemblies independent?', *NA*, No.18 (June 1874), p.22; [J. R. Caldwell], *W*, 18 (July 1888), p.vi; John Ritchie, *Assembly Privileges and Responsibilities* (Kilmarnock, n.d.), pp.7-8; cf. complaints about such letters not being used: C. M. Luxmoore, 'One', *NT*, 4 (1891-2), p.32; Editor's note [John Ritchie], 'Answers to special questions', *BM*, 15 (1905), p.72; also see below, pp.237-8.

109. See above, p.74.

110. W. W., 'A letter concerning Mr. Wesley's views of sanctification', *NW*, 5 (1875), pp.116-121; see above, pp.92-93.

111. For the views of Scottish Brethren on sanctification see below, pp.266-74.

112. For a fuller account of this eschatology, see below, pp.259-66.

113. A. J. H[oliday]. *et al.*, 'The coming of the Lord for His Church—will it be before or after the great tribulation?', *NT*, 2 (1889-90), pp.1-27.

114. Geo. Adam, 'The coming of the Lord', *W*, 34 (1904), pp.10-12.

most noted dissenter from Darby's 'any moment rapture' theory was the missionary Dan Crawford who held that there must be worldwide evangelism before the second advent.[115] Even in doctrine some diversity on its minutiae was tolerated.

Needed Truth

The Brethren kept organisation to the minimum. Possibly this was an adjunct of their adventism and their reaction against the institutionalism of existing denominations.[116] But their desire to preserve a quasi-mystical conception of the Church was probably more significant. Each assembly was individually responsible to the Lord, Glasgow preacher Thomas Cochrane maintained, and thus, while not being independent of the Word of God, they were independent of one another.[117] This was his version of Open Brethren independency which allowed for some diversity across the movement. But other strands which had existed within assemblies at least since the 1860s were to pull away from this position towards closer organisation. Donald Ross noted one of these elements in writing to a member of one of the new north-east meetings. The defect of such churches as his correspondent's one, he felt, was 'glorying in their purity'.[118] There were in addition those who had been deeply critical of the denominations which they had left.[119] At the first Inverurie conference of 1872 these criticisms had been so pronounced that the Glasgow preacher Robert Kerr publicly lamented that he would have liked to have heard 'more constructive along with the destructive truth'.[120] The drive for purity and negative perceptions of other churches led to demands for greater uniformity and increased separation from denominational Christianity to be achieved through greater organisation.

The central issue became 'the reception question', a debate over receiving non-Brethren Christians to the Lord's supper. Although the assembly was a gathered church it was not seen as being co-extensive with the universal Church in an area. The initial practice of most (though not all) assemblies was to allow fellow-Evangelicals to participate in the

---

115. Crawford, *Thirsting After God*, pp.135-43; rejection of the 'any-moment rapture' was usually combined with post-tribulationism, but it is not known if Crawford also held this view.

116. Bryan R. Wilson in *idem* (ed.), *Patterns of Sectarianism: organisation and ideology in social and religious movements* (London, 1967), pp.35, 244.

117. C[ochrane]., 'Are assemblies independent?' pp.21-2.

118. Donald Ross to 'one who had begun a meeting in the name of the Lord Jesus', 1 September 1871, quoted in R[oss]. (ed.), *Ross*, p.97.

119. See above, pp.69-70, 87.

120. Robert Kerr, quoted in 'Friday's Conference', p.74.

breaking of bread.[121] An early and influential statement of this position
was given in 1877 by Alexander Stewart. Stewart maintained that the
essential fellowship was with God and was the basis for communion with
other Christians. If it were established that a visitor from a 'religious
denomination' was a Christian, then 'the man's title to fellowship is
established':

> To have the Spirit is the fundamental condition of our communion with God and
> with each other as born of God and members of the Body of Christ. Fellowship
> therefore is the birthright privilege of all saints.[122]

This was Stewart's version of the Open Brethren maxim that 'life, not
light'—being born again rather than agreeing to a credal statement—was
the basis of intercommunion among Christians.[123] In 1872 when Donald
Ross's *Northern Evangelistic Intelligencer* listed a series of propositions
to govern the morning meeting, number seven stated 'all Christ's
members...are as free to come together with us for the breaking of bread,
as those already assembled...'.[124] A limited degree of cooperation with
other Evangelicals was also maintained in the early 1870s. During D. L.
Moody's Glasgow mission of 1874 assembly members in the city
attended services and assisted at after meetings, and others were willing to
accept preaching engagements in nondenominational missions.[125]

But there were those who were unhappy with these open practices.
Given the circumstances of their emergence, the north-east meetings were
particularly isolated from other Christian bodies and Ross criticised those
who attended services organised by other churches.[126] He also directed

---

121. For an exception, see above, p.87.

122. Alexander Stewart to Alexander Marshall, March 1877, quoted in John
Hawthorn, *Alexander Marshall: evangelist, author and pioneer* (Glasgow [1929]),
pp.127-132; this letter received wide circulation as *The Fellowship of the Saints of God*
(Glasgow, n.d.).

123. It was given its classic expression in A. N. Groves to J. N. Darby, 10 March
1836, in Mrs Groves (ed.), *Memoir of Anthony Norris Groves: compiled chiefly from his
journals and letters*, 3rd edn (London, 1869), pp.538-43; James Patrick Callahan has
termed this position 'soteriological unity', in *Primitivist Piety: the ecclesiology of the
early Plymouth Brethren* (Lanham, MA, 1996), pp.42-7.

124. Anon., 'Do this in remembrance of me', *NEI*, 2 (1872), p.103; cf. Mrs Code,
'The mystery of Christ', *NI*, 3 (1873), p.89; anon., 'The testimony', *NA*, No.7 (July
1874), p.20; T. C[ochrane]., 'A few hints to those meeting in the name of the Lord
Jesus', *NA*, No.10 (October 1873), p.41; anon, 'The great open meeting of Christianity',
NW, 5 (1875), p.151; J. S., 'William Stephen', *BP*, 54 (1933), pp.146-8.

125. An Old Disciple, 'Thoughts by an old disciple', *NA*, No.17 (1874), pp.17-18; T.
C[ochrane]., 'A word for the times', *NI*, 4 (1874), p.85; Alexander Marshall, *Holding
Fast the Faithful Word': or whither are we drifting?* (Glasgow [1908]), pp.24, 25.

126. [Donald Ross], 'Unequally yoked', *NA*, No.18 (June 1874), p.24.

criticism at Brethren from Edinburgh and England who preached or worshipped in other churches and did not keep to assemblies.[127] But even in Glasgow some Brethren had felt it was wrong to attend union prayer meetings during Moody's 1874 mission as they would be associated with the 'evils' they had fled.[128] Cooperation with other Christians was contentious.[129] In the 1870s there were tensions over the relationship to other Christians in Kilmarnock. The members of the town's second assembly complained that their fellow citizens had 'seldom heard the gospel'[130] and Kilmarnock Brethren were stopped attending services in other churches. George Müller, on his preaching tour in 1876 of various churches in places associated with Moody, broke bread with the meeting John Stewart had founded.[131] But Stewart's assembly was perceived as not observing 'the true Scriptural principles'[132] and was discontinued about 1879.[133] Stewart left the Brethren for the Free Church.[134] Ill-feeling between the Brethren and other churches was probably deepened by the works critical of the movement which were published by Scottish writers (mainly clergymen) during this period, and often these made no distinction between the Open and Exclusive sections.[135] In addition, the

---

127. [*Idem*], 'Religious shams', *NA*, Nos 14, 15 (February and March 1874), pp.7, 11.

128. J. S., 'Vessels unto honour', *NA*, No.16 (April 1874), pp.13-15; M., 'To the editor of the "Assemblies"', *NA*, No.17 (May 1874), pp.18-19; A. B. C., 'To the editor of "The Assemblies"', *NA*, No.19 (July 1874), pp.25-6; anon., '"Vessels unto honour"' *NA*, No.20 (August 1874), pp.29-30.

129. See the call for separation by [?J. A.] B[?oswell]., 'Letter to the editor', *NW*, 6 (1876), pp.43-4, 87-8, and supported by [?R. T.] H[?opkins]., to the editor, *ibid.*, pp.153-5; criticised by A. S[tewart]., to the editor, *ibid.*, pp.68-9; and T. C[ochrane]., to the editor, 7 June 1876, *ibid.*, pp.101-2.

130. *LR*, 6 (1873), p.118; in the next issue, this report was contradicted by an itinerant evangelist, *LR*, 6 (1873), p.133.

131. Beattie, *Brethren*, p.223; [Müller], *Narrative*, 4, 1st edn (London, 1886), p.390; for the founding of this assembly, see above, pp.43-4.

132. Beattie, Brethren, p.224; cf. the account of Stewart's principles which emphasises his ecumenicity in James Todd (ed.) *Words of Faith, Hope and Love from the Chamber of a Dying Saint: being a series of letters written by the late John Dickie, of Irvine, Scotland, during his last illness to his friend and brother in Christ, James Todd, Dublin*, 1 (London, 1900), p.xiii.

133. For the history of Kilmarnock Brethren in this period, see above, p.112 n.169.

134. 'The late Mr John Stewart of Shawhill', *KS*, 10 December 1887, p.3.

135. Anon., *Heresy Unveiled: the teaching of Plymouth Brethren contrasted with scripture: in four sections. I. Presidency and Ministry. II. The Divine Humanity of Christ. III Socinianism IV. The Righteousness of Christ* (Aberdeen [*c*.1870]); Hugh McIntosh, *The New Prophets: being an account of the operations of the Northern Evangelists* (Aberdeen, 1871); anon., *Prevalent Errors: a reply to a lecture by Mr C. J. Davis regarding the opinions of the party known as 'Brethren' by an elder* (Aberdeen, 1871); Alexander Burnet, *Plymouth Brethren is Antichrist* (Aberdeen, 1873); James Moir

increasing theological and social transformations within the Presbyterian churches in the later nineteenth century widened the gap between them and the Brethren and possibly, by way of counter reaction, had some influence on intensifying conservatism in the latter.[136] The way was led, however, in Shaw's 'tightening process' by Rice Hopkins and Albert Boswell, the critics of other denominations at the 1872 Inverurie conference. The first public indication of the move away from open principles was in 1873 at a conference held for evangelists in Sheffield. It was decided there that 'fellowship' applied not just to the breaking of bread but to all the activities of the assembly. This redefinition was a justification of stopping 'occasional fellowship', non-Brethren individuals sometimes participating in the Lord's supper.[137] The search was on for a more complete theory.

According to Alexander Marshall it was Hopkins who developed the distinction that membership of the universal Church did not automatically qualify one for membership of a local church.[138] J. R. Caldwell later dated the open emergence of the new thinking to April 1876 when Boswell anonymously asked some questions in *The Northern Witness* and

Porteous, *What is Plymouthism or Brethrenism? republished by request from the Government of the Kingdom of Christ* (London, 1873); R. H. Ireland, *Principles and Practices of 'Brethren': a word of warning to the churches* (Edinburgh [1873]); Duncan Macintosh, *The Special Teachings, Ecclesiastical and Doctrinal, of the Plymouth Brethren: compiled from their own writings. With Strictures* (Edinburgh [1873]); Peter Mearns, *Christian Truth Viewed in Relation to Plymouthism* (Edinburgh, 1874); William Reid, *Plymouth Brethrenism Unveiled and Refuted* (Edinburgh, 1875); James Moir Porteous, *Brethren in the Keelhowes*, 6th edn (London, 1876); I have been unable to trace anon., *Prevalent Errors*, and Burnet, *Plymouth Brethren* (see above p.98 n.52). There were in addition a number of such works published elsewhere in the United Kingdom (mainly in Ireland) which were widely available, see Crawford L. Gribben, '"The worst sect that a Christian man can meet": opposition to the Plymouth Brethren in Ireland and Scotland, 1859-1900', *Scottish Studies Review* (forthcoming).

136. For the changes see Andrew L. Drummond and James Bulloch, *The Church in Late Victorian Scotland 1874-1900* (Edinburgh, 1978); A. C. Cheyne, *The Transforming of the Kirk: Victorian Scotland's religious revolution* (Edinburgh, 1983); Donald C. Smith, *Passive Obedience and Prophetic Protest: social criticism in the Scottish Church 1830-1945* (New York, 1987), pp.215-313; Stewart J. Brown, 'Reform, reconstruction, reaction: the social vision of Scottish Presbyterianism c.1830-c.1930', *Scottish Journal of Theology*, 44 (1991), pp.489-517; James Lachlan MacLeod, *The Second Disruption: the Free Church in Victorian Scotland and the origins of the Free Presbyterian Church* (East Linton, 2000).

137. 'Conference at Sheffield', *NI*, 3 (1873), p.190.

138. CBA 2409, Alexander Marshall to P. F. Bruce, 12 October [1926/7], quoted in Neil Dickson, 'Scottish Brethren: division and wholeness 1838-1916', *CBRFJ*, No.41 (1990), p.28; Marshall dated the emergence of the new views to about 1873 in *Holding Fast*, p.10.

then answered them himself the following month.[139] Boswell's questions and answers were based on the distinction between the Church as the body of Christ and a local church and showed that it had important implications for fellowship with Christians from outside the Brethren.[140] He stated that as 'knowledge of sins forgiven is the ground on which we receive a young convert', it was reasonable that an acknowledgement of Christ as Lord should be 'required from those coming from that which is in rebellion against Him', that is a 'sect' or other Christian body.[141] This redefinition of fellowship subtly shifted the balance away from its earlier definition of shared life in Christ to some degree of knowledge being its basis. The acceptance of Brethren ecclesiology should govern relationships with other Christians. Boswell also argued that there was a responsibility on the assembly to 'receive' individuals, separate from the 'Lord bringing into the Church', and gave a more prominent role to elders in ruling the congregation. He had moved from the earlier, more mystical conception of Christian fellowship to a formally organised one.

In 1884 Hopkins restated these points in his *Fellowship Among Saints: what saith the Scriptures?*[142] But a more developed theory had been presented the previous year by the twenty-one-year-old Frederick Banks of Ipswich.[143] In *The Church and the Churches of God* (1883) Banks supplied exegetical support for the distinction between the universal Church and the local church, arguing that the New Testament distinguished two circles: 'the Body of Christ' and 'the church of God', the latter only 'used in the Word of God to designate a company of believers acting together in local accountability upon the earth'. There could be no allowing of 'casual communion' because along with the privilege of breaking of bread, the individual had to accept full responsibilities as a member of a church.[144] This meant in effect a closed communion, for those participating in the Lord's supper would have to

---

139. J. R. Caldwell, *A Revision of Certain Teachings Regarding the Gathering and Receiving of the Children of God* (Glasgow [1906]), p.6; the attribution of the questions to Boswell is made in: Thomas Stewart Veitch, *The Brethren Movement: a simple and straightforward account of the features and failures of a sincere attempt to carry out the principles of Scripture during the last 100 years* (London and Glasgow [1925]), p.96; and J. J. Park, *The Churches of God: their origin and development in the 20th Century* (Leicester, 1987), p.16.

140. [J. A. Boswell], 'Questions connected with fellowship', *NW*, 6 (1876), p.63.

141. [*idem*], 'Answers to questions connected with fellowship', *ibid.*, pp.78-9.

142. R. T. H[opkins]., *Fellowship Among Saints: what saith the Scriptures?* (Glasgow, 1884).

143. Hopkins's influence was probably strong in Ipswich as he had lived there from 1865 until 1875.

144. Frederick Arthur Banks, *'The Church', and the 'Churches of God' : a suggestive outline of truth* ([1883]), rpt. in *Spiritual Growth: and other writings of the late Frederick Arthur Banks*, 2nd edn (Bradford, 1947), pp.32-43.

leave their church and join an assembly before being received. The pamphlet found wide acceptance. At one conference in the north of Scotland a speaker, 'highly esteemed by many', failed to make the distinction that Banks insisted on. After the tea interval Banks expounded his views and the first speaker 'rose and publicly thanked F. A. B. for the clear and helpful way he had set forth these truths'.[145] There were many others in Scotland ready to listen.

Open dissension began to appear. In 1880 John Ritchie had refused to accept W. J. Grant and twelve others from Grant's Baptist flock into the assembly in Kilmarnock because they were being received as a group rather than individually. Ritchie forced a division when he proclaimed one Sunday morning, 'All those who want to follow the Lord, come with me to the Crown Inn Hall at 2 o'clock.'[146] About three years later open views caused a schism in Cathcart Road Gospel Hall, Glasgow, the leading strict assembly in the city, when a widower sought to bring his newly-wed second wife, an active Christian in another denomination, to the morning meeting. She was excluded from participating in the Lord's supper and made to sit in a back seat. A number of younger individuals who had been pressing for an open communion seceded (along with the bride and groom) to the recently formed Elim Hall, Crosshill.[147]

It was the restricted views which were winning over significant individuals. Ritchie issued Banks' pamphlet, as did Henry Pickering, then running a small printer's business in Newcastle.[148] Hopkins's pamphlet was issued by the Publishing Office in Glasgow and Banks took over control of this concern in 1886; it was he who appointed Pickering as his manager.[149] J. R. Caldwell, who was Boswell's brother-in-law, was also won over to these views, and for a while after 1879 a narrowing of viewpoint took place in his editorship of *The Northern Witness*.[150] Particularly prominent in Scotland in the promotion of the new views was John Brown, the owner of a large bakery business in Greenock, who expounded them in his published address *The Church: its constitution*

---

145. John Dorricot, 'Foreword', *ibid.*, pp.vii-viii.

146. Oral information, 14 April 1986; my interviewee's account came from a woman who witnessed the event as a teenager.

147. Crosshill Evangelical Church archive, 'Cathcart Road', undated MS; this incident apparently happened shortly after Elim Hall was founded in 1882.

148. A. T. Doodson, *The Search for the Truth of God* (Bradford, n.d.), p.41; Park, *The Churches of God*, p.19 (a facsimile of the Kilmarnock edition cover is shown on p.18).

149. *NW*, 16 (March 1886), cover; however see above, n.35 for evidence which suggests Caldwell might also have been involved in this change of ownership.

150. Park, *Churches of God*, p.86; CBA, Marshall to Bruce, quoted in Dickson, 'Scottish Brethren', p.28; [J. R. Caldwell], 'Forty-one years of witnessing', *W*, 30 (1910), p.196.

and government (1886).[151] Caldwell, however, had reservations about the novel teaching. In 1882 he claimed that to call an assembly 'the church of God' to the exclusion of other Christians 'is an assumption not warranted by Scripture'.[152] Articles by Banks and others in the emerging party were regularly printed in *The Northern Witness* throughout the 1880s. But it was later claimed that ones expounding his ecclesiology were refused by Caldwell.[153] It was possibly because of the lack of complete agreement between the two men that Banks's pamphlet was not issued by the Publishing Office. Banks died in 1887 and the following year Brown, along with Boswell and three English Brethren, established under their joint editorship a new journal, *Needed Truth*, to promote principles 'relating to the Churches of God'.[154] It was issued from the Glasgow Publishing Office and in the introduction it was stressed that its appearance was an example of 'specialization'.[155] Care was being taken not to be perceived as a rival to *The Witness* (from 1887 the title of *The Northern Witness*).[156] At first the tone of the new magazine was moderate and probably the proponents of the emerging ecclesiology hoped persuasion would bring everyone round to their thinking, something that they attempted through conference addresses and conversations.[157] Reform, they proclaimed, should be from within.[158]

There were other issues apart from those relating to intercommunion which troubled the emerging party. Thomas McLaren (son of the HFMF founder) later confessed to the embarrassment he had felt when someone would list the diversity of practices in the Open Brethren:

'Oh, the meeting at A—have a harmonium. The meeting at B—receives any Christian to 'the table'. The meeting a C—will admit an unbaptised believer. The meeting at D—are not so strait-laced towards the sects. The meeting at E—allows

151. John Brown, *The Church: its constitution and government* (1886), rpt in *idem*, *'Spoken Words' on Profitable Themes*, 2nd edn (Dundee & Edinburgh, 1938).

152. [J. R. Caldwell], 'QA', *NW*, 12 (1882), p.188.

153. Park, *Churches of God*, p.19; cf. Doodson, *Truth of God*, p.41.

154. *Circular Message*, quoted in Doodson, *Truth of God*, p.43; the English editors were: A. J. Holiday of Bradford, W. H. Hunter of Manchester and C. M. Luxmoore of Reading.

155. 'Needed Truth', *NT*, 1 (1888-9), pp.2-3.

156. See above n.33.

157. For examples, see the reports on J. A. Boswell, John Brown, W. J. Ervine, George Geddes, W. H. Hunter, and William Laing preaching in: *W*, 17 (September 1887), end pp.; *W*, 19 (September 1889), p.v; *ibid*., (October), p.v; Henry Pickering, 'What really constitutes a church of God?', *W*, 60 (1930), p.181; for an example of conversations, see Bruce to the writer, 26 April 1987, quoted in Dickson, 'Scottish Brethren', p.31.

158. [A. J. Holiday], 'Extract from a letter', *BP*, 7 (1886), pp.39-40; [*idem*], '"One accord"' *BP*, 9 (1888), pp.73-5; anon., 'Separation', *NT*, 1 (1888-9), p.154.

women to minister. The meeting at F—allows friends from the sects to minister among them.' etc., etc.[159]

Even if these were not practised in his assembly, McLaren had felt guilty of these 'loose' practices by association. Also a source of grievance was that no mechanism existed for judging who was in the right in a schism, both parties in a division being accepted as valid assemblies.[160] The source of the problem was seen to be the independency of the Open Brethren which allowed each meeting to practise according to its own understanding of scripture. Writers in *Needed Truth* began to turn their attention to the way assemblies could arrive at unanimity. Banks had felt that there was no 'definite guidance' in the New Testament about the 'intercommunion' of assemblies.[161] But now it was argued that just as churches in the administrative provinces of the Roman Empire had been grouped, so overseers within a district should come together.[162] In this way understanding would be achieved of the Lord's commandments and there would be mutual submission to one another and to godly leadership.[163] To eliminate 'looseness' some degree of formal organisation was being called for and this new doctrine provided the rationale.[164] Unity was to be provided by ecclesiology: in one illustration believers were said to be like staves in a barrel and Church truth the hoops which bound them together.[165] In a manner which was foreign to Open Brethren thinking, a representative capacity was also proposed for leaders. For Banks, the brother 'who says in the assembly, "Let *us* give thanks," ere he breaks the loaf *loses his individuality*, and is, for the time being, the mouthpiece of the church.' He should then publicly break the bread as a corporate act.[166] Similarly elders were representative of the assembly and could make decisions on its behalf.[167] There were moves to

---

159. Thomas McLaren Jnr, *Why I Left the Open Brethren* (London, 1893), p.16; however, it was in McLaren's interests to emphasise diversity and some of the practices listed were not necessarily very widespread.

160. J. A. Boswell, 'The kingdom present', *NT*, 4 (1891-2), pp.145-4.

161. Banks, '*The Church*', in *Spiritual Growth*, pp.41-2.

162. A. J. H[oliday]., *et al.*, 'The fellowship of assemblies', *NT*, 2 (1889-90), pp.49-76.

163. W. H. H[unter]., 'The fellowship of assemblies', *ibid.*, pp.28-40.

164. Gordon Willis and Bryan Wilson, 'The Churches of God: pattern and practice', in Wilson (ed.), *Patterns of Sectarianism*, pp.244-86.

165. Quoted in G. A[dam]., 'Thoughts on church government—IV', *W*, 21 (1891), p.103.

166. F. A. B[anks]., 'The feast of remembrance and testimony', *NW*, 16 (1886), p.74-5; cf. *ibid.*, 'Question CCXXV', p.80; *NW.*, 12 (1882), p.111; *BM*, 37 (1927), p.90.

167. H[unter]., 'fellowship of assemblies', pp.61-6.

increase the powers of district oversight meetings.[168] The erosion of independency, increased organisation, and the expansion of elders' roles were shifts towards greater institutionalisation.

The movement became polarised over these issues. Rice Hopkins was seen by many as the leader of the stricter party,[169] but in 1882 he had emigrated. Perhaps a more Scottish perspective on the leadership of the *Needed Truth* group was contained in the sneer that it was 'the house that John Brown built'.[170] From 1890 writers in the magazine became more outspoken. For Boswell, assemblies never had 'power', because they were not 'in the place which God would have His people occupy', instead 'place was given to the Devil.'[171] Articles discussed division.[172] Subsequently it became clear that feelings ran even deeper: Thomas McLaren Jnr later claimed that 'Open Brethren meetings have almost become a developed and elaborated system of lawlessness.'[173] Not everyone was persuaded of the *Needed Truth* thinking. Peter Hynd of Troon, a supporter of consultative district oversight meetings, stopped attending one held in an assembly hall because it seemed to be promoting 'exclusivism'.[174] Others turned back. From 1890 onwards articles began appearing in *The Witness* attacking the confederacy and exclusiveness which were felt to be implicit in *Needed Truth* teaching, most notably a series by George Adam, a Bible teacher who had joined the Brethren in Ross's north-east movement but by then was based in Stranraer.[175] The new prescriptions about representative capacities at the morning meeting also led to controversy in many assemblies.[176]

In an attempt to reconcile the differences a conference was held at Windermere in July 1891. It had representatives of the three different sections that were by now felt to exist in the Brethren: the open group, a middle one, and the strict party. However, the differences were too great

---

168. However, before 1892 writers in *Needed Truth* were careful to avoid granting them legislative powers: see the examples cited in Macdonald, 'Needed Truth Brethren', p.13.

169. Napoleon Noel, *The History of the Brethren*, 1 (Denver, CO, 1936), p.273; cf. Ian McDowell, 'Rice Thomas Hopkins 1842-1916': an open brother', *BAHNR*, 1 (1997-8), pp.24-30.

170. Quoted in Macdonald, 'Needed Truth Brethren', p.75; cf. writer's collection, II, F. F. Bruce to the writer, 8 June 1987.

171. J. A. B[oswell]., 'A transatlantic question', *NI*, 2 (1891-2), pp.146-7.

172. W. J. Ervine, 'Division', *NT*, 2 (1889-90), pp.135-7; *idem*, 'Divisions', *NT*, 3 (1890-1), pp.125-32.

173. McLaren Jnr, *Why I Left*, p.9.

174. Hynd to the editor, p.159.

175. G. A[dam]., 'Thoughts on church government', *W*, 21 (1891), pp.1-3, 18-20, 54-6, 102-4; *W*, 22 (1892), pp.35-7, 56-58, 70-1.

176. W. H. Clare, *Pioneer Preaching or Work Well Done* (London and Glasgow [1923]), p.88.

by this time and the conference only helped to emphasise them.[177] When in September 1891 George Adam published extracts from a letter in *The Witness* recounting how he had come to reject *Needed Truth* teaching,[178] the supporters of the latter maintained that it was an act of bad faith and future discussions were impossible.[179] Events in the Greenock assembly forced everyone's hand. There had been a period of disagreement in Greenock, principally it would appear between John Brown and Thomas Black, the tent manufacturer and the individual in whose home the meeting had commenced.[180] In February 1892 the latter was excommunicated for 'the sin of railing and covetousness'. The assembly had been equally divided on the merits of the charge and when Black gained control of the meeting hall, those who agreed with Brown were forced to seek new accommodation.[181] Ironically, for those who made consultation mandatory, the latter group had failed, as Caldwell pointed out, 'before pressing the matter to division to wait upon God for oneness of mind, and seek the help of brethren whose experience and discernment fitted them to give counsel at such a juncture'.[182] In the letters which Brown's assembly subsequently sent out, they justified their actions, claiming, in the words of one, that the point of division was separation from 'Open Brethrenism, known in some parts as "Loose" companies, which deny and oppose the plainest principles of the word of God'.[183] Individuals such as Boswell had condemned independency for allowing schisms to multiply[184] and the split in Greenock made others consider their future.[185] In October 1892 Boswell's own assembly in Edinburgh was the second secession, and he inveighed in the *Needed*

---

177. Doodson, *Truth of God*, pp.45-7.

178. George Adam, '"The Church of God" and "District Oversight"', *W*, 22 (1892), pp.140-2.

179. W. Laing, *The Present Crisis* (1892), cited by Park, *Churches of God*, pp.22-3.

180. 'Thomas Black', *W*, 35 (December 1905), end pp.

181. Norman Macdonald's collection, Newton Mearns: Duncan Colquhoun *et al.*, 'To overseeing brethren gathered into the name of the Lord Jesus Christ in Vancouver, 4 September 1893', typescript copy; J. R. C[aldwell]., 'The test question', *W*, 22 (October 1892), pp.164-5; Marshall, *Holding Fast*, p.12: neither Caldwell nor Marshall mention Greenock by name, but it is clearly the events there to which reference is being made. In Colquhoun *et al.*, there is an elision in the typescript where the excommunicated individual's name should occur; none of the other sources above mentions the protagonists who are identified in Chapman, *Hebron Hall Assembly*, pp. 37-8.

182. C[aldwell]., 'The test', p.164; Caldwell clearly doubted the merits of the charges.

183. Colquhoun *et. al.*, 'To...Vancouver'; MS copies of these letters are still preserved in a ledger in the possession of the Church of God, Greenock. I am indebted to Mr Gordon Farquhar for this information.

184. Boswell, 'The kingdom present', pp.145- 4.

185. Colquhoun *et. al.*, 'To...Vancouver'.

Truth against the 'great and increasing evils of Open Brethrenism'.[186] As one justification for their action, the seceders in Glasgow cited the existence of 'non-eternity' meetings.[187] Until 1894, 150 schisms took place throughout Britain, and the seventy divisions in Scotland were proportionally higher.[188] The faithful now had to 'outpurge' themselves from evil.[189]

The seceders took the formal name Churches of God (although they were popularly called 'the Needed Truth') and claimed to be the House of God in an area where Christ's will could alone be known and recognised. The new body developed into linked groups of churches governed by a hierarchy of oversights. They avoided the independency of the Open Brethren which, along with other churches was seen as 'Babylon', a system of human religion.[190] John Brown later remarked, 'We expected to carry all Scotland with us.'[191] But even if the estimate that a tenth of the Scottish Open Brethren membership seceded is correct, they failed to draw off anything like the numbers for which they had hoped:[192] only one Scottish evangelist, Frank Vernal of Ayr, defected.[193] There were a number of reasons why more did not leave. Henry Elson, an itinerant from Portsmouth who had seceded, was worried because of the stories concerning local incidents and alleged misconduct which were circulating. In his pamphlet *The Cause of the Separation* (1893) he reasserted the primacy of ecclesiology in the division.[194] Perhaps the initial schism at Greenock and other local troubles elsewhere had muddied the waters for some. Other reasons for not seceding were probably those cited by Thomas McLaren when he discussed those wavering: they felt that they still kept to the 'old paths'; their meeting

---

186. J. A. Boswell to 'my dear Brother in Christ', 14 November, 1892, quoted in *idem*, 'Open position', pp.77-8; *idem*, 'Take heed how ye hear', *NT*, 5 (1892-3), pp.45-9; if the chronology in the typescript of Colquhoun *et. al.*, 'To...Vancouver' is accepted (that Black was excommunicated in 'Feb. 1892'), then it is not clear why Boswell waited eight months, nor why Caldwell waited a similar time before publishing a denunciation. It is possible there has been a copyist's error.

187. W. Paterson *et al.*, in Chamings (compiler), 'Papers and Letters', p.23.

188. *Ibid.*, p.23.

189. McLaren Jnr, *Why I Left*, p.18; this expression was based on 2 Tim. 2: 20-1.

190. For the later development of the Churches of God see, Macdonald, 'Needed Truth Brethren', pp.25-75; C. A. Oxley, 'The "Needed Truth" Assemblies', *CBRFJ*, No.4 (April 1964), pp.21-32; Park, *Churches of God*, pp.27-68; and Willis and Wilson, 'Churches of God', pp.250-84.

191. Bruce to the writer, 26 April 1987, quoted in 'Scottish Brethren', p.31.

192. Macdonald, 'Needed Truth Brethren', p.23.

193. The same was true in England: of the five *Needed Truth* founding editors, only two, C. M. Luxmoore and John Brown, seceded and the latter later returned (see below, pp.211-12).

194. Henry Elson, *The Cause of the Separation* (London [1893]).

was not an open one; reform should be achieved from within; 'looseness' did not merit secession; and division was wrong.[195] Factors such as these probably explain the relative failure of the Churches of God to establish themselves in the north east.[196] According to Boswell, only in Aberdeen were Open tenets accepted but the leading Brethren in the north successfully shut out the Churches of God advocates during the Separation.[197] The assemblies in the region prided themselves in being preserved from the 'extremes of laxity and sectarian narrowness'.[198] They had no 'looser' practices from which to outpurge themselves.[199]

Others like Caldwell had the painful task of revising their thinking, something he compared to a schoolboy getting a sum wrong and having to work through the problem to find the point of departure.[200] He returned to his former open views of reception to the Lord's table. But for many others the Rubicon which they would not cross had been the powers granted to district oversights. This had been the case for George Adam, a former member of the Old Scots Independents, who reasserted a mystical conception of Christ's rule.[201] 'A uniformity of action may be brought about by an ecclesiastical combination,' he wrote 'but a oneness of mind and judgment, produced by the Lord Jesus being enthroned in every heart, is fundamentally a different thing.'[202] Unanimity was divinely produced whereas organisation was merely a human device. A charismatic conception of Christian unity had been reasserted against the more institutionalised procedures of the Churches of God.

---

195. McLaren Jnr, *Why I left*, pp.14-25; 'old paths' is a quotation of Jer. 6:16.

196. Churches of God came into existence in: Aberdeen, Boddam, Elgin, Cuminestown, Macduff and Orton: Neil Dickson, 'Open and closed: Brethren and their origins in the North East', in James Porter (ed.), *After Columba—After Calvin: religious community in North-East Scotland* (Aberdeen, 1999), p.168 n.61.

197. Boswell, 'Open position' p.75.

198. *BM*, 3 (1893), p.23.

199. Boswell, 'Open position' p.75; Bruce to the writer, 26 April 1987, quoted in Dickson, 'Scottish Brethren', p.31. Most probably this was also the reason for the lack of success of the Churches of God in Ulster where only two congregations were formed.

200. Caldwell, *Gathering and Receiving*, p.7.

201. For George Adam, see *W*, 18 (May 1888), p.vi; 'George Adam', *BM*, 17 (1907), p.60; 'George Adam', *CW*, 26 (1911), pp.114-5; 'George Adam', *W*, 60 (1930), p.15.

202. A[dam]., 'church government', (1891), p.55.

Holding Fast

One frequent complaint about the secessionists concerned the manner in which they had proselytised.[203] When the Edinburgh solicitor Ludovic W. G. Alexander, a later editor of *Needed Truth*, returned to the Open Brethren in 1906 he complained that many in the Churches of God were preoccupied with the supposed perfection of their ecclesiology, 'consequently a spirit of self-sufficiency is engendered, allied to a resting and glorying in their system, which is only equalled by the intolerance manifested towards any who dare to question those claims'.[204] Admittedly, such criticisms came from their opponents, but perhaps this was a further reason why many who were sympathetic did not join. Certainly the new movement continued to have schisms which suggested that the rebellious personality type was well represented among them. The largest of these secessions was in 1905 when Frank Vernal took most of the Scottish members with him over objections to the powers being granted to higher circles of overseers which enabled them to overrule decisions made at a lower level. The secessionists founded separate Churches of God that were popularly called 'the Vernalites'.[205] In some places quite sizable groups rejoined the Open Brethren.[206] John Brown too returned in 1905, apparently over the discipline which was to be imposed upon him after being declared bankrupt.[207] He proclaimed the Churches of God 'a fiasco'.[208] Most of the leaders who rejoined, such as Alexander, became advocates of more open practices, but Brown was

---

203. W. H. S[tancomb]., 'Independency', *W*, 21 (1891), p.41; W. H. B[ennet]., 'A warning from history', *ibid.*, p.82; A[dam]., '"The Church of God"', p.141; Caldwell, *Gathering and Receiving*, p.29; Bruce to the writer, 8 June 1987.

204. L. W. G. Alexander, *Discerning the Body* (Glasgow, 1907), pp.19-20; cf. Macdonald, 'Needed Truth Brethren', p.38-9.

205. Doodson, *Truth of God*, pp.55-63; Macdonald, 'Needed Truth Brethren', pp.44-8; Park, *Churches of God*, pp.27-8.

206. E.g., Edinburgh (Boswell to 'My...Brother', quoted in *idem*, 'Open position', pp.77-8); Govan (*BM*, 17 (May 1907), end pp.); Musselburgh (*W*, 37 (1907), p.184); Ayr (*BM*, 19 (February 1910), p.iv); Orton, Moray (*W*, 36 (March 1906) end pp.; and examples cited in Macdonald, 'Needed Truth Brethren', p.37-42.

207. Park, *Churches of God*, p.85; Macdonald, 'Needed Truth Brethren', p.39, is sceptical that bankruptcy alone was the cause for Brown's return and feels that there must have been doctrinal causes. Brown apparently thought that views which were more extreme than he had intended had pushed his principles too far, something he reputedly blamed on 'some of the brethren from Armagh' (William Gilmore, *These Seventy Years* (Kilmarnock [*c*.1952]), pp.51-2). However, F. F. Bruce noted that Brown retained many of the Churches of God principles in later life (Bruce to the writer, 8 June 1987). For Open Brethren attitudes to bankruptcy, see below, p.298.

208. Bruce to the writer, 8 June 1987: Brown also claimed that the Exclusives were 'a fraud' and the Open Brethren 'a failure'.

typical of others in that he maintained stricter (and, in his case, idiosyncratic) views.[209]

In 1901 when W. Blair Neatby wrote his *A History of the Plymouth Brethren*, he reported that those Open Brethren who 'are to the full as narrow and intolerant as the Exclusives at their worst' were strong in the north of England and Scotland.[210] The teaching of those who returned from the Churches of God and retained their narrower views, allied with the many remaining within Open Brethren assemblies who were sympathetic to aspects of *Needed Truth* teaching, meant that a separatist ecclesiology would continue to be promoted. One individual who had been expected to become a leader in the secession was John Ritchie.[211] But in 1889 at a conference in Glasgow he had spoken on Ahab, Elijah and Obadiah, examples of the 'broad man', the 'narrow man' and the 'middle man' respectively.[212] He evidently had begun to see himself as the last. When he founded *The Believer's Magazine* in 1891, he later claimed, it was because other magazines 'had changed their character and line of testimony'.[213] This was probably an allusion to the teaching on district oversights being adopted by *Needed Truth* writers and the more open communion being promoted in *The Witness* at the time. In 1891 during an address in the Marble Hall, Glasgow, he advocated assemblies supporting each other but not 'ordered and governed by a senate of men...who issue their *judicial* findings to an unwilling people' for this would issue in 'confusion and division'.[214] On the other hand Ritchie shared the *Needed Truth* concern over the 'looseness' of much Open Brethren practice. He agreed with the teaching of Hopkins on the Church and on the need to dissociate oneself entirely from other denominations either in receiving from them or preaching in them.[215] In 1907, after a correspondence on fellowship in *The Believer's Magazine*, he argued that 'a "Church of God" is a distinct and definite local circle' and those who wished to join it must 'share its privileges and responsibilities'. Consequently individuals had to be 'in and of the assembly' and could

---

209. Bruce to the writer, 26 April 1987 and 8 June 1987. For Brown's later disciples within the Open Brethren, see below, pp.234-6.

210. W. Blair Neatby, *A History of the Plymouth Brethren*, 1st edn (London [1901]), p.327.

211. HyP[ickering]., 'Death of a contemporary', *W*, 60 (1930), p.92.

212. *W*, 19 (November 1889), p.v.

213. [John Ritchie], 'The story of 'The Believer's Magazine'—1890-1908', *BM* , 18 (December 1908), end pp.; Ritchie dated the founding of the magazine to 1890 with the enlargement of the magazine taking place in 1899: he was a year out in both these dates.

214. John Ritchie, 'The fellowship of assemblies in the work of the Lord', *W*, 21 (1891), p.88.

215. Ian McDowell's collection, Chadstone, Australia: John Ritchie to W. H. Hopkins, 7 March 1916, quoted in Dickson, 'Scottish Brethren', p.41 n.117.

not be merely received to the Lord's table: to do so would be 'lawlessness'. He clearly intended an attack on the Churches of God when he criticised 'the opposite extreme' in which, 'safeguarding themselves against being "linked" through intermediate channels with "looseness", a sectarian position has been reached, excluding all who do not pledge themselves to separate from all who do not accept it.'[216] He represented a mediating position which combined the independency of the Open Brethren with the separatism of the Churches of God. It was one which proved attractive to many in the Scottish movement.

Open conflict between the two tendencies left within the movement emerged in the Edwardian period, and separation from other Evangelicals was again the central issue. Preaching in other Christian bodies, Ritchie justly claimed, was becoming more common.[217] Formerly, he argued, links with the Brethren had not been sought by other churches because of the opprobrium with which they were regarded.[218] But the numerous independent missions which had arisen towards the end of the nineteenth century regarded assemblies favourably and used their preachers.[219] Some assemblies welcomed fellow Evangelicals as preachers. The meeting in Pollokshaws, for example, had Peter McRostie and J. G. Govan as preachers, both prominent mission hall evangelists,[220] and in their 1895 Glasgow gospel campaign David Rea and Alexander Marshall had been assisted by a mission hall pastor and a Baptist minister.[221]

In 1906 J. R. Caldwell published a retraction of his narrower views entitled *The Gathering and Receiving of the Children of God*.[222] He recalled with nostalgia the presectarian days as assemblies emerged out of Victorian revivalism when 'we boasted that if Dr. Andrew Bonar came

---

216. [John Ritchie], 'A brief review of answers on "Church fellowship"', *BM*, 17 (1907), p.96.

217. [*idem*], '"Inter-Denominational"', *BM*, 10 (1900), p.12; [*idem*] 'Editor's note', *BM*, 15 (1905), p.12.

218. J. R[itchie]., 'Sectarian evangelists in Assemblies', *BM*, 12 (1902), pp.47-8.

219. *Ibid*; John R. Caldwell, 'Our "identification" with evangelistic efforts', *W*, 26 (1896), pp.165-6.

220. [Joseph L. G. Walker], *Centenary of the Pollokshaws Assembly 1873-1973* (n.pl. [1973]), [pp.7,8]; on J. G. Govan see: I. R. Govan, *Spirit of Revival: the story of J. G. Govan and the Faith Mission*, 3rd edn (Edinburgh, 1960); and on Peter McRostie see: Ena McRostie, *The Man Who Walked Backwards* (London, 1934).

221. Tom Rea (compiler), *The Life and Labours of David Rea, Evangelist: largely written from his own MSS.* (Belfast, 1917), p.139.

222. Caldwell, *Gathering and Receiving*: a version of the pamphlet also appeared as 'The Receiving of the Children of God', *W*, 41 (1911), pp.109-110, 125-6, 141-2; earlier Caldwell had also published the anti-Churches of God pamphlet: *District Oversight Meetings: their origin and their issues. [sic] and On Increase of Knowledge* (Glasgow n.d.), both of which had also appeared as articles in *The Witness* during 1890.

into the Marble Hall to break bread we would joyfully welcome him.'[223] In the pamphlet he formalised this period into a quasi-mystical doctrine of the Church. In the early Church, Caldwell argued:

> At first it was the attraction of a divine instinct, the power of a common object, the love of a new nature begotten of God, that drew together those who were or of one heart and of one soul, and 'of the rest durst no man join himself unto them.' Daily multitudes were added on the same principle of attraction, and the world was excluded by the same principle of expulsion.

If the Spirit again worked 'in a mighty power', Caldwell argued, then 'the attraction would be the same essentially'.[224] In a review pamphlet published by Ritchie this concept was criticised by W. H. Hunter of Manchester, a non-seceding founding editor of *Needed Truth*, for its 'vague indefiniteness'.[225] Hunter alleged that Caldwell had a tone of superiority, like someone making '*ex cathedra* statements from the throne of St. Peter, or even from an editorial chair.'[226] He asserted that reception into 'the fellowship of the assembly' was a separate act in Christian experience distinct from the new birth, and that those in a denomination were rebelling against the Lordship of Christ.[227] A more concrete conception of the local congregation was being opposed to Caldwell's charismatic concept of unity.

A direct attack on Ritchie's views on separation from fellow Evangelicals was offered in 1908 by Alexander Marshall in *Holding Fast the Faithful Word*.[228] Marshall, after evangelising in North America from 1879, had returned to Scotland in 1904. Initially he had accepted the stricter views but, like Caldwell, had come back to a more open position.[229] In his pamphlet he was primarily concerned with defending

---

223. J. R. Caldwell to Alexander Marshall, 30 August 1909, quoted in Hawthorn, *Marshall*, p.138.

224. Caldwell, *Gathering and Receiving*, pp.15-16.

225. W. H. Hunter, *The Gathering and Receiving of the Children of God: a review of a recent booklet* (Kilmarnock [*c*.1906]), p.8.

226. *Ibid*., p.16.

227. *Ibid*., pp.5-7, 10-11, 14.

228. The title is taken from Titus 1:9; the pamphlet evidently appeared in 1908 as the response by the Exclusive writer Alfred H. Burton, *What is Exclusivism? a review of Mr Alex. Marshall's 'Holding Fast the Faithful Word'*, has that year on its title page and internal evidence also places *Holding Fast* in 1908 (see chronology on p.11). The version used above incorporated a page of responses to the first printing.

229. Hawthorn, *Marshall*, p.137. Apparently Marshall revised the section on the Lord's supper in his *Straight Paths for the Children of God* (Glasgow, n.d.); in the edition of this pamphlet reprinted in the 1980s by Gospel Tract Publications, pp.32-3 argue for reception to assembly fellowship, but pp.29-30 of an edition held in the Christian Brethren Archive, Manchester (possibly dating from the early twentieth century), enjoin

open communion and speaking in mission halls. The target of his polemic was *The Believer's Magazine* whose editor Marshall felt was abusing his position.[230] Ritchie maintained of individuals who preached in other denominations that if those 'who see the evil effects on young believers of such persons being allowed to appear in assemblies as their instructors *would act firmly and unitedly, they would soon cease to trouble them.*'[231] Marshall felt that this was a call to war. He evidently thought that Ritchie had schismatic tendencies at this time.[232] In 1906 during moves towards unity by an Exclusive party he felt Ritchie would be of little help, noting privately to a friend that Ritchie 'has not broken bread in his own assembly for three and a half years'.[233] In the first draft of the pamphlet Marshall had avoided attributing quotations but eventually he inserted them in order to show 'when, where and how' open principles were being departed from.[234] Marshall's rhetoric was robust. He teased Ritchie because Ritchie published and sold non-Brethren works and by citing examples of Ritchie's attendance at services conducted by preachers whom Ritchie would not receive to the Lord's table.[235] Marshall pled for liberty on 'minor matters' which he listed as 'election, free will, predestination, baptism, church government, the Lord's coming, preaching in missions, &c.'[236] Many within Scottish assemblies welcomed the pamphlet but others accused Marshall of being divisive and Ritchie received a large number of expressions of support for *The Believer's Magazine*.[237] He did not reply to Marshall but complained that the truths the journal maintained had been 'traduced by others who have departed from them.'[238]

J. R. Caldwell had supplied a preface to Marshall's pamphlet. He rejected a rigid distinction between the universal Church and a local church, the latter being 'part of the whole'.[239] But his attitude to the

reception to the Lord's table—the distinction made in arguments for closed and open communion respectively. Presumably the former reprint is an earlier edition of the latter publication.

230. Marshall, *Holding Fast*, p.28.

231 [John Ritchie], 'Answers to correspondents', *BM*, 28 (1908), p.23, quoted in Marshall *Holding Fast*, p.29 [Marshall's italics].

232. *Ibid.*, p.28.

233. CBA 2356, Alexander Marshall to G. F. Bergin, 6 November 1906.

234. Note on end pp. insert in Marshall, *Holding Fast*.

235. Marshall, *Holding Fast*, pp. 20, 38; the preachers were the evangelists D. L. Moody and John McNeil and the Exclusive Brethren member W. P. T. Wolston.

236. *Ibid.*, p.27.

237. End pp. insert in *ibid*; [John Ritchie], 'Answers to correspondents', *BM*, 28 (1908), p.142.

238. [Ritchie], '"The Believer's Magazine"'; cf. [*idem*], 'Holding fast the truth', *BM*, 16 (1906), p.93.

239. 'QA', *W*, 38 (1908), pp.194-5.

relationship between the Brethren and denominational churches was an ambivalent one. Although he would not deny communion to someone 'on the sole ground of their church connection', yet, he wrote, 'the one introduced may not see his way to a full identification with the simple mode of assembling in the Name of the Lord'.[240] The Brethren still occupied higher ground to which the person might eventually be won. Marshall listed church government as a 'minor matter', but he gave as one of his reasons for preaching in missions the fact that through such contact many of them had been led to become assemblies.[241] Against one critic he defended his right to teach Brethren ecclesiology to those converted through his evangelism.[242] Both Marshall and Caldwell cited as the ideal (doubtless partly because of the participants' subsequent careers) the 1868 mission of Hopkins and Boswell in the Orkney churches, an episode which had left the congregations they visited depleted and relations embittered.[243] Those who argued for associating with Christians outside the movement, as well as their critics, argued from the premises that the Brethren possessed truth which it was their duty to teach to others and that denominations were 'sects'. The defence of liberty for preachers was not an expression of a simple pan-Evangelical ecumenism but could become an argument for a means of proselytising.

The Faithful Word

The divisions of the period are difficult to explain on socio-economic grounds. The *Needed Truth* leaders were of the same middle-class stratum as individuals such as J. R. Caldwell. Ritchie, too, became a successful businessman. Perhaps there were some elements of an urban-rural divide—one circular letter implied that stricter practices were harder to enforce in 'country districts'.[244] Certainly it was in areas of Scotland and in the north of England where the industrial working classes were strong that the Churches of God were most readily formed and the Glasgow Church of God was present in Townhead, Govan and Cathcart Street, working-class districts of the city. Undoubtedly important for the strongly doctrinal Brethren, however, were ideological factors. Exclusive teaching was one such influence. The theology of the movement had

240. Caldwell, *Gathering and Receiving*, p.19.

241. Marshall, *Holding Fast*, p.30.

242. [Alexander Marshall], *Wandering Lights: a stricture on the doctrines and methods of Brethrenism. A review by A. M.*, 3rd edn (Glasgow, n.d.), pp.17-18.

243. Caldwell to Marshall, 30 August 1909, quoted in Hawthorn, *Marshall*, pp.137-8; Marshall, *Holding Fast*, p.23. The former source provides the epigraph to Chpt. 3, p.597, above; for Hopkins and Boswell in Orkney see above, pp.83-4.

244. W. Paterson *et al.*, in Chamings (compiler), 'Papers and Letters', p.13.

been largely shaped by them as their writers were in the nineteenth century the most prolific and systematic ones that it possessed. Although Open Brethren using their writings kept quiet about it, undoubtedly Close Brethren literature was being utilised, particularly as preachers began looking for guidance to instruct the influx of new converts.[245] Readers turning to Exclusive publications encountered arguments hammered out in controversies earlier in the century which would influence them in a sectarian direction. The priority given to being separated from ecclesiastical evil would be reinforced by these works and the concept of district oversights was probably developed from Darby's argument that the various companies in London should comprise one assembly.[246] However, Exclusive writers were not cited openly because tradition was ostensibly disavowed and the Bible was claimed as the sole authority. Due to the place given to scripture, the concept of it which informed the debate was very significant in setting attitudes and influencing the movement in a more sectarian direction. All sides in the protracted reception question had to argue a difficult case. Writers in the *Needed Truth* and *The Believer's Magazine* maintained that the New Testament distinguished between entering the Church as the Body of Christ and being received into the local church as an institution, scripture also supplying the normative pattern for the latter. Caldwell and his allies wanted to retain the charismatic unity of the early Church while agreeing that the New Testament gave a clear church order for gathered congregations.[247] Both saw scripture as providing an ecclesiological model which had to be copied.

The Bible was accepted as being fully inspired by God: *Needed Truth* commenced with an article stressing its perfection.[248] The mode of inspiration was frequently stated as being that of dictation. For Caldwell the Psalmist wrote at 'the dictation of the Spirit of God', while for Rice

---

245. See below, p.256 n.14 for an example of R. T. Hopkins echoing the language of an early Brethren writing.

246. [J. N. Darby], *Letters of J. N. D.* (Kingston-on-Thames, n.d.), 1, p. 358; 2, pp.336, 338; 3, pp.381, 432; the lack of dates for this publication does not make it possible to correlate the emergence of the teaching on district oversights with the earliest edition of the letters, although it is probable that one was circulating soon after Darby's death in 1882; however, Exclusive influence could also have reached the Open Brethren through oral means or through membership transfers.

247. J. R. Caldwell, *The Charter of the Church: revised notes of an exposition of the First Epistle to the Corinthians*, 2 vols (Glasgow [1910]); 'The congregation of true believers in the Lord Jesus', in W. Hoste and R. M'Elheran (eds), *The True Church: what is it? who compose it?* (Glasgow [c.1915]), pp.32-6.

248. W. Laing, 'The Word of God', *NT*, 1 (1888-9), pp.10-18.

Hopkins the writers were 'so many pens in the one hand'.[249] A more sophisticated view was offered by physician David Anderson-Berry.[250] He rejected mechanical dictation but argued that inspiration was the result of men's selves coming into union with God who communicated his will to them. Though the style might be the writer's 'the matter is God's and the choice of expression is His'. Inspiration was 'plenary' and 'verbal',[251] and Anderson-Berry could still use the metaphor of the Holy Spirit using 'anonymous penmen'.[252] These ideas were derived from the high views of scripture propounded by some nineteenth-century Evangelicals.[253] Colonel Molesworth cited Robert Haldane as the source of his own views,[254] and the work of the Princeton theologians B. B. Warfield and Charles Hodge evidently lay behind Anderson-Berry's opinions. He echoed their thinking, rooted in Common Sense philosophy, that Scripture consisted of a 'collection of facts'.[255] In later discussion by others the language of dictation tended to be replaced by the Princeton translation of 'inspiration' as 'God-breathed'.[256] The Bible was completely reliable, historically and scientifically.[257]

These views of scripture gave rise to a literalist biblicism. There was no place for tradition but the appeal was to scripture alone which was the only confession of faith.[258] 'Will brethren at this point', Boswell

---

249. J. R. C[aldwell]., 'Inspiration of Scripture' *NW*, 10 (1880), p.82; R. T. H[opkins]., 'Thoughts on Deuteronomy', *NW*, 12 (1882), p.33; cf. John R. Caldwell, '"The Red Heifer"', *W*, 26 (1896), p.77; A. O. Molesworth, 'The inspiration of the Holy Scriptures', *W*, 35 (1905), pp.114, 119, 120; John Ritchie, *Lectures on the Book of Daniel with expository notes on 'The Times of the Gentiles' and prophetic subjects* (Kilmarnock, 1915), p.6.

250. David Anderson-Berry M.D., LL.D., F.R.S., a son of the manse and a relative of the Duke of Hamilton, was unique among earlier Scottish Brethren for his learning.

251. D. Anderson-Berry, 'The Holy Bible the Word of God', *W*, 41 (1911), pp.80, 81.

252. *Ibid.*, p.81; D. Anderson Berry, 'The return to Bethlehem', *W*, 44 (1914), p.106.

253. D. W. Bebbington, *Evangelicalism in Modern Britain: a history from the 1730s to the 1980s* (London, 1989), pp.86-91.

254. Colonel Molesworth, 'The inspiration of the Bible', *W*, 35 (1905), pp.174.

255. D. Anderson-Berry, 'After Death', *W*, 33 (1903), p.26. In this article Anderson-Berry was discussing how doctrines are constructed from the biblical evidence, and he does so by outlining 'the laws of thought', which are clearly the contemporary method for constructing a scientific theory. The Bible is 'the collection of facts' from which doctrines must be deduced. For the Princeton doctrine of scripture, see George M. Marsden, *Fundamentalism and American Culture: the shaping of twentieth-century evangelicalism 1870-1925* (Oxford, 1980).

256. E.g., J. R. Caldwell, 'The God-breathed Bible', *W*, 50 (August 1920), pp.305-7.

257. John Ritchie Jnr., *Is the Bible the Word of God?* (Kilmarnock, 1908).

258. T. C[ochrane]., 'A word for the times', *NI*, 4 (1874), p.85; J. R. C[aldwell]., 'Tradition and the Word of God', *NW*, 10 (1880), pp.65-7; Marshall, *Holding Fast*, p.2; [John Ritchie], 'Scripture and tradition', *BM*, 19 (1909), p.102.

challenged one waverer in 1892, 'go on with the Word of God, or will they take the traditions of Open Brethren as their guide?'[259] John Ritchie commended the man who stamped on the cover of his Bible 'Enquire Within about Everything'.[260] Brethren tended to allow only practices expressly commanded in scripture. After the interruption of the morning meeting at Lochore a special discussion was held at which the principal individuals agreed that musical practices not found in scripture should cease.[261] Daily, early Bible reading was recommended as the agent of practical sanctification.[262] The emphasis on every word of scripture being from God gave rise to the characteristic Brethren sermon which linked different phrases or images throughout the Bible, as in one of John Ritchie's subject outlines:

One thing thou lackest (Mark x. 21)—Salvation
One thing I know (John ix. 25)—Assurance
One thing is needful (Luke x. 42)—Communion
One thing I do (Phil iii. 13)—Devotion.[263]

New critical approaches to scripture were rejected and developments in theology, such as R. J. Campbell's modernist New Theology, were regarded with horror.[264] To their dislike of the institutionalism and mixed communions of the churches was added deep antipathy of the religious scepticism which was widely thought to characterise them. Against these trends the Brethren stressed the essentials of conservative Protestant Evangelicalism. By the first decade of the twentieth century the words 'fundamental' or 'foundation' were widely used among them: Caldwell wrote *Foundations of the Faith* (1903) and Ritchie *Foundation Truths* (1907); in 1907 *The Believer's Magazine* carried a series entitled 'Fundamental Truths' and in 1908 The *Witness* had 'Fundamental

---

259. Boswell to 'My...Brother', quoted in *idem*, 'Open position', p.78; cf. J. A. B[oswell]., 'Willingness to obey', *NW*, 10 (1880), p.168.

260. John Ritchie, 'The Lord's Supper', *BM*, 11 (1901), p.140.

261. Oral information, 19 November 1988, from a woman who was teenager at the time.

262. John Ritchie, 'The word of God: its place in the Christian's life', *BM*, 18 (1908), p.89; *idem*, 'The Bible and its daily use', *BM*, 21 (1911), p.37; *idem*, *From Egypt to Canaan*, pp.63-6.

263. John Ritchie, 'Four "One things"', in *idem*, *500 Gospel Subjects with outlines, divisions, and notes for preachers, teachers and Christian workers* (Kilmarnock, 1904), p.33.

264. J. R. Caldwell, 'The New Theology', *W*, 37 (1907), pp.57-9; [John Ritchie], '"The New Theology" and the foundations of the faith', *BM*, 17 (1907), p.25.

Facts'.[265] In advance of the later full-blown phenomenon, the Brethren were protofundamentalists.[266]

Practices had to be legitimated from scripture. The typical Sunday pattern in many assemblies was for a morning meeting, followed by in the afternoon a Sunday school, a ministry meeting and an open-air service, and finally in the evening a gospel meeting.[267] The Brethren did not acknowledge this as a pattern inherited from the Victorian Church, but maintained, as Alexander Stewart did, that worship before service was the biblical order.[268] One writer eliminated the pragmatic case for female preaching, which maintained it should be permitted because it was successful, by arguing that 'the one safe path is the path of obedience to the Word'.[269] The Bible was treated as being canon law. This created difficulty for those who tolerated diversity of practice. At the height of the *Needed Truth* agitation, J. R. Caldwell argued that there was a difference between a biblical '*precept* and a *principle*'. The former allowed 'little room for diversity of judgment' but the application of the latter, characteristic of the 'present dispensation', might not be apprehended by some 'who far excel their judges in grace and godliness.'[270] Marshall argued that:

> Scripture does not teach that differences of judgment on minor matters constitute a sufficient ground for the refusal or exclusion of fellow-saints. If God has permitted liberty and forbidden us to judge one another, and we insist on uniformity, thereby causing division, we shall not be blameless.[271]

These writers were pleading for the acceptance of diversity. But given the premises which the Brethren had concerning the Bible, those who felt that the scriptures legislated for every eventuality perhaps had an easier case to argue. It was natural that those who sat down with an open Bible in the

265. *BM*, 17 (1907), pp.37-40, 54-5, 61-3, 74-6, 85-7, 98-100; *W*, 28 (1908), pp.10, 48-9, 62, 80-1, 98, 111-12, 128-9, 145-6, 155-6, 171-2.

266. On the link between nineteenth-century protofundamentalism and the Brethren, see Ian S. Rennie, 'Fundamentalism and the varieties of North Atlantic Evangelicalism', in Mark A. Noll *et al.* (eds), *Evangelicalism: comparative studies of popular Protestantism in North America, the British Isles, and beyond 1700-1990* (New York, 1994), pp.333-50.

267. This is the pattern of services before World War I described in Alexander Rollo, *The Story of Innerleven Assembly* (n.pl., n.d.), p.8.

268. Alexander Stewart, untitled sermon in Henry Groves *et al.*, *Addresses Delivered at a Christian Conference Held at Paisley, April, 1877 by Mr Henry Groves, Kendal; Mr Henry Dyer, Bath; Mr Alex. Stewart, Glasgow. Subject: God's Holy Word* (Paisley [1877]), p.22.

269. W. F. H. N., '"Forbid him not"', p.115.

270. John R. Caldwell, 'On differences of judgment', *W*, 29 (1891), pp.177-9.

271. Marshall, *Holding Fast*, p.27.

manner described by William Shaw might become critical of those who failed to perceive what was plainly revealed to oneself.[272] Hopkins began his pamphlet *Fellowship Among Saints: what saith the Scriptures?* by arguing that 'individuality and independence' were the marks of the sinner, but in the assembly God had made Jesus as Lord 'and as a result expecting oneness of action in the church':

> No room then is left to speak of 'agreeing to differ' or for the suggestion that some things have been left open on which scripture is silent, as in that case we would have to take a path of our own choosing or follow one chosen by another.[273]

Scripture was incapable of teaching different things to different individuals about the Church.[274] The concept of a faultless, entirely sufficient Bible encouraged the Brethren to seek the perfect ecclesiology in scripture and to see other denominations as sinful for not accepting it.[275] It also made many feel that the toleration of diversity was implausible.

Assessments

The reception question left Scottish Brethren deeply divided. Although Henry Pickering, editor of *The Witness* from 1914, included Exclusive Brethren leaders in his collection of biographical profiles, *Chief Men Among the Brethren* (1918), Churches of God seceders were omitted. Among those who remained Open Brethren, the polemics had soured relations and the two tendencies differed in what constituted a church and which practices were acceptable within it. They also differed in assessing the state of assemblies. In 1916 with modest satisfaction, Ritchie felt that, although the movement was not 'THE Pentecostal or Apostolic Church reconstructed as at the beginning', it constituted a 'remnant' which had achieved 'actual and visible separation from the religious world'. While there never was any 'hope of gaining wide influence or great numbers', God had given power for 'holding fast'.[276] Caldwell, on the other hand,

---

272. See above, p.142.

273. Hopkins, *Fellowship*, p.4.

274. *NW*, 12 (1882), p.70.

275. Cf. John Ritchie, *'The Way, Which They Call Heresy: remarks on Mr. W. Blair Neatby's book, 'A History of the Plymouth Brethren'* (Kilmarnock [*c*.1901]), p.22.

276. John Ritchie, *Lectures on the Book of Revelation: with notes on 'Things which must shortly come to pass'* (Kilmarnock, 1916), pp.62-4: this was in the course of commentating on the Church at Philadelphia which he saw as being symbolic of the Brethren movement, cf. Andrew Miller, *Short Papers on Church History*, 1 (London, 1878), pp.632-8; for the theme of restoration in Brethren historiography, see above, pp.9-11.

felt it was the controversies which had hindered assembly growth. 'In many meetings', he lamented, 'there are two parties carrying on an internal strife, grieving to the Spirit and withering to souls'.[277] He wrote to Marshall:

> Had we gone where we were invited, and received all who loved the Lord, the Spirit would not have been grieved as He has, and the meetings would have grown to hundreds instead of tens.[278]

This assessment was echoed in 1916 by L. W. G. Alexander responding to a correspondence in *The Witness* concerning why many assemblies were being discontinued. The answer, Alexander felt, was the arguments over 'Church Truth'. He maintained that 'a deeply rooted and deadly disease in the history of meetings is openly manifesting itself' and that the next quarter century would determine whether it 'is to be rooted out or whether it will ultimately paralyse and destroy a movement that has been manifestly of God.'[279]

After the mid-1870s the movement became more conservative. The radical enthusiasms associated with democratised Christian groups in a nascent stage[280] had given way to a more settled, structured body. Most obviously the process of consolidation affected the role of women and theological exploration, and in this it reflected the emerging counter-culture of conservative Evangelicalism which decisively rejected the social and theological changes which were in evidence in the mainline churches.[281] However, although influences from wider Evangelicalism, such as theories of biblical inspiration, undoubtedly found their way into the Brethren, reaction to innovations among the churches had greater implications for Presbyterianism itself.[282] Within an increasingly introverted movement, which had an eschatology that already led it to expect departure from the truth in contemporary religion,[283] internal factors had more decisive effect in producing the intensification of sectarianism. R. S. Brown, the last provost of Pollokshaws before it was incorporated into Glasgow, was a rare example of someone who was engaged in society's affairs.[284] More characteristic of the period was the

---

277. J. R. Caldwell, 'Preface', in Marshall, *Holding Fast*, p.3.
278. Caldwell to Marshall, quoted in *Hawthorn*, Marshall, p.138.
279. L. W. G. Alexander, 'Decadence or revival', *W*, 46 (1916), p.136.
280. Nathan O. Hatch, *The Democratization of American Christianity* (New Haven, CT, 1989).
281. Bebbington, *Evangelicalism*, pp.184-91.
282. G. N. M. Collins, *The Heritage of Our Fathers: the Free Church of Scotland: her origin and testimony* (Edinburgh, 1974), pp.81-161; Drummond and Bulloch, *Late Victorian Scotland*, pp.298-322; MacLeod, *The Second Disruption*.
283. See below, pp. 263-4.
284. [Walker], *Pollokshaws Assembly*, [p.6].

withdrawal from association with other Evangelicals which took place
across the movement. The Brethren were moving into a more settled
phase of church life and differing emphases which had been latent within
assemblies struggled for dominance.[285] There was a strong desire for
order and biblical texts which counselled it became familiar parlance.[286]
Exclusive Brethren literature had an influence, but views of scripture were
probably the most powerful influence in shaping the eventual outcome.
Treating the Bible as revealing the mind of a single speaker without also
seeing it as the product of various authors tended to produce uniformity
rather than diversity. Although more nuanced readings of scripture
surfaced in the arguments of Caldwell and Marshall, probably the
majority saw unanimity as mandatory. The strong sense of doctrinal
orthodoxy which the movement carried over from its Evangelical
background was a powerful factor in ensuring virtually complete
agreement. But even here some differences of opinion were permitted
and inevitably individuals varied in how rigidly they applied principles
and practices. The autonomy of each assembly also made complete
conformity difficult to produce and the ecclesiology allowed variety. The
Needed Truth party wanted tighter organisation. By reconstituting the
perfect church pattern, they maintained, Christ's presence would be
guaranteed.[287] Some institutionalisation had been inevitable in the
movement as roles were defined more precisely and as orthodoxy was
established. But, as was apparent in the Churches of God, the creation of a
formal authority structure produced a more sectarian body.[288]

The only widespread schism to affect Scottish Open Brethren was
produced by the rejection of independency.[289] However, a quasi-mystical
view of the Church and the appeal of a charismatic order made the
majority resistant to institutional regulation. Formal structures and
official roles were kept to a minimum and administratively the Open
Brethren did not develop much beyond Moberg's stage of incipient
organisation.[290] John Ritchie was the most prominent supporter of the
open platform because it gave preachers liberty to deliver their
message.[291] He wanted to preserve the earliest phase of assembly life,

285. See above, pp.86-8.
286. For examples, see above, ns 9 and 83.
287. F. Roy Coad, *A History of the Brethren Movement: its origins, its worldwide
development and its significance for the present day*, 2nd edn (Exeter, 1976), p.218 n.
288. Cf. B. R. Wilson, 'An analysis of sect development', in *idem, Patterns of
Sectarianism*, p.33.
289. Willis and Wilson, 'Churches of God', in Wilson, *Patterns of Sectarianism*,
pp.244-50.
290. Moberg, *The Church as a Social Institution*, p.119.
291. [John Ritchie], 'Answers to special questions', *BM*, 10 (1900), pp.107-8;
[*idem*], 'Answers to correspondents', *BM*, 38 (1918), p.23.

something he was probably also attempting to do—given his origins in the north east—in resisting increased contact with fellow Evangelicals. Individuals such as Caldwell and Marshall were also appealing to an earlier, presectarian phase of the movement. The argument was about history.[292] Both sides could claim to be 'holding fast'.[293] Individuals such as Ritchie always wanted mechanisms to approve and uphold the judgment of individual assemblies:[294] Marshall could taunt him with what he felt was the latter's desire to excommunicate those who preached in mission halls, but he knew that congregational autonomy made this impossible for Ritchie.[295] Independency gave the movement considerable capacity to absorb such tensions without them leading to general schism.[296]

That the Brethren movement was privileged in being the custodian of a special truth was accepted by all. However a denominationalising tendency was present in those such as Marshall. He considered church government a minor matter, maintained interdenominational contacts, and opposed the open platform because it led to less orderly services. His attitude was a more pragmatic one. Diversity continued to exist, but increased conservatism, doctrinal orthodoxy, and the location of an ideal state in history—the emergence of a reified social order—made it more difficult for all assemblies to change and innovate. Probably, as Caldwell maintained, separatism did hinder Brethren growth to some degree. It made the movement less attractive to many potential recruits who wanted to retain links with interdenominational Evangelicalism.[297] But Alexander had been unduly pessimistic in his assessment that conflict might paralyse the movement. The Brethren were about to find that they could continue to grow in the twentieth century.

---

292. See above, pp.10-12.
293. See above, pp.173, 180.
294. Editor [i.e. John Ritchie], 'Answers to special questions', *BM*, 16 (1906), p.96; [*idem*], 'Answers to correspondents', *BM*, 18 (1908), p.47.
295. Marshall, *Holding Fast*, pp.28, 29, 38.
296. Neatby, *Plymouth Brethren*, p.325, cited in Willis and Wilson, 'Churches of God', p.246.
297. For two examples of Evangelicals who did join the Brethren (probably the Exclusives) because of their separatism, see M. M. Gordon, *Hay Macdowall Grant of Arndilly: his life, labours, and teaching* (London, 1876), pp.211-12; M. C. Lees, *A Scotch Jewel Newly Set: a brief memorial sketch of Nellie Drysdale* (Edinburgh and London, 1891), p.29; I am grateful to Mrs Alison Davies for the latter reference.

CHAPTER SIX

A Hearty, Happy Band:
Growth and Ethos 1914-1965

'But show me a company of "feeble folk", with little gift, less gold, yet with hearts aglow concerning the One whose "visage was so marred more than any man" (Isa. 52.14), and the love of Christ constraining them as ambassadors for Christ to beseech men "in Christ's stead to be reconciled to God" (2 Cor. 5.20), and you will behold a hearty, happy band bringing glory to God and goodwill to men. And, thank, God, many such there are.'
Henry Pickering, '"The Lord Himself"', *The Witness*, 46 (1916), p.6.

In 1943 the future missionary George Patterson was sent to work at a mechanical engineering plant which constructed military vehicles in Portobello, East Lothian.[1] The assembly in the town was composed of about eighty individuals, the men mainly fishermen and miners, and they met in a small room above a billiard hall in the Working Men's Institute. Serious and cerebral, belonging to the '"Tight" school of thought', they regularly met for animated discussions of the Bible. Once a week a conversational Bible reading was held when, after an introductory address, the passage in question was discussed through a 'verse-by-verse debate'. During the frequent visits to assembly members' homes, 'the talk would most of the time centre in the Word... Bibles would be brought out and an impromptu "Bible-reading" would continue for hours'.[2] Absorbed in the Brethren world which was self-sufficient in its provision for the lives of the members, many assemblies in the period discussed in the present chapter were similar to the Portobello one. Bible study and evangelism were the principal leisure pursuits and even industrial problems could be a means of pursuing them. In 1921 the 'Unemployed Preachers' appeared briefly in north Ayrshire,[3] and during the General

---

1. George N. Patterson, *Patterson of Tibet: death throes of a nation* (San Diego, CA, 1998), p.57.

2. *Idem, God's Fool* (London, 1956), pp. 38-40.

3. *W*, 51 (1921), p.74; *W*, 52 (1922), p.206.

Strike of 1926 miners engaged in Bible study and evangelistic missions.[4] During the second quarter of the twentieth century the internal life of the Brethren reached its high-water mark.

Two estimates of the size of the movement were produced in the period under consideration, one in 1933 and the other in 1960. In 1924 Henry Pickering, in an article for *The Witness*, had thought that Brethren numbers were increasing on a rising tide of enthusiasm,[5] and at the time of the 1960 estimate, the individuals who produced it also felt that assembly membership was larger than ever.[6] The movement, it was felt at these two different points in the twentieth century, was increasing in size. In an attempt to establish the reality which lay behind these impressions, the present chapter will examine these estimates and perceptions through the growth of assemblies and such statistics as are available. The period will be divided into two, using the two world wars as dividing lines. This is not merely a device. Both events had major consequences for society, and, as shall become apparent, this in turn meant they would also have important results for Scottish assemblies. An additional section will analyse several significant aspects of Brethren life and examine the ethos of the movement at a time when, as we have seen, contemporaries felt meetings were at their strongest. In an era when mainline churches were beginning to decline numerically, it will become clear that Scottish Brethren demonstrated several differences and similarities.

Growth 1914-39

Thinking that the Great War was sending millions of young men to hell apparently undermined the health of the Churches of God evangelist Frank Vernal and contributed to his early death.[7] The conflict gave the Brethren fresh incentive to evangelise.[8] Special tracts were issued and evangelists and assemblies attempted to take advantage of the large number of men brought together in the army.[9] Alexander Marshall spent

---

4. Oral information, 10 August 1997, from a Brethren member born into a mining community; writer's collection, I.L.2, W. Dunning, 'Assemblies in the South of Scotland. 1908-1947. Gatehouse of Fleet', typescript [1988].

5. HyP[ickering]., 'WW', *W*, 54 (1924), p.384.

6. See below, p.199.

7. J. J. Park, *The Churches of God: their origin and development in the 20th Century* (Leicester, 1987), p.28; Vernal had been an Open Brethren evangelist from 1888 until 1892.

8. For other Brethren attitudes to the war, see below, pp.220-7, 316-17.

9. *BM*, 24 (1914), p.120; *BM*, 24 (September 1914), pp.i, iv; 'Sergeant McAllister's Story', *HS*, 39 (January 1917); *BM*, 25 (January 1915), p.i; Alexander Rollo, *The Story of Innerleven Assembly* (n.p., n.d.), pp.11-12.

the war using the opportunities it provided for evangelism, visiting the German internment camps in Holland where he addressed the British prisoners of war and in 1918 spending several months at the front in France under the auspices of the Soldiers' Christian Association.[10] It was for his work with this last organisation during the war that James Anderson, a former missionary, was awarded an MBE.[11] Assemblies were formed at Nigg, Easter Ross (see Map 3),[12] Gretna, Dumfriesshire (see Map 14),[13] and, during the war probably, at Rosyth, Fife (see Map 7),[14] where naval bases with large concentrations of men—Brethren individuals among them—had come into existence. Nor was the home front neglected. In 1916 there was a brief ouburst of revivalism among some northern fisher girls who were staying at Lochee, Dundee, when some sixty to eighty of them were converted, and the following month it spilled over into the city's Hermon Hall where there were a further forty professions.[15] New assemblies were formed: in late 1914 a meeting was commenced in Old Kilpatrick, Dunbartonshire (see Map 12), where there had been a successful gospel campaign by Malcolm McKinnon two years earlier;[16] in 1915 one was formed at Livingstone Station, West Lothian (see Map 9) after evangelism by Arthur Gilmour;[17] the following year meetings were established in Golspie, Sutherland (see Map 3), aided, it seems, by the removal of a Brethren couple there,[18] and in Monifieth, Angus (see Map 6), where there had been an abortive attempt to found one before the war;[19] also probably during the war years, J. M. Nicholson succeeded in planting a second congregation on Lewis in Stornoway (see Map 3);[20] and the assemblies in Plantation Street, Glasgow (see Map 11),[21] and Chapelhall, Lanarkshire (see Map 10),[22] were founded by

---

10. John Hawthorn, *Alexander Marshall: evangelist, author and pioneer* (Glasgow [1929]), pp.142-6.

11. J. G[ray]., 'James A. Anderson, London', *BP*, 50 (1929), pp.34-6.

12. *BM*, 26 (May 1916), p.i; *BM* 38 (May 1918), p.i.

13. *BM*, 27 (May, 1917), p.i.

14. *BM*, 32 (June 1922), p.i, is the only reference to the Rosyth assembly and it was made close to its discontinuation when many were leaving the town because of reductions in the dockyards; cf. *BM*, 34 (July 1925), p.ii.

15. *W*, 46 (November 1916), p.143, end pp.; *ibid.*, (December), p.143, end pp.

16. *W*, 42 (1912), p.251; *BM*, 25 (January 1915), p.i.

17. *BM*, 25 (May 1915), p.i.

18. *W*, 46 (May 1916), p.60 endpp.

19. 'Mrs Wilson', *W*, 69 (1939), p.48; *W*, 40 (December 1910), end pp.; *BM*, 26 (August 1916), p.i.

20. *W*, 78 (1948), p.144, notes that the assembly was formed 'over 30 years ago', i.e. before 1918; cf. *W*, 49 (1919), p.145.

21. 'How it began: Harley Street, Glasgow', *BM*, 98 (1988), pp.104-5.

22. *W*, 48 (1918), p.27; however a note in *W*, 49 (1919), p.193, stated that 'Brethren of the district' had met on 25 October 1919 in Lauchope Hall, Chapelhall, to 'commend

Brethren individuals in 1915 and 1918 respectively. In 1917 an outreach by Larkhall assembly members succeeded in establishing a meeting in Ashgill.[23] Also probably during the war a small meeting was formed in Dunlop, Ayrshire (see Map 13), when Frederick Stanley Arnot's brother William began a breaking of bread service in his house[24] and further south in the county assemblies were re-formed in Ochiltree, mainly by members of Auchinleck meeting, in 1915[25] and Patna in 1918.[26] The internal conflict of the movement which had marked the early years of the century did not cease for the duration of hostilities,[27] and an additional five assemblies were formed through schism. Three of these were short-lived, which suggests that it was personalities rather than any fundamental principles which were involved. Rather different was the secession that took place in Hermon Hall, Govanhill, where it would appear there was dissatisfaction over the role of the leading elder, Fred A. Leith.[28] A dissenting group separated in 1917 to form a meeting in Dixon Halls, Govanhill,[29] and in 1920 Hermon affiliated to the Baptist Union.[30] One transfer of membership which favoured the Brethren movement was the merger of 1916 in Cowdenbeath of the town's gospel mission and its assembly.[31] Brethren continued their evangelism and concern for ecclesiological rectitude.[32]

Despite the effort, however, the war created difficulties for the movement. The conflict did not incline individuals to listen to the message the

---

them as a company': either the founding noted in January 1918 had failed or the surrounding assemblies were giving their blessing to it almost two years later. On the principle of not multiplying assemblies unnecessarily (see above p.15 n.86), the latter is the preferred solution.

23. *W*, 47 (1917), p.100.

24. 'William Arnot', *BM*, 34 (July 1925), p.v.

25. Writer's collection, I.C.6., John Hannah, interview with William Hannah, 18 April 1993, MS notes.

26. *BM*, 28 (1918), p.i; the earlier attempt to commence one in Patna had been in 1910, *BM*, 28 (May 1910), p.i.

27. See above, pp.171-5.

28. For the founding of this assembly, see above, p.125.

29. 'A. J. Fraser', *W*, 87 (1957), p.17; 'R. Hill', *W*, 96 (1966), p.116: this assembly eventually met in Victoria Hall, Govanhill.

30. Geo Yuille (ed.), *History of the Baptists in Scotland* (Glasgow, 1926), p.176: Leith had the unique position of being acclaimed in both Brethren and Baptist history as founding the same congregation.

31. Writer's collection, I.I.4., Robert Muir 'Union Hall, Broad Street, Cowdenbeath', typescript 1988; *BM*, 28 (April 1918), p.i; *W*, 48 (1918), p.27.

32. There was in addition an assembly at Stonefield, Lanarkshire, during these years (*fl.* 1916), but its cause of formation and precise date of origin are not known.

Brethren preached,[33] and in the absence of men, *The Believer's Magazine* advised, assemblies should use the sisters in inviting people to gospel meetings.[34] However, as Figures 6.1 and 6.2 suggest, membership remained fairly constant. The data in *The Witness* obituaries show fluctuations in recruitment with a growth peak in 1917 (Figure 6.1). The memberships of both Elim Hall, Glasgow, and Gospel Hall, Kilbirnie, increased slightly from 1914 until 1916 and dipped towards the end of the decade (Figure 6.2). But Figure 6.1 shows that in the early 1920s there was a marked increase in growth and further peaks on a lesser scale in the 1930s; however, it should be remembered that these data are less accurate after 1923.[35] Although during the 1930s the membership trend of three of the assemblies in Figure 6.2 was gently downwards, the inter-war years were at times favourable for Brethren growth. The membership of Kilbirnie assembly dipped in the early 1920s, probably due to out-migration—overseas emigration alone accounted for the loss of twenty-three members between 1919 and 1922; but on the other hand there was a steady number of additions, most notably in 1930 when there were on average 3.25 conversions per month (Figure 6.2).[36] The exception to much of this was Elim Hall, Crosshill, which finished the inter-war period with its highest levels of membership. Probably it had benefited in part from migration from the city centre. Three of the assemblies represented in Figure 6.2 ended the period with higher membership levels than those with which they began, and the exception, Gospel Hall, Newmilns, was reduced by only two individuals. Certainly by the end of the inter-war period growth was slowing considerably and complaints were being made that recruitment had ceased in many places.[37] But the evidence of the statistics in both figures suggests that although some assemblies suffered slight numerical decline on the eve of World War II, this was offset by gains elsewhere and that in the inter-war era there was a net increase.

Other evidence also suggests overall growth. The increase around 1920 in the membership of Elim Hall was largely due to the effects of revivalism. In 1920 some 2,000 conversions were claimed for a tent mission held by Fred Elliott in the Crosshill district of Glasgow and 120 were baptised in a specially dug baptistery with many of those immersed joining Elim Hall.[38] This scale of recruitment was approaching that of the

---

33. *BM*, 24 (October 1914), p.i; *BM*, 25 (August 1915), p.i; *W*, 45 (July 1916), p.84; *BM*, 26 (September 1916), p.i.

34. [John Ritchie], 'Gospellers', *BM* 27 (1917), p.47.

35. For the explanation of *The Witness* obituaries, see above, p.16 n.89.

36. Gospel Hall, Kilbirnie, roll book, 1928-30.

37. Montague Goodman, 'Why are there so few conversions to-day?', *W*, 57 (1937), pp.29-30; W. A. Beggs to the editor, *W*, 70 (1940), p.54; cf. Patterson, *Patterson of Tibet*, p.47.

38. *W*, 50 (1920), p.328.

nineteenth century and *The Witness* declared that 'Never since the days of Moody in '74, Richard Weaver, or David Rea in his best days have we seen the same interest and power'.[39] In the early 1920s the last spontaneous community-based revival of the British mainland affected Scottish Brethren assemblies.[40] In 1921 Jock Troup, a cooper turned evangelist, was involved in a revival in Great Yarmouth among the fishing people.[41] After an unusually depressed fishing season,[42] Troup moved north to Fraserburgh in November 1921 in response to what he believed had been a heavenly vision. Vast crowds attended his meetings and the town was stirred by his preaching.[43] The revival spread to other coastal fishing communities where it tended to be guided more by ministers.[44] In Fraserburgh the awakening took place mainly in non-Presbyterian dissenting churches, and the assembly there and in other places along the coast gained substantially from increased attendance at their services and in attracting the revival converts as members.[45] Brethren evangelists were drawn by the news of events: Alexander Marshall held evangelistic services and provided teaching for the new converts in the assembly at Peterhead where the revival had been less ecstatic.[46] By early 1922 *The Believer's Magazine* was able to report (probably referring to Brethren activity in each place) a 'general awakening' in Portessie, Peterhead, Fraserburgh, and Wick which was affecting many meetings elsewhere.[47]

The fishermen's revival led to the formation of new assemblies. The evangelist David Walker saw a large number of converts among the fishingfolk of Whinneyfold, Aberdeenshire (see Map 5), in the winter of 1921-2 and a meeting was formed there in 1923.[48] An evangelistic mission in 1925 by Murdo McKenzie also led to the planting of one at Hopeman, Moray (see Map 4),[49] and possibly the revivalist atmosphere in

---

39. *W*, 50 (August, 1930), p.315.

40. Donald E. Meek, 'Fishers of men': the 1921 religious revival, its cause, context and transmission', in James Porter (ed.), *After Columba—After Calvin: religious community in North-East Scotland* (Aberdeen, 1999), pp.135-42.

41. J. A. Stewart, *Our Beloved Jock* (Asheville, NC, 1964), p.8; Stanley C. Griffin, *A Forgotten Revival: East Anglia and NE Scotland—1921* (Bromley [1992]).

42. J. L. Duthie, 'The fisherman's religious revival', *History Today* (December, 1983), pp.23-4.

43. Griffen, *Forgotten Revival*, pp.67-8.

44. Duthie, 'Fisherman's Revival', p.25.

45. [William Noble], 'How it began: Fraserburgh', *BM*, 99 (1989), p.182.

46. Hawthorn, *Marshall*, p.151; Alex Marshall to the editor, 14 January 1922, *W*, 52 (1922), pp.166-7.

47. *BM*, 32 (January 1922), p.ii.

48. *W*, 52 (1922), pp.166-7; *W*, 76 (1946), pp.24-50; photograph of converts in Alex Stewart's collection, Hopeman, [Alex. Stewart (compiler)], 'A Record of Gospel Work. Christian Brethren. Moray & Nairn', MS, n.d.; *BM*, 33 (August 1923), p.i.

49. *BM*, 34 (February 1925) p.ii.

the fishing villages was a factor in the formation of the small assembly which existed at Cairnbulg near Fraserburgh (see Map 5) in 1927.[50] In Caithness, Angus Swanson, a Church of Scotland lay reader in Wick (see Map 3), who had been converted in 1919 through the Pilgrim Preachers—an organisation of revivalist itinerants founded in England by two Brethren individuals[51]—resigned his church membership after evangelising alongside Troup. When the two men were about to enrol as students at the Bible Training Institute, Glasgow, Swanson returned to Wick where he met two Brethren evangelists. In 1923 he and nine teenagers, who had also been influenced by the revival, began breaking bread.[52] Further south in St Monance, Fife (see Map 7), the same pattern of revival producing dissatisfaction with the institutional church was repeated. In the winter of 1921 some fishermen from the village had been trapped in the harbour at Great Yarmouth due to heavy gales, and a number of them were converted in the revival. Back in St Monance many of them went to the Congregational Church which had as its minister James Thomson, a former Brethren missionary.[53] In addition some of the fishermen had forged links with the movement when in various herring-fishing ports and three of them had joined the St Andrews assembly.[54] In 1923 when the evangelist Jack Roberts held a mission in St Monans, he taught Brethren ecclesiology, and the following year a meeting was established.[55]

The industrial troubles of 1921, it was lamented, 'do not induce large audiences...especially in mining districts'.[56] But many assemblies—particularly those with a mining constituency—found the early 1920s a fruitful time for recruitment. The membership of the one in Coatdyke, Lanarkshire, was doubled after a six-week mission by John McAlpine, commenced in November 1920, during which there were seventy conversions and twenty-eight baptisms,[57] while after a seven-week mission by Henry Steedman begun in the same month, the meeting in Shotts had

---

50. *W*, 57 (1927), p.76.

51. John W. Newton, *The Story of the Pilgrim Preachers: and their 24 tours throughout Britain with many stirring scenes, genuine conversions, peculiar positions, and soul-stirring experiences* (London [1938]).

52. Angus Swanson, 'Our heritage', *BM*, 82 (1972), pp.91-2; cf. *W*, 53 (1923), p.86; *H*, 1 (1923-4), p.82; 'Angus Swanson', *BM*, 100 (1990), p.121.

53. Oral information, 9 May 1987, from a former assembly member; cf. W. T. Stunt *et al.*, *Turning the World Upside down: a century of missionary endeavour*, 2nd edn (Bath, 1973), p.618.

54. 'How it began: St Monans', *BM*, 99 (1989), p.36; cf. *W*, 52 (July 1922), p.218.

55. *H*, 1 (1923-4), p.34; *W*, 54 (1924), p.407.

56. *BM*, 31 (June 1921), p.i.

57. *W*, 51 (1921), p.1; James McLachlan, *Ebenezer Hall Coatdyke* (n.p. [1946]), pp.11-12.

twenty added to it.[58] In 1921 the Brethren in Aberdeen witnessed emotional scenes in advance of the Moray coast revival when audiences of 2,000 on Sunday evenings and 6 to 700 at weeknight meetings attended an evangelistic campaign by two English evangelists.[59] The Irish missionary Tom Rea prolonged his stay in the city due to "'Christians singing, weeping, praying'",[60] and during Fred Elliott's tent mission in the spring there were a number of conversions, especially of men, with an estimated 2,500 present when he preached at its conclusion.[61] In 1924 Edinburgh Brethren saw their largest audiences since the 1890s when Rea had a mission at Bellevue Chapel and some thirty converts were made.[62] According to *The Witness* data, the peak years for Brethren growth in the immediate post-war period were 1921 and 1925 (Figure 6.1).[63] It was in this last year, for example, that forty individuals joined the meeting in Glengarnock, Ayrshire, after a mission by James Barrie,[64] while Cowdenbeath assembly had fifty new members added.[65]

The inter-war period remained relatively favourable for the formation of assemblies through evangelism. They had institutionalised awakenings in their evangelistic methods and were able to take advantage of factors, such as the troubled social and economic conditions of the period, conducive to advancing revivalism.[66] There was increased concern to establish the movement in virgin territory. In 1923 a new magazine, *The Harvester*, was founded as part of a move to publicise information about evangelism in districts with few assemblies,[67] and the following year an association entitled the Unreached Parts of Scotland was formed which organised support for evangelists, initially for those working in the northern Highlands and Argyll but later including the south west and Borders.[68] These events followed some success which had been achieved in the north-eastern Highlands when assemblies had been formed amongst scenes of revivalist fervour and some opposition in 1923 at

---

58. *W*, 51 (1921), p.14.
59. *Ibid.*, pp.37-8.
60. *Ibid.*, p.50.
61. *Ibid.*, p.74.
62. *H*, 2 (1923-4), p.136.
63. On 1925 cf. J. H., 'Half-Yearly Meetings of Christians', *W*, 55 (1925), p.215.
64. *W*, 55 (1925), p.76.
65. *H*, 2, (1925), p.79.
66. Cf. above, p.123.
67. J. A. J[udson]., 'Editorial', *H*, 1 (1923-4), p.26; 'Gordon Norie Davidson', *W*, 80 (1950), p.168. There had been, in addition, a short-lived newsletter, *Report of Pioneer Gospel Work in Scotland*, which was probably absorbed by the the new magazine; however, the publication in England of *The Harvester* told against it being used by Scottish Brethren to publicise their activities and by 1930 such news had virtually disappeared from it.
68. *H*, 1 (1923-4), pp.132-3, 157, 182-3; *W*, 56 (1926), p.260.

Embo, Brora, and Helmsdale, and the recently formed one in Golspie enjoyed some expansion (see Map 3).[69] Also during this period, slightly further south in Easter Ross, the evangelist George Bond broke bread in his house at Invergordon.[70] In Argyll the assembly had been re-formed in Campbeltown in 1919 when John Craig, a member of the Girvan meeting who had done his war service in the Royal Flying Corps at Campbeltown, moved there to establish a business.[71] Evangelism along the coast produced additional assemblies among the fishermen of Carradale in 1925[72] and Ardrishaig in 1929 where the removal of a Brethren individual to establish a business in the village assisted the process.[73] Two coastal communities in the south-west (see Map 14) also had assemblies formed in them: Port William meeting was re-formed in 1922 after a mission,[74] and the Kirkcudbright one was founded in 1933 after evangelism.[75] The Borders also received some attention and in 1928 a meeting was planted in Biggar, Lanarkshire (see Map 10), after a series of missions,[76] and one was re-formed at Moffat, Dumfriesshire (see Map 14), during a visit in 1931 of several evangelists with a gospel car.[77] There were, in addition, as a result of evangelism, assemblies founded on the islands of Trondra, Shetland (see Map 1), in 1924,[78] and re-formed on Papa Westray, Orkney (see Map 2), in 1933.[79] However, despite the energy expended on 'Unreached Parts', it was the industrial Lowlands in which Brethren missions created new assemblies most easily and some

69. *W*, 52 (1922), p.254; *H*, 1 (1923-4), pp.34-5, 61; Mr A. Stewart's collection, Hopeman, Moray: Mrs Murdo McKenzie to Alex Stewart, 14 February 1975, in [Alex Stewart (compiler)], 'A Record of Gospel Work. Christian Brethren. Moray & Nairn', MS, n.d.; *W*, 53 (1923), p.53.

70. *W*, 58 (1928), p.376; *W*, 60 (1930), p.214; *W*, 63 (1933), p.144.

71. *BM*, 29 (June 1919), p.i; *H*, 1 (1923-4), p.155; 'John Craig J.P.', *W*, 97 (1967), p.315; writer's collection, I.K.1., R. H. Craig to the writer, 4 July 1988; and 27 January 1989.

72. *H*, 2 (1924), pp.44-5, 107; *W*, 55 (1925), p.136.

73. *W*, 58 (1928), p.337; *W*, 59 (1929), p.120; 'William Holden', *BM*, 90 (1980), p.384.

74. *Report of Pioneer Gospel Work in Scotland*, No. 2 (November 1922), p.4; *W*, 52 (1922), p.242.

75. *W*, 63 (1933), p.192; it is possible that an assembly existed briefly in Whithorn, Wigtownshire, about 1924: *W, 54* (1924), p.247, noted a conference being held there, but perhaps it was for recent converts in the surrounding area; cf. *Report of Pioneer Gospel Work in Scotland*, No. 2 (November 1922), p. 4.

76. *BM*, 34 (September 1925), p.i; *W*, 56 (1926), p.396; *W*, 58 (1928), p.456.

77. *W*, 61 (1931), p.264.

78. *BM*, 34 (November 1924), pp.i-ii; *BM*, 34 (April 1924), p.i; *H*, 1 (1923-4), p.225.

79. *W*, 63 (1933), p.117; writer's collection, I.P.3., [Michael Browne], 'How It All Began—Papa Westray, Orkney', typescript [1977/8/9].

fourteen were formed in the region in this way.[80] Here, too, existing congregations were most readily able to plant further ones in neighbouring communities and at least thirteen additional meetings were established by this means.[81]

The Brethren also continued to attract members of other churches. The conversionism of the movement remained potent at a time when the mainline churches were competing in the provision of secular leisure.[82]

---

80. These were: Fife (see Map 7): Culross (1921): *BM*, 31 (June 1921), p.i; Kincardine (1922): *W*, 52 (1922), p.206; Methilhill (1933): Rollo, *Innerleven Assembly*, p.11; Stirlingshire (see Map 9): Denny (1935): *W*, 65 (1935), pp.261-2, 264; writer's collection, I.U.2., A. Comrie to the writer, March 1989; Kilsyth (refounded 1920): *W*, 50 (1920), p.242; Maddiston (1922): *W*, 52 (1922), p.254; writer's collection, I.U.4. Alexander Smith to the writer, 10 July 1989; Mid Lothian (see Map 8): Bonnyrigg (1928): *W*, 58 (1928), p.297; Gorebridge (c. 1928): *BM*, 38 (1928), p.i; West Lothian (see Map 9): Blackburn (1920): *W*, 50 (1920), p.336; writer's collection, I.N.2., Sam Thomson to the writer, 19 June 1988; Lanarkshire (see Map 10): Tannochside (1934): *W*, 64 (1934), p.237; Quarter (1921): *W*, 51 (1921), p.85; Glasgow (see Map 11 no. 19): New Central Tabernacle, George St. (1923): *W*, 53 (1923), pp.226-7; 'William Tytler', *W*, 60 (1930), p.168 (however, this congregation developed into an independent mission which joined the Elim Pentecostal Church in 1927); Ayrshire (see Map 13): Cumnock (1920): *BM*, 30 (October 1920), p.i; Hurlford (1933): *W*, 63 (1933), pp.213, 237.

Brethren individuals probably already lived in several of the above places: e.g. Denny (see next paragraph below). Kilsyth, Cumnock and Hurlford assemblies were re-formations; in addition, Loanhead assembly had originated in Bonnyrigg.

81. These were: Fife (see Map 7): Glencraig (1931): *W*, 61 (1931), p.236; Edinburgh (see Map 8, inset): Granton (1920s): 'George Wilson', *W*, 85 (1955), p.54; Stirlingshire (see Map 9): Falkirk (1937): *W*, 67 (1937), p.264; Lanarkshire (see Map 10): Bishopbriggs (1939): *W*, 69 (1939), p.260; Gavin McGregor, *The Bishopbriggs Assembly 1939-1989: the first fifty years* (n.p. [1989]); Bothwellhaugh (1921): *W*, 51 (1921), p.134; writer's collection, I.M.4. (i), David L. Cook to the writer 21 September, 1992, *ibid.*, L.4. (ii), M.A. Crooks, 'Relating the Commencement of the Gospel Effort in Bothwellhaugh', photocopy of holograph transcript, n.d.; Calderbank (1923): *W*, 53 (1923), p.4; Glassford (1922): oral information, 3 May 1987, from an assembly member; Glenboig (1938): *W*, 68 (1938), p.117; Holytown (1927): *W*, 27 (1927), p.56; writer's collection, I.M.15., Brian Young, untitled history of Holytown assembly, MS, 1988; Dunbartonshire (see Map 11): Hermon Hall, Clydebank (1931): *W*, 61 (1931), p.92; Renfrewshire (see Map 11): Newton Mearns (1930): *W*, 60 (1930), p.192; writer's collection, I.J.4., S. Bolton, 'A Short History of Newton Mearns Assembly', photocopy of MS, 1978; Ayrshire (see Map 13): Glenburn, Prestwick (1929): *W*, 59 (1929), p.238; writer's collection, I.C.4., John McCloy, '"O Glenburn Greatly Favoured", 1929-1959', typescript [1996]; Tarbolton (1922): 'James Frew', *W*, 46 (1937), p.140; oral information, 30 April, 1986, from a former assembly member.

Of the above, Falkirk, Bishopbriggs, Holytown, Newton Mearns and Tarbolton were re-formations.

82. Callum G. Brown, *The Social History of Religion in Scotland Since 1730* (London, 1987), pp.182-4.

One Brethren convert from a mining village with the nearest church five miles distant complained that his erstwhile minister was 'a man of the world, played golf most week days, had whist drives in his Kirk, and was as dark on eternal things as we were ourselves.'[83] A former pastor of Gourock Baptist church, Michael Grant, who had demitted his charge in 1915 after becoming dissatisfied with his ministerial role, joined the movement in 1921 and became an evangelist,[84] and his brother Edward, also a Baptist pastor, acted similarly about 1930.[85] Once more, it was from those churches which had most in common with the Brethren that large-scale transfers of membership came. The Ratho Baptist church had held an outreach about 1920 in the nearby village of Kirknewton and it had led to a regular gospel meeting there. The preaching supply at Kirknewton (see Map 8) was drawn from nearby Brethren meetings and in 1924 an assembly was formed out of the converts.[86] The meeting which was formed in Denny (see Map 9) after a mission in 1935 had as its nucleus a group who had left the Baptist church for Camelon assembly.[87] Several Exclusive Brethren congregations also transferred to the Open Brethren in the inter-war period. In Pitlochry the Glanton Party meeting associated with the Open movement in the 1930s,[88] and three Stuart Party assemblies transferred to the Open Brethren: the one in Fort William evolved into an Open meeting over the period 1919-22;[89] and Gospel Hall, Carluke, and Albion Hall, Larkhall, were accepted as Open Brethren in the 1930s.[90] It was, however, principally members of gospel missions who were attracted to the movement. In Fife (see Map 7) some members of the Railway Mission in Kettlebridge and of Pitlessie assembly used the former Railway Mission hall in Ladybank to form an assembly there in 1920.[91] The Miller Hall, Falkirk, lost about one third of its

---

83. *BM*, 34 (June 1924), p.v.

84. M. H. Grant, *Twice Delivered* ([1935]) rpt (Glasgow, n.d.); 'Michael H. Grant', *BM*, 68 (1958), p.264; Yuille (ed.), *Baptists in Scotland*, p.283.

85. 'Edward Hotchiss Grant (1894-1979)', in James Anderson (ed.), *They Finished Their Course* (Kilmarnock, 1980), pp.77-9; E. H. Grant had been pastor for a time at Hermon Baptist Church, Govanhill, the former assembly: Yuille (ed.), *Baptists in Scotland*, p.282.

86. Writer's collection, I.N.4., David Taylor to the writer, 13 April 1989; *BM*, 34 (May 1934), p.i.

87. Writer's collection, I.U.2., A. Comrie to the writer, March 1989; *W*, 65 (1935), pp.261-2, 264.

88. Oral information, 6 October 1994, from a Highland assembly member.

89. The process was evidently complete by 1922 when Fort William assembly was included in *List of Some Assemblies in the British Isles...* (London, 1922).

90. Oral information, 22 November 1988, from a Lanarkshire assembly member involved in the recognition process; for Exclusive parties, see above, pp.2-4.

members when in 1937 an assembly was re-formed in the town.[92] In Lanarkshire gospel missions in 1927 in Baillieston,[93] in 1935 in Salsburgh,[94] and in 1938 in Coatbridge[95] formed meetings. In Glasgow and Renfrewshire the process was well established, and the City Temple, Bedford Street, in 1923,[96] Johnstone Evangelistic Association, in 1925,[97] Sharon Hall, Ibrox, in 1937,[98] and Tabernacle Gospel Hall, Shettleston, in 1938[99] were accepted into the movement.[100]

This continued formation of assemblies suggests that membership remained high during the inter-war period. There were probably at least a further nine meetings formed during this period whose causes of origin are not known.[101] Out-migration of assembly members also led to new assemblies. Some twelve congregations, a few in northern Scotland but mainly in the industrial Lowlands, were created in this manner.[102] The

91. Writer's collection, I.I.8. (i). Catherine C. Bell to the writer, 1 April 1988; 8. (ii)., [Mr R. Mackay], untitled MS, n.d.; *ibid.*, I.I.8.(iii). Mr R. Mackay to the writer, 3 March 1988; and 9 April 1988; *BM*, 30 (July 1920), p.i.

92. Sally Herring, 'Dissent in Scotland', in Peter L. Sissons, *The Social Significance of Church Membership in the Burgh of Falkirk* (Edinburgh, 1973), pp.343-4.

93. Writer's collection, I.M.2., William S. Hutchinson, 'Baillieston Gospel Hall Assembly', typescript, 1988; *H*, 4 (1927), p.72.

94. Writer's collection, I.M.25., E. Long to the writer, 28 August 1988; *W*, 65 (1935), p.264.

95. Writer's Collection, I.M.9., Andrew Leggat, 'Hebron Hall, 20/22 Church St., Coatbridge', MS 1989.

96. *W*, 53 (1923), pp.226-7; 'Joseph A. Mitchell', *W*, 83 (1953), p.13; upon joining the Brethren this congregation changed its name to Bedford Hall (see Map 11, no.39).

97. *W*, 55 (1925), p.77.

98. *W*, 67 (1937), p.216, (see Map 11, no.36).

99. *W*, 68 (1938), p.288.

100. For attitudes to transfers from other Christian bodies in this period, see below, pp.232-3.

101. These were: Perthshire (see Map 3): Pitlochry (1933): *W*, 63 (1933), p.144; Angus (see Map 6): Broughty Ferry (by 1940): *W*, 70 (1940), p.44; Fife (see Map 7): Crossgates (by 1929): *W*, 59 (1929), p.47; East & Mid Lothian (see Map 8): Dunbar (1933): *W*, 63 (1933), p.117; Musselburgh (1923): *W*, 53 (1923), p.106; Ormiston (1924): *W*, 55 (1925), p.19; West Lothian (see Map 9): Westfield (1935): *W*, 65 (1935), p.264; Stirlingshire (see Map 9): Plean (1923): *W*, 53 (1923), p.28; Glasgow (see Map 11 no.16): Claremont Hall, Argyle St. (1930): *Post Office Glasgow Directory for 1930-1931* (Glasgow, 1930), p.178.

Of the above, Musselburgh and Pitlochry were re-formations; the latter assembly was a different one from that discussed above, p.194; in addition the meetings in Portmahomack, Tranent, Fallin, California, Cobbinshaw and Mossend, first mentioned in the 1921 address list, were possibly formed before World War I, see p.131 n.293.

102. These were: Highlands (see Map 3): Mallaig (c.1937): *W*, 67 (1937), p.213; 'Mrs William Simpson', *W*, 92 (1962), p.196; 'William Simpson', *W*, 93 (1963), p.76; Munlochy (1924): 'David Millar', *W*, 97 (1967), p.35; oral information, 2 April 1989,

mobility of fishermen had been an additional factor in the spread of the movement among their communities, and the migration of people in search of employment had a similar effect in diffusing the Brethren geographically. This cause in the planting of further assemblies makes explicit the social change which created favourable conditions for Brethren growth. The post-war mood was conducive to the advancement of a conversionist sect. By the years around 1930 the Brethren in Scotland were at their strongest numerically. The growth of the previous eighty years had increased the size of the membership and autogenous growth from among the relatively large families which were still the social norm had a similar effect. Geographically meetings were dispersed throughout Scotland and there was scarcely a community of substantial population in the Lowlands which did not have one. Even in Shetland, the Brethren had revived from their pre-war decline and in 1937 their five assemblies contained 190 members.[103] In 1933 the assembly address list contained 373 Scottish meetings, the largest reported number, and that same year it was calculated that there were 'considerably upwards' of 30,000 members—an average of some seventy-five per assembly, the highest estimated membership.[104]

---

from a former assembly member; Aberdeenshire (see Map 5): Tarland (1936): oral information, 13 July 1988, from a former assembly member; Fife (see Map 7): Blairhall: W, 67 (1937), p.192; writer's collection, I.I. 2., Thomas Rowan to the writer 10 June 1987; and 26 January 1988; Kinross-shire (see Map 7): Kinross (1925): W, 55 (May 1925), p.97; 'John Martin', W, 91 (1961), p.156; Lanarkshire (see Map 10): Carfin (1928): BM, 37 (February 1928), p.i; writer's collection, I.M.7., James H. Capie, 'Carfin Assembly—1988', typescript, 1988; Arunah Hall, Cambuslang (1925): W, 55 (1925), p.16; writer's collection, I.M.6. (i). David Wightman to the writer 18 September 1988; Glasgow: King's Park (1932) (see Map 11 no.53): W, 62 (1932), p.240; anon., 'Those Sixty Years 1890-1950', in *Elim Hall, 5 Prince Edward Street, Crosshill, Glasgow: 60th Annual Report 1st January to 31st December, 1949* (n.p. [1949]), p.6; Knightswood (1929) (See Map 11): W, 59 (1929), p.288; Renfrewshire (see Map 12): Elderslie (c. 1922): oral information, 13 October 1994, from an assembly member; Ayrshire and Bute (see Map 13): Kilmaurs (1920): W, 50 (1920), p.292; Millport (1934): W, 64 (1934), p.192.

Of the above, Tarland, Elderslie and Millport were re-foundations. In addition, during 1927-38 there was a breaking of bread service during the summer in Oban (W, 57 (1927), p136; oral information, 8 May 1990, from a Highland assembly member).

103. James Moar, 'Surveys of service. The Shetland Isles', BM, 47 (1937), pp.322-3, 326.

104. David P. Thomson (ed.), *The Scottish Churches' Handbook* (Dunfermline, 1933), pp.44-5; the anonymous estimate (probably by a Brethren member) was on the basis of about 400 assemblies; however, this calculation assumes that some 27 meetings were not included in the address list of the same year, probably too generous an estimate, and, in addition, those assemblies which did not enter their addresses tended to be very

Yet it would be erroneous to see the inter-war period as being entirely one of expansion. While numerical growth had continued, it was levelling off. Despite Brethren hopes, the Moray coast revival did not translate into a general awakening.[105] Fred Elliott's Glasgow mission of 1920 was the closest the city came to one, and even Jock Troup failed to ignite a movement of large-scale conversions when he moved there.[106] There was declining interest in the message the Brethren had to offer. A future missionary, Alec McGregor, who was active in evangelism in Renfrew after World War I noticed a hardening setting in during this period when, he felt, the preaching seemed too simple to the returning soldiers.[107] Perhaps throughout the inter-war period the appeal of the revivalist seemed too simple for increasingly more sophisticated audiences. Several of the new assemblies planted in the inter-war period were short-lived. This brief lifespan was especially true of those created through the Unreached Parts of Scotland movement. Apart from Wick, the new meetings of the northern Highlands had probably all been discontinued by 1939, as had the one at Carradale.[108] But declining numbers characterised other rural areas. In the 1920s John Ritchie felt that the movement in the landward parishes of Aberdeenshire had stagnated. Since its inception there in the 1870s, he lamented, 'Gospel work has been sluggish'.[109] In southern Scotland the new assemblies at Port William and Moffat were discontinued.[110] One writer noted of Wigtownshire assemblies in 1929 that they had suffered from emigration and 'the altered conditions of rural life during the past twenty years',[111] probably an allusion to the need for fewer farm workers and out-migration. More serious for the future of Brethren evangelism were the alterations noted in a perceptive comment in *The Believer's Magazine* in 1934. Cottage rows were being destroyed and populations were increasingly concentrated in housing schemes; improved bus services meant that on weekend evenings villages were emptied as people went to the towns.[112] The loss of community would have important implications for the ability of assemblies to recruit.

---

small. More serious for the estimate is the assumption of average size. If an average size of 50 is assumed for 373 assemblies, then the membership would have been 18,650.

105. Marshall to the editor, 14 January 1922, p.167.

106. Stewart, *Beloved Jock*, pp.15-17; cf. Duthie, 'Fisherman's Revival', p.27.

107. Oral information, May 1986, from Alec McGregor.

108. They were perhaps discontinued even earlier: none of them was listed in the 1933 address list.

109. *BM*, 34 (September 1925), p.i.

110. Moffat was discontinued in 1932 the year after its founding (*W*, 64 (1932), p.64) and Port William did not appear in the 1933 address list.

111. Hawthorn, *Alexander Marshall*, p.152.

112. *BM*, 44 (1934), p.80.

But despite these caveats, active decline for the movement as a whole was still some way off on the eve of World War II.[113] Revivalism might have declined as a significant factor in Brethren growth, but the routine evangelistic operations of the movement could still prove effective, and it was through these means that most of the enlargement had taken place. In addition, the increase of the early 1920s had been achieved against another period of high emigration in society which substantially affected Scottish Brethren.[114] Contemporary observers had felt that there were many more young people in assemblies.[115] The average age of conversion, extracted from *The Witness* obituaries, show that it was between 20 and 24 for the post-war period, while the average age of joining an assembly increased to 30.8 (Table 3.1). However, these data are at the limit of their accuracy in this period and both figures almost certainly should be lower because of childhood conversions and reception into fellowship not being recorded adequately.[116] Nevertheless, the high average age of reception into fellowship given in the data shows that adults were still being recruited into the 1930s. Attracting youth had had its disadvantages in Easter Ross where the young converts migrated to the cities.[117] But in the industrial areas of Scotland, the heartland of Brethren strength, the movement remained healthy. The influx of fresh, young blood in the early 1920s had promised vitality for a further number of years, and in the late 1930s Brethren were again commenting on the presence of many young people in assemblies.[118] Figure 6.1 also suggests some growth in this period, culminating in a peak in 1936-8.[119] One additional sign of the vigour of the movement was the formation in the inter-war years of at least twenty-three assemblies through schisms, many caused by the issues, which will be analysed in the next chapter, that were agitating the movement in this period.[120] The number of

---

113. Cf. Callum G. Brown, *The Death of Christian Britain: understanding secularisation* (London & New York, 2001), p.165.

114. See below, Fig. 9.1.

115. J. B. Watson, 'Dr. James Black on the "Plymouth Brethren"', W, 55 (1925), p.191; P[ickering]., 'WW',W, 54 (1924), p.384.

116. For the explanation of *The Witness* obituaries, see above, p.16 n.89.

117. Mrs Murdo McKenzie to Alex Stewart in [Stewart (compiler)], 'Moray and Nairn'.

118. D. J. Beattie, 'Let no man despise thy youth', W 68 (1938), pp.247-8; Andrew Borland, *Old Paths & Good ways in Personal, Family, and Church Life* (Kilmarnock, 1938), pp.7-8; F. A. Tatford, 'How can we keep our young people?', W, 68 (1938), p.29.

119. However, it should be remembered that the data on which it is based are at their most unreliable.

120. See below, pp.231-8.

secessions is a further indicator that it was a buoyant time for Scottish Brethren.[121]

Growth 1939-65

In 1960 two Glasgow Brethren, T. J. Smith and John Boyes, estimated for sociologist John Highet that there were 25,000 Brethren members throughout Scotland, an average of 71.4 per assembly.[122] This seems to indicate a decline since the calculation of 1933 had been made.[123] However, Smith and Boyes felt that there had not necessarily been a loss, but had the impression that Brethren membership was then at its peak.[124] The authors of *The Third Statistical Account* for Ayrshire reported that in 1951 there were in the county at a 'rough estimate' 2,000 Brethren members in thirty-nine assemblies (an average size of around fifty per congregation).[125] In Glasgow the *Account* had more accurate figures which also showed continuing Brethren strength. In 1955 the city's thirty-one assemblies contained 3,318 members, giving an average size of 107.[126] The traces for five of the assemblies of differing sizes in Figure 6.3 show their membership to have been fairly stable. Gospel Hall, Kilbirnie, after some fluctuations in the 1940s, grew in the 1950s, and Central Hall, Kilmarnock, after some decline in the post-war period saw a slight swelling in its membership in the early 1960s. Lesmahagow assembly had failed to recover from the effects of out-migration during the industrial troubles of the 1920s, and in 1960s there was a continuing reduction in its size. Although the Newmains meeting, set in another mining community, enjoyed some periods of growth in the 1960s, it too gradually contracted. The same was probably true of that of Newmilns in

---

121. For this view of schism, see above pp.119-20.

122. John Highet, *The Scottish Churches: a review of their state 400 years after the Reformation* (London, 1960), pp.36-8; the calculation was made on the basis of there being about 350 assemblies: this assumes that 26 assemblies did not report their existence in the 1959 address list, a figure which is probably too high (see above, n.104). The average size of assembly is perhaps over generous, and if one of 50 is assumed for 324 assemblies, then the membership would be 16,200.

123. See above p.196.

124. Dr John Boyes to the writer, 26 October 1988.

125. William Boyd and John Strawhorn, *TSA: County of Ayr* (Edinburgh and London, 1951), p.256; the information was supplied by an anonymous Brethren member. When the estimated 1,000 members of the other divisions of Brethren are added, then the Brethren were the fourth largest Christian body in the county.

126. John Highet, 'The Churches', in J. Cunnison and J. B. S. Gilfillan (eds), *TSA Glasgow* (Edinburgh, 1958), p.719; this represented 0.78% of the church-going population of Glasgow and 0.43% of the adult population, *ibid.*, p.726.

the decade before 1965.[127] Elim Hall, Glasgow, markedly declined, and probably this largely middle-class congregation was being eroded due to the suburbanisation of the city. In the suburbs, however, most Brethren would seek out another meeting thereby aiding growth there. But each of the assemblies represented in Figure 6.1 had years in the inter-war period when it had been larger. The decline in the number of congregations in the address lists, from 373 in 1933, to 339 in 1951, and 324 in 1959, also suggests some contraction. Any overall diminution in the movement was evidently slight enough not to trouble contemporary observers such as Smith and Boyes—some assemblies clearly could maintain numbers, even growing after depressed periods, and in the early 1960s post-war 'baby boom' offspring of Brethren parents helped swell membership. But by 1965 the movement had, to some degree it would appear, reduced in size.

World War II offered the same opportunities in evangelism as the First[128] and equally it presented assemblies with difficulties.[129] After the war there were expectations of revival among them.[130] The immediate post-war period was a favourable one for Evangelicals, and they were resurgent in the mainline Scottish churches.[131] It was the period of the interdenominational 'Tell Scotland' campaign, and as part of it the American evangelist Billy Graham was brought to Glasgow in 1955 for the 'All-Scotland Crusade'.[132] A leading figure in the initiative to bring Graham to Scotland was a Glasgow businessman John Henderson, the MP for Cathcart division and a member of Elim Hall, who had been on the Executive Committee of the evangelist's London mission.[133] Many other Brethren took an active role in the crusade and enthusiasm was particularly high among assemblies in Glasgow where during the year

127. Unfortunately the roll books for Gospel Hall, Newmilns, for 1956-67 have not been preserved; but there were 47 members in 1955 and 34 in 1968, suggesting that it decreased over the decade 1955-65.

128. James Anderson (compiler), *Willie Scott: 55+ years of service* (Glasgow, 1986), pp.15-34; 'Mrs Isabella Hopkins', *W*, 88 (1958), p.86; oral information, 18 April 1989, from an assembly member; oral information, 8 January 1991, from an assembly member.

129. *W*, 74 (1944), p.64; *W*, 78 (April 1948), p.iii; *W*, 88 (1958), p.214; letters to the editor, *BM*, 54 (1944), pp.94, 122-3, 151-2, 152, 186.

130. J. R. Rollo, 'In the beginning of the year', *W*, 76 (9146), pp.1-2; A. Borland, '"Revive Thy work"', *BM*, 57 (October 1947), p.iii; H. P. Barker *et al.*, 'Can Revival Come?', *ibid.*, pp.291-2.

131. Bebbington, *Evangelicalism*, p.254.

132. Highet, *Scottish Churches*, pp.86-8.

133. William Fitch, 'The story of beginnings and preparation', in Tom Allan (ed.), *Crusade in Scotland...Billy Graham* (London, 1955), pp. 30, 31; David Jeremy, *Capitalists and Christians: business leaders and the churches in Britain, 1900-1960* (Oxford, 1990), pp.398, 407; for Henderson, see below, pp.250-1, 322-4.

twenty-six city assemblies administered 196 baptisms.[134] To establish the new converts the Glasgow Summer Bible School was founded in 1955, an annual diet of services offering detailed biblical study,[135] and a similar aim lay behind the establishment in Motherwell of the Maranatha Centre that same year: it provided a games room, a library and a prayer room and was open every evening.[136] The English evangelist Peter Brandon witnessed emotional scenes in Maddiston, Stirlingshire (including a 'clockless prayer meeting' held on Friday nights), beginning in the month after the All-Scotland Crusade finished, and his mission produced a substantial number of converts.[137] The results claimed for Graham's style of crusade evangelism gave rise to imitation among the Brethren.[138] In Ayr during October 1956 over forty individuals, mainly brought in from surrounding districts by hired buses, were converted in a campaign entitled 'Faith is the Victory' which was held in a cinema by another English evangelist, Fred Whitmore.[139]

New assemblies were also formed in the post-war period. In 1945 two returning servicemen who had made contact with the Brethren formed an assembly in Gardenstown, Banffshire, joined by a former member of the Fraserburgh meeting who lived in a nearby village.[140] Through the outreach of existing congregations two further assemblies were formed in Shetland and five in new suburban areas including the Glasgow housing schemes of Drumchapel and Nitshill (see Map 11 nos 1 and 51).[141] The migration of Brethren members led to the formation of an additional eight meetings, among them ones in the new towns at East Kilbride,

---

134. Highet, 'Churches', p.719; this was the same number of baptisms *per capita* as the city's Baptist churches had.

135. Ian Ford, 'Glasgow Summer Bible School', *H*, 65 (July, 1986), p.11.

136. Oral information, 25 November 1990, from an individual who was a Lanarkshire teenager in the 1950s.

137. *W*, 85 (1955), pp.125, 166: the number of converts was not given, possibly due to a disapproval many Brethren had against numbering them; cf. above, p.16.

138. For the Crusade results see: Tom Allan 'The road ahead: results and lessons of the crusade', in *idem* (ed.), *Crusade in Scotland*, pp.106-128; Highet, *Scottish Churches*, pp.89-123.

139. *W*, 86 (1956), p.247.

140. 'How it began: Gardenstown, Banffshire', *BM* , 99(1989), pp.2-5.

141. The new assemblies were: Shetland (see Map 1): East Yell (1946): writer's collection, I.T.1., [James Moar], 'A Continued Survey of Service in the Shetland Isles from 1914 to 1976', photocopy of typescript, 1976; Scalloway (1951): *W*, 1951), p.197; Edinburgh (see Map 8 inset): Oxgangs: *W*, 94 (1964), p.116; Lanarkshire (see Map 10): Forgewood, Motherwell (1960): *W*, 90 1960), p.157 (this outreach was commenced in 1936, *W*, 66 (1936), p.213); Viewpark, Uddingston (1961): *W*, 91 (1961), p.436; Glasgow (see Map nos 1 & 51): Drumchapel (1959): *W*, 89 (1959), p.170; Nitshill (1962): oral information, February 1992, from a Glasgow assembly member.

Lanarkshire, in 1951 and Glenrothes, Fife, in 1956.[142] There were also several Christian bodies which transferred to the movement. The Motherwell independent mission, Hallelujah Hall, was recognised as an assembly in 1953,[143] as earlier in Glasgow had been London Road Gospel Hall in 1943[144] and Thornwood Hall in 1948 (see Map 11 nos 30 and 9).[145] Also in Glasgow Anniesland Hall decided to join the movement in 1942, and although the other three missions had associated with the Brethren when they were close to being discontinued, this last accession was a significant one because of the size and resources of the congregation.[146] In addition, a further two meetings were formed at Melrose in 1945 and Hopeman in 1951 whose origins are not known;[147] assemblies also existed at Beauly and Prestonpans in this last year;[148] and some eight schisms, all but two of them permanent, took place during the period. The new assemblies were signs of continuing vitality.

Children's services continued their traditional appeal. *The Third Statistical Account* reported that the Brethren Sunday schools in Glengarnock and Kilbirnie had 426 members between them, almost as many pupils as the 445 members the four Church of Scotland congregations had among them.[149] A later report of the churches in Falkirk in 1969 found that people with little or no connection to a church would send their children to a Brethren Sunday school, 'because they are respected as good people'. Although the parents regarded this as a preparation for joining a mainline church, it was noted, many of the

---

142. *W*, 81 (1951), p.131; *W*, 86 (1956), p.126. The others were: Orkney: <u>Shapinsay</u> (1940): *W*, 70 (1940), p.115; Highlands: <u>Oban</u> 1 (1941): *W*, (July 1941), p.iii; <u>Oban</u> 2 (1948): *W*, 71 (1948), p.iii; oral information 8 May 1990, from an assembly member; <u>Tain</u> (by 1951): *Assemblies in Britain...* (London, 1951), p.109; <u>Thurso</u> (1961): *W*, 71 (1961), p.476; Glasgow: <u>Craigton</u> (1943): *Post Office Glasgow Directory for 1943-1944* (Glasgow, 1943), p.2083; Dumfriesshire: <u>Sanquhar</u> (1952): writer's collection, I.F.1., Robert Lind to the writer, 3 May 1989.

Of the above, Oban and Thurso were re-formations; the assembly founded in Oban in 1941 was discontinued in 1945 and during 1945-7 there was a breaking of bread for the Glasgow Fair holidays only: *W*, 75 (May 1945), p.iv; in addition, for several years after 1957 there was a breaking of bread at North Berwick, East Lothian, during the summer: *W*, 87 (1957), p.132.

143. *BM*, 63 (1953), p.104; oral information, 15 November 1986, from a Motherwell assembly member.

144. *Glasgow Directory for 1943-1944*, p.2083.

145. *Post Office Glasgow Directory for 1948-1949* (Glasgow, 1948), p.2196.

146. Writer's collection, I.J.2., '19th September 1958', photocopy of anonymous MS.

147. *W*, 75 (December 1945), p.v; *BM*, 61 (1951), p.220.

148. These assemblies are known only from their inclusion in the 1951 assembly address list; they may, of course have been founded before the war.

149. Boyd and Strawhorn, *TSA: County of Ayr*, p.397.

pupils went on to enter the Brethren.[150] It was out of a Sunday school and a handicraft evening for young folk commenced in 1950 that the new post-war Edinburgh assembly had developed,[151] and the Uddingston one had grown from Bible teaching done in local schools since 1953.[152] Success in religious activities among the young provided new members. The children's evangelist Dan Cameron claimed that 1958 in particular had been a 'year of blessing among children' and that many 'teenagers had been won for Christ'.[153]

The word 'teenager' had been coined during the war. The growth of the inter-war era had largely been achieved by methods inherited from nineteenth-century revivalism,[154] but from the 1940s onwards new techniques increasingly began to be used. It was due to the rising awareness of the group which the new word represented that several of the innovations were adopted, not least because the offspring of assembly members were in it. During World War II the government encouraged young people to join a youth organisation. Many Brethren were suspicious. Young people had usually been discouraged from joining such groups, and an attempt at militarisation was suspected, but some were sufficiently pragmatic to take advantage of the situation.[155] A number of assemblies formed Christian Youth Centres (CYC) which attempted to provide physical, moral and spiritual training for the young.[156] A principal activity was an evening for teaching crafts, and during the summer a holiday camp was held which was mainly recreational. Such events were new for assemblies, but if the Brethren now had leisure activities they had an evangelistic purpose: both craft evenings and camps had a religious component.[157] Most of the CYC were discontinued after the war but holiday camps were continued. In north Ayrshire, for example, a camp was started by returning servicemen whose wartime experience of such life had made them realise its advantages.[158] Youth rallies, a type of event which originated in America and that had been introduced before the war, were also held at weekends for young

150. Sissons, *Burgh of Falkirk*, p.345.

151. Don Palmer, York: notes on interview with Mr Ron McColl and Mr and Mrs Bob McDonald, 13 May 1988.

152. *W*, 91 (1961), p.436.

153. *W*, 88 (1959), p.35.

154. For a survey of these, see above, pp.135-40.

155. G. N. Davidson to the editor, *W*, 72 (1942), p.51; J. B. W[atson]., 'WW', *ibid.*, p.52.

156. 'Registration for youth', *BM*, 51 (1942), p.80.

157. Oral information, 26 November 1990, from a CYC leader.

158. Oral information, 2 December 1990, from an Ayrshire assembly member.

people.[159] While these were often for those already Christian, one group of assemblies reported that thirty-four converts had been made in 1956 through such meetings held in a burgh town.[160] It is likely that much of this activity recruited the children of Brethren parents, but undoubtedly it also captured some young people from the wider community.

New methods of evangelism for adults were also considered. In 1955 a North American visitor at the Conference of Brethren at High Leigh, Hertfordshire, spoke of the transformation the morning family Bible hour had made in Vancouver,[161] and the following year Cecil Howley, the recently appointed editor of *The Witness*, was enthusing about them in a letter to a Scottish friend.[162] This advocacy of Sunday morning evangelistic services had some effect. There were, perhaps, a couple of assemblies who experimented with the new time from the 1950s onwards.[163] But it was Glenview Evangelical Church, Gartness, Lanarkshire, which probably was the first to adopt a morning family service permanently in 1964 because it was felt that non-churchgoers were more likely to attend a service on a Sunday morning.[164] In 1950 T. J. Smith became the first Brethren individual to preach on the radio when a service was broadcast from Ebenezer Hall, Coatdyke. This, it was felt, gave the 'unsaved' the opportunity of 'hearing the Gospel',[165] but the significance of the occasion probably lay more in its indication that new opportunities for evangelism were being considered.

Despite the effort and some attempt at innovation, assemblies saw fewer converts in the post-war period. Impressive as the All-Scotland Crusade had been, no awakening took place in the post-war mainland and revival on Lewis failed to spread.[166] The only meeting established through an evangelistic mission was one founded in 1942 at Eastfield, Lanarkshire.[167] The number of assemblies being founded was falling while those

---

159. *W*, 37 (1937), p. 36, is the first extant reference to them when a series of rallies was held in Greenock, Elim Hall, Glasgow, and Dundee; cf. Patterson, *Patterson of Tibet*, p.45.

160. *W*, 86 (1956), p.146: the town in question was not identified.

161. Anon. (ed.), *A New Testament Church in 1955* (Rushden, 1956), pp.83-4; for Scottish reactions to this conference, see below, pp.241-3.

162. OA, D27/6/4, G. C. D. Howley to Robert Rendall, 20 September 1956; cf. Touchstone [i.e. G. C. D. Howley], 'The Family Service', *W*, 93 (1963), pp.146-7.

163. Oral information, 17 May 1988, from a Lanarkshire assembly member.

164. Harry Morris to the editor, *A*, 69 (January 1991), p.23; this had been the argument used in their favour by H. L. Ellison, a Bible College lecturer in England, in his influential book, *The Household Church* (1963), 2nd edn (Exeter, 1979), pp.41-7; cf. below, p.336.

165. *W*, 80 (1950), p.164.

166. Bebbington, *Evangelicalism*, p.254.

167. *BM*, 52 (1942), p.159; however this does not include the seven assemblies discussed above, p.201, which were founded through the outreach of existing ones.

being discontinued was perceptibly rising. Rural areas were the worst affected.[168] The Highlands had fewer evangelists.[169] By 1959 inland Aberdeenshire had only eight assemblies and in the Borders, an area where the Brethren had always been weak, the movement had almost disappeared: meetings only remained in Hawick, Chirnside and Galashiels, and the last was discontinued soon after 1964.[170] In addition by the 1960s, although evidence is difficult to find, it would appear that there were few converts from outside Brethren families. Slightly later in 1970, of the twenty-four members of the Gospel Hall Bible class, Kirkintilloch, only three were from non-Brethren families and none of them remained with the assembly.[171] There were undoubtedly reasons in the wider society for this. Television was added to the earlier culprits for distracting people.[172] An additional reason for targeting young people in evangelism had been the growing indifference among adults. The large post-war housing schemes and the new suburbs, lacking the face-to-face nature of the communities which they replaced, were a less favourable context for Brethren recruitment. The new assemblies at Viewpark, and Drumchapel were soon discontinued, the latter after its hall was the subject of arson,[173] and inner-city Glasgow assemblies were heading for extinction due to the movement of Brethren members to the suburbs.[174] In the mining village of Drongan, Ayrshire, the only public amenities with which the gospel hall had to compete in the early twentieth century, were four shops, a school and an iron-clad public hall, but in the expanded post-war community, whose inhabitants came from several mining hamlets which had been demolished, there were, among other things, a community centre, a library, two churches (one Roman Catholic), two working-men's clubs, a bowling club, and an inn. The villagers were settled in housing schemes in which, it was complained, there had been a loss of cohesion.[175] This was, as Callum Brown has argued in the context of the city overspill, an environment in which

---

168. W. McInroy to the editor, *W*, 88 (1958), p.211.

169. W. McInroy to the editor, *W*, 91 (1961), p.112.

170. *Assemblies in Britain...* (London, 1959), pp.93-6; cf. W. Landles to the editor, *W*, 88 (1958), p.55.

171. Writer's collection, II, 'A sketch of the class', 'Enterprise' [magazine of Gospel Hall Bible class, Kirkintilloch] (May 1970), p.2.

172. W. K. Morrison, 'Christian of the sixties', *BM*, 74 (1964), pp.118, 121.

173. Oral information, 4 July 1999, from a Glasgow assembly member; for the new Nitshill assembly's later history, see below, p.361.

174. See below, pp.330, 331.

175. Gavin Wark, *The Rise and Fall of Mining Communities in Central Ayrshire in the 19th and 20th Centuries. Ayrshire Monographs No.22* (Darvel, 1999), pp. 35-9, Figures 2 and 3, pp.19, 38.

secularisation increased as religion lost its social role and the machinery of church growth struggled to cope with the new demographics.[176]

The Brethren were among those struggling and internal factors were also a cause for lack of additions. Families had been smaller from the later 1930s onwards. Although contraception was a taboo subject among Brethren and it would not be until the later 1960s that artificial methods were used, it would seem that a variety of natural means were used to reduce family sizes.[177] In addition to autogenous growth declining, so too was allogenous. Some evangelistic methods were proving ineffectual: in 1956 one individual pointed out that marquees were by then virtually useless in attracting people.[178] It was possibly difficult for individuals socialised into the Brethren world to imagine how more effective communication with the wider one might be achieved. But considerable suspicion existed of such changes as were suggested, undoubtedly the reason behind the reluctance to accept morning evangelistic services. One individual, in denouncing innovation, called for renewed emphasis in preaching on sin and hell.[179] Henry Pickering had criticised mass evangelism in the inter-war period as a possible form of mesmerism,[180] and after the war many Brethren continued his disapproval. CYC were regarded with suspicion for it was felt that they were too like other church youth organisations[181] and the Maranatha centre was shunned by the majority of Lanarkshire assemblies.[182] The introduction of techniques imported from America and the use of singing to attract young people were criticised because to the Brethren they seemed too much like entertainment.[183] The evangelist Isaac Ewan objected to the idea that teenagers might need their own forms of meeting and a lighter approach. 'The young', he declared, 'full of youthful exuberance in the things of everyday life, are generally very sober and serious in the things of God— if their elders will allow them.'[184] And perhaps most Brethren had lost

---

176. Callum G. Brown, 'The mechanism of religious growth in urban societies: British cities since the eighteenth century', in Hugh McLeod (ed.), *European Religion in the Age of the Great Cities 1830-1930* (London, 1995), p.258.

177. Oral information, 28 March 1999 and 10 April 1999, from female assembly members.

178. John S. Borland, 'How to speed the message, *BM*, 66 (1956), pp.101-2.

179. Hugh Borland to the editor, *BM*, 56 (1946), p.120.

180. *W*, 53 (1923), p.50; cf. the letters in support of him, *ibid.*, pp.81-2.

181. Oral information, 26 November 1990, from a CYC leader.

182. Oral information, 25 November 1990, from an individual who was a Lanarkshire teenager in the 1950s.

183. *BM*, 33 (1933), pp.42-3; [A. Borland], 'Latitudinarianism', *BM*, 51 (1941), p.19; [*idem*], 'Editor's comment', *BM*, 56 (1946), pp.57-8; W. Rodgers, 'Making a noise', *ibid.*, pp.57-8.

184. I. Y. E[wan]., 'Asahel, or the youth movement', *PT*, 9 ([194]), p.121-3.

contact with the wider society. 'Some members would of course require training in treating courteously an unfamiliar lady visitor who wore make-up or came without a hat', noted schoolteacher W. K. Morrison in an article on how gospel meetings might be made less alien to visitors.[185] The deep-seated conservatism of the movement in this period (to be discussed more fully in the following chapter) and its lack of sympathy with contemporary mores stifled adaptation.

Assembly Ethos

The movement in the post-Second World War period was not as yet—it was argued above—given over to serious decline. There was much vitality, young people were added and membership levels remained high. A warm afterglow continued from the inter-war years when the movement had probably reached its maximum strength. One sign of the continuing vigour was most assemblies acquiring their own halls. In 1922 some fifty-seven assemblies obviously met in rented accommodation and a further sixteen had a private house listed as an address, but by 1959 only eighteen were in the former position and none in the latter.[186] The upgrading of accommodation and the acquisition of new buildings was particularly marked after World War II—in 1955 the assembly which George Patterson had discovered in Portobello exchanged its rented room for Southfield Gospel Hall.[187] Most halls remained simple. The assembly in Bellevue Chapel, Edinburgh, was unique among Scottish Brethren in its choice of name and its acquisition in 1919 of a former Lutheran church resplendent with spire.[188] It was probably seen as one more indicator of Edinburgh Brethren being different. But the larger and more prosperous assemblies built bigger and grander halls than had been used formerly. One of the most impressive of these was the one which was opened in Kilmarnock in 1933 (Figure 6.4).[189] W. F. Valentine, a prominent local architect, designed the façade in the Italian Renaissance

---

185. Morrison, 'Christian of the sixties', p.117.

186. *List of Some Assemblies* (1922), pp.38-49; *Assemblies in Britain* (1959), pp.97-113. The figure for 1922 should probably be higher as only those places where rented accommodation is definitely indicated (e.g. Co-operative Hall, Masonic Hall etc.) have been counted; there were many assemblies which had buildings with names such as Wilson Hall or Eastburn Hall which may or may not have been rented; but in 1959 there were only two or three with such names.

187. *W*, 84 (1955), p.34.

188. Writer's collection, I.H.1., W. W. Campbell, 'Bellevue Chapel', photocopy of typescript, n.d.; however the assembly in Linlithgow called its building St John's Chapel for a while in the 1950s, *Assemblies in Britain* (1959), p.18.

189. *W*, 64 (1934), p.21.

style, its arched frontage based on the triumphal arch—a clearly non-Gothic manner popular in English Nonconformity.[190] The interior was spacious. It was designed to seat 450 with a balcony able to take a further 100. The lectern and baptistery were in an elliptical apse which was surmounted by an arch that echoed the shape of the ceiling.[191] Erected on one of the principal streets in the town, its name, Central Hall, indicated a greater confidence in the place the assembly had in the community.

The movement continued the pattern of intense activity which it had inherited from the nineteenth century. In addition to the usual three Sunday services (morning, afternoon and gospel meetings), assemblies also had Bible classes, Sunday schools, tract bands, and open-air meetings. Mid-week there were Bible readings, prayer meetings and children's meetings.[192] The sisters too were active in running women's gospel meetings, solo singing, and Dorcas work (hospital visitation).[193] Independent initiatives, such as that of Jimmy Black who ran religious services for the boys of Polmont Borstal, Stirlingshire, from 1935, were also undertaken by some Brethren.[194] Assemblies provided ample uses for the leisure time which its members increasingly enjoyed. An annual holiday had become a possibility for many, and Brethren piety occupied this fresh area. *The Witness* first carried notices of holiday accommodation in May 1926,[195] and by 1955 it listed 144 places, twenty-five of them in Scotland.[196] The establishments which were advertised (usually a 'Christian guest house') were maintained by fellow-Evangelicals, principally Brethren individuals. They allowed members of the movement to have their holidays in an environment insulated from worldliness and in the company of fellow Christians with an assembly to hand. The largest establishment of this type was Netherhall Christian Holiday and Conference Centre, the former mansion of physicist Lord

---

190. I am grateful to Prof. Sam McKinstry for this comment on the architecture.

191. 'The Central Hall', *KS*, 2 December 1933, p.5; in this article the feature which is described above as an 'apse' was described as a 'chancel': it clearly did not fulfil that function, but the use of the ecclesiastical term is significant.

192. Cf. the meetings listed for Bethany Hall, Camelon, in Patterson, *Patterson of Tibet*, p.19—there were five on a Sunday.

193. 'Mrs John Dalton', *W*, 94 (1964), p.36; 'Jane Helen Fraser', *W*, 106 (1976), p.115; 'Miss Sophia Hynd', *W*, 89 (1957), p.233; 'Mrs Agnes King', *W*, 88 (1959), p.59; 'Mrs Wallace Lee', *W*, 102 (1972), p.312; 'Mrs Euphemia McIntyre', *W*, 103 (1972), p.75; 'Cecilia H. Taylor', *W*, 108 (1978), p.125; 'Miss Helen Wright', *W*, 94 (1964), p.36.

194. James Anderson (ed.), 'Jimmy Black (1895-1975)', in *They Finished*, pp.25-8.

195. *W*, 56 (1926), p.340.

196. *W*, 85 (1955), pp.82-8.

Kelvin, in the Clyde coastal resort of Largs which was opened in 1927.[197] The initiative to acquire it was that of W. E. Taylor, a former household steward to aristocratic and wealthy families, who had helped in running a summer convention for young people at St Andrews.[198] This convention, commenced in 1919 and probably drawing upon the model of Keswick, was acclaimed as 'a solution to the problem of giving young men and women a holiday and a help Heavenward'.[199] Netherhall was purchased when university student accommodation was no longer available in St Andrews.[200] The new location continued the spirit of the earlier convention, extending it to adults and allowing for the use of invited resident preachers to provide devotional meetings for holidaymakers. Brethren also were counselled to use vacations for witnessing and a more directly religious holiday included evangelism.[201] The Green Tent Gospel Campers had been founded by two future missionaries in the Edwardian era and in the early inter-war period it continued to offer young men 'a profitable holiday, with opportunity for Gospel work',[202] mainly, it would appear, in the Ayrshire coastal resorts.[203] From 1947 the evangelist Willie Scott attracted many young men to Galloway for his 'Preaching Holiday Campaigns', based after 1953 at Machermore, the eventide home for assembly members which he had established in Wigtownshire. They provided practice for developing preachers and were fruitful in producing full-time Christian workers.[204] The activism of the Brethren and concern for the improvement in piety carried over into new opportunities for leisure.

Shorter working hours and increasing ease of travel allowed conferences to flourish after World War I. These were not for the faint-hearted—four to five preachers would give lengthy addresses (forty-five

---

197. *W*, 57 (1927), pp.16, 38.

198. 'W. E. Taylor', *W*, 70 (September 1940), p.iii.

199. *W*, 49 (1919), p.49; *W*, 50 (1920), p.316.

200. The St Andrews Convention was briefly revived during 1945-7: *W*, 75 (March 1945), p.iv; 'Mrs W. E. Taylor', *W*, 77 (1947), p.60.

201. William Balfour, 'Golden opportunities', *W*, 52 (1922), p.225; Leslie Randall, *Knowing the Scriptures*, No. 9 (March-April 1950), p.18.

202. *W*, 50 (1920), p.293; 'Peter Cochrane', *W*, 101 (1971), p.196, states the organisation was founded by 'former missionaries in Venezuela', naming them as S. B. Adams and J. N. Struthers; the former served in Venezuela 1910-40 and J. H. Struthers in 1915-26 (Stunt *et al.*, *Turning the World Upside Down*, pp.637, 638). The first extant reference to its existence is in *W*, 45 (1915), p.72, when it was in Largs, and given this date and the common Brethren pattern of independent initiatives in evangelism leading to missionary service, it seems likely that the organisation was founded in the Edwardian era before both men went to Venezuela.

203. *W*, 49 (1919), p.81; 'John Frame', *W*, 88 (1958), p.130.

204. Anderson (compiler), *Willie Scott*, pp.35-47; *W*, 85 (1955), p.125.

minutes being the usual time),[205] generally of an intellectually challenging nature[206]—but among the Brethren they were exceptionally popular. The Glasgow Half-Yearly Conferences had grown so large by their jubilee year of 1914 that the second largest venue in Glasgow, the City Halls, had to be used to accommodate the numbers attending— possibly about 2,000 individuals.[207] By 1950 it was reported that the Half-Yearly weeknight missionary rally, by then held in Glasgow's largest venue, St Andrews Halls, could draw about 2,700 attenders.[208] This gathering continued to fill the Halls until they were destroyed by fire in 1962. It had reached its apex two years earlier when, after the Missionary Exhibition held at Bellahouston Park Palace of Art which attracted 15,000 visitors, the final rally at the St Andrews Halls had to use the side halls for the audience of 3,000 and a further 1,500 were turned away.[209] The Glasgow Half-Yearly was the leviathan of the conferences, but others could achieve substantial numbers. The first day of 1925 saw a storm of exceptional violence, but it did not prevent there being New Year's Day conference audiences of 600 in Ayr, 900 in Kilmarnock, 500 in Glasgow, 700 in Hamilton, 1,000 in Motherwell, 750 in Edinburgh and 1,000 in Aberdeen—some 5,450 individuals in total.[210] Many Brethren Saturdays were spent in attending conferences.[211] The pattern established in the late nineteenth century for these gatherings was continued.[212] Public holidays, especially New Year's Day, were the favoured times for the larger ones held in the towns and cities.[213] The Saturday half-holiday was used for the smaller local ones with the months of April and September particularly popular. But they could be held at any time, as long as they

---

205. J. S. Borland to the editor, *BM*, 59 (1949), pp.185-6.

206. Cf. F. F. Bruce, *In Retrospect: remembrance of things past* (London and Glasgow, 1980), p.25.

207. J. G[ray]., 'The Fundamentals', *W*, 44 (1914), p.89. According to Joe Fisher, *The Glasgow Encyclopaedia* (Edinburgh, 1994), p.169, the City Halls held 3,500 at this period; it is unlikely, however, that this number was present. In 1921, when attendance was at its highest since the war, there were 2,000 attenders (*W*, 51 (1921), p.122), and it is probable that this figure held for the earlier occasion.

208. OA/D27/6/1, J. B. Watson to Robert Rendall, 4 October 1950; the capacity of St Andrews Halls was 2,500 at this time, both it and the City Halls having being reduced in seating capacity since 1914 for safety reasons, Fisher, *Glasgow Encyclopaedia*, pp.169, 170.

209. T. J. Smith, '"Operation overseas"', *BM*, 71 (1961), pp.324-6; the missionary James Caldwell's interview on television as a result of the exhibition was probably the first appearance on the medium by a Scottish Brethren individual on assembly affairs.

210. *W*, 55 (1925), pp.36-7.

211. Patterson, *God's Fool*, pp.18-19.

212. See above, p.145.

213. *BM*, 44 (1934), p.52; *BM*, 46 (1936), p.53.

did not conflict with another one in the district. In the typical year of 1934 some 182 conferences were held throughout Scotland.[214]

So popular was the institution that the Brethren developed variations on the theme. The traditional Bible class conferences, which probably included a fairly large number of older people, were replaced with ones billed as 'Youth Conferences' and by 1945 they were widespread.[215] They were one more inter-assembly event through which young people might find a suitable partner.[216] Missionary conferences became popular in the 1920s: an annual one was established in Ayrshire in 1920,[217] and five years later an annual open-air missionary conference was founded in the same county at Newmilns.[218] By 1938 a missionary conference for young people which was held in the grounds of the Livingstone Memorial, Blantyre, was attracting an audience of 400.[219] Doubtless this venue was chosen because it was felt that Scottish reverence for David Livingstone would intensify any challenge presented to the young, and the gathering was held annually from its initiation in July 1931 until 1952.[220] Residential conversational Bible readings spread over several days in May for men only were begun at Netherhall in 1935 and they continued, with a seven-year interruption caused by the war, until 1955.[221] Another series of Bible readings at Netherhall, which apparently grew out of the earlier one, was for a mixed-sex audience and in 1945 they transferred to Ayr.[222] These 'May Readings' became immensely popular, drawing visitors from throughout the country who would stay for their duration: in 1960, although attendance had fallen, there were still some 100 attending the morning sessions and 300 the evening ones.[223] From 1945 the pattern had been successfully copied by

---

214. *W*, 45(1935), *passim*; the number of conferences held per month were: January: 35; February: 17; March: 13; April: 23; May: 15; June: 1; July: 3; August: 9; September: 23; October: 17; November: 15; December: 11.

215. They were held in Troon, Ayrshire (from 1937, *W*, 70 (1940), p.56); Elim Hall, Glasgow (*BM*, 47 (1938), p.81); Innerleven, Fife (*W*, 69 (1939), p.69); Larkhall, Lanarkshire (*W*, 71 (1941), p.186); Assembly Hall, Aberdeen (*W*, 75 (February 1945), p.i), Paisley, Renfrewshire (*W*, 75 (March 1945), p.i); Hermon Hall, Dundee (*W*, 75 (April 1945), p.i); Cowdenbeath, Fife (*W*, 75 (August 1945), p.i).

216. For attitudes to courtship and marriage, see below, p.315.

217. *W*, 50 (1920), p.260.

218. *BM*, 42 (1932), p.i; cf. *W*, 56 (1926), p.396.

219. *BM*, 47 (1937), p.220.

220. *BM*, 41 (1931), p.ii; *W*, 83 (1953), p.108; on Livingstone's reputation in Scotland, see John M. Mackenzie, 'David Livingstone: the construction of a myth', in Graham Walker and Tom Gallagher (eds), *Sermons and Battle Hymns: Protestant popular culture in modern Scotland* (Edinburgh, 1990), pp.24-42.

221. *W*, 65 (1935), p.116; *W*, 78 (1978), p.72; *W*, 85 (1955), p.102.

222. *W*, 75 (1945), p.i.

223. *W*, 90 (1960), p.275.

September Bible readings in Aberdeen.[224] The period was one of conference-going for the Brethren.

The explicit aim of these gatherings was the inculcation of right doctrine and practice,[225] features which were eagerly embraced by those attending. In 1947 J. B. Watson, editor of *The Witness* (1941-55), enthused over the Ayr Bible Readings: 'Where else but in Scotland will one find three or four hundred men eager to gather for five successive weekday mornings with nothing to attract and hold them, but the desire to get to know the scriptures better?'[226] Other purposes can also be discerned in the conferences. The large gatherings provided support for those who were in small or isolated assemblies,[227] the community of believers helping to confirm the reality of the Brethren mental world. Also, like the magazines, in the absence of a formal organisation they were important for the cohesion of the movement.[228] One individual in the 1920s described conferences as providing 'an opportunity for happy reunion, social intercourse, mutual inquiries, as well as bringing together brethren from the homeland and far-away parts of the world'.[229]

Protestant Evangelical sects are sometimes perceived as being dull and lacking in festivals. However, assemblies had an annual cycle composed of the assembly social, the Sunday school trip, the Bible class trip, the annual conference and the Sunday school soirée [*sic*] which marked out the year.[230] Although Christmas was not celebrated within the assembly, the soirée was often near to it and served as a substitute, and socials might be held close to the commencement of the new year.[231] Conferences were certainly sober and solemn gatherings, but they too had a festal component. Audience expectation of the event, the anticipation of meeting others, the symbolic function of the singing (usually *a capella*),[232] and the satisfaction of having the Brethren world-view legitimated gave them a sense of occasion. They were festive events which punctuated the Brethren year. This was explicit in the north east where the conference circuit followed the rhythms of the farming year with (*inter alia*) Aberdeen Conference on New Year's Day, conferences in Dufftown and Buckie at Easter, a two-day one at Craigellachie in mid-

---

224. *Ibid.*, p.476.

225. J. McDonald, 'Do conferences justify their existence?', *W*, 58 (1928), p.451.

226. J. B. Watson, 'WW', *W*, 77 (1947), p.70.

227. J. G[ray]. to the editor, 'Glasgow Half-Yearly Conferences', *W*, 52 (1922), p.274.

228. See above, pp.146-8.

229. McDonald, 'Do conferences justify their existence?', p.451.

230. Cf. S. J. D. Green, *Religion in the Age of Decline: organisation and experience in industrial Yorkshire, 1870-1920* (Cambridge, 1996), pp.331-4.

231. *H*, 2 (1925), p.32; however, the stricter assemblies did not hold a social.

232. Cf. below, p.253.

July, and Harvest Thanksgiving ones in New Deer and Mosscorral in the autumn.[233] During the conference interval the speakers and audience shared a meal—usually a meat pie and a bag containing a roll and confectionery—and at the several-day ones the significance of this was most evident. At Craigellachie, in a scenic part of Speyside, the mid-day meal 'in Scotch-like fashion' of broth, pudding and tea was prepared and served by the local sisters, and visitors (some 600 by 1949, double the number of twenty years before)[234] were lodged with local Christians for the night.[235] One preacher at the conference, J. R. Rollo, a Fife headteacher, recalled the hospitality which was offered: 'the sense of unity was a throbbing reality... There and then we learned the meaning of the local term "couthie".'[236] For people used to arduous work, conferences, with their established rituals, were the festal holy days of the movement.

The Brethren in this period supported a number of full-time Christian workers. In 1920 there were thirty-six such individuals in Scotland,[237] and probably the number increased over the inter-war era. The evangelists were in the tradition of the working-class revivalist, strong-willed and forthright and possessing common sense and a quick wit.[238] Former miner Fred Elliott was described by one of his converts as having 'twinkling eyes, curly black hair and a broken nose. He was the sort of man a boy could trust...'.[239] Lengthy, sober sermons were expected of the gospel preacher.[240] The evangelist John McAlpine, a former journey-man printer, was praised for his methods which contained 'nothing flamboyant or sensational'.[241] The system of conferences was supported by some full-time Bible teachers. Two of the most prominent had

233. Bruce, *In Retrospect*, pp.20-2; Craigellachie conference was founded in 1889, J. B. Watson, 'WW', *W*, 79 (1949), p.100; and New Deer about 1878, *W*, 38 (December, 1908), end pp.

234. OA/D27/6/1, J. B. Watson to Robert Rendall, 27 July 1949; *W*, 59 (1929), p.213.

235. J. G[ray]., *W*, 53 (1923), p.149; *W*, 54 (1924), p.213.

236. Collection of Alex Stewart, Hopeman: J. R. Rollo to Alex Stewart, 6 November 1975, MS letter in [Alex Stewart, compiler], 'A Record of Gospel Work. Christian Brethren. Moray & Nairn', MS, n.d.

237. HyP[ickering]., *W*, 50 (1920), p.288.

238. Janice Holmes, *Religious Revivals in Britain and Ireland 1859-1905* (Dublin, 2000), pp.154-60.

239. Frederick Catherwood, *At the Edge* (London, 1995), p.13; cf. [Fred Elliott], *The Conversion and Call of Fred Elliott* (London and Glasgow, 1917).

240. J. G[ray]., 'United Tent Mission in Glasgow', *W*, 53 (1923), p.168; J. Ritchie, '"Ask for the old paths"', *W*, 57 (1927), p.210-1; *idem*, 'Plain advice for young preachers', *W*, 64 (1934), p.178.

241. A. B[orland]., 'Books to read', *BM*, 57 (1947), p.314; for McAlpine, see John McAlpine, *Forty Years Evangelising in Britain* (London, 1947).

seceded from moderate Exclusive parties: W. W. Fereday (1866-1959), an English preacher formerly with the Kelly Party, was resident in Scotland from 1936,[242] and W. F. Naismith (1896-1981), who had acceded with the Stuart Party assembly at Carluke, was in popular demand as a preacher on eschatological and devotional subjects.[243] For more mundane speakers Brethren publishers supplied an array of preaching aids. Henry Pickering and John Ritchie both produced several,[244] but also popular was *1200 Notes, Quotes and Anecdotes* (1963) by Archie Naismith, the missionary brother of the conference speaker. Unfortunately, few examples of Brethren preaching as it developed from the second quarter of the century are extant.[245] The allegorical, aphoristic, densely biblically-allusive style cultivated is quintessentially present in the transcript of a sermon by John Douglas, a Lanarkshire preacher who was a miner and market gardener, on the life of David in 1 Samuel:

> In Proverbs we read: 'A soft answer turneth away wrath.' David was innocent of this charge, the charge of Eliab and the question of his inability by Saul, brought out David's experiences with God. Public contest because of private communion. David knew his God in private. The defeat of the nation was the triumph of the individual who was in communion with his God. Pauline strength—Paul is the Caleb of the New Testament,—'I can do all things through the power of Christ which strengtheneth me.'[246]

The idiom is perhaps that of Douglas, but the tone and hermeneutic is representative of many Scottish Brethren preachers of the period.[247] The audiences were capable of following the multiple references: frequent

242. 'W. W. Fereday', *W*, 89 (1959), pp.182-3; *W*, 66 (1936), p.216.

243. James Anderson (ed.), 'A. Naismith W. F. Naismith', in *They Finished their Course in the Eighties* (Kilmarnock, 1990), pp.125-132.

244. Henry Pickering, *One Thousand Tales Worth Telling: mostly new/strictly true/suitable for you* (London and Glasgow [c. 1915]); *idem, 1000 Subjects for Speakers and Students* (Glasgow [1925]); *idem* (compiler), *Twelve Baskets Full of Original Outlines and Scripture Studies* (London and Glasgow, n.d.); John Ritchie, *500 Gospel Subjects with outlines, divisions, and notes for preachers, teachers and Christian workers* (Kilmarnock, 1904); *idem, 500 Gospel Illustrations: incidents, anecdotes, and testimonies for the use of evangelists, preachers and teachers* (Kilmarnock, 1912); *idem, 500 Evangelistic Subjects: with suggestive notes, outlines, and heads for evangelists, preachers, and teachers* (Kilmarnock, 1915); *idem, 500 Bible Subjects: with suggestive outlines and notes for Bible Students, preachers and teachers*, 2nd edn (Kilmarnock, 1926); see also below, p.278.

245. Some of the articles in *The Witness* and *The Believer's Magazine* began life as addresses.

246. John Douglas, *Lessons from the Kings of Israel and Judah* (Ashgill, 1997), p.13; cf. *idem*, 'Suffering', *BM*, 39 (1929), p.13.

247. For Douglas, see below, pp.234-6.

exposure to the Bible made assembly members intimately acquainted with its content. In this respect, as in much else, assemblies in this era dominated the lives of their members.

The Turning Tide

The period discussed in this chapter was a pivotal one for Scottish Brethren. In the judgment of James Hislop, a school headteacher who lived through the period, the years from the Miners' Strike of 1921 until the commencement of World War II were '"the great days" in the lives of Scottish assemblies'.[248] The epithet applied to the organisation of evangelism, but it could be usefully extended to the movement as a whole which achieved its most developed form during this era. It was the period to which the histories of Veitch and Beattie belong, evidence that the movement had reached an established phase.[249] The influences of the magazines, *The Witness* and *The Believer's Magazine*, were at their greatest and their circulation continued to rise—in the case of the former going from almost 20,000 per month worldwide about 1918 to some 30,000 in 1941.[250] But on the eve of World War II Andrew Borland, the newly appointed editor of *The Believer's Magazine*, detecting changes in the ethos of assemblies, had warned that they were entering the third phase of any movement—the long period of decline which followed inception and growth. They were now less vigorous, recruiting from families of believers who gave nominal assent to truths hard-won by previous generations.[251] After the war, the movement displayed signs of numerical contraction.

Until the inter-war period listening to open-air services had been a communal activity and crowds would gather, but in the post-war world new entertainments were more readily available. The writer Liz Lochhead (b.1947), a native of Lanarkshire, has described a Brethren open-air service of her childhood:

> Sunday, maybe later in the evening
> there'd be a Brethren Meeting.
> Plain women wearing hats to cover
> uncut hair. And

---

248. James Hislop to the writer, 19 January 1990.

249. For these histories, see above, pp.9-11.

250. End pp advert in Walter Scott, *Exposition of the Revelation of Jesus Christ*, 5th edn (London [*c*.1918]); supplement to *W*, 71 (March 1941); *BM*, 37 (1927), p.iv; *BM*, 41 (1931), p.iv.

251. Andrew Borland, *Old Paths & Good Ways in Personal, Family and Church Life* (Kilmarnock [1938]), pp.8-12.

singing, under lamp-posts, out in our street.
And the leader shouted the odds on Armageddon, he
tried to sell Salvation.
Everybody turned their televisions up...[252]

Brethren life-style in the post-war era looked old-fashioned. In 1956 Andrew Campbell, a Bible teacher from Leven, Fife, attempted to establish why Brethren gospel meetings were by then largely ineffective. The preacher, he felt, 'too often appears out of touch with modern life... Constant reference is made to Old Testament types, which anyone in touch with reality ought to know have no meaning for men and women of the world today'.[253] The assembly at Kelty in west Fife had shared in the post-war religious resurgence, rising from fourteen members in 1946 to forty in 1954.[254] It was probably the meeting described as being in a mining village which Campbell reported had doubled its membership in the previous five years through active evangelism. Such assemblies, he felt, were the exception, and he offered two reasons for the loss of evangelistic zeal. The first reason, repeating an old complaint, was that disputes over church order had preoccupied minds unduly, and his second reason was the materialism of Brethren members.[255] James Hislop concurred with this last cause of contraction in size: 'The spiritual and numerical declines came', he felt, 'with the Macmillan "you've never had it so good" years'.[256] The factors which led to ineffectiveness identified by these individuals may or may not be correct. But by the 1950s both the manner in which the movement appeared archaic and its increasing prosperity pointed to basic social changes which were affecting Brethren life and the ability to recruit new members.

The wave of the Brethren advance in Scotland probably reached its peak in the mid-1930s.[257] The sound of its long, withdrawing roar became more audible after World War II, but was perhaps hushed for contemporaries because the high-tide marks of Brethren life were so conspicuous and separate surges could still be detected. Membership probably reached its absolute peak around the same time as the Scottish Congregational and Baptist churches did in 1934 and 1935 respectively

252. Liz Lochhead, 'The Offering', in *Dreaming Frankenstein and Collected Poems* (Edinburgh, 1984), pp.60-1.
253. A. P. Campbell, 'Simplicity of testimony', in anon., *A Return to Simplicity: conference of Brethren at High Leigh, September 1956* (Rushden [1959]), pp.68-9.
254. Writer's collection, I.I.7., Helen B. Gallacher, 'The Story of Ebenezer Hall', typescript [1987].
255. Campbell, 'Simplicity of testimony', p.69.
256. Hislop to the writer, 19 January 1990.
257. Cf. J. A[nderson]., 'Editorial searchlight', *BM*, 90 (1980), p.65, which makes the same point.

and before the Church of Scotland did in 1956.[258] Growth, however, had slowed considerably and, as was argued in Chapter 4 above, like other denominations the Brethren had a membership *per capita* that had probably been falling since the turn of the century. On the other hand unlike the Church of Scotland, attendance kept pace with the membership longer.[259] In 1955 on average 31 per cent of the Church of Scotland's membership in Glasgow attended morning service on three census Sundays compared to 64 per cent of Brethren members, a figure which only the Baptists and the Free Church of Scotland (both at 62.9 per cent) could approach.[260] Nevertheless, the movement reached the same turning point in this period as the other churches did and about much the same time. This is evident in the contrast between the two post-war periods. Both were times which favoured assembly growth, but on the second occasion the expansion was on a noticeably lesser scale. Decline was most fully felt by Scottish churches in the early 1960s when the Brethren too were on the brink of substantial contraction.[261]

During the period from 1914 until 1965 the Brethren movement was in its most fully-developed form. Assemblies had grown initially and then retained their numerical strength and inner confidence. Although they had difficulties maintaining themselves in rural Scotland, they were by the mid-1960s thickly spread throughout the industrial Lowlands (see Maps 7-13). The movement had a rigid control over the lives of the members which can be seen in the way it completely provided for their leisure time. Brethren wanted to remain in this habitual world using the evangelistic strategies which had served them so well, and this did not make them responsive to change. The distaste for innovation could be clearly seen in their reaction to the transatlantic influences which were influencing Protestant Evangelicalism and to a significant subtext of the present chapter, the rising importance of youth. Those of a denomi-nationalising tendency had always pointed out that undue withdrawal

258. Robert Currie, Alan D. Gilbert and Lee Horsley, *Churches and Churchgoers: patterns of religious growth in the British isles since 1700* (Oxford, 1977), pp.134-5, 150-1.

259. See above, p.162; and Callum G. Brown, 'Religion and secularisation', in Tony Dickson and James H. Treble (eds), *People and Society in Scotland*, 3 (Edinburgh, 1992), pp.48-54.

260. Highet, 'Churches', pp.719, 731; however, the Brethren were not included in the census and it is not clear how the figure for them was arrived at; if it were supplied by a Brethren member then it is likely to be accurate since most Brethren would regard this as an under-estimate. In addition 1955 was possibly a better than average year for Church of Scotland attendance in Glasgow: as a percentage of membership it was 26.2% in 1954 and 28.4% in 1956; it is highly unlikely that Brethren attendance, being more closely related to membership levels, would fluctuate as much.

261. Brown, 'Religion and secularisation', p.54.

from society meant loss of contact with potential converts. But now the rate of change meant that society was leaving the Brethren behind as they remained devoted to the styles of a previous era. This had profound implications for a conversionist sect. The innovators were pragmatic enough to keep pace with the wider world, but the more sectarian wing of the movement resisted this process and by so doing became more introversionist. It was an era of increasing institutionalisation for the Brethren which hindered the ability to adapt to a changing world. This theme features prominently in the next chapter.

CHAPTER SEVEN

A Clear-Ring Testimony: Development 1914-1965

'Let the truth of God be turned up full blast, a clear-ring testimony given to God's truth and all of it without compromise, with a clear-cut line of separation from teachers, holders, and harbourers of error, and God will always use it to preserve and establish His own, as He has always delighted to do.'
John Ritchie, *The Believer's Magazine*, 32 (1922), p.ii.

Mary Gibson, a niece of the central African missionary Jeanie Gilchrist, intended to become a missionary in Africa when she matriculated at Glasgow University in 1915.[1] Once there, however, she fell in love with a fellow medical student who was a Roman Catholic, the future novelist A. J. Cronin. Through the character of Daniel Law in *Shannon's Way* (1948), a semi-autobiographical novel, Cronin gave a thinly veiled description of her father, Robert Gibson, a Hamilton master baker who was a leading individual in Baillies Causeway Gospel Hall.[2] Cronin did not see Law as the 'popular, slightly comic conception of the street-corner evangelist'. Rather he was like Paul, 'righteous and valiant', or one of the patriarchs who 'amidst the roar of the machine age, and the distracting blare of jazz, and the enticing flicker of the cinema...had raised his children in that tradition, not by fear, for he was no tyrant, but by a rule of tempered firmness'. He had saved his daughter 'from the iniquities of dances, card playing and the theatre, reduced her reading to *Good Words* and *Pilgrim's Progress*'. He makes her renounce Shannon

---

1. 'Robert Gibson', *BM*, 33 (1923), p.113; A. J. Cronin, *Adventures in Two Worlds* (London, 1952), p.8; writer's collection, II, University of Glasgow Archivist to the writer, 18 January 1990. Mary Gibson's mother and Jeanie Gilchrist were daughters of James Gilchrist, 'the Chapelton Baker' (for whom, see above, p.69); this also made her a niece-by-marriage of Mary Paterson, whose first husband was their brother and she too later became a missionary in Africa.

2. 'Robert Gibson', *W*, 53 (1923), p.168.

—the character which corresponds to Cronin—her 'unworthy lover'.[3] Cronin's not unsympathetic portrait shows that strains between acceptance of what society offered and the demands of the sect were perpetuated into the Jazz Age.[4]

World War I had the effect of increasing a sense of alienation from society among the Brethren. This was true not only of the movement during the inter-war period, but also of Evangelicalism as a whole, as the rise of Fundamentalism within it demonstrated. As a result, the second quarter of the twentieth century increased sectarian separatism within the Brethren. Yet Fundamentalism could also draw them into contact with those outside the movement, and the polarisation which had characterised it in earlier phases continued. This issued in a series of schisms, formal and informal, during the period, and while many in the movement were strongly hostile to trends in the wider world, others during this period were closely identified with aspects of culture and society. World War II repeated many of the patterns of the First and its aftermath, but towards the end of the later period the Brethren in Scotland were on the threshold of the most far-reaching changes in their history. The present chapter will examine the impact World War I had on the movement before turning to investigate in the inter-war era Fundamentalism and the movements which called for increased sectarian separation. Conservative reactions to post-World War II change will next be explored and aspects of the denominationalising counter trend will be surveyed in the final section.

Attitudes to War

A substantial section of Scottish Brethren, and certainly the majority in some areas, actively supported Britain's military campaign during World War I.[5] Most obviously there were the many Brethren who volunteered or

---

3. A. J. Cronin, *Shannon's Way* (1948) NEL edn (London, 1979), p.125; for identical attitudes in Charlotte Chapel, Edinburgh (a Baptist church similar in ethos to the Brethren), to comparable amusements in the 1930s as those listed by Cronin, see Eric Lomax, *The Railway Man* (London, 1995), pp.34-5.

4. Cf. HyP[ickering]., 'Jazz and other devilish dances', *W*, 50 (1920), p.259; for Pickering's disapproval of the cinema, see, *idem*, 'WW', *W*, 63 (1933), p.66; and, *idem*, 'WW', *W*, 78 (1948), p.58.

5. This view, based on Scottish evidence, differs from that advanced by Elisabeth K. Wilson, 'Brethren Attitudes to Authority and Government with Particular Reference to Pacifism' (University of Tasmania, Australia, thesis for Master of Humanities, 1994), pp.45-58; cf. John Rae, *Conscience and Politics: the British government and the conscientious objector to military service 1916-1919* (London, 1970), pp.74-5, which notes gradations of opinion among different sections of Brethren with the Open section least explicitly noncombatant.

later accepted conscription, serving their country with distinction, often at the cost of their lives. However, in view of the strong tradition of pacifism which there was in the Brethren,[6] *The Witness* took a neutral position as to whether individuals should join the armed forces.[7] In it Colonel Molesworth stressed the Christian's duty to be subject to the secular powers, but left the application of that principle to the individual's conscience.[8] There were hints that if conscription were introduced, then military service would be the preferred option, and the compromise solution of a noncombatant role was advocated by its editor Henry Pickering.[9] Many members were in reserved occupations such as coal mining and fishing, but when conscription was finally introduced in 1916 *The Witness* maintained its neutral stance.[10] Writers in the magazine perceived Britain as being in the right. Drawing upon anti-German propaganda, Pickering stated that the war was one of 'spiritual Principalities and Powers in league with the Passion and Pride of a group of men lusting to be conquerors of "all the world"', renewing the attack of Satan on believers which had been seen throughout Church history. Revival had flourished in the freedom of the English-speaking peoples while it had been repressed in Germany at the Counter-Reformation. It was this freedom which was under assault.[11] The balance of right was clearly tipped in Britain's favour. Others advocated joining the armed struggle more directly. At one conference the chairman had commented on the number of young men present and wished that a recruiting sergeant was in attendance.[12] In some assemblies a roll of honour was established at the entrance to the hall,[13] and prayers were offered for 'our cause'.[14]

There were those who joined in the jingoistic militarism of the early war years, using the language of civil religion which made them

6. Peter Brock, 'The peace testimony of the early Plymouth Brethren', *Church History*, 55 (1984), pp.30-45; Wilson, 'Brethren Attitudes to Authority', pp.30-42.

7. *The Witness*, quoted in Hunter Beattie, 'Mr Facing-Both-Ways', *Christian and War being 'The Word of the Cross'* (Glasgow, n.d.), p.133; I have been unable to trace this quotation in *The Witness*, possibly because it occurred in the cover pages which have not always been available to me; earlier, however, J. R. Caldwell, had been opposed to Christians voluntarily joining the army: see, J. R. Caldwell, 'The Christian's relation to the army', *W*, 28 (1898), pp.202-4; *idem*, 'QA', *W*, 33 (1903), pp. 67.

8. Col. Molesworth, 'Should Christians enlist?', *W*, 44 (1914), p.155.

9. Editor's Note, 'Conscription and enlisting', *W*, 45 (1915), p.34.

10. HyP[ickering]., 'On the watchtower', *W*, 46 (1916), p.33.

11. *Idem*, '"This solemn moment"', *W*, 45 (1915), pp.37-8.

12. Beattie, 'Facing-Both-Ways', *Christian and War*, p.134: however, this source should be treated with caution on this point: Beattie's antipathy to those Brethren who opposed him may have led him to exaggerate the speaker's comment.

13. *Ibid.*, p.100.

14. G. B. to the editor, *BM*, 26 (1916), p.95.

indistinguishable from the contemporary institutional church. David Beattie, the future historian of the Brethren, was most enthusiastic. In 1914 he wrote a hymn for the use of the British Expeditionary Force imploring the 'God of our nation' to 'Be our army's Head'.[15] His first book, *Oor Gate En'* (1915), was dedicated to those who had volunteered and it contained fourteen 'War Poems', which, among other themes, satirised the Germans, enjoined the USA to join the war, lamented how few volunteers there were, and castigated any 'slackers' who would 'His snivelling voice in discord raise / When death's red hand our manhood slays'.[16] Beattie was not alone in giving expression to such feelings in verse. When Edith Cavell was executed in 1915, William Shaw of Maybole apostrophised the national martyr (in strains which owed something to *Sacred Songs and Solos*) who had, he claimed, suffered under 'the lewd and murderous Huns'. 'We are coming Nurse Cavell' he cried in the title:

> And not one heart shall falter,
> And not one hand shall fail;
> Now tremble, all ye murdering hordes,
> For Right shall sure prevail.[17]

The implication of the capital in the last line above was clear: Britain would win because her cause was that of God. Even after the war was over Pickering was happy to use the language of civil religion by calling the 'loved lads mowed down in battle' a 'Sacrifice'.[18] How widespread support was can be seen from the thirty-four different places from which the seventy-five individuals recorded in *The Witness* obituaries as killed in action came.[19] In the pursuit of the war, many Brethren were more than willing to identify with the wider society.

---

15. Carlisle Library, G852, David Beattie, 'God of Our Nation' (Carlisle [1914]), reprinted in *idem*, *Songs of the King's Highway* (London and Glasgow, 1927), p.35.

16. D. J. Beattie, *Oor Gate En'* (Galashiels, 1915), pp.73-100.

17. William Shaw, 'We are Coming Nurse Cavell', in M. J. Finlayson (ed.), *An Anthology of Carrick* (Kilmarnock, 1925), pp.381-2.

18. Henry Pickering, 'One golden curl', in W. Hoste and R. McElheran (eds), *The Great Sacrifice: or what the death of Christ has wrought* (Kilmarnock [1927]), p.132; however, for Pickering sacrifice in his context did not have the potential for moral regeneration cf. Gavin White, 'The martyr cult of the First World War', *SCH*, 30 (Oxford, 1993), pp.383-8.

19. *W*, 44-9 (1914-19), *passim*; the places were: Aboyne, Bo'ness, Boddam, Burnbank, Cambuslang, Chryston, Craigellachie, Dalry, Dumfries, Edinburgh, Elgin, Evie, Falkirk, Gatehouse of Fleet, Glasgow (13 different assemblies), Halfway, High Blantyre, Holytown, Irvine, Kilbarchan, Kilmarnock, Kirkmuirhill, Larkhall, Leith, Milngavie, Motherwell, New Stevenston, Paisley, Portessie, Rothesay, Saltcoats, Stirling, Thornliebank, and Tillicoultry.

On the other hand there were those who resisted the call to arms and a number of future Brethren leaders served in the 2nd Scottish Company of the Non-Combantant Corps.[20] *The Believer's Magazine* opposed Christians joining the army.[21] Casuistically, John Ritchie allowed that soldiering was a matter of conscience, but that the Christian's 'enlightened' conscience could lead to only one conclusion: it was wrong for the believer to resist evil, for the Word of God 'will not lead one Christian to take one way and another the opposite, on a matter so vital to life and testimony as this'.[22] However, that the greater blame resided with Germany and that the Empire was to be preferred was not in dispute in *The Believer's Magazine* either,[23] and as the war progressed Ritchie modified his position. Although he continued to advocate non-resistance to evil,[24] when conscription was introduced he admitted that it was a genuine issue of conscience. 'Uniformity of judgment on such a matter is well-nigh impossible,' he conceded, 'under the diverse teachings which have been so widely given concerning it'.[25] He appeared to favour a noncombatant role[26]—though he did not rule out conscientious objection to even that—and he printed lists in the magazine of those on active duty.[27] Ritchie had developed some sympathy to the aims of his society during the war to the extent that he was prepared to admit that the Bible might be capable of more than one interpretation on this point.

More adamantine was an individual such as Hunter Beattie, the leading individual in Tylefield Gospel Hall in the Gallowgate, Glasgow, and an evangelist who became a homeopath. He was against the Christian enlisting and was even opposed to noncombatant work or service in the

---

20. 'A. Naismith W. F. Naismith', in James Anderson (ed.), *They Finished their Course in the Eighties* (Kilmarnock, 1990), pp.128-9.

21. [John Ritchie], 'Should a Christian become a soldier?', *BM*, 24 (1914), p.118; W. H. Hunter, 'Ought a Christian to join the forces of the crown?', *ibid.*, pp.122-5; the Editor [John Ritchie], 'The Christian and the state', *ibid.*, pp.125-6, 139; [*idem*], 'YBQB', *ibid.*, p.130; J. Ritchie, 'The Christian's place of separation and service', *BM*, 25 (1915), p.8; [*idem*], 'YBQB', *ibid.*, p.46.

22. [John Ritchie], 'Arguments n [*sic*] favour of Christians enlisting examined in the light of God's Word', *BM*, 25 (1915), pp.35-6.

23. W. H. Hunter, 'The Great War', *BM*, 24 (1914), pp.97-9; *ibid.*, The Editor [John Ritchie], 'The war in Europe', pp.97-9; [*idem*], 'The sinking of the "Luisitania"', *BM*, 25 (1915), pp.71-2; [*idem*], 'Notes on the rebellion in Ireland', *BM*, 26 (1916), pp.71-2.

24. [*Idem*], 'The Christian and the nation', *BM*, 26 (1916), pp.62-3, 76-7; [*idem*], 'The Christian's responsibility to the state', *BM*, 27 (1917), pp.131-2.

25. [*Idem*], 'The Military Service Act, and the Christian's relation thereto', *BM*, 26 (1916), pp.34-5.

26. [*Idem*], 'Compulsory military service', *BM*, 26 (1916), pp.46-7.

27. *BM*, 27 (January 1917), p.iv.

Medical Corps.[28] He claimed that the pacifist position was deliberately excluded from the Glasgow Half-Yearlies,[29] and in October 1915 he began an occasional periodical, *The Word of the Cross*, declaiming his opposition. The first issue he distributed outside a conference in Glasgow, which led, he claimed, to the threat of his arrest by a leading Glasgow brother, and the sixth issue—the most controversial thus far—outside the city's Elim Hall (Henry Pickering's assembly), following a week-night meeting.[30] After Beattie received unfavourable publicity in a Sunday newspaper, in a letter to the same publication Pickering and the HFMF treasurer, C. P. Watson,[31] denied that Beattie's views represented that of the majority of the Brethren.[32] Feelings were running high, and when Glasgow Brethren supplied the War Office with a list of regular preachers among them who might claim exemption from service, Beattie's name was not included. As a result he had to appear before a war tribunal where he succeeded in obtaining exemption.[33] Others were not so fortunate and a number went to prison as conscientious objectors.[34] The war confirmed, and perhaps widened, the distance between the polarities of the Brethren, and on the cessation of hostilities concern was expressed that 'the warring spirit' would continue among assemblies.[35] The significance of the above attitudes to war will require further analysis in Chapter 9 for what they reveal about the attitude of the Brethren to the state,[36] but in the present context it is enough to note that they confirmed some in their alienation from society.

There was, however, one response to the war in which combatant and conscientious objector were united: the conflict was an indication that the end of the age was near.[37] Walter Scott, a publisher and writer on eschatological topics, in the first article to appear in *The Witness* on the war's relationship to prophecy, dismissed any idea that it could be read as

---

28. Beattie, 'Christ again before the Tribunal', *Christian and War*, pp. 62, 64.

29. *Idem*, 'Gagging the Lord's servants', *ibid.*, pp.96-100.

30. Beattie, 'Preface', *ibid.*, p.7; 'The persecution', *ibid.*, p. 122.

31. For HFMF see above, pp.144-5.

32. Beattie, 'The persecution', *Christian and War*, p.123.

33. *Ibid.*, pp.123-4.

34. The Liddle Collection, Leeds University Library, Leeds, 'Experience of John Campbell, Brookfield, Fenwick, during the First World War, both as a volunteer and a conscientious objector' (undated typescript deposition); James Montgomerie, 'My Odyssey' (undated, unpublished typescript), in the possession of Mrs Nora Montgomerie, Edinburgh (James Montgomerie was an evangelist with the Vernalite party of the Churches of God).

35. *The Witness*, quoted in Beattie, *Christian and War*, p.133 (see above, n.7).

36. See below, pp.306-8.

37. Cf. Rae, *Conscience and Politics*, pp.74-5.

an indicator of the proximity of the second advent,[38] but by the following month J. R. Caldwell was arguing that the war showed that the time of Gentile domination was almost at an end and that Israel's restoration was close, both thought to be crucial indicators of the imminence of the *parousia*.[39] However it was held by all that the end was not yet; the war could not be Armageddon, for the wrong nations were involved.[40] Scott did admit that though the war was not an event of prophecy, nevertheless it might be a sign, and the frequency with which articles and series on prophecy appeared in both *The Witness* and *The Believer's Magazine* shows that it was indeed perceived as an indicator of the end. Between 1914 and 1919 Scott's *Exposition of the Revelation of Jesus Christ* went through three editions,[41] in 1915 William Tytler, a Glasgow preacher, published his lectures on prophecy[42] and John Ritchie did the same with his lectures on Daniel (1915) and Revelation (1916) because the war was 'turning the thoughts of many Christians toward the prophetic word'.[43] The Lord's certain coming might not be reliably indicated by the war, but the consensus was that it was one more sign that it was very near.

Allied to this sense of crisis was a profound feeling of pessimism at the course which society was taking. The causes of the First World War were quite clear to Brethren writers. It was God's judgment on the sins of the nations. In his initial response to the war in *The Witness* of August 1914 Henry Pickering had exempted Britain from any blame. On the contrary, it was Britain, along with the United States, which had done the most to disseminate the scriptures throughout the world and as a result both countries had been left in peace. He felt that the probable cause of the war was God's judgment on Russia, Germany and France for their respective persecution of Jews and Protestant sects, the production of higher criticism, and for the promotion of atheism.[44] Britain entered the war on 4 August, making his editorial anachronistic by the time many of his readers would see it, and in later comments Pickering was not so

---

38. Walter Scott, 'Prophecy and the coming crises', *W*, 44 (1914), p.136; cf. HyP[ickering]., 'WW', *W*, 47 (1917), p.99.

39. J. R. Caldwell, '"The times of the gentiles"', *W*, 44 (1914), p.152.

40. W. W. Fereday, 'The present crisis: its relation to the prophetic scripture', *W*, 44 (1914), p.154.

41. The third edition was published in 1914 and the fifth edition was published either in 1918 or 1919.

42. William Tytler, *Plain Talks on Prophecy or, the great prophetic cycles of time* (Glasgow [1915]), pp.77-8.

43. John Ritchie, *Lectures on the Book of Daniel with expository notes on 'The Times of the Gentiles' and prophetic subjects* (Kilmarnock, 1915), p.3.

44. HyP[ickering]., 'The European upheaval', *W*, 44 (1914), p.133.

sanguine about the nation.[45] Others too had no difficulty in identifying the sins which had brought the war upon Europe.[46] A further cause of pessimism was the bloodshed which the war had brought. From the beginning Pickering calculated the number slaughtered,[47] while Hunter Beattie deplored 'the dreaded vortex of war, with its unparalleled suffering and slaying of men'.[48] The cessation of hostilities only served to increase the despair. Writing in 1919 Pickering felt that due to modern communications the world was being 'welded together for the last great conflict', depravity—such as unbelief and the events of the war—was increasing, and economic and political uncertainty created the expectation of a 'superman', a figure of evil who would lead the nations against Christ.[49] Increased Jewish emigration to Palestine and the creation of the League of Nations—harbinger of a world union opposed to God— were also widely seen as presaging the end.[50] J. Muir Kelly, the founder of the Jewish Medical Mission, summed up the general mood of the immediate post-war years: 'The air is heavy with the threat of impending storm. Fears and forebodings are paralysing the industry of the people. Revolt is preached in public places, and the spirit of lawlessness is abroad.'[51] The eschatological pessimism of the movement will be discussed further in the next chapter.[52] In this period it dominated the thought of Brethren of different tendencies, uniting them in a chorus of gloom.

The war had important consequences for the Brethren *mentalité*. Attitudes had been polarised by the different stances which had been adopted to the fighting and was a further factor that added to the strains within the movement which issued in schisms in the inter-war years.[53] The sectarian and denominationalising tendencies which had been present in the Edwardian era were clearly marked out by the conflict.[54] World War I undoubtedly confirmed a sense of separateness in those who became

---

45. HyP[ickering]., 'The world at war', *ibid.*, p.166; *idem*, 'How the war proves the Bible true', *W*, 47 (1917), pp. 65-7.

46. L. W. G. Alexander, 'The night in Scotland', *W*, 46 (1916), p.146; Beattie, *Christian and War*, pp.74-82; The Editor [John Ritchie], 'The war in Europe', *BM*, 24 (1914), pp.97-9.

47. HyP[ickering]., 'The European War', *W*, 44 (1914), p.149; *idem*, 'The War of millions', *ibid.*, p.181; *idem.*, 'Six million casualties', *W*, 45 (1915), p.33; *idem.*, *W*, 46 (1916), p.32.

48. Beattie, 'A lost opportunity', *Christian and War*, p.16.

49. HyP[ickering]., 'WW', *W*, 49 (1919), p.84.

50. *Idem*, 'WW', *W* 49 (1919), pp.52, 100.

51. J. Muir Kelly, 'The cure of unrest', *W*, 50 (1920), p.329.

52. See below, pp.253-9.

53. Cf. Wilson, 'Brethren Attitudes to Authority', p.58.

54. See above, pp.166-71.

conscientious objectors; and both it and the succeeding instability had increased the sense of alienation from society of even those Brethren who actively supported the British military effort. To the Brethren, the war had justified what they had always felt to be true of society. The world was rapidly decaying and the second advent presented an imminent escape from the turmoil.[55] These several factors hardened Brethren resistance to changes in society of which they disapproved and led to a more intransigent expression of their own world view. In the post-war years they entered the era of Fundamentalism.

Fundamentalism

For the jubilee of the Glasgow Half-Yearly Conferences in 1914 the conveners took as their theme for both the spring and autumn diets 'the Fundamentals'. The series concentrated on basic doctrines and John Gray, one of the conveners, stated that these topics were chosen because 'it was thought wise, in these days of declension and departure from the faith, that there should be a restatement of those "things most surely believed amongst us"'. He felt that the large numbers attending showed that they had correctly read the interests and needs of the audience.[56] The term 'fundamentals', as already has been seen, had long been used among Brethren,[57] but is likely that on this occasion the conveners were also influenced by the series of transatlantic pamphlets of the same title, issued in the years 1910-15, which have been seen as giving rise to the term 'Fundamentalism' in the 1920s.[58] The reassertion of the basic doctrines of Brethren Evangelicalism on such a significant event was part of the response to new currents of thought which were instinctively felt to be hostile.

In his study of the American Fundamentalist movement of the 1920s George M. Marsden has argued that it was characterised by the intensity of its response to attempts by theological modernism to remould Christianity in accordance with contemporary thought. It was the militancy which was injected into the resistance that gave birth to it as a separate phenomenon within Protestant Evangelicalism. Marsden analyses it as having four key emphases: dispensationalist premillennialism, withdrawal from society fostered by the holiness movement, a robust

---

55. HyP[ickering]., 'WW', *W*, 47 (1917), p.122.

56. J. G[ray]., 'The Fundamentals', *W*, 44 (1914), p.89; the quotation is of Lk 1:1.

57. See above, p.178.

58. George M. Marsden, *Fundamentalism and American Culture* (Oxford, 1980), pp.118-123.

defence of the faith, and a negative assessment of culture.[59] It has already
been argued that the Brethren were proto-fundamentalists in the
nineteenth century,[60] and, as can be seen from Marsden's definition, the
two movements had close affinities.[61] Yet a note of caution was
expressed. Henry Pickering regretted the birth of one more 'ism' when
already assemblies were loyal to the word of God.[62] John Ritchie rejected
the new term outright as it would mean being associated with an
interdenominational movement,[63] and during his control of *The
Believer's Magazine* it did not reflect the specific issues of Fundamentalism. Both men, however (as were all other Brethren individuals
during this period), were Fundamentalists. Ritchie had long felt the
animus against modernism which characterised the new movement,[64] and
by the late 1920s, when his health was poor, articles raising the concerns
of Fundamentalism began to appear and they occurred more frequently
after his death in 1930.[65] Pickering was less inhibited about acknowledging outside influences. While commenting on an article by the American
Fundamentalist R. A. Torrey he noted that it showed assemblies were
'TRUE FUNDAMENTALISTS, although they prefer to abide by the
titles given by God',[66] and *The Witness*, which Pickering proudly claimed
was the longest continued magazine 'out and out on the Fundamentals of
the Faith',[67] regularly carried articles and comments which showed
familiarity with the issues that were agitating adherents of the new
movement.

It was not just the principal two magazines which disseminated the
Fundamentalist project. Sermons and special series of addresses also

---

59. *Ibid.*, pp.3-6; for Fundamentalism in Britain during this period, see D. W.
Bebbington, 'Baptists and Fundamentalism in inter-war Britain' *SCH: Subsidia*, 7
(Oxford, 1990), pp.297-326; *idem*, 'Martyrs for the truth: Fundamentalists in Britain',
SCH, 30 (Oxford, 1993), pp.417-452; Ian S. Rennie, 'Fundamentalism and the varieties
of North Atlantic Evangelicalism', in Mark A. Noll *et al.* (eds), *Evangelicalism:
comparative studies of popular Protestantism in North America, the British Isles, and
beyond 1700-1990* (New York, 1994), pp.333-50.
60. See above, p.179.
61. Cf. H. A. Ironside, *A Historical Sketch of the Brethren Movement* (1945) rpt.
(Neptune, New Jersey, 1985), p.7; Ian Randall, '"Outside the camp": Brethren spirituality
and wider Evangelicalism in the 1920s', *BAHNR*, 2 (2000), pp.122-3.
62. HyP[ickering]., 'Who are the true Fundamentalists?', *W*, 54 (1924), p.403.
63. [John Ritchie], 'What are the Fundamentals?', *BM*, 34 (1925), p.39; cf. *BM*, 34
(1925), p.153.
64. See the epigraph to the present chapter.
65. For examples, see below, n.74.
66. HyP[ickering]., 'Who are the "Fundamentalists?"', *W*, 53 (1923), p.129.
67. *Idem*, 'About "The Witness"', *W*, 57 (1927), p.213; cf. Bebbington, 'Martyrs for
the Truth', p.423.

communicated Fundamentalist concerns.[68] The St Andrews Summer
Convention for Young Men and Young Women took as its theme for
1924 'The Testimony of Christ to the Fundamentals'.[69] Alexander
Marshall went on the attack with *Christ or the 'Critics': whom shall we
believe?* (1923). Henry Pickering began the 'Handbooks of the
Fundamentals' series in 1926[70] and in addition he wrote *The Believer's
Blue Book* (1930) which, taking its title from Parliamentary reports,
surveyed the items which he considered to be essential truths for
assemblies,[71] Literary forms were also pressed into service. Andrew
Borland, an Ayrshire English teacher, wrote two children's novels which
controverted evolution and impressed the reliability of the Old Testament
on their readers through a series of tendentious conversations which the
characters have with a Christian schoolmaster.[72] David Beattie fused the
Scottish literary Kailyard with Fundamentalism in his poems about Betty,
who rebuts the mockery of her doctor concerning the improbability of
Jonah by claiming:

> For I'd believe't gin God declared
> That Jonah gulp'd the whale![73]

It was not only, as is evident from the above examples, the cardinal points
of Christian doctrine and the verbal inerrancy of the Bible and its plenary
inspiration which were stressed; but also modernism, critical biblical
scholarship and contemporary cults and trends in society were regularly
attacked.[74] Even the political unrest of the 1920s could be perceived as

---

68. *W*, 57 (1927), 36; J. G[ray]., 'Large gathering of Scottish saints', *W*, 58 (1928),
pp.351-2; *idem*, 'Glasgow spring conferences 1935', *W*, 55 (1935), pp.133-4.

69. 'Summer convention for Bible study', *W*, 54 (1924), p.385; for this convention,
see above, p.209.

70. For the first two works issued in this series, see above, p.9.

71. Henry Pickering, *The Believer's Blue Book* (Glasgow [1930]).

72. Andrew Borland, *The Cradle of the Race: the story of the world in its early days,
told for young folks* (Kilmarnock [1925]); *idem, The Cradle of the King: the story of the
birth and early days of Jesus, retold for young people* (Kilmarnock [1929]).

73. D. J. Beattie, 'Betty and the Critic', in *idem, Oor Ain Folk* (Carlisle, 1933),
pp.56-7; cf. 'Betty and the Squire', *ibid.*, pp.64-6.

74. HyP[ickering]., 'WW', 47 (1917), p.83; Alexander Marshall, 'Scheme of leading
Evangelical preachers on eternal punishment', *W*, 50 (1920), pp.233-4; HyP[ickering].,
'WW', 54 (1924), p.324; *idem*, 'Modernism or the old faith', *W*, 55 (1925), pp.181-3;
A. Borland, 'The kenosis theory', *BM*, 38 (1928), pp.107-8; J. G[ray]., 'Large gathering
of Scottish saints', *W*, 58 (1928), pp.351-2; E. W. Rodgers, 'Eternal punishment', *BM*,
39-40 (Dec. 1929-Jan. 1930); W. Hoste, 'Things most surely believed among us', *W*, 60
(1930), pp.241-3; F. A. Tatford, 'The Bible reliable', *BM*, 41 (1931), pp.86-9, 108-110;
D. J. Beattie, 'Authenticity of the Scriptures confirmed by the spade', *W*, 52 (1932),
pp.37-8.

being related to unorthodoxy in the churches.[75] A special place, however, was kept for evolutionary theory which, because of its influence on the young, was felt to be an especial danger.[76] Pickering maintained that it needed only the addition of an initial 'D' to 'indicate its origin and its destiny',[77] and even the encroachment of science into preaching was felt to be acceptable if it meant that 'mere theories like Darwinism' were condemned.[78] Fundamentalist concerns permeated every aspect of assembly life.

Other denominations were seen to be riddled with false teaching. Pickering maintained that there was not one 'that contends for the fundamentals of the Christian faith'[79] and that tolerance had been taken too far.[80] Both he and Marshall quoted the example of C. H. Spurgeon who when faced with those who rejected the fundamentals of the gospel stated that the 'bounden duty of the true believer' was 'to come out from among them'.[81] Fundamentalists should logically join the Brethren. But John Ritchie was right in maintaining that engagement with Fundamentalism could lead to a lessening of Brethren separateness.[82] Fundamentalist nondenominational preachers such as H. A. Ironside or A. W. Pink, were welcomed to address assemblies,[83] and a number of Brethren found the Gideons International, an organisation dedicated to placing Bibles in public places, congenial.[84] James Anderson, the wartime MBE, for a few years after 1921 became a lecturer at the theologically conservative Bible Training Institute, Glasgow.[85] Cooperation can be seen most clearly, however, in the role some Brethren individuals played in the formation of the Inter-Varsity Fellowship (IVF), the conservative Evangelical student body founded in 1923 in protest at the increasing

75. HyP[ickering]., 'WW', *W*, 53 (1923), p.66.

76. E.g., C. F. Hogg speaking in Aberdeen, *W* 58 (1927), p.276.

77. HyP[ickering]., 'WW', *W*, 57 (1927), p.194.

78. 'BQB', *BM*, 42 (1932), p.48.

79. HyP[ickering]., 'WW', 50 (1920), p.210.

80. *Idem*, 'WW', 55 (1925), p.94.

81. Marshall, *Christ or the 'Critics'*, pp.30-2; Henry Pickering, 'Modernism or the Old Faith', *W*, 55 (1925), pp.181-3 (later published as *Modernism versus the 'Old Faith'* (London and Glasgow [1926])).

82. Randall, '"Outside the camp"', pp.17-33; *idem*, *Evangelical Experiences: a study of English Evangelicalism 1918-1939* (Carlisle, 1999), pp.165-6.

83. E. S. English, *H. A. Ironside: ordained of the Lord* (Grand Rapids, Michigan, 1946), pp. 221-4; Iain H. Murray, *The Life of Arthur W. Pink* (Edinburgh, 1981), pp.93-4; for the view of the present writer that Ironside was effectively non-Brethren in this period, see above, p.7 n.34; however, Ironside's Scottish Brethren roots meant he could conveniently be regarded as a member by contemporaries.

84. 'Dr J. Brown-Hendry', *W*, 96 (1966), p.315; 'Mrs Wallace Lee' *W*, 102 (1972), p.312; 'William Martin', *BM*, 103 (1973), p.432.

85. J. G[ray]., 'James A. Anderson, London', *BP*, 50 (1929), pp.34-6.

liberalism of the Student Christian Movement (SCM).[86] At Glasgow University the first president of the new body was from the Brethren and others had key roles in the formation of societies at Aberdeen and Edinburgh.[87] At a national IVF conference John Rollo, then a recent graduate of St Andrews, inspired several students to found one at his *alma mater*.[88] An early president of Aberdeen IVF, the young Frederick F. Bruce, managed to combine it with membership of SCM.[89] Brethren involvement in IVF was to influence individuals such as William Still, a future Evangelical leader in the Church of Scotland,[90] and in turn assembly members associated with para-church bodies came to understand that the Christian world was broader than the Brethren. Nevertheless the general impression was that the churches were corrupt and events were moving to their eschatological conclusion. When in 1932 a speaker at the Keswick Convention allegedly posited that Christ could have come down from the cross, it was felt that this was 'but part of the world-wide apostasy that is ripening fast for the reception of the man of Sin'.[91] The influence of Fundamentalism, like that of the World War I, was to make the Brethren more pessimistic about the direction of society and, in a time of change, more profoundly conservative.

Sectarian Resurgence

As was noted in the previous chapter, at least twenty-three new assemblies came into existence due to schisms in the inter-war era with a further seven in the decade succeeding World War II.[92] Assemblies have always been prone to divisions, but their incidence in these years was high. Often the source of the strife was a conflict of personalities, but during this time the deep splits in determining the strictness of purity in practice continued and were intensified. Many assemblies were like the one at Campbeltown in this period, contended over by competing tendencies.[93]

---

86. *DSCHT*, p.432; Oliver Barclay, *Evangelicalism in Britain 1935-1995* (Leicester, 1997), pp.24-5.

87. W. R. Soutter *et al.*, to the editor, *W*, 53 (1923), pp.166, 169.

88. Douglas Johnson, *Contending For the Faith: a history of the Evangelical movement in the universities and colleges* (Leicester, 1979), p.133.

89. F. F. Bruce, *In Retrospect: remembrance of things past* (London and Glasgow, 1980), pp.45-6.

90. William Still, *Dying to Live* (Fearn, 1991), p.84.

91. W. H[oste]., *BM*, 42 (1932), p.286.

92. See above, pp.198-9, 202; one of the eight post-war ones was founded after 1955.

93. Campbeltown, Argyll, Springbank Evangelical Church: 'Minutes of Business Meetings in connexion with the Assembly of God's People meeting in Shore Street Hall, Campbeltown, Argyll 1925-31', 30 May 1929; 16 June 1930; 'Minutes of Business

Fundamentalist anxieties could be handy sticks with which to beat
opponents. Ritchie made the unlikely claim that 'simple Assemblies of
God...are being assailed with such subtleties and reasonings by men who
have "crept in unawares"' causing division.[94] This was the legacy of the
movement's profound unease over societal change which had been
expressed by its Fundamentalist concerns. The result was an increased
emphasis on sectarian distinctiveness.[95]

One issue which for many focused the singularity of Brethren
ecclesiology was the reception of other Christian bodies into the
movement. Mission halls had to give guarantees that they had
discontinued unacceptable practices, such as women preaching, and even
then some never found universal acceptance.[96] In Lanarkshire the
accessions from the Stuart Party Exclusives proved exceptionally
controversial. The one in Carluke (popularly known as 'the Scott
meeting' after its leading individual, jam manufacturer James Scott) and
the Open Brethren meeting in the town united in 1920.[97] Doubts were
raised about Scott's acceptance of believer's baptism[98] and several
months later the two congregations separated.[99] In 1921 a group of
seventy 'representative brethren of assemblies in Lanarkshire' met to
discuss this dispute and they upheld the decision to divide as it was felt
continued unity meant accepting 'unbeliever's baptism'.[100] Evidently
stung by accusations being levelled against them, the Scott meeting
published an outline of its beliefs, asserting Fundamentalist doctrines but
maintaining that no particular mode of baptism would be insisted upon as
it was not 'a foundational truth vital to the salvation of the soul'.[101] Olive
Hall, Hamilton, had been included in the Open Brethren address list since
1904,[102] but about 1930 when one of its members wanted to join another
Lanarkshire Open assembly, the latter meeting split over the issue, the

Meetings in Connexion with the Assembly of brethren meeting in Springbank Gospel
Hall, Campbeltown 4th February 1931 -1951', 30 June 1933; 22 June 1936.

94. [John Ritchie], *BM*, 34 (1925), p.24; the quotation is from Jude 4.

95. Roy Coad, 'Into a changing future: the evolution of a movement and coping with
change', (a paper presented at a conference in Regent College, Vancouver, British
Columbia, 1991), pp.5-6; Randall, *Evangelical Experiences*, p.143.

96. Oral information, 24 August 1987; 3 April 1989; 17 July 1989; and 29 November
1989, from various assembly members.

97. *W*, 51 (1921), p.38; 'James Scott', *W*, 88 (1958), p.260; James Anderson (ed.),
They Finished their Course in the Eighties (Kilmarnock, 1990), p.125.

98. Oral information, 15 November 1986, from the son of one of the protagonists.

99. *W*, 50 (1920), p.328; *BM*, 32 (1922), p.11.

100. CBA uncatalogued papers, Robert Chapman to Henry Pickering, 11 March 1921,
anon. MS transcript; it seems likely that this letter was intended for publication in *The
Witness* but it did not appear: cf. *BM*, 30 (Oct. 1921), p.i; and *BM*, 32 (1922), p.11.

101. T. C. Suffil *et al.*, *Gospel Hall. Carluke* (n.p., March 1923).

102. See above, p.127.

secessionists making appeal to the 1921 judgment.[103] They were accused of holding "'Needed Truth Dogma'",[104] presumably because a central decision was being insisted upon as binding, while those who left felt the others had 'embraced evil', presumably because they could tolerate the presence of a former member of Olive Hall.[105]

The accusations levelled in this last schism were significant for they focus the issues which were involved for the participants. Those who wanted greater uniformity of practice among assemblies welcomed consultation with others when a dispute threatened.[106] They also stressed careful purity of practice in the administration of church life. In much of this they had affinities with those who left in the Churches of God secession of the previous century. There were those who felt that accessions from the latter body and the Exclusives during this period had imported their practices,[107] and certainly many Brethren were widely read in Exclusive literature.[108] But it is more likely that these trends were already current within the Open Brethren which was the reason for their appeal. The other group tended to be more pragmatic. In the 1930s after a further consultation of representative Brethren failed, one leading preacher counselled the three Stuart Party assemblies to seek individual recognition from their nearest Open ones and to avoid public debate.[109] Both the Scott meeting in Carluke and Albion Hall, Larkhall, were able to be accepted as Open Brethren in this way;[110] and in 1951 Olive Hall was eventually recognised by Baillies Causeway Gospel Hall, allowing general acceptance by others.[111] Pragmatism could not commend itself, however, to those who wished a uniformly pure practice and among them there was an increasing strictness. The policy of welcoming paedobaptists to the Lord's supper was further eroded, as can be seen from the Carluke dispute, by being rejected or reinterpreted.[112] Customs that had been

---

103. Oral information, 15 November 1986, from the son of one of the protagonists.

104. CBA uncatalogued papers, circular letter, 18 March 1931, MS.

105. *Ibid.*, draft letter fragment, undated MS.

106. Cf. above, p.183.

107. Robert Barnett, '"Brethren" history and its lessons for us to-day', *W*, 57 (1927), pp.127-8.

108. See above Table 1.1.

109. Oral information from the individual concerned, 24 April 1986.

110. See above, pp.194; however, Albion Hall, Larkhall, did not appear in an address list until 1983.

111. *W*, 81 (1951), p.114; *BM*, 61 (1951), p.140; Gospel Hall, Newmains, 'Minutes of Half-Yearly Meetings and Annual Meetings of Gospel Hall, Newmains', 1951-66, 15 April 1961, and 11 November 1961; however, Olive Hall had continued to be included in the address lists of the inter-war period, probably an indication of the broader attitude at Pickering & Inglis which published them.

112. In a transcript of the constitution of Hebron Hall, Larkhall, made in 1940 the provision to receive those 'who have not been scripturally baptised' is glossed by the

formerly acceptable to all, such as 'tea meetings', at which John Ritchie, for example, had spoken, began to be regarded as frivolous entertainment. It was the latest phase of the conflict between the pragmatic denominationalising tendency and that of the institutionalised sect.

Two preachers who had large and admiring followings throughout the thirties and into the post-World War II period were John Douglas and Isaac Ewan. Both men concentrated on 'Church truth'—church government and practice. Douglas, who came from Ashgill, Lanarkshire, was an impressive public preacher and a skilled debater who preached largely in Lowland Scots.[113] The possessor of a fine memory and with a gift for the telling aphorism, his intense dynamism commanded respect. 'John Douglas', wrote his friend Jimmy Paton, 'hit the scene something like an Elijah, suddenly with short, sharp, solid ministry that hit its target with great force.'[114] His appeal lay mainly among those who wanted stricter practices, and a circle of assemblies, particularly in Lanarkshire, was deeply influenced by him. Isaac Ewan, an evangelist from Abernethy, Perthshire, who had developed conscientious scruples about fighting while a soldier during the war, appealed to a similar constituency, though his influence was felt mainly in eastern and central Scotland.[115] A versifier of some distinction (his favourite poet was George Herbert), there was a strain of poetry in his make up.[116] He resisted the elimination of the last vestiges of spontaneous preaching,[117] promoting a charismatic ministry with no prior arrangement.[118] His concept of worship at the breaking of bread dictated a carefully prescribed order and specific

---

transcriber as meaning 'Baptism not to be made a door to exclude any who may <u>have a disability</u>' (alluding to the difficulty immersion might cause): Writer's collection, II, [Cornelius Dickson], 'Excerpt of Disposition for Hebron Hall Academy Street Larkhall. 1924', holograph transcript [1940].

113. His name was habitually pronounced in Scots as 'Joan Dooglas'; for a quotation from a sermon by him, see above, p.214.

114. [James Paton], 'John Douglas (1891-1976)', in James Anderson (ed.), *They Finished Their Course* (Kilmarnock, 1980), p.67.

115. Oral information, 10 August, 1990, from an assembly member.

116. [Edwin Ewan (ed.)], *Caravanserai: a collection of poems by I. Y. Ewan* (Glasgow, 1980).

117. Cf. above, pp.179; for the erosion of the practice see: [John Ritchie], *BM*, (1926), pp.23, 120; *W*, 59 (1929), p.213; for those critical of the practice, see: L. W G. Alexander, 'QA',*W*, 50 (1920), p.202; HyP[ickering]., 'WW', *W*, 65 (1935), p.40; E. W. R[odgers]., 'BQB', *BM*, 49 (1939), p.106; for those supporting the practice, see: [John Ritchie], *BM*, (June 1926), p.i; [J. Charlton Steen], 'The ministry of the word at conferences', *BM*, 40 (1931), pp.52-6; T. Fitzgerald to the editor, *BM*, 49 (1939), pp.132-3; J. K. McEwan, 'Selection of conference speakers', *PT*, 9 ([1946]) pp.135-6.

118. I. Y E[wan]., 'God's order of ministry', *PT*, 9 ([1946]), pp.141-4.

symbolic actions,[119] and his interest in poetry and worship led him to produce his own hymn-book, *Remembrance Hymns* (1935), for use at the morning meeting.[120] This seeming oxymoron of a spontaneous liturgy led to accusations of ritualism.[121]

A feature of both men's emphases was their opposition to any association with other churches and both preserved the distinctiveness of the Brethren in their teaching. Douglas's favourite texts were in the Pastoral Epistles, where the governance of the church and the unalterable character of doctrine are seen as guaranteeing community stability. Margaret Macdonald has argued that they belong to a phase of the early church when the expanding tradition lessened possibilities for innovation as it was institutionalised.[122] This account of the Pastorals closely corresponds to Douglas's aims.[123] Although Ewan was developing new ideas (something his critics used against him),[124] paradoxically these emphases were also strongly present in his teaching. About 1930 he founded a magazine, significantly entitled *The Present Testimony*, as an outlet for his writing and that of his associates, and among its key words were 'order', 'faithfulness', and their cognates.[125] Ewan, in addition, had his own way of expressing the distinctiveness of assemblies. Being 'gathered together in my name' had a special place in the Brethren understanding of the Church.[126] Ewan argued that the preposition should be 'into': other churches might gather *in* the Lord's name, only

---

119. W. R. Lewis and E. W. Rodgers to the editor, 'Ritualism at the Lord's supper', *W*, 82 (1952), p.120; I. Y. E[wan]., 'When should the bread be broken?', *PT*, 6 (1940-1), pp.984-8.

120. I. Ewan, *Remembrance Hymns* (Abernethy, 1935).

121. Lewis and Rodgers, 'Ritualism', p.120; G. C. D. Howley, 'The church and its members', in anon. (ed.), *A New Testament Church in 1955* (Rushden, 1956), p.21.

122. Margaret Y. Macdonald, *The Pauline Churches: a socio-historical study of institutionalization in the Pauline and deutero-Pauline writings* (Cambridge, 1988), pp.203-44.

123. Cf. John Douglas, *Lessons from the Kings of Israel and Judah* (Ashgill, 1997).

124. HyP[ickering]., 'Strange doctrines', *W*, 68 (1938), p.186.

125. A linguistic analysis of 81 articles in *The Present Testimony* shows 'order' and its cognates ('regulating', 'pattern', etc.), and 'faithfulness' and its cognates ('perseverance', 'stand fast', etc) are the key words on 18 occasions; the most common other key words are: 'the Word of God' in 10 articles; 'departure' and its cognates ('evil day', 'disorder' etc.), and 'separation' with 9 articles each. These are rivalled only by ethical virtues (chiefly 'obedience', 'meekness' and its cognates, and 'service') in 19 articles; cf. I. Y. E[wan]., 'Reversion to type or conformity to pattern', *PT*, 6 (1940-1), pp.1035-9; A. G[ilmour]., 'Assembly features', *PT*, 9 ([1946]), pp.8-12.

126. Matt. 18:20; cf. above, pp.25 (epigraph), 58.

assemblies were gathered *into* the Lord's name.[127] Both men had clear antecedents in the earlier debates among Brethren: Douglas was an admirer of John Ritchie[128]—he followed his teaching on the Church— and Ewan was deeply influenced by John Brown—his quibble over the preposition, for example, came from Brown.[129] Douglas and Ewan did not agree with each other and had separate spheres of influence, but they both attempted to enforce greater uniformity through doctrine, thereby minimising the possibilities for change and diversity.

It might have been expected that the emergence of such well-defined positions as those held by Douglas and Ewan would develop into open division. Douglas was involved in an acrimonious schism in Ashgill[130] and other assemblies had to decide with which of the two meetings to associate.[131] Ewan's magazine acted as a focus and he was accused by some of being divisive.[132] A recognised circle of assemblies, mainly in eastern Scotland, were known as 'Ewanite' because of their adoption of his practices. But a formal division in the east never came, nor did one in Lanarkshire. A group of individuals from several meetings in the county raised the idea of establishing themselves as a separate circle of assemblies in order to be free from association with the 'looser' practices of others. But when they approached John Feely of Newmains, who was respected by all because of his personal sanctity, he refused to countenance the idea and it fell into abeyance.[133] The divisions of the period must not be over-emphasised. No formal breach took place in Lanarkshire, and the assemblies which practised Isaac Ewan's teaching did not accept the nickname which was thrust upon them. Individuals of different emphases continued to read *The Witness* and to advertise their services side-by-side in it. What they had in common was still greater than the issues which threatened to drive them apart. The independency of Brethren assemblies gave them considerable capacity to absorb strains without them becoming an open breach. No-one in this period was willing to take the critical step of sacrificing the principle of autonomy. As positions polarised across Scotland, the larger meetings of

---

127. I. Y. E[wan]., '"In" and "Into"', *PT*, 8 (n.d.), pp.43-6; cf. H. P. Barker, 'What is meant by being "gathered to the name"?', *W*, 61 (1931), pp.133-4; Bruce, *In Retrospect*, p.23.

128. Oral information, 15 April 1990, from a Lanarkshire conference attender.

129. Bruce, *In Retrospect*, p.26; I. Y. Ewan and his associates are not named by Bruce but are identified in F. F. Bruce to the writer, 26 April 1987.

130. [Paton], 'Douglas', in Anderson (ed.), *They Finished*, p.68.

131. 'Minutes...Gospel Hall, Newmains', 21 November, 1959; *ibid.*, 15 April, 1961.

132. Anonymous individual 'who knows Scotland well', quoted in HyP[ickering]., 'Strange doctrines', p.186.

133. Oral information from a friend of Feely, 14 June 1987; for Feely's disapproval of schism, see [J. Anderson], 'Why fewer assemblies?, *BM*, 91 (1981), pp.164-5.

'representative brethren' that had been held in some areas to resolve difficulties gradually fell into disuse. While consensus was by now difficult, overall unity could still be preserved by the pragmatic use of independency.

The events and movements surveyed in the present section did not affect all assemblies. 'Hobnobbing with sectarianism is now quite common', reported one disgusted north-east emigrant when he visited Scotland in 1920.[134] But the issues and personalities which have been examined above were symptomatic. The agitation inspired by Fundamentalism and the search for stability within assemblies had the undoubted effect of making everyone more cautious. The older leaders who had maintained traditions of openness were dying: Caldwell died in 1917, Alexander Stewart in 1923, William Shaw in 1927, Marshall in 1928. Although Henry Pickering did not die until 1941, he was no longer an immediate presence having moved to England in 1922.[135] Only L. W. G. Alexander lived on until 1951. As has already been noted above in discussing Fundamentalism, there were those who had interdenominational associations. In 1926 when one Edinburgh minister accused the Brethren of narrowness, an assembly member in the capital contradicted him by pointing to a recent mission held in a city church by an evangelist from the movement.[136] In Netherburn, a few miles away from Ashgill (see Map 11), a preacher from the Lanarkshire Christian Union had a successful campaign in the assembly in the 1930s,[137] while a number of mission halls in the north of the county were largely dependent on Brethren speakers.[138] The effect of the prominent English Brethren Bible teachers who came north to preach in this period, men such as C. F. Hogg (1861-1943), Harold St John (1876-1957), and J. B. Watson (1884-1955), was to direct individuals towards a more devotional faith.[139] But those who now represented the denominationalising tendency did not possess the wide influence of the earlier leaders. Letters of commendation for visitors, a testimony to assembly membership,

---

134. Charles B. Summers (compiler and ed.), *Return to Old Paths: the ministry of Charles Spurgeon Summers* (Tacoma, Wa, 1990), p.215.

135. J. B. Watson, 'Henry Pickering', *Witness Supplement, W*, 71 (1941).

136. Anon., *'The Brethren': with special reference to a recent article in 'The Record' of the United Free Church July 1925 by Rev. James Black D.D. of Free St George's, Edinburgh, by an Edinburgh Brother* (Edinburgh [1926]); Black's article was later reprinted in his *New Forms of the Old Faith: being the Baird Lecture delivered in 1946-47 under the title extra-church systems* (London, 1948), pp.138-158.

137. Oral information, 23 November 1989, from an assembly member.

138. *H*, 2 (1924-5), p.63.

139. C. F. Hogg and J. B. Watson, *The Promise of His Coming* (London, 1943); Robert Rendall, *J. B. Watson: a Memoir and Selected Writings* (London, 1957); Patricia St John, *Harold St John* (London, 1961).

became *de rigeur* in many meetings.[140] Whatever individuals might have thought privately, it was a much less troubled course if controversial behaviour was avoided. And this was true, not just in relationships with other churches, but in other issues too. Despite the exceptions which might be cited, in this period sectarian separatism increased throughout Scottish assemblies.

Post-World War II Conservatism

World War II saw a repetition of the attitudes displayed in World War I. From the early 1930s onwards there was renewed interest in prophecy.[141] Caution was again enjoined against seeing contemporary events as being signs,[142] but John Ritchie Jnr wrote *Impending Great Events* (*c*.1938),[143] and Willie Thomson, a prominent Glasgow preacher, published *God's Peace Plan* (1944), which was, the subtitle informed the reader, *His coming King*.[144] And again there was support for the non-combatant position. In 1938 at a special meeting in Glasgow, of which every assembly in Scotland had been notified, the audience of some 500 were counselled by the speakers to be separate from earthly forces.[145] Individuals such as John Douglas advocated pacifism,[146] while Andrew Borland, from 1938 editor of *The Believer's Magazine*, argued that the bearing of arms was wrong and the Christian's primary responsibility was

---

140. 'BQB', *BM*, 40 (1930), p.24; this is a point supported by the comments of those who did not think them necessary: HyP[ickering]., 'WW', *W*, 61 (1931), p.185; W. W. Fereday, 'QA', *W*, 97 (1947), p.105; cf. above, p.195.

141. Walter Scott, 'Signs indicating the near return of our Lord', *W*, 63 (1933), p.273; S. Lavery, 'Great events ahead', *W*, 66 (1936), p.11; selections from elder brethren, 'The Roman Empire in history and prophecy', *ibid.*, pp.12-14; J. B. Watson, 'The outlook in the world today', *W*, 66 (1936), pp.25-9; J. R. Caldwell, '"The times of the Gentiles"', *W*, 66 (1936), pp.81-2; Robert McPike, 'Notable characteristics of the Last Days', *W*, 67 (1937), pp.13-14; Hy Pickering, 'The certainty and immanence of the Coming', *W*, 67 (1937), pp.77-8; John Ritchie [Jnr], 'A message for these perilous times', *W*, 69 (1939), pp.247-8; W. E. Vine, 'The night far spent and the approaching day', *W*, 70 (1940), pp.1-2; W. W. Fereday, 'Europe's last dictator', *ibid.*, p.63; [J. B. Watson], 'WW', *W*, 75 (1945), p.48.

142. Robert Rendall, *History, Prophecy and God* (London, 1954), p.70.

143. John Ritchie, *Impending Great Events: addresses on the Second Coming of Christ and subsequent events* (London & Glasgow [*c*.1938]).

144. W. A. Thomson, *God's Peace Plan: His coming King* (London and Glasgow, 1944).

145. *BM*, 48 (1938), p.329.

146. [Paton], 'Douglas', p.67.

to preach the gospel.[147] Because of their conscientious objections, Brethren boats were among the few which fished continuously throughout the war in the north east.[148] Conscientious objectors were treated more sympathetically by the government.[149] Although some went to prison,[150] most Brethren pacifists enlisted in a non-combatant corps.[151] Many supported the war actively,[152] but perhaps the majority now were pacifists,[153] leading Robert Walker, a Glasgow assembly member, to write a tract against their position because he felt opposing views had insufficient prominence.[154] Although Germany was clearly felt to be in the wrong because of its treatment of Jews,[155] there was none of the jingoism that some Brethren had engaged in during the earlier war. It was, perhaps, a sign of their increased disaffection with society. There were fewer killed in action: *The Witness* recorded only four.[156] But the effect of the Second World War was the same as the First: to deepen the sense of eschatological pessimism.

After the war, the divisions that had been evident earlier continued. Some had wider Christian associations, but on the other hand, Willie Trew, an evangelist from Lanarkshire, spoke for many when in 1954 he delivered a talk in Motherwell which later received a wide circulation as a booklet entitled *My Reasons for Not Being Free to Engage in Inter-Denominational Service*.[157] It was noted in the previous chapter that new initiatives in the post-war era, especially in youth work, had their critics.[158] The older methods had proved their worth in their time—a

---

147. Editor [A. Borland], 'The Christian and the civil powers', *BM*, 49 (1939), pp.29-35; cf. Wilson, 'Brethren Attitudes', p.63 n.27, for a list of articles appearing in the *Believer's Magazine* on recommended attitudes to the war during this period.

148. Paul Thompson, *et al.*, *Living the Fishing* (London, 1983), p.207.

149. Rae, *Conscience and Politics*, pp.244-5.

150. Oral information, July 1990, from a Lanarkshire assembly member.

151. 'Advice for younger Brethren regarding military service', *BM*, 49 (1939), p.191; W. Martin to the editor, *ibid.*, p.206; cf. Wilson, 'Brethren Attitudes to Authority', p.59.

152. John Ritchie, 'A message for perilous times', *W*, 69 (1939), pp.247-8.

153. Again this view of Scottish Brethren differs from that advanced for Brethren in general in Wilson, 'Brethren Attitudes to Authority', pp.59-80, which sees the balance between the two positions as being evenly split.

154. Robert Walker, *The Christian and Warfare: an examination of the pacifist position* (Chryston, 1942); 'Robert Walker', *W*, 91 (1961), p.476.

155. I. Y. E[wan]., 'True perspective', *PT*, 6 (1940-1), pp.966-9.

156. *W*, 69-75 (1939-45), *passim*.

157. William Trew, *My Reasons for Not Being Free to Engage in Inter-Denominational Service* (Kilmarnock, 1954); in the earlier part of the meeting in which Trew delivered this address he had recommended conscientious objection to National Service: oral information, July 1990, from an attendee at the meeting.

158. See above, p.206.

powerful argument for maintaining them—but they had also come to be accepted as part of the way things were. To change them would be to sacrifice basic biblical principles—an unanswerable argument for those advancing it. In the 1950s when the Ayrshire Tent Committee was considering substituting its marquee for a gospel van, one individual impressively quoted, 'Remove not the ancient landmark.' The change was rejected.[159] Any young man, as George Patterson discovered in the 1950s, who was judged to be too radical, quickly stopped receiving preaching engagements.[160] In addition, opportunities for innovation were diminished by the way elders were appointed. According to Brethren theory, the Holy Spirit gifted elders who were to be recognised, not formally engaged.[161] However, this acknowledgement was in the hands of the existing ones,[162] effectively making the oversight a self-appointing oligarchy which tended to be, like all such bodies, resistant to change.[163] A deep conservatism continued to pervade Scottish Brethren assemblies.

The underlying conservatism of the movement in the post-war years can be seen most clearly in reactions within Scotland to the actions of a group of leading Brethren in England.[164] G. C. D. Howley, an itinerant Bible teacher and editor of *The Witness* (1955-79), had been dismayed at the effects of the restrictive practices of stricter individuals during visits to Scotland and the Antipodes.[165] What he saw convinced him that unless they were resisted, their thinking would triumph. Using a metaphor that provides an insight into his perception of the matter, he wrote to his friend Robert Rendall, a leading member of the Brethren community in Orkney, that 'the policy of appeasement never pays in ecclesiastical matters, any more than it did with Hitler...[*sic*]'.[166] He began preaching openly against 'legalism'—the treatment of the Christian faith as a set of codified rules—and he also began to advocate publicly an open reception at the Lord's Table, citing the precedent of J. R. Caldwell for doing so.[167]

---

159. Oral information, 15 April 1990, from an attendee at the meeting; the reference is to Prov. 22:28.

160. Meg Patterson, *Dr Meg* (Milton Keynes, 1994), pp.41-2.

161. See above, pp.149-50.

162. William Hoste and William Rodgers, *Questions and Answers* (Kilmarnock, 1957), William Bunting (ed.), pp.138-9.

163. Cf. T. C. F. Stunt, 'Two nineteenth-century movements', *The Evangelical Quarterly*, 37 (1965), p.229.

164. Harold H. Rowdon, 'The post-war background to Nantwich 1991', in *idem*, (ed.), *The Strengthening, Growth and Planting of Local Churches* (Exeter, 1993), pp. 127-141; Coad, 'Into a changing future', pp.10-18.

165. Geoffrey Robson's collection, Kent, G. C. D. Howley to A. T. Ginnings, 20 January 1978.

166. OA/D27/6/9, G. C. D. Howley to Robert Rendall, 26 March 1956.

167. *Ibid.*

The result of Howley's forthright expression was that Scottish assemblies stopped inviting him to preach. In 1960, when he was back in Aberdeen after a long absence, Howley learned 'that I was deliberately not invited to the city over that long time through the influence of the "tights"'.[168] His desire for change and Christian unity were not wanted by many in Scotland or were liable to cause too much difficulty if openly supported.

The event which focused the opposition to Howley and those who thought like him was a conference in 1955 (one of a series initiated in 1953)[169] at High Leigh, Hoddesdon, Derbyshire. Changes in the support and training of Bible teachers and evangelists, the issue which was preoccupying Howley at the time, was the main proposal raised at it. Several speakers advocated Bible school training for promising individuals,[170] and other issues, such as the public participation of women and attitudes to Christians outside the Brethren, were raised in passing.[171] Although High Leigh affirmed much of current Brethren practice, it caused a storm within Scotland when the conference proceedings were published the following year. Andrew Borland saw it as setting a new direction among assemblies and felt the changes which had been mooted would mean the end of Brethren distinctives. 'And whither is that process drifting,' Borland queried of proposals for training preachers, 'if not towards clerisy against which the very existence of assemblies is a continuing protest?'[172] The conference was also strongly criticised in another Ritchie publication, *The Christian Worker*, by the editor Arthur Gooding, an English preacher who was resident in Scotland and a director of John Ritchie Ltd, and an off-print was circulated around every British assembly.[173] He too felt that the conference seriously undermined what Brethren represented, and that the proposals of High Leigh were 'alterations that will lead away from the Scriptures into the realm of expediency'.[174]

The criticisms of the conference and the divisions that were revealed were the first general breach that had appeared in print among Open Brethren since the reception question in the early years of the century.

---

168. OA/D27/6/9, G. C. D. Howley to Robert Rendall, 17 October 1960.

169. G. W. Robson, 'Swanwick, 1958', *H*, 37, No.12 (December 1958), p.185.

170. G. C. D. Howley, 'The support of the home ministry', in anon (ed.), *A New Testament Church*, pp.78-81.

171. Anon (ed.), *A New Testament Church*, pp.20, 23-8, 37, 41, 51, 91.

172. Andrew Borland, 'High Leigh: whither? (2)', *BM*, 66 (1956), p.216.

173. For Gooding see William Houston *et al.*, 'Arthur M. S. Gooding 1915-1999', in Robert Plant (compiler), *They Finished Their Course in the 90s* (Kilmarnock, 2000), pp.131-41.

174. [A. M. S. Gooding], 'The Editor of the *Christian Worker* reviews "A New Testament Church in 1955"', *CW*, 71 (1956), p.2; cf. Geoffrey Robson's collection, Kent, A. M. S. Gooding to F. N. Martin, 9 November 1965.

Borland and Gooding both stated that their strictures had been difficult to make as many of the individuals they were criticising were personally known to them and both attempted to find statements from the conference with which they were in agreement.[175] They were not alone in Scotland in attacking the proceedings at High Leigh. Although Borland received letters criticising him, there were many more who supported him and sermons were preached in many areas against the conference which, freed from the restrictions of print, were often biting.[176] Even someone sympathetic to the call for an open communion such as Rendall had reservations about some of the conference's other aspects. He wrote to Howley about the 'tempest' which was 'raging' over High Leigh, regretting it had raised 'issues on which there may be strong opposing views on debatable matters (like women taking part audibly in prayer for example)'.[177] There were those in Scotland, however, who identified more openly with the series to which High Leigh belonged. F. F. Bruce, by then a university lecturer, had been one of the speakers of 1955, and over succeeding years there were a number of Scottish contributors.[178] Gooding had agreed that 'legalists' were 'extremists' but added, 'it is evident that the majority of those taking part at the conference belong to the other extreme'.[179] There had been throughout the inter-war years a gap between what were sometimes termed 'the Henry Pickering-type meetings' and 'the John Ritchie-type meetings'. But this perception of those associated with High Leigh demonstrates the chasm which lay between the majority of Scottish assemblies and those proposing radical change. For most Scottish Brethren in the 1950s, Rendall's conservatism was typical. The context in which they operated ensured that even those leaders who were sympathetic remained cautious and bound to accepted practices.

High Leigh represented the strong denominationalising tendency then at work in England. Significant here is the social differences which were reflected in the division of opinion. The conference speakers were middle-class individuals, a social grouping which was becoming better represented among English Brethren in the 1950s. Assemblies of a predominantly working-class composition, however, tended to remain conservative. In 1956 one of Andrew Borland's critics accused him of

---

175. Borland, 'High Leigh (5)', *BM*, 67 (1957), p.26; [Gooding], 'Reviews', p.8.

176. Oral information, 15 April 1990, from an attendee at west of Scotland conferences.

177. OA/D27/6/4, Robert Rendall to G. C. D. Howley, undated.

178. Writer's collection, II, G. W. Robson to the writer, 6 January 1990: Andrew Gray, a director of Pickering & Inglis, and T. J. Smith, a company director and chairman of the HFMF, chaired sessions at early conferences; and A. P. Campbell, a company director, Andrew Gray and the headteacher John Rollo spoke at later ones.

179. [Gooding], 'Review', p.2.

'seeking to curry favour with the working class sections in the assemblies', evidently because Borland's views had greater acceptance among them.[180] Gooding, too, saw a social dimension to High Leigh. He felt the demand for the further training of preachers slighted those individuals of little education who until then had been the leading speakers in many areas. He referred affectionately to the men 'whose delivery was halting, whose grammar was poor' who had taught him in his youth.[181] 'In these days', he complained of the 1950s, 'a good education, an eloquent tongue, a well-stocked library, a good memory and a striking personality may open up to a man more opportunities for ministry than he can fulfil and all that without spiritual gift.'[182] Those in Scotland who were most prominent in supporting the High Leigh conferences were also middle class and were looking for a diminished sectarianism.[183] Changes in the social composition of Scottish assemblies, which became increasingly evident in the rising prosperity of the post-war years, were to become the most significant factor in loosening their conservatism.[184]

Counterpoint

Currents within Scottish Brethren were complex in the period under review in the present chapter and one of its subtexts has been those who did not conform to a more standardised order. This complexity can be seen in the role played by women within the movement. Under the influence of Fundamentalism fears were expressed over the growing involvement of women in society and the pressure for change from women's movements.[185] Their altered roles were perceived as indicating the loosening of society's foundations, and many words were expended by the Brethren on issues relating to them. Tom Baird, a Scottish emigrant to the United States who wrote frequently for *The Witness*, opined that 'When the women of the world lead revolt and hurl defiance into the face of the Eternal God the race has reached the deepest depth of degradation.'[186] New women's fashions in hair were regarded with disapproval. In the 1920s Henry Pickering noted with satisfaction that one hairdresser had refused to bob a woman's hair, though he did

---

180. Borland, 'High Leigh (5)', p.26; for an example of the possible influence of class on sectarianism in this period, see below, pp.298-9.

181. Gooding, 'Review', p.8.

182. *Ibid.*, p.7.

183. See the listing of occupations given above in n.178.

184. See below, pp.344-7.

185. HyP[ickering]., 'WW', *W*, 47 (1917), p.91; *idem*, 'WW', *W*, 56 (1926), p.334.

186. Tom Baird, 'God's will for women', *W*, 56 (1926), p.451.

caution one questioner that a woman with her hair styled in this new fashion should not be excluded from the Lord's supper.[187] The later trend for women to attend church without a hat was likewise regarded with disapproval.[188] Brethren males wanted their women to preserve the Victorian preferences for long hair and having their heads covered in church, and Biblical teaching was adduced to that effect.[189] It was hotly debated whether a woman's long hair meant that it was uncut,[190] and both Pickering and William Hoste, an Irish preacher and editor of *The Believer's Magazine* (1931-8), claimed that her head should be covered when praying at home.[191] Women had to be seen to be in subjection.

Any form of leadership or public speaking to mixed audiences by women was firmly rejected, and their role was seen as being the ones of homemaking and child care.[192] In Brethren eyes women tended to gain their significance in relation to men. One Lanarkshire writer felt that 'In the divine economy the woman has not been given a public place in the assembly of God; but she has a great deal to do with shaping of the man, who has been given that place. It is a noble and honourable work...'.[193] Andrew Borland stated that the companionship of a young woman kept men attending meetings, and (with a revealing use of Scots) that women were good for working among "the bairns".[194] So strong was the emphasis on a woman remaining silent that women were not permitted to ask questions at Bible readings or assembly business meetings,[195] many did not approve of female solo singers,[196] and some felt that even sisters' meetings should not be permitted. 'Do you not think that a sister's place is one of obscurity?' queried one individual.[197] John Douglas strove to express these points as epigrammatically as possible. 'Two things God requires of women: hair and silence,' he said on one occasion;[198] and on

---

187. HyP[ickering]., 'WW', *W*, 58 (1928), p.334; *idem*, 'QA', *W*, 59 (1929), p.233.

188. J. B. Watson, 'WW', *W*, 72 (1942), p.100.

189. Baird, 'God's will', p.451.

190. P. Parsons, 'BQB', *BM*, 78 (1968), p.314.

191. W. Hoste, 'QA', *W*, 60 (1930), p.207; HyP[ickering]., *ibid.*, pp.230, 254.

192. HyP[ickering]., 'WW', *W*, 56 (1926), p.294; *idem*, 'WW', *W*, 59 (1929), p.140; Editor [J. C. Steen], 'BQB', *BM*, 41 (1931), p.71; 'Correspondence', *BM*, 42 (1932), p.166; Editor [A. Borland], 'The Church', *BM*, 68 (1958), pp.25-7, 49-50; G. M. Munro, 'Divine control', *PT*, 9 ([1946]), pp.49-53.

193. W. Prentice, 'Marriage', *BM*, 67 (1957), pp.31-2.

194. Editor [A. Borland], 'The service of sisters', *CW*, 58 (1941), p.49.

195. HyP[ickering]., 'QA', *W*, 59 (1929), p.89; 'BQB', *BM*, 37 (1937), p.182; W. A. Thomson, 'QA', *W*, 69 (1939), p.159.

196. 'BQB', *BM*, 41 (1941), p.142; [A. Borland], 'Making a noise', *BM*, 55 (1955), pp.133-4.

197. F. A., 'QA', *W*, 67 (1937), p.206; cf. 'QA', *W*, 67 (1937), p.206; but see 'BQB', *BM*, 43 (1933), p.24, for sisters' prayer meetings being supported.

198. Oral information, 3 August 1993, from an attendee at an Ayrshire conference.

another, 'God gave them fu' airms to keep their mooths shut.'[199] In the strictest assemblies there was segregated seating for men and women during participatory meetings.[200] Until the 1920s women could take part in mixed-sex prayer meetings in Strathaven,[201] but over the period the role of women was further constricted. Within assemblies it was thought to be that of permeating an ethereal mystique. 'The atmosphere of meetings, that intangible thing which means so much,' wrote Borland, 'is greatly determined by the godliness or otherwise of the sisters'.[202] In the north-east fishing communities the seasonal absences of men created a problem. With the men at sea the women would gather for the morning meeting but did not break bread. In such circumstances, Pickering felt, it would be appropriate for the women to pray together and for one of them to address the others.[203] *The Believer's Magazine*, on the other hand, counselled that 'the godly course would be for the sisters to wait silent before the Lord, as long as they felt able, and then quietly retire.'[204] It is difficult to resist the impression that most Brethren believed in the priesthood of male believers only during this period.

Yet against such discouragement there were women who achieved a more active role. There were some who were involved in their wider community, gaining its respect, such as Elizabeth Duff, an illiterate Irish immigrant of an unfailingly hospitable nature, who was held in such esteem that when she died in 1938 every blind in the village of Busby, Renfrewshire, was drawn as her cortege passed;[205] or Janetta Macdougall, a member of Union Hall, Uddingston, who was a maternity home matron and was awarded the MBE in 1956 for her distinguished service in that capacity.[206] A positive role model for women in Christian pursuits was offered by women missionaries:[207] it was they who spoke at the Young Women's Conference held in Elim Hall, Glasgow, in 1962.[208] But it was possible for women to achieve a more active role within some assemblies

199. Writer's collection II, John Boyes to the writer, 14 April 1990.

200. Oral information, 17 September 1991, from a female assembly member; for this practice in Christian history see Margaret Aston, 'Segregation in church', *SCH*, 27 (Oxford, 1990), pp.237-294.

201. Oral information, July 1990, from a attendee at a Strathaven prayer meeting.

202. [Borland], 'service of sisters', p.49.

203. 'HyP[ickering]., 'QA', *W*, 54 (1924), p.233.

204. W. H[oste]., 'BQB', *BM*, 42 (1932), p.119.

205. 'Mrs Duff', *BM*, 47 (1938), p.28; A. McAllister and J. Vernal (compilers), *Busby Gospel Hall: A Short History of Early Days, 1891-1964* (n.p., 1964), pp.2, 21-2.

206. 'Mrs Janetta Macdougall M.B.E.', *BM*, 93 (1983), p.32.

207. Pickering & Inglis published E[mma]. R. Pitman, *Lady Missionaries in Many Lands* (Glasgow [1929]); first published as *Lady Missionaries in Foreign Lands* (London, 1889). John Ritchie published [Frank Mundell], *Heroines of the Faith*, 1st edn (1898), 2nd John Ritchie edn (Kilmarnock, n.d), the stories of female martyrs.

208. *W*, 92 (1962), p.76.

of the less rigorous type. There were the many women involved in evangelism discussed in the previous chapter.[209] Women also continued to write. Mrs J. A. W. Hamilton of Glasgow and later Waterford, Ireland, contributed devotional verse regularly to *The Witness* and wrote the women's page in *The Christian Graphic*, a Pickering & Inglis magazine.[210] And there was the rare woman who could achieve a more dominant role within an assembly. In the mid-century when Chirnside meeting had no males, during the winter months the Lord's supper would be prepared in case a man arrived, but the elements would not be dispensed without one. However, the women used the occasion as a prayer meeting and maintained the assembly: one of them, Grace Stewart, was responsible for its organisation by, for example, arranging visiting male preachers during the summer.[211] Such a woman was achieving a more pastoral capacity, and it was also possible to reach this situation in larger assemblies with men present, albeit within a limited sphere. Ena Thomson of Elim Hall, Glasgow, was noted for her sound common sense and ability to size up both spiritual and physical problems quickly and deal with them. She had a special interest in missionary work, visiting some missionaries abroad and giving hospitality to others. When she died in 1959 her (doubtless male) obituarist in *The Witness* made the rare confession that she had skills which were uncommon in both men and women. 'Many, indeed,' he wrote, 'were indebted to her for kindly consideration, wise counsel, and that get-on-with-it encouragement which is so often needed but not often available.'[212] Although any official leadership position was denied to such women, they functioned in one *de facto*.

The achievements of such women in assemblies were, however, exceptionally modest. A parallel case might be those who held eschatological views which differed from the majority. One such individual was John Anderson from Rhynie, who returned to the north-east from China in 1920. He kept alive the earlier tradition of female preaching by advocating the public participation of women through his writings, and the other minority viewpoint he championed was post-tribulationism.[213] But on both issues he was perceived as a lonely and

---

209. See above, p.208.
210. 'Mrs J. A. W. Hamilton', *W*, 69 (1939), p.192.
211. 'Miss Grace Stewart', *W*, 95 (1975), p.396.
212. 'Mrs Robert Thomson', *W*, 89 (1959), p.36.
213. John A. Anderson, *Woman's Warfare and Ministry: what saith the Scriptures?* (Rhynie, n.d.); *idem, The Authority for the Public Ministry of Women* (Braemar, n.d.); *The Blessed Hope: a study in dialogue form on the coming again of the Lord Jesus* (London [*c*.1930]); *idem, The Chart: the Divine forecast of this age* (London, n.d.); *idem, Heralds of the Dawn* (Aberdeen [*c*.1934]); for post-tribulationism, see above pp.157-8, and for the majority eschatological view, see below, pp.259-66.

eccentric voice.[214] A more prominent exponent of post-tribulationism was the evangelist Peter Bruce, but he too failed to win adherents and at one large conference was publicly contradicted when he expounded his views.[215] Other dissidents met with a similar lack of success. In the 1950s Robert Rendall came to query the rigid dispensationalist scheme of the Brethren, but he was muted in his questioning,[216] and when Peter Bruce's son, F. F. Bruce, a postmillennialist, wrote an article on his prophetic views for *The Witness*, the then editor, J. B. Watson, declined to print it because, Watson felt, the magazine should carry articles on matters 'most surely believed among us'.[217] More success, both in numbers and influence, in resisting the formation of assemblies into a more regulated body attended those who innovated in evangelistic forms after World War II and those who were exceptions to the general rule of withdrawal from church and society. In the latter case there were the many individuals, men and women, who were involved in interdenominational ventures, discussed above and in the previous chapter. Such individuals kept the ecumenical vision of the Brethren movement alive and preserved it from becoming isolated from the larger Christian world.

F. F. Bruce was the most significant individual in this regard. Becoming the first Brethren Scot to be appointed to a university chair when he became professor of Biblical Studies at Sheffield University in 1955, Bruce was later appointed to the prestigious John Rylands Chair of New Testament Exegesis at Manchester University.[218] He spent most of

---

214. Bruce, *In Retrospect*, p.53-4.

215. Roy Coad's collection, Shropshire, A. M. S. Gooding to F. N. Martin, 9 November 1965; P. F. Bruce is not named in this letter, but it is clearly he who is intended.

216. Robert Rendall to William Barclay [c.1955], in Neil Dickson (ed.), *An Island Shore: selected writings of Robert Rendall* (Kirkwall, 1990), pp.53-4; *idem, History, Prophecy and God*, pp.68-9; cf. J. Stafford Wright, 'History, Prophecy and God', *Evangelical Quarterly*, 27 (1955), p.177.

217. F. F. Bruce, 'His writings', *W*, 85 (1955), p.199; the quotation is of Lk 1:1 (cf. above, pp.227, 229 n.74). For Bruce's postmillennialism, see his review of Iain H. Murray, *The Puritan Hope* (1971), in 'Book reviews', *W*, 106 (1976), p.432; and F. F. Bruce, *The Letter of Paul to the Romans: an introduction and commentary*, 2nd edn (Leicester, 1985), pp.199-212; Bruce also supported the public participation of women: he almost certainly, as the style shows, is the 'acknowledged authority on New Testament Greek' quoted by John Anderson in *Public Ministry of Women*, p.10, in support of Anderson's interpretation of 1 Tim. 2:8-9; cf. F. F. Bruce, 'Women in the Church: a biblical survey', *CBRJ*, 33 (1982), pp.7-14; and below, p.357.

218. On F. F. Bruce see: Bruce, *In Retrospect*; G. C. D. Howley, 'Frederick Fyvie Bruce: an appreciation', in W. W. Gasque and R. P. Martin (eds), *Apostolic History and the Gospel* (Exeter, 1970), pp.15-19; W. W. Gasque, 'A select bibliography of the writings of F. F. Bruce', in Gasque and Martin (eds), *Apostolic History*, pp.21-4; *idem,*

his professional life in England, but his reputation gave him considerable influence among Scottish Brethren. It is, however, for his influence on transatlantic Evangelicalism that he achieved greater significance.[219] Bruce brought to his studies a breadth of learning which had until then been rare within twentieth-century Evangelicalism. He was happiest pursuing his biblical studies in a university context where he found freedom from 'theological or sectarian bias',[220] and one obituarist commented that 'he personified catholicity'.[221] I. H. Marshall has argued that Bruce brought a rigorous scholarship to the study of the Bible doing much to counteract Fundamentalist attitudes to scripture which refused to engage with academic approaches. He stated that 1951, the year of publication of Bruce's *The Acts of the Apostles: the Greek text with introduction and commentary*, was 'the decisive date in the revival of evangelical scholarship and in its recognition by other scholars'.[222] Although many of Bruce's conclusions on textual and critical issues were conservative, this was because, he maintained, the evidence demanded it and not because of a predetermined position;[223] consequently he was prepared to accept more radical conclusions.[224] Writers on Fundamentalism comment on the role the Brethren have had in maintaining it.[225] Bruce's commitment to academic freedom meant that he was to have a key role in the eclipse of Fundamentalism within Evangelicalism and, eventually, in the minds of many Brethren.[226]

There were also a number of Brethren Scots who engaged significantly with culture and society. The work of David Beattie has already been

---

'A supplementary bibliography of the writings of F. F. Bruce', *CBRJ*, 22 (1971), pp.21-47.

219. Mark A. Noll, 'Evangelicals and the study of the Bible', in George Marsden (ed.), *Evangelicalism and Modern America* (Grand Rapids, Michigan, 1984), p.105; *idem*, 'C.T. at thirty', *Christianity Today*, 17 October 1986, p.21; *idem*, *Between Faith and Criticism: Evangelicals, scholarship and the Bible* (Leicester, 1991), pp.102-6, 123-4, 209-12.

220. Bruce, *In Retrospect*, p.140.

221. B. Drewery, 'His text was the Bible', *The Guardian*, 21 September 1990.

222. I. H. Marshall, 'F. F. Bruce as a biblical scholar', *CBRFJ*, 22 (1971), p.6.

223. Bruce, *In Retrospect*, p.311; cf. Iain H. Murray, *Evangelicalism Divided: a record of crucial change in the years 1950 to 2000* (Edinburgh, 2000), pp.180-1.

224. James Barr, *Escaping From Fundamentalism* (London, 1984) p.156; Barclay, *Evangelicalism in Britain*, p.129.

225. Ernest R. Sandeen, *The Roots of Fundamentalism: British and American millenarianism 1800-1930* (Chicago, Illinois, 1970), pp.59-80; James Barr, *Fundamentalism* (London, 1977), p.19; Rennie, 'Fundamentalism', in Noll *et al.* (eds), *Evangelicalism*, pp.333-47.

226. Roy Coad, 'F. F. Bruce: his influence on Brethren in the British Isles', *CBRFJ*, 22, pp.3-5.

mentioned.[227] He also produced a number of prose sketches which owe their inspiration to the Kailyard school of writing,[228] and it was in this period he wrote his two secular histories, his best non-religious work being *Lang Syne in Eskdale* (1950), a history of Langholm and its environs.[229] He was not alone. It was in the inter-war years that Robert Rendall made his archaeological discoveries in Orkney, including the Broch of Gurness, a well-preserved Iron Age fort.[230] In the two decades after World War II he produced dialect poetry on non-religious themes, a study of Orcadian mollusca, and historical and biographical writings. Although Rendall was the most significant figure in celebrating a local culture and becoming its literary spokesperson there were others. Tom Todd, a Borders shepherd and a Biggar assembly member, wrote dialect poetry under the pseudonym 'T. T. Kilbucho',[231] earning him Hugh MacDiarmid's accolade that his folk poems were 'the best of this kind in Scotland since Burns or Hogg'.[232] Also in the Borders, William Landles of Hawick, a poet and newspaper columnist, was awarded the MBE for his contribution to the literature of the region,[233] and another columnist, the journalist John S. Borland, brother of the editor of *The Believer's Magazine*, was known as the repository of the lore of the upper Irvine

---

227. For D. J. Beattie see: 'Founder of city firm is dead', *Cumberland News*, 3 August 1964, p.11.

228. Beattie, *Oor Gate En'*; *idem*, *Oor Ain Folk*.

229. *Idem*, *Langsyne in Eskdale* (Carlisle, 1950); also *idem*, *Prince Charlie and the Borderland* (Carlisle, 1925).

230. For Robert Rendall see: Neil Dickson, 'Robert Rendall: a life', in *idem* (ed.), *An Island Shore: the life and work of Robert Rendall* (Kirkwall, 1990), pp.17-49; George Mackay Brown, 'Robert Rendall', in *An Orkney Tapestry* (London, 1969), pp.163-71; 'A select bibliography of Robert Rendall's writings', in Dickson, *An Island Shore*, pp.218-19; Nora F. McMillan, 'Robert Rendall, 1898-1967', *Journal of Conchology*, 19 (1968), pp.273-4; see also below, pp.324-5.

231. For Tom Todd, see T. T. Kilbucho, *Sixty Rural Years* (Galashiels [1968]); *idem*, *My Rural Sojourn* (Edinburgh [1978]), pp.3-9; T. B. F., 'T. T. Kilbucho—poet, farmer and broadcaster', *Southern Recorder*, 10 January 1985, p.2. Todd's poetry books are: *Gathered in a Lowland Glen* (Glasgow [1954]); *Clachan and Countryside* (Glasgow [1956]); *A Shepherd's Years* (Glasgow, 1961); *From a Shiffoneer Drawer* (Thankerton [?1973]); and *Kilbucho's Latest* (Glenrothes [c.1974]).

232. Hugh MacDiarmid, 'An Appreciation', in T. T. Kilbucho, *Clachan and Countryside*.

233. For William Landles, see B. P., 'Death of devoted Christian and prolific writer', *Hawick News*, 1 January 1999, p.8. William Landles' poetry books are: *A Breath Frae the Hills* (Hawick, 1937); *Gooseberry Fair* (Hawick, 1952); *Penny Numbers* (Hawick [1961]); and *The Turn o' the Year* (Hawick, 1989); some of his journalism has been collected in: *I To the Hills* (Hawick, 1978); *All Good Gifts Around Us* (Hawick, 1982); *Roving Commission* (Hawick, 1992); he also wrote *Will H. Ogilvie: Poet of the Romantic Borderland* (n.p., 1993).

Valley in Ayrshire.[234] There were others who engaged in public service, such as David Warnock, the Chief Constable of Glasgow who died in 1943.[235] Trade union involvement was normally disapproved of strongly,[236] but there were a few who were active in union affairs, most notably James Barbour of Cowie, Stirlingshire. He became President of the National Union of Scottish Mineworkers as well as being active from 1922 in local government, first as an elected representative on Stirlingshire Education Authority and then from 1927, when these bodies were taken over by local authorities, as a councillor.[237] There were other individuals who served in this last capacity, two of whom had some significance. John Davidson, a businessman, joined Bathgate town council in 1919, becoming in succession a bailie, magistrate and police judge, before being elected provost in 1926.[238] Another businessman, John Henderson, in 1925 was first elected to Glasgow City Council for Langside Ward,[239] and in 1946 he became Conservative member of Parliament for Glasgow Cathcart division.[240] Involvement in society, rather than withdrawal, was acceptable to many Brethren during this period of the twentieth century.

At a time when the sectarian polarity of the Brethren movement had exercised a strong pull, the denominationalising tendency, which entailed a greater accommodation with society, was not without attraction. Fundamentalism, which displayed sect-like features, had in Britain nothing like the acrimony it possessed in America.[241] The Brethren in this period showed a similar moderation and in this respect are a classic British sect.[242] The archetypal individual of the epoch was Andrew Borland, a devout man who saw himself as treading a line between the stricter Scottish schools and that of High Leigh and its supporters. By no means blinkered in his thinking and of wide theological reading—

---

234. For J. S. Borland see, 'He carried his copy in his head', *KS*, 23 April 1971, p.3; 'A gifted Galstonian: tribute to 'Sifter', *KS*, 30 April 1971, p.6; also see below, p.324.

235. Crosshill Evangelical Church Archive, Glasgow, *Memorial Service to Mr. David Warnock.*

236. Cf. below, pp.310-11, 314, 319.

237. Mrs Sarah Campbell, Edinburgh, Cuttings scrapbook; this consists mainly of articles from *The Stirling Observer*, 1939-1956; cf. 'James Barbour O.B.E., J.P', *BM*, 96 (1985), p.157; see also below, pp.322-4.

238. 'Death of ex-Provost John Davidson', *West Lothian Courier*, 26 January 1945.

239. 'John Henderson (Langside Ward)', 'Glasgow Scrapbook', 13, Mitchell Library, Glasgow.

240. *Who Was Who 1971-1980*, 7, 2nd edn (London, 1989), pp.356-7; see below, pp.323-4.

241. Bebbington, 'Martyrs for the Truth', p.451.

242. Bryan Wilson, *Sects and Society: a sociological study of three religious groups in Britain* (London, 1961), p.2.

admiring particularly pietistic traditions of Christian writing[243]—his prudence gave rise to a profound conservatism. He counselled one assembly considering a change 'that any departure from customary procedure which is likely to cause dissension should be viewed with the utmost caution'.[244] While such moderation inhibited innovation, it also checked more acerbic reactions to society.

The issues discussed in the present chapter widened the polarities of the movement. Fears over contemporary secular trends, keenly felt during and after both world wars and deepened by a sense of eschatological pessimism, led to withdrawal, and these anxieties were expressed through Fundamentalism and the increased sectarian impulse of the mid-century. The effect of these was to make the movement cautious in case it should be accommodating the modern world. A renewed phase of sectarianism ensued, noticeably seen in the teaching of Isaac Ewan and John Douglas. Ewan displayed the paradox of the charismatic leader who innovates but does not allow any change once his practices have been accepted because they represent the purest form of church. Douglas was more content to accept mainstream Brethren traditions, but shared Ewan's desire for inflexibility in doctrine and practice. The resistance to innovation across Brethren of differing views was characteristic of the established sect. Yet despite a renewed phase of sectarian separatism, no-one was willing to take the crucial step of developing centralised control, perhaps because the Churches of God example was before them and they wished to be saved the accusation of importing their teaching. The Open Brethren principle of preserving uniformity through doctrine and not organisation was maintained.[245] It was through this means that the homogeneity of the movement was retained. But this policy preserved the independency of the Brethren and it permitted a number of individuals to develop a role within society. They could unbend a little: Rendall was a keen fisherman, Henderson was a bowling club president, and John Borland played golf. Those who involved themselves with society tended to be in the upper echelons of the more socially stratified society of Glasgow or the more homogeneous rural communities. In these localities a sectarian response to the anomie of modern life was not so compelling. A denominationalising strand continued throughout this period and its increase after World War II led to its burgeoning after the mid-1960s. It would

---

243. Andrew Borland, 'Books that have helped', *W*, 101 (1971), pp.296-7: among those listed are Thomas à Kempis and Brother Lawrence; the present writer also has in his possession a copy of Jeremy Taylor's *The Rule and Exercises of Holy Living* (1650) which Borland gave to a friend.

244. Writer's collection, II, Andrew Borland to Tom Dickson ([1956]).

245. Gordon Willis and Bryan Wilson, 'The Churches of God: pattern and practice', in Bryan R. Wilson (ed.), *Patterns of Sectarianism: organisation and ideology in social and religious movements* (London, 1967), pp.245-6; cf. above, p.182.

subsequently become apparent that a phase of Brethren life had come to an end.

CHAPTER EIGHT

Musing While We Sing:
Spirituality 1830s-1960s

Backward look we, drawn to Calvary,
  Musing while we sing;
Forward haste we to Thy coming,
  Lord and King.
Douglas Russell, *Songs of Salvation and Glory* (1927).[1]

Singing had an important place in Brethren life.[2] In 1922 one individual commented on the 'hearty' singing at the Glasgow Half-Yearly Conferences before noting, 'when by special request the thousands of voices sang, as only the Lord's people can sing, the 100th Psalm, we could not help thinking of the time when all the redeemed safely gathered home at last will sing without a discordant note the new song'.[3] For this observer the harmony of the singing was a symbol of the unity of Christian believers and its perfection in the world to come. Even the character of the metrical psalm had been transformed by its fervour. The movement had accepted the new hymns with their jaunty rhythms which entered Scotland with the awakenings of the second half of the nineteenth century. Hymn singing was a regular feature of Sunday evenings in many Brethren households,[4] and in the more prosperous twentieth century there were families which had at least one of its members, often a girl, learning to play the organ or piano to accompany these at home. Yet Brethren singing, particularly at the morning meeting, could have a different musical character. In an article pleading for 'more singing, and better, in our Assemblies', the historian and hymn writer David Beattie commented on the effects of music in different situations. 'Bright and

---

1. This hymn is no. 383 in *The Believers Hymn Book* (London and Glasgow [1885]).

2. Judith Adair, 'In the Splendour of His Holiness: a Study of the Musical Practices of the Christian Brethren' (University of Edinburgh, dissertation for Scottish Ethnology II, 1992), is a pioneering study of Brethren musical practice. It is examined through the mainly contemporary practice of Bellevue Chapel, Edinburgh.

3. *W*, 52 (1922), p.234.

4. Tom Morton, *Red Guitars in Heaven* (Edinburgh, 1994), pp.32-3.

cheerful singing' at gospel meetings was contrasted with the opening
hymn at the morning meeting, which 'at once concentrates our
thoughts'.[5] The movement had inherited two musical traditions, one
lively and emotional, deriving from revivalists such as Richard Weaver
and Ira Sankey, and the other more serious and reflective, deriving from
the slower rhythms of Presbyterian and Nonconformist worship.[6] Singing
displayed some of the complexities of Brethren spirituality and might
fittingly be taken as a metaphor for it as a whole.

Spirituality can be a word of vague meaning. It has usefully been
defined as 'those attitudes, beliefs, practices which animate people's lives
and help them to reach out towards super-sensible realities'.[7] The
spirituality of Scottish Brethren will be studied in this chapter through an
analysis of several key features of the movement: its distinctive worship;
its beliefs relating to eschatology and the Christian life; and the work of
publishers and hymn writers. The wider religious context of Brethren
spirituality was that of Evangelicalism. Studies of Evangelical spirituality
have found D. W. Bebbington's four defining characteristics of conversionism, activism, biblicism and crucicentricism to be central attributes
of the piety as well.[8] A more comprehensive account of the spirituality of
the Brethren than is possible here would have to consider these four
features.[9] The present discussion will concentrate on three other recurring
attributes. The Brethren held an immediate concept of faith which
expected the supernatural to be operative in daily life. There was an
insistence on separation from the secular world and, at its most rigorous,
from other Christian bodies. And there was a stress on right doctrine
which emphasised its apprehension and ordering by the mind. These
three features—supernaturalism, separatism and cerebralism—are vital in
understanding the movement and placing it in its historical and social
context.[10]

5. D. J. Beattie, 'What part should music or singing play in our Assemblies?', *W*, 57
(1937), pp.151-2.

6. Neil Summerton, 'The practice of worship', *CBR*, 39 (1988), pp.32-3, 36.

7. Gordon Wakefield (ed.), *A Dictionary of Christian Spirituality* (London, 1983),
p.361, quoted in J. M. Gordon, *Evangelical Spirituality: from the Wesleys to John Stott*
(London, 1991), p.vii.

8. Gordon, *Evangelical Spirituality*, pp.7, 311-29; David K. Gillett, *Trust and Obey:
explorations in evangelical spirituality* (London, 1993), p.8; Ian M. Randall,
*Evangelical Experiences: a study in the spirituality of English Evangelicalism 1918-
1939* (Carlisle, 1999); Linda Wilson, *Constrained by Zeal: female spirituality amongst
Nonconformists 1825-1875* (Carlisle, 2000), pp.43-59; cf. D. W. Bebbington,
Evangelicalism in Modern Britain (London, 1989), pp.2-17; and above, p.2.

9. Cf. Randall, *Evangelical Experiences*, pp.143-7, which uses Bebbington's
Evangelical characteristics to analyse Brethren spirituality in inter-war England.

10. Ian S. Rennie, 'Aspects of Christian Brethren Spirituality', in J. I. Packer and
Loren Wilkinson, *Alive to God: studies in spirituality* (Downers Grove, Illinois, 1992),

The Morning Meeting

Brethren spirituality found its fullest expression in the weekly breaking of bread or morning meeting.[11] John Ritchie's account of his first experience of one at Old Rayne in 1871 suggests why it proved such a focal point:

> The place was a country joiner's shop, with whitewashed walls, plank seats supported by cut clogs of wood, a plain deal table covered with a white cloth, on which the bread and wine stood near the centre; there was no platform, no chair, no chairman. We had often gone to hear the Lord's servants, and to seek His blessing on the Word spoken by them; here we had come to meet the Lord himself, to hear his voice, to see no man save Jesus only. The seats filled up, mostly by middle-aged country people, all plainly clad; there were no flowers or feathers, no gold ornaments or sparkling jewels there. When all had assembled, the door was shut, and we felt that we were shut in with God.

> Solemn silence prevailed. There was no haste, but a season of true waiting upon God. We had come there to worship God—not to *get*, but to *give*; and the Spirit was there to guide.

At the end of the meeting a hymn was sung which exhorted Christ to return. Ritchie wrote, 'it actually seemed as if we were on the move *upward*; we certainly were waiting for the call'.[12] The account juxtaposes the ordinariness of the surroundings with the supernaturalism of the event. Its language and imagery, doubtless coloured by memory, emphasise Jesus as the centre of the gathering and the exclusion of the world; simplicity, solemnity and the lack of ritual; an openness to the impulse of the Spirit; and an anticipation of the second advent. These were among the significant features of Brethren spirituality which were encompassed by the morning meeting.

The Brethren commemorated the Lord's supper weekly, an innovation in worship for those with a Presbyterian background. The service grew out of the movement's practice and theology. Many assemblies took advantage of the unfixed nature of the seats to form a square with the table carrying the elements in the middle (the pattern which Ritchie

pp.190-201, isolates four aspects of Brethren spirituality for his historical analysis: its bibliocentricism, separatism, charismaticism, and hyper-Calvinism; that the last was characteristic of the Brethren has been disputed by Randall, *Evangelical Experiences*, pp.143-4.

11. Neil Dickson, '"Shut in with Thee": the morning meeting among Scottish Open Brethren, 1840s-1960s', in R. N. Swanston (ed.) *SCH*, 35 (Woodbridge, 1999), pp.276-89.

12. John Ritchie, 'Revival times and work in Aberdeenshire', in C. W. R[oss]. (ed.), *Donald Ross: pioneer evangelist* (Kilmarnock [1904]), pp.170-1.

evidently observed at Old Rayne). It is a spatial arrangement that is not focused on one individual but which suggests the involvement and common status of the worshippers.[13] The men in assembly fellowship could freely participate in public prayer, choosing a hymn for congregational singing, reading the Bible or delivering extemporary sermons. In the Church all were clergy.[14] The absence of a chairman or presiding minister at the breaking of bread was stressed to emphasise that the centre of the gathering was Christ, and much was made by the Brethren of the promise in Matthew's Gospel that he would be 'in the midst' of those gathered in his name.[15] The use of the square pattern also suggested that he was the centre of the meeting. 'It was decided', noted the minutes of one assembly when this arrangement was adopted in the 1920s, 'to alter some of the seats to permit of the table being placed in the "midst" on Lord's Day mornings.'[16] The service was also rooted in the doctrine of the movement. Brethren theology tended to concentrate on the redemptive significance of the second Person of the Trinity to the exclusion of the relationships of the other Persons to the world. The death of Christ in particular had a central place. The cross was seen to be the foundation of the gospel just as salvation by blood was perceived as the central theme of the Bible.[17] In common with nineteenth-century Evangelicalism, its saving significance was seen to be the central concern, and debates over the extent of the atonement, which had recurred within Scottish theology, were marginalised.[18] The only permissible inter-

---

13. Neil Dickson, 'Brethren and their buildings', *H*, 68, no. 5 (October 1989), p.13.

14. R. T. Hopkins quoted in 'Friday's conference', *NEI*, 2 (1872), p.73; cf. [J. L. Harris], 'On Christian ministry', *The Christian Witness*, 1 (January 1834), rpt as *Scripture Subjects: truths for the Church of God* (London & Glasgow, 1882), p.9.

15. Matt. 18:20.

16. Tillicoultry, Bankfoot Evangelical Church, 'Minute Record of the Assembly & Oversight Business Meeting. From 1st Jan. 1925—Ann St. Gospel Hall, Tillicoultry', Half Yearly Business Meeting, 20 March 1926.

17. J. R. Caldwell, *From the Cross to the Kingdom* (n.d), rpt (Glasgow, 1983), p.188; Alexander Stewart, *Salvation Truths* (Kilmarnock, n.d.), p.10; John Ritchie, *From Egypt to Canaan* (Kilmarnock, n.d.), pp.21-3.

18. According to F. F. Bruce, 'Alexander Marshall', *SDCHT*, p.548, i, Marshall's adherence to universal atonement, carried over from his EU background, was 'in his day exceptional among Brethren preachers'. The majority view in the late nineteenth century was that of individuals, such as Donald Ross, who believed in a limited atonement. But over time (as Bruce's comment implies) the majority came to be that of universal atonement; so complete was the replacement that by 1998 limited atonement could be regarded as being unscriptural in J. R. Baker, 'Question box', *BM*, 108 (1998), p.107. For limited atonement, see Donald Ross, 'A clear statement', *W*, 69 (1939), pp.5-6; C. F. Hogg, 'QA', *W*, 57 (1927), p.73; and Henry Payne, *ibid.*; for universal atonement see, [John Bowes], 'What the death of Christ procured for mankind', *TP*, 1 (1849-51), pp.130-3; John Hawthorn, *Alexander Marshall: evangelist, author and pioneer* (Glasgow

pretation of the atonement was the penal substitutionary view. J. R. Caldwell thought that non-atoning views of Christ's death, current in nineteenth-century liberal theology, were signs of the heresy prophesied for the last days.[19] Ritchie was characteristically forthright on this point: 'a religion without *blood*', he wrote, 'is a sure title to the lake of fire.'[20] This primary focus in Brethren theology dictated the purpose of the morning meeting. 'The special object for which the Lord assembles His people thus, wrote Ritchie, 'is to "Remember Him" in the breaking of bread.'[21] The emphasis of the service therefore fell on commemorating the person of Christ, especially his death. It gave vital expression to the movement's Christocentricism and its liberty of ministry from among the men in fellowship.

It is because the morning meeting sprang from both the core of the movement's theology and its distinguishing practice that the characteristics of the spirituality can be clearly seen in it. In the pre-1860 period the Glasite influence on the gathering was strong.[22] But a greater stress on extemporary prayers and hymn singing, more suited to impulsive views of the Spirit current in contemporary revivalism rather than the Glasite practice of exhortation, came to predominate at the morning meeting.[23] It was the supernaturalism which was implicit in this understanding of the meeting which had appealed to the young Ritchie. Simplicity was perceived as an essential characteristic of the apostolic church,[24] and the word was frequently used with reference to the breaking of bread. 'It is a simple ordinance,' Caldwell noted, 'observed in a simple manner, and by a simple people.'[25] The New Testament gave no liturgy; therefore, it was argued, one should not be developed. The use of ecclesiastical art and architecture were strongly criticised, a point underlined by the plainness of the surroundings in which the Brethren worshipped.[26] Instrumental music at the morning meeting was also

---

[1929]), pp.22-3; and 'QA' from: A. M[arshall]., *W*, 53 (1923), p.13; HyP[ickering]., *W*, 57 (1927), p.131; George Goodman, *W*, 65 (1935), pp.278-9; and Robert Rendall, *W*, 76 (1946), p.23; cf. M. C. Bell, *Calvin and Scottish Theology* (Edinburgh, 1985); Bebbington, *Evangelicalism*, pp.16-17.

19. Caldwell, *Cross to Kingdom*, p.190.

20. Ritchie, *Egypt to Canaan*, p.21.

21. John Ritchie, *Assembly Privileges and Responsibilities* (Kilmarnock, n.d.) p.5; the allusion is to 1 Cor 11:24, 25.

22. See above, pp.47, 54.

23. Dickson, '"Shut in with Thee"', in Swanston (ed.), *SCH*, 35 pp.278-80; cf. above, p.153.

24. James Patrick Callahan, *Primitivist Piety: the ecclesiology of the early Plymouth Brethren* (Lanham, MD; 1996) pp.51-4.

25. J. R. Caldwell, 'Christ the sin offering', *W*, 24 (1894), p.56.

26. W., 'Herod and Jerusalem', *NI*, 3 (1873), p.164; J. R. Caldwell, 'Keeping the ordinances', *W*, 39 (1909), p.94; Dickson, 'Brethren and their buildings', pp.12-13.

eschewed. The stress on simplicity helped to heighten the sense of the supernatural. The divine was not mediated through material objects and rituals, as in the Old Testament, but God worked directly on the human spirit. The dispensation of ritualism was past and Christians lived in the dispensation of the Spirit. If the worship was directed, then it was the Holy Spirit 'as Guide and Sovereign Distributor of gifts' who was leading as he moved in the hearts of those present, using them as 'fit mouthpieces to express the assembly's worship'.[27] If there was a president, then it was the Lord himself who presided.[28] The direct faith that the Brethren had inherited from popular nineteenth-century Evangelicalism, with its strong sense of supernaturalism, lent itself to this understanding of the Lord's supper.

Separatism and cerebralism also had a place in perceptions of the morning meeting. The world was excluded, and all were agreed that it was for believers only. Judas had left the Last Supper, J. R. Caldwell was at pains to establish, before Christ broke bread, for it was a feast for disciples only.[29] The division of the Sunday services into a morning meeting for Christians and an evening one for unbelievers emphasised the separation.[30] It was captured in one of Alexander Stewart's hymns:

> Shut in with Thee far, far, above
> The restless world that wars below,
> We seek to learn and prove Thy love,
> Thy wisdom and Thy grace to know.[31]

The verse also makes plain that the key to the meeting was quietness so that there might be meditation on the love of Christ. It produced a leisurely service, in which it was expected there would be silences. Caldwell felt the ideal length of the morning meeting was two hours with the participation of the Lord's supper reasonably close to the start so that it 'might be lingered over in blessed meditation'.[32] Isaac Ewan wanted it nearer the end, moving towards it 'softly, reverently, meditatively'.[33]

---

27. J. R. Caldwell, 'QA', *W*, 24 (1894), p.84, John Ritchie, 'The Church in its worship', *BM*, 28 (1918), p.77; cf. *idem, Assembly Privileges*, p.4.

28. Alexander Marshall, 'The Lord's two ordinances', *W*, 19 (1889), pp.164-6.

29. J. R. Caldwell, 'The breaking of bread: the meaning, mode, and practical observance. Notes on I Corinthians xi. 23-6', *W*, 39 (1909), p.78; cf. John Ritchie, 'The Lord's supper', *BM*, 11 (1901), p.140 (later published as a pamphlet of the same title and as a chapter in *Early Paths for Young Believers* (1909); see below, n.130).

30. J. R. Caldwell, *Epitome of Christian Experience in Psalm XXXII with the development of the Christian life* (Glasgow [1917]), pp.104-5.

31. *Believers Hymn Book*, no. 129.

32. J. R. C[aldwell]., 'The object of the Lord's supper', *W*, 22 (1892), p.127.

33. I. Y. E[wan]., 'When should the bread be broken?', *PT*, 6 (1940-1), p.987.

Caution was advised against too vocal a service, for silence involved all those present, including the women. 'All should be exercised', counselled Ritchie, 'waiting upon God, meditating on Christ, during times of silence'.[34] The accounts which have survived of the earliest breaking of bread services bear testimony to the powerful awareness of the numinous that those present sensed. At Peterhead during the first morning meeting, it was remembered, the floor was wet with the tears of those present.[35] These gatherings when the movement was young could be emotional occasions.

The features of the morning meeting were formed by the piety of the participants, but other influences might be detected in them. The stress on simplicity and solemnity and the supernaturalism of the occasion arose out of the cultural context. They increased the state of awe prescribed by nineteenth-century Romanticism.[36] Paradoxically, the desire for separation was formed in part by strong negative reactions to nineteenth-century society which were continued into the twentieth.[37] The heavy reliance on meditation, like the adoption of an impulsive ministry, was possibly a Quaker influence on Brethren thinking, there having been an early influx of members of the Society of Friends into the movement in England.[38] But the use of meditation also pointed to the cerebralism of the movement which was that of lower middle-class and more articulate working-class individuals.[39] The features of the spirituality did not exist in isolation from their wider social and cultural context.

Eschatology

All three features of supernaturalism, separatism and cerebralism coexisted in Brethren eschatology, and through it some of their sources can be detected. From the beginning, the Brethren accepted the notion that the second advent would be premillennial and they became pioneers

---

34. Ritchie, *Assembly Privileges*, p.4.

35. Writer's collection, I.A.2., 'First Message in York Street Hall by Mr. Alex Buchan on 26th June, 1965', cyclostyled foolscap sheet, n.d; cf., anon., 'Assembly life experiences: letters of an octogenarian', *BM*, 29 (1919), p.55; Robert Chapman, *A Short History of the Inception, Progress and Personalities of Hebron Hall Assembly, Larkhall: 1866-1928* (Kilmarnock, 1929) p.12; anon., *How I was Led Outside the Camp* (Kilmarnock, n.d), p.3; Fordyce Hall, Insch, minute and account book of Insch assembly, 1873-1891, p.2.

36. Summerton, 'Practice of worship', p.36.

37. For Brethren attitudes to society, see below, pp.263-5, 309-25.

38. T. C. F. Stunt, *Early Brethren and the Society of Friends. CBRF Occasional Paper No.3* (Pinner, 1970), pp.23-5.

39. For Brethren social class, see below, pp.288-97.

in spreading this view at a popular level. In 1838 J. N. Darby had taught the Edinburgh church his prophetic views on his first visit to them.[40] John Bowes began as a postmillennialist but after 1851, influenced by Andrew Bonar's *Redemption Draweth Nigh* (1847), he became a premillennialist.[41] The view was taught to new converts and those joining the movement. At the nondenominational conference held in Hamilton to report on the success of the Lanarkshire revivals of 1866, J. R. Caldwell had addressed it on the second coming.[42] When the north-east assemblies were formed, he wrote a series on prophecy during 1873-4 for Ross's *The Northern Intelligencer*. 'The truth in them', wrote Caldwell later, 'was nearly all new to the natives of Aberdeenshire.'[43] At Larkhall in the early 1860s the second coming was one of the topics discussed, along with believer's baptism and the breaking of bread.[44] To identify with the Brethren was to adopt a distinctive premillennial expectation of the advent. To contemporaries it was one of the central identifying features of the movement.[45]

The variety of adventism accepted among the Brethren was dispensational premillennialism. This system had its origins in J. N. Darby's thought, and Scottish Brethren inherited it already formulated.[46] In 1867,

---

40. J. N. Darby to A. M. Foluquier, 6 Octobre 1838 (*Commencée en septembre*), 'Lettres de J. N. D.', *MÉ* (1897), p.294.

41. [John Bowes], 'The great mistake as to the second advent', *CM*, 1 (1844), pp.237-40; [*idem*], 'On the coming Kingdom', *TP*, 1 (1851), pp.257-260; however, Bowes had probably been influenced earlier by Robert Aitken's premillennialism, cf. Malcolm R. Thorp, 'Popular preaching and millennial expectations: the Reverend Robert Aitken and the Christian Society, 1836-40', in Malcolm Chase and Ian Dyck (eds), *Living and Learning: essays in honour of J. F. C. Harrison* (Aldershot, 1996), pp.103-117.

42. *R*, 16 (1867), pp.31-2; for this conference, see above, p.87.

43. J. R. Caldwell, 'Preface', in *Things to Come* (1875), rpt (Glasgow, 1983), p.311.

44. Chapman, *Hebron Hall Assembly*, pp.10-1.

45. William Reid, *Plymouth Brethrenism Unveiled and Refuted* (Edinburgh, 1875), pp.296-322.

46. For the origin of dispensational premillennialism in Darby's writings, see Clarence B. Bass, *Backgrounds to Dispensationalism: its historical genesis and ecclesiastical implications* (Grand Rapids, 1960); F. Roy Coad, *Prophetic Developments with Particular Reference to the Early Brethren Movement—C.B.R.F. Occasional Paper No.2* (Middlesex, 1966); Ernest R. Sandeen, *The Roots of Fundamentalism: British and American millenarianism 1800-1930* (Chicago, 1970); George M. Marsden, *Fundamentalism and American Culture: the shaping of twentieth century evangelicalism 1870- 1925* (Oxford, 1980), pp. 48-55; Kent Eaton, 'Beware the trumpet of judgement!: John Nelson Darby and the nineteenth-century Brethren', in Fiona Bowie and Christopher Deacy (eds), *The Coming Deliverer: millennial themes in world religions* (Cardiff, 1997), pp.119-62; Jonathan David Burnham, 'The Controversial Relationship

for example, D. T. Grimston's *A Diagram of Dispensations* was published by the Glasgow Exclusive Brethren publishers R. L. Allan and was available from their bookshop in the city. This work established the general principle that the history of the world was divided into different epochs, or dispensations, in which God dealt in various ways with humanity, each of which was concluded by judgement.[47] Darby belonged to the school which interpreted the book of Revelation in a futurist manner, believing that its prophecies had still to be fulfilled. He divided the second advent into two stages. There was a secret rapture of the Church, which could come at any moment, and then, after a period of tribulation on earth, a public return by Christ with his saints to institute his millennial reign. Within the prevailing premillennial view, as has already been noted in earlier chapters,[48] there were differences of interpretation and emphasis. The very small minority of post-tribulationists rejected the two-stage advent, but the Darbyite view was accepted by the vast majority.[49] Despite the shades of opinion, the Open Brethren in Scotland embraced the main outlines of dispensationalism wholeheartedly,[50] and three individuals from the movement played a significant role in spreading its teachings. Caldwell's articles were later published as *Things to Come* (1875) which the American prophetic teacher R. A. Torrey placed third in excellence on a list of books on the subject.[51] Robert McKilliam, the Aberdeenshire physician, after he moved to London, became the first editor of *The Morning Star*, founded in 1894 to spread 'futurist interpretation', a position he held for twenty-one years.[52] Most important of all was Walter Scott, who had been an accession from the Stuart Party of Exclusives and whose most substantial work was his *Exposition of the Revelation of Jesus Christ* (3rd edn 1914).[53] After 1893, Scott spent a period in America, and through his writings he gave dispensationalism its definitive terminology. He also had a decisive influence on C. I. Scofield and was one of only four individuals singled out by him as helping with *The Scofield Reference*

---

between Benjamin Wills Newton and John Nelson Darby' (University of Oxford D.Phil. thesis, 1999).

47. D. T. Grimson, *A Diagram of Dispensations: with key* (Glasgow, 1867).

48. See above, pp.12, 157-8, 246-7.

49. For the former view, see above, pp.157-8, 246-7.

50. However, for Robert Rendall's questioning of it, see above, p.307.

51. HyP[ickering]., 'John R. Caldwell', *idem* (ed.), *Chief Men Among the Brethren*, 2nd edn (London and Glasgow, 1931), p.152.

52. *The Morning Star*, 1 (1894), p.3; W. W. H., 'Dr. Robert McKilliam', Pickering (ed.), *Chief Men*, pp.175-7.

53. For the publishing history of this work, see above, p.225 n.41.

Bible (1909), a work which systematised dispensationalism into seven epochs and disseminated the scheme throughout the Evangelical world.[54] Premillennialism was marked by a strong supernaturalism. There was a constant expectation of sudden divine intervention in the affairs of history. Attempts to predict the date of the advent, a mark of historicist premillennialism, had discredited the idea that the time could be determined and the practice was condemned.[55] Christ's coming would be at any moment, and therefore could not be predicted. However, this did not stop individuals looking for signs that the end was near. Female preaching had been hailed as one indicator,[56] but there were others. In 1868 Bowes speculated that if Napoleon III were the Antichrist then the monarch's forthcoming sixtieth birthday must indicate the imminence of the advent (presumably because of the association with the number six).[57] The revivals of the nineteenth century were widely interpreted as a sign that the second coming was impending.[58] Even the appearance of the Brethren and the recovery of truths concerning the Church, it was suggested during the late-Victorian consolidation of the movement, was another sign.[59] The attempt to discern the times, the previous chapter has shown, was at its height during World War I, and there was renewed interest during World War II.[60] The Brethren lived in constant expectation of the cataclysmic interruption of human affairs and it determined their response to the events of history. Generations came and went in the belief that they would be living at the advent. Bowes's expectations had traces of the longing for status reversal which chiliasm often gave to the poor. The Church, he liked to think, was a school preparing the saints for ruling

---

54. 'Walter Scott', *W*, 63 (1933), p.282; C. I. Scofield, 'Preface', *The Scofield Reference Bible* (Oxford, 1909); David J. MacLeod, 'Walter Scott, a link in dispensationalism between Darby and Scofield?' *Bibliotheca Sacra*, 153 (1996), pp.155-78; Scott had been an Open Brethren member before joining the Stuart Party.

55. Anon., 'Must the Church pass through the tribulation?', *NW*, 10 (1880), p.106; A. O. M[olesworth]., 'The blessed hope of the Church', *W*, 23 (1893), p.55-6; J. R. C[aldwell]., 'On the fixing of dates for prophetic events', *ibid*., p.177; [John Ritchie], 'YBQB', *BM*, 14 (1904), p.94.

56. See above, p.76.

57. *TP*, 10 (1866-9), p.168.

58. [John Bowes], *The Twenty-First Report of the Means Employed by Several Churches of Christ to Proclaim the Glorious Gospel of God's Grace and promote unity, purity and activity in the church chiefly exhibited from J. Bowes's Journal. 1859-60* (Dundee, 1860), p.1; two English Brethren journals of the period were entitled *The Latter Rain* and *The Eleventh Hour*.

59. J. H., 'Habbakuk', *NW*, 5 (1875), p.59; Wm Lincoln, 'What is to be done?', *ibid*, p.102; anon., 'The influence of the Middle Ages on our Christian teachers', *ibid*., p.173; A. P. M[acdonald]., 'The house of God', *NW*, 22 (1882), p.71.

60. See above, pp.224-6, 238.

during the millennium.[61] But the dominant concern of Brethren eschatology was not of the insignificant of the earth becoming its rulers, but the instantaneous nature of the rapture and the marvels surrounding Christ's reign. In a scientific age, it provided a place for the supernatural. The apostolic era of miracles had passed away, Caldwell noted, 'and, to the outward sense, there is no apparent interference by the living God with the ordinary course of nature'. This was about to cease when Christ would exercise a 'personal, visible reign at Jerusalem', for the miraculous powers of the early church 'were but specimens of "the powers of the age to come", that will be committed to the saints'. It was confidently expected that Christians would ascend and descend from heaven, while in Jerusalem the Jewish sacrifices and rituals would be reestablished.[62] In the dispensationalist scheme, the age of signs and wonders was about to commence. In common with other nineteenth-century British adventists, it was the imminence of the supernatural within premillennial dispensationalism which attracted the Brethren.[63]

Nineteenth-century adventism was allied to a profoundly pessimistic view of the present.[64] John Bowes had shared the optimism of the Enlightenment and had detested gloomy views. He did not accept the concept of a secret rapture and at Christ's return, he maintained, the earth would be converted.[65] Nor did he see his views as a reason for retreating from hopes of improving society. 'We have long thought', he wrote, 'that our views of the church and Christ's second coming should not prevent us from doing all in our power to improve the condition of man in the world.'[66] Darby had taught that because each dispensation had ended in failure on the part of God's people, it might be expected that signs of decay would be detected in the contemporary church. True Christians should separate from the growing apostasy and form themselves into pure churches. This was a view that Bowes himself came to share in the 1850s, probably due to his reading of *Eight Lectures on Prophecy* (1852), a work which William Trotter, the former Methodist

61. *TP*, 2 (1852-3), pp.141-2.
62. J. R. C[aldwell]., 'Things to come', *NI*, 4 (1874), pp.34, 81-2; cf. *Walter Scott, Prophetic Scenes and Coming Glories: answers to numerous prophetic questions* (London, 1919), pp.61-83; [John Ritchie], 'YBQB', *BM*, 23 (1913), pp.58-9.
63. D. W. Bebbington, 'The advent hope in British Evangelicalism since 1800', *Scottish Journal of Religious Studies*, 9 (1988), pp.103-114; cf. *idem, Evangelicalism,* pp.83-5.
64. D. N. Hempton, 'Evangelicalism and eschatology', *JEH*, 31 (1980), pp.179-94.
65. [John Bowes], 'Preaching the gospel with gloomy views', *TP*, 1 (1849-51), pp.151-2.
66. *Idem, TP*, 8 (1861-2), p.189.

Brethren preacher, had produced in cooperation with Thomas Smith.[67]
'All false churches are Babylon and must soon fall,' Bowes wrote,
'should we not beware lest we be buried among the sins of the falling
city?'[68] Heterodoxy in the churches was keenly looked for on the part of
the Brethren, for it indicated the end.

The majority shared Darby's pessimistic outlook. Contrary to the
Victorian public myth, the world was not progressing. An optimistic hope
for worldwide conversions to Christianity attracted missionaries such as
Dan Crawford and John Anderson to query the prevailing eschatological
scheme.[69] But most did not expect the transformation of the world by the
gradualist efforts of the missionary movement, nor did they feel that
society could be improved. Rather, signs of decay were detected. 'What
we find previous to the Lord's return', wrote Walter Scott, 'is a rebellious
world and a *sleeping* Church.'[70] Developments in science and techn-
ology, Caldwell felt in 1882, were not leading to 'a triumphant church
and a converted world, but the culmination of Satan's schemes in the
Man of Sin'.[71] World War I demonstrated that faith in progress was ill-
founded.[72] Pessimism about society was reinforced by an other-worldy
conception of the nature of a Christian. Dispensationalism separated
Israel and the Church as belonging to different divine administrations.
The Church was God's heavenly people, to be caught up from the earth,
while Israel was his earthly people, to be reinstated after the rapture.[73] 'A
Christian has no more to do with the world's politics than with the
world's religion' declared Caldwell.[74] Duty was now narrowly defined.
Because of the Christian's heavenly calling, Bible teacher George Adam
argued, he should have nothing to do with the affairs of society: 'To
witness unto our absent and now rejected Lord is our *business* during our
sojourn on earth.'[75] Eschatology emphasised the necessity of separation
from the institutional church and from society and the real task of the
Christian, Brethren piety told them, was to convert others. Involvement in

---

67. [*Idem*], 'On the second advent', *TP*, 2 (1852-3), pp.25-9; cf. William Trotter and
Thomas Smith, *Eight Lectures on Prophecy: from shorthand notes* (1852), edn (London,
1881); for Trotter, see above p.41.

68. [John Bowes], 'The perils of the times', *TP*, 3 (1854), p.173.

69. Dan Crawford, *Thirsting After God* (London [1927]), pp.135-43; John A.
Anderson, *The Blessed Hope: a study in dialogue form on the coming again of the Lord
Jesus* (London [c.1930]), p.11.

70. Scott, *Prophetic Scenes*, p.9.

71. J. R. Caldwell, *NW*, 12 (1882), p.113.

72. L. W. G. Alexander, 'Heaven's hope versus Earth's hopelessness', *W*, 46 (1916),
pp.55-6.

73. Coad, *Prophetic Developments*, p.28.

74. J. R. C[aldwell]., '"Things to come"', *NI*, 3 (1873), p.51.

75. George Adam, 'The heavenly calling of the Church', *W*, 28 (1898), p.160.

the world or the acquisition of its comforts was futile. 'Brethren,' Donald Ross would thunder, 'we are just God's pickings out of this wretched world, and when He has got all His own out of it, He'll burn up the whole concern like so much kindling-wood.'[76] Dispensationalism was an essentially separatist scheme because of its pessimism about the course of the Church and the world, and it led to the rejection of both.[77] Such attitudes to society will call for further analysis in the next chapter.

The central attraction of the dispensationalist scheme for many was its ability to organise the scriptural data and its presentation of an apparently incontrovertible scheme of the future. 'Reverent and prayerful study of the prophetic Word, in the Old and New Testament,' Ritchie counselled, 'will be found a means of godly edification and a safeguard against the many speculations concerning the future'.[78] Brethren members pored over the apocalyptic and prophetic books of the Bible. 'The Word of God is like a complicated puzzle,' wrote one individual, 'much of its truth seems disconnected, the one part from the other, and it is only the Holy Spirit of God that can teach us to put it together so as to make a lovely and harmonious whole.'[79] Dispensationalism was the key that had been given. Scripture was reduced to a system, and lengthy discussions sought to establish how difficult texts could be accommodated. Charts were produced as a guide to its complexities. Ritchie designed one which connected eschatology with the feasts of the book of Leviticus, rituals which were seen to have typological significance, thus relating one difficult area of interpretation to another (Figure 8.1). Brethren eschatology expressed the separatism and the heightened supernaturalism of their spirituality, but perhaps more clearly than any other aspect of their belief, it demonstrated their respect for ideas and a love of organising the facts. This intellectual trait has been traced to the role of Scottish Common Sense philosophy in the development of Fundamentalism.[80] Scottish Brethren were philosophically naive, yet nevertheless, they had an empiricist's regard for the facts and their systematic arrangement. This pursuit of the 'statement of Bible facts' (in the phrase of the evangelist Henry Steedman) contained in scripture led to a rigid

76. R[oss]. (ed.), *Ross*, p.16.

77. Rennie, 'Aspects of Brethren spirituality', pp.196-200; Bass, *Backgrounds to Dispensationalism*, pp.127, 149; T. C F. Stunt, 'Irvinginte pentecostalism and the early Brethren', *CBRFJ*, 10 (1965), p.41.

78. John Ritchie, 'Signs of the end', *BM*, 19 (1909), pp.13-14.

79. F. Brodie, 'The bride of the Lamb—who is she?', *NI*, 4 (1874), p.129.

80. Marsden, *Fundamentalism and American Culture*, pp.55-62; cf. James Barr, *Fundamentalism*, (London, 1977), pp.270-9.

fixing of them in a system of knowledge, and it can be seen in areas other than dispensationalism.[81]

The Way of Holiness

It is apparent from the discussion of Brethren eschatology that their spirituality had diverse sources which were not always easily accommodated to each other. Nineteenth-century supernaturalism sat alongside a cerebralism which had its roots in earlier habits of thought. Separatism, too, could act as a counterforce on other aspects of the spirituality. The fault lines which ran through Brethren piety can be perceived in their concepts of sanctification. Early Brethren writings have been seen as among the sources of nineteenth-century holiness teaching.[82] In Scotland, as earlier chapters have shown, Brethrenism did actually lead to the adoption of perfectionism in the 1860s and of higher-life teaching in the 1870s.[83] Although neither of these holiness schools was eventually accepted, concepts of an exalted state of Christian living continued to have an influence. The higher-life movement held a distinctive interpretation of Romans 7:14-25, a passage in which the Apostle Paul depicts himself as having an internal struggle against sinning. Darby thought that this passage showed the individual learning through experience of the power of sin. Once this had been lived through, the individual could know 'complete deliverance from the whole power of sin' through realising 'his perfect acceptance in Christ, described in Romans chapters 6 and 8, and the 'only normal state of the Christian then is unclouded fellowship' with God.[84] Darby claimed that it was due to his comments that Robert Pearsall Smith, the seminal American holiness teacher, accepted these chapters as the key biblical passage for teaching victory over sin.[85] Among the Open Brethren

---

81. Writer's collection, II, Henry Steedman quoted in 'The divine and eternal Sonship of the Lord Jesus Christ', notes on an address in James K. Jack, Prestwick, holograph annotations in The Holy Bible, Authorised Version, interlinear edn (Oxford, n.d.), end pp. As a systematising of scripture in areas other than dispensationalism, Steedman's address is a case in point; for the view of scripture as 'fact', cf. David Anderson-Berry, quoted above, p.177; and Robert Rendall, *History, Prophecy and God* (London, 1954), pp.17-25.

82. Bebbington, *Evangelicalism*, pp.157-9.

83. See above, pp.74, 95.

84. J. N. Darby, 'Letter on Mr R. P. S.'s "Holiness through Faith"', in William Kelly (ed.), *The Collected Writings of J. N. Darby*, 23 (London, n.d.), pp.320-358

85. J. N. Darby to a 'Brother', 20 February 1875, *Letters of J. N. D.*, 2 (London, n.d.), p.335; *idem* to a German 'Brother', 1875, *ibid.*, p.354. In a letter in which he criticised Henry Varley's *Trust in the Living Father* (1873), Darby claimed that he had

Donald Munro accepted this exegesis,[86] and Munro's convert, John Ritchie also adopted and promoted it in his later writings.[87] Romans 7, in Ritchie's view, was not a 'normal picture of Christian life' but of an individual 'who has life but not liberty'. By using the might of Christ, portrayed by Paul in the following chapter, it was possible to leave this 'phase of the Christian life' and 'to live a life of power and of victory'.[88] Ritchie's view is that of Darby, but his vocabulary shows that it has been refracted through the teachings of the higher-life movement. His terms are those which came to be associated with the Keswick Convention.[89] The desire to exalt the power of Christ and for an enhanced purity of life were common to both Brethren views and higher-life teaching. The supernaturalism of Brethren spirituality gave it significant affinities with holiness movements.

Ritchie's views, however, were by no means identical with those of Keswick. He differed on how the victory over sin could be achieved. It was not through a special act of consecration but through realising the power of the indwelling Christ.[90] In maintaining this Ritchie was again

experienced the struggle described in Romans 7 'fifty years ago' and that he had 'treated it as a non-Christian state' (J. N. Darby, 23 December 1873, *ibid.*, p.245)—this is an allusion to his experience in 1826-7, described in J. N. Darby to Prof. Tholuck, 1855, *Letters*, 3, pp.299-300. By this phrase he appeared to mean, not that it was the experience of a non-Christian, but that it was not the state which might be expected of a Christian. He noted, however, that 'It may come after pardon, and in these free gospel days often does' (May, 1867, *Letters*, 1, p.500). In some of his letters Darby counsels non-Christians to 'have gone through' Romans 7 into the liberty of Romans 6 and 8 (Darby to Mr Governor, May 1863, *ibid.*, pp.355-6), and in others he counsels Christians similarly (11 June 1878, *Letters*, 2, pp.452-4; 11 May 1881, *Letters*, 3, pp.155-8). See also *Letters*, 15 February 1875, 2, p.328; February 1875, *ibid.*, p.333; March 1875, *ibid.*, p.337.

86. [John Ritchie], *Donald Munro 1839-1908: a servant of Jesus Christ* ([1908]), rpt (Glasgow, 1987), p.72.

87. There are striking verbal parallels between the writings of Ritchie and: anon., 'Loose him, and let him go', *NEI*, 2 (1872), pp.13-4; W. H. W., 'Answers', pp.7-10; L[?undin]. B[?rown]., 'Notes on the Epistle to the Romans', *NW*, 12 (1882) pp.12-4. Ritchie evidently learned his interpretation from his early contact with the movement in the north east. For example, Ritchie states that some Christians are in legal bondage and need to enter the liberty of the gospel: 'Like Lazarus raised to life, but bound with grave clothes, they need to be "loosed" and "let go"' (John Ritchie, *Notes on Paul's Epistle to the Romans* (Kilmarnock, n.d.), p.104); this analogy provided the basis of the anonymous article 'Loose him, and let him go'.

88. Ritchie, *Romans*, pp.105, 101, 104.

89. J. C. Pollock, *The Keswick Story* (London, 1964), pp.74-5; Charles Price and Ian Randall, *Transforming Keswick* (Carlisle, 2000), pp.228-44; David Bebbington, *Holiness in Nineteenth-Century England: the Didsbury Lectures* (Carlisle, 2000), pp.73-90.

90. Ritchie, *Romans*, pp.105-6.

following the Calvinist Darby who criticised Pearsall Smith's views for magnifying human ability, something Darby blamed on the Wesleyan influence on Smith.[91] Ritchie also accepted Darby's view that sanctification primarily referred to an accomplished fact at conversion, the believer being sanctified or 'set apart' in Christ.[92] 'There is no "higher life" than this' Ritchie caustically observed.[93] His stress on the believer's perfect standing in Christ, or 'positional sanctification', was combined with the traditional Evangelical view that the believer is also in constant warfare with sin.[94] This combination was Ritchie's version of what H. H. Rowdon has shown to be the Open Brethren concept of sanctification.[95] In Scotland, it received its clearest expression in J. R. Caldwell's writings. Caldwell also held that the 'positional' aspect of sanctification was the primary one.[96] In emphasising the believer's perfection in Christ at conversion the Brethren were attempting to abandon the close examination of one's actions which in Reformed teaching was held to be necessary for the individual to be assured of salvation.[97] This was intimately connected to Brethren concepts of instant salvation and the propositional assurance which had been inherited from early nineteenth-century hyper-Calvinism.[98] Salvation was attained as soon as the individual concurred with the propositions of scripture relating to it, and likewise the acceptance of the biblical statements formed the basis of the assurance of salvation.[99] Caldwell was typical in

91. J. N. Darby, 'Review of R. Pearsall Smith on "Holiness through Faith"', in Kelly (ed.), *Collected Writings*, pp.277-319.

92. Ritchie, *Egypt to Canaan*, pp.11-12.

93. John Ritchie, 'The tabernacle in the wilderness', *NW*, 12 (1882), p.54; cf., G. F. G., '"The higher life"', *NW*, 8 (1878), pp.155-9; Stewart, *Salvation Truths*, p.77.

94. Ritchie, *Egypt to Canaan*, p.77; Ritchie had been strongly influenced by W. P. Mackay, a Congregational minister and revivalist, who also emphasised this point, see W. P. Mackay, *'Grace and Truth' under Twelve Aspects*, 2nd edn (Edinburgh, 1875), 64th edn (London, 1905), pp.172-218.

95. H. H. Rowdon, 'The Brethren concept of sainthood', *Vox Evangelica*, 20 (1990), pp.91-102.

96. J. R. Caldwell, 'Sanctification', *W*, 33 (1903), pp.29-30, 45-7.

97. Rowdon, 'Sainthood', pp.96-7.

98. Rennie, 'Brethren spirituality', p.205; Donald M. Lewis, *Lighten Their Darkness: the evangelical mission to working-class London* (Westport, CT, 1986), pp.30-1; propositional or contractual assurance was diffused in Scotland by revivalists such as Brownlow North and instant salvation by ones such as Hay Macdowall Grant and Reginald Radcliffe.

99. See above, pp.98, 110, 117 n.25; Alexander Marshall was criticised by an anonymous Scottish Methodist for expounding these views, see [Alexander Marshall], *Wandering Lights: a stricture on the doctrines and methods of Brethrenism. A review by A. M.*, 3rd edn (Glasgow, n.d.), pp.6-12; a parallel controversy between Methodists and Brethren also took place in Canada, cf. Phyllis D. Airhart, '"What must I do to be saved?"

arguing that the individual should not look for any other corroboration of salvation other than God's bare word that he is forgiven. To do so would be to make God a liar.[100] However, despite his rejection of evidential assurance, Caldwell also stressed that sanctification was 'conditional' or progressive.[101]

Both Ritchie and Caldwell were influenced by Darbyite thinking and were accepting an already formulated concept. Counter to the views of sanctification which had been established by the early writers of the movement were perfectionism and, later, the Pentecostal experience of baptism of the Spirit. Subsequent authors were unanimous in rejecting the possibility of either.[102] Doctrinal conservatism was strong in the Brethren. Despite the obvious affinities Ritchie's views had with Keswick teaching, he and his associates explicitly rejected it.[103] Yet there were others, apart from Ritchie, whose teaching showed influences from it. Most prominent was W. J. Grant, the former Baptist pastor, who believed, according to one obituarist, that the 'great need among assemblies was the Keswick message of holiness.'[104] John Ritchie Jnr accepted the

---

Two paths to evangelical conversion in late Victorian Canada', *Church History*, 59 (1990), pp.372-85.

100. Caldwell, *Christian Experience*, p.30; cf. John Ritchie, *Assurance: or how I know I am saved* (Kilmarnock, n.d.).

101. J. R. Caldwell, 'Sanctification', *W*, 33 (1903), pp.45-7, 61-2; *idem*, 'The meat offering', *W*, 24 (1894), pp.168-9; *idem*, 'The red heifer', *W*, 26 (1896), pp.53-4, 76-7, 85-7; *idem*, 'Epitome of Christian experience', *W*, 38 (1908) pp.5-6, 23-5, 55-7, 73-4, 88-90, 118-20, 135-7, 151-2; *idem*, 'The old and new within', *W*, 41 (1911), pp.157-8; *idem*, 'Union with Christ', *ibid.*, pp.77-8, 93-5. Of these articles, the following were published in books: 'Sanctification' as *Sanctification* (Glasgow, 1903); 'The meat offering' in *Christ in the Levitical Offerings* (Glasgow, n.d.); 'The red heifer' in *Shadows of Christ in the Old Testament* (Glasgow, n.d.); and *Epitome of Christian Experience* (Glasgow, 1917).

102. W. H. W., 'Answers to "Twenty-six questions concerning the old man, &c."', *NI*, 3 (1873), pp.7-10; W. W., 'A Letter Concerning Mr. Wesley's views of sanctification', *NW*, 5 (1875), pp.116-121; John Ritchie, 'The tabernacle in the wilderness', *NW*, 12 (1882), p.82; 'QA', *ibid*, pp.95, 128; J. R. C[aldwell]., 'Christ the sin offering', *W*, 24 (1894), p.39; [*idem*], 'Sanctification', *W*, 33 (1903), p.61; [John Ritchie], 'Answers to correspondents', *BM*, 10 (1900), p.36; [*idem*], 'YBQB', *BM*, 18 (1908), p.142; George Adam, 'The Christian armour', *W*, 36 (1906), p.132; William Hoste, 'Operations of the Holy Spirit', *BM*, 18 (1908), pp.139-40; 'QA', *W*, 41 (1911), pp.18-19; 'YBQB', *BM*, 31 (1921), pp.28-9.

103. John Ritchie, 'The tabernacle in the wilderness', *NW*, 12 (1882), p.54; *idem*, *Egypt to Canaan*, p.77; *BM*, 41 (1932), pp.143-4.

104. J. G[ray]., 'William J. Grant, Kilmarnock', *BP*, 51 (1930), pp.98-101; HyP[ickering]., 'Home-call of W. J. Grant, M.A., Kilmarnock', *W*, 60 (1930), pp.187-8. Pickering described Grant's teaching as 'the safe side of the Keswick teaching on the higher life.' He added, 'This he often gave, with general acceptance.' (p.187); cf. W. J.

Darbyite exegesis of Romans 7 and went further, stressing there must be a moment of consecration, of 'definite, cleancut surrender'.[105] For Andrew Borland, although he rejected any notion of a 'second blessing' and thought consecration was a daily act, 'Complete victory is assured for every genuine Christian now over the power of sin...'. He supported his assertion with Charles Wesley's words, 'He breaks the power of cancelled sin'.[106] In the more open wing of the movement, Keswick teaching itself was tolerated or accepted by some Brethren especially in England.[107] Its concept of consecrated faith lacked the objectionable element of sinlessness which perfectionism promoted.[108]

Yet in Scotland it was eventually only a few individuals, who were mainly on the fringes, who actually adopted it. Keswick's stress on experience and feeling made doctrine seem less real.[109] The Brethren, on the other hand, made the claims of truth paramount. Here was a crucial reason why holiness teaching was not accepted. Like higher-life teaching, the Brethren movement had grown out of the influence which Romanticism, with its emphasis on feeling and transformed states, had on

---

Grant, 'Excelsior' and other Addresses (Goodmayes, 1928), pp. 64-9; idem, 'The great mission of the Holy Spirit', W, 61 (1931), pp.105-8.

105. John Ritchie, The Bulwarks of the Christian Faith as Expounded in the Epistle to the Romans (London and Glasgow [1939]), pp.107-111, 144-5; Ritchie added, however, that this was a private transaction, not to take place in a 'consecration meeting' (p.101).

106. Andrew Borland, Romans Chapter Eight (Kilmarnock, 1964), pp.39, 43, 55.

107. Hawthorn, Marshall, p.38; G. E. Tilsley, Dan Crawford: missionary and pioneer in central Africa (London [1929]), pp.26-9; Percy Beard, A Neglected Aspect of the Cross (Airdrie, 1910); writer's collection, I.I.8. (iii), Mr R. Mackay to the writer, 9 April 1988; for Keswick influence among Brethren in England, see: W. B. Sloan, These Sixty Years: the story of the Keswick Convention (London and Glasgow, 1935) pp.87, 94, 95, 97; Fay Inchfawn, Those Remembered Days (London, 1963), pp.15-63; Randall, Evangelical Experiences, pp.15, 37; Price and Randall, Transforming Keswick, pp.98-9. The book which gave the most scholarly exposition of the Keswick view of Romans 7 and 8, H. C. G. Moule's The Epistle of Paul to the Romans (London, 1894), was reprinted by Pickering & Inglis, c.1928, and they also published Sloan's history of Keswick. For the role of Brethren in spreading Keswick teaching to other areas of the English-speaking world see: 'C. A. Spratt', W, 91 (1961), p.36; and Brian Dickey, 'Evangelical Anglicans compared: Australia and Britain', in George A. Rawlyk and Mark A. Noll (eds), Amazing Grace: Evangelicalism in Australia, Britain, Canada, and the United States (Montreal, 1994), p.234.

108. Cf., C[aldwell]., 'the sin offering', pp.38-9. When W. H. Bennett, the editor of The Golden Lamp, criticised the writings of the South African exponent of Keswick teaching, Andrew Murray, he commended Murray's desire for holiness and his target was instead Murray's view of Christ's human nature: Bennett, 'The relation of the Lord Jesus to "fallen nature"', W, 25 (1895), p.167-9; 183-4; cf. the criticisms by the English preacher George Goodman, later a Keswick speaker himself, W, 49 (1919), p.160, but cf. idem, 'Attainment: what may be expected', W, 50 (1920), pp.334-5.

109. Bebbington, Evangelicalism, pp.170-1.

Evangelicalism.[110] The Brethren, however, also insisted on the careful statement and ordering of doctrine. Ritchie rejected the 'rest of faith' advocated by Keswick as being not only 'one-sided' but also 'sentimental'.[111] It ultimately separated the Brethren from holiness movements which were orientated towards experience. The cerebralism of the Brethren made them emphasise doctrine. It was a powerful conservative force which kept them within the boundaries established by early Brethren thought.

The influence of cerebralism was also marked in the role the morning meeting had in the Brethren practice of holiness. The breaking of bread was the most significant moment of the week, 'the greatest privilege,' Ritchie wrote, 'and the highest form of fellowship with God and His people, to which the believer is called upon earth'.[112] It was the service above all others at which attendance was obligatory.[113] The need for careful preparation of the soul was stressed.[114] Because of the worshippers' dependence on the promptings of the Spirit, it was important that the individual's life was also kept open to his influence. 'If there is to be spirituality in worship on the first day of the week,' wrote Ritchie, 'there must be spirituality in life and godliness in walk, on the six days that precede it.'[115] The Brethren, as extreme anti-ritualists, explicitly propounded the commemorative, Zwinglian view of the Lord's supper,[116] but most approached the Calvinist position, maintaining that the believer at the Lord's table fed by faith on Christ—a stance that was perhaps given its fullest statement by Andrew Borland.[117] 'That will make better Christians of us,' claimed Caldwell, 'it will separate us from the world and its ways, bind us together in divine love and unity, and give us victory over sin and Satan.'[118] A link was made between the holiness of the occasion and the members' lives.[119] The Brethren were unique

---

110. *Ibid.*, pp.86, 94-6, 165-7.

111. Ritchie, *Egypt to Canaan*, p.77.

112. Ritchie, 'The Lord's Supper', *BM*, pp.140-1.

113. HyP[ickering]., 'WW', *W*, 60 (1930), p.114.

114. J. A. Ireland, 'The breaking of bread', *W*, 78 (1948), pp.43-4; R. Eadie, 'The Lord's supper', *W*, 87 (1957), pp.102-7; John Ritchie, 'Hints for behaviour in the assembly', *BM*, 16 (1906), p.32; *idem*, 'The church in its worship', *BM*, 28 (1918), p.76; A. Borland, 'The Lord's supper', *BM*, 61 (1951), pp.1-2, 99; *BM*, 62 (1952), pp.1-2; *BM*, 63 (1953), pp.17-19.

115. John Ritchie, 'worship', p.76.

116. Peter Manson, 'A Sunday morning meditation', *W*, 78 (1948), pp.17-18; Ireland, 'breaking of bread', pp.43-4.

117. A. Borland, 'The Lord's supper', *BM*, 60 (1950), pp.97-8; *ibid.*, 61 (1951), pp.49-51; *idem*, 'The Lord's supper', in J. B. Watson (ed.), *The Church: a symposium* (London, 1949), pp.75-6; cf. Ritchie, 'The Lord's supper', *BM*, p.141.

118. J. R. C[aldwell]., 'Christ the peace offering', *W*, 24 (1894), p.137.

119. G. A[dam]., 'The holiness of the Lord's table' *W*, 30 (1900), p.154.

among Evangelicals in the central place they gave to the ordinance.[120] Regarded as the crucial means by which spirituality was advanced, the breaking of bread became (to borrow a phrase from the Salvation Army) the holiness meeting of the movement, the core of the members' devotion.[121]

But cerebralism came to be dominant in the spirituality. The morning meeting had suited higher-life spirituality admirably for both stressed surrender to the Spirit. The pseudonymous 'Crucified Man' (possibly Ross himself) criticised those who were too active during the service for 'Doing! Doing Doing!'. Using an image favoured by Romantic writers and holiness teachers alike, he wrote that believers at the breaking of bread 'ought to be like the Aeolian harp, on which the winds of heaven play sweet music—the Holy Ghost playing sweet music on their soul to the glory of God, and His grace'.[122] Yet it was the intellectualism of the Brethren which eventually prescribed how the morning meeting should be conducted. The opening hymn set a theme for each service and participants were expected to follow it,[123] leading one individual to complain in 1964, with some rhetorical exaggeration, that the young 'find themselves concentrating on recognising the theme, seeking to link each hymn, prayer or meditation together, sometimes by a process of mental gymnastics little short of Olympic standard'.[124] It was presumed that the more intelligent contributions would show some familiarity with the typological significance of the Old Testament offerings,[125] and this expectation perhaps reached its zenith in Isaac Ewan's codification of the service.[126] The objective focus of the meeting required a capacity for abstract thought, and this need for intellectual understanding acted also as a brake on emotionalism.[127] Cerebralism produced a less spontaneous, more restrained service. The development of a detailed theology of the occasion concentrated minds on it, in the process exposing the

---

120. Dickson, '"Shut in with Thee"', in Swanston (ed.), *SCH*, 35, p.289.

121. J. A. Ireland, 'Why I sit at the Lord's table', *W*, 70 (1940), pp.121-3; T. A. Kirkby, 'Why we prize the morning meeting', *W*, 71 (1941), pp.203-4; Andrew Borland, 'The Lord's supper', in Watson (ed.), *The Church*, pp.77-8.

122. A Crucified Man, 'Worship meetings', *NA*, no. 2 (February 1873), pp.5-6: the attribution to Ross is made on stylistic grounds; for the Aeolian harp, cf. George M. Marsden, *Fundamentalism and American Culture: the Shaping of Twentieth-Century Evangelicalism 1870-1925* (New York, 1980), pp.76-7.

123. J. R. C[aldwell]., 'Praise', *NW*, 15 (1885), p.48; *idem*, 'Ministry at the Lord's table', *W*, 41 (1911), pp.33-4.

124. W. E. Howie to the editor, *W*, 94 (1964), p.230.

125. Ella [Jack]., *Central View* [the magazine of Central Evangelical Church], no. 20 (March, 1994), pp.10-11; Dickson, '"Shut in with Thee"', in Swanston (ed.), *SCH*, 35, p.281.

126. See above, pp.234-5.

127. Cf. Summerton, 'practice of worship', p.35.

differences between the Brethren and the nineteenth-century holiness movement.

Separatism also had a prominent place in Brethren concepts of holiness. During the process of regulation at the end of the nineteenth century an important modification to ideas about sanctification became evident. The key to progress in holiness, it was held, was obedience to the ecclesiology and practices which the Brethren detected in the New Testament. The way to 'spiritual growth and power', maintained F. A. Banks, was believer's baptism and fellowship in an assembly.[128] In an address, later published as a pamphlet by Ritchie, Donald Munro argued that the way to ensure that Christians grew spiritually was to gather them into an assembly with baptism the first step of obedience for the new convert.[129] Ritchie's own *Early Paths for Young Believers* (1909) showed that for him too the signs of holiness meant an adherence to Brethren distinctives. The book, which began life as a series of addresses to new converts in Glasgow, was intended to show 'the early steps' that Christians should take. It consists of chapters on Bible reading, separation from the world, baptism, the Lord's supper, the correct church, and the necessity of joining an assembly.[130] Christians outside the Brethren had a lesser degree of holiness, for they either lacked knowledge of God's will or were disobedient.[131] Ritchie was not alone in this belief, for, although he was later to reject it, as late as 1903 J. R. Caldwell was arguing as much in a series of articles, which was later published as a booklet entitled *Sanctification*.[132] The institutional separatism of the Brethren found ideological form here. Separation was the connecting thread which ran through Ritchie's views on holiness. The believer was set apart in Christ, the victorious life made him separate from sin, and the Christian life consisted of separation from the world's pursuits and religion.

It was not the guiding thought for all. Like Caldwell, the Bible teacher George Adam stressed the continuing battle with sin and the need for progression in holiness. He held the traditional Reformed view of

---

128. F. A. B[anks]., 'Spiritual growth', *NW*, 15 (1885), p.6; this article was later reprinted by John Ritchie in Frederick Arthur Banks, *'The Church' and the 'Churches of God'* (Kilmarnock, 1883).

129. Donald Munro, 'How shall we order the child?', *BM*, 11 (1901), pp.109-110, 127-8, 136-8.

130. Ritchie's chapter titles are: 'The word of God', 'The unequal yoke', 'Baptism', 'The Lord's supper', 'What church should I join?', and 'The footsteps of the flock'; each chapter had a separate existence as a booklet before being brought together in *Early Paths*.

131. Ritchie, *Early Paths*, pp.93-6.

132. Caldwell, 'Sanctification', *W*, p.62.

Romans 7, that it described the condition of an advanced believer.[133] The Brethren view of holiness was diverse and it allowed differing emphases. Yet the need for separation had an important place in all views. That holiness meant accepting Brethren ecclesiology and practices became orthodoxy for sections of the Scottish movement in the nineteenth century, and the evidence suggests that they became increasingly larger sections as the twentieth century progressed. Separation, however, is a negative concept. Not only did it succeed in directing attention away from perfectionism and holiness teaching, it often diverted effort away from moral development altogether. The Christian life was concerned with maintaining the separated community. Both cerebralism and separatism led the movement along a route which drew it away from its earlier affinities with higher-life teaching.

Publishers and Hymn Writers

The cerebralism of Scottish Brethren suggests that they were an élitist movement, and in some senses this was true. Alluding to Neatby's comment that the favourite form of recreation for the Brethren was the conversational Bible reading, Ian S. Rennie has noted that 'Brethren spirituality appears restricted, cerebral and serious'.[134] This can be seen if they are contrasted with the Pentecostal churches which appealed to similar social classes, but were without the intellectualism of the

---

133. G. A[dam]., 'God's remedy for indwelling sin', *NW*, 16 (1886), pp.33-4, 72-4; cf. *idem*, 'Communion with God', *W*, 24 (1894), pp. 7-8, 25-6, 37-8; *idem*, 'The knowledge of Christ', *ibid.*, pp. 80-2; *idem*, 'God's provision for keeping people right with himself', *W*, 29 (1899), pp.144-6, 175-7; *idem*, 'God himself the source of all real power', *W*, 33 (1903), pp.9-12; *idem*, 'The Christian armour', *W*, 36 (1906), pp.111-12, 132-3.

134. Rennie, 'Brethren Spirituality', p.195; cf. W. Blair Neatby, *A History of the Plymouth Brethren* (London, 1901), p.278; on cerebralism within Evangelicalism, see D. J. Tidball, *Who Are the Evangelicals?* (London, 1994), p.205. Patricia Beer, the Devon poet and literary critic and herself the child of Brethren parents, has criticised the Brethren for their inability to think. She has written: 'One can work one's way down the long column in the OED which defines philosophy, from 1 to 9b, without coming across anything which sounds like a mental process engaged in by the Brethren.' (Patricia Beer, 'Happy Few', *London Review of Books*, 23 May 1991, p.12). Certainly after the mid-nineteenth century, the British Brethren movement was a popular one. Its members were unaware of philosophy and undoubtedly their expression of their piety was in popular terms. Differences between Beer's south-west England and Scotland must be allowed for, but nevertheless the movement, among people who were, in the main, not highly educated, was one in which intellectualism was prominent. Their cerebralism was not of an academic type, but of those with longings for self-improvement; cf. below, pp.308-9; and Morton, *Red Guitars*, pp.31-2.

Brethren.[135] The movement was built on men such as John Miller (d.1933) who worked in Broomloan Shipyard, Rutherglen, and who rose at 4 a.m. to read the Bible before starting work at 6 a.m..[136] However, the radical disjunctions in Brethren spirituality and the lack of integration evident in concepts of holiness serve as reminders that the movement was a popular one. Their cerebralism was not of an academic variety, but that of those who had been newly affected by advances in basic literacy.

This can be seen from the work of Brethren publishers. Evangelicals in the nineteenth century took advantage of increased rates of literacy and new methods of distribution to disseminate their message.[137] The pattern which emerges among Brethren publishers is of individuals utilising print to promote the issues which they saw as significant. The two publishing houses which proved to be the most successful were Pickering & Inglis of Glasgow and, later, London, and John Ritchie Ltd of Kilmarnock.[138] In his study of these two publishing enterprises, J. A. H. Dempster has explained their ability to prosper economically in terms of what has been

---

135. Bryan Wilson, *Sects and Society: a sociological study of three religious groups in Britain* (London, 1961), pp.63-75.

136. 'John Miller', *BP*, 55 (1934), p.36; for similar examples, cf. Jimmy Paton, above pp.7-8; and coalminer Isaiah Stewart in Neil Dickson, '"The Church itself is God's clergy": the principles and practices of the Brethren', in Deryck W. Lovegrove (ed.), *The Rise of the Laity in Evangelical Protestantism* (London, 2002), p.226.

137. Richard D. Altick, *The English Common Reader: a social history of the mass reading public, 1800-1900* (Chicago, 1957), pp.99-128; Patrick Scott, 'The business of belief: the emergence of 'Religious' publishing', in Derek Baker, *SCH*, 10 (1973), pp.213-24; Michael J. Cormack, *The Stirling Tract Enterprise and the Drummonds* (Stirling, 1984).

138. For the founding of these firms, see above, pp.146-7. Arnold D. Ehlert, *Brethren Writers: a checklist with an introductory essay and additional lists* (Grand Rapids, MI, 1969), p.73-9, claims to have found 28 Scottish Brethren publishers or those who published at least one Brethren work. A random search by Dr David Brady in the British Library catalogue of four of those listed by Ehlert (R. L. Allan, R. M. Cameron, A. Walker and C. Zeigler), revealed only one, R. L. Allan, as mainly a Brethren publisher (David Brady to the writer, 1 May 1992). The other three may have published a few items by Brethren authors (although none were listed in the BL catalogue) and it is likely that most others on Ehlert's list are in an identical position. The present writer has established the following Open Brethren publishers which have existed in Scotland: Hunter Beattie, Glasgow; Bible and Tract Room, Aberdeen (transferred to City Bible House, Edinburgh); Percy Beard, Airdrie; Bowes Bros, Dundee; John Brown, Edinburgh; City Bible House, Edinburgh (later subsumed under the Publishing Office, Glasgow); Edwin Ewan, Abernethy; Isaac Ewan, Abernethy; Gospel Tract Publications, Glasgow; Pickering & Inglis, Glasgow and London; The Publishing Office, Glasgow (later became Pickering & Inglis, Glasgow); John Ritchie Ltd, Kilmarnock; John Ritchie [Jnr], Kilmarnock; Alex Ross, Aberdeen; W. M. Ross, Dundee; Wm Shaw, Maybole; David Taylor, Kirknewton. A number of these, however, only published works written by themselves.

called the Pontifex factor.[139] Pontifex was a character in *The Way of All Flesh* (1903) who, according to Patrick Scott, knew that 'the number of people who might buy any book is limited, but the number to whom it may be given away is almost unlimited'.[140] Both Pickering & Inglis and Ritchie published in large quantities tracts outlining the message of salvation which were distributed indiscriminately by their customers. The scale of this circulation might be seen from Alexander Marshall's immensely popular pamphlet *God's Way of Salvation* ([1888]). On one occasion a Glasgow professional employed someone to disseminate 250,000 copies throughout the city. By 1928 it had been translated into fourteen languages, including Gaelic, and it was claimed that almost five million copies had been distributed. Before Christmas that same year, advertisements in the Christian and secular press led to a further 8,000 being sent out.[141] Individuals devoted themselves to dispersing tracts with extravagance. David Frew of Plann, Ayrshire, gave away 10,000 annually, and another tract distributor managed to dispense 27,000 in one year.[142] The magazines published for gratuitous circulation have already been noted in Chapter 4,[143] and in this largesse children were not overlooked. Donald Ross had founded the short-lived *The Northern Youth* in 1873.[144] More enduring were John Ritchie's *The Young Watchman* begun in 1883, and *Our Little One's Treasury*, begun in 1888 for very young children, and also commenced in this last year, Pickering & Inglis' *Boys and Girls*. These magazines were given free of charge to children attending Brethren Sunday schools.

Particularly in the inter-war period both publishers also issued a large number of 'gift and reward' books for children which were used as prizes for attending Sunday school or children's meetings. Many of them were reprints of nineteenth-century works and were mainly books of Bible stories or the biographies of those, such as Florence Nightingale

---

139. J. A. H. Dempster, 'Aspects of Brethren publishing enterprise in late nineteenth century Scotland', *Publishing History*, 20 (1986), pp.91, 95-6.

140. P. G. Scott, 'Richard Cope Morgan, religious periodicals, and the Pontifex Factor', *Victorian Periodicals Newsletter*, 5, no. 16 (June 1972), p.1.

141 Hawthorn, *Marshall*, pp.116-123; *W*, 59 (1928), p.46. Alexander Marshall, *God's Way of Salvation, set forth by illustration, comparison and contrast* ([1888]), was formed by the merging of two earlier tracts by Marshall. Unfortunately no publishing figures are available after 1928, but its circulation continued to be considerable and the tract is still in print at the time of writing. As recently as 1985 a copy was given to every household in Whitehead, County Antrim: Bernie Reid, *No Greater Joy: the story of Bobbie Wright* (Belfast, 1989), p.109.

142. 'David Frew', *W*, 69 (1939), p.45; 'Andrew Jamieson', *W*, 89 (1959), p.56; cf. above, p.138.

143. For these tracts, see above, p.138.

144. *NI*, 3 (1873), p.80.

and David Livingstone, whose lives were considered worthy of emulation.[145] However, fiction was permissible for children provided it taught a suitably edifying religious lesson.[146] In the three Scottish novels by M. B. Paxton published by Pickering & Inglis, the heroine faces temperamental shortcomings and danger from the sea which she is enabled to confront through her conversion earlier in the narrative. The heroine dies in two of them (and a boy she befriends in the third), but the other characters are reconciled to the deaths through knowing that the departed is in heaven.[147] Each child attending the numerous and large Brethren Sunday schools was given a book, making them one of the principal sources of revenue for the publishers. Andrew Borland in one of his novels described the profusion of children's books in John Ritchie's shop as it appeared before a Christmas in the early 1920s:

> What a feast met their eyes! They stood almost spellbound as they gazed at shelf after shelf filled with books of every description. How they wished to possess a copy of each!—Christmas books, books of travel, missionary books, picture books and what not.[148]

Ritchie and Pickering & Inglis serviced a movement whose members were intent on converting their fellows through print. Their economic success was due in part to the zeal with which the Brethren pursued that goal.

---

145. Andrew Borland (ed.), *The Bible and Its Doctrines: original outlines on the great themes* [*The Christian Worker* for 1930 in one volume] (Kilmarnock, 1930), end pp. adverts; Pickering & Inglis also published A. Montefiore-Brice, *David Livingstone: his labours and his legacy* (1890) Pickering & Inglis edn (London [1938]).

146. Cf. the novels by Andrew Borland, *The Cradle of the Race: the story of the world in its early days, told for young folks* (Kilmarnock [1925]) and *The Cradle of the King: the story of the birth and early days of Jesus, retold for young people* (Kilmarnock [1929]). In the first half of the twentieth century Pickering & Inglis published The 'Red Cord' Series which carried novels by Maria L. Charlesworth, Charlotte Murray, and M. E. Drewsden; and the 'Excelsior Library' carried novels by M. E. Drewden and *Uncle Tom's Cabin* (end pp. adverts in Maria L. Charlesworth, *Ministering Children* (1854), Pickering & Inglis edn (London and Glasgow [1925])). In the same period John Ritchie published the 'Young Folks Story' series, with novels by, *inter alia*, Charlotte Murray and John Bunyan; the 'Boys and Girls' series with novels by Robert Pollok, Mary L. Code, and Leigh Richmond; and 'Schoolday Stories' Series which included *The Pilgrim's Progress* and Louisa Alcott's *Little Women* and *Good Wives* (end pp. adverts in John Ritchie, *Among the Cannibals: peeps at the South Sea Islands and their savage inhabitants with life stories of their missionary heroes*, revised edn (Kilmarnock [1930])); on Brethren attitudes to fiction, see below, pp.311-12; cf. Dempster, 'Brethren publishing', pp.88-9.

147. M. B. Paxton, *Only a Gipsy: a story of Caithness* (London [1920]); *idem, In an Isle of the Sea: a story of the Shetland Isles* (London [1920]); *idem, Astur: a waif of the sea* (London [1924]).

148. Borland, *Cradle of the King*, p.62.

Yet the Pontifex factor is only a partial explanation of the prosperity of both publishing firms. Much of the material that they printed was for internal consumption by the Brethren. An intensive writing project went into the magazines and books which fuelled the interest in biblical doctrine and interpretation. What is remarkable, too, as Dempster points out, is that Pickering & Inglis and Ritchie largely duplicated each other's efforts and interests. They produced parallel popular expository and devotional literature. Both produced books of sermon outlines and children's talks, aids for those engaged in preaching and youth work.[149] There were monthly magazines containing similar material: Pickering & Inglis possessed *The Believer's Pathway*, commenced by William Shaw in 1880, while from 1886 Ritchie had *The Christian Worker*.[150] Both publishers' flagships, the biblical magazines *The Witness* and *The Believer's Magazine*, also showed strong resemblances in the features they carried.[151] They had a heavy emphasis on doctrine and the necessity of this was reiterated continually by the editors. Caldwell claimed that he only published material for 'the profit and edification of the general body of readers', while Ritchie avowed his intention of 'keeping back nothing profitable to the general edification'.[152] Certainly there were differences. Articles in *The Believer's Magazine* tended to be shorter and less weighty than those in *The Witness*; and the magazines appealed to different constituencies, Ritchie's publication to the stricter section and Pickering & Inglis' to the more open. However, the dissimilarities must not be exaggerated. *The Witness* did not neglect the populist touch. 'When considering articles remember those rows of miners' cottages!' was the advice of Henry Pickering to his successor as editor.[153] And individuals continued to take both magazines. A limited market supported two overlapping publishing concerns. Dempster concludes that it was possible for them to prosper because 'the Brethren were a reading people, positively encouraged to turn constantly to print for spiritual enlightenment and upbuilding.'[154] The predilection for print as a means of converting others and for self edification were the marks of a people who had gladly embraced the opportunities offered by mass literacy.

Because the Brethren movement was a popular one, there was no internal impulse to make its spirituality intellectually cohesive. Cerebralism did not overwhelm supernaturalism. This is clear from the

149. For examples, see above, pp.136 n.324, 325; 214.

150. The latter was originally *The Sunday School Worker's Magazine and Bible Student's Helper*.

151. For the history of these magazines, see above, pp.146-7, 1713.

152. *W*, 41 (1911), p.196; *BM*, 19 (December 1909), endpp.

153. Robert Rendall, *J. B. Watson: a memoir and selected writings* (London, 1957), p.68.

154. Dempster, 'Brethren Publishing', p.97.

work of Brethren hymn writers. Certainly, concern for sound doctrine was evident in attitudes towards hymns. When *The Believers Hymn Book* was produced in 1885, J. R. Caldwell announced that hymns which used 'Jesus' too frequently had been amended. To address Christ as such was not scriptural.[155] But although the necessity of observing theological exactitude was conceded by Brethren, writing in verse among them expressed the demands of the heart as much as the head. A substantial body of devotional verse was produced which appeared regularly in the magazines. Most of these effusions failed to rise above the level of doggerel, and the best of the versifiers were Isaac Ewan and J. M. S. Tait, a solicitor from Lerwick, who could both attain a more lyrical note.[156] Perhaps the most popular poet, however, was William Blane, a mines engine-keeper from Galston, Ayrshire, and emigrant, whose 296-line poem in rhyming couplets, 'The Atonement', was an exposition in verse of the universal efficacy of the death of Christ.[157]

The hymn writers worked within the prevailing atmosphere of Victorian hymnody. The hymns of the singing evangelist, R. F. Beveridge, being intended for use in missions, express the emotional satisfaction which was felt to accompany salvation. In one hymn by Beveridge, the appeals of the revivalist can be heard. It demonstrates the sentimentality, which could easily lurch into bathos, that was endemic to the contemporary popular hymn:

> Eternity! O dreadful thought
> For thee a child of Adam's race,
> If thou shoulds't in thy sins be brought
> To stand before the awful Face
> From which the heaven and earth shall flee,
> The Throned one of Eternity.
>
> To-night may be thy latest breath,
> Thy little moment here be done,
> Eternal woe—'the second death',
> Await the grace-rejecting one,
> Thine awful destiny foresee—

---

155. J. R. C[aldwell]., 'Praise', *NW*, 15 (1885), p.48.

156. [Edwin A. Ewan (ed.)], *Caravanserai: a collection of poems by I. Y. Ewan* (Abernethy, 1980); J. M. S. Tait, *Bells and Pomegranates* (London, 1946).

157. William Blane, 'The Atonement', in *idem, Lays of Life and Hope* (c.1890), rev. edn (Kilmarnock & London, 1938), pp.9-17; this book is still in print at the time of writing. On Blane's later life, see below, pp.375-6.

Time ends,—and then Eternity![158]

A more common theme than the evangelistic one was the Christian life. The evangelist William Sloan had one hymn that passed into general use which assured the singer that by trusting God,

> We shall find the promised blessing
> Daily strength till Jesus come.[159]

It was William Blane, however, who best conveyed the immediacy of Brethren faith and the perils that the world posed:

> Kept, safely kept;
> My fears away are swept;
> In weakness to my God I cling,
> Though foes be strong I calmly sing,
> Kept, safely kept.
>
> Through simple faith,
> Believing what He saith,
> Unshaken on my God I lean,
> And realise his power unseen,
> But known to faith.[160]

One significant gap in the hymn themes is the confession of sin, and in an article on Brethren hymnology John Andrews attributed this to the strain of perfectionism in their thought.[161] What the hymns do demonstrate is how central to Brethren devotion the morning meeting was. The evangelist Douglas Russell, who in 1868 emigrated to North America, produced his best hymn for use in this setting (a verse from it provides the epigraph to the present chapter).[162] David Beattie, who wrote evangelistic and children's hymns, also wrote a hymn for use at the Lord's supper which encapsulated the mystical Christocentricism of the occasion:

---

158. R F. Beveridge (compiler), *Celestial Songs: a collection of 900 choice hymns and choruses* (London [1921]), no.513; the best-known revivalist hymn to which Beveridge contributed verses was 'Homeward Bound for Glory', *ibid.*, no. 586.

159. *Believers Hymn Book*, no. 229.

160. *Ibid.*, no. 121.

161. J. S. Andrews, 'Brethren Hymnology', *Evangelical Quarterly*, 28 (1956), p.213.

162. *Believers Hymn Book* no. 383; in this collection it first appeared in *The Believers Hymn Book Supplement* (London and Glasgow [1959]), no. 383.

O help us, Lord, while gathered here,
 That we none else may see;
Keep Thou our thoughts graced with Thy love,
 And wholly stayed on Thee.[163]

Isaac Ewan managed to conjure a hymn out of the meat offering, the Jewish sacrifice involving flour, to evoke devotion at a morning meeting:

In smooth and silken whiteness,
 Without a rough'ning grain,
In clear, unbroken brightness,
 Without a speck or stain
The fine flour in its beauty
The Perfect Man portrays
In all his path of duty
In all his heavenly ways.[164]

The conception is not very hymnic, but its statement of Christ's perfection is redolent of the way he was set apart from soiled humanity in the Brethren imagination.

One of Alexander Stewart's hymns for use at the Lord's supper which made clear the separation from the secular world that was felt to characterise the occasion has already been quoted above.[165] Stewart's other hymn which passed into general use was probably the best produced by a Scottish Brethren hymn writer:

O Lamb of God, we lift our eyes
 To Thee amidst the throne;
Shine on us, bid Thy light arise,
 And make Thy glory known.

Yet would we prove Thine instant grace,
 Thy present power would feel;
Lift on us now Thy glorious face,
 Thyself, O Lord reveal.

---

163. *Ibid.*, no. 367; Beattie's hymns and choruses can be found in David J. Beattie, *Songs of the King's Highway* (London and Glasgow, 1927), and Beveridge, *Celestial Songs*.

164. I. Ewan, *Remembrance Hymns* (Abernethy, 1935), no. 14.

165. See above. p.258; it also provides the epigraph to the next chapter.

From Thy high place of purest light,
O Lamb, amidst the throne,
Shine forth upon our waiting sight
And make Thy glory known.[166]

The imagery of height and light, and the allusions to the exaltation of
Christ in Revelation chapter five, emphasise the transcendental.[167] The
potential immediacy of the divine is conveyed through the supplicants'
invocations. Vowel quality, evoking the numinous, and the simple diction
make the hymn technically more satisfying than the others. Brethren
hymnody made too ready use of a debased, archaic diction and syntax
for it to be a consistently good corpus. What the hymns do demonstrate is
the immediacy of Brethren faith which exalted the sense of the
supernatural and made the sacred seem present. The literary productions
of the Brethren demonstrate the divergent tendencies of a movement
which used the language of feeling in its worship yet which had a desire
for the careful ordering and statement of truth.

Critics and Saints

Brethren spirituality was not without its difficulties, and criticisms were
addressed at it from within the movement. In 1905 Alexander Marshall
accused his fellow-Brethren of a censorious and supercilious attitude
towards other Christians.[168] In addition, George Adam felt, the stress on
the Christian's perfect sanctification in Christ could lead to a neglect of
present sin.[169] Holiness as separation from the secular and ecclesiastical
worlds led to a concept of morality which was divorced from ethics. After
the phases when ecclesiology had been stressed in the later nineteenth
century and the inter-war years of the twentieth century, concerned voices
could be heard. In 1894, after the Churches of God secession, J. R.
Caldwell deplored the neglect of ethical growth, lamenting that 'one of
our deepest errors...[is] that we have received increased light from God
without corresponding humiliation and confession'.[170] Caldwell liked to
preach on the Old Testament regulations concerning the red heifer, an
apparently abstruse subject which was actually concerned with the

---

166. *Believers Hymn Book*, no. 346.
167. Rev. 5:6.
168. Alexander Marshall, 'Hindrances to progress in the gospel', W, 35 (1905),
p.167.
169. G. A[dam]., 'God's provision for keeping his redeemed people right with
himself', W, 29 (1899), pp.144-5.
170. J. R. Caldwell, 'Christ the sin offering', W 24 (1894), p.70.

necessity of continual repentance.[171] The zeal for exactitude which was to the fore in the inter-war years showed that cerebralism also brought its problems. In 1956 Robert Rendall produced an incisive critique of the way progress in the Christian life was often measured in terms of biblical and theological knowledge. He reminded the Brethren of their earlier reputation for practical holiness and recalled them to 'the good life'— the ethical one. He criticised the definition of doctrine 'as abstract truth, subscribed to intellectually, and capable of theological expression'. Doctrine, he pointed out, was used in the New Testament 'for teaching that bears on the practical life of the believer'. Alluding to the common practice of using the term 'saint' for assembly members, he warned: 'If assemblies today, cease to produce those whose lives are characterized by..."saintliness", all claims of "sainthood" will not secure continuance of vital testimony'.[172] These writers felt that separatism and cerebralism could destroy the potency of the movement.

Yet despite these indications of aridity, the spirituality did allow development. Not all of its strands were equally prominent in every member. As in other things, an individual's temperament lent a distinctive colouring, and the various emphases contained within the movement caused some aspects rather than others to predominate within individuals. The spirituality was practised by women. When Mary Crombie of Irvine died aged 100, it was noted of her, 'She had a wonderful memory, and a mind steeped in the Word of God.'[173] Or there was the missionary Jeanie Gilchrist who received the accolade of a biography by John Ritchie.[174] Both these women were single, but married women too could be activists.[175] However, the most characteristic products of Brethren spirituality were men. An individual such as W. J. Grant was widely respected for his sanctity,[176] but perhaps a more typical product was Alexander Marshall. A vigorous controversialist, he devoted most of his considerable energies to proclaiming an uncomplicated

---

171. J. R. Caldwell, 'The red heifer', *W*, 26 (1896), p.53; HyP[ickering]., 'John R. Caldwell', *W*, 47 (1917), pp.17-20.

172. Robert Rendall, *The Greatness and Glory of Christ* (London, 1956), p.102; for a similar point, cf. Andrew Borland, *Old Paths & Good Ways in Personal, Family and Church Life* (Kilmarnock [1938]), pp.15-17.

173. 'Miss Mary Crombie', *W*, 108 (1978), 253; cf. Linda Wilson, 'Women and personal devotions in nineteenth-century English Nonconformity', *Christianity and History Newsletter*, no.18 (summer 1999), pp.22-45; *idem, Constrained by Zeal*, pp.116-22.

174. J[ohn]. R[itchie]., *Jeanie Gilchrist: pioneer missionary to the women of Central Africa* (Kilmarnock [1927]).

175. For examples, see above, p.208 n.190.

176. P[ickering]., 'Grant', p.188; G. G[ray]., 'W. J. Grant, M.A., of Kilmarnock', *CW*, 45, no. 535, (July 1930), [pp.98-9].

fundamentalist gospel. His restless activity took him on punishing itineraries throughout the United Kingdom and around the world and left him with recurring bouts of insomnia. He was what the Brethren termed 'an aggressive worker'.

This chapter has focused on three significant features of Brethren spirituality: its supernaturalism, separatism and cerebralism. If to them is added a fourth feature, the devotedness which led to a life of intense activity, then the distinctive features of Brethren spirituality might fairly have been defined.[177] Such activism could become another focus for the individual's life. 'Loved the Lord,' it was noted of Daniel Lennox, a member of Kilbirnie assembly, when he died after preaching at an open-air service, 'and lived a life of Christian activity.'[178] It could lead to tension with other aspects of the piety. The missionary Jamie Clifford was impatient with those British Brethren who immersed themselves in Old Testament typology while there was a need for evangelism.[179] The other strands of the spirituality did not always lie easily together. The paradox which was noted in the singing was present. An emotional revivalism was in an unresolved tension with a drier intellectualism.[180] Among stricter Brethren, singing on Sunday evenings was supplanted by discussion of the Bible.[181] Brethren spirituality, growing as it did out of the nineteenth-century emphasis on spontaneous feeling, had sought new channels in which to run. The morning meeting, which was so central to the piety, was an innovative service and the emotionalism of revivalism was given an outlet here. Yet the need to guard and organise truth with care was a brake on innovation and ultimately on emotionalism. The cerebralism of Brethren spirituality was a profoundly conservative force. Separatism made clear that not only did the spirituality have implications for the ability to adapt, but it also had for self-definition too. Perceiving advance in the Christian life in terms of Brethren distinctives which several influential individuals adopted, is characteristic of a separatist, sectarian tendency as the boundaries of the sect are established. Those who resisted this pressure and stressed ethics as the heart of the Christian life were voicing a denominationalising tendency that possessed a pan-Evangelical impetus.

History and society were not irrelevant to the spirituality. Over time its expression changed. There was a shift from the optimistic views in the

---

177. F. Roy Coad, *A History of the Brethren Movement*, 2nd edn (Exeter, 1976), pp.263-7, singles this out as the most attractive feature of early Brethrenism.

178. 'Daniel Lennox', *W*, 57 (1927), p.178.

179. A. C. T[homson]., *Un Hombre Bueno: vida de Jaime Clifford* (Argentina, 1957), p.27; this was when Clifford was resident in the UK during World War I.

180. Cf. Marsden, *Fundamentalism and American Culture*, pp.43-4, 61; Barr, *Fundamentalism*, pp.17-18.

181. For an example, see above, p.185.

period before 1860 to the more pessimistic thinking of those later individuals who espoused J. N. Darby's dispensationalism. This led to a retreat from the social involvement characteristic of individuals, such as John Bowes and John Stewart, who entered the movement before 1859 to the withdrawal which was typical of the succeeding one hundred years. Teaching on holiness changed. During the course of the twentieth century, sectarian ideology was tacitly accepted by the majority. Even the morning meeting altered as a widespread pattern of service developed and as cerebralism had an increasing effect in its regulation. The three features of Brethren spirituality that have been isolated also suggest a wider link with societal features. Their supernaturalism grew out of cultural trends, their separatism arose in part out of a pessimism about the course of society, and the cerebral strain in their piety was that of individuals who had been affected by mass literacy. The spirituality of the movement demonstrates significant features about the emergence and development of the Brethren and it must be taken into account in a historical analysis. However, issues of class and society need further examination.

CHAPTER NINE

The Restless World:
Culture and Society 1830s-1960s

Shut in with Thee far, far, above
   The restless world that wars below,
We seek to learn and prove Thy love,
   Thy wisdom and Thy grace to know.
Alexander Stewart, *The Believers Hymn Book* ([1885]), No.129.

At the age of twelve John Gray was left fatherless. When he was thirteen, in 1884/5, he started work with the Glasgow & South-Western Railway Company as a telegraph boy; he then became a railway clerk in Hurlford, Ayrshire, and eventually won promotion to be Goods Manager in nearby Kilmarnock, transferring in 1897 to the equivalent, but larger, office at St Enoch's Station, Glasgow. Shortly after he had started work he had had an Evangelical conversion and had become a member of Kilmarnock Baptist Church, but due to the witness of a Brethren railway guard he had later joined an assembly in the town. In 1908 on the death of William Inglis, he became a partner in Pickering & Inglis and he removed to Glasgow, taking the main responsibility for printing and publishing after Henry Pickering retired to London in 1922.[1] When Gray died in 1936 there were about 500 mourners at his funeral, and *The Witness* thought worthy of note the presence of some seventy motor cars.[2] For Gray, Brethren membership and involvement in its institutions had been no bar to upward social mobility.

The societal role of religion has been of interest to historians and sociologists, and the present chapter will examine the relationship of the Brethren to culture and society. One overtly political function for religion is that proposed by E. P. Thompson in his discussion of the influence of Methodism on the development of the English working

---

1. 'Notable Kilmarnock man: the late Mr John Gray', *KS*, 8 February 1936, p.5; H., 'Mr. John Gray of Glasgow', *BP*, 57 (1936), pp.34-5. The assembly Gray joined met in the Wellington Hall, Kilmarnock, which places his membership at some point after 1888.
2. 'John Gray', *W*, 66 (1936), p.66.

class.[3] Thompson alleged that Methodism produced a disciplined and compliant workforce and enforced political passivity, and it might be argued that Brethrenism had a similar effect on its members. This imputed subservience would serve the interests of the dominant classes within society and therefore the role of these groups within the Brethren will be examined to determine whether they used the movement to further the interests of their own class. The Weber-Tawney hypothesis, first propounded by sociologist Max Weber and later broadly supported by economic historian R. H. Tawney, that ascetic Protestantism provided the mental environment for the rise of modern rational capitalism, proposes a further potential role of the Brethren which will be discussed.[4] Members of the movement believed in their chosen status and had a strong sense of calling to fulfil the will of God within the world, factors which the Weber-Tawney thesis sees as being of significance. The ethos of the movement might therefore seem to promote the spirit of rational capitalistic enterprise. Not only has the the role of religion in relation to society received attention, but so too has its societal function in the life of its adherents. The Brethren movement grew as Scottish society underwent profound economic and industrial changes. One function proposed by writers such as Bryan Wilson and A. D. Gilbert for religion in these conditions was that it lessened anomie for its adherents.[5] This proposed latent function of religion will be examined as a possible social role for the movement in the life of its members.

However, any interpretation of the function of the movement will need to take account of the social class of its members. For this reason the social status of the membership will be analysed first as a basis for exploring the topic raised in the previous paragraph, the relationship of the Brethren to society. The third area which the present chapter will discuss is attitudes within the movement to culture and society. The prescriptive position of the Brethren was that involvement in both should be avoided so far as possible. But they did not withdraw into vicinal segregation, and so considerable accommodation was necessary. Attitudes which allowed such negotiation to take place will be examined. That the movement had a societal role, most of its members would have regarded as surprising. Yet the analysis of its social class and function and its

---

3. E. P. Thompson, *The Making of the English Working Class*, 1963 edn (London, 1980), pp.385-440.

4. Max Weber, *The Protestant Ethic and the Spirit of Capitalism* (1904-5); Eng. trans. 1930; rpt (London, 1992); R. H. Tawney, *Religion and the Rise of Capitalism* (1922), Penguin edn (Harmondsworth, 1975).

5. Bryan Wilson, *Sects and Society: a sociological study of three religious groups in Britain* (London, 1961), p.343-5; *idem, Religious Sects* (London, 1970), p.242; Alan D. Gilbert, *Religion and Society in Industrial England: church, chapel and social change* (London, 1976), pp.59-67.

attitude to culture and society will illuminate not only the Brethren movement, but also the community of Victorian and twentieth-century Scotland.

Table 9.1. **Social class of eight Brethren assemblies, 1863-1937**

Social class[1]	I	II	III	IV	V	W	X	U
Chapelton (1863)								
Membership 20								
Number	0	3	6	1	0	(2)[3]	0	10
%[2]	(0)	(30)	(60)	(12.5)	(0)	(40)	(0)	(50)
Strathaven (1881)								
Membership 56								
Number	2	14	18	7	0	(14)[3]	(1)[3]	14
%[2]	(4.8)	(33.3)	(42.8)	(16.7)	(0)	(42.9)	(2.4)	(25)
Hebron Hall, Glasgow[4]								
(1913)								
Membership 118								
Number	2	20	64	6	10	-	-	16
%[2]	(2)	(19.6)	(62.7)	(5.9)	(9.8)			(13.6)
Dumfries (1913)								
Membership 23								
Number	1	6	13	3	0	(8)[3]	0	0
%	(4.3)	(26)	(56.5)	(13)	(0)	(61.5)	(0)	(0)
Kirkintilloch (1917)								
Membership 22								
Number	0	3	6	5	1	(4)[3]	1	6
%[2]	(0)	(20)	(40)	(33.3)	(6.7)	(50)	(6.25)	(27.2)
Kirkwall (1919)								
Membership 49								
Number	0	7	20	4	0	3 (+8)[3]	2 (+3)[3]	13
%[2]	(0)	(22.6)	(64.5)	(11.8)	(0)	(61.1)	(13.9)	(24.5)
Kilbirnie (1931)[4]								
Membership 280								
Number	0	16	172	12	25	-	12	37
%[2]	(0)	(7.1)	(76.4)	(3.3)	(11.1)	-	(5)	(13.2)
Newarthill (1937)								
Membership 32								
Number	0	5	18	2	0	5 (+7)[3]	2 (+3)[3]	0
%[2]	(0)	(20)	(72)	(8)	(0)	(66.7)	(15.6)	(0)

Notes for Table 9.1:

1. Classes I-V = social groups A-E (see Appendix 4); W = housewives (married women not in employment); X = unwaged (retired, students, disabled, and unemployed); U = unidentified; where possible, the social class of those not in employment has been allocated to that of the head of household in columns I-V.

2. Percentages in a social class are those of the total number to whom it is possible to allocate one; percentages of housewives are those of all identified women; percentages of unwaged are those of all identified individuals; and percentages of unidentified are those of the total membership.

3. The number in brackets is of those also allocated to a social class.

4. Occupations based on valuation rolls in which housewives are not listed.

Sources for Table 9.1: East Kilbride Free Church, 'Minutes of Kirk Session', 2 (1848-83); 'Roll of Members of Strathaven Assembly 1876-1897'; *Hebron Hall, 16 Wilton Street: List of Members* (Glasgow, 1913); oral information, Bethany Hall, Dumfries (1989); Kirkintilloch Account Book, 1922-49; OA D/27, Robert Rendall papers; Kilbirnie Roll Book 1931; oral information, Gospel Hall, Newarthill (7 September 1988).

Social Class

Table 9.1 gives the social class of eight assemblies in the period 1863 until 1937. The Brethren were not interested in collecting such data, and how difficult they were to gather can be seen from the number of unidentified individuals: some 50 per cent in the case of Chapelton, and around a quarter of the membership in the assemblies in Strathaven, Kirkintilloch, and Kirkwall. In addition, Chapelton, Dumfries, Kirkintilloch and Newarthill were very small, possibly—with the exception of Chapelton—below average assembly size for the periods in which they existed. These difficulties mean that conclusions are often being projected from a very small base. Nevertheless the picture which emerges is a consistent one which suggests that it is reasonably accurate.

It can be seen from Table 9.1 (a total of 504 individuals to whom it was possible to allocate a social class)[6] that the largest social class in Scottish Brethren assemblies tended to be that of the skilled working class

---

6. Where possible, the social class of those not in employment has been allocated to that of the head of household in order to provide consistency of classification as in the valuation rolls the employment of the head of household only is given. Occasionally (as in one family in the Strathaven sample), a woman whose husband was class III worked as a domestic (class V). But in cases such as these the combined incomes would make them more prosperous members of class III. A more difficult example is when family offspring living at home belonged to a higher social class than the parental one. Cases such as these are noted in the discussion below, pp.294, 295.

(class III).[7] Unskilled workers (class V) were a very small proportion of the whole. There were apparently no members in this class in Chapelton, Strathaven, Dumfries, Kirkwall and Newarthill. However, in Hebron Hall, in the North Kelvinside district of Glasgow, and the Ayrshire steel town of Kilbirnie, they attained a moderately sized proportion of the membership—11.1 per cent and 9.8 per cent respectively. A larger group than the unskilled were semi-skilled workers (class IV) who had a percentage total somewhere between 33.3 in the case of Kirkintilloch and 3.3 in that of Kilbirnie. The table, however, almost certainly under-represents both class IV and V individuals. A number from these classes were almost definitely among the single individuals whom it was not possible to identify in Hebron Hall, Strathaven and Kilbirnie as they were hard to trace in valuation rolls or census returns. They probably belonged to such occupations as domestic or farm servants and moved frequently.

Table 9.2. **Social class of Scottish Brethren members with occupation given in an obituary in** *The Witness*

Social class[1]	I	II	III	IV	V
All obituaries	67	136	142	5	0
%	(19.1)	(38.9)	(40.6)	(1.4)	(0)
Born 1826-60	15	30	32	1	0
%	(19.2)	(38.5)	(41)	(1.3)	(0)
Born 1861-1898	24	54	59	2	0
%	(17.3)	(38.8)	(42.4)	(1.4)	(0)
Born 1899-1916	10	10	13	1	0
%	(29.4)	(29.4)	(38.2)	(2.9)	(0)
Born 1917-1942	2	6	4	0	0
	(16.7)	(50)	(33.3)	(0)	(0)

Note for Table 9.2:
1. Classes I-V = social groups A-E (see Appendix 4).

Source for Table 9.2: 'With Christ', *The Witness*, 33-108 (1903-78).

7. See Appendix 4 for an explanation of the analysis of the social classification employed and for a listing of the employments encountered.

But it is clear that the social class with the most substantial representation, was that of skilled workers with apparently between 76.4 (Kilbirnie) and 40 per cent (Kirkintilloch) of the membership in each assembly. Of these the largest group—10.5 per cent of this sample—was that of skilled tradesmen: joiners, bakers, house decorators and the like, comprising 16.7 per cent of all class III individuals. The second largest group was steel workers, a figure skewed by the inclusion of the large assembly in Kilbirnie where much of the male work force was dependent on that industry. However, the proportion of them in the meeting suggests that there was social congruence between the predominant working-class occupation in a community and an assembly.[8] But of those whose employment was noted in an obituary in *The Witness* (350 individuals: Table 9.2),[9] 23.1 per cent in class III were miners and fourteen per cent were fishermen. This latter group was evidently important, but was by no means dominant except in eastern coastal communities where uniformity between the employment of assembly members and that of the wider society ensured their preponderance in assemblies.[10] *The Witness* sample suggests almost ten per cent of the entire membership from 1870 until 1939 (roughly the period covered by the obituaries) were miners. However, these obituaries need to be treated with caution here for obviously an individual's employment was more likely to be stated if it had been prestigious, and such individuals would often be widely known in the movement and thus more likely to be the subject of an obituary.[11] In addition the occupations of miners and fishermen were most often given because of fatal accidents at work and, because of the high casualty rate among the latter, the obituaries probably exaggerate their numbers. As a result, the percentage of miners was almost certainly higher than *The Witness* figure suggests, for it was in the coal mining districts of the Lowlands that Brethren strength lay (see Maps 7-10, 13). Again the social congruence between community and

---

8. Cf. Mark Smith, *Religion in Industrial Society: Oldham and Saddleworth 1740-1865* (Oxford, 1994), pp.124-34.

9. Evangelists and missionaries have not been included in this number.

10. Gillian Munro, 'Reconciling difference: religious life as an expression of social, cultural and economic survival', in James Porter (ed.), *After Columba—After Calvin: religious community in North-East Scotland* (Aberdeen, 1999), p.175, reports the oral tradition in the Moray coast village of 'Balnamara' (an ethnologist's pseudonym which was identified by the researcher at a conference the present writer attended) that before World War II only the poorest of the fishing folk belonged to the Brethren; as the village in question did not have an Open Brethren assembly until after the war, this comment evidently applied to the Exclusives, for which the community was a stronghold. It is possible that this socio-economic condition might have been true of the Open Brethren in similar communities, but there is no evidence for or against the proposition.

11. For explanation of *The Witness* obituaries, see above p.16 n.89.

assembly supports a larger percentage of miners in the membership: in the large assembly at Larkhall after 1870 most of the assembly members were miners,[12] and one individual recollected that in Lochore, Fife, in the years before World War I all the men in the assembly except one were similarly employed.[13] Given the importance of those in skilled manual occupations in the Brethren, skilled tradesmen and miners evidently formed a substantial proportion of the membership.

A significant part of the membership belonged to the intermediate stratum (class II), the lower-middle class. This ranges in Table 9.1 from 33.3 per cent of the membership in Strathaven to 7.1 per cent in Kilbirnie. Of these many were small businessmen: the member who was the exception in Lochore owned a shop. In Table 9.1 small businessmen comprised 31.5 per cent of those in this class and 47 per cent in Table 9.2. The next largest group of those in this class in the latter table with 14.1 per cent was the health associate professionals (such as nurses and opticians), but this group accounted for only 8.6 per cent of those in this class in Table 9.1, the same percentage as that of tenant farmers. There were, as Table 9.2 demonstrates, a number of individuals who belonged to the professional, merchant-manufacturing and manager class (class I). However, because of the over-representation of classes I and II in *The Witness* sample, Table 9.1 undoubtedly gives a more accurate picture of their relative proportions to the working classes. Nevertheless, there were class I individuals present in some assemblies. In Strathaven in 1881 these were John Frew, one of the rising men of the town, and his wife. Frew was the owner of John Frew & Sons Ltd, silk manufacturers, founded in 1876. By 1881 he employed 130 workers and eventually became Strathaven's largest employer in the early twentieth century.[14] In Dumfries in 1913 the individual in class I was lawyer Alex Milroy and in Hebron Hall, Glasgow, in 1917 this group was represented by William Patrick, the prosperous proprietor of a produce merchant's business, and his wife. But it was doctors who were, apparently, the largest group in this class, composing 30.4 per cent of all individuals in class I in *The Witness* sample.

---

12. Robert Chapman, *The Story of Hebron Hall Assembly, Larkhall, 1866-1928: a short history of the inception, progress and personalities of the assembly* (Kilmarnock, 1929), pp.24-5.

13. Oral information, 19 November 1988, from an assembly member.

14. Strathaven Assembly Roll Book; Census Return (1881); William Fleming Downie, *A History of Strathaven and Avondale* (Glasgow, 1979), pp.89-90, 194ff.

Table 9.3. Social class of three Brethren assemblies, 1937-1963

Social class[1]	I	II	III	IV	V	W	X	U
Kirkintilloch (1917)								
Membership 22								
Number	0	3	6	5	1	(4)[3]	1	6
%[2]	(0)	(20)	(40)	(33.3)	(6.7)	(50)	(6.25)	(27.2)
Kirkintilloch (1935)								
Membership 46								
Number	1	4	29	5	0	2 (+11)[3]	3	2
%[2]	(2.6)	(10.3)	(74.4)	(12.8)	(0)	(29.5)	(6.8)	(4.3)
Kilbirnie (1931)[4]								
Membership 280								
Number	0	16	172	12	25	-	18	37
%[2]	(0)	(7.1)	(76.4)	(3.3)	(11.1)	-	(7.4)	(33.6)
Kilbirnie (1960)								
Membership 210								
Number	5	32	128	16	0	6 (+42)[3]	8 (+9)[3]	15
%[2]	(2.8)	(17.7)	(70.7)	(8.8)	(0)	(38.9)	(8.7)	(7.1)
Newarthill (1937)								
Membership 32								
Number	0	5	18	2	0	5 (+7)[3]	2 (+3)[3]	0
%[2]	(0)	(20)	(72)	(6.7)	(0)	(66.7)	(15.6)	(0)
Newarthill (1953)								
Membership 33								
Number	0	8	13	4	0	1 (+8)[3]	6	1
%[2]	(0)	(32)	(52)	(16)	(0)	(58.8)	(18.75)	(3)
Newarthill (1963)								
Membership 41								
Number	0	16	15	0	2	4 (+8)	4 (+5)[3]	0
%[2]	(0)	(48.5)	(45.5)	(0)	(6)	(42.8)	(22)	(0)

Notes for Table 9.3:
1. Classes I-V = social groups A-E (see Appendix 4); W = housewives (married women not in employment); X = unwaged (retired, students, disabled, and unemployed); U = unidentified; where possible, the social class of those not in employment has been allocated to that of the head of household in columns I-V.
2. Percentages in a social class are those of the total number to whom it is possible to allocate one; percentages of housewives are those of all identified women; percentages of unwaged are those of all identified individuals; and percentages of unidentified are those of the total membership.
3. The number in brackets is that of those also allocated to a social class.

4. Occupations based on the valuation roll in which housewives are not listed.

Sources for Table 9.3: Kirkintilloch Account Book, 1922-49; Kilbirnie Roll Books, 1931 & 1960; oral information, Gospel Hall, Newarthill (7 September 1988).

Table 9.4.   **Social class of Brethren assemblies aggregated according to period, 1863-1963**

Social class[1]	I	II	III	IV	V	X	U
1863-81	2	16	23	8	0	(1)[3]	24
%[2]	(4)	(32.7)	(47)	(16.3)	(0)	(2)	(32.9)
1913-1919	3	36	103	12	11	6	41
%[2]	(1.8)	(21.8)	(62.4)	(7.2)	(6.7)	(3.5)	(19.3)
1931-7	1	25	219	19	25	17 (+3)[3]	39
%[2]	(0.3)	(8.7)	(75.8)	(6.6)	(8.7)	(6.5)	(11.3)
1960-63	5	61	174	22	2	20 (+17)[3]	16
%[2]	(1.9)	(23.1)	(65.9)	(8.3)	(0.8)	(13)	(5.3)

Notes for Table 9.4:
1. Classes I-V = social groups A-E (see Appendix 4); X = unwaged (retired, students, disabled, and unemployed); U = unidentified.
2. Percentages of a social class are those of the total number to whom it is possible to allocate one; percentages of unidentified are of those of the total membership.
3. The number in brackets is that of those also allocated to a social class.

Sources for Table 9.4: Tables 9.1 and 9.3.

The data in *The Witness* obituaries also show that those in class I tended to be concentrated in certain areas with some 48.5 per cent of them found in Glasgow, Edinburgh, Aberdeen, or suburban districts such as Cambuslang. Their general presence can be seen if the 27.9 per cent who lived outside these places is contrasted with the 68.3 per cent of small businessmen who lived in large and small towns. In addition a further 23.5 per cent of class I individuals in *The Witness* sample moved at some point in their life to England. Typical of this was David Stone, the Strathaven member listed in column X in Table 9.1. The son of James Stone, the farmer and preacher, he was a school pupil in 1881, later graduating in medicine from Glasgow University in 1887. After a spell as a ship's surgeon, he spent the remainder of his life in Northampton.[15] *The Witness* obituaries show that individuals in classes I and II were also apparently a slightly more mobile group, each group making on average 2.1 removals to new places, compared to those in class III who moved on average 1.6 times. In most assemblies, class I individuals were simply not to be found, a point supported by Table 9.1.

Tables 9.2 to 9.4 examine the changes in social class over time. It is possible to calculate the year of birth of 264 individuals in *The Witness* sample. In Table 9.2 the data have been grouped into four periods, with individuals being allocated to the one in which he or she was 21. The cut-off date for each period is the final year in each of the intervals in Table 9.4 when individuals would attain that age. It shows the relative proportions of classes as remarkably constant in the nineteenth century, but the paucity of obituaries for the later periods makes generalisations from it about the twentieth century difficult. Tables 9.3 and 9.4 suggest that class remained fairly constant until the 1930s with, if anything, an increase in the skilled working-class occupations (class III). This may be because the three assemblies on which much of the later data in Table 9.3 is based—Kirkintilloch, Kilbirnie and Newarthill—had a larger proportion of working-class members than was true nationally, a possibility supported by the smaller proportion in class II. On the other hand it is more probable that these assemblies in industrialised communities were more typical of Scottish ones than others in Table 9.1 and may therefore give a truer picture of the balance of classes in the overall movement. It was not until after World War II that social change began to be felt, as can be seen from Table 9.3. By 1937 in Kirkintilloch, East Dunbartonshire, one individual, the son of assembly members, had become a chartered accountant, moving into class I, but the assembly maintained its working-class character, even increasing it from 1917. Post-World War II change can be seen in Kilbirnie assembly, where in 1960 some 79.5 of the members still belonged to classes III and IV. However, the representation of classes I and II had markedly increased, something which was set to continue as a further three members, the offspring of working-class Brethren parents and classified in Table 9.3 under class III,[16] were teachers and another two individuals were at university and would later enter the same profession. In the steel village of Newarthill, Lanarkshire, the upward rise in social class by the early 1960s is also marked with a decrease in class III and a corresponding increase in class II. In addition the rise in members classified in column X in Newarthill is also due to the number who were still at school, as in

---

15. 'Dr David Stone', *W*, 78 (1948), p.72.
16. For this classification, see above, n.6.

Kilbirnie, a sign of future increased upward mobility, a point which shall be discussed in the next chapter.[17]

One group which showed some fluctuations in size was the proportion of women who were housewives (calculated as a proportion of all identified females).[18] Women constitute 60.2 per cent of all members whose sex it is possible to determine in Table 9.1 and 61.2 per cent of Table 9.4.[19] Given the high correlation between membership and attendance in the movement, men were probably prominent by their presence at Brethren meetings whereas women with young children could not always attend. These factors probably made the preponderance of females in membership less noticeable. In the 1901 Dundee church census, women composed 49.6 per cent of Brethren attenders at morning service compared to 53.4 per cent for other churches.[20] It would appear that the proportion of females in the movement was only slightly below that of English Nonconformity and that of other Scottish churches such as the Baptist ones, but those men the movement did attract were more visibly active especially in attendance at the morning meeting at which they could participate.[21] Half of the ten congregations profiled in Tables 9.1 and 9.3 had, seemingly, a preponderance of women in employment with housewives ranging from a majority of 66.7 per cent in Newarthill in 1937 (Table 9.1) to a minority of 29.5 in Kirkintilloch in 1935 (Table 9.3). However, married women were mainly housewives: in 1935 in Kirkintilloch 92.3 per cent were housewives and in 1960 in Kilbirnie 74.2 per cent were also housewives. Until the 1960s, it would appear, the fluctuations in the number of women in employment were due to the proportion of single women in an assembly.

A persistent minority in social classes II-IV consisted of those engaged in agricultural occupations, ranging from large tenant farmers, such as James Stone of Ardochrigg, tenant of one of the Earl of Eglinton's

---

17. See below, pp.344-7.

18. However, it should be noted that women (particularly single women or ones with husbands not in fellowship) were more likely to be unidentified, making generalisations about them based on the available data more unreliable.

19. Women constitute 45.5% of obituaries in *The Witness*; but as a reflection of their membership this figure is probably too low as they were much less likely to receive an obituary (see above, p.16 n.89).

20. *The Dundee Advertiser*, 1 April 1901, p.5; this figure is for all sections of the Brethren movement included in the survey.

21. D. W. Bebbington (ed.), *A History of the Baptists in Scotland* (Glasgow, 1988), p.85; Clive D. Field, 'Adam and Eve: gender in the English Free Church constituency' *JEH*, 44 (1993), pp.63-74; Peter Hillis, 'The 1891 membership roll of Hillhead Baptist Church', *RSCHS*, 30 (2000), pp.183-4, Table 8, p.122; the average female membership of nineteenth-century Presbyterian churches given in Hillis, Table 8, is 62.7%; Field deduces from his evidence that the fewer demands on men, the greater their numbers.

largest Lanarkshire farms,[22] to small-holding proprietors such as William Adams in Kirkintilloch. The Brethren were a remarkably pervasive force throughout Scottish society. However, the principal Brethren strength in Scotland was among occupations in industrialised communities. Before World War II the social profile of the movement was similar to that of late nineteenth-century English Nonconformity.[23] The core of the membership lay in the skilled working class with a significant representation of both the lower strata of society and the intermediate class before World War II, but with some upwards social movement in favour of the last group in the post-war period. The presence of these classes had great importance for the way in which assemblies interacted with their societies.

Social Functions: Society

R. Q. Gray has argued that the intermediate class in the late nineteenth- and early twentieth-century Edinburgh churches supported the hegemonic ideology of society and provided a significant role in mediating these values to the strata below them.[24] It might be argued that, given the presence of this group within the Brethren and in the light of the social conservatism of the movement (to be discussed more fully below),[25] it performed a similar function for society within assemblies. A symbol for this putative role might be found in *Sound Speech* (1927), a series of lessons written by schoolteacher R. D. Johnston to teach the basics of grammar to preachers with poor education.[26] Middle-class cultural values were apparently being transmitted to the lower social strata.[27] Undoubtedly the Brethren moulded a compliant workforce as the demands of the sect produced dependability for the industrial routine and this was coupled with the strong emphasis on submission to authority,

---

22. *Valuation Roll for the County of Lanark for the Year 1891-2—Parish of East Kilbride*, p.621.

23. Hugh McLeod, *Class and Religion in the Late Victorian City* (London, 1974), pp.309-311; Gilbert, *Religion and Society*, pp.59-67; Clive D. Field, 'The social structure of English Methodism: eighteenth-twentieth centuries', *BJS*, 28 (1977), pp.199-225; Michael R. Watts, *The Dissenters. Volume II: the expansion of Evangelical Nonconformity* (Oxford, 1995), pp.303-27.

24. R. Q. Gray, 'Religion, culture and social class in late nineteenth and early twentieth century Edinburgh', G. Crossik (ed.), *The Lower Middle Class in Britain 1870-1914* (London, 1977), pp.134-58.

25. See below, pp.316-24.

26. R. D. Johnston, *Sound Speech: studies in English for Christian workers* (Kilmarnock, 1927).

27. Cf. Thompson, *English Working Class*, pp.385-440.

including (as will emerge below) not striking.[28] Assemblies, it might
further be argued, were run in the employers' interests. J. R. Caldwell, in
a sermon on masters and servants published in 1892, primarily
emphasised the duties of the latter which included responsibility,
obedience and honesty (incorporating not cheating in time-keeping).[29] It
might be maintained more cynically that business values could be found
controlling practice. Both J. R. Caldwell and John Ritchie promoted
sympathy towards bankrupts, probably because of their own background
in trade and an awareness of its vicissitudes, and Henry Pickering advised
mercy during the depression of the early 1920s.[30] In giving this advice
they were reacting to others who took a harder line, similar to the more
sectarian Churches of God which John Brown of Greenock left when his
business failed through its incompetent management by relatives.[31] There
were even hints of class antagonism between the middle class and others.
Assemblies could split along class lines, a more relaxed, open position
appealing to middle-class individuals and a more sectarian line to
working-class ones. In Glasgow in the 1880s the polarity between these
two sections of the movement was displayed in the disparity between
Cathcart Road Gospel Hall, on the edge of the Gorbals and the skilled
working-class area of Govanhill, and Elim Hall in Crosshill with its
housing for the middle classes;[32] and in the mid-twentieth century such
divisions have already been noticed in the arguments over High Leigh.[33]
John Douglas warned against, 'Three signs of the world: the cigarette in
the mouth, the ring on the finger, the stick in the hand.'[34] It is highly

---

28. See below, p.314.

29. J. R. Caldwell, 'Masters and servants' *W*, 22 (1892), pp.132-6, 155-7; reprinted
as a chapter in *idem, Earthly Relationships of the Heavenly Family* (n.d.), rpt. (Glasgow,
1983).

30. [J. R. Caldwell]., 'QA', *NW*, 12 (1882), pp.47-8; J. R. C[aldwell]., 'On
discipline in the assembly', *W*, 19 (1889), p.36; [John Ritchie], 'BQB', *BM*, 21 (1911),
p.71; HyP[ickering] 'QA' *W*, 53 (1923), p.103; [*idem*], 'QA', *W*, 54 (1924), p.263; cf.
David Jeremy, *Capitalists and Christians: business leaders and the churches in Britain,
1900-1960* (Oxford, 1990), p.53.

31. J. J. Park, *The Churches of God: their origin and development in the twentieth
century* (Leicester, 1986), p.85; see also above, p.170.

32. See above, p.163; Crosshill was incorporated into Glasgow in 1891.

33. See above, pp.242-3.

34. Writer's collection II, quoted in Max Wright to the writer, 11 February 1992;
Douglas was also echoing a general disapproval of modishness in male dress: cf. John
Justice's dislike in 1872 of trousers as being too 'foppish' (M. K[err]., *Memoir of John
Justice* (Ayr, 1875), p.79); J. R. Caldwell's distaste in 1908 for white umbrellas with
green lining (J. R. Caldwell, *The Epitome of Christian Experience in Psalm XXXII with
the development of the Christian life* (Glasgow [1917]), p.97); and Andrew Borland's
comment in 1923 that 'The supercilious coxcomb is almost as common within some

unlikely that his caricature dandy existed among Brethren business people, but Douglas's animus against a more genteel image which could be cultivated among them is clear.[35]

But despite the variety of social classes and the examples which might be cited as evidence of social control and class antagonism within assemblies, homogeneity of attitude marked them. The more prosperous lower-middle class members of Kilbirnie assembly in 1931 (Table 9.1) might be owner-occupiers in Stoneyholm Road and Largs Road, streets which opened into the countryside, but they shared the same industrial small-town culture and within the assembly were united by the same religious values. What was of greater importance was the division of the community into 'saved' and 'unsaved'. The individuals from class I, who, as was seen above, tended to be found in the cities or middle-class suburbia, similarly promoted salvation. In comparison, social distinctions were minor.[36] They used their abilities in pursuit of the same objectives as their working-class fellow Brethren and were the leading individuals in many of the most flourishing assemblies.[37] Along with members of the intermediate class, they performed a valuable role in being assembly trustees and in staffing such committees as the Brethren possessed. James Robertson (1842-1926), owner of the largest coachbuilding firm in Glasgow, was chairman of the Glasgow Half-Yearly Conferences and a trustee of both HFMF and the charitable Aitchison Trust; Gordon Davidson (d.1950), a wealthy sausage manufacturer, was a director of Netherhall and a convener of the Half-Yearlies; and probably the leading pluralist among committee members was T. J. Smith (d.1966), a director of Colvilles Ltd, the iron and steel manufacturers.[38] Trustees of assembly halls also tended to be individuals drawn from a higher social strata. Table 9.5 shows the social class of the founding trustees of two

churches as is the dandified fop in many a theatre' (Andrew Borland, *Love's Most Excellent Way: or Christian courtship* (London & Edinburgh [1923]), p.64).

35. Cf. the aphorisms expressing suspicion of wealth of Alex Easton, a Grangemouth preacher, cited in George N. Patterson, *Patterson of Tibet: death throes of a nation* (San Diego, CA, 1998), p.53.

36. Cf. P. L. M. Hillis, 'Education and evangelisation: Presbyterian missions in mid-nineteenth century Glasgow', *SHR*, 66 (1989), pp.46-62.

37. For a similar comment on England, cf., Roy Coad, 'The influence of Brethrenism on English business practice', *Biblioteca Storica Toscana*, 11 (Firenze, 1988), p.110.

38. 'James Robertson, *W*, 56 (1926), p.299; 'Gordon Norie Davidson', *W*, 80 (1950), p.168; cf. 'John A. Ireland' *W*, 92 (1962), p.436; W. B. Scott, 'Thomas James Smith', *W*, 96 (1966), p.228: at the time of his death Smith was Senior Treasurer of HFMF, chairman of the Retired Missionary Aid Fund, treasurer of the Widows and Orphans Fund, vice-chairman of the Stewards' Company Ltd., vice-president of the National Bible Society of Scotland, an honorary vice-president of the Scottish Evangelistic Council, council member of the Scripture Gift Mission, and trustee of several charitable Christian trusts; on Smith see below, p.302.

Kilmarnock assemblies in the 1930s. Given the proportion of middle-class individuals in both groups, probably all of the male members in the higher social strata in both assemblies were acting as trustees. Even in Elim Hall, noticeably lower-class, four of the class III individuals were non-employing self-employed individuals. Sometimes, perhaps, a more organisation-oriented mentality could be detected among businessmen. When being interviewed about his missionary prospects George Patterson, an *enfant terrible* of the movement, found the Glasgow missionary committee members dubious of his enthusiasm for an absolute form of living by faith and on the side of financial husbandry. For Patterson it was a conflict between the charismatic and the institutional mentalities.[39] In common with their equivalents in other churches, businessmen had, it would appear, more influence within the movement than they had on controlling their employees or in proselytising them.[40] But among assemblies their talents were at the service of the common object of the salvation of their fellows, not the furtherance of business interests.

Table 9.5. **Social class of the founding trustees of two Kilmarnock assemblies**

Social class[1]	I	II	III	IV	V	X
Elim Hall (1931)	1	3	7	1	0	0
Central Hall (1934)	3	3	4	0	0	1

Note for Table 9.5:
1. Classes I-V = social groups A-E (see Appendix 4); X = retired.

Sources for Table 9.5: 'Christian Brethren, originally holding meetings in the Co-operative Hall, John Dickie St., Kilmarnock, then in Princes St., Kilmarnock, and presently in Cuthbert Pl., Kilmarnock. Statement of the Constitution and Government. Section II—Government', typescript, 1931; 'Disposition to the Trustees of Christian Brethren meeting in Central Hall, John Finnie St., Kilmarnock', typescript, 1934.

Brethren literature, in addition, was remarkably free from social propaganda.[41] In the several magazines which were issued for children, even teaching on morality was avoided for the Brethren were very firmly

39. George N. Patterson, *God's Fool* (London, 1956), pp.58-60.
40. Jeremy, *Capitalists and Christians*, pp.245-408.
41. J. A. H. Dempster, 'Aspects of Brethren publishing enterprise in late nineteenth century Scotland', *Publishing History*, 20 (1986), pp.84-5.

of the opinion that conversion was the only solution to social problems.[42] It was a simple religious message which was disseminated through their children's work. This is not to deny that there were latent functions in the Sunday schools and children's meetings. A fairly typical Brethren Sunday school was probably being depicted in the story 'Heaven's Roll' (1938) in which the majority of those attending 'belonged to the poorer class, and were scantily clad.'[43] For such children they aided literacy: in giving a recitation at a soirée or memorising the Bible—one non-Brethren nonagenarian recalled receiving a prize in Wellington Hall, Kilmarnock, for reciting all of Isaiah 53.[44] As Mark Smith has argued for similar activities in Lancashire, they also prepared children for associational leisure activities through soirées, outings and the entertaining 'action choruses' (in which the singers mimed the key words) with which the Brethren liked to sugar the religious pill.[45] More significantly for class relations, they could provide children with role models from their own social class, who were respectable, disciplined and prosperous. But if so, then they were also deeply religious ones. The Brethren strove to inculcate transcendental belief, not social propaganda.

It is also for this reason that the Brethren do not support the Weber-Tawney hypothesis. They appear to conform to Weber's ideal type of the inner-worldy ascetic in which Christian austerity 'undertook to penetrate just that daily routine of life', one of the principal foundations for his case that Protestantism fostered the spirit of capitalism which he found to be shown very clearly in the Protestant sects.[46] Certainly the movement promoted the values of temperance, discipline and financial prudence which gave the members a relatively prosperous life in comparison to many of their neighbours. Capitalism, too, was acceptable. Caldwell argued that it was the duty of the Christian businessman to buy in the cheapest market and sell in the dearest.[47] Investment was also permissible,

42. Fred Elliott, 'The gospel and its blessings', in W. Hoste and R. McElheran (eds), *The Great Sacrifice: or what the death of Christ has wrought* (Kilmarnock [1927]), p.61.

43. M. M'L., 'Heaven's Roll', *Boys and Girls* , No.609 (October, 1938), [p.16].

44. Oral information, 10 July 1997, from the individual concerned; cf. Robert Moore, *Pit-Men, Preachers and Politics: the effects of Methodism in a Durham mining community* (Cambridge, 1974), pp.109-113.

45. Smith, *Religion in Industrial Society*, pp.258-9, cf. children in Larkhall singing a religious chorus in accompaniment to their games, Chapman, *Hebron Hall*, p.33.

46. Weber, *Protestant Ethic*, p.154; *idem*, 'The Protestant sects and the spirit of capitalism', in H. H. Gerth and C. Wright Mills (eds), *From Max Weber: essays in sociology* (1948) Routledge edn (London, 1970), pp.302-22. In a probably unconscious echo of Weber, James Black, *New Forms of the Old Faith: being the Baird Lecture delivered in 1946-47 under the title extra-church systems* (London, 1948), p.148, stated of the Brethren: '*Ideally, they are monks without a monastery!*'

47. J. R. C[aldwell]., 'Honesty', *NW*, 10 (1880), p.2.

being clearly distinguished from gambling.[48] But, as Roy Coad has shown through a study of English Brethren businessmen, the Weber-Tawney thesis does not fit the movement, for they were without the ruthlessness which Weber attributes to the Protestant entrepreneur.[49] R. H. Campbell has noted that Christian businessmen were frowned upon for using wealth for social advancement rather than philanthropy.[50] Their Brethren counterparts, however, were definitely of the opinion that profits should be used in the Lord's service.[51] Charles A. Aitchison, whose family owned a bakery firm which supplied the upper classes, 'lived in a plain home on the plainest of fare' and gave largely to home and foreign missions. When he died in 1906 he left £150,000 to found a trust for the support of religious objects.[52] In the twentieth century, one of the most significant businessmen was T. J. Smith, from 1958 a director of Colvilles Ltd, one of the 100 largest companies in Britain. Again he was a massive benefactor of foreign missions and, as was noted above, used his business acumen for the benefit of interdenominational Evangelical agencies.[53] In addition, investing in joint-stock companies was frowned upon because it drew the Christian into association with unbelievers or might be a sign of avarice.[54] The concept of labour as a calling was also drastically modified by the Brethren. As among the Anabaptists, employment as a vocation was weakened through it being perceived as a necessary condition of life, merely enabling the believer to be financially independent.[55] Henry Pickering approvingly retailed the reply of the Glasgow worker when asked his occupation: 'To wait for His Son from Heaven, and to fill up

---

48. 'YBQB', *BM*, 30 (1920), p.51.

49. Coad, 'English business practice', pp.107-8; cf. *idem, Laing: the Biography of Sir John W. Laing, C.B.E. (1879-1978)* (London, 1979).

50. R. H. Campbell, 'A critique of the Christian businessman and his paternalism', in David Jeremy (ed.), *Business and Religion in Britain* (Aldershot, 1988), p.38-9.

51. 'Stewardship', *NW*, 12 (1882), pp.26-30; cf. 'Luxury among Christians', *TP*, 1 (1849-51), p.237.

52. 'Charles A. Aitchison', *W*, 36 (September 1906), end pp.; 'Charles A. Aitchison', *BM*, 16 (September 1906), end pp.; 'James Robertson', *W*, 56 (1926), p.299; John Hawthorn, *Alexander Marshall: evangelist, author and pioneer* (Glasgow [1929]), pp.63-4; Coad, 'English business practice', p.111; the Aitchison Trust is still operative at the time of writing.

53. Scott, 'Smith', p.228; see also above, n.38; Duncan Ferguson, who had transferred to the Brethren in 1936 from the independent mission Hallelujah Hall, Motherwell, was Chairman and Managing Director of Colvilles Ltd: 'Duncan Ferguson', *W*, 100 (1970), p.156.

54. 'QA', *W*, 29 (1899), pp.115-16; 'Answers to correspondents', *BM*, 10 (1900), p.47: an exception could be made, however, for one consisting entirely of Christians.

55. Weber, *Protestant Ethic*, p.150.

the time making buttons.'[56] But the concept of employment was further modified in that it was to evangelism in the workplace the individual was called, not to the dignity of labour. As J. R. Caldwell advised his hearers, when 'God has called you as serving in a mason's yard, or a joiner's shop, or at a mill loom, or as a household servant, He has called you for the very purpose that *there* you should let your light shine.'[57] Witnessing, not work, was the true sign of God's grace. Caldwell was also firmly against working for any motive of personal profit. To start a business on borrowed capital was for him a sign that it was not God's will.[58] Money and secular success were inimical to spirituality.[59] Unlike English Dissenters such as the Quakers, the Brethren did not develop business family dynasties, either through a failure to produce heirs or through younger members of the family leaving the movement.[60] The predominance of the working classes remained absolute until World War II, after which the Brethren rose socially as improved prospects were more widely available throughout society. The movement did provide a social function for the community. It reinforced working-class self-improvement values of discipline, temperance and responsibility and it encouraged articulacy and literacy. These values, which the middle-class Caldwell was cited above as promoting in 1892,[61] were not the property of his class alone. Nor did the spirit of capitalism reside within the Brethren.

Social Functions: Membership

One potential explanation of the social function assemblies fulfilled for their members was that they helped assuage anomie, replacing the hopelessness induced by a fractured society with the confident security of the sect.[62] If this were a primary societal role of the Brethren, it might be expected that they would flourish in communities which were particularly subject to a breakdown of purpose. That assemblies were formed in communities which had undergone rapid social change has been noted in

56. Hy Pickering, *One Thousand Tales Worth Telling: mostly new/strictly true/suitable for you* (London and Glasgow [1918]), p.37.

57. J. R. Caldwell, 'Masters and servants, p.134; the italicisation of 'there' is from the book version *Earthly Relationships*, p.390.

58. *Idem*, 'Honesty', p.2.

59. W. Shaw, 'Why the singing ceased', *W*, 28 (1898), pp.153-4.

60. Whether those who left were more successful businessmen because of a Brethren upbringing (and therefore support the Weber-Tawney hypothesis) is beyond the scope of the present study.

61. See above, p.298.

62. Gilbert, *Religion and Society*, pp.87-93.

previous chapters.[63] Rural areas in which meetings were formed, such as Orkney and Aberdeenshire, had been subject to such alterations, but the change most often took the form of industrialisation. Most of the assemblies in the period before 1859 were established in textile communities or in cities. The industrial exception here was Newmains, the village which grew around the Coltness Iron Works. In the decade after 1859 the movement began to appear in communities undergoing this second phase of industrialisation such as Larkhall and Dalmellington. But even here Brethren assemblies were mainly formed in communities which had an experience of industrialisation that went back to the eighteenth century. The Lanarkshire cotton industry began in East Kilbride in 1783,[64] and a number of the other smaller towns and villages in which assemblies were formed—Strathaven, Lesmahagow, and Larkhall—had been weaving communities since the late eighteenth century. In places such as Rutherglen and Dalmellington, there was a mixture of weaving and mining which went back to the previous century.[65] These communities had experienced several decades of industrialisation.

Assemblies were not planted in the Lanarkshire parishes which were undergoing the most rapid industrial and demographic growth in the 1860s. The most intense revivals out of which assemblies grew initially occurred in communities, such as Strathaven, Lesmahagow, and Larkhall, which had undergone change, but which had achieved (or, in the case of rural areas, such as Orkney, had not entirely lost) some stability and homogeneity. This is not to say, however, that the Brethren could not grow in communities undergoing rapid expansion, for in places such as Glasgow and Greenock social change was continuous. Nevertheless, in Lanarkshire assemblies were not established in the new burghs of Airdrie, Motherwell and Wishaw, places which were being deeply transformed, until either assembly members migrated to them or, in the last instance, through the outreach of a nearby meeting. By the 1890s the movement had so penetrated industrial society that assemblies tended to be transplanted by the migration of labour (such as during the development of the west Fife coalfield)[66] and suburbanisation (as happened most obviously in Glasgow).[67] The pattern of Brethren growth within Scotland suggests that anomie was not the principal factor behind the increase of the movement. In Lerwick the Brethren emerged in a time of prosperity when a period of economic difficulties had passed.[68] Arguably, the

---

63. See above, Chpts 2, 3, 4, and 6.

64. *TSA: County of Lanark*, p.29.

65. *TSA: County of Ayr*, p.732.

66. See above, pp.111 n.161, 126-7, 195 n.102.

67. See above, pp.107 n.137, 125 n.259.

68. J. W. Irvine, *Lerwick: the birth and growth of an island town* (Lerwick, 1985), pp.51-72.

revivalism which aided their emergence in the Shetland countryside in the 1870s and 1880s was due to a continuation of communal coherence rather than its fragmentation.[69] When out-migration both there and in Aberdeenshire had passed its peak the Brethren entered a period of decline in these places.[70] Undue social fragmentation seemed to produce paralysis.[71]

Industrialisation, too, could create community where there had been none,[72] such as was the case in the industrial villages of the Lowlands in which much of Brethren strength resided. The inhabitants of Larkhall, a town in which the Brethren were singularly successful, were aware of the tranquillity of their community and the transition from weaving to mining was made without any civic tensions.[73] Miners had a strong sense of solidarity which, as John Bowes found in Carluke, Lanarkshire, in 1855, could be a hindrance to recruitment[74] and they were aware of themselves being a separate group.[75] The problem for the Brethren was not that miners were members of a fragmented society, but rather that members of the movement had to penetrate tightly-knit communities, and the opposition they faced initially showed that this entrance was not accomplished easily.[76] Social change was important for the emergence of assemblies, but the evidence suggests that some communal stability was necessary for recruitment to be successful. It was not the case that assemblies were formed among rootless people searching for stability amidst social fragmentation.

Scottish Brethren support the contention of Hugh McLeod on working-class converts in London that they were 'drawn mainly from those with ideas, in search of meanings, systems, explanations or from those in revolt against the way of life of their neighbours'.[77] Brethrenism was not, as has been stated of it in the context of the north-east fishing communities, a religion 'of the disinherited, providing, for those who

69. See above, pp.101-2, 113; for the argument that revivals are dependent on community coherence, see Donald E. Meek, '"Fishers of men": the 1921 religious revival, its cause, context and transmission', in Porter (ed.), *After Columba*, pp.135-42.

70. See above, pp.113-14.

71. Cf. Hugh McLeod, *Class and Religion*, p.282.

72. Cf. Smith, *Religion in Industrial Society*, p. 32; for the view that in the second half of the nineteenth century there was a consolidation of a sense of community in large factory towns cf. Patrick Joyce, *Work, Society and Politics: the culture of the factory in later Victorian England* (Brighton, 1980), pp.103-23.

73. Alan B. Campbell, *The Lanarkshire Miners: a social history of their trade unions, 1775-1874* (Edinburgh, 1979), pp.133-37, 159-160.

74. *TP*, 4 (1855-6), pp.119-20.

75. Gavin Wark, *The Rise and Fall of Mining Communities in Central Ayrshire in the 19th and 20th Centuries: Ayrshire Monographs No.22* (Darvel, 1999), pp.10-16.

76. For persecution of the Brethren, see below, pp.313-14.

77. McLeod, *Class and Religion*, p.283.

were losing hope in the present, a future in the world beyond.'[78] The type of individual who belonged to an assembly can be seen from the effects emigration exerted (Figure 9.1). The peak and troughs in national emigration and Brethren emigration largely coincide.[79] Comparison of the two sets of statistics has been achieved through expressing each as a percentage deviation from an eighty-eight-year mean (the period covered by the data). It can be seen from this that while assembly members tended to emigrate at the same time as others, they were more likely to emigrate.[80] It seems probable that, given their status as members of the intermediate or working classes, the Brethren were no more subject to 'push' factors (such as industrial depression) than the general population. But 'pull' factors (such as the opportunities offered over-seas) operated more powerfully on Brethren. They were more likely to be aware of conditions abroad through the network of contacts established there by earlier meeting members[81] and assemblies provided a ready-made network of support.[82] Brethren were also offered extra inducements to emigrate, which legitimated the enterprise, such as opportunities to evangelise or establish assemblies.[83] Indeed, John Bowes argued, it was

---

78. Paul Thompson, *et al*, *Living the Fishing* (London, 1983), p.258; cf. Thompson, *English Working Class*, p.427.

79. No figures are available for national emigration 1914-17.

80. The data for Scottish national emigration are those of total emigration from Scottish ports (Marjory Harper, *Emigration from North-East Scotland*, 1 (Aberdeen 1988), pp.35-6); the data for Brethren emigration are those of 720 individuals whose year of emigration can be determined, mainly from an obituary in *The Witness* or *The Believer's Magazine*. Reliance on these last data raises the usual difficulties associated with using them as a source (see above p.16 n.89), especially in determining which years Brethren emigration was at its highest. In particular the inter-war period may be underestimated because it falls in the period when obituaries are less reliable as a source; the same holds for the earlier nineteenth century. The Brethren statistics also do not take account of those who returned, as often a brief period overseas was not mentioned or dated in an obituary. Obituaries of those who died overseas became less common in British magazines as Brethren journals were established in the host countries. The general result of these factors is that Scottish Brethren emigration is likely to be underestimated in the available statistics. What is clear is that the peaks in Brethren emigration are higher than those of the general population.

81. James Wisely to the ed., 10 June 1851, *TP*, 1 (1850-1), p.239; T. H. Maynard to the ed., *W*, 56 (1926), p.471; C. Innes to the ed., *W*, 59 (1929), p.88; however, note the warnings in, 'Observations of an emigrant', *BM*, 22 (1912), p.36; *BM*, 33 (1923), p.36; and G. Arden to the ed., *W*, 55 (1925), p.92.

82. *W*, 25 (1925), p.140; *W*, 57 (1927), p.57; *BM*, 34 (1934), p.26; *W*, 77 (1947), p.35; J. Merridar to the ed., *BM*, 67 (1957), p.120.

83. Alex Marshall to the ed., *W*, 41 (1911), p.82; E. H. Broadbent, 'Christians and missionary service', *W*, 59 (1929), p.35; *W*, 57 (1927), p.179; *W*, 61 (1931), p.288; A. E. Brown to the ed., 9 August 1962, *W*, 42 (1962), pp.391-2; for attitudes among

the Christian's duty to emigrate so that New Testament churches might multiply.[84] Emigration could have a missionary purpose. These latter factors loosened the hold which loyalty to place had on Brethren. In the phrase of Bernard Aspinwall their beliefs were 'portable'[85]—a point supported by the significant number of missionaries that the movement produced which *The Witness* obituaries indicate was 1.7 per cent of the membership from 1876 until 1980. This percentage figure is perhaps too high as missionaries were more likely to receive an obituary,[86] and the same data were possibly more accurate in suggesting that 10.6 per cent of the Scottish membership emigrated over the period 1860 until 1967, a substantial proportion.[87] This last statistic shows that assembly members were eager for individual social improvement, a further reason which made them prepared to be mobile. The movement attracted independent and self-directed individuals and in turn reinforced such traits by providing a structure through which to express them.

That it was as a system of meaning that the Protestant Evangelicalism represented by the Brethren appealed can be seen from miners and fishermen. Both were engaged in dangerous occupations. Fishing communities were noted for their religious enthusiasm,[88] and stories of sudden deaths were intertwined with themes of religious conversion and experience.[89] In mining communities accidental death was also used as an appeal: the evangelist Charles Reid was converted through listening to a miner whose friend had been killed in a pit give his testimony.[90] Brethren miners themselves died in pit accidents from the Udston disaster in

Scottish Christians to emigration in the inter-war period see Marjory Harper, *Emigration from Scotland between the Wars: opportunity or exile?* (Manchester, 1998), pp.157-93.

84. [John Bowes], 'On the duty of the Christian to emigrate', *TP*, 2 (1851-3), p.103; cf. similar inducements for Mormon converts in P. A. M. Taylor, *Expectations Westward: the Mormons and the Emigration of their British Converts in the Nineteenth Century* (Edinburgh, 1965).

85. Bernard Aspinwall, *Portable Utopias* (Aberdeen, 1984)

86. Although the figure probably does not exaggerate the number of missionaries by much: Harold Rowdon, 'The Brethren contribution to world mission', in *idem* (ed.), *The Brethren Contribution to the Worldwide Mission of the Church* (Carlisle, 1994), p.38, suggested that 1% of the entire UK membership of the Brethren served as an overseas missionary.

87. These dates are for the first and last dates of emigration given in an obituary in *The Witness*; for the explanation of this data, see above p.16 n.89.

88. Thompson, *et al*, *Living the Fishing* , p.203.

89. For examples drawn from the stories of mainly Brethren fishermen from the 1860s until the late twentieth century, see Graham Mair (compiler), *The Fisherman's Gospel Manual* (London, 1994).

90. 'Chums!', *OLOT*, No. 255 (March 1909).

Lanarkshire of 1887 to the Kames one in Ayrshire of 1955.[91] The drama of salvation helped to make sense of a precarious existence and provide hope in the face of the imminence of death. An egalitarian independence was also a feature of these communities. The common ownership of fishing boats meant that they were 'societies of petty entrepreneurs' which bred individuality.[92] Autonomy was also a value of the miners. The historical development of the industry in Scotland gave rise to the 'independent collier', a status which was jealously guarded.[93] In Larkhall miners continued the local tradition of the weavers owning their own houses and were celebrated as 'The Lairds o' Larkie'.[94] In such mining communities self-help flourished in the form of the Co-operative movement and building and friendly societies, the last a form of material protection for those in dangerous occupations. An egalitarian sect such as the Brethren reinforced the values of autonomy and self-improvement.

Within the movement, miners were renowned for their Bible knowledge. Among such working-class groups as they represented, the autodidact, a figure who flourished in Scotland and was often nurtured by Evangelicalism, was a respected individual.[95] The origin of R. D. Johnston's *Sound Speech* was frequent expressions of regret made to the author by preachers on their inability to avoid grammatical mistakes. 'With many', he wrote of these converts, 'former days of opportunity were neglected, but with new life came new ambition'.[96] As T. W. Laqueur has noted in the context of Sunday schools, the social values which were transmitted were those of the working-class adherents themselves.[97] Their aspirations were a desire for respectability, improvement, and a regulated life.[98] Some of the independent individualism of

---

91. *W*, 19 (October 1889), v; 'James Marshall' and 'William Smith', *W*, 88 (1958), pp.15-16.

92. Thompson, *et al.*, *Living the Fishing* , pp.214-33; N. Dickson, 'Open and closed: Brethren and their origins in the north east', in Porter (ed.), *After Columba*, pp.160-2.

93. Campbell, *The Lanarkshire Miners*, pp.26-48.

94. Jack McLellan, *Larkhall: its historical development* (Larkhall, 1979), p.36-7; anon., 'The Lairds o' Larkie', *ibid.*, Appendix 17, pp.110-11.

95. Jonathan Rose, *The Intellectual Life of the British Working Classes* (New Haven, CT, 2001), pp.12-91; cf. the experience of one Churches of Christ evangelist who found that a Brethren individual in the late 1860s at Crofthead, West Lothian, who tended to despise education, was rather more poorly educated than the other assembly members in the village: James Anderson, *An Outline of My Life: or selections from a fifty years' religious experience* (Birmingham, 1912), p.39-40; I am indebted to Dr David Brady for the latter reference. For Brethren attitudes to tertiary education, see below, p.345.

96. Johnston, *Sound Speech*, p.3.

97. T. W. Laqueur, *Religion and Respectability: Sunday schools and working-class culture 1780-1850* (New Haven, CT; 1976), pp.239-40, 227-39.

98. R. Q. Gray, *The Labour Aristocracy in Victorian Edinburgh* (Oxford, 1976); Brian Harrison, *Peaceable Kingdom: stability and change in modern Britain* (Oxford, 1982),

the Brethren can also be seen in their liking for alternative medicines, particularly homeopathy. There were a number of homeopathic practitioners (including Hunter Beattie) among them,[99] and many Brethren homes contained a copy of *The Homeopathic Vade Mecum* (2nd edn 1905) or Professor Kirk's *Papers on Health* (1897), a work consisting largely of folk remedies.[100] The 'do-it-yourself doctor', T. C. F. Stunt has argued, was the 'acme of individualism'.[101] The cerebralism of the movement was discussed in the previous chapter.[102] Scottish Brethren attracted the autonomous sections of the working classes, desirous of self-advancement and capable of taking opportunities for social melioration.[103] As the sociologist Steve Bruce has argued, presumed latent functions of religion, such as assuaging anomie, or psychological compensation, cannot explain its adoption without making its adherents appear manipulators or fools.[104] It was as part of the innate human desire for meaning that the movement appealed to the classes from which its members came.

Attitudes to Culture and Society

The congruence of Brethren civic virtues and those of the classes to which they belonged must not be overemphasised. The prescriptive teaching of the movement was strongly opposed to engagement in the

pp.157-190; W. W. Knox, *Industrial Nation: work, culture and society in Scotland, 1800-present* (Edinburgh, 1999), pp.94-103; Michael Lynch (ed.), *The Oxford Companion to Scottish History* (Oxford, 2001), pp.522-3.

99. 'Dr. James Wardrop', *CW*, 30 (1915), pp.130-1; Henry Beattie, 'My father: Hunter Beattie 1875-1951', *BM*, 87 (1977), pp.196-7; and for Dr Brown Henry, see William Still, *Dying to Live* (Fearn, 1991), p.26; for herbalists, see the obituaries of two widows for their husbands' work: 'Mrs Thomas Anderson', *W*, 39 (1939), p.92; and 'Mrs W. C. Muir', *W*, 97 (1967), p.116.

100. E. Harris Ruddock, *The Homeopathic Vade Mecum of Modern Medicine and Surgery*, 2nd edn (London, 1905); Edward Bruce Kirk (ed.), *Papers on Health by Professor Kirk, Edinburgh* (1899), one-vol. edn (London, Glasgow and Philadelphia, PA, 1921). The author of the latter work was John Kirk, the EU minister out of whose labours the Newmains/Wishaw meeting had grown (see above, pp.46-7); for the use of 'Professor Kirk's Cure' by the evangelist Walter Anderson see Mr Alex. Stewart, Hopeman, Moray, [Alex. Stewart (compiler)], 'A Record of Gospel Work. Christian Brethren. Moray & Nairn', MS, n.d.

101. T. C. F. Stunt, 'Homeopathy and the Brethren', *W*, 103 (1973), pp.127-8.

102. See especially pp.274-5.

103. Cf. Gilbert, *Religion and Society*, pp.82-5; McLeod, *Religion and the Working Class in Nineteenth-Century Britain* (London, 1984), pp.22-5.

104. Steve Bruce, 'Social change and collective behaviour: the revival in eighteenth-century Ross-shire', *BJS*, 34 (1983), pp.554-72.

affairs of culture and society. They were, in Richard Niebuhr's typology, proponents of 'Christ-against-culture'.[105] Involvement was to be avoided. Believers were to exclude themselves from politics, and their only relation to government should be to obey it.[106] Voting was frowned on by most, sometimes on the grounds that the Christian had nothing to do with earthly affairs, or that one might be found voting against God's will or, more facetiously, because the believer's representative was in heaven.[107] John Bowes was an admirer of the Co-operative Society, but most later Brethren were opposed to even such modest forms of association with unbelievers.[108] Even as pioneer missionaries in Central Africa appalled by pagan ethics, they avoided influencing society through involvement in its affairs but remained passive spectators.[109] In a much quoted phrase Dan Crawford referred disparagingly to any (presumably non-Brethren) missionary who did adopt secular powers as 'a little Protestant Pope'.[110] The principle at stake, in Brethren eyes, was the need to separate from the world.[111] For this reason many of the institutions developed by working people to promote their interests or self-improvement were eschewed. Not only Co-operative shops, but friendly societies, the temperance movement, YMCA, mechanics' institutes, and union membership were all to be

105. H. Richard Niebuhr, *Christ and Culture* (London, 1952), pp.58-92.

106. C[aldwell]., 'Honesty', p.1.

107. C., 'Resurrection-life', *NW*, 6 (1876), p.152; J. R. Caldwell, 'Subject and rulers', *W*, 22 (1892), pp.179-81; *idem*, 'The general election', *W*, 89 (1929), p.85; K[err]., *John Justice*, pp.70-1; W. F. Naismith, *Faith's Radiant Path* (London, 1930), p.18.

108. [John Bowes], 'Co-operative societies', *TP*, 7 (1860-1), pp.209-11; 'QA', *W*, 29 (1899), pp.115-16; 'QA', *W*, 33 (1903), pp.162-4, 180, 194-5; [John Ritchie], 'Answers to special questions', *BM*, 14 (1904), pp.47-8; HyP[ickering]., 'QA', *W*, 62 (1932), p.191.

109. Robert I. Rotberg, 'Plymouth Brethren and the occupation of Katanga, 1886-1907', *The Journal of African History*, 5 (1964), pp.285-97.

110. Dan Crawford, *Thinking Black: 22 years without a break in the long grass of Central Africa* (London, 1912), p.324; however, Crawford himself had reluctantly to accept some civil powers from the Belgian authorities after the death of the African chieftain Msiri in 1891; for a more proactive Brethren attitude to an obstructive neighbouring chief, see Robert I. Rotberg, *Christian Missionaries and the Creation of Northern Rhodesia 1880-1924* (Princeton, NJ, 1965), pp.68-9; and for the example of the English Brethren missionary C. A. Swan helping the Quaker George Cadbury expose slave labour in cocoa production in Angola, see Jeremy, *Capitalists and Christians*, pp.145-52.

111. J. R[itchie]., 'The tabernacle in the wilderness', *NW*, 12 (1882), p.37; *idem*, *From Egypt to Canaan*, 6th edn (Kilmarnock, n.d.), pp.17-18; A. M[arshall]., 'Separation from the world', *W*, 19 (1889), pp.123-4; Naismith, *Faith's Radiant Path*, pp.11-14.

shunned.[112] Other popular organisations such as Masonic Lodges and the Orange Order were also to be avoided.[113] As a rule-of-thumb, one writer quoted the terse advice, 'Join nothing.'[114] Combinations were seen as preparing for the rule of the antichrist whose will would override the individual's.[115] Even the League of Nations was perceived as a harbinger of his tyranny.[116] Separation included business partnership with unbelievers or marriage to them and the stricter individuals advised endogamy.[117] After she joined an assembly, Jeanie Gilchrist, the future African missionary, broke off her engagement because her fiancée, a Free Church minister, would not leave his denomination.[118] A firm line was also taken against recreational activities. Evangelical disapproval of dancing, the theatre and novels had increased during the nineteenth century,[119] and the Brethren, from John Bowes onwards, continued it on these issues.[120] New converts were commended for their zeal in burning novels,[121] particularly suspect because as fiction they were a form of lying and for their effects which included becoming 'a silly sentimentalist', promoting 'unwholesome excitement', and encouraging prostitution.[122] Some were even unhappy with the notion that Christ's

112. W. H. Broom, 'Objections to a Christian joining temperance societies', *NEI*, 3 (1873), pp.122-6; anon., 'Concentration', *NW*, (1876), pp.133-8; 'QA', *NW*, 10 (1880), p.95; 'QA', *NW*, 12 (1882), pp.79-80; 'YBQB', *BM*, 30 (1920), pp.12, 63-4, 'Answers to questions', *ibid.*, pp.135-6; 'YBQB', *BM*, 31 (1921), pp.65-6; W. Scott, 'Things as they are to-day', *W*, 51 (1921), pp.75-7.

113. 'QA', *NW*, 10 (1880), p.62.

114. E. W. R[odgers]., 'BQB', *BM*, 49 (1939), p.191: this, too, in the context of stating that it was permissible to join the Co-operative Society.

115. J. C. Stein, 'The Antichrist: his appearing', *W*, 50 (1920), p.333; [John Ritchie], 'Answers to questions', *BM*, 30 (1920), pp.65-6; HyP[ickering]., 'WW', *W*, 79 (1949), p.164.

116. HyP[ickering]., 'WW', *W* 49 (1919), pp.52, 100.

117. [A. J. Holiday], 'Only in the Lord', *BP*, 7 (1886), pp.182-3.

118. J[ohn]. R[itchie]., *Jeanie Gilchrist: pioneer missionary to the women of Central Africa* (Kilmarnock [1927]), pp.15-16.

119. Michael Hennell, 'Evangelicalism and worldliness', in G. J. Cuming and Derek Baker (eds), *SCH*, 8 (Cambridge, 1972), pp.229-236.

120. [John Bowes], 'Preface', *TP*, 1, (1849-52), p.2; 'Should Christians attend the theatre?', *TP*, 2 (1852-3), p.116; [*idem*], 'Novels excluded from a library', *TP*, 9 (1863-6), p.291-2; J. R[itchie]., 'Letters to a young convert', *NI*, 4 (1874), p.180; HyP[ickering]., WW', *W*, 67 (1937), p.114.

121. 'The novel reader', *LR*, 1 (1866), p.43; W. H. Clare, *Pioneer Preaching or Work Well Done* (London and Glasgow [1925]), pp.58-9.

122. [John Bowes], 'Female prostitution: its effects and remedies', *TP*, 1 (1849-51); 'QA', *NW*, 15 (1885), p.64; L. W., 'The novel reader', *BP*, 41 (1920), p.75; W. J. McClure, 'Novel reading, and its disastrous consequences', *BM*, 35 (1926), p.34; M. G. Stickley to the ed., *W*, 95 (1965), pp.348-9; cf. Neil Dickson, 'Fiction's wicked lies', *A*, 70 (June 1991), pp.21-2; and Doreen Rosman, '"What has Christ to do with Apollo?":

parables were fictional.[123] As the mainline churches engaged in increasing use of recreation and the arts, the Brethren expressed disapproval.[124] Their condemnation of amusements was extended to new ones as they appeared: cinema, radio, television and popular music were all in turn denounced.[125] Especially to be avoided was football.[126] Glasgow Rangers had expressed an interest in John Douglas, but when he was converted in 1913 he forswore an interest in the game, even ceasing to read a newspaper in case it tempted him.[127] Such leisure activities were perceived as being in competition with the life on which the convert had embarked. It was this which made one writer warn young Christians against seemingly innocuous movements for self-improvement.[128] The Christian belonged to heaven,[129] and the 'world is a waste, howling wilderness'.[130] The proper use of time was in striving for the conversion of others and in working for the assembly.[131]

The Brethren were in revolt against the way of life of their neighbours. Ritchie paraphrased the argument of those who counselled some accommodation:

> You may be a Christian and sing an innocent worldly song, take a dance or enjoy a bit of pleasure. There are a good many Christian people who see no harm in doing these things.[132]

But he put the advice into the mouth of Satan. Such rejection of community mores could mean refusing the signs of status. Schoolteacher

---

evangelicalism and the novel 1800-30', in Derek Baker (ed.), *SCH*, 15 (1977), pp.301-12.

123. William Tytler, *Plain Talks on Prophecy: or, the great prophetic cycles of time* (Glasgow [1915]), pp.50-1.

124. HyP[ickering]., 'WW', *W*, 54 (1924), p.264.

125. *Idem*, 'WW', 53 (1923), p.104; *idem*, 'WW', 63 (1933), p.66; 'Wireless entertainments', *BM*, 46 (1937), p.271; Andrew Borland, *Old Paths & Good Ways in Personal, Family and Church Life* (Kilmarnock [1938]), p.22; W. Shaw, 'Our position in the world', *W*, 55 (1935), pp.57-8; J. B. Watson, 'WW', 78 (1948), p.58; *W*, 81 (1951), p.71; J. K. Duff, 'Television and the Christian home', *BM* 67 (1957), pp.130, 134-5; D. Cook, 'James Cuthbertson (1903-1981)', *BM*, 91 (1981), p.371.

126. *W*, 58 (1928), p.372; W. S., 'Black Saturday', in A. Marshall (ed.), *They Shall Shine as the Stars* (Glasgow, n.d.), [no pagination].

127. [Jimmy Paton], 'John Douglas (1891-1976)', in James Anderson (compiler), *They Finished Their Course* (Kilmarnock, 1980), pp.65-6; cf. 'James McLean', *BM*, 92 (1982), p.96; 'David Annal', *BM*, 93 (1983), p.288.

128. Anon., 'Concentration', pp.133-8.

129. J. R. C[aldwell]., 'What amusements are innocent?', *NW*, 5 (1875), pp.61-2.

130. Ritchie, *Egypt to Canaan*, p.56; cf. Naismith, *Faith's Radiant Path*, p.23.

131. *BM*, 20 (1920), pp.38-9.

132. Ritchie, *Egypt to Canaan*, p.18.

Andrew Borland did not own a car and lived in a local authority house.[133] It could bring persecution.[134] Some antagonists were those with opposing opinions, such as those in Fife from the Dunfermline universalist church in 1870 or the communists in Lumphinans in 1934.[135] But more often it came from the general community: ministers preaching sermons against Brethrenism, assemblies being ejected from meeting places in rented accommodation or stopped street preaching, or members being subjected to mockery and calumny.[136] In one Deeside town the beginning of gospel meetings accompanied by a soup kitchen were satirised by a local balladeer:

> In Ballater a plan's been launched
> Tae wean folks frae the pub—
> A hybrid, double-barrelled scheme,
> Half kirk, half Dorcas club.[137]

This confrontation with rough culture, resistant to the entrance of respectability, was also evident at Plains, Lanarkshire, when during the first open air in the 1880s miners dipped earth sods in the open drain and threw them at the meeting members.[138] Sometimes the opposition appeared to be directed at a novel arrival that disturbed family and community life.[139] Some new converts were forbidden by their parents from attending assembly services.[140] Individuals were ostracised by

---

133. The editors, 'An appreciation: the late Andrew Borland 1895-1979', *BM*, 101 (1991), p.101.

134. Cf. McLeod, *Class and Religion*, pp.72-3.

135. *LR*, 3 (1870), p.241; *W*, 64 (1934), p.237.

136. James Stone to the ed., 20 May 1863, *TP*, 9 (1863-6), p.39; *ibid.*, p.79-80; John Graham to the ed., 2 January 1866, *ibid.*, p.288; C. J. [*sic*] Miller to the ed., *TP*, 10 (1866-9), p.240; K[err]., *Justice*, p.31; David J. Beattie, *Brethren: the story of a great recovery* (Kilmarnock [1939]), p.215; James Anderson, 'A Brief Record Concerning the Early Days of the Assembly in Lesmahagow' (unpublished MS, 1960), pp.27-8, 38-9, 59-60; *NEI*, 3 (1973), pp.14-15; 'Should open-air testimony cease?', *BM*, 26 (1916), p.83.

137. 'An anonymous poem', F. F. Bruce, *In Retrospect: remembrance of things past* (London and Glasgow, 1980), Appendix 2, pp.318-19.

138. 'How it began—in Plains Lanarkshire', *BM*, 90 (1980), p.226; cf. the opposition at Ayr, Inverurie and Huntly, above pp.85, 95-6, 99: for rough culture, see Lynch (ed.), *Scottish History*, pp.531-2.

139. Cf. D. W. Bebbington, 'Mission in Scotland, 1846-1946', in David Searle (ed.), *Death or Glory* (Fearn and Edinburgh, 2001), p.35.

140. HyP[ickering]., 'Archibald McLay of Cardiff', *BP*, 43 (1922), pp.38-41; 'Roderick Shaw', *W*, 103 (1973), p.316.

former friends or church members upon joining an assembly.[141] In Aberdeenshire this took a particularly cruel turn when the livelihood of some businessmen was threatened through the withdrawal of trade from them.[142] Conflict between assembly members and their communities was especially acute during industrial strikes. As part of their refusal to join a trade union, the Brethren also discountenanced striking. The bitter 1897 laceworkers' strike in Newmilns was a 'testing time for believers'.[143] In the Ayrshire mining village of Dreghorn, where the assembly members continued working during the strikes of the 1920s, the conflict was especially fierce. Stones were thrown through their windows and a scurrilous poem was circulated mocking them.[144] In one later industrial dispute three Brethren miners in Midlothian had to leave their jobs because of their opposition to the closed shop.[145] Religious values transcended class loyalty and membership of an assembly drove a wedge between the individual and the community.

Nevertheless, like other sects, the Brethren had to arrive at some accommodation with the institutions of society. Their cavalier attitude to record keeping caused some annoyance for the Inland Revenue. One exasperated official noted in 1927 concerning the finances for erecting a hall in Kilmarnock:

> There seems to be no formal constitution of these bodies and an absence of formality about their records of meetings and accounting arrangements. In this case we have no proper accounts of the Building Fund and from correspondence it seems unlikely that a detailed account could be obtained.[146]

However, the evidence is that they managed a rapprochement with the state without undue tension. Marriage was one of the first issues to be resolved. To accept solemnisation from a minister would be acknowledging sectarianism and so 'leading brethren' officiated and signed the schedule.[147] Charles Miller of Lesmahagow trumpeted after one such occasion that it 'shows we are clear of the sects...and yet obey the

141. Chapman, *Hebron Hall*, p.13; anon., *How I was Led Outside the Camp* (Kilmarnock, n.d.), [p.4]; for other examples of persecution, see above, p.85 n.192.

142. C. W. R[oss]. (ed.), *Donald Ross: pioneer evangelist* (Kilmarnock [1903]), p.159.

143. *BM*, 7 (1897), p.132; James Mair, *A Community Rent Asunder: the Newmilns laceweavers' strike of 1897. Ayrshire Monographs No.21* (Darvel, 1999); cf. *BM*, 1 (1891), p.23, for the 1891 Railway strike.

144. Oral information, 19 July 1992, from an assembly member.

145. J. B. W[atson]., 'WW', *W*, 79 (1949), p.148.

146. Edinburgh, Scottish Record Office, IRS 21/1811; I am indebted to Dr Elizabeth C. Sanderson for this reference: see also above p.1.

147. 'James Murray', *W*, 49 (1919), pp.196; 'Marriages in Scotland', *W*, 57 (1927), p.114; 'Mrs Agnes Wright', *W*, 60 (1930), p.168.

marriage law of Scotland'.[148] From 1927 the Registrar-General required proof that the celebrant was a 'Minister or Pastor of a Christian Congregation'.[149] This the Brethren were quite happy to do, often using the formula 'Pastor, Christian Brethren', two expressions which in other circumstances would be anathema to them. Where the marriage should take place was also a problem, but a registry office, the solution adopted by the Exclusive Brethren, proved unacceptable.[150] In 1923 Andrew Borland, in a book on courtship, approved of the Scottish custom of marriage in a house but recommended the 'Church Marriage' because of its more serious atmosphere.[151] Although the tradition of home marriages apparently lingered longest in strict assemblies,[152] in the course of the twentieth century assembly halls eventually came to be used by all for weddings. The legal requirements of title deeds for halls was willingly undertaken, for, given the struggle many assemblies had to obtain property, they were aware of its value and having it properly secured. For such legal purposes the name 'Christian Brethren' was again adopted.[153] Advantage was taken of the law governing charities in several cases, most notably with the HFMF, which were regulated by trustees from 1908,[154] and the Lord's Work Trust, founded by John Ritchie, which was incorporated in 1947, allowing it to hold and administer heritable property (in this instance, homes for missionaries on furlough).[155] The administration of title deeds was aided by the establishment of the Scottish Stewards Trust, a company incorporated in 1922 and limited by guarantee which was administered by prominent Brethren appointed as directors.[156] It was unique in being the only agency the Brethren developed to negotiate with the institutions of society. Many assemblies (though not all) also framed constitutions which included a statement of faith as part of the legal deeds. Sufficient pragmatism was maintained by the Open Brethren to compromise four of their most cherished principles—the avoidance of a denominational name, the use of a pastor, no credal statement, and the autonomy of each assembly—to safeguard their legal interests and to accommodate the government. Possibly this

---

148. C. T. Miller to the ed., 20 December 1868, *TP*, 10 (1866-9), p.264.

149. 'Marriages in Scotland', p.114.

150. [A. J. Holiday], 'Where should we get married?', *BP*, 7 (1886), pp.135-7.

151. Borland, *Love's Most Excellent Way*, pp.83-7.

152. This is the pattern suggested by the weddings of the grandparents of the present writer and his wife.

153. For two examples, see the sources above to Table 9.5, p.300.

154. See above, pp.144-5.

155. A. B[orland]., 'The Lord's Work Trust', *BM*, 87 (1977), p.347.

156. Edinburgh, Scottish Company House, SC12163; I am indebted to Mr Campbell Fullarton, Mackintosh & Wylie, Solicitors, Kilmarnock, for this reference. For the example of T. J. Smith's vice-chairmanship, see above, n.38.

was partly due to the practical approach of the businessmen who administered these settlements. But for its part, the modern, secularising British state was only too ready to extend toleration which allowed assemblies not to feel threatened.

Despite their apolitical stance, there was a strong streak of conformity to the state within the Brethren. This can even be seen in the area which brought them into pronounced conflict with civil society, their attitudes to war.[157] In the early stages of World War I, the impression given by both *The Witness* and *The Believer's Magazine* was that the introduction of conscription might mean service in the armed forces, even if only in a non-combatant role.[158] There was a nervousness about defying the government because the force of the biblical injunctions to submit to the secular power was so strongly felt. The 'submission to this authority ordained by God' was the climax of Robert Walker's argument in his pamphlet, *The Christian and Warfare* (1942), written in support of the believer bearing arms.[159] After World War I when it was debated if the two minutes' silence should be observed in assemblies, Henry Pickering argued for this commemoration because it was a command of the King who should be obeyed. Not to submit might 'be begotten of that "lawlessness" of these last days.'[160] Despite this, most assemblies in Scotland did not observe a silence. However, even those individuals who opposed serving in the armed forces did so on the grounds of what Neil Summerton has termed 'vocational pacifism': they maintained that Christians should not participate in fighting while accepting that the state may legitimately engage in war.[161] This was the position held by John Ritchie.[162] In a pastiche of Faithful's trial at the town of Vanity, Hunter Beattie had his pilgrim state before a tribunal:

> I wish to say that I have no strictures to pass on this war, or on any war—nor on the nation for engaging in war. I fully acknowledge that the nation has authority accorded to it by God to repress evil and inflict punishment on the evildoers...[163]

157. For discussion of conscientious objectors during the two world wars, see above pp.220-4, 238-9.

158. HyP[ickering]., 'The European war', *W*, 44 (1914), p.149; [*idem*], 'Editor's note', *W*, 45 (1915), p.34; [John Ritchie], 'YBQB', *BM*, 24 (1914), p.118.

159. Robert Walker, *The Christian and Warfare: an examination of the pacifist position* (Chryston, 1942), p.45.

160. *W*, 59 (1929), p.41.

161. Neil Summerton, 'The just war: a sympathetic critique', in O. R. Barclay (ed.), *Pacifism and War* (Leicester, 1984), pp.196-9.

162. The editor, 'The Christian and the state', *BM*, 24 (1914), pp.125-6, 139.

163. Hunter Beattie, *Christian and War being 'The Word of the Cross'* (Glasgow, n.d.), p.49.

Even in resisting the wishes of the state, the Brethren were willing to allow it considerable powers over the rest of the population. They were firmly in favour of strong civil government.

Expressions of social radicalism were rare in the Brethren. For even John Bowes, socialism, because of the link he made between it and infidelity, was seen as an enemy.[164] John Ritchie felt that those who advocated Christian socialism, such as Keir Hardie, were being disingenuous.[165] It was fatally allied to atheism and deluded people with a false heaven-upon-earth achieved through revolution.[166] In 1921 Walter Scott, the publisher and prophetic writer, felt that the Labour Party was incapable of government which 'requires special training for which many of the labour working classes are unfitted'.[167] The Brethren were not even enamoured of democracy. It has been noted in previous chapters that Brethrenism represented a democratised form of Christianity.[168] It had begun in the 1820s among the the upper classes but was the expression of a profoundly democratic spiritual ideal. This equality of the spirit had allowed it to become downwardly socially mobile, and it had appealed to those seeking for a democratised church order.[169] In common with Victorian popular Protestant Evangelicalism, it fitted the mass democracy of the emerging modern world.[170] But egalitarianism, like socialism, was flawed in the eyes of the Brethren because of its association with radical political movements which were antipathetic to Christianity. Their eschatology told Brethren to fear the emerging world order which would be that of antichrist,[171] and the rise of popular democracy they perceived as being manipulated by sinister forces. It was viewed as being the lowest form of government (an allusion to the clay feet of the statue in Nebuchadnezzar's dream),[172] expressing man's self-

164. John Bowes, 'Discussion on Socialism between the editor and John Esdaile', *CMHU*, 1 (1843-4), pp.49-57; Bowes also wrote a pamphlet against Socialism: the Mitchell Library, Glasgow, holds a copy (the only one the present writer has been able to trace), but it cannot be located.

165. John Ritchie, *Socialism: an enemy of God and the gospel* (Kilmarnock, n.d.), p.2.

166. *Ibid., passim.*

167. Walter Scott, 'Things as they are to-day', *W*, 51 (1921), p.75.

168. See above, pp.37-41, 94-5.

169. Neil Dickson, '"The Church itself is God's clergy": the principles and practices of the Brethren', in Deryck W. Lovegrove (ed.), *The Rise of the Laity in Evangelical Protestantism* (London, 2002), pp.222-6.

170. For this view of popular Victorian Evangelicalism, see John Coffey, 'Democracy and popular religion: Moody and Sankey's mission to Britain, 1873-1875', in Eugenio F. Biagini (ed.), *Citizenship and Democracy: Liberals, radicals and collective identities in the British Isles, 1865-1931* (Cambridge, 1996), pp.93-119.

171. For eschatological views, see above, pp.259-66.

172. Dan. 2: 33, 40-1.

will.[173] Alexander Stewart was emphatic that liberty of ministry in the assembly was 'not a radicalism in which every man does his own will, but an absolute monarchy where God rules as He will.'[174] In this sense the Brethren were not a democratic sect. Church government was successional, residing in the elders who were a self-appointing oligarchy.[175] Pickering lumped democracy with communism and anarchy.[176] The social upheavals of the 1920s, he felt, presaged its collapse.[177] In 1931 he printed in *The Witness* an extract from a paper by J. N. Darby lamenting the effects of the 1832 Reform Bill which, in Darby's opinion, exalted '"*the will of the people*"' (Pickering's italics) and made 'the poor masters'. 'The general public effect', Darby wrote, 'will be a great and rapid increase of centralisation or despotic power, and loss of personal liberty.'[178] That Pickering, a self-made man from Newcastle-upon-Tyne, could identify with the sentiments of Darby, a product of the upper-middle classes who regretted power being transferred from the land to the boroughs, demonstrates how a movement which had been allied to some of the emerging social forces of the modern world began to appear profoundly conservative once these forces took political shape in the twentieth century. Nineteenth-century premillennialism which the Brethren adopted had been, in part, a pessimistic reaction to the development of the secular British state and the condition of society.[179] The rising tide of the popular will was regarded by Brethren of all social classes with dismay.

The fear of social upheaval meant that by the twentieth century Brethren writers supported a conservative political programme. The late

173. J. R. C[aldwell]., 'Things to come', *NI*, 3 (1873), p.50; G. A[dam]. to the editor, *W*, 29 (1899), pp.64-5; John Ritchie, *Lectures on the Book of Daniel with Expository Notes on 'The Times of the Gentiles' and Prophetic Subjects* (Kilmarnock, 1915), pp.35-6; Steen, 'The antichrist', pp.332-3.

174. Alexander Stewart, *Salvation Truths* (Kilmarnock, n.d.), p.198; cf. J. A. B[oswell]., 'Holiness in the House', *NT*, 1, (1888), p.35; G. A[dam]., 'Thoughts on church government', *W*, 21 (1891), p.20; John Ritchie, *'The Way which They Call Heresy': remarks on a book by W. Blair Neatby entitled 'A History of the Plymouth Brethren'* (Kilmarnock [c.1901]), p.15.

175. See above, p.240.

176. HyP[ickering]., 'WW', *W*, 51 (1925), p.194.

177. *Idem*, 'WW', *W*, 50 (1924), p.304.

178. J. N. Darby, 'The progress of democratic power', *W*, 61 (1931), pp.125-6; printed in Darby's works as: [*idem*], 'Progress of democratic power and its effect on the moral state of England', William Kelly (ed.), *Collected Writings of J. N. Darby*, 32 (London, n.d.), pp.506-511.

179. D. N. Hempton, 'Evangelicalism and eschatology', *JEH*, 31 (1980), p.190; Malcolm R. Thorp, 'Popular preaching and millennial expectations: the Reverend Robert Aitken and the Christian Society, 1836-40', in Malcolm Chase and Ian Dyck (eds), *Living and Learning: essays in honour of J. F. C. Harrison* (Aldershot, 1996), p.110.

Victorian marriage of morality and politics was long regarded as the ideal. Gladstone was the one politician quoted with approval on religious matters[180] and, in common with other Christians, Queen Victoria was perceived as being the ideal monarch,[181] she and Albert being the only non-Brethren individuals to have gospel halls named after them.[182] For J. R. Caldwell speaking in 1892, his listeners were 'subjects under the best government that ever existed in the world—the government under which is found most liberty and most repression of evil'.[183] Sometimes the policies supported were those of Gladstonian Liberalism. Liberty of the individual, free trade and private enterprise were admired. An additional reason for disapproving of trade unions was that such combinations opposed the first two,[184] and in 1947 large business corporations were criticised for hindering the last.[185] More markedly Tory in his opinions was Walter Scott. His eschatological interpretation found that the divine enemies were those of Britain. Writing in 1919 he opined that Gog (Russia) would come to dominate Gomer (Germany) and they would clash with the western nations in Palestine, liberated by a friendly maritime power (Great Britain probably).[186] His vision of the millennium, when Christ 'in irresistible might will roll back the rushing tide of a lawless, godless democracy and rule with a rod of iron', was totalitarian.[187] The monarchy provided an opportunity for more overt expressions of loyalty to the British state. When Pickering reproved younger members of the royal family for lack of Sabbath observance, he prefaced his reproach with the boast that 'Brethren (so-called) are among the most loyal of Christians; and the *Witness* has ever stood for loyalty to King and Country'.[188] Brethren magazines vied with one another to express devotion to the monarch. The search for evidence that they were

---

180. Alexander Marshall, '"A full salvation"', *W* 41 (1911), pp.127-8; 'Gladstone and the Bible', *BM*, 57 (1947), p.338.

181. John Wolffe, 'The end of Victorian values? Women, religion and the death of Queen Victoria', W. J. Sheils and Diana Wood (eds), *SCH*, 27 (Oxford, 1990), pp.481-504.

182. One later exception is Arnot Gospel Hall, which the assembly in Kennoway, Fife, removed to in 1977: it was a former church named after a ministerial uncle of Frederick Stanley Arnot, and the name was kept in honour of the latter.

183. Caldwell, 'Subjects and rulers', *W*, 22 (1892), p.166; cf. Scott, 'Things as they are', p.75; Andrew Borland, 'The Christian and the permissive society', *BM*, 82 (1972), p.225.

184. J. R. Caldwell, 'Parents and children', *W*, 22 (1892), p.115.

185. W. F. Naismith, 'The degeneration and regeneration', *BM*, 57 (1947), pp.39-41.

186. Walter Scott, *Prophetic Scenes and Coming Glories: answers to numerous prophetic questions* (London, 1919), pp.49, 57-9.

187. *Ibid.*, p.10.

188. HyP[ickering]., 'WW', *W*, 54 (1929), p.211.

'saved' was taken to absurd lengths.[189] This conservative acceptance of
the British state shifted as the working class was included in government.
In 1924 Henry Pickering cautiously admitted that Labour might alleviate
social hardship and on Ramsay MacDonald's death speculated that he
might have been 'born again'.[190] These Scottish Brethren supported the
central institutions of Britain.

The writers cited above, however, belonged to the middle or lower-
middle classes. Most of them also belonged to the less sectarian wing of
the movement which was more ready to identify with nationhood. For the
attitudes of Brethren in lower social classes there is difficulty with the
evidence as the lack of written evidence makes them less accessible to the
historian. However, the conservative impulse was probably found among
them too. If the emphases of preachers such as John Douglas and Isaac
Ewan on rule, order and discipline are transposed into a political key then
a very reactionary programme emerges.[191] The Unionist Party had
considerable Protestant working-class support in Scotland, and it is to be
expected that endorsement of its sentiments should be found among the
Brethren.[192] The anti-Catholicism of the movement alone gave it a bias
towards Unionism.[193] The missionary George Patterson, who grew up in
Laurieston, Stirlingshire, claimed that in the 1930s many Brethren
sympathised with and even voted for the Conservatives, although he felt
this was especially true of those belonging to the middle classes.[194]

But more radical loyalties probably also existed, particularly during the
deep class division between the middle and working classes in inter-war

189. *BM*, 11 (February 1901), end pp.; HyP[ickering]., 'Britain's King and the
Bible', *HS*, No. 345 (September 1907); *idem*, 'Britain's new King and Queen', *HS*, No.
33 (June 1911); *OLOT*, No 282 (June 1911), cover; *ibid.*, No 557 (May 1935), cover;
ibid., No. 581 (May 1937) cover; *W*, 55 (1935), p.41; *BM*, 47 (February 1936), end pp.
Attempts to prove the monarch was 'saved' reached their zenith in those who asserted
that Queen Mary of Teck had been converted through a Brethren tract: *W*, 59 (1929),
pp.241, 235, *W*, 60 (1930), p.17; for the concern of early nineteenth-century
Evangelicals for the monarch's conversion, cf. Ian Bradley, *The Call to Seriousness: the
Evangelical impact on the Victorians* (London, 1976), pp.35-6.
190. HyP[ickering]., 'WW', *W*, 54 (1924), p.264; *idem, ibid.*, *W*, 67 (1937), p.281.
191. See above, p.235.
192. J. T. Ward, 'Some aspects of working-class Conservatism in the nineteenth
century', in John Butt and J. T. Ward (eds), *Scottish Themes* (Edinburgh, 1976), pp.141-
57; Graham Walker and Tom Gallagher, 'Protestantism and Scottish politics', *idem* (eds),
Sermons and Battle Hymns: Protestant popular culture in modern Scotland (Edinburgh,
1990), pp.91-2.
193. For the roots of nineteenth-century Protestant anti-Catholicism in the
Evangelicalism, which was predominantly Tory in sympathy, out of which the Irish and
English Brethren emerged, see John Wolffe, *The Protestant Crusade in Great Britain
1829-1860* (Oxford, 1991).
194. Patterson, *Patterson of Tibet*, p.33; cf. Bruce, *In Retrospect*, p.54.

society. Ritchie was aware that Christian socialism might tempt those who 'recognise the common brotherhood of the children of God and the equality grace has given to all'.[195] John Bowes, from a poor agrarian background, sympathised with reform.[196] In Kilbirnie Jamie Clifford, the future missionary to Argentina, was a pit-pony boy by the age of twelve and during industrial troubles in the 1890s he was recruited by the Independent Labour Party as a potential MP because of his oratorical skills. He remained a life-long sympathiser with socialism. Working people, he later said, were *'tratados como animales* [treated like animals]'.[197] Another Brethren mining convert who agreed with this opinon noted of working men: 'No wonder that socialists and communists sprang up to defend their cause.'[198] Other radical opinions could be expressed. The voice of one oral witness, a nonagenarian woman from Lochore, Fife, shook with emotion recalling how the government 'took a' the miners' sons' during World War I.[199] Even John Ritchie refused to apportion blame during the 1921 miners' strike.[200] More forthright opinions, it might be imagined, were held by Brethren in mining communities. In the 1920s George Patterson's father (also George Patterson), a fiery socialist before his conversion, refused promotion as a mine inspector, believing it would associate him with the exploitation of his fellow-workers. He declared cryptically, 'A mine manager may be a Christian, but a Christian cannot be a mine manager.'[201] Tom Todd, the Selkirkshire shepherd and poet, was dismissive of the landed classes, having 'a decided "scunner" against anything, even a tattie-bogle, in knickerbockers'.[202] Perhaps his finest poem was a macabre *memento mori* which depicts the grave as a social leveller:

---

195. [John Ritchie], 'Religious radicalism', *BM* 18 (1908), p.141.

196. See above, pp.37-9.

197. A. C. T[homson]., *Un Hombre Bueno: vida de Jamie Clifford* (n.p., Argentina, 1957), pp.15-17, 24-5; in Spanish the expression is apparently a strong one.

198. Writer's collection, II, [Robert Morrison], 'A few notes on old Kilwinning Town and the biography of Robert Morrison, Crosshouse', typescript, *c*.1939; for Morrison's conversion, see above, p.135.

199. Oral information, 19 November 1988, from the individual concerned.

200. [John Ritchie], 'Answers to correspondents', *BM 31* (1921), pp.88-9.

201. Patterson, *Patterson of Tibet*, pp.7-9, 39.

202. T. T. Kilbucho [i.e. Tom Todd], *Sixty Rural Years* (Galashiels [1968]), pp.15-16.

Gin death descends on man's pursuits
What's for the gangril's for the laird.[203]

Despite these attitudes, however, working-class Brethren generally persisted in a non-political stance. George Patterson senior remained a shop steward after conversion and in the early 1960s his son was adopted as the Liberal candidate for Edinburgh West, but Jamie Clifford was more typical in coming to believe that he should not engage in politics.[204] Abe Moffat, a Fife Communist Party member, had a Brethren father, also Abe Moffat, who was a preacher and a regular reader of the Communist Party newspaper the *Daily Worker*. The son noted of the father that he was 'a good fighter for his rights within the colliery, and feared no official or employer', but that 'he stopped his activity when he came to the pit top because of his religious beliefs'.[205] Most usually those involved in politics left the Brethren. Despite upbringings within the movement, which influenced their later attitudes, three prominent left-wing activists did not become members: Thomas Dickson, Labour MP for Lanark (1923-4; 1929-31)[206] and Abe Moffat and his brother Alex, also a Communist Party member, both of whom became Scottish area presidents of the National Union of Mineworkers (1942-61 and 1961-7 respectively).[207] Brethren refused to be deflected from the pursuit of religious objectives.

In spite of the different political and social stances, the movement did not pull apart, and nor, ultimately, did Scottish society. Both remained moderate. This can be seen in the contrasting careers of James Barbour and Sir John Henderson. James Barbour, the President of the National Union of Scottish Mineworkers, was a socialist—on one occasion almost standing for Parliament as a Labour candidate but instead making way

---

203. 'Death and the Gangril [i.e. tramp]', in *idem, A Shepherd's Years* (Glasgow, 1961), p.11; this poem was singled out for its merit by critic and poet Douglas Young in his introduction to the book.

204. Patterson, *Patterson of Tibet*, pp.9, 349-40; T[homson]., *Clifford*, p.25; for the example of another individual active in Liberal politics, see George Younie in Bruce, *In Retrospect*, pp.18-19.

205. Abe Moffat, *My Life with the Miners* (London, 1965), p.9; the Moffats' parents were in Lochgelly assembly, Fife.

206. William Knox (ed.), *Scottish Labour Leaders 1915-39: a biographical dictionary* (Edinburgh, 1984), pp.87-9; Tom Dickson, *Was Moses a Bolshevist? The Hebrew law-giver on land, interest and direct action* (Glasgow, n.d.); Dickson, a native of Cleland, Lanarkshire, is described by Knox as being brought up in 'the close Plymouth Brethren'; this description may indicate he was raised among the Exclusives or Churches of God rather than the Open Brethren.

207. For Abe Moffat see: Abe Moffat, *My Life*; for Alex Moffat see: 'Death of miners' leader', *The Dunfermline Press*. 9 September 1967; cf. Stuart Macintyre, *Little Moscows: Communism and working-class militancy in inter-war Britain* (London, 1980), p.58.

for a friend[208]—and he was in favour of a command economy. He began as a pit boy in 1902 earning three shillings a day and continued his education through nightschool. As the miners' agent for Stirlingshire in the inter-war period, Barbour promoted negotiation. He was a disciple of Bob Smillie, Keir Hardie's ally, and aligned himself with the anti-communist stance of miners' leader Andrew Clarke.[209] Probably the contemporary moral ethos of trade unionism made his involvement easier.[210] During World War II Barbour advocated that trade unionists should unite in the anti-Nazi cause. He was a member of the joint consultative committee, its mining members nominated for their skill and experience in negotiating with the owners, that formulated amendments to the 1942 white paper which outlined proposals for the government taking control of the mines,[211] and he also served from 1942 as Director of Labour for the Scottish region for the Ministry of Fuel and Power, being awarded the OBE by Churchill's government for his work. In 1947, when the coal mining industry was nationalised, he was appointed the first Labour Director of the Scottish Divisional Coal Board, and much of the welfare provision which took place until his retiral in 1956, such as pithead baths and medical centres, was due to his efforts.[212] Like the Methodist union leaders of Durham, the tendency of his leadership was to negotiate with, rather than conflict with, authority.[213] On the other hand, Sir John Henderson was a Conservative member of Parliament. He was the chairman of his own produce importer business and from 1926 until 1946 he was involved in the administration of Glasgow's civic amenities —streets, libraries, public assistance and, most notably, the prestigious committee responsible for the city's water supply of which he was convener.[214] Never a very vocal backbencher, nevertheless he was eloquent in advocating improved housing conditions for slum dwellers in the post-war House of Commons.[215] Knighted on retiring as an MP in

---

208. Oral information, April 1997, from his daughter.

209. For Clarke, see Knox (ed.), *Scottish Labour Leaders*, pp.77-8.

210. W. W. Knox, 'Religion and the Scottish Labour Movement c.1900-39', *Journal of Contemporary History*, 23 (1988), pp.607-30.

211. R. Page Arnot, *The Miners in Crisis and War: a history of the Miners' Federation of Great Britain* (New York, 1961), p.340.

212. Edinburgh, Mrs Sarah Campbell, Cuttings scrapbook; this consists mainly of articles from *The Stirling Observer*, 1939-1956.

213. Moore, *Pit-Men, Preachers and Politics*, pp.161-195.

214. *Who Was Who 1971-1980*, 7, 2nd edn (London, 1989), pp.356-7; Candidus, 'No.XII—John Henderson', *Glasgow Evening News*, 24 April 1933.

215. *Hansard*, 5th Series, vol. 432 (1947), pp.842-3.

1964, he was a one nation Tory. Both Barbour and Henderson, from their respective political positions, were drawn to a moderating stance.[216]

That both men could exist within the Brethren movement despite its decided apolitical stance, is a mark of how it allowed for diversity. It could incorporate different tendencies. Others participated in their local cultures and were seen as being representative of it.[217] The journalist John Borland became identified with his tightly-knit local community, the three industrial towns of the upper Irvine Valley in Ayrshire. Under the pseudonym 'Sifter' he conducted in the local newspaper a weekly column which was a *pot pourri* of humorous anecdotes, pawky sayings, eccentric incidents, notes on local landmarks, superstitions and emigrants, and much else that captured the contemporary Scottish small-town spirit. He also contributed articles on local history under the pen-name of 'John Loudoun' and when he died his editor claimed: 'No more kenspeckle figure ever trod the streets of the three sister towns... And few were more thoroughly steeped in their traditions and lore'.[218] The tone of Borland's output was similar to that of David Beattie who found the literary Kailyard congenial in his writings on Langholm.[219] In contemporary popular fashion, Beattie also made eclectic use of Scottish history, delivering a lecture which was an act of piety to the Covenanters (1915) and producing a work of sentimental Jacobitism, *Prince Charlie and the Borderland* (1928).[220] He was untroubled by appropriating early-twentieth century Scottish popular culture. A more significant example was Robert Rendall, still commemorated in Orkney for being the quintessential Orcadian.[221] 'Half a dozen lyrics from *Orkney Variants*', wrote George Mackay Brown of Rendall's finest poetry book, 'hold most of the essence of Orkney.'[222] Rendall also made some attempts to integrate his cultural and natural history interests with his faith despite the absence of a Brethren theology of culture and creation. Towards the end of his life he developed a form of Christian Platonism. The natural world could speak of realities which lay beyond it, and its mathematical order reflected that which existed in 'a Creative Intelligence', a proof of God's

---

216. For the theme of moderation and cooperation in British society in the nineteenth and twentieth centuries, see Joyce, *Work, Society and Politics*, pp.50-82; Harrison, *Peaceable Kingdom*, pp.309-77; Ross McKibbin, *The Ideologies of Class: social relations in Britain, 1880-1950* (Oxford, 1990), pp.1-42.

217. See above, pp.248-9.

218. 'He carried his copy in his head', *KS*, 23 April 1971, p.3.

219. D. J. Beattie, *Oor Gate En'* (Galashiels, 1915); *idem, Oor Ain Folk* (Carlisle, 1933); *idem, Langsyne in Eskdale* (Carlisle, 1950).

220. *Idem, Psalm Singing among the Scottish Covenanters* (Carlisle, 1915); *idem, Prince Charlie and the Borderland* (Carlisle, 1928).

221. R. J. Berry and H. N. Firth (eds), *The People of Orkney* (Kirkwall, 1986), p.2.

222. George Mackay Brown, *An Orkney Tapestry* (London, 1969), p.3.

existence.[223] The invisible world would suddenly shine out, and 'man made in the image of God,' he noted in a reverie, 'has the power to view Nature in an eternal and non-temporal way...apprehending in some way how the world must have looked in Eden.' The poet as 'the priest of nature' was especially susceptible to this vision.[224] However, because of the conceptual background he inherited in Protestant Fundamentalism, Rendall was not wholly successful in integrating his thinking on culture, science and faith.[225] The individuals who engaged in their local culture, were to be found in districts with a strong sense of community. Society was more homogeneous in these areas and Brethren individuals, despite their loyalty to the sect, were able to absorb their local culture. However Scottish society as a whole within the Union was moderate, eventually able to accommodate different interests and be tolerant of divergence. As Barbour and Henderson (both living within the industrial Lowlands) demonstrate, they too did not feel threatened and could collaborate with the state.

Continuity, Growth and the Sect

Scottish Brethren displayed both continuity and discontinuity with culture and society. They largely belonged to the lower-middle and working classes and the movement reflected aspects of the culture of these strata. Brethren social life, such as tea-meetings and Sunday school soirées, was that of their fellows.[226] The movement reinforced the aspirations of these classes after improvement, respectability and a more regulated life. Cultural continuity can be seen at a regional level. The fierceness of loyalties among Lanarkshire Brethren and the closeness of their assembly life, particularly until the mid-twentieth century, continued features of the mining community. During the strikes of 1921 and 1926 it would appear that most Brethren miners withheld their labour and organised Bible study or engaged in evangelism to avoid embittering relations within their communities.[227] Along with the strikers, they too needed financial assistance.[228] One of the reasons for the pervasiveness of the movement was its success in participating in the life of the society

223. Robert Rendall, *Orkney Shore* (Kirkwall, 1960), pp.121-9.
224. Kirkwall, OA, D27/2/8(3), [Robert Rendall], 'Dwarme'.
225. Neil Dickson, 'Littoral truth: the mind of Robert Rendall', unpublished paper delivered at the Orkney Science Festival, 1998.
226. Gray, *Labour Aristocracy*, pp.100-1.
227. Oral information 10 August 1997, from a Brethren member born into a mining community; cf. Moore, *Pit Men, Preachers and Politics*, pp.202-13.
228. *W*, 56 (1926), p.419; *W*, 59 (1929), p.21.

which it penetrated.[229] The worst persecution tended to happen when the Brethren were new to a district and before they were accepted into it. Some, such as John Borland and Robert Rendall, were able to achieve a thorough immersion in their local culture and came to be regarded as representative of it. There were those who participated in civic administration: local government officials, policemen and even the occasional justice of the peace. However, the movement preferred revivalist activity over cultural activity or social improvement. There were those, such as John Wardrop and W. J. Grant, who advocated a more active support for the temperance movement.[230] But although the Brethren were strict teetotallers, more narrowly religious pursuits were always exalted over moral crusades. As with class, identity with society was just one of the rivalling allegiances and the principal loyalty was with the community of believers.[231] This often led to a more forceful rejection by the Brethren of certain aspects of their neighbours' way of life. Unlike village Methodism in England, the Brethren movement never became communal, an integral element of a wider self-contained social structure, but remained associational as a voluntary society.[232] Although it had a strong appeal for those in dangerous occupations, ultimately the large demands the movement made on its members severely limited the attraction of assemblies within Scottish society.

If national growth was finally limited, the Brethren did permit individual development. Although the point is not amenable to proof, psychologically the movement probably helped alleviate some degree of anomie, but more importantly it provided a framework of meaning for those questing after it. The civic values of Brethren of all classes tended to be those of Victorian Evangelicalism. The movement promoted a disciplined life that valued honesty, literacy and financial prudency which were aspirations shared with others in society. It often led to the recognition of Brethren as 'good people'.[233] As was the case with other sects, the movement aided social integration.[234] The limitations on recreation undoubtedly could prove irksome, particularly to the young,[235] but even here they were not applied uniformly and the less

---

229. Dickson, 'Open and closed', in Porter (ed.), *After Columba*, pp.160-2.

230. 'Death of Mr John Wardrop', *HA*, 3 September 1892, p.6; W. J. Grant, 'The Christian in relation to strong drink', *W*, 50 (1920), p.323.

231. Smith, *Religion in Industrial Society*, p.30.

232. Moore, *Pit Men, Preachers and Politics*, pp.121-132.

233. For an example, see above, p.252.

234. Wilson, *Religious Sects*, p.242.

235. For the example of a son of Brethren parents at senior secondary school in the early 1950s, see William McIlvanney's semi-autobiographical novel, *The Kiln* (London, 1996), pp.180-1; in the novel the character's family is described as being 'Close Brethren', but in a speech McIlvanney gave at the centenary dinner of Kilmarnock

strict individuals allowed some leeway. This was also true of other issues. The permissibility of voting was allowed to be a matter of conscience by some.[236] Before World War I, one financially hard-pressed Brethren woman in the mining hamlet of Fergushill, Ayrshire, joined the Co-operative when she discovered a fellow assembly member had accumulated £70 through her membership.[237] The prescriptions of the stricter individuals were not always followed.

Sectarianism was not uniform across the movement. The continued working-class status of Brethren undoubtedly maintained it,[238] and it was stronger in periods of social unrest. On the other hand, as younger members of the movement were able to take advantage of increased educational opportunities some of the strictures on the novel, for example, were relaxed. Many women in the movement read Annie Swan, approved because her fiction promoted self-help and Christian fortitude.[239] One Brethren schoolteacher argued in 1926 that reading novels was permissible in the interests of education, a position echoed in 1954 by a Brethren young people's discussion.[240] This point of view was evidence of a more denominational attitude.[241] Withdrawal was also limited by the conversionist need to remain in contact with society. Alexander Stewart felt that football was not harmful and the prohibition on it cut assembly members off from their neighbours.[242] Sectarianism also varied with social class. Many of the businessmen and professional people had a more pragmatic approach which made for moderation. Possibly Brethren splits of the inter-war period and after were reinforced to some degree by increasing class division within the movement, a sign of the breakdown of the identity of interest among social groups which had marked it.[243] But the hold which the Brethren had over the minds of

Academy in November 1998, he identified the individual on whom the character was based: the son of members of one of Kilmarnock's Open Brethren assemblies.

236. L. W. G. Alexander, 'QA', *W*, 75 (1945), p.15.

237. Oral information, 10 August, 1997, from a granddaughter of the woman in question who was the wife of Robert Morrison, see above, n.198.

238. Cf. Liston Pope, *Millhands and Preachers: a study of Gastonia* (New Haven, CT, 1942), pp.117-120.

239. Beth Dickson, 'Annie S. Swan and O. Douglas: legacies of the Kailyard', in Douglas Gifford and Dorothy McMillan, *A History of Scottish Women's Writing* (Edinburgh, 1997), pp.329-46.

240. A. Bayne, 'QA', *W*, 56 (1926), p.333; David Haxton *et al.* (eds), *Discipleship: a record and report of a week-end discussion at Netherhall, Largs* (Edinburgh, 1954), p.14.

241. Valentine Cunningham, *Everywhere Spoken Against: Dissent in the Victorian novel* (Oxford, 1975), p.52.

242. Alexander Stewart, 'Half-yearly meetings of Christians at Glasgow', *Eleventh Hour*, 11 (January 1887), p.11; *idem*, 'Strangers and pilgrims', *W*, 35 (1905), p.169.

243. Most of the evidence cited in the present chapter of such class tension as existed in the movement belongs to the inter-war period and after; cf. above, pp.342-3.

its members was never totalitarian. The voluntaryism of the movement was one reason why the middle classes could not use it to further their own interests even if they had been disposed to do so,[244] and Open Brethren independency was an additional factor which resisted any single group winning absolute dominance. Mainly because of this autonomy, it is difficult to present a simple coherent account of Brethren attitudes to society. Although the majority withdrew, a more open, denomination-alising tendency was always present which allowed some to participate in culture and society. Nevertheless, despite these variations in attitude, the general social tendency of all shades of opinion within the movement was to cultivate cooperation between employer and employee and to promote a centrist loyalty to the British state. Scottish Brethren, like the society in which they existed, had been ultimately able to accommodate a number of tendencies without fragmenting.

244. Cf. Gilbert, *Religion and Society*, p.87.

CHAPTER TEN

Some Organic Disintegration:
Growth and Development 1965-2000

'I think I would have to say, rather sadly, that as I have seen it, there
has been some organic disintegration within the local assembly.'
W. K. Morrison speaking in 1990.

At secondary school Merjorie Sneddon won the Mysie Thomson Inglis
prize for excellence in art three years running. But she was not allowed to
attend art school because her mother was 'Plymouth Brethren'. Instead
she went to Brussels as a bilingual secretary where she 'loved the
lifestyle' and later died through choking on a truffle. Merjorie Sneddon
is a comic creation in a monologue by the Lanarkshire writer Liz
Lochhead, but as an invention she symbolises the transition among
Brethren from the mid-twentieth century to the *fin de siècle*.[1] During this
period members of the movement found it harder to isolate themselves
from societal pressures which were not congenial to a separatist faith. In
consequence, within Brethren assemblies a complex series of changes
occurred which was to transform a number of them radically. In many
places the patterns passed on from previous generations were modified,
while others regarded the alterations within the Brethren world with
increasing dismay.

The present chapter will examine the changes which affected Brethren
during the final quarter of the twentieth century. The decline in the
numerical strength of the movement will be noted first. There were,
however, signs of continuing vitality, including new initiatives in
evangelism and changes in attitude to society, and these will be examined
next. This modernisation was in part the result of far-reaching social
alterations in the composition of the movement which will subsequently
be analysed. Many individuals could be found expressing discontent with
features of assemblies and some of these dissatisfactions will be noted.
Discussion will then turn to how the innovations of the period and the

---

1. Liz Lochhead, 'Meeting Norma Nimmo', in *Bagpipe Muzak* (Harmondsworth,
1991), p.34; I am indebted to Mrs Ella Jack for this reference.

changing class profile of the movement increased the polarisation of the sectarian and denominationalising tendencies and left it more fragmented than it had ever been. The chapter will conclude by noting in what ways the Brethren movement in Scotland was facing a crisis which at the time of writing is as yet unresolved.

Decline and Growth

From about 1970 until the 1990s membership fell considerably. The number of assemblies rose slightly from 296 in 1970 to 299 in 1975, but after then it fell to 274 in 1984 and 226 in 1997.[2] But the contraction of the membership is undoubtedly sharper than these figures suggest, for the closure of meetings considerably lags behind the fall in numbers within them. The rapid reduction in membership could be seen from the figures for five individual assemblies during this period (Figure 10.1). The overall trend in each case had been downwards. The decline in numbers was not just restricted to smaller village ones such as Newmains, Lanarkshire, but could also be seen in larger city congregations, such as Crosshill Evangelical Church (formerly Elim Hall), Glasgow. In 1966 it was the largest assembly among those represented in the figure, but its membership steadily fell due to suburbanisation leading to its discontinuation in 1991. Lower numbers also had more serious consequences for the smaller ones as the reduction in size meant that there were fewer active members and it placed a greater burden on those individuals. In 1995 it was estimated that there were about 10,530 Open Brethren members throughout Scotland,[3] the number of assemblies falling by one quarter after 1951 and the total membership by perhaps as much as a third after 1960.[4]

---

2. Neil Summerton, 'Christian Brethren growth', in Peter Brierley *et al.*, *The Christian Brethren as the Nineties Began* (Carlisle, 1993), p.90; *The Assemblies Address Book: useful addresses and other information for Christians*, 4th edn (Bath, 1997), pp.156-92.

3. A calculation done by the present writer for Peter Brierley *et al.* (eds), *UK Christian Handbook 1994/5 Edition* (London, 1994), Table 9.4.2; cf. the calculation of 12,500 members which the present writer did for *Telling the Good News Together in Scotland: a Report to the B.C.C.* (London, 1989), p.8. These figures were arrived at by calculating an average size for assemblies in populous districts (100) and one for smaller assemblies, often in less populous districts (28). The averages were then used to calculate the number of assembly members in a region.

4. Neil Dickson, '"Brethren" in Scotland: the present situation', in Harold H. Rowdon (ed.), *The Strengthening, Growth and Planting of Local Churches* (Carlisle, 1993), pp.109-110

With this decline in numbers there was an accompanying redistribution of where many Brethren members lived. They were increasingly to be found in the suburban areas, such as those of Glasgow and Edinburgh, where employment and the social ambience attracted the middle classes. Most of the large Brethren assemblies in Scotland were now to be found in residential towns near Glasgow and Aberdeen, places such as Milngavie or Milltimber. The growing strength of assemblies in middle-class areas and the decline of those in working-class areas was not limited to the cities, but could also be seen in the larger towns. By the late 1980s one of the largest assemblies in Britain with some 300 members was Riverside Evangelical Church (EC), Ayr, situated in the traditional county town which had a substantial middle-class population.[5] It was in communities like this one that the larger concentrations of Brethren were increasingly to be found. The numerical strength of congregations in areas with a large middle class was often at the expense of the smaller ones as younger people moved into the more prosperous districts of the larger towns. The building in Hamilton of a Wimpey housing estate in the 1960s virtually doubled the membership of one of the town's assemblies.[6] A corollary of the growth in affluent areas was the decline in industrialised areas. Inner-city Glasgow assemblies continued to fall in number from twenty-two meetings in 1966 to thirteen by 1994. Industrial villages suffered too. Due to the decline of the steel industry and the closure of mining in Newarthill, Lanarkshire, for example, employment prospects were poor and there was little work for businessmen and professional people. In addition the village was not a residential area for the middle classes. The assembly was seriously depleted, and the single largest factor in the decline was the transfer-out of members, which was particularly the case among the young. As a result membership had fallen from thirty-two in 1963 to thirteen by 1988, leading to the discontinuation of the assembly in the early 1990s.[7] The drift from rural villages continued: in Shetland, for example, Lerwick assembly grew at the expense of country meetings.[8] There always had been a disparity in size between assemblies in larger towns and those in surrounding villages, but the depletion of numbers within the movement had brought many assemblies in smaller communities close to discontinuation.

5. Anon., 'Leadership at Ayr', *H*, 68 (April 1989), pp.15-6; this assembly was formed in 1906, *W*, 36 (April 106), endpp.

6. Oral information, 25 November 1990, from an assembly member.

7. Oral information, 7 September 1988, from Newarthill assembly; cf. the statistics for Alloa assembly in Kenneth J. Panton, 'The Church in the community: a study of patterns of religious adherence in a Scottish burgh', in Michael Hill (ed.), *A Sociological Yearbook of Religion in Britain*, 6 (1973), pp.183-206; Alloa was discontinued in 1980.

8. L. Wilson, 'Witnessing in Shetland', *H*, 61 (February 1981), pp.2-5.

There were various reasons for these changes. All churches in Scotland suffered a fall in membership over this period, and some suffered more than others. A census of Scottish churches in 1994 reported that only fourteen per cent of the adult Scottish population were in church on census Sunday, representing a fall of three per cent since the previous survey ten years before.[9] John Highet pointed out that, although there are difficulties in the comparison, in 1959 he had found twenty-six per cent of Scottish adults attended church, and that over the intervening years the Church of Scotland and the Roman Catholic Church had suffered the sharpest decline.[10] Secularisation affected the Brethren in common with other churches. Some causes of the changes, however, can be traced to internal factors within the movement. The innate conservatism of the Brethren was one such cause. Many meetings persisted with the evangelistic forms that had served them so well in the past, and sometimes in exactly the same manner. Fred Stallan, one of the editorial committee responsible for *The Believer's Magazine* from 1974 until 1999, described his amazement when an open-air service he attended one Sunday evening faced an unlit office building. It was a traditional stance, and at one time, it appeared, there had been houses there.[11] The archaisms hindered contact with people.[12] There were, however, several other reasons why the Brethren both declined and were to some extent redistributed within Scotland. In two perceptive articles written in 1981, James Anderson, a college history lecturer and another member of *The Believer's Magazine* editorial committee, puzzled over why fifteen assemblies had been discontinued in the previous five years. He pointed to industrial decline, the movement of members into 'desirable areas' to live (which he attributed to 'material ambition'), individuals moving for employment or education, schisms within assemblies, and the lack of evangelism.[13]

It was not all decline, however, in this period. As Figure 10.1 shows, some assemblies, such as Central EC, Kilmarnock, managed to increase. A survey of UK assemblies conducted in 1998 by the Brethren support agency Partnership drew responses from fifty-one Scottish ones. Although this number represented only some twenty-two per cent of those 226 Scottish congregations which were solicited, the data contained

9. Peter Brierley and Fergus Macdonald, *Prospects for Scotland 2000: trends and tables from the 1994 Scottish Church Census* (Edinburgh and London, 1995), p.16; *idem*, *Prospects for Scotland: report of the 1984 census of the Scottish churches* (Edinburgh, 1984), p.60.

10. John Highet, 'Trends in attendance and membership', in *ibid.*, pp.8-10.

11. F. E S[tallan]., 'Editorial searchlight', *BM*, 99 (1989), p.1.

12. John Allan, 'The local church and evangelism', *H*, 58 (1979), pp.16-17, 20.

13. J. A[nderson]., 'Why fewer assemblies?', *BM*, 91 (1981), pp.132-3, 196-8.

a fairly broad sample of ones of different type.[14] The survey showed that the sample grew on average by 2.7 members over the previous two years, which compared favourably with the 1.2 members the previous survey of fifty-five Scottish assemblies had shown for 1986-8[15] and the UK average which showed the 322 responding assemblies growing on average by 1.76 individuals over 1996-8. The growth, however, was not evenly spread, and the majority of congregations in the sample had actually experienced no growth or were in decline, a pattern that was apparently more marked since the previous survey (Figure 10.3).[16] Size was clearly a factor in growth as can be seen by dividing the data into large, medium and small congregations (Figures 10.3 and 10.4).[17] Large assemblies increased on average by 5.2 individuals, medium by 4.5 and small by 0.25. However, in addition, only three of the thirteen large assemblies in the sample reported they were smaller than they had been five years before, while only six of the twenty-four small ones had experienced any growth. Although these last statistics show that larger assemblies were more likely to increase in size and smaller ones decrease, evidently size was not the sole determinant of growth or decline. The ten most rapidly growing churches, which had experienced an average growth of 16.9 individuals over two years, had an average size of 146 and the ten most rapidly decreasing ones, declining on average by 7.7 individuals over the same period, had an average size of ninety-eight, both above the average membership size of fifty-three members for the total sample. In small meetings, however, individuals were more likely to transfer out or to leave a meeting—on average 3.4 and 7.9 individuals respectively (Figure 10.4). If these trends continue into the present century, then many smaller assemblies are likely to decline to such an extent that they will be discontinued.

It was clear from the survey that there were congregations which were growing, and in larger and medium-sized assemblies net growth was happening partly through conversions—a net increase of 1.4 and 1.6 individuals respectively if losses for reasons other than death or transfer out are set against conversions (Figures 10.3 and 10.4). But growth was also partly through the transfer of members from other churches with a net increase of 2.4 individuals in large churches and 1.6 in medium-sized ones (Figures 10.3 and 10.4). Most of these transfers came from other Brethren assemblies: in small meetings it accounted on average for two of all transfers and for 8.6 of all transfers in large ones (cf. Figure 10.3).

---

14. Separate figures for Scotland were supplied to the writer by Graham Brown whose help is gratefully acknowledged.

15. Brierley *et al.*, *Christian Brethren*, p.14-15.

16. The two surveys are not directly comparable, for although the majority of respondent assemblies are in both surveys, there are some differences in the two samples.

17. Defined as: large = 90+; medium = 40-89; small = -39.

Although much of this congregational growth was at the expense of other assemblies, non-Brethren individuals were joining the movement, and this increase was principally true of large churches. The survey suggested a considerably fluid situation within the Brethren movement in Scotland, with transfers among assemblies and some large ones suffering considerable membership losses while some small ones enjoyed growth. Although the movement declined overall after the mid-1960s, this had not characterised all individual congregations. It is to an analysis of the complex circumstances of this period to which we must turn.

Continued Vitality

As can be seen from the numerical analysis of the movement, the period after the mid-1960s was not entirely one of decline. In the later 1960s the Irish evangelist Hedley Murphy held a number of large crusade-style missions,[18] but the tendency over the period was to move away from revivalist-type services and to explore new and more informal methods of recruitment. Younger individuals within assemblies debated the manner in which their meetings might be reformed.[19] Some assemblies adapted in response to the changing conditions around them, and a series of new institutions and fresh initiatives showed that the period was paradoxically also one of continued vitality for Scottish Brethren. Even the causes of decline could become a source of renewal as individuals responded to the challenges they posed.

Meetings aimed at teenagers became more common in the 1960s. The approach was sometimes timid—as late as 1970-1 among the programme titles at the Ayrshire youth rallies were 'Is Chastity Outmoded?' and 'Is Authority Necessary?' (subtitled 'The Christian and Rule in His [*sic*] Church').[20] The Brethren world isolated individuals to some extent from the societal pressure of separate activities for adults and youth. At a rally in Kilmarnock in 1968 it was reported that there had been 250 people present 'of which a good proportion was young people'.[21] But new forms did establish themselves and youth events increasingly dealt with young people on their own terms. By 1976 Tom Morton, later to become a full-time Christian rock evangelist, was pleading in *The Witness* for

---

18. *W*, 95 (1965), p.435; *W*, 96 (1966), p.196; *W*, 97 (1967), p.36; *W*, 98 (1968), p.275; *W*, 100 (1970), p.355; *W*, 103 (1973), p.195; *W*, 104 (1974), p.115; *W*, 105 (1978), p.35.

19. George Moffat, *Yet Will I Rejoice* (London, 1982), pp.45-6.

20. Writer's collection, II, Ayrshire Christian Youth Rallies committee minutes, 1964-1987, 29 September 1969.

21. *Ibid.*, 20 January 1969.

Christians to be involved in performing secular rock music.[22] One of the two individuals behind the Dundee Street Level Festivals that were begun in 1979 and which were to have a significant influence on the development of Christian rock throughout Scotland, was Brethren musician Ricky Ross.[23] The rising power of youth subculture and the impossibility of isolating Brethren young people from it did not seem to leave any other option open for many but to run separate youth activities with their own forms. The more radical the form, the less adults were attracted. Increasingly in many assemblies youth work came to appeal to young people in their own terms.

One organisation which attempted to use the number of young people within Brethren assemblies in the 1960s was the Scottish Counties Evangelistic Movement (SCEM). Founded in 1965, it took teams of young people to the rural areas of Scotland on summer missions to support small assemblies and to plant new ones.[24] SCEM successfully harnessed the energy of young people and enabled them to be more closely involved in the life of their home church after the summer missions.[25] It was an attempt to pass the Brethren enthusiasm for evangelism on to a new generation. The evangelists who supervised the teams also provided training for their members, and some of them, such as John Robb and John Clunas, were very much in the mould of the extravert evangelist. They appealed to young people's sense of adventure. Youthful groups arriving in an area also created an impression. One SCEM convert, talking about his perception of Brethren, derived from seeing them at open-air services in the late sixties, felt that 'I couldn't relate to them in any way. The women looked like something out of the 1930s, 40s.'[26] It was his contact with teenagers of a summer SCEM team which changed his perceptions. From the beginning SCEM also employed new techniques in evangelism, such as the youth coffee bars which were then the fashion among Evangelicals, and as such it became a source of much needed new thinking. George Russell, a businessman who was one of SCEM's founders, thought it was 'quite revolutionary at the time', for it employed contemporary music and to many teenagers coming from traditional assemblies this was heady

---

22. Tom Morton, 'Should the Devil have all the best music?', *W*, 106 (1976), pp.21-3, cf. John Allan, 'Youthtrack', *H*, 67 (October 1988), pp.12-13, *ibid.*, (November), pp.12-13, 26; the first half of Tom Morton's novel, *Red Guitars in Heaven* (Edinburgh, 1994), is the fullest account of these developments.

23. *DSCHT*, p.615, ii.

24. George Russell, 'How it all began', *SCEM Gen*, (1990), p.2.

25. 'What after SCEM?', *ibid.*, p.3.

26. Quoted in writer's collection, II, [Neil Dickson], 'Twenty-Five Years of Change', typescript narration for Scottish Counties Evangelistic Movement audio-visual, 1990.

material.[27] The movement successfully pioneered inter-assembly evangelistic cooperation on a national scale, and it continued to introduce new techniques in evangelism—largely moving away in the 1980s, for example, from campaign evangelism to more informal techniques.

Eventually several of the younger men who had initiated some of the more adventurous youth work of the fifties, and teenagers who had grown up in it, came to positions of responsibility within assemblies. The approach in youth work might often have been uneven and tentative, but the informality of atmosphere of these activities began to make itself felt in the adult services of some assemblies. In the 1980s a number of them adopted hymn-books, especially *Mission Praise* (1983), with music and lyrics which used contemporary forms.[28] Praise bands incorporating guitars and drums began to appear in the later part of the decade. Other changes were made which showed that some Scottish assemblies felt the need to adapt to altered conditions. One of the most basic innovations that a number of congregations introduced was the morning family service which had been recommended in the fifties and sixties.[29] In 1978 a morning family service was introduced at Victoria Hall, Ayr, probably making it the second assembly in Scotland to have one continuously.[30] A number of interested visitors came to witness it, and by 1988 the Partnership survey showed that twenty-six of the fifty-five Scottish Brethren respondent assemblies had one.[31] The new type of service aimed to attract families, and children were usually made an important focus in it.[32] The effect was to make it more lively and less sombre than the evening gospel meeting. In 1990 when the artist and writer Mairi Hedderwick visited the morning service at St John's EC, Linlithgow, she found:

> A young and very handsome preacher from Chicago, Illinois, dripped humid sweat as he preached the sermon. His theme was the 'love letter' of Genesis, *God's word*, illustrated with passionate intensity. He and his fiancée had lived four hundred miles apart during their engagement. Letters were read and re-read. Meanings searched and found between the lines, 'And always the joy of reading again and again at the end of each letter the "I LOVE YOU!"' Pretty teenage girls at my side giggled...
>
> Somewhere below in the bowels of the church thumps indicated a very active Sunday School session.

---

27. Russell, 'How it all began', p.2.

28. Neil Young, 'Singing or worship?', *H*, 63 (Jan. 1984), pp.19-20.

29. See above, p.204.

30. Oral information, 25 November 1990, from an assembly member.

31. Figure supplied by Graham Brown.

32. Alastair Noble, 'Family Services at Crosshill Evangelical Church, Glasgow', *H*, 69 (October 1990), pp.16-7.

> At the end of the service tea, coffee, juice and biscuits were served as we sat in maroon velour padded chairs easily nudged round to form spontaneous groups. 'We got rid of the pews. Too formal,' a chummy elder told me.[33]

As this not entirely sympathetic account also shows, the new service pointed to a change in the ambience of an assembly.

In 1978 Victoria Hall, Ayr, had also changed its name to Riverside Evangelical Church. Underlying the change of ethos was a rejection of sectarianism and this alteration was perhaps most clearly shown in the willingness to adopt the word 'church' in place of 'assembly'.[34] By 1990 thirty-one assemblies were calling themselves churches, and a further four were calling themselves 'chapel' or 'fellowship'.[35] The new generation of assembly buildings which began to appear from the mid-1960s onwards rejected the traditional box-like gospel hall. Typical of them was the Evangelical Church, Hamilton (Figure 10.5), which, when the town centre was redeveloped, replaced Baillies Causeway Gospel Hall in 1968. Designed by Brethren architect James Hyslop, the building contained several side halls of varying sizes which could accommodate different types of activities. The sanctuary's sharply peaked roof (emphasised by the slope on which the building was placed) was an unmistakable allusion to ecclesiastical architecture and the façade carried the plaque 'Evangelical Church'. The buildings were apprehended in a different manner from the Gospel halls and they signalled this change in a contemporary manner.

Another sign that some Brethren were losing their sectarian isolation was the use of resident full-time workers.[36] They differed from pastors—although by the 1990s this terms was increasingly being used to describe them—in that they were not ordained, preaching was not confined to them, and they had considerably less authority, sometimes not even being appointed as an elder. Nevertheless they represented a significant break with the Brethren distaste for a resident ministry. The first Scottish initiative of this kind was in Campbeltown where from 1971 to 1975 John Carrick, an evangelist working with SCEM, was based in the assembly. For the first year of his work he was assisted by a youth evangelist.[37] In 1978 the Swanwick conference (the new venue for the series of English

---

33. Mairi Hedderwick, *Highland Journey: a sketching tour of Scotland retracing the footsteps of Victorian artist John T. Reid* (Edinburgh, 1992), p.9; Mrs Hedderwick is a granddaughter of the Brethren missionary Dan Crawford.

34. The first two assemblies to use the name 'Evangelical Church' were St John's Chapel, Linlithgow, and Gospel Hall, Gartness, Airdrie, in the early 1960s.

35. *Assemblies Address Book* (Bristol 1990), pp.73-92; cf. Neil Dickson, 'Brethren and their buildings', *H*, 68 (October 1989) p.13; Morton, *Red Guitars*, p.38.

36. The phrase is that suggested in *CBRFJ*, 37 (1988), *passim*.

37. Anon., 'Wanted—full-time worker', *H*, 68 (October 1989), p.16.

Brethren conferences which had formerly met at High Leigh) promoted the use of resident full-time workers, and after it more began to be used.[38] The second assembly in Scotland to have one was the Old Schoolhouse, a Glanton Exclusive meeting in Edinburgh which was increasingly forming links with the Open Brethren. In 1981 it appointed a full-time youth worker.[39] But the most ambitious experiment in the use of resident full-time workers in the 1980s was at Riverside EC. In 1984 a youth worker was appointed to be followed by two other individuals, one of them a former Baptist minister, to teaching and pastoral ministries.[40] In the 1998 Partnership survey fifteen of the fifty-one respondent Scottish assemblies had full- or part-time resident workers. Some of the appointments of such workers were fairly short-lived, suggesting that the process of grafting on a full-time congregational ministry to a lay movement was not without its difficulties. This development, however, showed that a number of assemblies were willing to consider radically new patterns.

There were also individuals who led the way in attempting to recover a social conscience. The evangelist Alex Allan began working in penal institutions in 1966, and he founded a rehabilitation centre at Longriggend, Lanarkshire, in 1976 to help smooth the transition between prison and society, and in 1999 another evangelist, John Locke, established a similar ministry in Cumbernauld.[41] In 1977 Ashbank House was opened in Dumfries to provide long- or short-term care for mentally or physically handicapped children.[42] In the 1980s a number of assemblies started mothers' and toddlers' groups, to which women could bring young children and receive support meeting and talking with other mothers. At Cartsbridge EC, Busby, a female full-time worker was appointed in 1988 to run one such group and to provide additional support for a number of single parents through home visitation.[43] In Edinburgh Gwen McDowell established in 1985 a Christian counselling service, dealing with a range of problems from depression to sexual

---

38. John Polkinghorne, 'Ministry', in Alan G. Bamford (ed.), *Where Do We Go From Here? The Future of the Brethren: report of addresses and discussions at the Swanwick Conference of Brethren, September 1978* (Worthing, 1979), p.55.

39. John Storey, 'Local church full-time workers: a Scottish experience', *H*, 62 (January 1982), pp.2-3; the Old Schoolhouse was included among Open Brethren in *The Assemblies Address Book: useful information for Christians*, 2nd edn (Bristol, 1991), p.92, but was removed in subsequent editions.

40. Anon., 'Leadership at Ayr', *H*, 68 (April 1989), pp.15-16.

41. A. G. Allan, 'Real Life', *H*, 67 (July 1987), pp.15-16; *BM*, 109 (1999), p.158.

42. Miss C. Dick, 'Ashbank House Dumfries', *H*, 66 (October 1987), p.15.

43. Anon., 'Cartsbridge Evangelical Church', *H*, 67 (July 1988), p.17; Ewan Cathcart, *H*, 70 (April 1991), p.16.

abuse.[44] Deprived urban areas had received little attention from the Brethren during the period under consideration,[45] but one exception was the Viewpark Project. In 1974 Gospel Literature Outreach (GLO), founded in Australia in 1965 to send young people on international summer missions, had established its British training centre at Motherwell, giving the Scottish movement its first Brethren-based training centre.[46] The initial impact on Scottish assemblies was limited as most of trainees went to other countries.[47] In 1989 GLO—true to its principle of working in urban areas—in association with Bothwell EC, began a project in Viewpark, Uddingston, a Strathclyde Region area for priority treatment. A group of full-time Christian workers rented a local authority house in the scheme and from it did a mixture of social work and evangelism. The aim of the project was 'to bridge the widening gap between Church and community' by living in a working-class area and serving it.[48] Another outreach to the disadvantaged, in this case to the homeless, was commenced in Dundee by a married couple in 2000.[49] After a period of isolation from the sharper social pressures, attempts were being made by some individuals and assemblies to combine their faith with social action.

More conventional Brethren forms also led to new initiatives in evangelism. The energy of the sixties extended traditional evangelism into new and neglected rural areas, and by 1975 James Anderson was commenting on the 'two dozen younger men' who had become evangelists from the early 1960s.[50] One of them, Ian Munro, had moved into Easter Ross in 1961 to itinerate within the area, and others had followed him into the eastern Highlands.[51] In 1967 John Campbell went to live in Perth to evangelise rural Perthshire, an area of Scotland which the Brethren had rarely touched.[52] Several other individuals followed him by moving into the north-east Lowlands, and a number of evangelists moved into the Borders, too, during this period. This was following a well-established Brethren tradition of evangelising remoter rural areas where there were few assemblies, though it was probably on a scale not

---

44. Gwen McDowell, *'Homework'* (December/January 1990).

45. J. A[nderson]., *'Assemblies in Britain and Other Parts'*, *BM*, 85 (1975), p.373.

46. Colin B. C. Tilsley, *Through the Furnace* (Newtown, NSW, Australia, 1979), pp.59, 75.

47. J. Brown and Ray Cawston, 'Gospel Literature Outreach', *H*, 66 (December 1987), p.17.

48. Graham Poland, 'Bridging the gap', *H*, 68 (November 1989), pp.6-7; David Buchan, 'Viewpark: one year on', *H*, 69 (December 1990), pp.6-7; anon., 'Update on Viewpark', *H*, 70 (January 1991), p.26

49. *BM*, 110 (2000), p.383.

50. J. A[nderson]., *BM*, 85 (1975), p.65.

51. *BM*, 91 (1981), p.30.

52. *BM*, 97 (1967), p.315.

seen since the inter-war period. Marquees were used less by Scottish Brethren itinerants. They tended to be subject to arson attempts, and they were too commodious for the reduced numbers attending evangelistic missions. Portable halls proved more comfortable and compact, and they were increasingly used by the new generation of evangelists.[53] By 1973 there were thirty-three itinerant evangelists based in Scotland,[54] and although special missions had decreased in frequency, in 1990 there were still some twenty-three, one of them, a children's evangelist, a woman.[55]

The activity of the period led to at least twenty-seven assemblies being formed after 1966. Three Scottish cities gained new assemblies: an assembly was formed in 1966 in Gilmerton, Edinburgh (see Map 8, inset), the result of a post-war outreach commenced by the evangelist Rice Alexander;[56] in 1967 Aberdeen gained an additional assembly in Fernilea (see Map 5, inset);[57] and in Dundee (see Map 6, inset) the assembly in Lochee, which had been discontinued in 1950 was re-formed in 1971.[58] Several assemblies were planted in this period due to the movement of Brethren members. At Bishopton, Renfrewshire (see Map 12), after the building of new housing, an assembly was formed in 1977,[59] and the opening of the Brethren-run Maranatha conference centre in Biggar (see Map 10) led in 1988 to the re-formation of the assembly which had been discontinued five years earlier.[60] In the Borders (see Map 14) when some Brethren families moved to Peebles, the assembly there, which had been discontinued in 1948, was recommenced in 1968;[61] and the removal of another family to Kelso, where there had been no assembly since the nineteenth century, led to the re-founding of one in 1990.[62] Another post-war outreach in the Strutherhill district of Larkhall (see Map 10) had resulted in an assembly being formed there in 1972.[63] The new evangelistic initiatives of the mid-1960s and after also led to the formation of some assemblies. It was after a SCEM mission in Annan (see Map 14) in the early sixties that an outreach was begun in the area which issued in the formation of a meeting there, and another one

---

53. R. Miller 'Robert M. McPheat (1933-1990)', *BM*, 99 (1990), p.311.

54. Collection of Mr Alex. Stewart, Hopeman, Moray: [Alex. Stewart (compiler)], 'A Record of Gospel Work. Christian Brethren. Moray & Nairn', MS, n.d.

55. Figure calculated from *'Homework'* in 1990.

56. 'R. H. Alexander', *W*, 88 (1958), p.214; *W*, 98 (1968), p.436.

57. *BM*, 77 (1967), p.192.

58. *W*, 80 (1950), p.88; *BM*, 81 (1971), p.62.

59. *W*, 107 (1977), p.213.

60. *'Homework'* (August/September 1990).

61. *W*, 78 (September 1948), p.iii; *W*, 99 (1969), p.276.

62. Oral information, 7 September 1991, from an assembly member.

63. *BM*, 79 (1969), p.158; oral information, 11 March 1990, from a former assembly member.

was begun in Gretna in the late 1960s.[64] In the north of Scotland, the increased attention being given to the eastern Highlands resulted in an assembly being formed in Kingussie (see Map 3) in 1971 by Brethren individuals who had moved into the area.[65] In Luthermuir, Angus (see Map 6), a mission was held by Dan Gillies, one of the evangelists who was based in the north-east. As a result a group of eight individuals left the parish church to form an assembly in 1975.[66] A further gain from another Christian body occurred in neighbouring Perthshire when in 1997 the former London Exclusive assembly in Blairgowrie, which had seceded from the parent body after 1970, reported its existence in the Open Brethren address list.[67] In 1992 the GLO Viewpark Project in Uddingston (see Map 10) led to the commencement of a breaking of bread service.

Those assemblies listed above which were in areas remote from Brethren strength remained small, however, and the ones at Annan and Gretna were eventually discontinued. Among the most thriving assemblies planted in this period were the result of urban expansion in towns which already had one. This happened in Ayr (1970), Milltimber, Aberdeen (1975), East Kilbride (1978), Livingston (1981), Inverness (1982), Kirkcaldy (1985), and Cumbernauld (1990).[68] Being in areas with new housing, many of them were formed predominantly by young married couples, and all these new congregations adopted the name 'church' or 'fellowship'.

The continued vitality of the period was also seen in other ways. A number of Brethren became more closely involved with society. Headteacher W. K. Morrison welcomed comprehensive schools for it meant that Brethren children would not be separated from 'rough lads and girls of average and below average intelligence.'[69] From 1965 until the end of the century, eleven Brethren members were appointed to chairs in Scottish universities, and one individual went on to become university vice-principal. The chairs held were in science and practical disciplines (four were in medicine, two in engineering and one each in accountancy, biology, business policy, computing and statistics), perhaps demonstrating a Brethren inclination towards the utilitarian. There were, however, individuals from the 1980s onwards who made contributions

64. Oral information, December 1989, from a member of a south-west assembly.

65. *BM*, 81 (1971), p.30.

66. *BM*, 85 (1975), p.271.

67. *The Assemblies Address Book: useful addresses and other information for Christians*, 4th edn (Bath, 1997), p.182; for the London Exclusives, see above, pp.2-4.

68. *W*, 81 (1971), p.96; *W*, 105 (1975), p.435; *W*, 103 (1973), p.396; *BM*, 91 (1981), p.93; *BM*, 100 (1991), p.383.

69. W. K. Morrison, 'Comprehensive education: a headmaster's personal view', *W*, 103 (1973), pp.142-4.

towards the arts, in Scottish history and literature and the history of architecture,[70] and a number of other individuals could also be found in public service. Areas of entertainment which the Brethren had shied away from began to be accepted, albeit cautiously at first: in the 1960s many Brethren homes acquired a television and some tentatively visited the cinema for the first time.[71] Some forty years later, even *The Believer's Magazine* was tacitly accepting that Brethren young people would have access to a number of types of home amusements forbidden by previous generations as well as forms of entertainment in the wider society.[72] By the early 1990s, Brian Irvine, a Scottish international football player, was a member of Deeside Christian Fellowship, Aberdeen;[73] and Brethren individuals were commenting to the news media on the appropriateness of teaching the controversial novelists Irvine Welsh and James Kelman.[74] Articles on literature and the arts began to appear in *The Witness*, and W. K. Morrison could broach the subject of contraceptives in *The Believer's Magazine*.[75] Increasingly open to comment on politics, science and the arts was *Harvester* magazine, which changed its name to *Aware* in 1991. From 1992 it had an Anglo-Scot, John Allan, as its editor and a

---

70. For the historical works of the period, see above, p.14 n.76; for Scottish literature, see: Beth Dickson, 'Foundations of the modern Scottish novel', in Cairns Craig (ed), *The History of Scottish Literature*, 4 (Aberdeen, 1987), pp.49-60; Neil Dickson (ed.), *An Island Shore: selected writings of Robert Rendall* (Kirkwall, 1990); Beth Dickson, 'Class and being in the novels of William McIlvanney', in Gavin Wallace and Randall Stevenson (eds), *The Scottish Novel Since the Seventies* (Edinburgh, 1993), pp.54-70; William Landles, *Will H. Ogilvie: poet of the romantic Borderland* (n.p., 1993); Beth Dickson, 'Annie S. Swan and O. Douglas: legacies of the Kailyard', in Douglas Gifford and Dorothy McMillan, *A History of Scottish Women's Writing* (Edinburgh, 1997), pp.329-46; *idem*, 'An ordinary little girl': Willa Muir's *Mrs Ritchie*', in Carol Anderson and Aileen Christianson (eds), *Scottish Women's Fiction 1920s to 1960s: journeys into being* (East Linton, 2000), pp.97-108.

71. For television, see: Tom Morton, *S*, 2 December, 1992, p.12; *idem*, *Red Guitars*, p.38; Peter L. Sissons, *The Social Significance of Church Membership in the Burgh of Falkirk* (Edinburgh, 1973), p.344; but for an earlier use of television in 1961, see above p.210 n. 209; for cinema, see: Tom Morton, *W*, 106 (1976), pp.58-60; *idem*, *S*, 13 April 1994, p.12; *idem*, *S*, 30 November 1994, p.15.

72. J. G[rant]., 'Editorial', *BM*, 111 (2001), p. 290.

73. Andrew Wingfield Digby and Stuart Weir, 'Brian Irvine', in *idem*, *Winning is not Enough* (London 1991), pp.98-112.

74. For the opinions of two Brethren individuals see: Ken Cunningham quoted in Jackie Kemp, '"Radical" literature for Highers', *Scotland on Sunday*, 3 September 1995, p.3; and Beth Dickson quoted in Iain Martin and Jean West, 'Lessons to swear by', in *The Sunday Times*, 10 November 1996, p.18. I am indebted to Mrs Val Wells for the former reference.

75. Jonathan C. Inglesby, 'A plea for the reading of fiction', *W*, 95 (1965), pp.264-5; H. E. Freeston, 'The voice of the poet', *W*, 101 (1971), pp.378-80; W. K. Morrison, 'The Christian family', *BM*, 92 (1982), pp.296-7.

substantial number of the contributions came from Scottish writers. When Green politics were at their height in the early 1990s, one of them, Beth Dickson, contributed a regular column on environmental issues. Change was affecting every aspect of Brethren life. In 1989 Interface was founded to run a series of national and local conferences to provide a forum for discussing the innovations which had taken place within Scottish assemblies and the complex issues which confronted them.[76] The adaptations of secular youth culture, the changes in assembly practice, and the involvement in society and its problems all showed that many Brethren were shedding some of their sectarian features.

There was also continued activity in transmitting traditional Brethren doctrines. Individuals such as Robert McPheat, a mines manager who became an itinerant evangelist in 1968, continued the pattern of combining evangelism with Bible teaching.[77] There were others active solely in Bible teaching, and until the 1990s Scottish Brethren had probably as many full-time Bible teachers as at any other point in their history. The concern for teaching could also be seen in the programmes of Brethren publishers. It was from 1981 that the newly-founded Gospel Tract Publications began reprints of earlier works of Brethren theology and biographies.[78] In 1983-98 John Ritchie Ltd published *What the Bible Teaches*, an ambitious ten-volume devotional and homiletical commentary on the New Testament under the editorship of Tom Wilson, a Scottish further education lecturer and an editor of *The Believer's Magazine*. The commentary was written by a number of Brethren Bible teachers from throughout the English-speaking world. The theological standpoint of the commentary was strictly defined to preserve Brethren distinctives. The editor's statement of the theological basis emphasised 'the verbal and plenary inspiration of the Scriptures' and their 'inherent and infallible teachings'.[79] Ritchie also launched in 1996 the Family Series, booklets, written by the evangelist John Grant (in 1999 to become the sole editor of *The Believer's Magazine*) and illustrated by a *Beano* cartoonist. They tackled issues such as courtship and parenting, applying traditional teaching to the contemporary setting of these issues.[80] The publishing enterprises were attempting to ensure that conventional Brethren patterns and thought would not be lost in the changes affecting

---

76. [Beth Dickson], 'Working for change in Scotland', *H*, 70, (September 1991), p.5; in 2001 Interface merged with Partnership.

77. Miller 'McPheat', *BM*, p.311; see Robert Miller *et al.*, 'Robert M. McPheat 1933-1990', in Robert Plant (compiler), *They Finished Their Course in the 90s* (Kilmarnock, 2000), pp.207-13.

78. See above, pp.12-13.

79. Tom Wilson 'Preface', *idem*, (ed.), *What the Bible Teaches*, 1 (Kilmarnock, 1983), p.vii; in 2001 an Old Testament series of commentaries was commenced.

80. E.g., John Grant, *Let's Talk about Courtship* (Kilmarnock [1996]).

assemblies from within and without. Like the traditional evangelism, they demonstrated that considerable strength remained in customary Brethren ethos.

Social Change

Underlying the activity and changes of the late twentieth century were alterations in the social composition of the Brethren which had profound implications for the movement. In the post-war era a number of Brethren businessmen had been able to take advantage of the new economic opportunities to establish substantially-sized businesses.[81] The boom in car ownership and road use, in particular, enabled several Brethren members to build up businesses in the motor and haulage industries. There always had been businessmen among the Brethren, but after the war they were present in greater numbers. Also more members increasingly belonged to the professions, particularly the medical and educational ones. Scottish Brethren began to lose their principally working-class identity and be composed of the middle classes.[82]

Table 10.1. **Educational performance of children of working-class Brethren parents and other children**

	Selected for 5 yr secondary course	At school after leaving age	Completing secondary course	Entering higher education
	%	%	%	%
Skilled manual	18	8	7	4
Middle-class	45	36	27	19
Brethren manual	58	52	47	20

Source: Ian G. D. Ford, 'Religious affiliation and educational achievement: a note on the "Brethren" in western Scotland', *Scottish Educational Studies*, 3, No.1 (May 1971), pp.20-4.

It was the affluence of the period which also led to an increase in individuals being able to take advantage of an extended education. In the late 1960s (before Scottish secondary education became comprehensive) Ian Ford, a lecturer at Jordanhill College of Education and himself a Brethren member, did a study of the educational attainment of Brethren

---

81. Oral information from several Brethren businessmen; however, Brethren businesses for this period would technically be classified as small businesses.
82. For the Brethren social class in earlier periods, see above, pp.288-97.

children.[83] He limited his study to the children of manual workers,
looking at four points in their educational career: selection for a five-year
secondary course, remaining in school beyond the leaving age (then 15),
completing the secondary course, and entrance to higher education.
Among these children, he found, not only did a higher percentage
perform better educationally than both the children of skilled manual
workers (according to national Scottish figures), but also better than the
children of middle-class parents did. They functioned like 'a superior
middle-class sample' until university entrance when the Brethren children
still had figures equivalent to a normal middle-class sample (Table
10.1).[84] Ford was surprised by his results, for they showed to a marked
degree that in the Brethren children he studied, religious affiliation was a
more potent factor than socio-economic class in determining educational
success.[85] Only in the considerable drop-off in those going on to higher
education, Ford felt, might class still be having an effect. However, as he
pointed out, this must be a relatively small factor as it was obvious that the
determining factor in educational performance was religious affiliation. It
may be that the fall was partly due to a Brethren suspicion of the effects
of higher education. In the late 1960s sermons could still be heard in
some assemblies warning of the dangers of education and its corrupting
influence on the mind.[86] In the late 1960s Ford had some difficulty
finding enough manual workers among Scottish assemblies to do his
research, and of these only 23.3 per cent had belonged to classes IV and
V.[87] Obviously the same processes found in his sample would be at work
to a more marked degree with the children of parents in the higher social
classes.

   The post-war period was a crucial one for the children of Brethren
parents taking advantage of educational opportunities. The result was that
by the 1990s the Brethren contained a substantial number of
professionals. The occupations of the members of Central EC (formerly

---

83. Ian G. D. Ford, 'Religious affiliation and educational achievement: a note on the
"Brethren" in western Scotland', *Scottish Educational Studies*, 3, No.1 (May 1971),
pp.20-4; cf. an interview with Ford on his research, P. K[imber]., 'Clever Christians?',
W, 100 (1970), pp.100-1.
84. Ford's classification of occupations was that of the Registrar General's
Classification of Occupations, 1966 (the same system used in the present work). Of his
sample, only 21 of the families belonged to Classes IV and V, and 69 belonged to Class
III. Any returns from the higher social classes were rejected.
85. This was similar to what researchers had discovered among New York Jewish
communities, Ford, 'Religious affiliation', p.21.
86. The present writer's memories.
87. Ford quoted in K[imber]., 'Clever Christians?', p.101; *idem*, 'Religious
affiliation', p.22; see above, n.82.

Central Hall), Kilmarnock, in 1993 demonstrate the movement into the higher social classes (Table 10.2).

Table 10.2. **Social classification of the membership of Central Evangelical Church, Kilmarnock, 1993**

Social class[1]	I	II	III	IV	V	W	X	U
Central EC								
Membership 157								
Number	24	77	28	0	0	1 (+16)[3]	25 (+25)[3]	2
%[2]	(18.6)	(59.7)	(21.7)	(0)	(0)	(20.2)	(32.3)	(1.3)
Brethren members								
1961-3[4]								
Sample size 251								
Number	5	48	143	16	2	10 (+50)	12 (+14)[3]	15
%[2]	(2.3)	(22.4)	(66.9)	(7.5)	(0.9)	(39)	(10.4)	(6)

Notes for Table 10.2:
1. Classes I-V = social groups A-E (see Appendix 4); W = housewives (married women not in employment); X = unwaged (retired, students, disabled, and unemployed); U = unidentified; where possible, the social class of those not in employment has been allocated to that of the head of household in columns I-V.
2. Percentages in a social class are those of the total number to whom it is possible to allocate one; percentages of housewives are those of all identified women; percentages of unwaged are those of all identified individuals; and percentages of unidentified are those of the total membership.
3. The number in brackets is that of those also allocated to a social class.
4. The data are for two assemblies: Kilbirnie (1961) and Newarthill (1963), see Appendix 1 Table 9.3.

Sources for Table 10.2: Prayer List and Address Book, Central Evangelical Church, Kilmarnock, 1993 (n.p. [1993]); Appendix 1 Table 9.3.

Kilmarnock is a socially mixed community but despite this, the balance of membership of the congregation had swung heavily in favour of social classes I and II with over three-quarters of the members belonging to them: over half belonged to the latter, the intermediate lower middle-class. In Table 10.2 the social class of the church membership is set against aggregated figures for two other assemblies, Kilbirnie in 1960 and Newarthill in 1963. This comparison has its limitations as Kilmarnock is the type of larger town in which assemblies always had a greater representation of the higher classes than did smaller industrial communities such as Kilbirnie and Newarthill.[88] Nevertheless the upward social movement of the membership of Central EC is marked in comparison to earlier periods of Brethren history and teachers composed the largest number in any one occupation. This last factor could be explained on socio-economic grounds, as teaching tends to be the profession most readily chosen by the children of working-class parents. It is one additional pointer to upwards social movement. That this trend is set to continue can be seen from the rise in numbers in column X which was mainly due to the number in secondary or tertiary education (18.1 per cent of all identified individuals compared to 5.1 per cent in the two assemblies in 1960 and 1962). This also seems to indicate that Brethren children were now more likely to enter higher education than they were when Ford did his research. Because of several factors in their ethos, it seems likely that the Brethren will continue to profit from expanded economic opportunities in society.

Discontents

Social change had implications not only for the way in which Brethren interacted with society, but it also had important consequences for the internal life of assemblies. The continuing conservatism of many of them became a cause of disaffection. A snapshot of how individual assemblies were being affected is provided by the study of the churches of Falkirk done between September 1968 and August 1970 by researchers from Edinburgh University under the supervision of Peter L. Sissons.[89] Among the churches of Falkirk, two of the town's assemblies, Bethany Hall, Camelon, and Olivet Hall (as well as the town's mission, the Miller Hall), were studied. Olivet Hall, Sissons reported, was 'the much more progressive and "modern" of the two assemblies'.[90] The membership was about 100, younger and more middle-class than that of Bethany Hall. It was, Sissons wrote, 'a well heeled congregation... The roads outside the building are usually lined with very clean and mostly new cars'.[91] Attendance at the evening service was high and the membership of the assembly consisted of 'some of the more affluent and more mobile lower

88. Cf. above, Table 9.5, for the social class of the founding trustees of Central Hall, Kilmarnock .

89. Sissons, *Burgh of Falkirk* (Edinburgh, 1973). The study is not as useful as it might have been for present purposes as the two Brethren assemblies and the Miller Hall were counted as 'Protestant minority' churches along with the Congregational Church and the Scottish Episcopal Church. It is therefore impossible to disentangle information on the Brethren in much of the anecdotal and all of the tabulated data.

90. Sally Herring, 'Dissent in Scotland', in *ibid.*, p.344.

91. Sissons, *ibid.*, p.46.

middle-class people with a number of schoolteachers, college lecturers, proprietors of local businesses and the headmaster of one of the town's comprehensive schools'.[92] Bethany Hall, the report stated, was 'very much in the tradition of the Gospel Hall, old-fashioned and sombre'.[93] It had a membership of about eighty, but there were fewer than that in attendance at the services. The membership was 'predominantly middle-aged and elderly, with very few young members', and it was composed of mainly manual workers and their families. The houses which once surrounded the hall in Camelon (a working-class area of Falkirk) had disappeared and it was not by then in the centre of the area's population. The social differences between the two assemblies could be seen, it was felt, in the leadership: 'The elders of Olivet Hall include two insurance agents, two company representatives, a bank clerk and the owner of a motor business; the elders of Bethany Hall are foundry workers, a master baker and a clerk'.[94]

Bethany Hall and Olivet Hall provide an interesting comparison, for Olivet Hall had been founded by Bethany Hall members in 1935, and the latter was at one time the largest assembly in the district.[95] The two assemblies were close in emphases at the time of Olivet's formation. But by the late 1960s, as well as being socially different, the researchers found increasing divergence in the assemblies' practices and attitudes. These could be related to the socio-economic differences between them. Much of the contrast was focused by views on the young people's activities. Olivet Hall had a flourishing youth fellowship which had formed a folk-song group that had toured North American assemblies. Sectarian separation from secular leisure pursuits were being relaxed and some members belonged to sports and golf clubs, one individual even playing regularly at the socially prestigious Gleneagles course.[96] In Bethany Hall, and in the Miller Hall, on the other hand, it was reported that there were tensions between age groups. The older members were reluctant to change and the services consisted of 'long extempore prayers and extended preaching of the Gospel'. The elders were suspicious of the use of guitars and disapproved of the activities of the younger members.[97] For their part the young were 'impatient with such traditions

92. *Ibid.*, p.46.

93. Herring, *ibid.*, 344-5. Shortly after the study was made, Bethany Hall was demolished and another building was acquired (cf. *ibid.*, p.345).

94. *Ibid.*, p.345.

95. Peter McIntyre, 'How it began: Camelon', *BM*, 98 (1988), pp.261-2.

96. Sissons, *Burgh of Falkirk*, p.344.

97. For criticism of new musical trends, cf. W. F. N[aismith]., 'QA', *BM*, 80 (1970), p.27.

as the silence of women in meetings and the long sermons of speakers who do not always have the gift of preaching.'[98]

Those Brethren members who belonged to the higher classes had often been through social change in their own lives, and they tended to be more concerned to seek change within their assemblies. This process was most acute among the young who were most affected by the alterations. After the 1950s teenagers increasingly had also formed their own subculture which gave them, in varying degrees, a different lifestyle from their parents, and the cultural shifts which began to be explicit in Britain throughout the sixties had their most marked effects among young people. One Brethren father might be overheard asking, 'Who is Bob Dylan anyway?', but his son received one of the rock musician's albums as a Christmas present.[99] Many of the young were now impatient with forms that had been inherited from the past which could not immediately justify themselves in the present. The division was not just one of social class, but also one of age. The greatest source of dissatisfaction with the assemblies in Falkirk, Sissons reported, was not change (as it was among the Roman Catholics interviewed), but conservatism.[100] The picture that the study gave could be seen in many Scottish Brethren assemblies.

For many who felt that innovation in Brethren practices was not rapid enough, dissatisfaction continued to mount. There were, as was noted above, some who joined assemblies from other churches during this period,[101] but more common, it would appear, was discontent making a small but significant number of Brethren members transfer into Baptist churches. In 1988 one of the pastors of a Baptist church in the west of Scotland calculated that some twenty-six per cent of the membership (about eighty individuals) had at one time been Brethren.[102] Although this might be unrepresentative of most Baptist churches in Scotland, it could be paralleled elsewhere. A survey in 1988 of thirty-six individuals who had left a Brethren assembly for a Baptist church showed that twenty-six of the respondents (or seventy-two per cent of the sample) had left the Brethren within the previous two decades.[103] This might partly be a function of age, but it confirms impressions that these years had seen a greater movement into Baptist churches.

The respondents in the survey emerged as being dissatisfied in general with a number of features of the Brethren. In 1986 Nathan DeLynn

---

98. Sissons, *Burgh of Falkirk*, p.346.

99. Ricky Ross, 'The fall and rise of His Bobness', *S*, 14 November 1992, p.13.

100. Sissons, *Burgh of Falkirk.*, p.172.

101. See above, p.334; cf. K. Taylor, 'Why I am in the local assembly', *BM*, 92 (1982), pp.228-30; Robert Marshall, 'Why I am in the local assembly', *ibid.*, pp.311-2; N. J. Gourlay to the editor, *H*, 73 (November 1994), pp.20-1.

102. Neil Dickson, 'Brethren and Baptists in Scotland', *BQ*, 33 (1990), p.380.

103. *Ibid.*, p.380.

Smith interviewed individuals who had left the movement in the USA, and he found that the most common reasons for leaving were five negative features of the Brethren which they had identified: lack of positive leadership, lack of vitality, listless worship services, women's role marginalised, and narrowness.[104] In the Scottish sample there were seven individuals who had left their assembly because of a life-change (having, for example, married a Baptist, or moved to a different town), but it is clear that the sense of dissatisfaction was the main reason for even these individuals leaving. When asked how much weight the factors identified by Smith had in their decision, half of the Scottish sample indicated that three or more of these features had exerted a strong influence (Figure 10.6).[105] The chief source of dissatisfaction in leaving was the perception of the narrowness of the Brethren, on which educated assembly members in Sissons's survey had also commented.[106] Several individuals noted the limitations their meetings had placed on Christian fellowship, and on the 'legalistic attitudes and unwritten but strict rules'.[107] It would appear that for many 'narrowness' was closely connected to the sense of conservatism that several respondents identified, and probably also related to the poor quality of youth work or Sunday schools that they claimed to have found. The discontents felt most strongly were ethical and sectarian narrowness and the lack of willingness to change which affected the young most. Marginalisation of a woman's role was the second largest cause of dissatisfaction in the 1988 survey, but significantly, the worship at the breaking of bread ranked as the least strong source of dissatisfaction. The service continued to have a special place in Brethren spirituality. However, even here the number who indicated that the quality of worship had some influence on their decision to leave far outnumbered those upon whom it had no influence (Figure 10.6).

Their conservatism made it difficult for many assemblies to cope with the social and cultural changes affecting younger members after the 1960s. The haemorrhaging of members to Baptist churches became an additional cause of decline in numerical strength. In the early sixties one of the causes of the growth in size had been the increase in the numbers of young people within assemblies.[108] The survey of former Brethren in 1988 showed that it was mainly those in this age group who left in the seventies and eighties for Baptist churches.[109] It was a crucial group to lose as it meant not only a loss of numbers but also of their energy and

---

104. Nathan DeLynn Smith, *Roots and Renewal* (Pasadena, CA, 1986), pp.47-65.
105. Dickson, 'Brethren and Baptists', p.380.
106. Sissons, *Burgh of Falkirk*, pp.46, 94, 115.
107. Dickson, 'Brethren and Baptists', p.382.
108. See above, p.200.
109. Dickson, 'Brethren and Baptists', p.380.

the young families that they themselves in turn were rearing. Many who left an area did not join an assembly in the new district to which they went, an indication they had lost the sense of the importance of the Brethren that earlier generations possessed. Of the thirteen individuals who had left Gospel Hall, Newarthill, after 1963 six joined another denomination or abandoned Christian practice, while of those who remained in the village another six joined another church or lapsed.[110] The Brethren had previously achieved notable success in retaining the children of members, but now assemblies began to lose young people to other churches or from the faith altogether. Despite the continuing signs of vitality already noted, the steady attrition pointed to an underlying malaise.

Innovation and Conservation

The new initiatives within assemblies, altering attitudes to culture, the social changes which had affected Brethren, and the continuing conservatism of a section of the movement had significant consequences for the coherence of Brethrenism. Particularly from the mid-1970s onwards, some of the strains within the movement could be seen in the formation of new assemblies in towns which already had one.[111] The ostensible cause of their establishment was that new congregations were being created in an area without an assembly.[112] But most of these later plantings were by individuals concerned to innovate and they felt that the meetings which they had left were more conservative. The emergence of some of these new congregations was a sign of the increasing tension between the two different elements within the Brethren. The tension in these cases was resolved amicably by a group moving out to a new area of a town to arrange their affairs as they wished. Six of the new assemblies of the period were formed through schisms, all of them after 1970, and several more large-scale transfers of membership took place. The ferment could be seen more clearly here. Some of the transfers of membership were due to a group meeting resistance when seeking innovation, and some of them were due to a relatively moderate group finding an increasing conservatism uncomfortable. Others of the splits were for the opposite reason: a conservative minority who were uneasy with an assembly which was open to change. The more widespread acceptance of large-scale transference, however, had an additional significance. There had always been individuals who changed assemblies

---

110. Oral information, 7 September 1988, from Newarthill assembly.
111. See above, p.341.
112. 'Deeside Christian Fellowship', *H*, 68 (April 1989), p.16.

because of various causes of discontent. Occasionally, if a difficulty arose within an assembly, other ones nearby accepted a large number of people from the troubled assembly,[113] but usually they were reluctant to do so in case relationships between the two were damaged. The more general acceptance of large-scale transfer of members was a sign that the cohesion of the Brethren world had undergone some disintegration.

The changes which had followed the mid-1960s had not only resulted in a fresh outburst of activity, but also in a deepening division. Opinions were polarised due to the severity of the crisis facing assemblies and what seemed to some the radical nature of the innovations which were being proposed. Many of the changes, from the use of resident full-time workers to the use of new Bible translations and hymn-books, were criticized,[114] as was the development of 'large central assemblies, drawing their numbers from a wide area where other small assemblies exist.'[115] Those who wished to conserve the practices and thinking they had inherited saw the more radical changes as being for the worse and felt those pressing for them were being potentially divisive. *The Believer's Magazine*, felt that the notion of 'keeping up with the times' needed to be fought as 'the door has opened to "NEW INVENTIONS" within the pale of the local church with disastrous results.'[116] Many of the innovations were, however, an expression of the denominationalising tendency of the Brethren movement which was now more powerfully at work during this period than at any other. The acceptance of a religious professional within an assembly, the use of the word 'church', and the openness to society and its problems showed a marked slackening of sectarian isolation. It was not to be expected that such a process would take place without a reaction from those who wished to preserve separation from the church and the world. The result of the innovations was the strongest polarisation that the movement had experienced between the sectarian tendency and the denominationalising one.

The changes first became obvious among the Brethren in England and the severest strictures from the conservative critics in the decade after the late 1960s were reserved for the movement there. But gradually, during the succeeding two decades, the same innovations came to characterise a substantial section of Scottish assemblies, modifying them, as has already been seen, in significant ways. Change also affected them in other ways. When G. C. D. Howley, F. F. Bruce and H. L. Ellison edited *A New*

---

113. For an example of large-scale transfer happening, see above, p.163.

114. G. P. Waugh, 'Must we have a resident pastor?' *BM*, 87 (1977), pp.260-1; R. McP[ike]., 'The Household Church', *BM*, 90 (1980), p.152; F. E. S[tallan]., 'Editorial searchlight', *BM*, 97 (1987), p.2.

115. John Grant, 'Living for God: *What about assembly fellowship?*', *BM*, 102 (1992), p.48; cf. J. A[nderson]., 'Editorial searchlight', *BM*, 87 (1977), p.193.

116. R. McP[ike]., 'Editorial searchlight', *BM*, 90 (1980), p.129.

Testament Commentary (1969), it was warmly reviewed by a Swanwick speaker, the Fife headmaster, J. R. Rollo.[117] But others in Scotland criticised it for departing from traditional Brethren interpretations at a number of points.[118] Andrew Borland, still at that point the editor of *The Believer's Magazine*, felt the contributors were confined to a 'particular field of thought' within Brethren—an allusion to the more open perspective of the writers—and that the editors had ignored those who differed from them in Scotland and Ireland, the more conservative areas of Brethren.[119] Among the issues for which the commentary was criticised in Scotland was its departure from dispensational pre-millennialism. F. F. Bruce's contribution on the book of Revelation was from a mainly preterist perspective, instead of the futurist interpretation favoured among Brethren, and his eschatology made no reference to premillennialism.[120] But the erosion of traditional Brethren eschatology happened in Scotland too. Robbie Orr, a Scottish missionary in Pakistan published a commentary on Revelation, *A Victory Pageant* (1972), which interpreted the book from a non-dispensational premillennial view-point.[121] Others went further. During the Gulf War in 1991, which had potentially serious consequences for Israel, *The Believer's Magazine* made reference to the putative eschatological implications of the conflict, but the Scottish writer in the *Harvester* concentrated on the injustice of the Iraqi cause.[122] By 1993 Alex McIntosh, a retired university lecturer, was expounding an amillennialist position at the national Interface conference, and there was no dissent from those attending.[123] Possibly because of the erosion of traditional Brethren eschatology, the most fully-developed section of the doctrinal statement in *What the Bible Teaches* was the one stressing dispensational premillennialism.[124] Quietly but surely, however, a significant section of Scottish Brethren had moved away from a once widely-held part of the movement's world view.

The lack of comment about the major changes affecting the world at the end of the twentieth century, such as the ending of the Cold War, from those who continued to maintain dispensationalism might also suggest that for them too millennialism had lost some of its force. But for

---

117. John R. Rollo, 'A New Testament Commentary', *W*, 100 (1970), p.109.

118. W. F. Naismith, 'New Testament Commentary', *BM*, 80 (1970), pp.141-2.

119. A. B[orland]., 'A New Testament Commentary', *BM*, 80 (1970), pp.89-90.

120. F. F. Bruce, 'The Revelation to John', in G. C. D. Howley, *et al.* (eds), *A New Testament Commentary* (London, 1969), pp.629-666; for Bruce's eschatological views, see above, p.247.

121. R. W. Orr, *Victory Pageant* (London, 1972).

122. F. E. S[tallan]., 'Editorial searchlight', *BM*, 99 (October 1990), p.2; [Beth Dickson], 'Saddam rules OK?' *H*, 70 (October 1990), p.28.

123. Personal observation of the present writer.

124. Wilson, *What the Bible Teaches*, 1, p.vii.

those who wished to continue in separation there were precise limits to change. In *Our Heritage* (1973) James Anderson quoted with approval a sociological definition of sectarianism and argued that 'the maintenance of such bodies of people requires continued devotion to the same convictions'. Although some assemblies were shedding some sectarian features, the majority would have agreed with Anderson that continuing sectarianism showed that they were 'the direct descendants of primitive Christianity'.[125] With a significant use of imagery Tom Wilson proclaimed 'Conservation is the cry of our day in the polluted environments of the western hemispheres. Let it be our cry in the Assemblies as well.'[126] But even those who were modifying sectarian attitudes felt that innovation should proceed only so far and Scottish Brethren still remained cautious. This could be seen in their attitudes to other churches. A small section of English Brethren had achieved some rapprochement with the British Council of Churches. When a representative from the Council had been present at Swanwick in 1964, A. M. S. Gooding had criticized the conveners heavily. The use of 'Brethren', apparently as a denominational title, caused him to exclaim, 'These extremists take too much upon themselves these days.'[127] Scottish assemblies, however, did not participate in ecumenical dialogue in the 1960s and only two congregations in the 1998 Partnership survey took part in the Churches Together initiative of the 1990s.[128] Any association with theological liberalism or Roman Catholicism was enough to scare most away. New developments in Evangelicalism could be regarded with suspicion too. As the Charismatic movement emerged from the 1960s onwards, Scottish Brethren gave it a few leaders, individuals such as Raymond Wylie and Bob Gordon. But unlike English Brethren, those in Scotland who became Charismatic had to leave their assemblies and even these were only a handful of individuals.[129] In the 1998 Partnership survey none of the respondent assemblies practised speaking in tongues and only one claimed it allowed prophecy or exercised a healing ministry.[130] While not all would have been as hostile to the Charismatic movement as Tom Wilson who claimed that it was 'a Satanic imitation of

---

125. James Anderson, *Our Heritage* (Kilmarnock, 1973), p.47.

126. Tom Wilson, 'Conservation', *BM*, 85 (1975), pp.316-7.

127. A. M. S. Gooding, 'Christian unity', *BM*, 75 (1965), p. 218.

128. Partnership Survey (1998).

129. Oral information, 23 October 1994, from a former Brethren pastor of a Charismatic church; cf. Dickson, 'Brethren and Baptists', p.382; for English Brethren, see: *W*, 95 (1965), pp.384-6, 427-30; Andrew Walker, *Restoring the Kingdom: the radical Christianity of the house church movement* (London, 1985), pp.35-49; Harold H. Rowdon, 'The Post-War Background to Nantwich 1991', in *idem* (ed.), *Strengthening, Growth and Planting*, pp.138-9; Brierley *et al.*, *The Christian Brethren*, pp.49, 59.

130. Partnership survey (1998).

Pentecostal blessing',[131] Scottish Brethren of all complexions proved resistant to it and it had little impact among them.

Yet contact with other Christians played a significant part in broadening some Brethren. There were those willing to cooperate on an interdenominational basis. After a series of successful inter-assembly summer missions in Glasgow during the 1970s, Alastair Noble, a schools inspector, held two interdenominational missions in north-eastern Scotland[132]—leading the assembly in one town in the area to dissociate itself publicly from his mission.[133] He was also National Coordinator of Billy Graham's Scottish mission of 1991, and it was noted at the time that Brethren were proportionately better represented in its organisation than were other churches.[134] The increasing numbers of Brethren children who remained at school or went to university or college were often deeply influenced by Scripture Union and the Universities and Colleges Christian Fellowship (formerly IVF), interdenominational Evangelical agencies active within educational institutions.[135] Brethren churches also became members of the Evangelical Alliance when a Scottish branch was formed in 1992.[136] These contacts, however, were within Evangelicalism, and any wider contact with Christians from other traditions was in general shunned. Even the more open Brethren wished to remain a protest movement against institutionalised Christianity; yet at the same time they had accepted that their movement was but one more Christian denomination. The Brethren no longer appeared as being the sole upholder of true Christianity.

Table 10.3. **Educational performance of Brethren children by sex**

	Selected for 5 yr secondary school course	At school after leaving age	Completing secondary course	Entering higher education
	%	%	%	%
Boys	63	61	55	28
Girls	52	44	38	11

131. T. Wilson, 'BQB', *BM*, 85 (1975), p.284.

132. Oral information, 29 September 1991, from Alastair Noble.

133. *BM*, 80 (1970), p.189; *BM*, 90 (1980), p.158.

134. [Beth Dickson], 'Preaching in Paradise', *H*, 71 (May 1991), p.27.

135. John Chapman, 'So you're going to college this autumn', *H*, 59 (1980), p.321; Neil Dickson, 'Thanks for the memory: W. K. Morrison', *A*, 70 (April 1991), pp.9-10; John Mackinnon, 'The Church's mission in Scotland: a para-church perspective', in David Searle (ed.), *Death or Glory* (Fearn and Edinburgh, 2001), pp.100-7.

136. Oral information, 18 April 2000, from a Brethren Evangelical Alliance Council member.

Source for Table 10.3: Ian G. D. Ford, 'Religious affiliation and educational achievement: a note on the "Brethren" in western Scotland', *Scottish Educational Studies*, 3, No.1 (May 1971), pp.20-4.

The assemblies in Scotland which did innovate during the years after 1980 were perhaps only a fifth of all assemblies, and at times the innovations proceeded very slowly. The complexities of the balance between innovation and conservation within churches and across the movement as a whole, and the issues which underlay them, can be seen particularly clearly from the role and status accorded to women among Scottish Brethren over this period. Male membership remained high— forty-seven per cent of the membership of Central EC in 1993—and men continued to dominate the movement.[137] Ian Ford found during his research in the late 1960s into the educational performance of the children of Brethren parents that the influence of their background was clearly seen in the poorer performance of girls from Brethren families (Table 10.3). Here the sharply defined roles of men and women in assemblies, Ford felt, was having an effect. In 1971 Scottish women were doing rather better than the national British ratio for university entrance of 3:2 in favour of the men. But among Brethren women the ratio was not even 5:2.[138] One consequence of the fall-off in women entering higher education was that while there were a number of male Brethren members with second degrees, until the mid-1980s it was possible to find only two native Scottish women with doctorates. Particularly in conservative circles, a woman's role continued to be defined negatively as one of silence.[139] New fashions were also the subject of much un- favourable comment,[140] and the wearing of a hat to assembly meetings came increasingly to be regarded as a litmus test of orthodoxy.[141] Changes in women's roles were felt to be motivated by 'a broad spirit of liberalism that conforms to the spirit of the age, instead of bowing

---

137. Given that membership and attendance have a high correlation in the Brethren, this figure might reasonably be compared with the 37 per cent of all Scottish churchgoers who were male in 1984: Brierley and Macdonald, *Prospects for Scotland*, p.30.

138. Ford, 'Educational Achievement', pp.22-3.

139. Andrew Stenhouse, 'The service of sisters', *BM*, 88 (1978), pp.214-5; anon, 'Why not equal rights', *BM*, 90 (1980), pp.56-8, 88-9, 116-7; James Anderson, 'A reply to a letter on women's ministry', *BM*, 90 (1980), pp.267-8; in addition J. R. Caldwell's *Ministry of Women* was reprinted in 1970 (*BM*, 80 (1970), pp.202-4).

140. Andrew Stenhouse, 'Christian women and modern fashion', *BM*, 80 (1970), pp.88-9.

141. D. O. Murray, 'The covering of the head', *BM*, 88 (1978), pp.54-6; N. J. Gourlay, *Church Symbols for Today: the water, the head, the bread and wine* (Kansas City, KA, 1999), pp.139-78; A. Sinclair, 'Does it matter where I go for fellowship?', *BM*, 109 (1999), pp.77-8; John Dunlop, 'A partner in marriage', *ibid.*, p.228.

humbly to the word of God.'[142] Some women found the restrictions and negative pronouncements irksome.[143] The lower status accorded to women among the Brethren was remarked on by several respondents in the 1988 survey of those who had left an assembly for a Baptist church. Some commented on the scope there was for women praying publicly in Baptist churches, a practice that was forbidden in most Brethren assemblies. This discontent can be related to social differences between Brethren assemblies and Baptist churches. One individual who had left in the 1980s commented, 'There is more scope in a Baptist church for the professional woman to use her gifts & more provision is made for the single woman'.[144] The difference in attitudes within Scottish Brethren to males and females which Ian Ford had found some ten years earlier were still having an effect.

But changes came to the role of women too. The other main controversial proposal of the Swanwick conference of 1978 at which resident full-time workers had been advocated was the public participation of women. The Brethren historian Roy Coad argued in his lecture that the biblical teaching on the subject needed some cultural adaptation, a position maintained by F. F. Bruce in a paper delivered before a Brethren audience earlier in that same year.[145] The promotion of a public speaking role for women was strongly rejected by the conservative individuals and it was felt that such a proposal could never prove acceptable. A. M. S. Gooding, by then editor of *Assembly Testimony*, saw that the potential effect of Swanwick would be 'more likely to cause disunity in local assemblies than anything that has taken place in the last 50 years'.[146] His criticisms arose out of his attitude to the Bible. He did not like the idea that its message might need cultural adjustment and asserted that God 'knew all about the days in which we live and that his word is sufficient for all time, even unto the end of the age'.[147] Yet a public role for women came to be accepted among some

---

142. Andrew Borland, *Women's Place in the Assembly* (Kilmarnock, 1969).

143. S. Westbury, 'Women in the church', *H*, 71 (March 1992), pp.17-18.

144. Dickson, 'Brethren and Baptists', p.382.

145. Roy Coad, 'Where is "here"?', in Bamford (ed.), *Where Do We Go From Here?*, pp.10, 21-4; F. F. Bruce, 'Women in the church: a biblical survey', *CBRFJ*, 33 (1982), pp.7-14; on the 1978 Swanwick Conference see, Rowdon, 'Background to Nantwich', pp.127-141.

146. A. M. S. Gooding, 'Review of Swanwick Conference of Brethren', *AT*, No.160 (September/October 1979), p.101. Gooding also quoted an individual who made a similar point during discussion at the conference, see Bamford (ed.), *Where Do We Go From Here?*, p.76.

147. Gooding, 'Review of Swanwick', p.103.

Scottish assemblies, a process aided by Bruce's arguments.[148] When in 1983 a series of articles in the *Harvester* also advocated the public participation of women, two letters in response came from Scotland, one from a man, the other from a woman. The former disapproved, declaring that 'The prospect is now before us of one the most serious divisions among so-called "Christian Brethren" that has been seen'. The woman's letter commended the articles.[149] In the 1998 Partnership survey fifteen assemblies reported permitting various public roles for women, from leading the church in prayer to announcing hymns and songs.[150] As well as the women who were in full-time service within Scotland, there were at least two other churches which had appointed deaconesses.

Change came in other ways for women. It is doubtful that if Ford's research into the educational performance of Brethren children had been repeated in the 1990s that there would have been the imbalance between the sexes which he had found. Girls were probably encouraged to go on to tertiary education as much as boys.[151] More Brethren women now worked, as can be seen from the sharp drop in the number of housewives in Central EC, Kilmarnock. These females had ranged from 66.7 per cent of all identified women to 29.5 per cent in earlier periods but consisted of only 15.5 per cent in the case of Central EC (Tables 9.1, 9.3, and 10.2). However, the changes for women were slow in coming, and in some places where women were allowed to participate publicly individuals left their assemblies. In the 1998 Partnership survey only two of the respondent assemblies stated that women expounding scripture was permitted and there were no assemblies which had women elders. Willingness to change the role of women, however, showed that some were edging away from Fundamentalism. Although *The Believer's Magazine* regretted the pejorative connotations 'Fundamentalism' had acquired,[152] the move away from it among other sections of the movement could also be seen in a new openness to differing interpretations on issues such as biblical inerrancy, creation and hell.[153] 'Conservative

---

148. Neil Dickson, 'Modern prophetesses: women preachers in the nineteenth-century Scottish Brethren', *RSCHS*, 25 (1993), p.117.

149. J. McDerment, *H*, 63 (April 1984), p.22; E. S. Dickson to the editor, *H*, 63 (January 1984), p.23.

150. Partnership survey (1998).

151 Of the fourteen students in tertiary education in Central EC, Kilmarnock, in 1993, eight were male and six were female.

152. F. E. [Stallan]., 'Editorial', *BM*, 105 (1995), p.322.

153. [John Allan], 'The Bible's changing fortunes', *H*, 70 (June 1991), pp.4-6; A. A. Wilson, 'The six days of creation', *H*, 72, (March 1993), pp.12-14; [John Allan], 'A question of judgment', *H*, 73, (November 1993), pp.3, 6-7; Neil Dickson, 'The unevangelized', *ibid.*, pp.4-5; Cecil Steer to the editor, *H*, (January 1994), pp.16-7.

evangelical' became the preferred term for many.[154] The change in terminology represented a less strident approach,[155] but it also demonstrated that although Scottish Brethren were innovating, they did so cautiously.

The End of a Movement?

The picture of Scottish Brethren after the mid-sixties was a diverse one.[156] Societal trends and the Brethren world view pulled apart imposing strains. Issues such as women's participation or the Charismatic movement showed the underlying conservatism of Scottish Brethren. They most easily introduced changes when they felt it would have a beneficial effect in evangelism or on their own families. Most of the resident full-time workers which were appointed were evangelists or youth workers. In 1956 A. P. Campbell, the Fife lay Bible teacher, had claimed that 'modernistic teaching has found no place in our assemblies',[157] and the statement was still largely true forty years later. Theological conservatism remained one of the marks of the Brethren. When changes had theological implications, such as the difficult hermeneutical and doctrinal problems raised by women's participation, then they were less readily accepted. This caution made for a strong conservatism across all types of Scottish Brethren. Consequently Brethren identity held up better in Scotland than it did in England where the fragmentation was greater.[158] The elder of one large innovating assembly when questioned during a religious programme on television in 1988 as to why women did not participate publicly replied that there was no such demand from among the women.[159] As Ford had found in his research on educational performance, a Brethren upbringing was a more powerful influence than social factors. It is this which does not make it possible to analyse the

---

154. David Clarkson, 'The authority of the Scriptures', *BM*, 80 (1970), pp.7-8; cf. Touchstone [i.e. G. C. D. Howley], *W*, 85 (1955), p.227.

155. For the distinction between Fundamentalism and conservative Evangelicalism see D. W. Bebbington, 'Martyrs for the truth: Fundamentalists in Britain', *SCH*, 30 (Oxford, 1993), pp.419-20; in 1995 the present writer heard the term 'fundamental Evangelical' used to describe Brethren theology by a preacher from the innovative wing of the movement.

156. Rowdon, 'Background to Nantwich', pp.133-4.

157. A. P. Campbell, 'Simplicity of testimony', *A Return to Simplicity: Conference of Brethren at High Leigh, September, 1956* (Rushden [1959]), p.66.

158. Harold H. Rowdon, *Who Are the Brethren and Does It Matter?* (Exeter, 1986), pp.7-18.

159. 'High Spirits', STV religious affairs programme, August 1988.

Brethren solely in socio-economic terms. University lecturers and wealthy businessmen were also found among more conservative assemblies.

The division between those who were concerned to innovate by introducing new practices and those who wanted to conserve the practices they had inherited from the inter-war years became the most significant and widespread issue facing Scottish assemblies after the mid-1960s. It was among those Evangelical churches and Christian fellowships which innovated in more radical measures that the loss of a wider Brethren consciousness was most marked. They often wanted to dissociate themselves from the Brethren because of the negative features they perceived in assemblies. New churches, such as Tayside Christian Fellowship, Perth, although largely Brethren in practice, claimed to be interdenominational fellowships,[160] and others, such as the Deeside Christian Fellowship, wrote their history omitting any reference to the Brethren.[161] The consequent historical rootlessness had its perils, but that such groups were not Brethren was something with which some conservative individuals were ready to agree. One writer felt that 'The Scriptures are being applied in a different way to accommodate the present state of culture' with the result that 'In many instances it would be difficult to recognise assembly features.'[162] There were those who tried to keep themselves clear of the developing polarities. Throughout the period, W. K. Morrison built bridges across assemblies of different traditions by having 'tolerance and respect...for stances which one does not personally adopt'.[163] Others desired a middle ground between the more radical innovators and the more intransigent conservatives. James Anderson pled for assemblies to be 'firm on fundamentals and lax on incidentals'. The issues he listed, however, showed how difficult it was to define what fell into each category: he regarded no public role for women as a fundamental, and the use of contemporary hymn-books and translations and meeting times (an allusion to family services) as

---

160. H. N. Pope, 'Renewal in Scotland', *H*, 63 (March 1984), p.19; *idem*, 'Tayside Christian Fellowship', in Roger Foster (ed.), *Ten New Churches* (Harrow, 1986), pp.96-7; 'Deeside Christian Fellowship', p.16; Rowdon, *Who Are the Brethren?*, pp.17-18.

161. 'History of the Church', *Deeside Christian Fellowship Church Diary*, 5 September 1993; it is this interdenominationalism which makes it difficult to categorise: the congregation is Brethren according to the criteria adopted in the present work (see above, pp.5-6); nevertheless, although the footballer Brian Irvine was mentioned above (p.342), another former member of the church when he was the Professor of Celtic at the University of Aberdeen, Donald E. Meek, was excluded from the list of those Brethren holding chairs (see above, p.341) because of his continuing commitment during his membership to the study of Baptist churches, his own ecclesiastical background.

162. C. D. Pollard, 'The Lord's Assembly', *BM*, 100 (1991), p.38.

163. W. K. Morrison, 'Who are the Brethren?', in F. A. Tatford, *That the World May Know*, 7 (Bath, 1985), p.486; Dickson, 'Thanks for the memory', pp.9-10.

incidentals.[164] Each of these had significant bodies of opinion opposed to them.

The late twentieth-century division between conservationists and innovators is bound to get deeper in the future as social change continues and more assemblies adopt radical changes such as resident full-time workers and the public participation of women. The ensuing polarisation will make the desired middle ground increasingly hard to find. And the ground had imperceptibly shifted underfoot. The issues which divided assemblies were no longer those concerning degrees of strictness in practice, but responses to social change. The fundamental differences between one tendency among Brethren and the other were not solely, in a phrase of G. C. D. Howley, 'matters of procedure'[165] but were also social and cultural ones. Unity had often been a problem for a movement as diverse as the Brethren, and it seems clear that in the future preserving it will be even more difficult. Innovating assemblies and conservative ones increasingly functioned as discrete groups with their own circles of preachers.

Numerically the Brethren were in overall decline, and rural and village assemblies suffered particularly. The pressures of society were strong and some of those who had pioneered new strategies were lost to the movement. Ricky Ross left before finding fame with the rock band Deacon Blue,[166] while Tom Morton left for a Charismatic community and then renounced Evangelicalism before achieving prominence as a journalist and broadcaster.[167] Some of the prominent conservative pioneers of the sixties also became casualties.[168] An increased openness to Evangelicalism brought its losses for the movement too. Nitshill EC, Glasgow, transferred to Glasgow City Mission in the early 1970s and the Holm EC, Inverness, affiliated to the Baptist Union of Scotland in 1991.[169] The publishers, Pickering & Inglis, was acquired in the 1980s by another Christian publishing firm and was lost to the movement and in 1999 their Glasgow shop was absorbed into a national chain of Christian bookshops. Morale was at a low, and there was an alarming collapse of institutions which had served the Brethren well. Special Saturday conferences were less well attended. The Glasgow Half-Yearly Meetings had to reduce drastically the scale of their operations in 1981 due to

164. J. A[nderson]., 'Editorial searchlight', *BM*, 89 (1979), p.193.

165. OA, D27/ 6/4, G. C. D. Howley to Robert Rendall, 17 October 1960.

166. Ricky Flynn, 'Ricky sings the blues', *The Scotsman Weekend*, 1 June 1991, p.17.

167. Tom Morton, *Spirit of Adventure* (Edinburgh, 1992), p.150; *idem*, 'Saved by a fall from grace', *The Scotsman Weekend*, 21 March 1992, p.2.

168. *BM*, 91 (1981), p.30.

169. Oral information, February 1992, from a Glasgow assembly member; Norman Cordiner to Alan Campbell, 13 January 1992.

falling attendance, shedding the meetings for Bible teaching which had been the main feature of the gatherings since their inception in 1865.[170] The Lesmahagow Camp Meeting was discontinued in 1984 after 116 years of existence.[171] In 1988 Netherhall, the large guest house and conference centre in Largs, closed, a casualty not only of changing holiday patterns, but also of the movement's loss of cohesion.[172] Brethren magazines also suffered. Because of falling circulation numbers, *The Witness* merged with *The Harvester* in 1980. Ten years later the latter had a UK circulation of around 2,000 and was in severe financial difficulties which led to its demise in 1995.[173] It was a victim of what some saw as its overly *avant-garde* approach,[174] changing reading patterns and the innovative churches identifying more readily with a wider Evangelicalism than with the Brethren.[175] The journal of the traditionalists, *The Believer's Magazine*, avoided these trends more successfully, and its total circulation was 6,000 by 1994,[176] with perhaps some two-thirds of that number distributed within Scotland. Revivalist-type gospel missions were increasingly ineffective.[177] Even the zeal for evangelism which had been such a marked feature of the Scottish movement was waning and the appetite for church planting had radically diminished. By 1990 George Russell was commenting that 'the overall wish and desire to evangelise our own country has been lost. There is a distinct lack of enthusiasm for evangelism'.[178] Some felt that everything the Brethren represented could well disappear.[179]

The innovations, too, were not always successful. A creative family service failed to save Crosshill EC, Glasgow (discontinued 1991),[180] or the appointment for a while of a resident full-time worker Oxgangs EC, Edinburgh (discontinued 1992). The larger congregations had grown initially by the transfer of Brethren members rather than by the recruitment of individuals from outside the movement. The reluctance of

---

170. For the Glasgow Half-Yearly Conferences, see above, p.86.

171. *BM*, 95 (1985), p.156; cf., above, p.74.

172. For Netherhall, see above, pp.208-9.

173. Neil Summerton, 'Goodbye Harvester?' *H*, 69 (September 1990), pp.1-2; [John Allan], 'Comment', *A*, 74 (February/March, 1995), p.1.

174. James Oliver to the editor, *A*, 70 (January 1991), p.21.

175. Beth Dickson, 'Goodbye to George Flett', *A*, 74 (February/March, 1995), p.15.

176. Brierley *et al.* (eds), *UK Christian Handbook 1994/5 Edition*, p.465.

177. Cf. the contrasting experiences of the Irish evangelist Jim Hutchinson in one Glasgow assembly in 1952 and 1987 in James G. Hutchinson, *Something of My Life: whose I am, and whom I serve Acts 27:23* (Glasgow, 1997), pp.44, 103.

178. Quoted in 'Twenty-Five Years of Change'.

179. The worst of three potential futures for the Brethren suggested by F. E. S[tallan]., 'Editorial searchlight', *BM*, 99 (1990), p.2; the other two were 'division' and 'a closer identity with denominationalism'.

180. Noble, 'Crosshill Evangelical Church', pp.16-7.

assemblies to cooperate made it difficult for many of the problems
arising out of social issues to be dealt with adequately and some of those
who engaged in work among the socially disadvantaged complained that
their efforts received little support.[181] It led to some of the new social
enterprises ceasing or not remaining entirely in Brethren hands. Politics
were still avoided by the Brethren. William Craig, was unique in this
period, holding office as provost of Campbeltown from 1971 until his
sudden death the following year.[182] Also mixed was the success of
Brethren young people's work. In 1984 John Allan, then a widely-
travelled youth worker, reported that he had been in contact with one
Scottish Brethren youth group 'of which any church would be proud'
but that overall 'we're not doing too well'.[183] The paucity of numbers
made running inter-assembly youth events difficult by the mid-1980s.
Only in Glasgow did larger young people's meetings continue to be held,
and even there the annual Bible School founded after the All Scotland
crusade ceased.[184] Several larger churches had an adventurous youth
work for their own young people, but they tended not to involve
themselves with other assemblies. SCEM missions suffered from reduced
numbers. It was, like the Glasgow Bible School, a victim of the loss of a
wider Brethren consciousness among the larger congregations.

The changes threw up several profound problems for the movement.
The experiments in new patterns of ministry had yet to achieve stability
within the lay-led Brethren. Their increasing middle-class membership
meant that they tended to lose contact with the social groups and urban
areas where their recruitment was formerly most successful. This upward
social mobility also had its dangers. In 1970 Ian Ford noted that if the
Brethren followed the pattern of other religious movements then they
would become 'materialistic'.[185] Several public scandals affecting
Brethren members or former members in the 1990s, widely reported in
the news media, might be seen as evidence that the prophecy was being
fulfilled. The separatism of its spirituality was what many individuals
within it were eager to leave behind, while the cerebralism of much of its
piety, rooted in the vanishing traditions of working-class self-education,
appeared anachronistic under late twentieth-century cultural trends which

181. A. G. Allan, 'Real Life', pp.15-16; Dick, 'Ashbank House Dumfries', p.15.

182. 'Many people at the funeral of the late Mr W. S. G. Craig', *The Campbeltown Courier*, 2 September 1972, [p.1]; the Labour MSP for Glasgow Govan, Gordon Jackson QC, left the movement before entering politics.

183. John Allan, 'Understanding young people', *H*, 63 (January 1984), p.6.

184. See above, p.201.

185. Cited in K[imber]., 'Clever Christians?', p.101.

stressed non-rationalism.[186] The conjunction of an increasing immersion in society and the loss of vitality in its spirituality had serious consequences for the movement.

No voluntary body is guaranteed a permanent place within a society, but there were signs in the period under survey that the Brethren in Scotland will endure for some time further. Although the conversion of forty individuals during a mission in Coatdyke, Airdrie, in 1989 was exceptional[187] and traditional evangelism increasingly found a few hearers only, the children of members in conservative assemblies continued to be added. The congregations which responded to social changes might have been few, but some of them were the largest in Scotland, giving them a substantial percentage of the total Brethren membership. The innovating churches were obviously well represented in the 1998 Partnership survey, shown by the 54.9 per cent (or twenty-eight congregations) in the sample which had a family service, and it was the presence of these churches which produced an overall increase in membership in the statistics.[188] Small rural assemblies, too, sometimes managed to reverse decline through a bold initiative, such as happened at Strathaven through the reconstituting of the congregation as an Evangelical Church, or at Tillicoultry and Chirnside through the appointment of resident full-time workers.[189] The increased contact with wider Evangelicalism, itself resurgent within the Christian Church, was also a source of renewal for the movement. It lay behind the social concern found among some late twentieth-century Brethren.[190] Given the energy which had often been a marked feature of the movement, it is likely that, despite the problems, many individuals and assemblies will rise to further challenges.

The latent denominationalising tendency within Scottish Brethren was long in being fulfilled. During the period that has been surveyed in the present chapter it had begun to be realised. A significant section of the

---

186. Jonathan Rose, *The Intellectual Life of the British Working Classes* (New Haven, CT, 2001), pp. 11, 455-64; for the earlier Brethren spirituality, see Chpt. 8 *passim*.

187. 'Ebenezer Hall', *'Homework'* (April/May 1989).

188. Cf. the survey for 1992-3 of sixteen innovating churches with an average membership of 130 in Peter Brierley, *Some Scottish Brethren* (London, 1994), p.1, which found that seven had had a five per cent increase in membership, three had seen it decline by a similar amount and the other six had been static.

189. David Shields, 'How we started again', *H*, 71 (March 1992), pp.23-4; H. N. Pope, 'Watch this space', *H*, 73 (October 1993), pp.20-1; writer's collection, I.B.1, Kenneth Brown to the writer, 29 November 1994.

190. David Bebbington, 'The decline and resurgence of Evangelical social concern', in John Wolffe (ed.), *Evangelical Faith and Public Zeal: Evangelicals and society in Britain 1780-1980* (London, 1995), pp.175-97.

movement no longer wished to continue in separation from the wider Evangelical world nor from society and culture. The acceptance of literature by some Brethren, for example, was one consequence of the increasing numbers of professionals.[191] The open emergence of denominationalising tendency, however, had finally been dependent not on any inherent dynamic of sect development, but on wider social changes from which the movement, because of aspects of its ethos, had been able to profit. The acceptance of the Brethren as one more of the denominations of Christianity had been accompanied with a resurgence in the innovative side of the movement. Once more its churches were pioneering appropriate forms of service and congregational patterns. They had seen modest growth, which was against the trend in late twentieth-century Britain. It might have been slight and the innovations achieved slowly, but they had happened nevertheless. Brethren churches of this type displayed the pragmatic and individualistic features which David Martin has claimed are characteristic of the denomination. They adopted utilitarian approaches to organisation and they valued moderation: the congregation did not dominate the life of the individual.[192] These trends provoked a reaction from those who wished to remain in sectarian isolation from church and society. Feelings ran deep on both sides and the polarisation of the late twentieth century among Scottish Brethren was probably irreversible. Only the independency of the movement saved it from a formal split, but one existed *de facto*. The loss of cohesion and the diversity among Brethren might suggest that the concept of one 'movement' might no longer apply.[193] However, the division in the 1990s between conservationist and innovator was but the latest manifestation of the tension between sect and denomination which had marked the Brethren throughout their history.

191. Cf. Valentine Cunningham, *Everywhere Spoken Against: Dissent in the Victorian novel* (Oxford, 1975), p.57.
192. David Martin, 'The denomination', *BJS*, 13 (1962), pp.1-14.
193. Cf. Rowdon, 'Background to Nantwich', pp.139-141.

CHAPTER ELEVEN

Nothing Static: Conclusion

'Time and again in the history of the people of God a similar call has
come when a new advance must be made into the unknown and
unfamiliar, to occupy fresh territory under the leadership of Jesus.
There is nothing static about Him or His cause; to stand still is to fall
behind Him.'
F. F. Bruce, *Commentary on the Epistle to the Hebrews* (1964),
p.404.

In the early 1950s Robert Rendall visited St Andrews where he met David
Melville, a retired stonemason and the mainstay of the small Brethren
assembly for much of the previous half century. In a letter to Ernest
Marwick, the Orcadian journalist and folklorist, Rendall described him:

> he is deeply versed in local history & seems to know every stone about the place,
> besides having (I could see) the respect of his fellow townsmen. I've never met a
> more engaging guide who was warmly human. He recited to me old poems & ballads
> also with evident enjoyment & was enthusiastic on Samuel Rutherford, whose
> house & grave we visited, as well as as [sic] past civic notables of the place. A real
> human man & yet withal a good 'brother'. I wish we had more such![1]

Rendall's description raises several questions about the nature of the
Brethren. Melville could identify with Protestant Evangelical tradition,
Scottish culture and local society; yet the assembly in St Andrews was
small, the preserve of a few. His membership of the Brethren had
evidently allowed him to maintain wide interests and to develop into a
sympathetic human being; yet the rarity of these attributes among
contemporary Scottish Brethren is conceded. Not least among the
ambiguities of the passage is that Rendall was addressing Marwick, a
Presbyterian by upbringing who had converted to Episcopalianism,
simultaneously glossing the Brethren favourably and lamenting their
failures. The movement's relationship to its social and religious contexts
was often complex. The present chapter will attempt to draw together the

---

1. OA, Kirkwall, N21/34/1, Robert Rendall to Ernest Marwick, Sunday night, St
Andrews; (internal evidence shows that this letter was written some time between 1950
and 1956); 'David G. Melville', *W*, 90 (1961), p.275.

central polarities in relation to society of this study—integration and withdrawal, continuity and change, growth and decline—and seek to draw some conclusions.

Integration and Withdrawal

Aspects of the Brethren do not always fit easily into the ideal-type of the sect. B. R. Wilson has used the concept of sectarianism as a measure of the rejection of society by religious groups and their separation from it.[2] The variable relationships the movement had with other churches and society, from an identification with many of their aspects to a rigorous isolation from them, makes it difficult to identify a single degree of Brethren protest. Like the nineteenth-century Quakers, it contained both sectarian and denominationalising tendencies.[3] The study of the movement supports the use of carefully refined models in the analysis of sects.[4] Although the Brethren are a conversionist sect, they also have elements of the introversionist sect which directs attention away from society towards the community of believers, particularly the distinctive values it possesses, and have no special ministerial caste.[5] There was in addition a strong adventism within the movement which encouraged them to withdraw from society. Despite this, the Brethren would not fit Wilson's typology of the adventist sect which elevates understanding of its eschatological teachings above the experience of conversion.[6] The difficulty in categorising the Brethren demonstrates the problems in constructing theoretical models. But it also shows that within the movement there were diverse understandings of its nature and purpose which arose from the emphasis given to the various strands of its doctrine.[7]

---

2. Brian R. Wilson, *Sects and Society: a sociological study of three religious groups in Britain* (London, 1961), p.326; *idem*, 'An analysis of sect-development', in *idem* (ed.), *Patterns of Sectarianism* (London, 1967), pp.23-4; *idem*, *Religious Sects* (London, 1970), pp.7, 26-8.

3. Elizabeth A. Isichei, 'From sect to denomination in English Quakers', in Wilson (ed.), *Patterns of Sectarianism*, pp.161-81; E. A. Isichei, *Victorian Quakers* (Oxford, 1970), pp.10-24, 280.

4. See above, p.20.

5. Wilson, 'An analysis', in *idem* (ed.), *Patterns of Sectarianism*, pp.28-9.

6. *Ibid.*, pp.27-8.

7. Wilson, 'Introduction', *idem* (ed.), *Patterns of Sectarianism*, pp.13-4, notes that the Brethren 'tolerate some diversity both in doctrine and local practice' having as the basis of association 'a common acceptance of scriptural life'. However, this is to state the matter from the point of view of the more open tendency; as will have been evident, not all within the Open Brethren would accept this statement of their position.

It is the variegated nature of the Brethren which makes them difficult to generalise about. Their variety was reinforced by them not developing any organisation for the regulation of affairs among assemblies, a product of their belief in the proximity of second advent and a quasi-mystical conception of the Church.[8] They did not even adopt a credal statement to which members must subscribe.[9] This independency ensured there would be considerable disparities between different geographical regions and also a range of views and practices across the entire movement.[10] It also meant that diversity could be absorbed without producing schism. If disagreement did arise, quarrels were localised without involving the entire movement in the dispute.[11] The only large-scale schism to occur was the result of the push for greater regulation through more institutionalised procedures.[12] The Churches of God separatists were quick to point out that those who abhorred 'loose' practices merely avoided association with those practising them and did not seek a formal split. The secession of the new body became one further reason for not developing central organisations as individuals wanted to avoid the imputation of importing 'Needed Truth' doctrine. The Open Brethren did not become a single unified entity, but remained a movement. Discussion of it must be differentiated and nuanced.

Evangelicalism, in common with other strands within Christianity, has had a constant tension between isolation and integration.[13] Within Brethrenism disengagement from Church and society was marked and is most usually attributed to its premillennial dispensationalism, a form of adventism in which withdrawal from religious and secular communities is strong.[14] However, also of significance was the conversionism which Brethren inherited from nineteenth-century revivalism. It magnified individual salvation above the redemption of society to such an extent that the latter disappeared from vision. Such revivalism promoted separatism.[15] During periods of growth sustained by the awakenings, sectarianism intensified. The Churches of God separation arose during

---

8. See above, p.158.

9. Wilson, 'Introduction', *idem* (ed.), *Patterns of Sectarianism*, pp.13-4. There were, however, some assemblies which had a list of their beliefs in their constitution; see above, p.315.

10. For an example, see F. F. Bruce, *In Retrospect: remembrance of things past* (London and Glasgow, 1980), pp.7-11.

11. W. Blair Neatby, *A History of the Plymouth Brethren*, 1st edn (London [1901]), p.325.

12. See above, pp.158-69.

13. For a contemporary example, cf. Paul A. Bramadat, *The Church on the World's Turf: an evangelical group at a secular university* (Oxford, 2000).

14. See above, pp.264-5.

15. See above, pp.69-70, 89.

the greatest percentage increase in Brethren membership and there was increased sectarianism after the post-World War I growth.[16] The need to educate and discipline large numbers of new converts and to resist the uniformity of the movement being eroded by them, brought an increased stress on Brethren distinctives and led to a search for a more rigorous formulation of them. Its corollary was that schism accompanied expansion as formerly concealed disagreements became evident when individuals accentuated different strands within the movement.[17] However, since the mid-1960s—a period of overall decline—emphasis on the distinctiveness of the sect has been a product of the perceived internal threat to its identity;[18] and the perception of external threats could also lie behind sectarian intensification in earlier periods, as happened, it was argued above, during the Fundamentalist agitation of the inter-war period.[19] Although for certain personality types intensifying autism had an attraction, introversion did not increase by any internal dynamic in sectarianism. It was produced by the action of historical circumstances on principles which the movement inherited from its original religious environment.

There was a continuing strand of engagement with Church and society in the Brethren. The birth of the movement through nondenominational revivalism was of significance here. The acceptance of conservative Evangelical theology meant that the separatism of the most rigorous was modified. Even when they despised its churches, they read its preachers' books.[20] There always was an awareness of a wider Christian world. The early ecumenical vision of unity on the basis of shared life in Christ outside denominational boundaries was deeply embedded in Brethren thinking. It was because conversion not doctrine—'life not light'—was regarded as the test of fellowship that no credal test was adopted. Those of a sectarian tendency subtly altered the formula to make it an exclusive one, but its inclusive potential was maintained or continually being revived. The continuity with Evangelicalism was a significant denominationalising force within the Brethren.[21] Not that the traffic here was all one way. The movement continued to have an influence on conservative Evangelicalism out of all proportion to its size. The piety of the former isolated it from wider secular and religious trends preserving Fundamentalist emphases which constantly reinvigorated the latter

---

16. See above, Chpts 4 and 6.
17. See above, pp.117-18, 198-9.
18. See above, p.352.
19. See above, pp.227-38.
20. See above, pp.7-8.
21. Cf., Wilson, 'An analysis', in *idem* (ed.), *Patterns of Sectarianism*, p.30.

particularly after World War II.[22] Another denominationalising tendency was conversionism as contact had to be maintained with potential recruits. Consequently, the Open Brethren never adopted extreme forms of separation, such as that eventually adopted by the main body of British Exclusive Brethren.[23] The enduring importance of evangelism also ensured that 'preaching the gospel' would offer another polarity from the introversionist stress on 'church truth'. A similar pull was exercised by an emphasis on Christian ethics as opposed to ecclesiastical purity.[24] These strands within Brethrenism enabled its adherents to identify sympathetically with Christians outside the movement. They also sympathised with aspects of the British state which additionally enabled Brethren members to associate with many of its aspirations. They were in favour of strong civil government, and many found much to admire in British society. These factors were probably most evident during World War I when even those who argued for conscientious objection to fighting did not question the right of the state to pursue its war aims.[25] The Brethren were not uniformly marked by withdrawal.

Some managed to achieve a remarkable degree of integration with their communities and came to be accepted as its representative individuals.[26] The Brethren did not encourage a missionary engagement with culture—their faith generally encouraged its rejection, not its transformation.[27] For figures such as David Beattie and John Borland mediation between faith and culture was probably provided by the literary Kailyard, with its Christian roots and its idealisation of the Scottish peasantry.[28] It enabled them to feel they were obeying the Pauline injunction to think on things that were true, pure, and of good report.[29] Robert Rendall rejected the sentimentality of the Kailyard nor, despite his affinities with it, did he look for inspiration to the contemporary Scottish Literary Renaissance, with its modernist origins and antipathy to Evangelicalism, but drew on 'the perennial urge in man's heart towards a life in the country' encouraged by Georgian and

---

22. For a similar point about premillennialism, cf. D. W. Bebbington, 'The advent hope in British Evangelicalism since 1800', *Scottish Journal of Religious Studies*, 9 (1988), p.110.

23. See above, pp.3-4.

24. See above, pp.274, 282-3.

25. See above, pp.316-17.

26. For one of the most remarkable interactions between a Scottish missionary and a non-Western culture, see Dan Crawford, *Thinking Black: 22 years without a break in the long grass of Central Africa* (London, 1912).

27. For these motifs in Christian history, see H. Richard Niebuhr, *Christ and Culture* (London, 1952), pp.58-92, 192-228.

28. See above, pp.229, 249, 324.

29. Phil. 4:8.

classical poetry.[30] The influences from popular and high culture gave these individuals a way of perceiving Scotland—in many ways a premodern Scotland before its invasion by contemporary hostile forces—which highlighted areas common to faith and Scottish culture and that allowed integration with the latter. A denominationalising tendency was also a consequence of geography. Those individuals who engaged in interdenominational cooperation or the affairs of society or their local culture, tended to be found in cities or remoter areas. Nondenominational revivalism flourished in the city, and often these individuals belonged to its middle classes, while in some rural areas society was more homogeneous and the protest against it was milder. However, moderate sectarianism was a feature of the movement in general. Although it certainly displayed withdrawal, it avoided the more extreme measures of isolation and in this regard is a typical British sect.[31] The largest such body in Scotland for much of the twentieth century, it reflected the temperate nature of the community in which it subsisted.[32]

Continuity and Change

Identification with Evangelicalism and with aspects of culture and society gave the Brethren continuity with their religious and secular background. This continuity was evident in something as seemingly remote from the setting as Brethren spirituality.[33] Yet because of the withdrawal from Church and society, a convert entering the movement was probably more aware of the change from his former life.[34] Alteration also marked Brethrenism over its history. Successive phases can be detected: the pre-1859 Bowesite movement, the expanding body after the mid-nineteenth century revivals, the established sect of the later nineteenth and early twentieth centuries, and the post-1960s renovations. The changing roles offered to women demonstrate how marked these successive phases were.[35] Change within the movement often tended to be in a sectarian direction. The presectarian Bowesite phase, recapitulated in the aftermath of the awakenings of the 1860s, was surpassed by an intensification of

---

30. Robert Rendall, dustjacket flyleaf of *Country Sonnets and Other Poems* (Kirkwall, 1946); see also, Neil Dickson, 'Robert Rendall: a life', in idem (ed.), *An Island Shore: selected writings of Robert Rendall* (Kirkwall, 1990), pp.17-49.

31. Wilson, *Sects and Society*, p.2.

32. This generalisation could be modified by examining the Brethren regionally: perhaps the more rigid Lanarkshire and west Fife Brethren reflected less temperate industrial and social relations.

33. See above, Chpt 8 *passim*.

34. However, an Evangelical proselyte might be less conscious of change.

35. See above, pp.74-7, 151-3, 243-6, 356-8.

sectarianism in the later nineteenth century. The secession of the Churches of God was because of the desire for increased sectarianism.[36] But, as the lament of J. R. Caldwell hankering after the earlier nondenominational phase showed,[37] the balance had also shifted within the Open Brethren. Those who wished to maintain the initial presectarian condition had been successfully resisted. In the second quarter of the twentieth century there was further intensification of sectarianism. The things that those who called for an increased purity were objecting to, such as interdenominationalism or the acceptance of newer evangelistic forms adopted from contemporary Evangelicalism, showed that they were resisting a potentially denominationalising tendency. Those who were in favour of increased sectarianism within the various types of Brethren appealed to the movement's first principles and saw themselves as being in continuity with them. Institutionalisation proceeded, not through the adoption of structures, but by a firmer application of doctrine and ideology. Within the Brethren change often meant increasing rigidity rather than increasing flexibility.[38]

The development of the movement was produced by both external circumstances acting on it and the necessity for internal organisation. Novel patterns and ideas were accepted in the early years of the movement, some of which arose out of the fresh light that it thought it had discovered in scripture. This new interpretation was itself the product of the cultural and religious background out of which the movement had grown, and other novel practices and attitudes of the Brethren can be directly traced to this setting.[39] After the initial creative burst, however, innovation was not welcomed. The emergence of a reified social order having an apparently objective existence as part of the nature of things made innovation difficult to justify.[40] It was continuity with the Brethren past that was stressed. Both the denominationalising tendency and the sectarian one found support for its case in history; both used the text 'Holding fast the faithful word'.[41] The fixed understanding of scripture which the appeal to this particular text and others like it demonstrated showed how difficult change was for all forms of Brethren.[42] When first principles are perceived as being divinely given, modification is

---

36. See above, pp.158-69.

37. See above, pp.172-3, 180-1.

38. Cf. Isichei, 'English Quakerism', p.161.

39. See above, pp.69-73.

40. Cf. Peter L. Berger and Thomas Luckmann, *The Social Construction of Reality: a treatise in the sociology of knowledge* (1966), Penguin edn (Harmondsworth, 1967), pp.65-109.

41. See above, p.183 n.293.

42. See above, pp.176-80.

impossible.[43] Brethren ideology also reinforced resistance to innovation. In the late nineteenth and early twentieth centuries optimism in human capabilities was high, giving birth to liberal theology in the mainline denominations. The Brethren belonged to a popular groundswell which felt pessimistic about society's direction, and the notion of progress was regarded with hostility. In addition, the mindset of Brethren, with its roots—albeit very long ones—in Scottish Common Sense philosophy led to a delight in categorisation of doctrine and practice which inhibited innovation.[44] The movement had a predisposition towards conservation.

The exception in much of this inherent caution was evangelism. The need to keep in contact with potential recruits meant that change was more readily accepted here than in any other area. The Brethren had kept organisation to a minimum, but the need to organise for evangelism eroded open gospel meetings and allowed inter-assembly committees to emerge.[45] Apart from the Stewards Trust, the central institutions which the Brethren developed, HFMF and SCEM, were for foreign mission and evangelism respectively.[46] Continuous social alterations in the twentieth century shifted attitudes to change. The emergence of increasing pragmatic innovations after the 1960s demonstrated how the denominationalising tendency had been strengthened, but this trend did not unfold as a necessity of sect development. It is as Brethren members shared in the general prosperity of post-war Scotland, and found themselves able to take advantage of it because of factors contained in their ethos, that accommodation to society increased. However, it should be noted that this process was not uniform and many whose socio-economic position had improved still displayed sectarian features. The alterations had again been most readily undertaken in evangelism, but they began to affect other areas of assembly life. Those who innovated often did not see themselves in continuity with the Brethren past but identified their church as one within the wider Evangelical world, something that those who disagreed with them concurred. Brethren denominational potential was long in being fulfilled, dependent finally on societal trends. The late-twentieth century movement underwent profound changes which raised difficulties over continuity.[47]

43. Wilson, 'Introduction', in *Patterns of Sectarianism*, p.11
44. See above, pp.265, 271.
45. See above, pp.143-4.
46. For the Stewards Trust, see above, p.315, for HFMF, see above, pp.144-5, and for SCEM, see above, pp.335-6.
47. John Allan, '"A new shape, though unformed"', in Kevin G. Dyer, *Must Brethren Churches Die?* (Exeter, 1991), pp.7-21.

Growth and Decline

By the early twentieth century the Brethren were pervasive enough within Scottish society to turn up in novelistic backgrounds as diverse as an Orkney agricultural fair or the churchgoers of Montrose.[48] The popular nature of their piety often made them appear comic, even to themselves.[49] It became the subject of criticism by writers commenting on Scottish society: the domination of their life by the assembly; the rigid division of humanity into the saved and the damned; their hell-fire preaching and fissiparous nature; the drabness of their abstemiousness; their peculiarities which were forced on the young; and their repression of the individual.[50] They became a by-word for religious oddity or awkwardness. In his autobiography Eric Linklater described an eccentric neighbour and Brethren member, Billy Pin-Leg, famed for his meanness among the generous Orcadians.[51] The Brethren member in A. A. Thomson's novelistic portrait of Yorkshire small-town life who resists the installation of an organ in the assembly and refuses to return when he loses, is a Scotsman.[52] These rebellious personality types were not alone: they were attracted by the relative autonomy of action which the movement gave them and they became a further cause of the numerous schisms.[53]

---

48. Eric Linklater, *White Maa's Saga* (1929) Penguin edn (Harmondsworth, 1963), p.85; Willa Muir, *Imagined Corners* (1935) Cannongate edn (Edinburgh, 1987)), p.67.

49. For examples, see Bruce, *In Retrospect*, pp..23-4; Tom Morton, *Red Guitars in Heaven* (Edinburgh, 1994), pp.26-42, 55-75.

50. For this list, see respectively: J. M. Porteous, *Brethren in the Keelhowes*, 6th edn (London, 1876), p.136; Molly Hunter, *A Sound of Chariots* (New York, 1972; London, 1973); Christopher Rush, 'Me and my St Monans', in *Peace Comes Dropping Slow* (Edinburgh, 1983), p.7; William McIlvanney, *A Gift From Nessus* (1968) Mainstream edn (Edinburgh, 1990), pp.60-1; Morton, *Red Guitars*; William McIlvanney, *The Kiln* (London, 1996), pp.180-1.

51. Eric Linklater, *The Man On My Back* (London, 1941), p.11. 'Billy Pin-Leg' was Billy Robertson, a member of the Harray Open Brethren assembly who was regarded by his fellow members as an eccentric and whose contributions in the morning meeting were often felt to be tiresome. After one such occasion, when a piece of plaster fell from the hall roof narrowly missing him, it was humorously seen as a judgement: oral information, August, 1989, from an Orkney assembly member; see also the encounter, apparently with the English Brethren preacher Robert Broadbent described in H. V. Morton, *In Scotland Again* (London, 1933), pp.91-4; cf. [William Cochrane], *Excerpt from Mr. H. V. Morton's Book, entitled 'in Scotland Again' Re Mr. R. Broadbent, Evangelist. With copy of letter sent by Mr. W. Cochrane, Newmilns, and letter of acknowledgement from Mr. H. V. Morton* (n.p., n.d.).

52. A. A. Thomson, *The Exquisite Burden* (1935), rpt, (London, 1962), pp.185-199.

53. Cf. the experience of two itinerants in Scotland, G. H. Lang, *An Ordered Life* (London, 1959), pp.176-7; and James G. Hutchinson, *Something of My Life: whose I*

Other criticisms were levelled at the Brethren. There was the boredom that the young felt during lengthy meetings. The poet William Montgomerie, son of a Vernalite Churches of God evangelist, described the breaking of bread of his boyhood:

> together we watch the cover glass
> sweat over the wine
> and drip
> twice every weary hour[54]

There were those within it who criticised facets of the movement.[55] Perhaps, given the restrictions placed on their activities for much of its history, many women found some of its aspects constricting.[56] But whether Brethrenism could assist individual growth was most acute for those facing change in their own lives. Despite the hesitations of Mary Gibson, the prospective missionary, over her romance with A. J. Cronin, she eventually gave up her ambition and in 1922 married him.[57] In *Shannon's Way* Cronin has the character whose situation corresponds to hers come to a crisis during which she realises that the Brethren worldview is too narrow in not embracing Roman Catholics. She asks if God intended 'that one should live in the darkness of lies, and the other in the light of truth? If so, Christianity was meaningless.'[58] Her faith is broadened. Before the 1980s the best known of those who left was William Blane, the hymnwriter.[59] After his emigration in 1883 to South Africa he helped establish the assembly in Johannesburg and became a highly successful manager in the goldmines.[60] He found the country a place of 'strange new temptations'[61] and later a much-loved daughter died. His poems hint darkly at aridity and alienation.[62] When he returned

am, and whom I serve Acts 27:23 (Glasgow, 1997), p.103; cf., Wilson, *Sects and Society*, p.352.

54. William Montgomerie, 'Breaking of Bread', in *idem, From Time to Time: selected poems* (Edinburgh, 1985), p.11.

55. See above, pp.282-3.

56. See above, pp.153, 244-5, 356-7.

57. See above, pp.219-20; Elizabeth Robertson, 'Doctor despair', 6 July 1996, *The Herald Weekend Extra*, p.10.

58. A. J. Cronin, *Shannon's Way* (1948), NEL edn (London, 1979), p.287.

59. See above, pp.279, 280.

60. *The Weekly Supplement for Galston, Newmilns Darvel and Hurlford*, 14 January 1883; 'James Goch', *W*, 64 (1934), p.48; J. S. Borland, 'Humble Galston boy won fame as engineer: a tribute to William Blane', *Irvine Valley Times*, 28 May 1964, p.6.

61. William Blane, 'Returning by the book', *W*, 22 (1892), p.132; cf. *idem*, 'South Africa' *BP*, 5 (January 1884), pp.8-11.

62. Cf. *idem*, 'The Silent Land: a Dream', in *The Silent Land and Other Poems* (London, 1906), pp.1-13.

to Britain in 1911 he did not rejoin the Brethren, and it would appear he had become a believer in a Tennysonian wider hope.[63] His poetry shows that the experience of leaving was difficult, as it was for many others.[64] Abandoning the security of the sect was often a painful step in self-development.

Whatever might have been true for individuals, however, the Brethren did attain considerable popularity within Scotland. Despite the prohibitions, women composed the majority of the membership and evidently a number of them joined without the imposition of male authority, being either single or having husbands who were not members.[65] If the Brethren had been as completely destructive of fulfilment as the critics suggested, it is hard to see why they achieved substantial numerical strength or won respect within their communities. However, the extent of Brethren membership must not be exaggerated. If the calculation of 30,000 members in 1933 (one of their years of maximum strength) is accepted as accurate,[66] then at that point they comprised only some 1.95 per cent of all Protestant church members[67] and some 0.62 of the Scottish population.[68] Nevertheless, their growth and wider influence through Sunday schools and children's meetings lends support to the growing body of evidence that working-class adherence to religion has been seriously underestimated.[69] Both ideological and socio-economic factors were important for this growth. The nineteenth-century Protestant churches attempted to re-Christianise Scotland, and the initial growth of the Brethren was due to the crusade promoted by them. Revivalism entered deeply into the soul of Brethrenism. It became a movement directed towards expansion. Evangelicalism has from its inception contained an international dimension, and in nineteenth-century revivalism were transmitted currents in popular

---

63. *Idem*, "'These Three'", in *The Verse of William Blane* (Oxford, 1937), p.92; [W. Hoste], 'The Verse of William Blane, C.B.E.', *BM*, 46 (1937), p.272.

64. William Blane, 'The Castaway' , in *Silent Land*, pp.42-3.

65. See above, p.296.

66. See above, p.196 n.104 for discussion of this figure.

67. This calculation is based on figures given in David P. Thomson, *The Scottish Churches' Handbook* (Dunfermline, 1933), supplemented by more accurate figures, where available, in Robert Currie, Alan D. Gilbert and Lee Horsley, *Churches and Churchgoers: patterns of religious growth in the British isles since 1700* (Oxford, 1977); if the estimated Roman Catholic population in 1934 is included (none is available for 1933), then the percentage of Brethren members becomes 1.39 per cent of all orthodox Christian church members.

68. Based on size of the Scottish population in 1931, Michael Flinn (ed.), *Scottish Population History from the 17th Century to the 1930s* (Cambridge, 1977), p.302. Table 5.1.1.

69. For the literature, see above pp.21-2 ns 112 and 113.

ideology which were transatlantic in scope.[70] The Brethren in Scotland were a product of trends which drew the Scottish churches into a wider British religious life.[71] The emergent movement expressed a greater faith in lay agency, a zeal for restored communities and a heightened supernaturalism which were contained within nineteenth-century religious life.[72] The movement grew best where change had undermined traditional social controls most, and this largely meant industrialised communities (see Maps 7-13). Change allowed new ideas to penetrate society and it also provoked a flight towards a new meaning and security for life. Both factors produced Brethren growth. The pattern of that growth supports the model developed by Callum Brown.[73] The major period of increase for the movement was the late nineteenth century with Brethren advancement slowing against that of the population probably in the mid-1890s.[74] Absolute growth peaked in the mid-1930s, but serious decline did not set in for another thirty years.[75] Within the general pattern smaller peaks and troughs can be detected: surges in additions during 1845-51 and 1920-5, and some declension due to emigration before World War I.[76] Although internal factors of the movement were behind this growth pattern, its correspondence with that of other Protestant churches in Scotland demonstrates that external societal factors operated on the Brethren in common with other Christian bodies. As a conversionist sect, they were not isolated from trends affecting religious adherence.

---

70. Richard Carwardine, *Transatlantic Revivalism: popular Evangelicalism in Britain and America, 1790-1865* (Westport, CT, 1978); John Kent, *Holding the Fort: studies in Victorian revivalism* (London, 1978); Bernard Aspinwall, *Portable Utopias: Glasgow and the United States 1820-1920* (Aberdeen, 1984); *idem*, 'Hands Across the Sea: the english speaking transatlantic religious world (1820-1920) *Hispania Sacra*, 40 (1988), pp.853-66; *idem*, 'The Scottish religious identity in the Atlantic World 1880-1914', in Stewart Mews (ed.), *SCH*, 18 (1982), pp.505-18; Mark Noll, David W. Bebbington, George A. Rawlyk (eds), *Evangelicalism: comparative studies of popular Protestantism in North America, the British Isles, and beyond 1700-1990* (New York, 1994); George A. Rawlyk and Mark A. Noll (eds), *Amazing Grace : Evangelicalism in Australia, Britain, Canada, and the United States* (Montreal, 1994); T. C. F. Stunt, *From Awakening to Secession: radical evangelicals in Switzerland and Britain 1815-35* (Edinburgh, 2000); Janice Holmes, *Religious Revivals in Britain and Ireland 1859-1905* (Dublin, 2000); for the eighteenth century see W. R. Ward, *The Protestant Evangelical Awakening* (Cambridge, 1993).

71. Brown, *Social History of Religion in Scotland*, pp.14-9; cf., D. W. Bebbington, 'Religion and national feeling in nineteenth-century Wales and Scotland', in Stuart Mews (ed.), *SCH*, 18 (Oxford, 1982), pp, 489-503.

72. See above, Chpt, 2 *passim*, pp.72-3, 94-5.

73. For the literature, see Brown's works listed above, p.22 ns 113, 114.

74. See above, p.131.

75. See above, pp.216-7.

76. See above, pp.47-53, 131-3, 185-91.

One further cause of Brethren growth is the manner in which aspects of the movement correlated with the communities of Lowland Scotland. The Bowesite movement was a democratised Christianity, rejecting secular and religious and establishments, empowering ordinary people and longing for a transformed order.[77] The later Brethren movement was also the expression of a more demotic faith, and it was a modernising force, reflecting the new nineteenth-century order of mass democracy. However, eventual fear of the emergent political system, which seemed about to unleash anarchy to Brethren eyes, made their apolitical stance a fundamentally conservative one.[78] The rejection of politics also meant that they failed to develop a social critique, although members such as James Barbour and Sir John Henderson attempted on an individual level to ameliorate the conditions of the working classes.[79] However, the separatism of the movement, its remoteness from centres of power, and extreme independency did not make it amenable to political control. Instead the movement continued to reflect aspirations of the lower-middle and working classes. It promoted values which made individuals productive members of their society, supported community equability, and assisted individual development. It aided the stability of British society. The Brethren appealed to individuals with longings for autonomy and self-improvement. It was among them that the movement grew rather than the indigent, and in turn it provided opportunity for their self-development. This appeal can be seen in Brethren eschatology. Although an element of chilialism as the disinherited of society seeking compensation in a future where they became rulers might occasionally be detected in Brethren views, it primarily had an ideological function for them. It provided its exponents with a total system by which to understand society and gave almost endless scope for intellectual exploration and speculation. It was as a system of meaning, not compensation, that it appealed.[80] The pronounced streak of cerebralism in Brethren spirituality, fuelled by the productions of their publishers, gave ample scope to the Scottish desire for self-improvement through learning, although their piety ensured that such learning was usually of a strictly religious character. The movement belonged to the lower-middle and more prosperous working classes and it continued aspects of their culture. Its early gospel halls, especially, the self-built ones, qualify as John Betjeman's 'true architecture of the people',[81] and the social life of

---

77. See above, Chpt 3, *passim*.

78. See above, pp.317-18.

79. See above, pp.322-4.

80. See above, pp.305-9.

81. John Betjeman, 'Nonconformist architecture', *The Architectural Review*, 88 (1940), pp.161-174.

assemblies reflected that of the groups to which they belonged.[82] Their ethos cultivated a form of individual growth that continued features of the social strata in which it flourished. The conjunction between Brethren culture and that of Lowland communities partly explains the growth of the movement.

This conjunction was probably not unique to Scotland, but most likely in many respects characterised Brethren in other industrial areas of Britain and Northern Ireland.[83] Nevertheless, the regionalism of the movement ensured that in Scotland it did possess its own flavour, as difficult to define as Scottishness itself, but which possibly included its love of precise argumentation, the passion with which opinions were held and opposed, and the vigour with which religious duty was pursued.[84] However, the strict behavioural boundaries set by Brethrenism always made the movement's growth self-limiting within Scotland at any point in its history. After the 1960s membership fell sharply. Psychologically, in a movement whose mechanisms are designed to produce recruitment, the declension created frustrations which Brethren of all shades of opinion could be found expressing. There are, however, problems specific to the different wings of the movement. The change in the conditions of society from those in which the movement flourished creates a difficulty for those who wish to conserve traditional patterns. The continuity which the Brethren showed with their environment was what made them successful within it. The contemporary conservative assemblies, however, do not find any clear correspondence between the values latent in their practices and their social setting. This makes recruitment difficult. As they become smaller sectarianism has intensified as identity is threatened. The danger is that ossification will lead to terminal decline.[85] There are also obstacles for those who wish to innovate. Their churches are the products of cultural and social forces which are either obsolete or from which they have become isolated through social mobility. The dilemma for them is how to transmute into new forms which are authentic expressions of their members' lives— although in the process they may have ceased to be Brethren. The future of the movement is uncertain. Whatever course events take, they will continue to show a complex interplay with a constantly shifting culture and society which has been the mark of Scottish Brethren history.

---

82. See above, p.325.

83. Unfortunately the absence of social history of the Brethren in general and studies of the movement in south Wales, northern England and Northern Ireland do not make it possible to make a fruitful comparison.

84. These characteristics may also be true of the Brethren in Northern Ireland, which has a strong Ulster Scots component.

85. Cf. Wilson, 'Introduction' in *idem* (ed.), *Patterns of Sectarianism*, p.11.

APPENDIX 1
Figures

Figure 3.1. **Brethren Growth 1859-70**

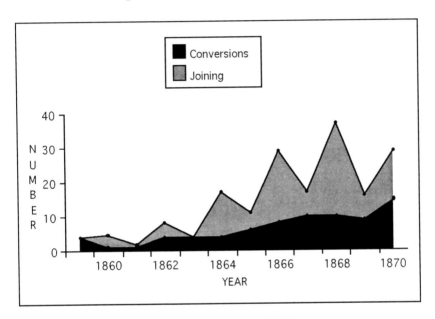

Source: 'With Christ', *The Witness*, 33-108 (1903-78).

Figure *3.2.* **The growth of three Lanarkshire assemblies 1862-71**

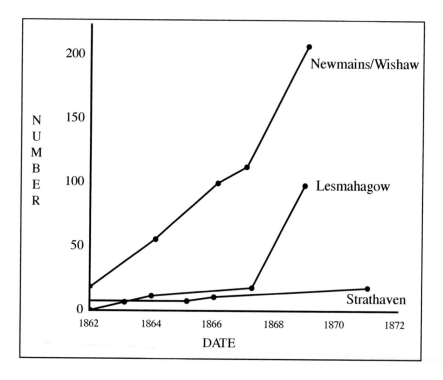

Sources: *The Truth Promoter*; 'List of the Members of the Strathaven Brethren'; writer's collection, I.M.28., untitled history of Ebenezer Gospel Hall, Wishaw, photocopy of MS, n.d.

Figure 4.1. **Lesmahagow Gospel Hall, growth 1876-1891: gross membership with net gains and losses through lapse in membership**

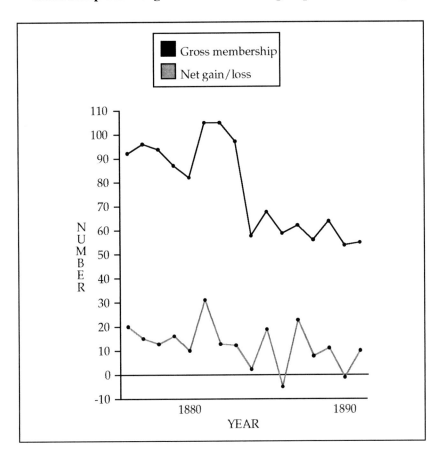

Source: Gospel Hall, Lesmahagow, roll book 1876-1907.

Figure 4.2. Brethren growth 1871-91

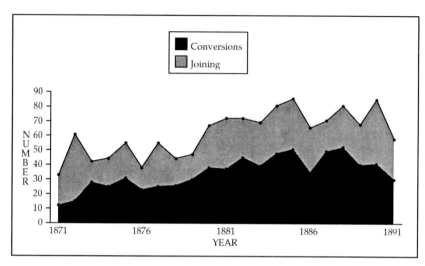

Source: 'With Christ', *The Witness*, 33-108 (1903-78).

Figure 4.3. Brethren growth 1892-1914

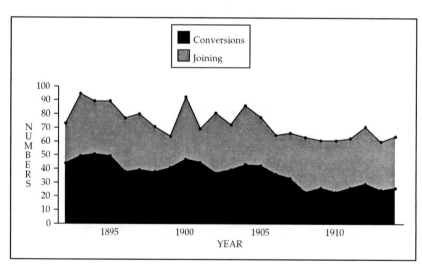

Source: 'With Christ', *The Witness*, 33-108 (1903-78).

Figure 4.4. **Lesmahagow Gospel Hall, growth 1892-1914: gross membership growth against net gains and losses through lapses in membership**

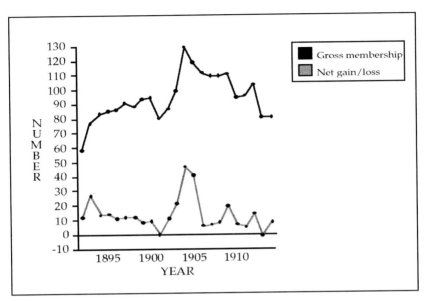

Source: Hope Hall, Lesmahagow, Gospel Hall roll books, 1876-1907 & 1908-29.

Figure 4.5 Elim Hall, Crosshill, Glasgow, 1890-1914: membership

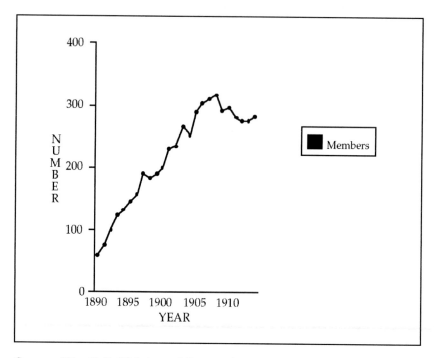

Source: *Elim Hall, 98th Annual Report, 1st January to 31st December, 1981* (n.p. [1981]).

Figure 4.6. Plan for Gospel Hall, Kirkintilloch, 1897

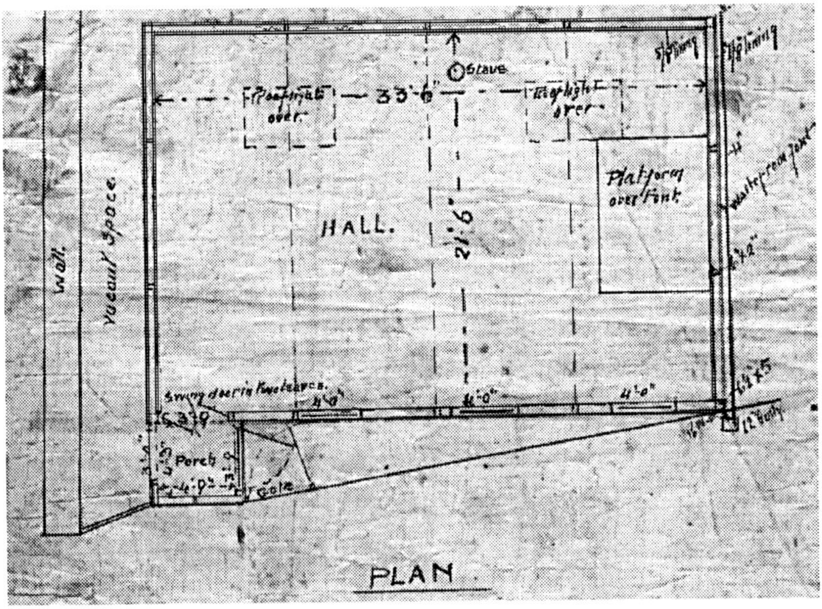

Source: Writer's collection, I.G.3.(ii), drawings by John Shanks, 'Proposed meeting house for Christian Brethren at East High Street', November 1897.

Figure 6.1. Brethren growth 1914-39

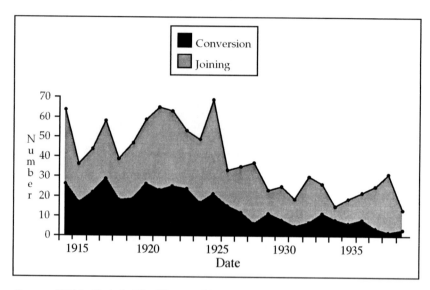

Source: 'With Christ', *The Witness*, 33-108 (1903-78).

Figure 6.2. The growth of four assemblies: Elim Hall, Glasgow, 1914-39; Gospel Hall, Kilbirnie, Ayrshire 1914-39; Gospel Hall, Newmains, Lanarkshire, 1923-39; Gospel Hall, Newmilns, Ayrshire, 1919-39

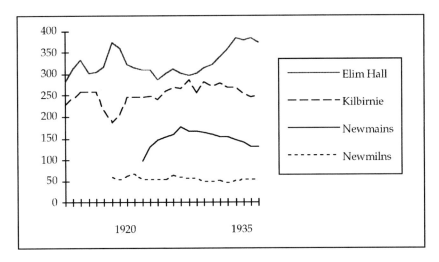

Sources: *Elim Hall 5 Prince Edward Street Crosshill Glasgow 60th Annual Report 1st January to 31st December, 1949* (Glasgow [1949]), [p.12]; Kilbirnie roll books, 1913-15, 1916, 1919-21, 1925-6, 1928-30, 1931-3, 1934-6, 1937-40; 'Minutes of Half-Yearly and Annual Meetings of Gospel Hall Newmains', 1923-51; 'Assembly Register of Believers Meeting in the Name of the Lord Jesus Christ in Drygate Street Gospel Hall Newmilns', 1907-1933; Sam Hill, untitled summary of membership of Gospel Hall, Newmilns, 1929-51, MS notes.

Figure 6.3. Membership of six assemblies: Elim Hall, Glasgow, 1939-65;
Central Hall, Kilmarnock, 1939-65; Gospel Hall, Kilbirnie, 1939-62;
Gospel Hall, Newmains, 1939-65; Gospel Hall, Newmilns, 1939-55; Hope
Hall, Lesmahagow, 1950-65

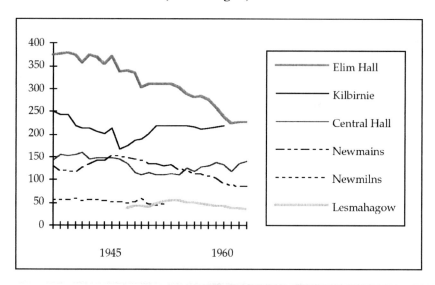

Sources: *Elim Hall 5 Prince Edward Street Crosshill Glasgow 108th Annual
Report 1st January to 31st December, 1949* (Glasgow [1991]), [p.12]; Central
Hall, Kilmarnock, 'Minutes of Annual Business Meeting', 1932-1989; Gospel
Hall, Kilbirnie, roll books, 1937-40, 1941-44, 1945-6, 1947-8, 1949-52, 1957-
60, 1961-2; 'Minutes of Half-Yearly and Annual Meetings of Gospel Hall
Newmains', 1923-51; 'Assembly Register of Believers Meeting in the Name
of the Lord Jesus Christ in Drygate Street Gospel Hall Newmilns', 1951-1955;
Sam Hill, untitled summary of membership of Gospel Hall, Newmilns, 1929-
51, MS notes; Hope Hall, Lesmahagow, roll books, 1950-60, 1961-71.

Figure 6.4. **Central Hall, Kilmarnock, 1933**

Source: drawing by Gordon Weir, *c*.1985, Central Evangelical Church, Kilmarnock.

Figure 8.1. **A chart relating eschatology and typology**

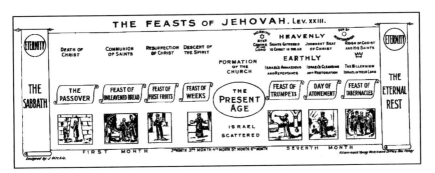

Source: John Ritchie, *The Feasts of Jehovah: bright foreshadowings of grace and glory* (Kilmarnock, 1895).

Figure 9.1. Emigration of Scottish assembly members against Scottish national emigration, 1851-1938 (expressed as a percentage of an eighty-eight- year mean)

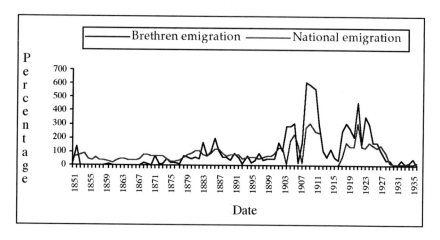

Sources: Marjory Harper, *Emigration from North-East Scotland*, 1 (Aberdeen, 1988), pp.35-6; *The Truth Promoter*, volumes 1-10 (1849-69); *The Witness*, volumes 3-119 (1873-1980); *The Believer's Magazine* volumes 1-107 (1891-1997); Gospel Hall, Kilbirnie roll books, 1903, 1909-16, 1919-21, 1925-6, 1928-62.

Figure 10.1. **Membership of five assemblies 1966-90: Elim Hall/Crosshill Evangelical Church, Glasgow, 1966-90; Central Hall/Central Evangelical Church, Kilmarnock, 1966-90; Gospel Hall, Newmains, 1965-83; Gospel Hall, Newmilns, 1968-90; Gospel Hall, Tillicoultry, 1965-90**

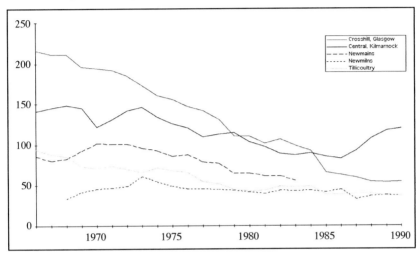

Sources: Crosshill Evangelical Church, Glasgow; Central Evangelical Church, Kilmarnock; Gospel Hall, Newmains; Gospel Hall, Newmilns; and Gospel Hall, Tillicoultry.

Figure 10.2. **Assembly increase/decrease, 1983-98**

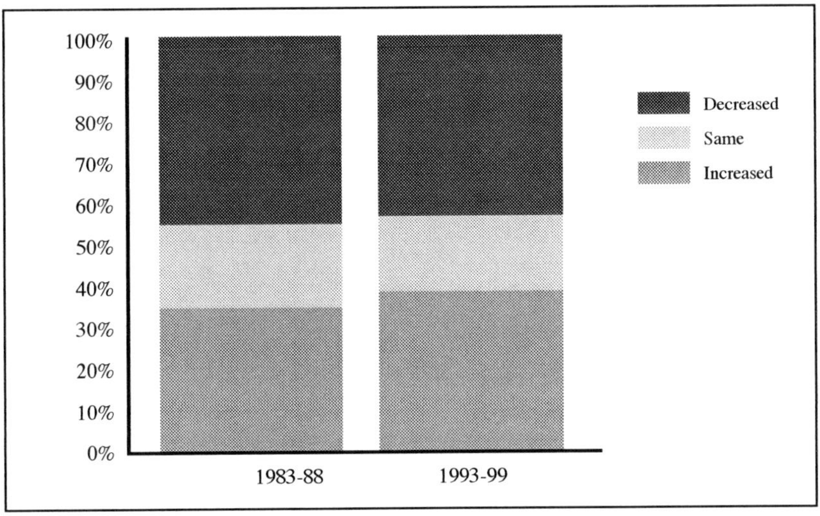

Source: Partnership survey of UK Brethren assemblies (1998).

Figure 10.3. Average assembly gains, 1996-8

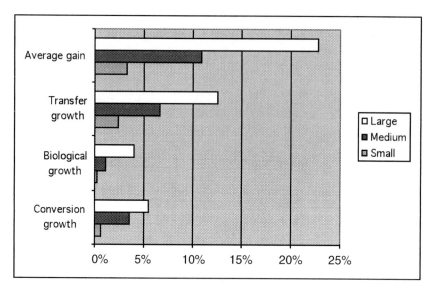

Source: Partnership survey of UK Brethren assemblies (1998).

Figure 10.4. Average assembly losses, 1996-8

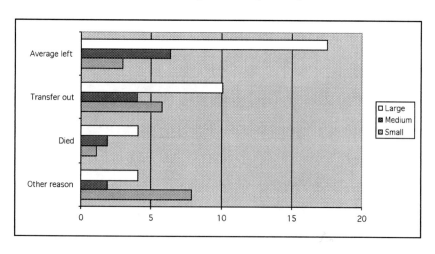

Source: Partnership survey of UK Brethren assemblies (1998).

Figure 10.5. **Evangelical Church, Hamilton, 1968**

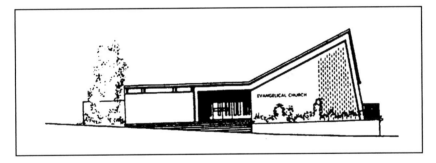

Source: Evangelical Church, Selkirk Street, Hamilton.

Figure 10.6. **Response of former Scottish assembly members in Baptist churches to Nathan DeL. Smith's respondents' reasons for leaving an assembly (USA, 1986)**

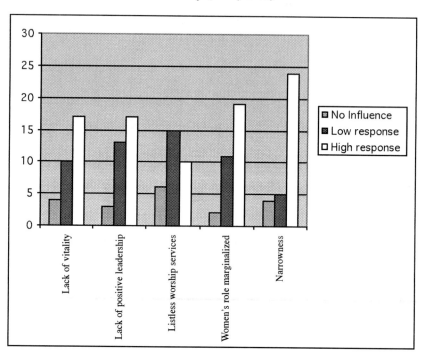

Source: Neil Dickson, 'Brethren and Baptists in Scotland', *BQ*, 33 (October 1990), p.380.

APPENDIX 2
Maps

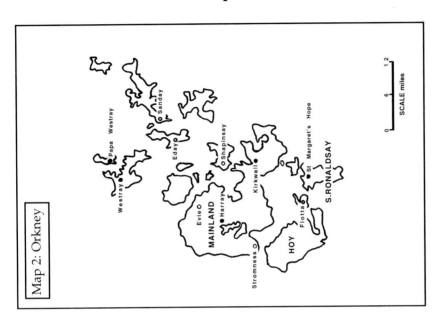

Map 2: Orkney

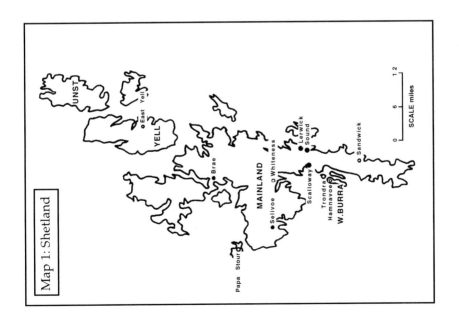

Map 1: Shetland

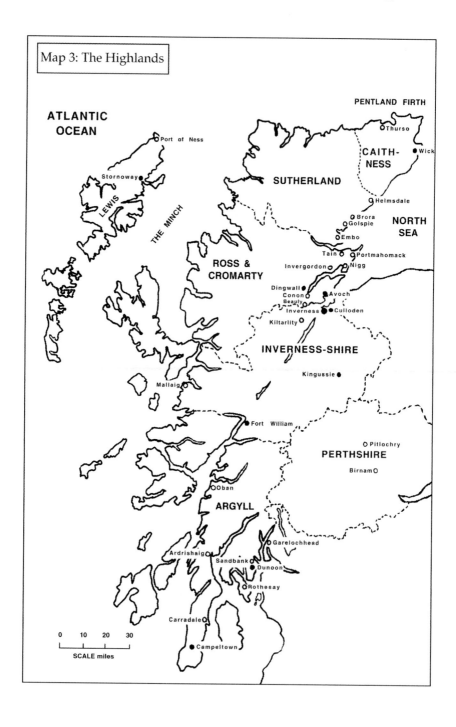

Map 3: The Highlands

ATLANTIC
OCEAN

PENTLAND FIRTH

Port of Ness

Thurso

CAITH-
NESS

Wick

SUTHERLAND

Stornoway

LEWIS

THE MINCH

Helmsdale

Brora
Golspie

Embo

NORTH
SEA

ROSS &
CROMARTY

Tain
Portmahomack

Invergordon
Nigg

Dingwall
Conon
Beauly
Inverness
Kiltarlity

Avoch
Culloden

INVERNESS-SHIRE

Kingussie

Mallaig

Fort William

Pitlochry

PERTHSHIRE

Birnam

Oban

ARGYLL

Garelochhead

Ardrishaig
Sandbank
Dunoon

Rothesay

Carradale

0   10   20   30

SCALE miles

Campeltown

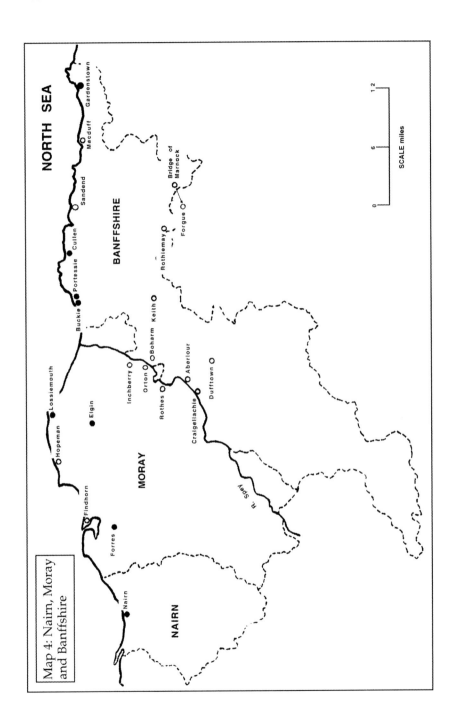

Map 4: Nairn, Moray and Banffshire

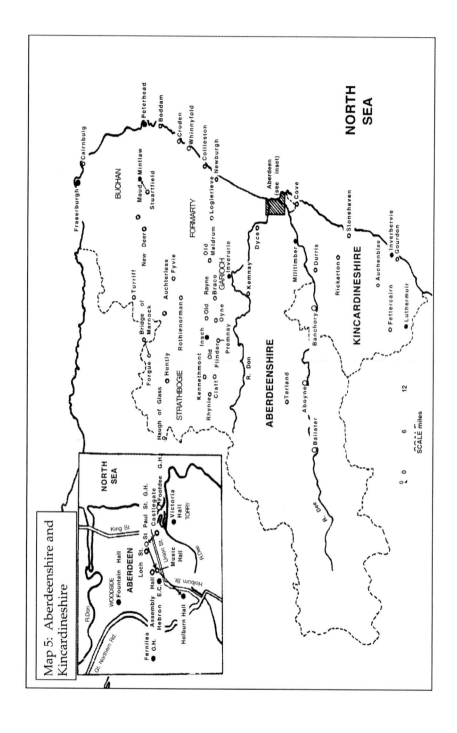

Map 5: Aberdeenshire and Kincardineshire

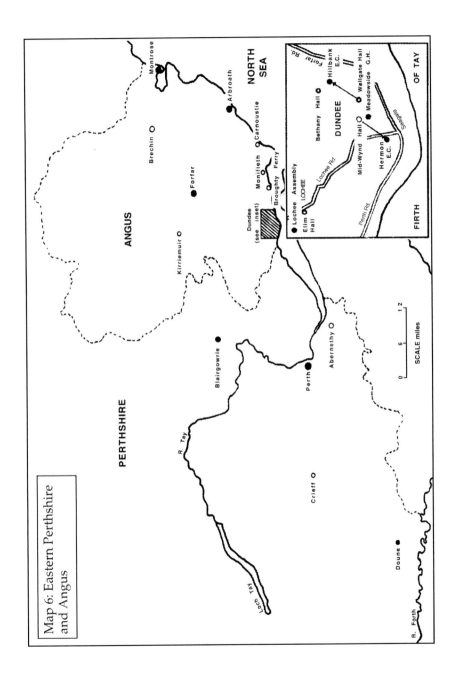

Map 6: Eastern Perthshire and Angus

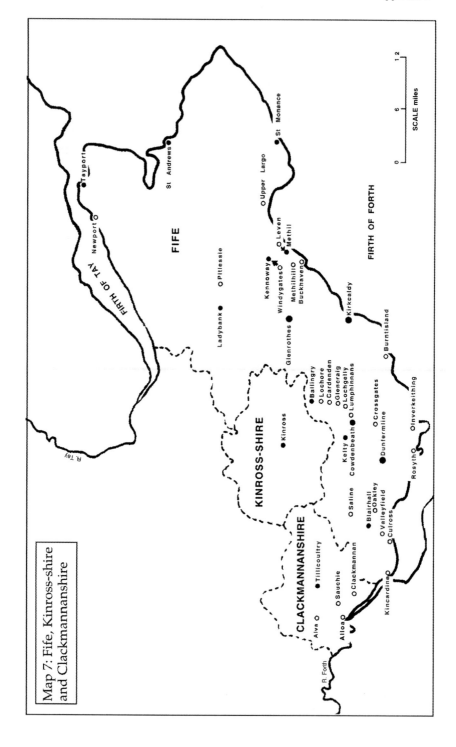

Map 7: Fife, Kinross-shire and Clackmannanshire

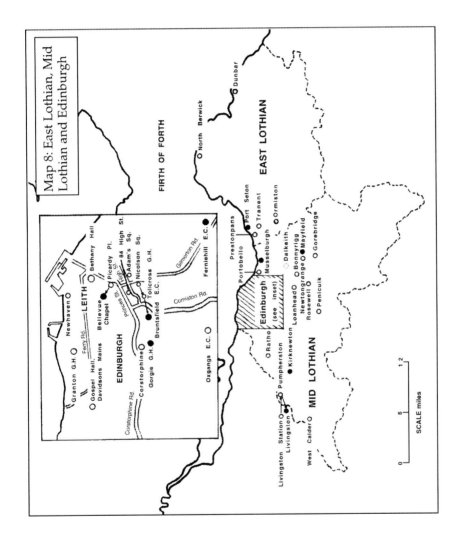

Map 8: East Lothian, Mid Lothian and Edinburgh

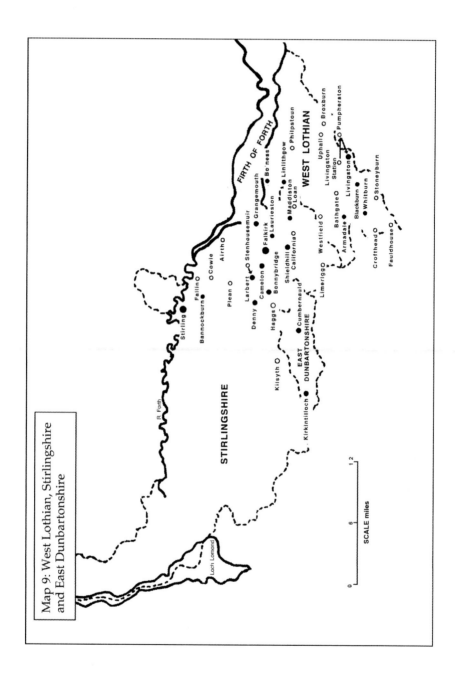

Map 9: West Lothian, Stirlingshire and East Dunbartonshire

Map 10: Lanarkshire

Key to Central North Lanarkshire

1. Coatdyke
2. Chapelhall
3. Gartness
4. Roughrigg
5. Salsburgh
6. Kirkwood
7. Calderbank
8. Tannochside
9. Uddingston
10. Bellshill
11. Mossend
12. Holytown
13. Bothwell
14. New Stevenston
15. Carfin
16. Newarthill

SCALE miles

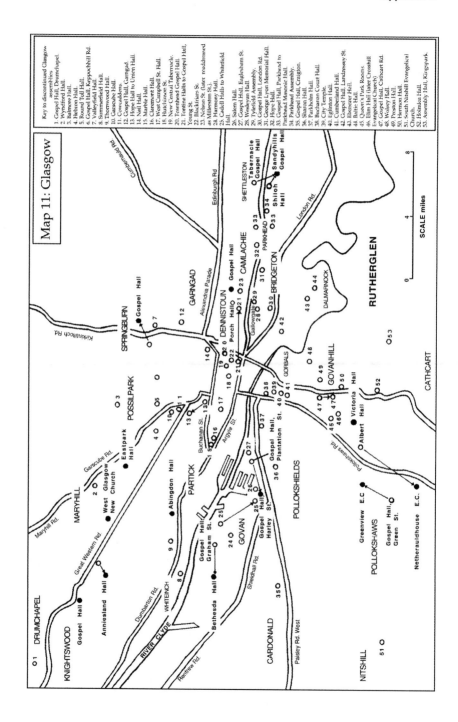

Map 11: Glasgow

Key to discontinued Glasgow assemblies
1. Gospel Hall, Drumchapel.
2. Wyndford Hall.
3. Balmore Hall.
4. Hebron Hall.
5. Round Toll Hall.
6. Gospel Hall, Keppochhill Rd.
7. Valleyfield Hall.
8. Summerfield Hall.
9. Thornwood Hall.
10. Garscube Hall.
11. Convaulden.
12. Gospel Hall, Garngad.
13. Hope Hall to Union Hall.
14. Neil Hall.
15. Marble Hall.
16. Claremont Hall.
17. West Campbell St. Hall.
18. Hutchison St.
19. New Central Tabernacle.
20. Townhead Gospel Hall.
21. Torrance Halls to Gospel Hall, Young St.
22. Blackfriars St.
23. Nelson St. (later rould dressed as Millennium St.).
24. Harmony Hall.
25. Cadell Halls to Whitefield Hall.
26. Salem Hall.
27. Gospel Hall, Eaglesham St.
28. Wesleyan Hall.
29. Tyefield Assembly.
30. Gospel Hall, London Rd.
31. George Lyon Memorial Hall.
32. Hope Hall.
33. Gospel Hall, Parkhead to Parkhead Masonic Hall.
34. Parkhead Assembly.
35. Gospel Hall, Craigton.
36. Sharon Hall.
37. Parkholm Hall.
38. Buchanan Court Hall.
39. City Temple.
40. Eglinton Hall.
41. Cumberland Hall.
42. Gospel Hall, Landressy St.
43. Ebenezer Hall.
44. Baltic Hall.
45. Queen's Park Rooms.
46. Elim Hall (later Crosshill Evangelical Church).
47. Gospel Hall, Cathcart Rd.
48. Wolsey Hall.
49. Preston Hall.
50. Herman Hall.
51. South Nitshill Evangelical Church.
52. Holmlea Hall.
53. Assembly Hall, Kingspark.

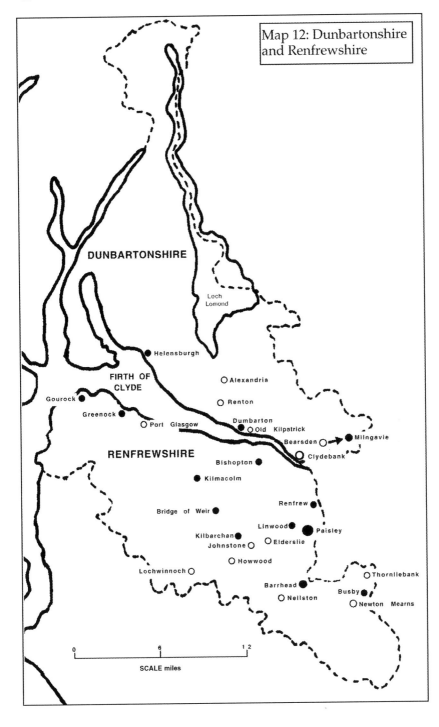

Map 12: Dunbartonshire and Renfrewshire

DUNBARTONSHIRE

Loch Lomond

Helensburgh

FIRTH OF CLYDE

Gourock

Greenock

Port Glasgow

Alexandria

Renton

Dumbarton
Old Kilpatrick

Bearsden

Milngavie

Clydebank

RENFREWSHIRE

Bishopton

Kilmacolm

Bridge of Weir

Renfrew

Linwood

Paisley

Kilbarchan

Eldersile

Johnstone

Howwood

Lochwinnoch

Barrhead

Thornlebank

Busby

Neilston

Newton Mearns

0   6   1 2

SCALE miles

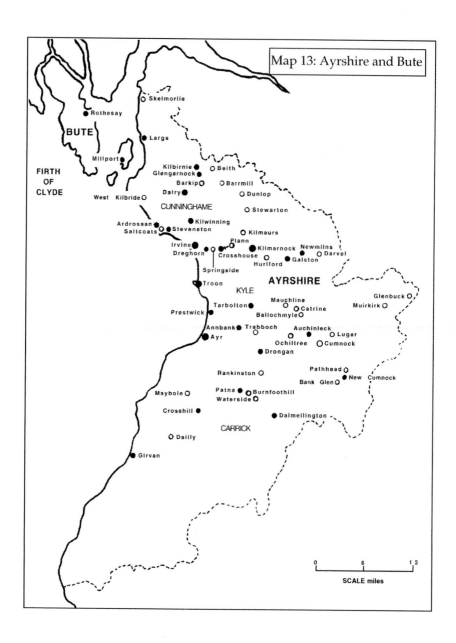

Map 13: Ayrshire and Bute

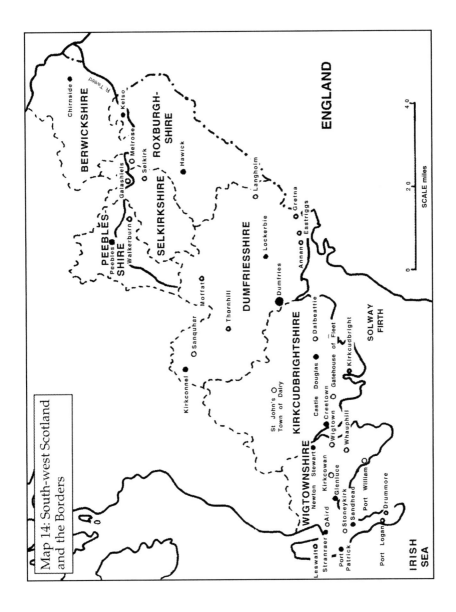

Map 14: South-west Scotland and the Borders

APPENDIX 3

A Historical List of Scottish Open Brethren Assemblies

Contents

Introduction

The historical list of Scottish Open Brethren assemblies below records all those found in the course of the present research. Assemblies are listed alphabetically within regions, but when a community has had more than one assembly, then they are listed in chronological order under their most recent or final name or address. A number of meetings shifted from one town or village to another and these assemblies are listed under their original locations which are cross referenced under the later locations.

The dates listed are those for an assembly's year of formation and (if applicable) its discontinuation. Where no founding date is available, the earliest date by which an assembly is known to have existed is given (indicated by the use of 'by' before the date); if no date is known for its discontinuation, then the last year in which it was known to exist is given (indicated by the use of 'after' before the date): in most cases these dates are probably close to the actual year of an assembly being founded or discontinued. When an assembly's existence is known from only a few mentions or even a single mention in extant sources, then the dates around which it existed are noted by giving the Latin abbreviation for 'flourished'. However, this convention is not entirely appropriate here, for far from prospering most of these assemblies remained small and were short lived. While every effort has been made to ensure that the list is accurate at the time of going to print, the lack of central records and the transience of many assemblies make the writer all too aware that it is impossible to attain infallibility.

Abbreviations

assy	—	assembly
BUS	—	Baptist Union of Scotland
c.	—	*circa* (about)
C	—	century
CG	—	Churches of God
disc.	—	discontinued
E.C.	—	Evangelical Church
f.	—	founded
fl.	—	*fleurit* (flourished)
n.d.	—	no date
OB	—	Open Brethren
s.o.	—	summer only

Shetland

Brae: see Northmavine.
East Yell (1946-after 1959).
Lerwick:
    1. Ebenezer Hall (f. 1864).
    2. Sound Gospel Hall (f. 1983).
Northmavine (f. 1906; to Brae
    1976).
Papa Stour (by 1884-1950s).
Sandwick (1878-1980).
Scalloway (f. 1951).
Selivoe:
    1. *Fl.* 1875.
    2. Gospel Hall (f. 1887).
Trondra (1923-83).
West Burra (*fl.* 1904).
Whiteness (*c.*1887-after 1959).

Orkney

Eday (1876-1974).
Flotta (1910-*c.*1945).
Mainland:
    1. Harray (f. *c.*1868).
    4. Stromness (*c.*1868-1989).
    3. Evie (*c.*1868-1956).
    4. Kirkwall (*c.*1873).
Papa Westray:
    1. *Fl.* 1910.
    2. Gospel Hall (f. 1933).
Sanday (1887-*c.*1918).
Shapinsay (1935-56).
South Ronaldsay (*c.*1868).
Westray (f. 1868).

The Highlands

Ardenadon: see Sandbank.
Ardrishaig (1929-78).
Avoch: see Munlochy.
Beauly (*fl.* 1951-59).
Brora (*fl.* 1923).
Campbeltown:
    1. *Fl.* 1904.
    2. Springbank E.C. (f. 1919).
Carradale (*fl.* 1925).
Conon (*fl.* 1873).
Culloden: see Inverness.
Dingwall (f. 1907).
Dunoon:
    1. Masonic Hall (1882-1971).

    2. Park Hall (f. 1972).
Embo (*fl.* 1922).
Fort William (to OB *c.*1922).
Golspie:
    1. *Fl.* 1916-23.
    2. *Fl.* 1951 (s.o.).
Helmsdale: 1923-*c.*1965.
Invergordon (*fl.* 1928-33).
Inverness:
    1. Gospel Hall (f. 1884; to CG
    1894).
    2. Ebenezer Hall (f. 1911).
    3. Culloden Assembly (f.
    1980; to Culloden 1983).
    4. The Holm E.C. (f. 1982; to
    BUS 1991).
Kiltarlity (*fl.* 1911).
Kingussie (f. 1971).
Mallaig (*c.*1937-63).
Munlochy (f. 1924; to Avoch
    1927).
Oban:
    1. Unionist Club (by 1884-
    1916).
    2. Masonic Hall (*fl.* 1922-38,
    s.o.).
    3. Gospel Hall (1941-47, s.o.).
    4. Gospel Hall (1948-84).
Pitlochry:
    1. Mr English's house (1907-
    after 1922).
    2. Moulin Reading Room
    (1935-6).
Portmahomack (*fl.* 1921-2).
Sandbank (by 1887-after 1922).
Lewis:
    1. Port of Ness (*c.*1894-
    *c.*1920s).
    2. Stornoway (f. *c.*1918).
Nigg (1916-*c.*1918).
Tain (by 1951-64).
Thurso:
    1. G. Robertson's house (by
    1904-after 1922).
    2. Thurso Christian Fellowship
    (1961-6).
Wick:
    1. New Rifle Drill Hall (*fl.*
    1897-1911).
    2. Bethany Hall (f.1923).

Nairn, Moray & Banffshire

Aberlour (1872-1960s).
Boharm (f. *c*.1872; ? to Orton by 1892; ? to CG *c*.1894).
Bridge of Marnock (f. 1890; to Forgue 1910-*c*.1959).
Buckie (f. 1879).
Craigellachie (by 1889-*c*.1930).
Cullen (f. by 1904).
Dufftown (f. 1872-1980s).
Elgin (f. 1872).
Findhorn (*fl.* 1874).
Forres:
    1. *Fl. c*.1873.
    2. Gospel Hall (f. *c*.1883).
Gardenstown (f. 1945).
Hopeman:
    1. 1925-*c*.1930.
    2. Gospel Hall (1951-82).
Inchberry (1909-13).
Keith (1873-*c*.1963).
Lossiemouth (f. 1902).
Macduff (1904-1998).
Nairn:
    1. *Fl.* 1872.
    2. J. E. Meiklejohn's house (*fl.* 1894-7).
    3. Gospel Hall (f. 1899).
Orton:
    1. See Boharm.
    2. *Fl.* 1906.
Portessie (f. 1901).
Portsoy: see Sandend.
Rothes (*c*.1873-after 1933).
Sandend (1894-1997).

Aberdeenshire

Aberdeen:
    1. Bowesite church (1841-*c*.1850).
    2. Holburn Hall (f. 1868).
    3. Footdee (1879-1980s).
    4. Woodside (f. 1881).
    5. Hebron Hall (f. 1889).
    6. Victoria Hall, Torry (f. 1900).
    7. Assembly Hall (1918-late 1970s).
    8. Gospel Hall, Fernilea (f. 1967).

    9. Deeside Christian Fellowship Church: see Milltimber.
Aboyne (1872-*c*.1927).
Auchterless (*c*. 1872-after 1904).
Ballater (1906-70).
Blackpool: see Millbrex.
Boddam (by 1881-*c*.1944).
Braco (1872-after 1904).
Cairnbulg (*fl.* 1927).
Clatt (1845-62).
Collieston (*c*.1892-after 1904).
Cruden Bay (by 1897-after 1933).
Dyce (*fl.* 1897-1904).
Forgue: see Bridge of Marnock, Banffshire.
Fraserburgh:
    1. Bethel Hall (*fl.* 1872).
    2. Gospel Hall, Albert St. (f. by 1897).
    3. Gospel Hall, The Cross (*c*.1939-42).
Fyvie: see Millbrex.
Haugh of Glass (*fl.* 1897-1904).
Huntly (1873-*c*.1978).
Insch:
    1. Bowesite church (1845-63).
    2. Fordyce Hall (f. 1873).
Inverurie (f. 1871).
Kemnay (1871-after 1904).
Kennethmont (1871-2).
Kirkerton (*fl.* 1904).
Logierieve (1901-60s).
Maud (*fl.* 1991-5).
Millbrex (1880-after 1926).
Milltimber (f. 1975).
Mintlaw (f. by 1904; to Stuartfield after 1922; to Mintlaw 1950s).
Mosscorral: see Bridge of Marnock, Banffshire.
Newburgh (*c*.1871-after 1904).
New Deer (1871-*c*.1975).
Northaven (*fl.* 1897).
Old Flinder (*fl. c*.1872).
Old Meldrum (1872-after 1904).
Old Rayne (1871-*c*.1890).
Oyne (1871-*c*.1884).
Peterhead (f. 1868).
Port Errol: see Cruden Bay.
Premnay (1878-1920).
Rhynie (1873-*c*.1926).
Tarland:
    1. Ferrier Sq. (1871-1932).

2. *Fl.* 1936.
Turriff (1872-after 1922).
Whinnyfold:
   1. Gospel Hall (*fl.* 1897-1904).
   2. Assembly Hall (1923-70).

Kincardineshire, Angus & Perthshire

Abernethy (1901-92).
Arbroath:
   1. Bowesite church (*fl.* 1841).
   2. Exchange Hall (*fl.* 1897-1904).
   3. Springfield Gospel Hall (f. 1911).
   4. Gospel Hall, Park St. (1950-2).
Auchenblae (*c.*1911-31).
Banchory (*fl.* 1873).
Bervie: see Inverbervie.
Birnam (*fl.* 1864).
Blairgowrie (to OB 1990s).
Brechin (1891-1984).
Broughty Ferry (by 1940-62).
Carnoustie (1910-*c.*1963).
Cove (*fl.* 1888).
Crieff (by 1897-1940s).
Doune (f. 1903).
Dundee:
   1. Hermon E.C. (f. 1866).
   2. Hillbank E.C. (f. 1878).
   3. Bethany Hall (1887-9).
   4. Gospel Hall, Nelson St. (*fl.* 1897).
   5. Elim Hall, Lochee (1907-50).
   6. Lochee Assembly (f. 1971).
   7. Meadowside Gospel Hall (1981-2000).
Durris (*fl.* 1897-1904).
Fettercairn (*fl.* 1862).
Forfar:
   1. Gospel Hall (f. *c.*1901).
   2. East High St. (*fl.* 1911).
Gourdon (1904-after 1922).
Inverbervie (1873-2001).
Kirriemuir (1873-after 1903).
Luthermuir (f. 1975).
Monifieth (1910-26).
Montrose (f. *c.*1872).

Perth:
   1. Good Templar's Hall (1873-*c.*1886).
   2. Gospel Hall (f. 1900).
Rickarton (*c.*1884-1903).
Stonehaven:
   1. See Rickarton.
   2. Mission Hall (1914-41).

Fife

Auchterderan (f. 1905; to Bowhill by 1908; to Cardenden 1956-80s).
Ballingry: see Glencraig.
Blairhall (f. 1935).
Bowhill: see Auchterderan.
Buckhaven (1870/1-after 1933).
Burntisland: (by 1887-1922).
Cardenden: see Auchterderan.
Cowdenbeath (f. 1897).
Crossgates (by 1929-after 1959).
Culross (*fl.* 1922-33).
Dunfermline:
   1. Abbot Hall (f. 1869).
   2. Gospel Hall, Randolph St. (by 1904-7).
   3. St. Margaret's Hall (by 1922-32).
   4. Gospel Hall, Hospital Hill (f. 1935).
Glencraig (f. 1931; to Ballingry 1968).
Glenrothes (1956-2001).
High Valleyfield: see Low Valleyfield.
Inverkeithing (1910-2001).
Kelty (f. *c.*1880).
Kennoway:
   1. See Upper Largo 1.
   2. Arnot Hall: see Windygates.
Kincardine (*fl.* 1922).
Kirkcaldy:
   1. Pathhead (1886-89).
   2. Dunnikier Evangelistic Hall (*c.*1890-1978).
   3. Hebron Hall (f. *c.*1929).
   3. Newcraigs E.C. (f. 1985).
Ladybank (f. 1920).
Leven: see Upper Largo, Innerleven Gospel Hall.
Lochgelly (1880s-1970s).

Lochore (f. *c*.1910; to OB 1913-91).

Low Valleyfield (f. 1910; to High Valleyfield 1953-8).

Lumphinnans (*fl.* 1904).

Methilhill (1933-89).

Methil:
1. Lindsay Sq. Hall (*fl.* 1904).
2. See Upper Largo 1.

Newport (*c*.1888-*c*.1927).

Oakley (*fl.* 1905).

Pitlesssie (1888-after 1933).

Rosyth (*fl.* 1922).

St Andrews (f. 1888).

St Monance (f. 1924).

Saline (*fl.* 1905).

Sinclairton (*fl.* 1897).

Tayport (f. 1873).

Upper Largo:
1. Innerleven Gospel Hall (f. by 1880; to Kennoway; to Leven *c*.1880; to Methil 1907).
2. Mission Room (1909-after 1922).

Valleyfield: see Low Valleyfield.

Windygates (f. 1914; to Kennoway 1977).

Stirlingshire, Clackmannanshire & Kinross

Airth (1905-after 1933).

Alloa (1904-80).

Alva (*fl.* 1905).

Bannockburn (f. 1905).

Bonnybridge (f. 1902).

California (f. by 1922-after 1959).

Camelon (f. 1913).

Clackmannan (*fl.* 1897-1904).

Cowie (1895-1989).

Denny (f. 1935).

Falkirk:
1. Bowesite church (*fl.* 1867).
2. Gospel Hall (1889-after 1934).
3. Olivet Hall (f. 1937).
4. Thornhill Gospel Hall (f. 1945).

Fallin (*fl.* 1921-2).

Grangemouth:
1. Albert Hall (f. 1866).
2. Bethany Hall (*fl.* late C19).

Haggs (1902-late 1990s).

Kilsyth:
1. Good Templars' Hall (by 1897-1911).
2. Gospel Hall (1920-1980).

Kinross (f. 1925).

Larbert: see Stenhousemuir.

Laurieston:
1. Gospel Hall (f. 1909).
2. 1926-*c*.1947.

Limerigg (*fl.* 1888-97).

Maddiston (f. 1922).

Plean (1923-70s).

Sauchie (1936-96).

Shieldhill (f. *c*.1890).

Stenhousemuir (f. 1885; to Larbert 1990).

Stirling (f. by 1882).

Tillicoultry (f. *c*.1859).

Edinburgh

City:
1. Darbyite assy (f. 1838; ?1848 to Exclusive Brethren).
2. Bowesite church, Adam's Sq. (*fl*. 1851).
3. Phoenix Hall (f. *c*.1866-72).
4. Good Templars' Hall (*fl.* 1872).
5. Bruntsfield E.C. (f. 1874).
6. Bellevue Chapel (f. 1891).
7. Gospel Hall, Jamaica St. (1891-*c*.1894).
8. Gospel Hall, Nicolson Sq. (*fl.* 1905).
9. Juniper Green (*fl.* 1909).

Corstorphine (1935-*c*.1958).

Davidsons Mains (1911-51).

Gilmerton (f. 1966).

Gorgie:
1. Gospel Hall (f. 1908).
2. Ardmillan Hall (*fl.* 1912).

Granton (1920s-1980s).

Leith (*c*.1900-94).

Newhaven (*fl.* 1887).

Oxgangs (1964-92).

The Lothians

Armadale (f. *c.*1868).
Bathgate (*c.*1906-after 1930).
Blackburn (f. 1920).
Bo'ness:
  1. Hebron Hall (f. *c.*1883).
  2. Bethany Hall, Grangepans (by 1933-mid-1950s).
Bonnyrigg:
  1. Hermon Hall, Loanhead (f. 1875; to Loanhead *c.*1890-1991).
  2. Gospel Hall (1928-63).
Broxburn:
  1. Gospel Hall (*c.*1880-1908).
  2. Gospel Hall, Uphall (f. by 1904; to Uphall 1976-2001).
  3. Lesser Public Hall (by 1933-mid-1950s).
Cockenzie (f. 1882; to Port Seton 1922).
Crofthead (*fl.* 1868).
Dalkeith (f. 1902; to mission hall 1995).
Dunbar:
  1. Charles Spence's house (1895-1924).
  2. Masonic Hall (1933-1970).
Edgehead (1908-*c.*1955).
Fauldhouse:
  1. Co-op Hall (1913-80s).
  2. *Fl.* 1918.
Gorebridge (*c.*1928-45).
Kirknewton (f. 1924).
Linlithgow (f. by 1897).
Livingston:
  1. Gospel Hall, Deans: see Livingston Station.
  2. Almondale Gospel Hall, Dedridge (f. 1981).
Livingston Station (f. 1915).
Loan (*fl.* 1897).
Loanhead: see Bonnyrigg 1.
Mayfield
  1. *Fl.* 1868.
  2. See Newtongrange.
Musselburgh:
  1. Dickson's Halls (*fl.* 1907).
  2. Millholm Hall: see Portobello 1.
  3. Gospel Hall (f. 1923).
Newtongrange (f. 1913; to Mayfield 1970).

North Berwick:
  1. Forresters' Hall (*fl.* 1907-8).
  2. Hope Rooms (1957-60s, s.o.).
Ormiston (*fl.* 1924).
Penicuik:
  1. Hawthornbank Hall, Shottstown (1875-1933).
  2. Gospel Hall (1916-after 1933).
Philpstoun (1895-*c.*1940).
Portobello:
  1. Working Men's Institute (f. 1905; to Musselburgh 1908-after 1909).
  2. Southfield Gospel Hall (1910-after 1959).
  3. Gospel Hall, Working Men's Institute (*fl.* 1959).
Pumpherston: see Livingston Station.
Prestonpans (*fl.* 1951).
Ratho (1911-after 1963).
Rosewell (*fl.* 1875).
Shottston: see Penicuik.
Stoneyburn
  1. Welfare Hall (*c.*1905-after 1930).
  2. 1918-19.
Tranent (by 1922-after 1959).
Uphall:
  1. Ross Hall (1905-39).
  2. Gospel Hall: see Broxburn 2.
West Calder (*c.*1879-1952).
Westfield (*fl.* 1935).
Whitburn (f. *c.*1901).

Lanarkshire

Airdrie:
  1. Bowesite church (*fl.* 1850).
  2. Gospel Hall, Cullen St. (*fl.* 1881).
  3. Hebron Hall (f. 1883).
  4. Ebenezer E.C.: see Coatdyke.
  5. Glenview E.C.: see Gartness.
  6. Gospel Hall, Mill Rd (1954-*c.*1991).
Annathill (1910-66).

Ashgill:
1. Gospel Hall (1917-*c*.1990).
2. Bethany Hall (f. 1948).
Auchentibber (1885; to Blantyre 1916-23).
Baillieston:
1. Band Hall (*fl.* 1897).
2. Gospel Hall (f. *c*.1924; to Baillieston 3, 2001).
3. Baillieston Gospel Church (f. 1952).
Bellshill:
1. Evangelistic Hall (by 1867-1911).
2. Gospel Hall (f. 1887).
Biggar:
1. Gospel Hall (1928-83).
2. Bethany Hall (f. 1988).
Bishopbriggs:
1. Gospel Hall (*fl.* 1913).
2. Woodhill E.C. (f. 1939).
Blackwood: see Kirkmuirhill.
Blantyre:
1. See High Blantyre.
2. See Auchentiber.
Bothwell (f. 1884).
Bothwellhaugh (1921-78).
Burnbank (f. 1895).
Burnside: see Rutherglen 3.
Calderbank:
1. Gospel Hall (1922-98).
2. Bethany Hall (*c*.1931-*c*.1950).
Caldercruix (1893-1964).
Cambuslang:
1. Westcoats E.C. (f. 1866).
2. Ebenezer Hall: see Halfway.
Carfin (f. 1928).
Carluke:
1. Bowesite church (*fl.* 1850).
2. Gospel Hall (f. 1867; to OB 1930s).
3. Templars' Institute (*fl.* 1920).
4. Templars' Institute (*fl.* 1921-2).
Chapelhall (f. 1918).
Chapelton (f. 1863; to East Kilbride 1864; disc. by 1880s).
Chryston: see Muirhead.
Coalburn (1905-81).
Coatbridge:

1. Shiloh Hall (*c*.1874-1984).
2. Hebron Hall (to OB 1938).
Coatdyke (f. 1896; to OB 1913).
Cobbinshaw (*fl.* 1921-2).
Crossford (*fl.* 1904).
Douglas:
1. Bowesite church (1847-60s).
2. Gospel Hall (1883-1997).
Douglas Water (*c*.1909-58).
Dykehead (f. by 1889; ? to CG *c*.1893).
Eastfield (1942-after 1959).
East Kilbride:
1. See Chapelton.
2. Gospel Hall (1889-1947).
3. Threshold Church (f. 1951).
4. Westwoodhill E.C. (f. 1973).
Forth: see Haywood.
Gartness (f. 1934).
Glassford (f. 1922).
Glenboig (*fl.* 1938).
Glengowan (by 1904-after 1933).
Greengairs (to OB 1908).
Halfway (1906-early 1990s).
Hamilton:
1. Bowesite church (*c*.1850-*c*.1856).
2. Evangelical Church, Selkirk St. (f. 1863).
3. Kensington Hall (*fl.* 1897).
4. Low Waters Gospel Hall (f. 1899).
5. Cadzow Bridge Hall (*fl.* 1909).
6. High Parks Gospel Hall (f. 1884; to OB 1930s).
Harthill (*fl.* 1904-5).
Haywood (f. 1883; to Wilsontown *c*.1930; to Forth 1936).
High Blantyre (by 1878-1997).
Holytown:
1. 1867-89.
2. Gospel Hall (f. 1927).
Kirkfieldbank (*fl.* 1868).
Kirkmuirhill (f. 1884).
Kirkwood (by 1897-*c*.1933).
Lanark:
1. Bowesite church (*fl.* 1850).
2. Gospel Hall (f. 1868).

Larkhall:
1. Gospel Hall, Hareleeshill (f. *c*.1866).
2. Albion Hall (f. 1874; to OB 1950s).
3. Gospel Hall, Strutherhill (f. 1972).
Leadhills (f. 1879).
Lesmahagow:
1. Hope Hall (f. *c*.1864).
2. Good Templars' Hall (1918-24).
3. Gospel Hall (1932-3).
Longriggend:
1. *c*.1873-1905.
2. Gospel Hall (1908-30).
Morningside (f. *c*.1893; to Newmains 1903).
Mossend (*fl*. 1921-2).
Motherwell:
1. Bowesite church (*fl*. 1847).
2. Roman Rd Gospel Hall (f. *c*.1868).
3. Sheilds Rd Gospel Hall (f. 1908).
4. Ebenezer E.C. (f. *c*.1911).
5. Hallelujah Hall (to OB 1953-*c*.1963).
6. Forgewood Gospel Hall (1960-93).
Muirhead (f. 1892; to Chryston *c*.1892).
Netherburn (*c*.1866-2000).
Newarthill:
1. Bowesite church (*fl*. 1851).
2. Gospel Hall (by 1878-early 1990s).
New Lanark (*fl*. 1897).
Newmains:
1. Ebenezer Hall, Wishaw (f. 1847 to Wishaw 1847; to Newmains *c*.1855; to Wishaw, 1869-1905).
2. Gospel Hall: see Morningside.
New Stevenston:
1. Gospel Hall (1897-1991).
2. Assembly Hall (f. *c*.1930).
Overtown (f. 1905).
Plains (f. 1882).
Ponfeigh (*fl*. 1883).
Quarter (*fl*. 1921).
Rosebank (*fl*. 1867).

Roughrigg (*fl*. 1873-88).
Rutherglen:
1. Bowesite church (*fl*. 1848).
2. Hebron Hall (1864-1982).
3. Gospel Hall, Burnside (f. 1925).
Salsburgh:
1. Gospel Hall (by 1882-early C20).
2. Gospel Hall (f. early 1920s; to OB 1935).
Shotts:
1. See Dykehead
2. Gospel Hall (1902-2002).
Stonefield (*fl*. 1916).
Stonehouse:
1. Bowesite church (*fl*. 1872).
2. Gospel Hall (late 1880s-*c*.1981).
Strathaven:
1. Bowesite church (*fl*. 1854).
2. Strathaven E.C. (f. 1862).
Tannochside (*fl*. 1934).
Tarbrax (1908-50).
Uddingston:
1. Gospel Hall (f. *c*.1895).
2. Viewpark (*fl*. 1961).
3. Viewpark E.C. (f. 1992).
West Benhar (1888-after 1904).
Wilsontown: see Haywood.
Wishaw:
1. Victoria Hall: see Newmains 1.
2. Bowesite church (*c*.1850-*c*.1855).
3. Ebenezer Hall (f. *c*.1904).

Glasgow

Anniesland:
1. Anniesland Hall (f. 1868; to OB 1942).
2. West Glasgow New Church (f. 1989).
Bridgeton:
1. Ebenezer Hall (by 1876-1976).
2. Gospel Hall, Landressey St.: see Dalmarnock 1.
3. Gospel Hall, London Rd (to OB 1942 -51).

Camlachie:
1. Camlachie Assembly (*fl.* 1866-7).
2. Lyon Hall (f. c.1873; to OB 1890s-1962).

Cathcart:
1. Homelea Hall (1911-30).
2. Co-operative halls (1914-17).

City:
1. Two Bowesite churches (*fl.* 1843).
2. Bowesite church (f. 1850; to Cowcaddens 1851-after 1855).
3. Blythswood Hall, West Campbell St. (1860-after 1882).
4. Bell's Hall, Trongate (*fl.* 1863-6).
5. Blackfriar's St. (*fl.* 1863-8).
6. Annfield Hall, Gallowgate (f. 1866; to Gallowgate 1874-after 1905).
7. Union Hall (1860s-1970).
8. New Central Tabernacle (f. 1923; to Elim Pentecostal Church 1927).
9. City Temple (to OB 1923-45).

Cowcaddens: see City 2.
Craigton (1943-early 1960s).
Crosshill:
1. Queen's Park Rooms (*fl.* 1876).
2. Elim Hall (1882-1991).

Dalmarnock:
1. Gospel Hall (*fl.* 1897-1904).
2. Baltic Hall (1911-58).

Dennistoun (c.1873; to OB 1887).
Drumchapel (*fl.* 1959).
Eglinton:
1. Buchanan Ct (1874-90s).
2. Eglinton Hall (1892-1946).
3. Cumberland Hall (by 1908-16).

Finnieston:
1. Marble Hall (1866-1925).
2. Claremont Hall (1930-48).

Gallowgate:
1. Nelson St. (readdressed as Millerston St.) (*fl.* 1866-7).
2. Annfield Hall: see City 6.

3. Tylefield Assembly (by 1897-1974).
Garngad (f. 1889; to OB 1892-1945).
Garscube (*fl.* 1904).
Gorbals: Cathcart Rd (c.1877-1930).
Govan:
1. Bethesda Hall (f. 1874; to Whiteinch, 1902).
2. *Fl.* 1888.
3. Harmony Hall (by 1889-1938).
4. *Fl.* 1900.
5. Gospel Hall, Graham St. (to OB 1909-13).
6. Whitefield Hall (1926-44).
7. Parkholm Hall: see Paisley Rd.

Govanhill:
1. Preston Hall (by 1904-19).
2. Hermon Hall (1904; to BUS 1920).
3. Victoria Hall (f. 1917).

Ibrox:
1. Salem Hall (1903-20).
2. Gospel Hall, Harley St.: see Plantation 1.

Kelvinside North (f. by 1886; to Maryhill 1, 1961).
Keppochhill (1908-56).
King's Park (1932-82).
Knightswood (f. 1929).
Linthouse: see Govan, Bethesda Hall.
Maryhill:
1. Hebron Hall Eastpark (f. by 1877).
2. Wyndford Hall (by 1897-1961).

Nitshill (f. 1962; to Glasgow City Mission c.1972).
Oatlands
1. Wolsley Hall (1882-1975).
2. Mathieson St. Hall (*fl.* 1907).

Paisley Rd: Parkholm Hall (f. 1876; to Govan 1947-mid-1950s).
Parkhead:
1. Bowesite church (*fl.* 1864).
2. Hope Hall (1886-1939).
3. Gospel Hall (1896-1902).

4. Parkhead Assembly (1925-92).

Partick:
1. Abingdon Hall (f. 1874).
2. Thornwood Hall (to OB 1948-mid-1950s).

Plantation:
1. Gospel Hall, Harley St. (f. 1915).
2. Gospel Hall, Eaglesham St. (1921-35).
3. Sharon Hall (to OB 1937-40).

Pollokshaws:
1. Greenview E.C. (f. 1874).
2. Netherauldhouse E.C.: see Shawlands.

Possilpark:
1. Round Toll Assembly (1888-1926).
2. Balmore Hall (1910-c.1958).

Sandyhills: see Shettleston 1 & 3.
Shawlands (f. 1909; to Pollokshaws 1994).

Shettleston
1. Shiloh Hall (f. 1884; to Sandyhills 1972).
2. Co-operative Hall (*fl.* 1904).
3. Tabernacle Gospel Hall (f. c.1904; to OB 1938; to Sandyhills 1972).

Springburn:
1. Gospel Hall (f. 1881).
2. Valleyfield Hall (*fl.* 1907).

Townhead:
1. Townhead Gospel Hall (1875-1965).
2. Neil Hall (f. by 1913-31).

Whiteinch (1902-1986).

Dunbartonshire

Alexandria:
1. Bowesite church (*fl.* 1851).
2. Ebenezer Hall (c.1875-1981).

Bearsden (f. c.1885; to Milngavie 1892/3).

Clydebank:
1. Gospel Hall (c.1882-1993).
2. Hope Hall (*fl.* 1901).

3. Victoria Hall (1913-95).
4. Hermon Hall (1931-41).

Cumbernauld:
1. Mossknowe Gospel Hall (f. 1913).
2. Eastfield E.C. (f. 1990).

Dumbarton:
1. Bowesite church (*fl.* 1864).
2. Lennox E.C. (f. mid-1860s).

Garelochead (*fl.*1904).
Helensburgh (f. 1847; to OB 1860s).
Kirkintilloch (f. by 1876).
Milngavie: see Bearsden.
Old Kilpatrick (1914-after 1931).
Renton (1868-after 1904).

Renfrewshire

Barrhead (f. 1884).
Bishopton (f. 1977).
Bridge of Weir (to OB 1903).
Busby (f. 1891).

Elderslie:
1. 1908-13.
2. Gospel Hall (c.1922-94).

Gourock (f. 1887).

Greenock:
1. Ardgowan Sq. E.C. (f. 1862).
2. Bogston Hall (1915-68).

Johnstone:
1. Ebenezer Hall (by 1892-2000).
2. Gospel Hall, Dimity St. (f. 1907; to OB 1925-82).

Howwood (by 1897-1946).
Kilbarchan (to OB 1884).
Kilmacolm (to OB 1887).
Linwood (to OB 1904).
Lochwinnoch (c.1886-1982).
Neilston (1854/5-c.1980).

Newton Mearns:
1. Gospel Hall (1886-after 1897).
2. Maple E.C. (1930-1991).

Paisley:
1. Kilnside E.C.: f. 1867; to OB c.1870).
2. Bethany Hall (by 1897-after 1930).
3. Wellmeadow/Bethany Hall: (f. 1919).

Port Glasgow:
1. Old Town Hall (c.1876-1941).
2. Hebron Hall (c.1928-99).
Renfrew:
1. Albert Hall (f. by 1886).
2. Gospel Hall, Moorpark (fl. 1914-20).
Thornliebank (1902-38).

Ayrshire & Bute

Annbank (f. 1883).
Ardrossan (1888-2001).
Auchinleck (f. c.1874).
Ayr:
1. Gospel Hall (f. 1864).
2. Late 1860s-1874.
3. Riverside E.C. (f. 1906).
4. Woodpark E.C. (f. 1970).
Ballochmyle (1891-1929).
Barkip (1906-36).
Barrmill (1902-mid-1950s).
Beith:
1. Gospel Hall (c.1890-c.1904).
2. Bethany Hall (1922-95).
Burnfoothill (f. by 1874; to Patna 1951).
Catrine (c.1885-1978).
Crosshill (f. 1902).
Crosshouse: see Plann.
Cumnock (Old):
1. Bowesite church (fl. c.1846).
2. Town Hall (by 1892-after 1911).
3. Gospel Hall (1920-95).
Dailly (c.1881-1973).
Dalmellington:
1. Fl. 1866.
2. Bethany Hall (1870-2002).
Dalry:
1. Gospel Hall, Townend (1864-1913).
2. Gospel Hall, North St. (f. by 1908).
3. Gospel Hall, Townend (1961-1990).
Darvel:
1. Bowesite church (1846-c.1852).

2. Gospel Hall (1880-late 1950s).
Dreghorn:
1. Gospel Hall (by 1887-c.1907).
2. Ebenezer Hall: see Springside.
Drongan (f. by 1885).
Dunlop (late 1910s-1925).
Galston (f. 1871).
Glenbuck (1887-1954).
Glengarnock (f. by 1891).
Hurlford:
1. Evangelistic Hall (1877-after 1904).
2. Gospel Hall (1933-1970s).
3. Bridgend Hall (fl. 1951).
Girvan (f. 1886).
Irvine (f. c.1862).
Kilbirnie:
1. Fl. 1867.
2. Gospel Hall (f. 1889).
Kilmarnock:
1. Nelson St. (1842-c.1879).
2. Bowesite church (1844-mid-1850s).
3. Strand St. Hall (c.1870-1910).
3. Central E.C. (f. 1880).
4. Ebenezer Hall (f. 1880-c.1898).
5. Elim Hall (f. 1926).
Kilmaurs (1920-1960s).
Kilwinning (f. 1874).
Knockentiber: see Plann.
Largs (f. 1865).
Lugar (fl. 1875-93).
Mauchline:
1. Bowesite church (fl. 1847).
2. c.1877-1903.
Maybole:
1. Gospel Hall (1877-1960s).
2. Town Hall (fl. 1895-7).
Millport:
1. Miss McAlister's house (1887-1933, often s.o.).
2. Lesser Town Hall (1934-48, s.o.).
3. Millport E.C. (f. 1949).
Muirkirk (by 1878-1978).
New Cumnock:
1. Pathhead (f. c.1882).

2. Burnfoot (f. *c*.1893; to New Cumnock 1, 1956).
3. Bank Glen (f. 1897; to New Cumnock 1, 1956).
Newmilns (f. 1878).
Ochiltree:
   1. *fl.* 1904.
   2. 1915-1920s.
Patna:
   1. *Fl.* 1904.
   2. Ebenezer Hall (1918-39).
   3. Ebenezer Hall: see Burnfoothill.
Plann (f. 1882; to Crosshouse 1966).
Prestwick:
   1. Bute Hall (f. 1877).
   2. Gospel Hall, Glenburn (f. 1929).
Rankinston (by 1879-1991).
Rothesay:
   1. West End Hall (by 1879-1970s).
   2. Ebenezer Hall (1961-*c*.1996).
Saltcoats:
   1. Gospel Hall (1888-1915).
   2. Bethany Hall (1896-1994).
   3. Ebenezer Hall (by 1911-53).
Skelmorlie (*fl.* 1887).
Springside (f. *c*. 1886; to Dreghorn n.d.; to Springside 1894; to Dreghorn 1904).
Stevenston:
   1. Loan Hall (f. *c*.1867).
   2. Bethany Hall (f. *c*.1906).
   3. Gospel Hall, Hayocks (f. *c*.1930).
Stewarton (f. 1898-after 1910).
Tarbolton:
   1. Mr Gibson's house (*c*.1880-1904 occasional).
   2. *Fl.* 1919.
   3. Gospel Hall (f. 1922; disc. 1999; f. 1999).
Troon (f. 1868).
Trabboch (1900-*c*.1945).
Waterside (*fl.* 1895-7).
West Kilbride (1914-54).

Dumfries & Galloway

Aird (*c*.1881-*c*.1917).

Annan:
   1. See Lowtherton.
   2. Central Hall (1907-after 1913).
Castle Douglas (f. 1891).
Creetown (f. *c*.1874).
Dumfries (f. by 1889).
Drummore (*c*.1883-1970s).
Eastriggs: see Lowtherton.
Gatehouse of Fleet (by 1889-1940s).
Glenluce (f. *c*.1887).
Gretna:
   1. N1 West (1917-20).
   2. 1969-*c*.1980.
Kirkconnel (f. 1910).
Kirkcowan (1892-1943).
Kirkcudbright:
   1. Town Hall (*fl.* 1933).
   2. Gospel Hall (1942-after 1953).
Leswalt (1888-1965).
Lockerbie (f. 1897).
Lowthertown (f. 1873; to Annan n.d.; to Eastriggs early C20-*c*.1968).
Newton Stewart (f. *c*.1879).
Port Logan (*fl.* 1871).
Portpatrick (f. 1909).
Port William:
   1. Oddfellows' Hall (by 1897-after 1908).
   2. Mr Grier's house (1922-after 1933).
St John's Town of Dalry (*fl.* 1897).
Sandhead (f. 1887).
Sanquhar:
   1. Town Hall (f. by 1904-1938).
   2. Gospel Hall (1952-85).
Stoneykirk (*fl.* 1902).
Stranraer:
   1. Gospel Hall, Lewis St. (f. *c*.1866).
   2. Gospel Hall, St John St. (1938-53).
Thornhill (*fl.* 1890).
Whauphill (*fl.* 1895-1905).
Wigtown (*c*.1882-1920s).

The Borders

Chirnside (f. early 1870s).

Dalbeattie (1887-after 1904).
Galashiels (1870-1950).
Hawick (f. 1877).
Innerleithen: see Walkerburn.
Kelso:
    1. *Fl.* 1881.
    2. Bowmont St. (f. 1990).
Langholm (f. *c.*1884-1940s).
Melrose (1945-*c.*1950).
Moffat:
    1. *c.*1877- *c.*1927.
    2. Masonic Hall (1931-32).

Peebles:
    1. Gospel Hall (by 1888-1948).
    2. Peebles E.C. (f. 1968).
Selkirk:
    1. Gospel Hall (1878-1910).
    2. Masonic Hall (1911-after 1964).

Walkerburn (by 1886-1952).

APPENDIX 4

Occupational Classification

Because of the period (1863-1993) covered by the tables showing socio-economic groups, the classification adopted is based on the ones which the Registrar General issued in conjunction with the national census as it allows for comparability. This approach has been modified as suggested by W. A. Armstrong, 'The use of information about occupation', in E. A. Wrigley (ed.), *Nineteenth-Century Society: essays in the use of quantitive methods for the study of social data* (Cambridge, 1972), pp.198-310. Armstrong particularly recommends the consideration of individual cases rather than applying a general grid before allocating someone to a particular social class. Where possible this was done in the list below which consists of all the occupations encountered in the course of the research. The classification in the present study required a uniform approach and the system adopted seemed best suited to provide one. Religious lay people, such as itinerant evangelists, have been allocated to group C below as that class tended to be the one from which they were recruited and it also best reflects the level of skill needed for this particular occupation in the Brethren. Where occupations were encountered frequently they were allocated to a sub-group, allowing for finer analysis, but ones only encountered once were usually grouped together.

A. Professional etc. occupations, merchant manufacturers, administrators, etc.

1. Professional occupations

architect, chartered accountant, civil engineer, dentist, doctor, lawyer, mechanical engineer, polytechnic principal, solicitor, structural engineer, surgeon, university lecturer.

2. Merchant-manufacturers

cabinet manufacturer, linen manufacturer, silk manufacturer, produce merchant; sailmaker and ships' chandler.

3. Administrators, directors, managers
chief electrical engineer (NCB), company director (large).

4. Commissioned officers
major-general, lieutenant colonel.

B. Intermediate occupations
1. Teachers
college lecturers, headteacher (junior secondary), headteacher (primary), secondary teacher, primary teacher.

2. Sales occupations
company agent (Scotland), commercial agent, commission agent, fish salesman (employing), medical representative, regional marketing manager, sales manager, timber salesman (employing).

3. Small manufacturers
factory owner (unspecified), lemonade manufacturer, toilet manufacturer.

4. Employing tradesmen, shop managers, company directors (small)
advertising agency owner, bookseller, businessman (unspecified), cabinet works manager, chemist, company director (small), coppersmith, fishmonger, draper, grocery manager, general store owner, hairdresser, haulage operator, hotel manager, master baker, master builder, master grocer, master joiner, master painter, master plumber, master stonemason, motor garage owner, restaurateur, publisher, ship's chandler, woodmill owner, shipbuilder, fishing boat owner, quarrymaster, undertaker.

5. Health associate professionals
nurse (qualified), nursing matron, nursing superintendent, optician, pharmicist.

6. Farmers
tenant farmer (large).

7. Managers

bank manager, industrial production manager, mine manager, mines undermanager, shipping company manager, shoe factory manager.

8. *Others*

aeroplane inspector, artist, burgh assessor and registrar, carriage hirer, carpet designer (self-employed), chauffeur, chartered surveyor, chief constable, chief petty officer, civil servant, computer technician, environmental health officer, inspector of the poor, journalist, museum curator, orphanage manager, police inspector, public assistance officer, quantity surveyor, ship's captain, sample passer, social worker, postmaster, city stationmaster.

C. Skilled occupations

1. Clerical workers and secretaries

bank cashier, company cashier, office worker (unspecified), police clerk, postal clerk, railway office worker, secretaries (typists).

2. Commercial travellers etc.

commercial traveller, firm's representative, insurance agent, insurance salesman.

3. Religious lay people

army scripture reader, Bible woman, colporteur, lay evangelist.

4. Protective services

policeman, sailor (RN), soldier.

5. Non-employing self-employed tradesmen and shopkeepers

bookseller, boarding-house proprietor, confectioner, hairdresser, herbalist, fishmonger, general store proprietor, grocer, photographer, tailor.

6. Foremen

foreman cooper, foreman dyer, foreman grocer, foreman joiner, foreman networker, foreman plater, foreman (unspecified), housekeeper (large establishment), provincial station master, timber-yard foreman.

7. Skilled tradesmen

baker, blacksmith, bootmaker, builder, cabinet maker, coach painter, cooper, decorator, electrician, grocer, hairdresser, joiner, lithographer, motor mechanic, plumber, sadler, shoemaker, slater, stone carver, tailor, upholsterer.

8. Mine-workers

miner (unspecified), mines' fireman, pit bottomer.

9. Iron and steel employees

boiler maker, foundry blacksmith, foundry gasman, foundry worker (unspecified), furnaceman, iron-works worker (unspecified), moulder, pinner, rollingmill engine driver, smelter, steel worker (unspecified).

10. Weavers and textile workers

bleacher, cotton weaver, flax dresser, hackle maker, mill worker (unspecified), networker, pattern-maker, ruffer, sowing machine operator, tenter, silk weaver, wool weaver.

11. Fishermen and seamen

diver, fisherman, fishing boat skipper, master mariner, sea-going engineer, quarter-master.

12. Shop assistants

butcher shop assistant, draper's assistant, grocery shop assistant, window dresser.

13. Railway workers

locomotive driver, railway guard, railway worker (unspecified), signalman.

14. Skilled agricultural workers

miller, tenant farmers (small).

15. Others

ambulance attendant, ambulance driver, assistant manager, beltman, boilermaker, cable runner, chef, crane man, dental assistant, draughtsman, driller, engine man, engineer (unspecified), factory worker (unspecified), hospital worker, homeopathic practitioner, laboratory technician, lorry driver, machine man (unspecified), milliner, motor man, nursing assistant, omnibus driver, orphanage worker (unspecified), platelayer, postman, postal worker (unspecified), preserve maker, shipyard worker (unspecified), small-holding proprietor, steamroller driver, stocktaker, quarryman, sub-postmistress, telephonist.

D. Semi-skilled occupations

1. Agricultural workers

farm servants, herd.

2. Domestic servants

child minder, home-help, housekeeper, launderer, servant.

3. Factory labourers

cabinet works labourer, female factory worker (unspecified), iron foundry labourer, mill labourer, steel works labourer.

4. Others

builder's labourer, canteen worker, caretaker, carter, foreman porter, gardener, gas works stoker, gravedigger, janitor, packer, pirn winder, roadman, sorter, stableman.

E. Unskilled Occupations

1. General labourer

2. Scavenger

3. Char women

BIBLIOGRAPHY

1. Primary Sources

(i) Manuscript Primary Sources (including typescript primary sources)

(A) ASSEMBLY AND CHURCH COLLECTIONS (IN THE POSSESSION OF THE
RELEVANT ASSEMBLY OR CHURCH)

Campbeltown, Argyll, Springbank Evangelical Church: 'Minutes of
Elders Meetings', 2 vols, 1925-64.
East Kilbride, Lanarkshire, Moncrieff Parish Church:
East Kilbride Free Church, 'Minutes of Kirk Session', vol. 2, 1848-83.
Glasgow, Crosshill Evangelical Church:
'Elim Hall, Crosshill, Glasgow: copy letter intimating commencement
of gathering for breaking of bread', anonymous holograph transcript.
A. Bruce, 'Gather My Saints Together Unto Me', typescript [c.1931].
anon., 'Cathcart Road Hall', MS.
anon., 'Lodging House Work', MS.
Insch, Aberdeenshire, Fordyce Hall:
Minute and account book of Insch assembly, 1873-1891.
Kilbirnie, Gospel Hall:
Roll books, 1903, 1909-16, 1919-21, 1925-6, 1928-62.
Kilmarnock, Ayrshire, Central Evangelical Church:
Central View [the magazine of Central Evangelical Church].
'Disposition to the Trustees of Christian Brethren meeting in Central
Hall, John Finnie St., Kilmarnock', typescript, 1934.
'Minutes of Annual Business Meeting', 1932-1989.
Kilmarnock, Ayrshire, Congregational Church:
'Communicants' Roll Book; or Names, Designations, etc., of Members
belonging to Clerk's Lane Congregation, Kilmarnock 1840-1950'.
Kilmarnock, Ayrshire, Elim Hall:
'Christian Brethren, originally holding meetings in the Co-operative
Hall, John Dickie St., Kilmarnock, then in Princes St., Kilmarnock, and
presently in Cuthbert Pl., Kilmarnock. Statement of the Constitution
and Government', typescript, 1931.
Lesmahagow, Lanarkshire, Hope Hall:
James Anderson, 'A Brief Record Concerning the Early Days of the
Assembly in Lesmahagow', MS, 1960.
Gospel Hall, Lesmahagow, roll books, 4 vols, 1876-1926; 1950-71.

Newmains, Lanarkshire, Gospel Hall:
'Minutes of Half-Yearly Meetings and Annual Meetings, Gospel Hall, Newmains', 3 vols, 1924-84.

Newmilns, Ayrshire, Gospel Hall:
'Assembly Register of Believers Meeting in the Name of the Lord Jesus Christ in Drygate Street Gospel Hall Newmilns', 1907-1933; 1951-1955.
J. R. Caldwell to a 'Brother', 14 September 1892.
William Cochrane's duplicate notebook, 1902-3.
Sam Hill, untitled summary of membership of Gospel Hall, Newmilns, 1929-51, MS notes.

Strathaven, Lanarkshire, Strathaven Evangelical Church:
'Roll of Members of Strathaven Assembly 1876-1897'.

Tillicoultry, Clackmannanshire, Bankfoot Evangelical Church:
'Minute Record of the Assembly & Oversight Business Meeting. From 1st Jan. 1925- Ann St. Gospel Hall, Tillicoultry', 1925-39.

(B) ARCHIVES

Christian Brethren Archive, University Library of Manchester, Manchester:
CBA 2356 2357, 2364, 2385, 2409, correspondence of Alexander Marshall to G. F. Bergin.
CBA 2409, Alexander Marshall to P. F. Bruce, 12 October [1926/7].
CBA 5710 (2), 5710 (10) correspondence of Harold St John to Robert Balloch.
CBA 7049, Fry MS.
CBA GC46349 *This Way'*, 1 October 1909.
Uncatalogued material, Robert Chapman to Henry Pickering, 11 March 1921; anon. MS transcript; circular letter, 18 March 1931, MS; draft letter fragment, undated MS.
Uncatalogued box of Robert Rendall papers.

Liddle Collection, Leeds University Library, Leeds:
[John Campbell], 'Experience of John Campbell, Brookfield, Fenwick, During the First World War, both as a Volunteer and a Conscientious Objector', typescript, n.d..

Orkney Archive, Kirkwall:
OA/D/27, Robert Rendall papers.
OA/D31/34, Ernest Marwick papers.

Scottish Record Office, Edinburgh:
IRS 21/1811, Correspondence with Thomas Caldwell.

University of Stirling Library:
MS50, Peter Drummond, 'The Stirling Tract Enterprise: its rise and progress', MS 1860.

(C) PUBLIC LIBRARIES

Carnegie Library, Ayr, ACL 671 BL, Hugh L. Allan, 'Ayr Half a Century Ago and Since' (series from *Ayr Advertiser*, 1889).

Dundee City Library, Lamb Collection, Box 398, 'Newspaper Cuttings, Biographical Notices of Dundee Men', pp.51-8.

Carlisle Library, Carlisle, G852, David Beattie, 'God of Our Nation' (Carlisle [1914]).

Mitchell Library, Glasgow, 'Glasgow Scrapbook', vol. 13.

(D) PRIVATE COLLECTIONS

Mrs Sarah Campbell, Edinburgh:
Cuttings scrapbook.

Mr Roy Coad, Church Stretton, Shropshire
A. M. S. Gooding to F. N. Martin, 9 November 1965.

Mrs Helen Gordon, Kennethmont:
Helen Gordon, MS notebook on history of Insch assembly.

Mr Ian McDowell, Chadstone, Australia:
J. A. Boswell to R. T. Hopkins, 25 July 1889.
W. H. Hopkins, untitled typescript on the early life of R. T. Hopkins, n.d.
John Ritchie to W. H. Hopkins, 7 March 1916.

Mr Norman Macdonald, Newton Mearns, Glasgow:
Duncan Colqhuhoun *et al.*, to overseeing brethren gathered into the name of the Lord Jesus Christ in Vancouver, B.C., 4 September 1893, typescript copy.

Mrs Elizabeth McKinnon, Crosshouse, Ayrshire:
John Ferguson, holograph flyleaf inscription in anon., *The Gospels: why are there four, why do they differ and are they fully inspired?* (London, n.d.).

Mrs Nora Montgomerie, Edinburgh:
John Montgomerie, 'My Odyssey', typescript, n.d..

Mr R. W. Orr:
F. F. Bruce to Robbie Orr, 13 January 1988, typescript letter.

Mr Don Palmer, York:
Notes on interviews with:
Mrs Norman Aitken, Brian Lightbody and Robert Lightbody, 29 May 1988.
Mr Gordon Birss, June 1988.
Mr Jim Harkness, December 1988.
Mr Ron McColl and Mr and Mrs Bob McDonald, 13 May 1988.
Mr Alex Webb, December 1988.

Mr Geofrrey Robson, Brenchley, Kent:
Swanwick Conference Papers.

Dr Margaret H. B. Sanderson, Linlithgow, West Lothian:

Robert McPike, 'Annbank Assembly - 1883-1875 [*sic*]', holograph MS [1975].

'Milngavie per Mr Daisley, Eastbourne', holograph MS, [1974].

J. Waugh, 'Cowie Assembly', holograph MS, 26 November 1974.

Mr Alex. Stewart, Hopeman, Moray:

[Alex. Stewart (compiler)], 'A Record of Gospel Work. Christian Brethren. Moray & Nairn', MS, n.d.

(E) WRITER'S COLLECTION

(I) Material relating to individual assemblies

I.A. Aberdeenshire

1. Fraserburgh: William Noble, 'Fraserburgh', typescript 1989.
2. Peterhead: 'First Message in York Street Hall by Mr. Alex Buchan on 26th June, 1965', cyclostyled foolscap sheet, n.d..

I.B. Angus

1. Arbroath: (i). John Beattie, 'History of Arbroath Assembly', MS 1989.
   (ii). Nicol Millar to the writer, 17 April 1989.
2. Dundee: (i) James Burton-Smith to the writer, 4 March 1998.
   (ii). Hillbank Evangelical Church: William Mills, 'Extracts from "News and Views", November 1980 to June 1981. A History of Hillbank by W. Mills', A4 typescript [1980].
3. Forfar: Charles Pollard to the writer, 4 September 1989.
4. Montrose: Robert I. Taylor to the writer, 6 January 1990.

I.C. Ayrshire

1. Auchinleck: James McCombe, 'A History of Auchinleck Assembly', A4 typescript, 1981.
2. Barrmill: David Bell, 'A Short History of the Christian Brethren Movement with Special Reference to the Origin of the Barrmill Assembly', typescript, 1986.
3. Crosshill: (i). James McBirnie to the writer, 11 April 1989.
   (ii). H. Wright, 'Crosshill Assembly's Diamond Jubilee', photocopy of typescript poem [1962].
4. Glenburn, Prestwick: John McCloy, '"O Glenburn Greatly Favoured", 1929-1959', typescript [1996].
5. Largs: anon., 'Recollections & Reports of Largs Assembly in Bath Hall', MS [1986].
6. Ochiltree: John Hannah, interview with William Hannah 18 April 1993, MS notes.

I.D. Banffshire

1. Portessie: Tom Morrow to the writer, 8 December 1988.

2. Portsoy: James Merson to the writer, 28 November 1988.

I.E. Berwickshire
1. Chirnside: Kenneth Brown to the writer, 29 November 1994.

I.F. Dumfriesshire
1. Kirkconnel: Robert Lind to the writer, 3 May 1989.
2. Lockerbie: [Alex S. Traill], 'Lockerbie Assembly', typescript, 1987.
3. Sanquhar: Robert Lind to the writer [1989].

I.G. Dunbartonshire
1. Cumbernauld: [Willie Barr], 'Cumbernauld Assembly' MS, 1989.
2. Dumbarton: Robert Boyd to Alex McIntosh, 21 April 1987, photocopy of holograph letter.
3. Kirkintilloch: (i). Account book of Gospel Hall, Kirkintilloch, 1922-1949.
   (ii). 'Proposed meeting house for Christian Brethren at East High Street', draughtsman's drawings by John Shanks, November 1897.
3. Milngavie: [Clem Round], 'Milngavie Assembly', typescript [1988].

I.H. Edinburgh
1. Edinburgh: W. W. Campbell, 'Bellevue Chapel', photocopy of typescript, n.d..
2. Leith: (i). anon., 'Blackburn Hall, Leith', photocopy of MS, n.d..
   (ii). anon., 'The Leith Assembly', photocopy of MS, n.d..

I.I. Fife
1. Ballingry: Kenneth A. Munro to the writer, 9 June 1988.
2. Blairhall: Thomas Rowan to the writer 10 June 1987; and 26 January 1988.
3. Cardenden: Dr James Runcie to the writer 12 April 1989.
4. Cowdenbeath: Robert Muir 'Union Hall, Broad Street, Cowdenbeath', typescript 1988
5. Dunfermline: John Orr to the writer [1987].
6. Inverkeithing: (i). [Archie Carmichael], untitled MS [1988].
   (ii). Harry Edwards to the writer [1987]; 1 September [1987]; and 15 August [1988].
7. Kelty: (i). Helen B. Gallacher, 'The Story of Ebenezer Hall', typescript [1987].
   (ii). Helen B. Gallacher to the writer, 30 June 1987.
8. Ladybank: (i). Catherine C. Bell to the writer, 1 April 1988.
   (ii). [Mr R. Mackay], untitled MS, n.d..
   (iii). Mr R. Mackay to the writer, 3 March 1988; and 9 April 1988.

9. Lochore: James Innes, 'Assembly at Lochore, Fife, Scotland', MS [1988].
10. St Andrews: Ian Ross to the writer, 29 June 1988.

I.J. Glasgow

1. Albert Hall, Shawlands: anon., 'Albert Hall, Shawlands Cross', photocopy of typescript, n.d..
2. Anniesland Hall, Anniesland: anon., '19th September 1958', photocopy of MS.
3. London Road Gospel Hall: 'Gospel Hall, 1059 London Rd.', Sunday school business meeting minute book, 1938-42.
4. Newton Mearns: S. Bolton, 'A Short History of Newton Mearns Assembly', photocopy of MS, 1978.

I.K. Highlands

1. Campbeltown, Argyll: R. H. Craig to the writer, 4 July 1988; and 27 January 1989.
2. Rothesay, Bute: D. C. Muir to the writer, 11 April 1989.

I.L. Kircudbrightshire

1. Creetown: 'Creetown Assembly Since 1920 (as remembered by W[illiam]. D[unning].)', photocopy of typescript, n.d.
2. Gatehouse of Fleet: W. Dunning, 'Assemblies in the South of Scotland. 1908-1947. Gatehouse of Fleet', typescript [1988].

I.M. Lanarkshire

1. Airdrie: Willie Dickson, 'What I Remember about the Assembly in Hebron Hall, Airdrie - May 1981', photocopy of typescript, 1981.
2. Baillieston: William S. Hutchinson, 'Baillieston Gospel Hall Assembly', typescript, 1988.
3. Bellshill, Jim Lewis, 'Some Notes re. History of Bellshill Assembly', MS 1989.
4. Bothwellhaugh: (i). David L. Cook to the writer, 21 September 1992.
(ii). M. A. Crooks, 'Relating the Commencement of the Gospel Effort in Bothwellhaugh', photocopy of holograph transcript, n.d..
5. Burnbank: John Donaldson, history of Burnbank assembly on cassette tape, 1973.
6. Cambuslang: (i). Arunah Hall, Burnside: David Wightman to the writer, 18 September 1988.
(ii). Ebenezer Hall, Halfway: John Griffen 'Ebenezer Hall, Halfway, Cambuslang', MS 1989.
(iii). Westcoats Evangelical Church: T. A. Roy, untitled history of Westcoats Evangelical Church, typescript 1989.
7. Carfin: James H. Capie, 'Carfin Assembly - 1988', typescript, 1988.

8. Carluke: T. C. Suffil *et al.*, *Gospel Hall, Carluke* (n.p., March, 1923).
9. Coatbridge: Andrew Leggat, 'Hebron Hall, 20/22 Church St., Coatbridge', MS 1989.
10. Forth: (i). Tom Aitken, untitled history of Forth assembly, MS, 1988.
   (ii). James McCallum, 'The Roll Call', MS transcript of a poem [*c*.1914].
11. East Kilbride: David Wightman to the writer, 5 August 1988.
12. Gartness: Harry Morris, 'Glenview Evangelical Church Gartness', MS 1988.
13. Greengairs: (i). anon., 'Assembly of God, Greengairs', MS [1989].
   (ii). anon., untitled history of Greengairs assembly, typescript, n.d..
   (iii). John Rae to the writer, 29 May [1989].
14. Hamilton:
   (i). Gospel Hall, High Parks: Alfred Brown to the writer [March 1989]; and 6 May 1989.
   (ii). Gospel Hall, Low Waters: Andrew Mathie to the writer, 5 May 1986.
15. Holytown: Brian Young, untitled history of Holytown assembly, MS, 1988.
16. Lanark: Alex Reid to the writer [November 1988].
17. Larkhall: [Cornelius Dickson], 'Excerpt of Disposition for Hebron Hall Academy Street Larkhall. 1924', holograph transcript [1940].
18. Law: Thomas Finlay to the writer, 13 January 1989.
19. Leadhills: (i). Robert R. McCall to the writer 10 May 1987; 21 May 1987 and 30 May 1987.
   (iii). 'Lines composed by William Lindsay on the Opening of the New Hall at Leadhills on 10th November, 1905', cyclostyled typescript.
20. Netherburn: James McAulay, 'A Minor Survey of "The Assembly"', n.d., typescript copy, 1964.
21. Newmains: James P. Aitken, 'Newmains Assembly', MS 1988.
22. New Stevenston: David Wilson, 'A Brief History of the Assembly of Christian Brethren Meeting in Gospel Hall, Hall St., New Stevenston, Motherwell', MS [1989].
23. Overtown: [James Hislop], '"Seventy Years On" or "These Seventy Years": the story of Overtown Assembly of Christian Brethren', photocopy of MS [1971].
24. Rutherglen: Arunah Hall, Burnside: David Wightman to the writer, 18 September 1988.
25. Salsburgh: E. Long to the writer, 28 August 1988.
26. Strathaven: (i). 'List of the Members of the Strathaven Brethren', MS notebook, 1862-75.
   (ii). James S. Macfarlane to the writer, 19 August 1988.
27. Uddingston: Andrew McNeish to the writer, May 1988; and 7 June 1988.

28. Wishaw: anon., untitled history of Ebenezer Gospel Hall, Wishaw, photocopy of MS, n.d..

I.N. Lothians

1. Armadale: JRRL, 'A Short History of the Assembly of Christian Brethren in Armadale', typescript 1982.
2. Blackburn: Sam Thomson to the writer, 19 June 1988.
3. Bo'ness: Andrew Ferguson to the writer, 15 August, 1988.
4. Kirknewton: David Taylor to the writer, 13 April 1989.
5. Port Seton: J. S. Blackie, 'Viewforth Gospel Hall Port Seton; a short history', cyclostyled A4 sheet [1982].

I.O. Moray

1. Forres: J. Paterson to the writer, 8 April 1989.
2. Lossiemouth: Jim Gault to the writer, 15 February 1989.

I.P. Orkney

1. Orkney: [John Oddie], untitled account of the history of Orkney assemblies, typescript [1989].
2. Harray: [John Oddie], untitled account of Harray Meeting House centenary conference, typescript [1979].
3. Papa Westray: [Michael Browne], 'How It All Began - Papa Westray, Orkney', typescript [1977/8/9].
4. Westray: E. B. Bromiley to Robert Rendall, 31 January 1944, photocopy of holograph letter.

I.Q. Perthshire

1. Abernethy: [J. A. Wilkie], 'Abernethy Gospel Hall', typescript, 1990.
2. Perth: Wm Walker to the writer, 13 April 1989.

I.R. Renfrewshire

1. Bridge of Weir: (i). Tom Kent to John Hamilton, 1 March 1978, photocopy of holograph letter.
(ii). Tom Kent to the writer, 10 April 1989.
2. Barrhead: Jim McLatchie to the writer, 16 April 1989.
3. Greenock [S. K. Church], 'Assembly at Greenock, Renfrewshire, Now Meeting at Ardgowan Square Evangelical Church', typescript, 1988.
4. [William Geddes], '100 Years Ago..', *Link* [the magazine of Shuttle Street Hall Assembly, Paisley] (1978), pp.1-18.
5. Renfrew: Wm Loudoun, 'Renfrew Assembly', MS 1988.

I.S. Roxburghshire

1. Hawick: [autograph page missing] to William Landles, 29 July 1955, photocopy of holograph letter.

I.T. Shetland
1. Shetland: (i). [James Moar], 'A Continued Survey of Service in the
   Shetland Isles from 1914 to 1976', photocopy of typescript, 1976.
   (ii). [James Moar], 'Experience on Foula', photocopy of typescript
   [1952].
   (iii). George Peterson to the writer [March 1989]; and 27 April 1992.
2. Selivoe: [James Moar], 'The Work of the Lord in Connection with
   Selivoe Assembly in Country Districts', photocopy of typescript, n.d..

I.U. Stirlingshire
1. Cowie: Danny Sharp to the writer, 13 August 1988.
2. Denny: A. Comrie to the writer, March 1989.
3. Haggs: Russell Turnbull to the writer, 30 October 1988.
4. Maddiston: Alexander Smith to the writer, 10 July 1989.
5. Stirling: James Hislop, 'The Story of Christian Brethren Assembly,
   Stirling', MS [1989].

I.V. Wigtownshire
1. Glenluce: William Henry, untitled history of Glenluce assembly, MS
   [1989].

(II) Miscellaneous
Ayrshire Christian Youth Rallies committee minutes, 1964-1987.
Andrew Borland to Tom Dickson, MS letter [1956].
John Cowan, Motherwell, holograph annotations in Thomas Newberry
   (ed.), *The Englishmen's Bible* (London, 1884).
[Neil Dickson] 'Twenty-Five Years of Change', typescript narration for
   Scottish Counties Evangelistic Movement audio-visual, 1990.
'Enterprise' [magazine of Gospel Hall Bible class, Kirkintilloch] (May
   1970).
James K. Jack, Prestwick, holograph annotations in *The Holy Bible*,
   Authorised Version, interlinear edn (Oxford, n.d.).
Peter Jack, Shotts, holograph annotations in *The Holy Bible*, Revised
   Version (Oxford and Cambridge, 1903).
Malcolm Leslie to George Budge, tape cassette, 1979.
[Robert Morrison], 'A few notes on old Kilwinning Town and the
   biography of Robert Morrison, Crosshouse', typescript, *c*.1939.
Jas. Paton, 'Where Is It?', MS notebook, *c*.1950.
Charles Smith, Kirkwall, papers:
   Charles Smith, 'Water and Spirit', MS notebook.
   J. R. Caldwell to Charles Smith, 18 March 1909.
   W. H. Bennet to Charles Smith, 18 July 1910; 13 August 1910; and 21
   January 1911.
   Charles Smith to W. H. Bennet, 15 July 1910, holograph copy.

Charles Smith to W. H. Bennet, n.d., draft holograph copy.
Charles Smith to W. H. Bennet, 15 August 1910, holograph copy.
James Stephen to Charles Smith, 30 November 1910; 19 December 1910; and 20 February 1911.
W. E. Vine to Charles Smith, 22 December 1910.
Letters to the writer:
John Boyes to the writer, 14 April 1990.
F. F. Bruce to the writer, 26 April 1987; and 8 June 1987.
John S. Fisher to the writer, 3 September 1990.
James Hislop to the writer, 19 January 1990.
G. W. Robson to the writer, 6 January 1990.
University of Glasgow Archivist to the writer, 18 January 1990.
Max Wright to the writer, 11 February, 1992.

(ii) Printed Primary Sources

(A) BRETHREN PERIODICALS

Assembly Testimony
The Believer's Magazine (*Believer's Magazine* from 1992)
The Believer's Pathway
The Believer's Treasury
The Christian Graphic (*Faithful Words* until 1921; *Our Monthly Magazine* incorporated 1936)
The Christian Magazine and Herald of Union
The Christian Witness
The Christian Worker and Bible Student's Helper (*The Sunday School Worker and Bible Student's Helper* until 1911)
Eleventh Hour
'*Homework*'
The Harvester (*The Witness* incorporated 1980; *Aware* from 1991)
The Herald of Salvation
Knowing the Scriptures
The Latter Rain
Le Messager Évangélique
Newsletter - Partnership (from 1995 *Partnership Perspectives*)
Needed Truth
The Northern Assemblies (*The Assemblies* from March 1874)
The Northern Trumpet
Our Little One's Treasury
The Present Testimony
Report of Pioneer Gospel Work in Scotland
The Truth Promoter (founded as *The Truth, the only Way to the Freedom. Elevation and Happiness of Man*)

The Witness (successively *The Northern Evangelistic Intelligencer* (1871-1878); *The Northern Intelligencer* (1873-4); *The Northern Witness* (1875-87); and *The Witness* (1888-1980))
The Young Watchman

(B) NON-BRETHREN PERIODICALS
The Christian
The Primitive Methodist Magazine
The Presbyterian Quarterly and the Princeton Review
The Revival
The St Andrews University Magazine
The Wynd Journal

(C) NEWSPAPERS
Aberdeen Free Press
The Aberdeen Journal
The Alloa Advertiser
The Campbeltown Courier
Cumberland News
The Dundee Advertiser
The Dunfermline Press
The Glasgow Herald
The Guardian
Hamilton Advertiser
Hawick News
Kilmarnock Standard
The North Star
The Orcadian
The Orkney Herald
Scotland on Sunday
The Sunday Times
The Scotsman
Southern Recorder
The Weekly Supplement for Galston, Newmilns, Darvel and Hurlford
West Lothian Courier
Wigtown Free Press

(D) ASSEMBLY ADDRESS BOOKS
The Assemblies Address Book: useful addresses for Christians (Bristol, 1990).
The Assemblies Address Book: useful information for Christians, 2nd edn (Bristol, 1991).
The Assemblies Address Book: useful addresses and other information for Christians, 3rd edn (Bath, 1995).

The Assemblies Address Book: useful addresses and other information for Christians, 4th edn (Bath, 1997).
Assemblies in Britain and Other Parts: where believers gather in the name of the Lord Jesus Christ on the first day of the week for breaking of bread (London, 1951).
Assemblies in Britain and Other Parts: where believers gather in the name of the Lord Jesus Christ on the first day of the week for breaking of bread (London, 1959).
Christian Brethren Assemblies Round the World (Basingstoke, 1983).
J. W. Jordan, *List of Some Meetings in the British Isles and Regions Beyond* (Greenwich, 1897).
—, *List of Some Meetings in the British Isles and Regions Beyond* (London, 1904).
List of Some Assemblies in the British Isles: where believers professedly gather in the name of the Lord Jesus for worship and breaking of bread in remembrance of him upon the first day of the week (London and Glasgow [1921]).
List of Some Assemblies in the British Isles: where believers professedly gather in the name of the Lord Jesus for worship and breaking of bread in remembrance of him upon the first day of the week (London, 1922).
References (January 1884) (n.p., 1884).
References (January 1885) (n.p., 1885).

(E) AUTOBIOGRAPHICAL AND BIOGRAPHICAL MATERIAL ON BRETHREN INDIVIDUALS

Robert Allison and Lois Fleming, *Leaves from the African Jungle: the life story of Robert Crawford Allison* (Kilmarnock, 1999).
James Anderson (ed.), *They Finished Their Course* (Kilmarnock, 1980).
— (ed.), *They Finished their Course in the Eighties* (Kilmarnock, 1990).
— (compiler), *Willie Scott: 55+ years of service* (Glasgow, 1986).
John S. Anderson, *Heroes of the Faith in Modern Italy* (Glasgow, 1914).
Anon., *How I was Led Outside the Camp and Gathered in the Name of the Lord Jesus* (Kilmarnock, n.d.).
Ernest Baker, *The Life and Explorations of Frederick Stanley Arnot: the authorised biography of a zealous missionary, intrepid explorer, & self-denying benefactor amongst natives of Africa* (London, 1921).
Samuel Blow, *Reminiscences of Thirty Years' Gospel work and Revival Times* ([c.1890]) rpt (Glasgow, 1988).
John Bowes, *The Autobiography: or the history of the life of John Bowes* (Glasgow, 1872).
George Mackay Brown, 'Robert Rendall', in *An Orkney Tapestry* (London, 1969), pp.163-71.

F. F. Bruce, *In Retrospect: remembrance of things past* (London and Glasgow, 1980).

W. H. Clare, *Pioneer Preaching: or work well done* (Glasgow [1923]).

Roy Coad, *Laing: the biography of Sir John W. Laing CBE (1879-1978)* (London, 1979).

Ransome W. Cooper, *James Lees: shepherd of lonely sheep in Europe* (London, 1947).

Neil Dickson, 'Robert Rendall: a life', in *idem* (ed.), *An Island Shore: selected writings of Robert Rendall* (Kirkwall, 1990), pp.17-49.

William P. Douglas *et al.*, *John Ferguson: evangelist and teacher*, 2nd edn ([Detroit, MI, 1940]).

Andrew Wingfield Digby and Stuart Weir, 'Brian Irvine', in *Winning is not Enough* (London, 1991), pp.98-112.

[Editors of *Echoes of Service* (eds)], *Selected Letters with Brief Memoir of J. G. M'Vicker* (London, 1902).

[Fred Elliott], *The Conversion and Call of Fred Elliott* (London and Glasgow, 1917).

J. J. Ellis, *Dan Crawford of Luanza* (Kilmarnock [1927]).

E. S. English, *H. A. Ironside: ordained of the Lord* (Grand Rapids, MI, 1946).

C. F. Geddes, *Love Lifted Me* (Glasgow, 1986).

William Gilmore, *These Seventy Years* (Kilmarnock [c.1952]).

Michael Grant, *Twice Delivered* [1935] rpt (Glasgow, n.d.).

Mrs [Harriet] Groves (ed.), *Memoir of Anthony Norris Groves: compiled chiefly from his journals and letters*, 3rd edn (London, 1869).

John Hawthorn, *Alexander Marshall: evangelist, author and pioneer* (Glasgow [1929]).

G. C. D. Howley, 'Frederick Fyvie Bruce: an appreciation', in W. W. Gasque and R. P. Martin (eds), *Apostolic History and the Gospel* (Exeter, 1970), pp.15-19.

James G. Hutchinson, *Something of My Life: whose I am, and whom I serve Acts 27:23* (Glasgow, 1997).

— (ed.), *Sowers, Reapers, Builders: a record of over ninety Irish evangelists* (Glasgow, 1984).

Fred Kelling, *Fisherman of Faroe: William Gibson Sloan* (Göta, Faroe Islands, 1993).

M[ark]. K[err]., *Memoir of John Justice* (Ayr, 1875).

G. H. Lang, *An Ordered Life* (London, 1959).

— *Anthony Norris Groves: saint and pioneer* (London, 1939).

John McAlpine, *Forty Years Evangelising in Britain* (London, 1947).

James McKendrick, *Seen and Heard During Forty-Six Years' Evangelistic Work* (London [1933]).

[George Müller], *A Narrative of Some of the Lord's Dealings with George Müller, written by Himself*, 6 vols, 9th edn (London, 1895).

George Moffat, *Yet Will I Rejoice* (London, 1982).

George N. Patterson, *God's Fool* (London, 1956).

— *Patterson of Tibet: death throes of a nation* (San Diego, CA, 1998).

Meg Patterson, *Dr Meg* (Milton Keynes, 1994).

Henry Pickering, 'Brief life of the author', in John R. Caldwell, *Epitome of Christian Experience in Psalm XXXII with the development of the Christian life* (Glasgow [1917]), pp.ix-xxxiv.

— (ed.), *Chief Men Among the Brethren*, 1st edn (Glasgow, 1918); 2nd edn (London, 1931).

Robert Plant (compiler), *They Finished Their Course in the 90s* (Kilmarnock, 2000).

Robert Rendall, *J. B. Watson: a memoir and selected writings* (London, 1957).

[John Ritchie], *Donald Munro 1839-1908: a servant of Jesus Christ* ([1909]), rpt (Glasgow, 1987).

J[ohn]. R[itchie]., *Jeanie Gilchrist: pioneer missionary to the women of Central Africa* (Kilmarnock [1927]).

John Ritchie [Jnr], *'Feed My Sheep': memorials of Peter Hynd, of Troon* (Kilmarnock [1904]).

Tom Rea (compiler), *The Life and Labours of David Rea, Evangelist: largely written from his own MSS* (Belfast, 1917).

Bernie Reid, *No Greater Joy: the story of Bobbie Wright* (Belfast, 1989).

C. W. R[oss]. (ed.), *Donald Ross: pioneer evangelist of the North of Scotland and United States of America* (Kilmarnock [1903]).

Patricia St John, *Harold St John* (London, 1961).

James Stephen, 'Alexander Marshall', in *idem, Twelve Famous Evangelists with incidents in their remarkable lives* (London [*c*.1935]), pp.50-7.

Charles B. Summers (compiler and ed.), *Return to Old Paths: the ministry of Charles Spurgeon Summers* (Tacoma, WA, 1990).

[Ebenezer Tainsh (compiler)], *Whither Bound? How God saved eight well-known veterans* (East Kilbride, 1943).

W. Elfe Tayler, *Passages from the Diary and Letters of Henry Craik of Bristol* (London, 1866).

C. B. C. Tilsley, *Through the Furnace* (Newtown, NSW, Australia, 1979).

G. E. Tilsley, *Dan Crawford: missionary and pioneer in Central Africa* (London [1929]).

A. C. T[homson], *Un Hombre Bueno: vida de Jaime Clifford* (n.p., Argentina, 1957).

W. G. Turner, *John Nelson Darby: a biography* (London, 1926).

John Wilson and James McClelland, *Impossible with Men* (Belfast, 1996).

Max S. Weremchuk, *John Nelson Darby* (1988) Eng. edn (Neptune, NJ, 1992).

(F) PRINTED MATERIAL BY BRETHREN WRITERS

John Allan, *The Evangelicals: an illustrated history* (Exeter, 1989).
— '"A new shape, though unformed"', in Kevin G. Dyer, *Must Brethren Churches Die?* (Exeter, 1991), pp.7-21.

L. W. G. Alexander, *The Breaking of Bread* (Glasgow [1907]).
— *Discerning the Body* (Glasgow, 1907).

David Anderson-Berry, *Pictures in the Book of Acts: or the unfinished work of Jesus* (Glasgow [c.1910]).
— *The Seven Sayings of Christ on the Cross* (Glasgow [1904]).

James Anderson, *Our Heritage* (Kilmarnock, 1973).

James A. Anderson, *The Authority for the Public Ministry of Women* (Braemar, n.d.).
— *The Blessed Hope: a study in dialogue form on the coming again of the Lord Jesus* (London [c.1930]).
— *The Chart: the Divine forecast of this age* (London, n.d.).
— *Heralds of the Dawn* (Aberdeen [c.1934]).
— *Passion Week Retold: last days of Christ's public ministry* (Rhynie [1946]).
— *Woman's Warfare and Ministry: what saith the scriptures?* (Rhynie, n.d.).
— Sir Robert Anderson, *The Gospel and Its Ministry: a handbook of evangelical truth* ([c.1870]), 13th edn (Glasgow [c.1905]).

Anon., *'The Brethren': with special reference to a recent article in 'The Record' of the United Free Church July 1925 by Rev. James Black D.D. of Free St George's, Edinburgh, by an Edinburgh Brother* (Edinburgh [1926]).

Anon., (ed.), *A New Testament Church in 1955* (Rushden, 1956).

Anon., (ed.), *A Return to Simplicity: Conference of Brethren at High Leigh, September, 1956* (Rushden [1959]).

Alan G. Bamford (ed.), *Where Do We Go From Here? The Future of the Brethren: report of addresses and discussions at the Swanwick Conference of Brethren, September 1978* (Worthing, 1979).

F. A. Banks, *The Bishops of Scripture: their qualification and their work* (Kilmarnock, n.d.).
— *Spiritual Growth: and other writings of the late Frederick Arthur Banks*, 2nd edn (Bradford, 1947).

Percy Beard, *A Neglected Aspect of the Cross* (Airdrie, 1910).

David J. Beattie, *Langsyne in Eskdale* (Carlisle, 1950).
— *Oor Ain Folk* (Carlisle, 1933).
— *Oor Gate En'* (Galashiels, 1915).
— *Prince Charlie and the Borderland* (Carlisle, 1925).
— *Psalm Singing Among the Scottish Covenanters. A lecture delivered to the Carlisle Adult School, Fisher Street, on Wednesday, June 30th, 1915* (Carlisle [1915]).

— *The Romance of Sacred Song* (London, 1931).
— *Stories and Sketches of our Hymns and their Writers* (London, 1931).
— *Songs of the King's Highway* (London and Glasgow, 1927).
Hunter Beattie, *Christian and War being 'The Word of the Cross'* (Glasgow, n.d.).
— *Jesus the Divider: a devotional meditation on the Son of God whose claims on the souls of men send fire and a sword and division unto this day* (Kilmarnock, n.d.).
The Believers Hymn Book (Glasgow [1885]).
The Believers Hymn Book Supplement (London [1959]).
R. F. Beveridge (compiler), *Celestial Songs: a collection of 900 choice hymns and choruses* (London [1921]).
[Caroline S. Blackwell], *A Living Epistle: or gathered fragments from the correspondence of the late Caroline S. Blackwell* (1873) John Ritchie edn (Kilmarnock, n.d).
William Blane, *Lays of Life and Hope* ([c.1890]), rev. edn (Kilmarnock and London, 1938).
— *The Silent Land and Other Poems* (London, 1906).
— *The Verse of William Blane* (Oxford, 1937).
Andrew Borland, *By This Conquer: studies in the Epistle to the Philippians* (Kilmarnock, 1930).
— *The Cradle of the King: the story of the birth and early days of Jesus, retold for young people* (Kilmarnock [1929]).
— *The Cradle of the Race: the story of the world in its early days, told for young folks* (Kilmarnock [1925]).
— *Crusaders for Christ in Heathen Lands: short biographies of six noble men and women who went forth into the dark places of the earth with the light of the gospel (with original poems)* (Kilmarnock, 1928).
— 'The Lord's Supper', in J. B. Watson (ed.), *The Church: a symposium* (London, 1949), pp.66-81.
— *Love's Most Excellent Way: or Christian courtship* (London and Edinburgh [1923]).
— *Old Paths & Good Ways in Personal, Family and Church Life* (Kilmarnock [1938]).
— *Romans Chapter Eight* (Kilmarnock, 1964).
— *Women's Place in the Assembly* (Kilmarnock, 1969).
Andrew Borland (ed.), *The Bible and Its Doctrines: original outlines on the great themes* [*The Christian Worker* for 1930 in one volume] (Kilmarnock, 1930).
John Bowes, *Christian Union: showing the importance of Unity among real Christians of all Denominations, and the Means by which it may be effected* (Edinburgh, 1835).
— *A Hired Ministry Unscriptural* (Manchester [c.1843]).

— *Mormonism Exposed in its Swindling, Polygamy, & Licentious Abominations, Refuted in its Principles, and in the Claims of its Head, the Modern Mohammed, Joseph Smith, who is proved to have been a Deceiver and no Prophet of God. Addressed to the serious consideration of the 'Latter-Day Saints', and also to the friends of mankind*, 2nd edn (Cheltenham, 1854).

— *The New Testament translated from the purest Greek* (Dundee, 1870).

— and Joseph Barker, *The Report of the Public Discussion, at Stockport between Mr John Bowes of Cheltenham, editor of 'The Truth Promoter', &c. and Mr Joseph Barker, of Ohio, America: the question for debate:- 'Are the Scriptures of the Old & New Testaments of Supernatural Origin and Divine Authority; are the Doctrines Contained therein Conducive to Morality and Virtue?'* (London, 1855).

— and Woodville Woodman, *Report of a Public Discussion between the Rev. Woodville Woodman and Mr John Bowes on the Doctrines of the New Jerusalem Church concerning Heaven and Hell, the Trinity, Justification, and the Resurrection* (Bolton, 1858).

— *The Twenty-First Report of the Means Employed by Several Churches of Christ to Proclaim the Glorious Gospel of God's Grace and promote unity, purity and activity in the church chiefly exhibited from J. Bowes' Journal. 1859-60* (Dundee, 1860).

John Brown, *Something or Nothing: which?* (London, 1893).

— *'Spoken Words' on Profitable Themes* (1886), rpt (Dundee and Edinburgh, 1938).

F. F. Bruce, *Commentary on the Epistle to the Hebrews* (London, 1964).

— 'Church history and its lessons', in J. B. Watson (ed.), *The Church: a symposium* (London, 1949), pp.178-195.

— *History of the Bible in English*, 3rd edn (Guildford and London, 1979).

— *Israel and the Nations: from the Exodus to the fall of the Second Temple* (Exeter, 1963).

— *The Letter of Paul to the Romans: an introduction and commentary*, 2nd edn (Leicester, 1985).

— *New Testament History*, 3rd edn (London and Glasgow, 1980).

— *The Spreading Flame: the rise and progress of Christianity from its first beginnings to the conversion of the English* (Exeter, 1961).

— 'Women in the Church: a biblical survey', *CBRJ*, 33 (1982), pp.7-14.

Alfred H. Burton, *What is Exclusivism? a review of Mr Alex. Marshall's 'Holding Fast the Faithful Word'* (London, 1908).

John R. Caldwell, *'Because Ye Belong to Christ': or the responsibilities of believers to each other* (Glasgow [1899]).

— *The Charter of the Church: revised notes of an exposition of the First Epistle to the Corinthians*, 2 vols (Glasgow [1910]).

— *Christ in the Levitical Offerings* (Glasgow. n.d.).

— 'The congregation of true believers in the Lord Jesus', in W. Hoste and R. M'Elheran (eds), *The True Church: what is it? who compose it?* (Glasgow [1922]), pp.32-6.

— *District Oversight Meetings: their origin and their issues* [sic] *and On Increase of Knowledge* (Glasgow, n.d.).

— *The Earthly Relationships of the Heavenly Family* (Glasgow [c.1890]).

— *Epitome of Christian Experience in Psalm XXXII with the development of the Christian life* (Glasgow [1917]).

— *Exclusivism: a letter by J. R. C.* (Glasgow, 1882).

— *Foundations of the Faith Once for all Delivered to the Saints* (Glasgow [1903]).

— *From the Cross to the Kingdom*, rpt (Glasgow, 1983).

— *Leaven* (Glasgow [1883]).

— *A Revision of Certain Teachings Regarding the Gathering and Receiving of Children of God* (Glasgow [1906]).

— *The Ministry of Women* (Glasgow [1895]).

— *Separation from the World: Jehoshophat and other papers* (Glasgow [1883]).

— *Shadows of Christ in the Old Testament* (Glasgow, n.d.).

— *Sanctification* (Glasgow, 1903).

— *Things to Come: being a short outline of some of the great events of prophecy* ([1875]) rpt (Glasgow, 1983).

Dan Crawford, *Back to the Long Grass: my link with Livingstone* (London [1922]).

— *Thinking Black: 22 years without a break in the long grass of Central Africa* (London, 1912).

— *Thirsting After God* (London [1927]).

— 'What is the gospel?', in W. Hoste and R. McElheran (eds), *The Great Sacrifice: or what the death of Christ has wrought* (Kilmarnock [1927]), pp.29-37.

[J. N. Darby], *Collected Writings of J. N. Darby*, 33 vols (ed.) William Kelly (Kingston-on-Thames, n.d.).

— *Letters of J. N. D.*, 3 vols (Kingston-on-Thames, n.d.).

[C. J. Davis], *Aids to Believers: being all the writings for the Lord's people of the late Dr. C. J. Davis* (Glasgow [1912]).

John A. H. Dempster, *The T. & T. Clark Story: a Victorian publisher and the New Theology with an epilogue covering the twentieth-century history of the firm* (Durham, 1992).

John Dickie, *The Story of Philip Sharkey, the Kilmarnock blacksmith* (Kilmarnock, n.d.).

— *The Story of William Cochrane: or knowing about it, and yet not saved* (Kilmarnock, n.d.).

— *Words of Faith, Hope and Love from the Chamber of a Dying Saint: being a series of letters written by the late John Dickie, of Irvine, Scotland, during his last illness to his friend and brother in Christ, James Todd,* Dublin, 2 vols (ed.) James Todd (London, 1900).

Beth Dickson, 'Annie S. Swan and O. Douglas: legacies of the Kailyard', in Douglas Gifford and Dorothy McMillan, *A History of Scottish Women's Writing* (Edinburgh, 1997), pp.329-46.

— 'Class and being in the novels of William McIlvanney', in Gavin Wallace and Randall Stevenson (eds), *The Scottish Novel Since the Seventies* (Edinburgh, 1993), pp.54-70.

— 'Foundations of the Modern Scottish Novel', in Cairns Craig (ed.), *The History of Scottish Literature,* 4 (Aberdeen, 1987), pp.49-60.

— '"An ordinary little girl": Willa Muir's *Mrs Ritchie'*, in Carol Anderson and Aileen Christianson (eds), *Scottish Women's Fiction 1920s to 1960s: journeys into being* (East Linton, 2000), pp.97-108.

W. H. Dorman, *Principles of Truth on the Present State of the Church addressed to all Denominations: also reasons for retiring from the Independent or Congregational body, and from Islington Chapel* (London, 1838).

John Douglas, *Lessons from the Kings of Israel and Judah* (Ashgill, 1997).

Kevin G. Dyer, *Must Brethren Churches Die?* (1990) UK edn (Exeter, 1991).

H. L. Ellison, *The Household Church* (1963), 2nd edn (Exeter, 1979).

Fred Elliott, 'The gospel and its blessing', in W. Hoste and R. McElheran (eds), *The Great Sacrifice: or what the death of Christ has wrought* (Kilmarnock [1927]), pp.60-8.

I. Y. Ewan, *Remembrance Hymns* (Abernethy, 1935).

— *Caravanserai: a Collection of Poems by I. Y. Ewan* [(ed.) Edwin Ewan] (Glasgow, 1980).

N. J. Gourlay, *Church Symbols for Today: the water, the head, the bread and wine* (Kansas City, KA, 1999).

John Grant, *Let's Talk about Courtship* (Kilmarnock [1996]).

W. J. Grant, *'Excelsior' and other Addresses* (Goodmayes, 1928).

[Anthony Norris Groves], *Journal of a Residence at Bagdad, during the Years 1830 and 1831 by Mr. Anthony N. Groves, Missionary* (ed.) A. J. Scott (London, 1832).

D. T. Grimson, *A Diagram of Dispensations: with key* (Glasgow, 1867).

David Haxton *et al.* (eds), *Discipleship: a record and report of a week-end discussion at Netherhall, Largs* (Edinburgh, 1954).

R. T. H[opkins]., *Fellowship Among Saints: what saith the scriptures?* (Glasgow, 1884).

— *Remarks on a Letter: what does 'separation' mean?* (Melbourne, 1888).

William Hoste and William Rodgers, *Questions and Answers* (Kilmarnock, 1957), William Bunting (ed.).

W. H. Hunter, *The Gathering and Receiving of Children of God: a review of a recent booklet* (Kilmarnock [c.1906]).

C. F. Hogg and J. B. Watson, *The Promise of His Coming* (London, 1943).

G. C. D. Howley, *et al.*, (eds), *A New Testament Commentary* (London, 1969).

Fay Inchfawn, *Those Remembered Days* (London, 1963).

R. D. Johnston, *The Man who Moved Multitudes: and the secret of his success* [D. L. Moody] (London [1937]).

— *Resurrection: Myth or Miracle* (Kilmarnock, n.d.).

— *The Solace of Shadowland* (London, 1948).

— *Sound Speech: studies in English for Christian workers* (Kilmarnock, 1927).

W. Kelly, *Lectures on the Church of God* (London, n.d.).

T. T. Kilbucho [i.e. Tom Todd], *Clachan and Countryside* (Glasgow [1956]).

— *From a Shiffoneer Drawer* (Thankerton [?1973]).

— *Gathered in a Lowland Glen* (Glasgow [1954]).

— *Kilbucho's Latest* (Glenrothes [c.1974]).

— *My Rural Sojourn* (Edinburgh [1978]).

— *Sixty Rural Years* (Galashiels [1968]).

— *A Shepherd's Years* (Glasgow, 1961).

William Landles, *All Good Gifts Around Us* (Hawick, 1982).

— *A Breath Frae the Hills* (Hawick, 1937).

— *Gooseberry Fair* (Hawick, 1952).

— *I To the Hills* (Hawick, 1978).

— *Penny Numbers* (Hawick [1961]).

— *Roving Commission* (Hawick, 1992).

— *The Turn o' the Year* (Hawick, 1989).

— *Will H. Ogilvie: poet of the romantic Borderland* (n.p., 1993).

John Mackinnon, 'The Church's mission in Scotland: a para-church perspective', in David Searle (ed.), *Death or Glory* (Fearn and Edinburgh, 2001), pp.100-7.

Sam McKinstry, *Rowand Anderson: 'Scotland's premier architect'* (Edinburgh, 1991).

— *Sure as the Sunrise: a history of Albion Motors* (Edinburgh, 1997).

— and Gavin Stamp (eds), *'Greek' Thomson* (Edinburgh, 1994).

[C. H. Mackintosh], *Miscellaneous Writings of C. H. M.*, 5 vols (London, n.d.).

Thos McLaren (Jnr), *Why I Left the Open Brethren* (London, 1893).

Graham Mair (compiler), *The Fisherman's Gospel Manuel: a collection of true stories from the sea* (London, 1994).

Alexander Marshall, *The Exclusive Position Tested* (Glasgow, n.d.).

— *God Says I Am Saved: true and telling illustrations of how to be saved and sure* (Glasgow, n.d.).

— *God's Way of Salvation: set forth by illustration, comparison and contrast* (Glasgow [1888]).

— *'Holding Fast the Faithful Word': or whither are we drifting?* (Glasgow [1908]).

— *Christ or the 'Critics': whom shall we believe?* (Glasgow [1923]).

— *New Tests of Fellowship* ([?Chicago] n.d.).

— 'Repentance: what it is and what it is not', in W. Hoste and R. McElheran (eds), *The Great Sacrifice: or what the death of Christ has wrought* (Kilmarnock [1927]), pp.115-121.

— *Straight Paths for the Children of God* (Glasgow, n.d.).

— *Will a God of Love Punish Any of His Creatures for Ever?: a plain answer* (Glasgow, n.d.).

[Alexander Marshall], *Wandering Lights: a stricture on the doctrines and methods of Brethrenism. A review by A. M.*, 3rd edn (Glasgow, n.d.).

A. B. Miller, *What is God's Path for His People: a review of the origin, progress and development of what is known as 'The Brethren Movement' with an examination of modern teachings as to the Church* (Glasgow [1909]).

Andrew Miller, *Short Papers on Church History*, 3 vols (London, 1873-8).

John Montgomerie, *Open Brethren Principles: an examination and a review; also a brief statement of 'Needed Truth' error, with an appeal for a return to the old paths* (Inverness, n.d.).

W. K. Morrison, *God's Authority in a Permissive Age: Beacon Bible Studies Annual Lecture 1968* (n.p. [1968]).

— 'Who Are the Brethren?', in F. A. Tatford, *That the World May Know*, 7 (Bath, 1985), pp.484-9.

Donald Munro, *Oversight and Rule* (Kilmarnock, n.d.).

G. M. Munro, *The Glories of Christ* (Kilmarnock [1950]).

Archie Naismith, *1200 Notes, Quotes and Anecdotes* (London and Glasgow, 1963).

— and W. Fraser Naismith, *God's People and God's Purpose: or the hope of Israel and the Church* (Kilmarnock, 1949).

W. Fraser Naismith, *Faith's Radiant Path: from grace to glory as illustrated in the Book of Ruth* (London and Glasgow, 1930).

John W. Newton, *The Story of the Pilgrim Preachers: and their 24 tours throughout Britain with many stirring scenes, genuine conversions, peculiar positions, and soul-stirring experiences* (London [1938]).

Robbie W. Orr, *Journey with the New Testament as Guide: an aid for individuals, small groups and churches*, 2 vols (Edinburgh, 1995).
— *Victory Pageant: a commentary on Revelation* (London, 1972).
[E. C. P.], *A Reply by E. C. P., to Fellowship Among Saints, by R. T. H.* (n.p. [1884]).
Harold S. Paisley, *The Believers Hymn Book Companion* (Glasgow, 1989).
Hy Pickering, *The Believer's Blue Book* (Glasgow [1929]).
— *How to Make and Show 100 Object Lessons: suitable for Sunday schools, annual treats, seaside services, open-air gatherings, happy evenings, at home, Bible classes and all work among young or old* (Glasgow, 1922).
— *Modernism versus the 'Old Faith'* (London and Glasgow [1926]).
— *1000 Subjects for Speakers and Students* (Glasgow [1925]).
— 'One golden curl', in W. Hoste and R. McElheran (eds), *The Great Sacrifice: or what the death of Christ has wrought* (Kilmarnock [1927]), pp.132-6.
— *One Thousand Tales Worth Telling: mostly new/strictly true/suitable for you* (London and Glasgow [1918]).
— (compiler) *Twelve Baskets Full of Original Outlines and Scripture Studies* (London and Glasgow [1936]).
Robert Rendall, 'The Church: what is it?', in J. B. Watson (ed.), *The Church: a symposium* (London, 1949), pp.15-27.
— *Country Sonnets and Other Poems* (Kirkwall, 1946).
— *The Greatness and Glory of Christ* (London, 1956).
— *History, Prophecy and God* (London, 1954).
— *An Island Shore: the life and work of Robert Rendall,* (ed.) Neil Dickson (Kirkwall, 1990).
— *Orkney Shore* (Kirkwall, 1960).
— *Priests and Preachers* (London [1956]).
John Ritchie, *Among the Cannibals: peeps at the South Sea Islands and their savage inhabitants with life stories of their missionary heroes,* revised edn (Kilmarnock [1930]).
— *Assembly Privileges and Responsibilities* (Kilmarnock, n.d.).
— *Assurance: or how I know I am saved* (Kilmarnock, n.d.).
— *A Brief Sketch of Church History* (Kilmarnock, n.d.).
— *Baptism: the subjects, the mode, the meaning* (Kilmarnock, n.d.).
— *Early Paths for Young Believers* (Kilmarnock, 1909).
— *From Egypt to Canaan* (Kilmarnock, n.d.).
— *The Feasts of Jehovah: bright foreshadowings of grace and glory* (Kilmarnock, 1895).
— *500 Bible Subjects: with suggestive outlines and notes for Bible Students, preachers and teachers,* 2nd edn (Kilmarnock, 1926).

— *500 Children's Subjects: with outlines of blackboard and emblematic gospel address for workers amongst the young*, 2nd edn (Kilmarnock, 1911).

— *500 Evangelistic Subjects: with suggestive notes, outlines, and heads for evangelists, preachers, and teachers* (Kilmarnock, 1915).

— *500 Gospel Illustrations: incidents, anecdotes, and testimonies for the use of evangelists, preachers and teachers* (Kilmarnock 1912).

— *500 Gospel Subjects with outlines, divisions, and notes for preachers, teachers and Christian workers* (Kilmarnock, 1904).

— *Foundation Truths of the Faith* (Kilmarnock, 1907).

— *How to Teach and Win the Young: a practical handbook for Sunday school teachers and all evangelistic workers amongst young folks* (Kilmarnock [1924]).

— *Lectures on the Book of Daniel with Expository Notes on 'The Times of the Gentiles' and Prophetic Subjects* (Kilmarnock, 1915).

— *Lectures on the Book of Revelation: with notes on 'Things which must shortly come to pass'* (Kilmarnock, 1916).

— *The Lord's Supper* (Kilmarnock, n.d.).

— *Man's Future State: an examination of Scripture testimony on this great subject I. - in life and at death II. - in the intermediate state III. - at the resurrection and for eternity* (Kilmarnock, 1912).

— *Marriage Scenes of Scripture: a series of gospel addresses to young men and women* (Kilmarnock, 1904).

— *Notes on Paul's Epistle to the Galatians* (Kilmarnock, n.d.).

— *Notes on Paul's Epistle to the Romans* (Kilmarnock, n.d.).

— *The Second Advent of the Lord Jesus with Subsequent Events in Heaven and on Earth* (Kilmarnock [*c*.1908]).

— *Socialism: an enemy of God and of the gospel* (Kilmarnock, n.d.).

— *The Tabernacle in the Wilderness* (Kilmarnock, 1889).

— *'The Way, Which They Call Heresy': remarks on Mr. W. Blair Neatby's book, 'A History of the Plymouth Brethren'* (Kilmarnock [*c*.1901]).

[John Ritchie], *Association with the World in Its Philanthropic Schemes* (Kilmarnock, n.d.).

John Ritchie ([Jnr]), *The Bulwarks of the Christian Faith as Expounded in the Epistle to the Romans* (London [1939]).

— *Impending Great Events: addresses on the Second Coming of Christ and subsequent events* (London [*c*.1938]).

— *Is the Bible the Word of God?* (Kilmarnock, 1908).

J. R. Rollo, 'Church life and fellowship', in J. B. Watson (ed.), *The Church: a symposium* (London, 1949), pp.39-48.

Alex. Ross, *'Fifty Years in Christ': meditations, messages, ministry, miscellaneous* (Aberdeen, 1972).

— *'Musings from the Heart'* (Aberdeen, 1980).

— *Stories of Amazing Grace* (Stonehaven [c.1970]).

Douglas Russell, *Songs of Salvation and Glory* (Glasgow [1927]).

Elizabeth C. Sanderson, *Women and Work in Eighteenth Century Edinburgh* (London, 1996).

Margaret H. B. Sanderson, *Ayrshire and the Reformation: people and change, 1490-1600* (East Linton, 1997).

— *Cardinal of Scotland: David Beaton c.1494-1546* (Edinburgh, 1986).

— *Robert Adam and Scotland: portrait of an architect* (Edinburgh, 1992).

— *Mary Stewart's People* (Edinburgh, 1987).

— *Scottish Rural Society in the Sixteenth Century* (Edinburgh, 1982).

Walter Scott, *Bible Words and Biblical Notes* (London, 1917).

— *The Coming Great Tribulation and the Partial Rapture Theory* (Goddmayes, n.d.).

— *Exposition of the Revelation of Jesus Christ*, 5th edn (London [c.1918]).

— *The Lord's Supper: some of its privileges and responsibilities* (Hamilton, n.d.).

— *Prophetic Catechism and Millennial Glories and Blessings* (London and Glasgow, n.d.).

— *Prophetic Scenes and Coming Glories: answers to numerous prophetic questions* (London, 1919).

— *Signs Indicating the Near Return of Our Lord* (Hull, n.d.).

— *The Tabernacle: its structure, vessels, coverings, sacrifices, and services* (Goodmayes, n.d.).

— *The Two Trees of Paradise: or God's grace and man's responsibility*, 3rd edn (Kilmarnock, 1898).

[William Scott *et al.*], *Machermore Castle Eventide Home* (n.p., n.d.).

William Shaw, *Fellowship Among Saints: reprinted from 'The Believer's Treasury', February, 1895* (Belfast, n.d.).

— *The Fulness of the Blessing* (Glasgow, n.d.).

— *The Fulness of God* (Glasgow, n.d.).

— *The Lord's People. Fellowship, being selections from 'The Believer's Pathway'* (Glasgow, n.d.).

— *This Do in Remembrance of Me* (London, n.d.).

— 'Sunset on Carrick Shore' and 'We are coming, Nurse Cavell', in Malcolm J. Finlayson (ed.), *An Anthology of Carrick* (Kilmarnock, 1925), pp.380-4.

— *This Do in Remembrance of Me* (London and Glasgow, n.d.).

Alexander Stewart, *The Fellowship of the Saints of God* (Glasgow, n.d.).

— *Israel: a sketch of their past, present, future* (Glasgow, n.d.).

— 'On Christ dwelling in the heart by faith', in Dr Anderson-Berry *et al.*, *Heart Preparation for the Lord's Return: a series of address*

delivered at a conference in Caxton Hall, Westminster (London [1904]), pp.59-67.
— 'On Redemption', in Denham Smith *et al., Fundamental Truths: being a series of addresses delivered at conferences of Christians at Clapton Hall, Alkham Road, Stoke Newington on Wednesday, May 9th, and Thursday, May 10th, 1888* (London [1888]), pp.166-73.
— *Outside the Camp* (Kilmarnock, n.d.).
— *Salvation Truths* (Kilmarnock, n.d.).
— untitled sermon in Henry Groves *et al., Addresses Delivered at a Christian Conference Held at Paisley, April, 1877 by Mr Henry Groves, Kendal; Mr Henry Dyer, Bath; Mr Alex. Stewart, Glasgow. Subject: God's Holy Word* (Paisley [1877]), pp.17-22.
[John Stewart], 'Mr John Stewart', in anon. (ed.), *Jubilee of the Rev. Wm. Orr* (Kilmarnock, 1880), pp.78-80.
James Tait, *Bells and Pomegranates* (London and Glasgow, 1946).
W. A. Thomson, *God's Peace Plan: His coming King* (London and Glasgow, 1944).
William Trew, *My Reasons for Not Being Free to Engage in Inter-Denominational Service* (Kilmarnock, 1954).
W. Trotter, *The Justice and Forbearance of the Methodist New Connexion Conference, as they were illustrated in the case of W. Trotter* (London, 1841).
— *The Origin of the (So Called) 'Open Brethren': a letter by W. Trotter giving the whole case of Plymouth & Bethesda* (London, n.d.).
— and Thos Smith, *Eight Lectures on Prophecy: from shorthand notes* (London, 1852).
William Tytler, *Plain Talks on Prophecy: or, the great prophetic cycles of time* (Glasgow [1915]).
John Waddell *et al., Scripture Action Pieces for Young Folks: book no.2* (London, 1951).
R. Walker, *The Christian and Warfare: an examination of the pacifist position* (Chryston, 1942).
Tom Wilson (ed.), *What the Bible Teaches*, 11 vols (Kilmarnock, 1983-98).
A Younger Brother [i.e. Arthur Rendle Short], *The Principles of Open Brethren* (Glasgow [1913]).

(G) NON-BRETHREN MATERIAL PUBLISHED BY BRETHREN PUBLISHERS
Anon., *In Scotia's Wilds: the story of how the gospel entered the land of the thistle and wrought its wonders among the ancient dwellers there* (Kilmarnock [1927]).
Anon. (ed.), *Letters Concerning their Principles and Order from Assemblies of Believers in 1818-1820* (1820) rpt (London, 1889).

Anon., *Tales and Sketches of the Covenanters* (1880), John Ritchie edn (Kilmarnock, n.d.).

Anon., *Martin Luther: the reformer* ([1883]), John Ritchie edn (Kilmarnock [1928]).

T. D. Barnard, *The Progress of Doctrine in the New Testament* (1866), Pickering & Inglis edn (Glasgow [1926]).

Maria Louisa Charlesworth, *Ministering Children* (1854), Pickering & Inglis edn (London and Glasgow [1925]).

Dora Enock, *'Druggers All'* (Kilmarnock [1938]).

J. L. Erk, *Through Peril and Flame: the story of the English Bible* (Kilmarnock [1929]).

Alexander Gammie, *In Glasgow's Underworld: the social work of the Salvation Army* (London [1943]).

— *Pastor D. J. Findlay: a unique personality* (London, 1949).

— *Preachers I Have Heard* (London [1946]).

— *Romance of Faith: the story of the orphan homes of Scotland and the founder William Quarrier* (London [?1940]).

J[ohn]. H[awthorn]. and Jennie Chappell, *They Who Comforted: the life stories of Fanny Crosby and Agnes Weston* (London [1935]).

Edward Bruce Kirk (ed.), *Papers on Health by Professor Kirk, Edinburgh* (1899), one-vol. edn (London, Glasgow and Philadelphia, PA, 1921).

H. P. Liddon, *The Divinity of Our Lord and Saviour Jesus Christ* (1866), Pickering & Inglis edn (Glasgow [1926]).

A. Montefiore-Brice, *David Livingstone: his labours and his legacy* (1890) Pickering & Inglis edn (London [1938]).

K. Moody-Stuart, *Brownlow North: the story of his life and work*, 2nd edn (Kilmarnock, 1904).

H. C. G. Moule, *The Epistle of Paul to the Romans* (1894), Pickering & Inglis edn (London [c.1928]).

[Frank Mundell], *Heroines of the Faith*, 1st edn (1898), 2nd John Ritchie edn (Kilmarnock, n.d).

Andrew Murray, *With Christ in the School of Prayer: thoughts on our training for the ministry of intercession* (1886), Pickering & Inglis edn (London [1957]).

M. B. Paxton, *Astur: a waif of the sea* (London [1924]).

— *In an Isle of the Sea: a story of the Shetland Isles* (London [1920]).

— *Only a Gipsy: a story of Caithness* (London [1920]).

E. R. Pitman, *Lady Missionaries in Many Lands* (1889), Pickering & Inglis edn (London and Glasgow [1929]).

Robert Pollok, *Tales of the Covenanters* (1833), John Ritchie edn (Kilmarnock [1928]).

John Shearer, *Old Time Revivals* (Glasgow [1930]).

W. B. Sloan, *These Sixty Years: the story of the Keswick Convention* (London, 1935).

James Smith and Robert Lee, *Handfuls on Purpose for Christian Workers and Bible Students*, 13 vols (London, 1923-36).

Harriet Beecher Stowe, *Uncle Tom's Cabin* (1852), Pickering & Inglis edn (London [1923]).

J. H. Thomson, *The Martyr Graves of Scotland*, (ed.) Matthew Hutchison, 2nd series (1877), John Ritchie edn (Kilmarnock, n.d.).

(H) CONTEMPORARY NON-BRETHREN PRINTED MATERIAL

William Adamson, *The Life of Principal Morison D.D.* (London, 1898).

Aliquis [William Henderson], *Letters Philological, Theological and Harmonological addressed to Hugh Hart, minister of Shiprow Chapel on his embracing and Preaching the Sabellian Heresy* (Aberdeen, 1838).

Tom Allan (ed.), *Crusade in Scotland...Billy Graham* (London, 1955).

James Anderson, *An Outline of My Life: or selections from a fifty years' religious experience* (Birmingham, 1912).

Anon., *Ayrshire Christian Union: a century of witness 1878-1978* (Beith [1978]).

Anon., *Heresy Unveiled: the teaching of Plymouth Brethren contrasted with scripture: in four sections. I. Presidency and Ministry. II. The Divine Humanity of Christ. III Socinianism IV. The Righteousness of Christ* (Aberdeen [c.1870]).

Anon. (ed.), *Reminiscences of the Revival of Fifty-Nine and the Sixties* (Aberdeen, 1910).

I. T. Armstrong, *Plea for Modern Prophetesses* (Glasgow, 1866).

Anne Arnott, *Wife to the Archbishop* (London, 1976).

G. F. Barbour, *The Life of Alexander Whyte* (London, 1923).

J. Barker and W. Trotter, *A Brief report of the Proceedings of the Conference of the Methodist New Connexion in the case of Joseph Barker and Wm. Trotter* (Newcastle [1841]).

James A. Begg, *The Condition in Which All Men Are Placed: being an examination of the sentiments of Dr. Wardlaw of Glasgow and Mr. Russell of Dundee, regarding the atonement, forgiveness, and justification of faith* (Glasgow, 1834).

— *A Connected View of Some Scriptural Evidence of the Redeemer's Speedy Personal Return, and Reign on Earth with His Glorified Saints, during the Millennium; Israel's Restoration to Palestine, and the Destruction of Antichristian Nations with Remarks on Various Authors who oppose these Doctrines* (1829), 3rd edn (Paisley, 1831).

— *An Examination of the Authority for a Change of the Weekly Sabbath at the Resurrection of Christ: proving that the Practice of the Church in Substituting the First day of the Week, for the Appointed*

Seventh day is Unsanctioned by the New Testament Scriptures (Glasgow, 1850).

— *Summary of Doctrines Taught in the Christian Meeting House, 90 Norfolk Street, Laurieston, Glasgow* (Glasgow 1869).

James Black, *New Forms of the Old Faith: being the Baird Lecture delivered in 1946-47 under the title extra-church systems* (London, 1948).

W. E. Boardman, *The Higher Christian Life* (1858) UK edn (Edinburgh, 1859).

Andrew A. Bonar, *James Scott: a labourer for God* (London [1885]).

Horatius Bonar, *Life of the Rev. John Milne of Perth* (1868), 5th edn (London [1868]).

Robert Braithwaite (ed.), *The Life and Letters of Rev. William Pennefather, B.A.* (London, 1878).

John Bremner, *Hoy: the dark enchanted isle* (Kirkwall, 1997).

Robert Brown, *Paisley Poets with brief memoirs of them and selections from their works*, 2 (Paisley, 1890).

N. W. Bryson (compiler), *History of the Lanarkshire Christian Union: instituted 1882* (Strathaven, 1937).

Alexander Campbell, *An Essay on Domestic and Church Order* (London, 1838).

Frederick Catherwood, *At the Edge* (London, 1995).

Thomas Croskery, 'The Plymouth Brethren', *The Presbyterian Quarterly and the Princeton Review* (New Series), 1 (1872), p.48.

A. J. Cronin, *Adventures in Two Worlds* (London, 1952).

— *Shannon's Way* (1948) NEL edn (London, 1979).

Tom Dickson, *Was Moses a Bolshevist? The Hebrew law-giver on land, interest and direct action* (Glasgow, n.d.).

[Thomas Erskine], *Letters of Thomas Erskine of Linlathen* (Edinburgh, 1878), William Hanna (ed.).

Thomas Evans, *Christian Policy, the Salvation of Empire: being a clear and concise examination into the causes that have produced the impending, unavoidable national bankruptcy, and the effects that must ensue, unless averted by the adoption of this only real and desirable remedy, which would elevate these realms to a pitch of greatness hitherto unattained by any nation that ever existed*, 2nd edn (London, 1816).

Charles G. Finney, *Lectures on Revivals of Religion* (1835), introduction and notes by W. H. Harding (New York and London, 1910).

— *The Memoirs of Charles G. Finney: the complete restored text*, (eds) Garth M. Rosell and Richard A. G. Dupuis (Grand Rapids, MI, 1989).

John Fleming, *A Testimony for a Universal Church* (Edinburgh, 1826).

Gordon Forlong, *Inspiration of the Bible: considerations addressed to the deist and the agnostic and a manual for young believers* (London, 1897).
— *Principles of a Bank of Character and Skill*, 2nd edn (Glasgow, 1847).
H. I. G., *In Memoriam: Jessie McFarlane a tribute of affection* (London, 1872).
James Gall, *The Carrubers Close Mission: its planting and first fruit* (Edinburgh, 1860).
Alexander Gammie, *Pastor D. J. Findlay: a unique personality* (London, 1949).
— *Rev. John McNeill: his life and work* (London [1934]).
W. Gordon-Gorman, (ed.), *Converts to Rome during the XIXTH Century*, 5th edn (London, 1884).
M. M. Gordon, *Hay Macdowall Grant of Arndilly: his life, labours, and teaching* (London, 1876).
James Alex. Haldane, *A View of the Social Worship and Ordinances Observed by the First Christians, drawn from the Sacred Scriptures Alone: being an attempt to enforce their divine obligation; and to represent the guilt and evil consequences of neglecting them*, 2nd edn (Edinburgh, 1806).
Hugh Hart, *A Diversity of Theological Subjects scripturally stated, illustrated, and defended - calculated under the benediction of the Great Head of the Church amicably to compose the religious differences existing among biblical Christians, and respectfully designed not only as a Compendium of Faith to assist in repairing the breaches occasioned by schism, in the organic walls of the Militant Jerusalem, but also as an assistant to ministers and students in their theological pursuits* (Aberdeen, 1833).
— *An Outline and a Defence of Consultative Presbyterian Government designed to assist in repairing the disciplinary breaches, and building up the organic walls of the militant Jerusalem to which is subjoined, an epitome of the faith of the members constituting the churches in fellowship with the Original United Relief Association* (Aberdeen, 1833).
— *A Dissertation Theological and Philological in which the doctrine of the Holy Trinity is scripturally stated, illustrated, and defended* (Aberdeen, 1834).
— *William Henderson, A.M. Rebuked for the ignorance, impudence misrepresentation, and falsehood, contained in a pamphlet entitled 'Letters to Hugh Hart', and published under his authority* (Aberdeen, 1840).

A. J. Hayes and D. A. Gowland (eds), *Scottish Methodism in the Early Victorian Period: the Scottish correspondence of the Rev. Jabez Bunting* (Edinburgh, 1981).

Mairi Hedderwick, *Highland Journey: a sketching tour of Scotland retracing the footsteps of Victorian artist John T. Reid* (Edinburgh, 1992).

George Herod, *Biographical Sketches of some of those Preachers whose Labours Contributed to the Origination and Early Extension of the Primitive Methodist Connexion* (London, n.d.).

G. Joseph Holyoake, *The History of Co-operation in England: its literature and its advocates*, 2 vols, 2nd edn (London, 1875-77).

J. Hunter, *Funeral Sermon for the late Rev. Hugh Hart pastor of Zion Chapel, Aberdeen, preached on Lord's Day May 4, 1862* (Aberdeen, 1862).

Molly Hunter, *The Dragonfly Years* (London, 1984).

— *A Sound of Chariots* (New York, 1972; London, 1973).

R. H. Ireland, *Principles and Practices of 'Brethren': a word of warning to the churches* (Edinburgh [1873]).

[Peter King], *An Enquiry into the Constitution, Discipline, Unity and Worship of the Primitive Church, That Flourish'd within the first Three Hundred years after Christ. Faithfully collected out of the extant writings of these ages. By an impartial hand*, 2nd edn (London, 1713).

Helen Kirk, *Memoirs of Rev. John Kirk D.D.* (Edinburgh, 1888).

M. C. Lees, *A Scotch Jewel Newly Set: a brief memorial sketch of Nellie Drysdale* (Edinburgh and London, 1891).

Eric Linklater, *White Maa's Saga* (1929) Penguin edn (Harmondsworth, 1963).

— *The Man On My Back* (London, 1941).

Liz Lochhead, *Bagpipe Muzak* (Harmondsworth, 1991).

— *Dreaming Frankenstein and Collected Poems* (Edinburgh, 1984).

Dugald MacColl, *Among the Masses: or work in the wynds* (Glasgow, 1867).

Jessie Macfarlane, *Scriptural Warrant for Women to Preach the Gospel* (Peterhead [1864]).

Ena McRostie, *The Man Who Walked Backwards* (London, 1934).

William McIlvanney, *A Gift From Nessus* (1968), Mainstream edn (Edinburgh, 1990).

— *The Kiln* (London, 1996).

E. McHardie, *James Turner: or how to reach the masses* (London, 1889).

Duncan Macintosh, *The Special Teachings, Ecclesiastical and Doctrinal, of the Plymouth Brethren: compiled from their own writings. With Strictures* (London, 1873).

Hugh McIntosh, *The New Prophets: being an account of the operations of the Northern Evangelists* (Aberdeen, 1871).

W. P. Mackay, *'Grace and Truth' under Twelve Aspects*, new edn (Edinburgh, 1875), 64th edn (London, 1905).

John Macpherson, *Life and Labours of Duncan Matheson: the Scottish evangelist* (London, n.d.).

John Macmurray, *Search for Reality in Religion* (London, 1965).

Peter Mearns, *Christian Truth Viewed in Relation to Plymouthism* (Edinburgh, 1874).

Abe Moffat, *My Life with the Miners* (London, 1965).

K. Moody-Stuart, *Brownlow North, B.A., Oxon: records and recollections* (London, 1878).

William Montgomerie, *From Time to Time: selected poems* (Edinburgh, 1985).

George E. Morgan, *R. C. Morgan: his life and times* (London and Glasgow, 1909).

H. V. Morton, *In Scotland Again* (London, 1933).

Tom Morton, *Red Guitars in Heaven* (Edinburgh, 1994).

— *Spirit of Adventure* (Edinburgh, 1992).

Ian H. Murray, *The Life of Arthur W. Pink* (Edinburgh, 1981).

Willa Muir, *Imagined Corners* (1935) Cannongate edn (Edinburgh, 1987).

Brownlow North, *'I Feel': a word to the anxious* (London, 1866).

James Paterson, *Richard Weaver's Life Story* (London [1897]).

James Moir Porteous, *Brethren in the Keelhowes*, 6th edn (London, 1876).

— *What is Plymouthism or Brethrenism? republished by request from the Government of the Kingdom of Christ* (London, 1873).

[Jane Radcliffe], *Recollections of Reginald Radcliffe by his wife* (London [1896]).

William Reid, *Plymouth Brethrenism Unveiled and Refuted* (Edinburgh, 1875).

James Riddell, *Aberdeen and its Folk* (Aberdeen, 1868).

R. M. Robertson (ed.), *William Robertson of the Carruber's Close Mission* (Edinburgh and London, 1914).

Thomas Rosie, *Statement and Appeal of the Extension of Home Mission Agency to the Towns and Villages on the Coast from Montrose Northwards* (Aberdeen, 1858).

E. Harris Ruddock, *The Homeopathic Vade Mecum of Modern Medicine and Surgery*, 2nd edn (London, 1905).

Christopher Rush, *Peace Comes Dropping Slow* (Edinburgh, 1983).

C. I. Scofield, *The Scofield Reference Bible* (Oxford, 1909).

W. Graham Scroggie (ed.), *The Story of a Life in the Love of God: incidents collected from the diaries of Mrs James J. Scroggie* (London [1938]).

Oliphant Smeaton, *Principal James Morison: the Man and His Work* (Edinburgh, 1902).

J. A. Stewart, *Our Beloved Jock* (Asheville, NC, 1964).

William Still, *Dying to Live* (Fearn, 1991).

Mrs Seth Sykes and Seth A. G. Sykes, *A Great Little Man: a biography of evangelist Seth Sykes* (Glasgow, 1958).

A. A. Thomson, *The Exquisite Burden* (1935) rpt (London, 1962).

David P. Thomson, *The Scottish Churches' Handbook* (Dunfermline, 1933).

Henry Varley, *Henry Varley: the powerful evangelist of the Victorian era* (London [*c*.1913]).

John Weir, *The Ulster Awakening* (1860) rpt (Belfast, 1987).

Christian Watt, *The Christian Watt Papers*, (ed.) David Fraser (Edinburgh, 1983).

C. E. Woods (ed.), *Memoirs and Letters of Canon Hay Aitken with an introductory memoir of his father by the Rev. Robert Aitken of Pendeen* (London, 1928).

Max Wright, *Told in Gath* (Belfast, 1991).

(I) MISCELLANEOUS

British Parliamentary Papers: Census of Great Britain, 1851: religious worship and education, Vol. 11 (1852-4), pp.509-42.

Annual Report of the North-East Coast Mission: with list of subscriptions and donations (Glasgow and Aberdeen), 1856-61.

2. Secondary Sources

(i) Brethren history

(A) ASSEMBLY HISTORIES

Anon., 'A Brief History', in *Elim Hall Centenary 1882-1982* [n.p. [1982]).

Anon., *1833-1983: Annbank Gospel Hall centenary campaign* (n.p. [1983]).

Anon., 'Those Sixty Years 1890-1950', in *Elim Hall, 5 Prince Edward Street, Crosshill, Glasgow: 60th Annual Report 1st January to 31st December, 1949* (n.p. [1949]).

Anon., 'History of the Church', *Deeside Christian Fellowship Church Diary*, 5 September 1993.

John S. Borland, *History of the Brethren Movement in Galston* (Kilmarnock [1948]).
— [and May Young], *History of Galston Assembly* (n.p. [1998]).
[Hannah Brown], *Gospel Hall Kilbirnie Centenary Year 1889-1989* (n.p. [1989]).
James Cordiner, *Fragments from the Past: an account of people and events in the assemblies of northern Scotland* (London, 1961).
Robert Chapman, *The Story of Hebron Hall Assembly, Larkhall, 1866-1928: a short history of the inception, progress and personalities of the assembly* (Kilmarnock, 1929).
[Robert Fulton], *Bethany Hall Troon: a hundred years of Christian witness* (n.p. [1970]).
Thomas G. Galbraith (compiler), *These are my Brethren [sic]: a record of God's faithfulness to His people. Linwood Gospel Hall 1953* (n.p., 1953).
Stephen Lennox Johns, *The Gospel Hall Tillicoultry: a short history* (n.p., 1990).
A. McAllister and J. Vernal (compilers), *Busby Gospel Hall: a short history of early days, 1891-1964* (n.p. [1985]).
Gavin McGregor, *The Bishopbriggs Assembly 1939-1989: the first fifty years* (n.p. [1989]).
James McLachlan, *Ebenezer Hall Coatdyke* (n.p. [1946]).
[George Peterson], *A Century of Witness in Ebenezer Hall, Lerwick 1885-1985* (Lerwick, 1985).
Alexander Rollo, *The Story of Innerleven Assembly* (n.p., n.d.).
Alex. Strang (compiler), *Centenary of Hebron Hall Assembly Larkhall 1866-1966* (n.p. [1966]).
[Sam Thomson], *The Springburn Assembly 1881-1981* (n.p. [1981]).
[John Waddell], *Roman Road Hall Motherwell: centenary 1875-1975* (Lanark, 1975).
[Joseph L. G. Walker], *Centenary of the Pollokshaws Assembly 1873-1973* (n.p. [1973]).

(B) PRINTED GENERAL MATERIAL ON BRETHREN HISTORY

Phyllis D. Airhart, '"What must I do to be saved?" Two paths to evangelical conversion in late Victorian Canada', *Church History*, 59 (1990), pp.372-85.
J. S. Andrews, 'Brethren hymnology', *Evangelical Quarterly*, 28 (1956), pp.208-229.
Robert Baylis, *My People: the story of those Christians sometimes called Plymouth Brethren* (Wheaton, Il, 1995).
David J. Beattie, *Brethren: the story of a great recovery* (Kilmarnock [1939]).

Patricia Beer, 'Happy Few', *London Review of Books*, 23 May 1991, p.12.

David Brady and Fred J. Evans, *Christian Brethren in Manchester and District: a history* (London, 1997).

E. H. Broadbent, *The Pilgrim Church: being some account of the continuance through succeeding centuries of churches practising the principles taught in the New Testament* (London and Glasgow, 1931).

Peter Brock, 'The peace testimony of the early Plymouth Brethren', *Church History*, 55 (1984), pp.30-45.

Peter Brierley, *Some Scottish Brethren*, (London, 1994).

Peter Brierley *et al, The Christian Brethren as the Nineties Began* (Carlisle, 1993).

[Matthew S. R. Brown], *Aberdeen Christian Conference Centenary 1874-1973* (Aberdeen, 1972).

James Patrick Callahan, *Primitivist Piety: the ecclesiology of the early Plymouth Brethren* (Lanham, MD; 1996).

F. Roy Coad, 'F. F. Bruce: His influence on Brethren in the British Isles', *CBRJ*, 22, pp.3-5.

— *A History of the Brethren Movement: its origins, its worldwide development and its significance for the present day*, 2nd edn (Exeter, 1976).

— 'The influence of Brethrenism on English Business Practice', *Biblioteca Storica Toscana*, 11 (1988), pp.107-114.

— *Prophetic Developments with Particular Reference to the Early Brethren Movement - C.B.R.F. Occasional Paper No.2* (Middlesex, 1966).

J. A. H. Dempster, 'Aspects of Brethren publishing enterprise in late nineteenth century Scotland', *Publishing History*, 20 (1986), pp.61-101.

Neil T. R. Dickson, 'Brethren and Baptists in Scotland', *BQ*, 33 (1990), pp.372-87.

— '"Brethren" in Scotland: the present situation', in H. H. Rowdon (ed.), *The Strengthening, Growth and Planting of Local Churches* (Carlisle, 1993), pp.109-110.

— '"The Church itself is God's clergy": the principles and practices of the Brethren', in Deryck W. Lovegrove (ed.), *The Rise of the Laity in Evangelical Protestantism* (London: Routlege, 2002), pp.217-35.

— 'Scottish Brethren: division and wholeness 1838-1916', *CBRFJ*, No.41 (1990), pp.5-41.

— 'Modern prophetesses: women preachers in the nineteenth-century Scottish Brethren', *RSCHS*, 25 (1993), pp.89-117.

— 'Open and closed: Brethren and their origins in the North East', in James Porter (ed.), *After Columba - After Calvin: religious community in North-East Scotland* (Aberdeen, 1999), pp.151-170.

— '"Shut in with Thee": the morning meeting among Scottish Open Brethren, 1830s-1960s', in R. N. Swanston (ed.), *SCH*, 35 (Woodbridge, 1999), pp.276-89.

A. T. Doodson, *The Search for the Truth of God* (Bradford, n.d.).

Kent Eaton, 'Beware the trumpet of judgement!: John Nelson Darby and the nineteenth-century Brethren', in Fiona Bowie and Christopher Deacy (eds), *The Coming Deliverer: millennial themes in world religions* (Cardiff, 1997), pp.119-62.

Arnold D. Ehlert, *Brethren Writers: a checklist with an introductory essay and additional lists* (Grand Rapids, MI, 1969).

Peter L. Embley, 'The early development of the Plymouth Brethren', in *Patterns of Sectarianism: organisation and ideology in social and religious movements* (London, 1967), pp.213-43.

Ian G. D. Ford, 'Religious affiliation and educational achievement: a note on the "Brethren" in western Scotland', *Scottish Educational Studies*, 3, No.1, (May, 1971), pp.20-4.

W. W. Gasque, 'A select bibliography of the writings of F. F. Bruce', in *idem* and R. P. Martin (eds), *Apostolic History and the Gospel* (Exeter, 1970), pp.21-4.

'A supplementary bibliography of the writings of F. F. Bruce', *CBRJ*, 22 (1971), pp.21-47.

Crawford L. Gribben, '"The worst sect that a Christian man can meet": opposition to the Plymouth Brethren in Ireland and Scotland, 1859-1900', *Scottish Studies Review* (forthcoming).

H. A. Ironside, *A Historical Sketch of the Brethren Movement* (1945) rpt. (Neptune, NJ, 1985).

Timothy Larsen, '"Living by faith": a short history of Brethren practice', *BAHNR*, 1 (1997-8), pp.67-102.

Peter J. Lineham, *There We Found Brethren: a history of assemblies of Brethren in New Zealand* (Palmerston North, NZ, 1977).

Ian McDowell, 'The influence of the "Plymouth Brethren" on Victorian society and religion', *Evangelical Quarterly*, 55 (1983), pp.211-22.

— 'Rice Thomas Hopkins 1842-1916: an open brother', *BAHNR*, 1 (1997-8), pp.24-30.

David J. MacLeod, 'Walter Scott: a link in dispensationalism between Darby and Scofield?', *Bibliotheca Sacra*, 153 (1996), pp.155-78.

Nora F. McMillan, 'Robert Rendall, 1898-1967', *Journal of Conchology*, 19 (1968), pp.273-4.

I. H. Marshall, 'F. F. Bruce as a biblical scholar', *CBRJ*, 22 (1971), pp.5-12.

W. Blair Neatby, *A History of the Plymouth Brethren*, 1st edn (London [1901]).

Napoleon Noel, *The History of the Brethren*, 2 vols (Denver, CO, 1936).

C. A. Oxley, 'The "Needed Truth" Assemblies', *Christian Brethren Research Fellowship Journal*, No.4 (April 1964), pp.21-32.

J. J. Park, *The Churches of God: their origin and development in the 20th Century* (Leicester, 1987).

C. J. Pickering *et al.*, *1865-1965: the Half-Yearly Meetings of Christians in Glasgow* (n.p. [1965]).

Ian Randall, '"Outside the camp": Brethren spirituality and wider Evangelicalism in the 1920s', *BAHNR*, 2 (2000), pp.17-33.

Ian S. Rennie, 'Aspects of Christian Brethren spirituality', in J. I. Packer and L. Wilkinson (eds), *Alive to God: studies in spirituality* (Downers Grove, Illinois, 1992), pp.190-201.

Robert I. Rotberg, 'Plymouth Brethren and the occupation of Katanga, 1886-1907', *The Journal of African History*, 5 (1964), pp.285-97.

Harold H. Rowdon, 'The concept of "living by faith"', in Antony Billington, Tony Lane, Max Turner (eds), *Mission and Meaning: essays presented to Peter Cotterell* (Carlisle, 1995), pp.339-56.

— 'The early Brethren and the ministry of the Word', *JCBRF*, No.14 (1967), pp.11-24.

— 'The Brethren concept of sainthood', *Vox Evangelica*, 20 (1990), pp.91-102.

— 'The Brethren contribution to world mission', in *idem* (ed.), *The Brethren Contribution to the Worldwide Mission of the Church* (Carlisle, 1994).

— *The Origins of the Brethren 1825-1850* (London, 1967).

— 'The post-war background to Nantwich 1991', in *idem* (ed.), *The Strengthening, Growth and Planting of Local Churches* (Exeter, 1993), pp.127-141.

— 'The problem of Brethren identity in historical perspective', *Biblioteca Storica Toscana*, 11 (Firenze, 1988), pp.159-174.

— *Who are the Brethren and Does it Matter?* (Exeter, 1986).

Roger Shuff, 'Open to Closed: the growth of exclusivism among Brethren in Britain 1848-1953', *BAHNR*, 1 (1997-8), pp.10-23.

Nathan DeL Smith, *Roots and Renewal* (Pasadena, CA, 1986).

T. C. F. Stunt, 'Article review: Patterns of Sectarianism, *JCBRF*, No.19 (March 1969), pp.35-9.

— *Early Brethren and the Society of Friends. CBRF Occasional Paper No.3* (Pinner, 1970).

— 'Evangelical cross-currents in the Church of Ireland, 1820-1833', in W. J. Shiels and Diana Wood (eds), *SCH*, 25 (Oxford, 1989), pp.215-221.

— 'Irvingite pentecostalism and the early Brethren', *CBRFJ*, 10 (1965), pp.40-8.

— 'Leonard Strong: the motives and experiences of early missionary work in British Guiana', *CBRJ*, 34 (1983), pp.95-105.

— 'Two nineteenth-century movements', *Evangelical Quarterly*, 37 (1965), pp.221-31.

W. T. Stunt *et al.*, *Turning the World Upside down: a century of missionary endeavour*, 2nd edn (Bath, 1973).

Neil Summerton, 'The practice of worship', *CBR*, 39 (1988), pp.29-52.

Thomas Stewart Veitch, *The Brethren Movement: a simple and straightforward account of the features and failures of a sincere attempt to carry out the principles of Scripture during the last 100 years* (London and Glasgow [1933]).

Gordon Willis and Bryan Wilson, 'The Churches of God: pattern and practice', in Bryan Wilson (ed.), *Patterns of Sectarianism: organisation and ideology in social and religious movements* (London, 1967), pp.244-86.

B. R. Wilson, 'The Exclusive Brethren: a case study in the evolution of a sectarian ideology', in *idem* (ed.), *Patterns of Sectarianism: organisation and ideology in social and religious movements* (London, 1967), pp.287-342.

J. Stafford Wright, 'History, Prophecy and God', *Evangelical Quarterly*, 27 (1955), p.177.

(C) UNPUBLISHED MATERIAL ON BRETHREN HISTORY

Judith Adair, 'In the Splendour of His Holiness: a Study of the Musical Practices of the Christian Brethren' (University of Edinburgh dissertation for Scottish Ethnology II, 1992).

Jonathan David Burnham, 'The Controversial Relationship between Benjamin Wills Newton and John Nelson Darby' (University of Oxford D.Phil. thesis, 1999).

A. D. Buchanan. 'Brethren Revivals 1859-70' (University of Stirling B.A. dissertation, 1991).

Arthur Chamings (compiler), 'Some Papers and Letters in Connection with the Separation of the 1880's and 1890's', typescript, 1987.

[William Cochrane], *Excerpt from H.V. Morton's Book entitled 'In Scotland Again' Re Mr. R. Broadbent, Evangelist. With copy of letter sent by Mr. W. Cochrane, Newmilns, and letter acknowledgement from Mr. H. V. Morton* (n.p., n.d.).

Roy Coad, 'Into a changing future: the evolution of a movement and coping with change', Lecture 4, unpublished paper presented at Regent College, Vancouver, BC, 1990.

Shih-An Deng, 'Ideas of the Church in an age of reform: the ecclesiological thoughts of John Nelson Darby and John Henry Newman, 1824-1850' (University of Minnesota Ph.D. thesis, 1994).

Neil T.R. Dickson, 'God's glory in dandelions: the work of Robert Rendall', in 'Papers on the Christian Brethren Movement', 1 (papers presented at a conference in Regent College, Vancouver, BC, 1990), pp.28-46.

— 'Littoral truth: the mind of Robert Rendall', unpublished paper delivered at the Orkney Science Festival, 1998.

Norman S. Macdonald, 'One Hundred Years of Needed Truth Brethren 1892 to 1992: a historical analysis', typescript [1992].

Ross H. McLaren, 'The Triple Tradition: the Origin and Development of the Open Brethren in North America' (Vanderbilt University, M.A. thesis, 1982).

Kenneth J. Newton, 'A History of the Brethren in Australia with particular reference to the Open Brethren' (Fuller Theological Seminary, CA, Ph.D. thesis, 1990).

Elisabeth K. Wilson, 'Brethren Attitudes to Authority and Government with Particular Reference to Pacifism' (University of Tasmania, Australia, thesis for Master of Humanities, 1994).

(ii) General printed material

Richard D. Altick, *The English Common Reader: a social history of the mass reading public 1800-1900* (Chicago, 1957).

Olive Anderson, 'Women preachers in mid-Victorian Britain: some reflexions on feminism, popular religion and social change', *The Historical Journal*, 12, (1969), pp.467-84.

R. Page Arnot, *The Miners in Crises and War: a history of the Miners' Federation of Great Britain from 1930 onwards* (New York, 1961).

W. A. Armstrong, 'The use of information about occupation', in E. A. Wrigley (ed.), *Nineteenth-Century Society: essays in the use of quantitive methods for the study of social data* (Cambridge, 1972), pp.198-310.

Margaret Aston, 'Segregation in church', *Studies in Church History*, 27 (Oxford, 1990), pp.237-294.

Bernard Aspinwall, 'A fertile field: Scotland in the days of the early missions', in R. I. Jenson and M. R. Thorp (eds), *Mormons in Early Victorian Britain* (Salt Lake City, 1989), pp. 104-117.

— 'Hands across the sea: the english speaking transatlantic religious world (1820-1920)', *Hispania Sacra*, 40 (1988), pp.853-66.

— *Portable Utopias: Glasgow and the United States 1820-1920* (Aberdeen, 1984).

— 'The Scottish religious identity in the Atlantic World 1880-1914', in Stewart Mews (ed.), *SCH*, 18 (1982), pp.505-18.

Oliver Barclay, *Evangelicalism in Britain 1935-1995: a personal sketch* (Leicester, 1997).

James Barr, *Fundamentalism* (London, 1977).

— *Escaping From Fundamentalism* (London, 1984).

Clarence B. Bass, *Backgrounds to Dispensationalism: its historical genesis and ecclesiastical implications* (Grand Rapids, MI, 1960).

Donald Beaton, 'The Old Scots Independents', *RSCHS*, 3 (1929), pp.135-45.

D. W. Bebbington, 'The advent hope in British Evangelicalism since 1800', *Scottish Journal of Religious Studies*, 9 (1988), pp.103-114.

— 'Baptists and Fundamentalism in inter-war Britain', in Keith Robbins (ed.), *SCH: Subsidia*, 7 (Oxford, 1990), pp.297-326.

— 'The decline and resurgence of Evangelical social concern 1918-1980', in John Wolffe (ed.), *Evangelical Faith and Public Zeal: Evangelicals and society in Britain 1780-1980* (London, 1995), pp.175-97.

— *Evangelicalism in Modern Britain: a history from the 1730s to the 1980s* (London, 1989).

— 'Evangelicalism in modern Scotland', *Scottish Bulletin of Evangelical Theology*, 9 (1991), pp.4-11.

— (ed.), *A History of the Baptists in Scotland* (Glasgow, 1988).

— *Holiness in Nineteenth-Century England: the 1998 Didsbury Lectures* (Carlisle, 2000).

— 'Martyrs for the truth: Fundamentalists in Britain', in Diana Wood (ed.), *SCH*, 30 (Oxford, 1993), pp.417-452.

— 'Mission in Scotland, 1846-1946', in David Searle (ed.), *Death or Glory* (Fearn and Edinburgh, 2001), pp.32-53.

— 'Religion and national feeling in nineteenth-century Wales and Scotland', in Stuart Mews (ed.), *SCH*, 18 (Oxford, 1982), pp. 489-503.

— *Victorian Nonconformity* (Bangor, 1992).

Oliver A. Beckerlegge, 'Early Methodism in Paisley', *PWHS*, 29 (1953), pp.76-83.

— 'In search of forgotten Methodism', *PWHS*, 29 (1954), pp.160-1.

— 'The Methodist New Connexion in Scotland', *PWHS*, 29 (1954), pp.160-61.

— *The United Methodist Free Churches: a study in freedom* (London, 1957).

M. C. Bell, *Calvin and Scottish Theology* (Edinburgh, 1985).

Peter L. Berger and Thomas Luckmann, *The Social Construction of Reality: a treatise in the sociology of knowledge* (1966), Penguin edn (Harmondsworth, 1967).

R. J. Berry and H. N. Firth (eds), *The People of Orkney* (Kirkwall, 1986).

John Betjeman, 'Nonconformist architecture', *Architectural Review*, 88 (1940), pp.161-74.

Eugenio F. Biagini and Alastair J. Reid, 'Currents of radicalism, 1850-1914', in *idem* (eds), *Currents of Radicalism: popular radicalism, organised labour and party politics in Britain, 1850-1914* (Cambridge, 1991), pp.1-19.

Clyde Binfield, 'Jews in Evangelical Dissent: the British Society, the Herschell connection and the pre-millennarian thread', in Michael Wilks (ed.), *SCH: Subsidia*, 10 (Oxford, 1994), pp.225-70.

W. G. Blaikie, *After Fifty Years: 1843-1893* (Edinburgh [1893]).

Ian Bradley, *The Call to Seriousness: the Evangelical impact on the Victorians* (London, 1976).

Paul A. Bramadat, *The Church on the World's Turf: an evangelical group at a secular university* (Oxford, 2000).

Peter Brierley and Fergus MacDonald, *Prospects for Scotland: report of the 1984 census of the Scottish churches* (Edinburgh and London, 1984).

— *Prospects for Scotland 2000: trends and tables from the 1994 Scottish Church Census* (Edinburgh and London, 1995).

Peter Brierley *et al.* (eds), *UK Christian Handbook 1994/5 Edition* (London, 1994).

— (ed.), *UK Christian Handbook Religious Trends No.1- 1998/99* (London and Carlisle, 1997).

British Council of Churches, *Telling the Good News Together in Scotland: a Report to the B.C.C.* (London, 1989).

Donald Bridge and David Phypers, *The Meal that Unites* (London, 1981).

Callum G. Brown, 'The cost of pew-renting: church management, church-going and social class in nineteenth-century Glasgow', *JEH*, 38 (1987), pp.347-61.

— *The Death of Christian Britain: understanding secularisation 1800-2000* (London and New York, 2001).

— 'Did urbanization secularize Britain', in Richard Rodger (ed.), *Urban History Yearbook 1988* (Leicester, 1988).

— '"Each take off their several way"? The Protestant churches and the working classes in Scotland', in Graham Walker and Tom Gallagher (eds), *Sermons and Battle Hymns: Protestant popular culture in modern Scotland* (Edinburgh, 1990), pp.69-85.

— 'Faith in the city?', *History Today*, 40 (1990), pp.41-7.

— 'The mechanism of religious growth in urban societies: British cities since the eighteenth century', in Hugh McLeod (ed.), *European Religion in the Age of the Great Cities 1830-1930* (London, 1995), pp.239-62.

— *The People in the Pews: religion and society in Scotland since 1780* (Dundee, 1993).

— *Religion and Society in Scotland since 1707* (Edinburgh, 1997).

— 'Religion, class and church growth', in W. Hamish Fraser and R. J. Morris (eds), *People and Society in Scotland: II 1830-1914* (Edinburgh, 1990), pp.310-335.

— 'Religion and secularisation', in Tony Dickson and James H. Treble (eds), *People and Society in Scotland: III 1914-1990* (Edinburgh, 1992), pp.48-79.

— 'Religion and social change', in T. M. Devine and Rosalind Mitchison (eds), *People and Society in Scotland: I 1760-1830* (Edinburgh, 1988), pp.143-62.

— 'A revisionist approach to religious change', in Steve Bruce (ed.), *Religion and Modernization: sociologists and historians debate the secularization thesis* (Oxford, 1992), pp.31-58.

— *The Social History of Religion in Scotland Since 1730* (London, 1987).

— 'The Sunday school movement in Scotland, 1780-1914', *RSCHS* 21 (1981), pp.3-26.

— '"To be aglow with civic ardours": the "Godly Commonwealth" in Glasgow, 1843-1914', *RSCHS*, 26 (1996), pp.169-95.

— and Jane D. Stephenson, '"Sprouting Wings?": women and religion in Scotland c.1890-1950', in Esther Breitenbach and Eleanor Gordon (eds), *Out of Bounds: women in Scottish society 1800-1945* (Edinburgh, 1992), pp.95-120.

Stewart J. Brown, 'The Disruption and urban poverty: Thomas Chalmers and the West Port operation in Edinburgh, 1844-47', *RSCHS*, 20 (1978), pp.65-89.

— 'Reform, reconstruction, reaction: the social vision of Scottish Presbyterianism c.1830-c.1930', *Scottish Journal of Theology*, 44 (1991), pp.489-517.

— *Thomas Chalmers and the Godly Commonwealth in Scotland* (Oxford, 1982).

— and Michael Fry (eds), *Scotland in the Age of the Disruption* (Edinburgh, 1993).

Steve Bruce (ed.), *Religion and Modernization: sociologists and historians debate the secularization thesis* (Oxford, 1992).

— 'Social change and collective behaviour: the revival in eighteenth-century Ross-shire', *BJS*, 34 (1983), pp.554-72.

George B. Burnet, *The Story of Quakerism in Scotland 1650-1850* (Edinburgh, 1952).

Alan B. Campbell, *The Lanarkshire Miners: a social history of their trade unions 1775-1974* (Edinburgh, 1974).

R. H. Campbell, 'A critique of the Christian businessman and his paternalism', in David Jeremy (ed.), *Business and Religion in Britain* (Aldershot, 1988), pp.29-41.

E. H. Carr, *What is History?* (1961), Penguin edn (Harmondsworth, 1964).

Grayson Carter, *Anglican Evangelicals: Protestant Secessions from the via media, c.1800-1850* (Oxford, 2000).

Richard Carwardine, 'The Religious Revival of 1857-8 in the United States', in Derek Baker (ed.), *SCH*, 15 (Oxford, 1978), pp.393-406.

— *Transatlantic Revivalism: popular Evangelicalism in Britain and America, 1790-1865* (Westport, CT, 1978).

— 'The Welsh Evangelical community and "Finney's Revival"', *JEH*, 29 (1978), pp.463-80.

Ian Carter, *Farmlife in Northeast Scotland 1840-1914: the poor man's country* (Edinburgh, 1979).

A. N. Cass, 'Developments in Dundee Methodism, 1830-1870', *Journal of the Scottish Branch of the Wesleyan Historical Society*, 2 (1973), pp.3-7.

Owen Chadwick, *The Secularization of the European Mind in the Nineteenth Century* (Cambridge, 1975).

John H. Chamberlayne, 'From *sect* to *church* in British Methodism', *BJS*, 15 (1964), pp.139-49.

Don Chambers, 'Prelude to the last things: the Church of Scotland's mission to the Jews', *RSCHS* 19 (1975), pp.43-58.

Olive Checkland, *Industry and Ethos Scotland 1832-1914* (London, 1984).

A. C. Cheyne, *The Transforming of the Kirk: Victorian Scotland's religious revolution* (Edinburgh, 1983).

John Coffey, 'Democracy and popular religion: Moody and Sankey's mission to Britain, 1873-1875', in Eugenio F. Biagini (ed.), *Citizenship and Democracy: Liberals, radicals and collective identities in the British Isles, 1865-1931* (Cambridge, 1996), pp.93-119.

G. N. M. Collins, *The Heritage of Our Fathers: the Free Church of Scotland: her origin and testimony* (Edinburgh, 1974).

Robert Colls, 'Primitive Methodists in the northern coalfields', in Jim Obelkevich *et al.* (eds), *Disciplines of faith: studies in religion, politics and patriarchy* (London, 1987), pp.323-34.

Michael J. Cormack, *The Stirling Tract Enterprise and the Drummonds* (Stirling, 1984).

Jeff Cox, *English Churches in a Secular Society: Lambeth 1870-1930* (Oxford, 1982).

Valentine Cunningham, *Everywhere Spoken Against: Dissent in the Victorian novel* (Oxford, 1975).

Robert Currie, Alan D. Gilbert and Lee Horsley, *Churches and Churchgoers: patterns of religious growth in the British isles since 1700* (Oxford, 1977).

E. T. Davies, *Religion in the Industrial Revolution in South Wales* (Cardiff, 1965).

Grace Davie, *Religion in Britain since 1945: believing without belonging* (Oxford, 1994).

N. D. Denny, 'Temperance and the Scottish churches, 1870-1914', *RSCHS*, 23 (1988), pp.217-39.

T. M. Devine (ed.), *Scotland's Shame: bigotry and sectarianism in modern Scotland* (Edinburgh, 2000).

— 'The paradox of Scottish emigration', in *idem* (ed.), *Scottish Emigration and Scottish Society* (Edinburgh, 1992), pp.1-15.

— 'Scottish farm labour in the era of agricultural depression, 1875-1900', in *idem*, (ed.), *Farm Servants and Labour in Lowland Scotland 1770-1914* (Edinburgh, 1984).

— *The Scottish Nation 1700-2000* (Harmondsworth, 1999).

Gordon Donaldson, *The Faith of the Scots* (London, 1990).

Hugh Douglas, 'Roderick Lawson of Maybole', *Ayrshire Collections*, 12 (1978), pp.75-100.

William Fleming Downie, *A History of Strathaven and Avondale* (Glasgow, 1979).

Andrew L. Drummond, *Edward Irving and His Circle* (London [1938]).

— and James Bulloch, *The Scottish Church 1688-1843: the church of the Moderates* (Edinburgh, 1973).

— *The Church in Victorian Scotland 1843-1874* (Edinburgh, 1975).

— *The Church in Late Victorian Scotland 1874-1900* (Edinburgh, 1978).

Robert Duncan, *Wishaw: life and labour in a Lanarkshire industrial community 1790-1914* (Motherwell, 1986).

J. L. Duthie, 'The fisherman's religious revival', *History Today* (December, 1983), pp.23-7.

— 'Philanthropy and evangelism among Aberdeen seamen, 1814-1924', *SHR*, 63 (1984), pp.155-73.

David Englander, 'The Word and the world: Evangelicalism in the Victorian city', in Gerald Parsons (ed.), *Religion in Victorian Britain Volume II: controversies* (Manchester, 1988), pp.15-38.

Harry Escott, *A History of Scottish Congregationalism* (Glasgow, 1960).

Richard J. Evans, *In Defence of History* (London, 1997).

Arthur Fawcett, 'Scottish lay preachers in the eighteenth century', *RSCHS*, 12 (1955), pp.97-119.

— *The Cambuslang Revival* (London, 1971).

Clive D. Field, 'Adam and Eve: gender in the English Free Church constituency', *JEH*, 44 (1993), pp.63-74.

— 'The social structure of English Methodism: eighteenth-twentieth centuries', *BJS*, 28 (1977), pp.199-225.

Klaus Fiedler, *The Story of Faith Missions: from Hudson Taylor to present day Africa* (Oxford, 1994).

Michael Flinn (ed.), *Scottish Population History from the 17th Century to the 1930s* (Cambridge, 1977).

Le Roy Edwin Froom, *The Conditionalist Faith of Our Fathers*, 2 vols (Washington DC, 1965).

Tom Gallagher, *Edinburgh Divided: John Cormack and No Popery in the 1930s* (Edinburgh, 1987).

— *Glasgow: The Uneasy Peace: religious tension in modern Scotland* (Manchester, 1987).

Alexander Gammie, *The Churches of Aberdeen* (Aberdeen, 1909).

Mary Gebbie, *Sketches of the Town of Strathaven and Parish of Avondale* (Edinburgh, 1880).

Alexander Goodfellow, *Birsay and Harray Church History* (Kirkwall, 1903).

James M. Gordon, *Evangelical Spirituality: from the Wesleys to John Stott* (London, 1991).

I. R. Govan, *Spirit of Revival: the story of J. G. Govan and the Faith Mission*, 3rd edn (Edinburgh, 1960).

Andrew Gibb, *Glasgow: the making of a city* (London, 1983).

Alan D. Gilbert, *The Making of Post-Christian Britain: a history of secularization of modern society* (London, 1980).

— *Religion and Society in Industrial England: church, chapel and social change, 1740-1915* (London, 1976).

Robin Gill, *The Myth of the Empty Church* (London, 1993).

David K. Gillett, *Trust and Obey: explorations in Evangelical spirituality* (London, 1993).

D. A. Gowland, *Methodist Secessions: the origins of Free Methodism in three Lancashire towns: Manchester, Rochdale, Liverpool* (Manchester, 1979).

Malcolm Gray, *The Fishing Industries of Scotland 1790-1914* (Oxford, 1978).

— *Scots on the Move: Scots Migrants 1750-1914* (Edinburgh, 1990).

Robert Q. Gray, *The Labour Aristocracy in Victorian Edinburgh* (Oxford, 1976).

— 'Religion, culture and social class in late nineteenth and early twentieth century Edinburgh', in G. Crossick (ed.), *The Lower Middle Class in Britain 1870-1914* (London, 1977).

S. J. D. Green, *Religion in the Age of Decline: organisation and experience in industrial Yorkshire 1870-1920* (Cambridge, 1996).

Stanley C. Griffin, *A Forgotten Revival: East Anglia and NE Scotland - 1921* (Bromley [1992]).

Henry Harcus, *The History of the Orkney Baptist Churches* (Ayr, 1898).

Marjory Harper, *Emigration from North-East Scotland*, 2 vols (Aberdeen, 1988).

— *Emigration from Scotland between the Wars: opportunity or exile?* (Manchester, 1998).

Brian Harrison, *Peaceable Kingdom: stability and change in modern Britain* (Oxford, 1982).
— and Patricia Hollis (eds), *Robert Lowery: Radical and Chartist* (London, 1979).
Nathan O. Hatch, *The Democratization of American Christianity* (New Haven, CT, 1989).
George Hay, *History of Arbroath to the Present Time* (Arbroath, 1876).
Alan J. Hayes, *Edinburgh Methodism 1761-1975: the mother churches* (Edinburgh, 1976).
— 'A Warrenite secession in Edinburgh', *Journal of the Scottish Branch of the Wesleyan Historical Society*, 10 (1977), pp.3-18; *ibid.*, 11 (1978), pp.3-6.
D. N. Hempton, 'Evangelicalism and eschatology', *JEH*, 31 (1980), pp.179-94.
Michael Hennell, 'Evangelicalism and worldliness', in G. J. Cuming and Derek Baker (eds), *SCH*, 8 (Cambridge, 1972), pp.224-36.
John Highet, *The Churches in Scotland Today* (Glasgow, 1950).
— *The Scottish Churches: a review of their state 400 years after the Reformation* (London, 1960).
Peter L. M. Hillis, 'Presbyterianism and social class in mid-nineteenth century Glasgow: a study of nine churches', *JEH*, 32 (1981), pp. 47-64.
— 'Education and evangelisation: Presbyterian missions in mid-nineteenth Century Glasgow', *SHR*, 66 (1989), pp.46-62.
— 'The 1891 membership roll of Hillhead Baptist Church', *RSCHS*, 30 (2000), pp.170-92.
— 'The sociology of the Disruption', in Stewart J. Brown and Michael Fry (eds), *Scotland in the Age of the Disruption* (Edinburgh, 1993), pp.44-62.
Janice Holmes, *Religious Revivals in Britain and Ireland 1859-1905* (Dublin, 2000).
J. T. Hornsby, 'John Glas: his life and work', *RSCHS*, 7 (1940), pp.94-113.
David G. Horrell, *The Social Ethos of the Corinthian Correspondence: interests and ideology from 1 Corinthians to 1 Clement* (Edinburgh, 1996).
James Hutchinson, *Weavers, Miners and the Open Book: a history of Kilsyth* (Cumbernauld, 1986).
Paul Hyland, *The Black Heart: a voyage into Central Africa* (London, 1988).
K. S. Inglis, *Churches and the Working Classes in Victorian England* (London, 1963).
James W. Irvine, *Lerwick: the birth and growth of an island town* (Lerwick, 1985).

Elizabeth A. Isichei, 'From sect to denomination among English Quakers', in Bryan R. Wilson (ed.), *Patterns of Sectarianism: organisation and ideology in social and religious movements* (London, 1967), pp.161-181.

— *Victorian Quakers* (Oxford, 1970).

Kenneth S. Jeffrey, *When the Lord Walked the Land: the 1858-1862 Revival in the north east of Scotland* (Carlisle, 2002).

Douglas Johnson, *Contending For the Faith: A history of the evangelical movement in the universities and colleges* (Leicester, 1979).

Wayne J. Johnson, 'Piety among "The Society of People": the witness of Primitive Methodist local preachers in the North Midlands, 1812-1862', in W. J. Sheils and Diana Wood (eds), *SCH*, 26 (Oxford, 1989), pp.343-56.

Patrick Joyce, *Work, Society and Politics: the culture of the factory in later Victorian England* (Brighton, 1980).

David Jeremy, *Capitalists and Christians: business leaders and the churches in Britain, 1900-1960* (Oxford, 1990).

David S. Katz, 'The phenomenon of philo-semitism', in Diana Wood (ed.), *SCH* (Oxford, 1992), pp.327-62.

H. Bickerstaffe Kendall, *The Origin and History of the Primitive Methodist Church*, 2 vols (London, 1906).

John Kent, *Holding the Fort: studies in Victorian revivalism* (London, 1978).

R. Buick Knox, 'Dr John Cumming and Crown Court Church, London', *RSCHS*, 22 (1984), pp.57-84.

W. W. Knox, *Industrial Nation: work, culture and society in Scotland, 1800-present* (Edinburgh, 1999).

— 'Religion and the Scottish Labour Movement c.1900-39', *Journal of Contemporary History*, 23 (1988), pp.607-30.

W. R. Lambert, 'Some working-class attitudes towards organized religion in nineteenth-century Wales', in Gerald Parsons (ed.), *Religion in Victorian Britain Volume IV: interpretations* (Manchester, 1988), pp.96-114.

Ned Landsman, 'Evangelists and their hearers: popular interpretation of revivalist preaching in eighteenth-century Scotland', *Journal of British Studies*, 28 (1984), pp.120-49.

T. W. Laqueur, *Religion and Respectability: Sunday schools and working-class culture, 1780-1850* (New Haven, CT, 1976).

D. W. Lovegrove, 'Unity and separation: contrasting elements in the thought and practice of Robert and James Alexander Haldane', in Keith Robbins (ed.), *SCH: Subsidia*, 7 (Oxford, 1990), pp.153-77.

Donald M. Lewis, *Lighten Their Darkness: the evangelical mission to working-class London* (Westport, CT, 1986).

— '"Lights in Dark Places": women evangelists in early Victorian Britain, 1838-1857', in W. J. Sheils and Diana Wood (eds), *SCH*, 27 (Oxford, 1990), pp.415-28.

Dane Love, *The History of Auchinleck: village and parish* (Cumnock, 1991).

David Luker: 'Revivalism in theory and practice: the case of Cornish Methodism', *JEH*, 37 (1986), pp.603-19.

Joseph McAleer, *Popular Reading and Publishing in Britain 1914-1950* (Oxford, 1992).

Michael A. McCabe, 'A question of culture? Evangelicalism and the failure of socialist revivalism in Airdrie, *c*. 1890-1914', *RSCHS*, 29 (1999), pp.107-118.

Iain McCalman, *Radical Underworld; prophets, revolutionaries and pornographers in London, 1795-1840* (Cambridge, 1988).

Lesley Orr Macdonald, *A Unique and Glorious Mission: women and Presbyterianism in Scotland 1830-1930* (Edinburgh, 2000).

— 'Women in the Scottish Churches', in Women's Claim of Right Group (eds), *A Woman's Claim of Right in Scotland* (Edinburgh, 1991), pp.77-94.

Margaret Y. Macdonald, *The Pauline Churches: a socio-historical study of institutionalization in the Pauline and Deutero-Pauline writings* (Cambridge, 1988).

Alex McEwan and Earl Robinson, 'Evangelical beliefs, attitudes towards schooling and educational outcomes', *Research in Education* No.52 (November 1994), pp.65-74.

John MacInnes, 'The origin and early development of the "The Men"', *RSCHS*, 8 (1942), pp.16-41.

Stuart Macintyre, *Little Moscows: Communism and working-class militancy in inter-war Britain* (London, 1980).

Archibald McKay, *The History of Kilmarnock* (Kilmarnock, 1864).

William MacKelvie, *Annals and Statistics of the United Presbyterian Church* (Edinburgh, 1893).

John M. Mackenzie, 'David Livingstone: the construction of a myth', in Graham Walker and Tom Gallagher (eds), *Sermons and Battle Hymns: Protestant popular culture in modern Scotland* (Edinburgh, 1990), pp.24-42.

Ross McKibbin, *The Idealogies of Class: social relations in Britain, 1880-1950* (Oxford, 1990).

H. McLachlan, *The Story of a Nonconformist Library* (Manchester 1923).

Jack McLellan, *Larkhall: its historical development* (Larkhall, 1979).

Hugh McLeod, *Class and Religion in the Late Victorian City* (London, 1974).

— *Religion and Irreligion in Victorian England: how secular was the working class?* (Bangor, 1993).

— *Religion and Society in England, 1850-1914* (Basingstoke, 1996).
— *Religion and the Working Classes in Nineteenth-Century Britain* (London, 1984).
— 'New perspectives on Victorian working-class religion: the oral evidence', *Oral History Journal*, 14 (1986), pp.31-49.

James Lachlan MacLeod, *The Second Disruption: the Free Church in Victorian Scotland and the origins of the Free Presbyterian Church* (East Linton, 2000).

John McLeod, *By-Paths of Highland Church History*, (ed.) G. N. M. Collins (Edinburgh, 1965).

A. Allan McLaren, *Religion and Social Class: the Disruption years in Aberdeen* (London, 1974).

Archibald MacWhirter, 'The Church of the New Jerusalem in Scotland', *RSCHS*, 12 (1956), pp.202-219.
— 'Unitarianism in Scotland', *RSCHS*, 13 (1959), pp.101-143.

James Mair, *A Community Rent Asunder: the Newmilns laceweavers' strike of 1897. Ayrshire Monographs No.21* (Darvel, 1999).

George M. Marsden, *Fundamentalism and American Culture: the shaping of twentieth-century evangelicalism 1870-1925* (Oxford, 1980).

David Martin, 'The denomination', *BJS*, 13 (1962), pp.1-14.
— *A Sociology of English Religion* (London, 1967).

William H. Marwick, 'Studies in Scottish Quakerism', *RSCHS*, 16 (1969), pp.89-98.

Donald E. Meek, 'Evangelical missionaries in the early nineteenth-century Highlands', *Scottish Studies*, 28 (1987), pp.1-34.
— '"Fishers of men": the 1921 religious revival, its cause, context and transmission', in James Porter (ed.), *After Columba - After Calvin: religious community in North-East Scotland* (Aberdeen, 1999), pp.135-42.

Stuart Mews, 'Reason and emotion in working-class religion, 1794-1824', in Derek Baker (ed.), *SCH*, 9 (1972), pp.365-82.

David O. Moberg, *The Church as a Social Institution: the sociology of American religion* (1962) 2nd edn (Grand Rapids, MI, 1984).

Robert Moore, *Pit-Men, Preachers and Politics: the effects of Methodism in a Durham mining community* (Cambridge, 1974).

Ian A. Muirhead, 'The revival as a dimension in Scottish church history', *RSCHS*, 20 (1980), pp.179-96.

Gillian Munro, 'Reconciling difference: religious life as an expression of social, cultural and economic survival', in James Porter (ed.), *After Columba - After Calvin: religious community in North-East Scotland* (Aberdeen, 1999), pp.171-81.

Derek B. Murray, 'The influence of John Glas', *RSCHS*, 22 (1984), pp.45-56.

— 'The Scotch Baptist tradition in Great Britain', *BQ*, 33 (1989), pp.186-198.

— *Scottish Baptist College: centenary history 1894-1994* (Glasgow, 1994).

Iain H. Murray, *Evangelicalism Divided: a record of crucial change in the years 1950 to 2000* (Edinburgh, 2000).

Jocelyn Murray, 'Gender attitudes and the contribution of women to evangelism in the nineteenth century', in John Wolffe (ed.), *Evangelical Faith and Public Zeal: Evangelicals and society in Britain 1780-1980* (London, 1995), pp.97-116.

Norman Murray, *The Scottish Hand Loom Weavers 1790-1850* (Edinburgh, 1978).

Jeremy N. Morris, 'Church and people thirty-three years on: a historical critique', *Theology*, 94 (1991), pp.92-101.

— *Religion and Urban Change: Croyden 1840-1914* (Woodbridge, 1992).

Stephen Neill, *A History of Christian Missions* (Harmondsworth, 1964).

H. Richard Niebuhr, *Christ and Culture* (London, 1952).

— *The Social Sources of Denominationalism* (1929), New American Library edn (New York, 1975).

Mark A. Noll, *Between Faith and Criticism: Evangelicals, scholarship and the Bible* (Leicester, 1991).

— 'Evangelicals and the study of the Bible', in G. M. Marsden (ed.), *Evangelicalism and Modern America* (Grand Rapids, MI, 1984), pp.103-122.

— and David W. Bebbington, George A. Rawlyk (eds), *Evangelicalism: comparative studies of popular Protestantism in North America, the British Isles, and beyond 1700-1990* (New York, 1994).

James Obelkevich, *Religion and Rural Society: South Lindsay 1825-1875* (Oxford, 1976).

W. H. Oliver, *Prophets and Millennialists: the uses of biblical prophecy in England from the 1790s to the 1840s* (Auckland and Oxford, 1978).

J. Edwin Orr, *The Second Evangelical Awakening* (London, 1949).

Gerald Parsons, 'Emotion and Piety: revivalism and ritualism in Victorian Christianity', in *idem* (ed.), *Religion in Victorian Britain Volume I: traditions* (Manchester, 1988), pp.214-34.

— 'A question of meaning: religion and working-class life', in *idem* (ed.), *Religion in Victorian Britain Volume II: controversies* (Manchester, 1988), pp.64-87.

Kenneth J. Panton, 'The Church in the community: a study of patterns of religious adherence in a Scottish burgh', in Michael Hill (ed.), *A Sociological Yearbook of Religion in Britain*, 6 (1973), pp.183-206.

Martyn Percy, *Words, Wonders and Power: understanding contemporary Christian fundamentalism and revivalism* (London, 1996).

Paul T. Phillips, *The Sectarian Spirit: sectarianism, society and politics in Victorian cotton towns* (Toronto, 1982).

Stuart Piggin and John Roxborogh, *The St Andrews Seven: the finest flowering of missionary zeal in Scottish history* (Edinburgh, 1985).

J. C. Pollock, *The Keswick Story* (London, 1964).

Harry N. Pope, 'Tayside Christian Fellowship', in Roger Foster (ed.), *Ten New Churches* (Harrow, 1986), pp.90-102.

Liston Pope, *Millhands and Preachers: a study of Gastonia* (New Haven, CT, 1942).

Charles Price and Ian Randall, *Transforming Keswick* (Carlisle, 2000).

David Pride, *A History of the Parish of Neilston* (Paisley, 1910).

John Rae, *Conscience and Politics: the British government and the conscientious objector to military service 1916-1919* (London, 1970).

George A. Rawlyk and Mark A. Noll (eds), *Amazing Grace : Evangelicalism in Australia, Britain, Canada, and the United States* (Montreal, 1994).

Ian M. Randall, *Evangelical Experiences: a study in the spirituality of English Evangelicalism 1918-1939* (Carlisle, 1999).

Ian S. Rennie, 'Fundamentalism and the varieties of North Atlantic Evangelicalism', in Mark A. Noll *et al.* (eds), *Evangelicalism: comparative studies of popular Protestantism in North America, the British Isles, and beyond 1700-1990* (New York, 1994), pp.333-50.

Gerald T. Rimmington, 'Methodism and society in Leicester, 1881-1914', *The Local Historian*, 30 (2000), pp.74-87.

Keith Robbins (ed.), *Protestant Evangelicalism: Britain, Ireland, Germany and America C.1750-C.1950: SCH Subsidia*, 7 (Oxford, 1990).

D. R. Robertson, 'The relationship of church and class in Scotland', in David Martin (ed.), *A Sociological Yearbook of Religion in Britain*, 1 (London, 1968), pp.9-31.

Geoffrey Robson, 'Between town and countryside: contrasting patterns of churchgoing in the early Victorian Black Country', in Derek Baker (ed.), *SCH*, 16 (Oxford, 1979), pp.401-14.

— 'The failure of success: working class evangelists in early Victorian Birmingham', in Derek Baker (ed.), *SCH*, 15 (Oxford, 1978), pp.381-91.

Jonathan Rose, *The Intellectual Life of the British Working Classes* (New Haven, CT, 2001).

Doreen Rosman, '"What has Christ to do with Apollo?": evangelicalism and the novel 1800-30', in Derek Baker (ed.), *SCH*, 15 (1977), pp.301-12.

Andrew C. Ross, 'Scottish missionary concern 1874-1914: a golden era?', *SHR*, 51 (1972), pp.52-72.

Kenneth R. Ross, 'Calvinists in controversy: John Kennedy, Horatius Bonar and the Moody Mission of 1873-74', *Scottish Bulletin of Evangelical Theology* (1991), pp.51-63.

Robert I. Rotberg, *Christian Missionaries and the Creation of Northern Rhodesia 1880-1924* (Princeton, NJ, 1965).

Harold H. Rowdon, 'Secession from the Established Church in the early nineteenth century', *Vox Evangelica*, 3 (1964), pp.76-88.

Geoffrey Rowell, *Hell and the Victorians: a study of the nineteenth-century theological controversies concerning eternal punishment and the future life* (Oxford, 1974).

Kenneth B. E. Roxburgh, 'George Whitefield and the Secession Church in Scotland: an unpublished Letter from Ralph Erskine', *Journal of the United Reformed Church History Society*, 5 (1995), pp.375-382.

Ernest R. Sandeen, *The Roots of Fundamentalism: British and American millenarianism 1800-1930* (Chicago, 1970).

Laurance J. Saunders, *Scottish Democracy 1815-1840: the social and intellectual background* (Edinburgh, 1950).

Patrick G. Scott, 'The Business of Belief: the Emergence of "Religious" Publishing', in Derek Baker (ed.), *SCH*, 10 (Oxford, 1973), pp.213-224.

—— 'Richard Cope Morgan, religious periodicals, and the Pontifex factor', *Victorian Periodicals Newsletter*, 15 (1972), pp.1-14.

—— '"Zion's Trumpet": Evangelical enterprise and rivalry, 1833-5', *Victorian Studies*, 13 (1969), pp.199-203.

Raymond J. Scott, *History of Mid Wynd International Investment Trust PLC* (Dundee, 1987).

Peter L. Sissons, *The Social Significance of Church Membership in the Burgh of Falkirk* (Edinburgh, 1973).

Donald C. Smith, *Passive Obedience and Prophetic Protest: social criticism in the Scottish Church 1830-1945* (New York, 1987).

Hance D. Smith, *Shetland Life and Trade 1550-1914* (Edinburgh, 1984).

Mark Smith, *Religion in Industrial Society: Oldham and Saddleworth 1740-1865* (Oxford, 1994).

T. C. Smout, *A Century of the Scottish People 1830-1950* (London, 1986).

K. D. M. Snell, *Church and Chapel in the North Midlands: religious observance in the nineteenth century* (Leicester, 1991).

Colin Spencer, *The Heretic's Feast: a history of vegetarianism* (London, 1993).

Harry Sprange, *Kingdom Kids: the story of Scotland's children in revival* (Fearn, 1994).

John Strawhorn, *A New History of Cumnock* (Glasgow, 1966).

T. C. F. Stunt, *From Awakening to Secession: radical evangelicals in Switzerland and Britain 1815-35* (Edinburgh, 2000).

Wesley F. Swift, *Methodism in Scotland: the first hundred years* (London, 1947).

R. H. Tawney, *Religion and the Rise of Capitalism* (1922) Penguin edn (Harmondsworth, 1975).

P. A. M. Taylor, *Expectations Westward: the Mormons and the emigration of their British converts in the nineteenth century* (Edinburgh, 1965).

Barbara Thatcher, 'The Episcopal Church in Helensburgh in the mid-nineteenth century', in John Butt and J. T. Ward (eds), *Scottish Themes* (Edinburgh, 1976), pp.98-123.

David M. Thompson, *Let Sects and Parties Fall: a short history of the Association of Churches of Christ in Great Britain and Ireland* (Birmingham, 1980).

— *Nonconformity in the Nineteenth Century* (London, 1972).

Dorothy Thompson, *The Chartists: popular politics in the Industrial Revolution* (Aldershot, 1984).

E. P. Thompson, *The Making of the English Working Class* (1963), Penguin edn (Harmondsworth, 1968).

Paul Thompson *et al.*, *Living the Fishing* (London, 1983).

W. P. L. Thompson, *History of Orkney* (Edinburgh, 1987).

Malcolm R. Thorp, 'Popular preaching and millennial expectations: the Reverend Robert Aitken and the Christian Society, 1836-40', in Malcolm Chase and Ian Dyck (eds), *Living and Learning: essays in honour of J. F. C. Harrison* (Aldershot, 1996), pp.103-117.

Derek J. Tidball, *Who Are the Evangelicals?* (London, 1984).

John Torrance, 'The Quaker Movement in Scotland', *RSCHS*, 3 (1929), pp.31-42.

Ernest Troeltsch, *The Social Teachings of the Christian Churches* (1911), Eng. trans., 2 vols (New York, 1931).

Christopher B. Turner, 'Revivalism and Welsh society in the nineteenth century', in Jim Obelkevich *et al.* (eds), *Disciplines of Faith: studies in religion, politics and patriarchy* (London, 1987), pp.311-22.

Dorothy Valenze, *Prophetic Sons and Daughters: female preaching and popular religion in industrial England* (Princeton, CT, 1985).

Andrew Walker, *Restoring the Kingdom: the radical Christianity of the house church movement* (London, 1985).

Graham Walker and Tom Gallagher, 'Protestantism and Scottish politics', in *idem* (eds.), *Sermons and Battle Hymns: Protestant popular culture in modern Scotland* (Edinburgh, 1990), pp.90-3.

John T. Ward, 'Some aspects of working-class Conservatism in the nineteenth century', in John Butt and J. T. Ward (eds), *Scottish Themes* (Edinburgh, 1976), pp.141-157.

W. R. Ward, *The Protestant Evangelical Awakening* (Cambridge, 1993).
— 'Revival and class conflict in early nineteenth-century Britain', in *idem, Faith and Faction* (London, 1993).
— 'Scottish Methodism in the age of Jabez Bunting', *RSCHS*, 20 (1979), pp.17-63.
Gavin Wark, *The Rise and Fall of Mining Communities in Central Ayrshire in the 19th and 20th Centuries. Ayrshire Monographs No.22* (Darvel, 1999).
Hugh Watt, 'The praying societies of the early eighteenth century', *Original Secession Church Magazine*, 5th series, 1 (February 1934), pp.49-53.
Michael R. Watts, *The Dissenters. Volume II: the expansion of Evangelical Nonconformity* (Oxford, 1995).
Max Weber, *The Protestant Ethic and the Spirit of Capitalism* (1904-5) Eng. trans. 1930; Routledge edn (London, 1992).
— 'The Protestant sects and the spirit of capitalism', in H. H. Gerth and C. Wright Mills (eds), *From Max Weber: essays in sociology* (1948), Routledge edn (London, 1970), pp.302-22.
Gavin White, 'The martyr cult of the First World War', *SCH*, 30 (Oxford, 1993), pp.383-8.
E. R. Wickham, *Church and People in an Industrial City* (London, 1957).
C. R. Williams, 'The Welsh religious revival, 1904-5', *BJS*, 3 (1962), pp.242-59.
Donald J. Withrington, 'The churches in Scotland, *c*.1870-*c*.1900: towards a new social conscience?', *RSCHS*, 19 (1977), pp.155-68.
— 'The 1851 Census of Religious Worship and Education: with a note on church accommodation in mid-nineteenth century Scotland, *RSCHS*, 18 (1973), pp.133-48.
— 'Non-church going, *c*.1750-*c*.1850': a preliminary study', *RSCHS*, 17 (1970), pp.99-113.
— (ed.), *Shetland and the Outside World 1469-1969* (Oxford, 1983).
Alexander Wilson, *The Chartist Movement in Scotland* (Manchester, 1970).
A. Skevington Wood, 'Methodism in Scotland', in Rupert Davies, George A. Raymond and Gordon Rupp (eds), *A History of the Methodist Church in Great Britain*, 3 (London, 1983), pp.272-3.
Bryan R. Wilson, (ed.), *Patterns of Sectarianism: organisation and ideology in social and religious movements* ((London, 1967).
— *Religion in Secular Society* (Harmondsworth, 1966).
— *Religion in Sociological Perspective* (Oxford, 1982).
— *Religious Sects* (London, 1970).
— *Sects and Society: a sociological study of three religious groups in Britain* (London, 1961).

— *The Social Dimensions of Sectarianism: sects and new religious movements in contemporary society* (Oxford, 1990).

John Wilson, 'The sociology of schism', in Michael Hill (ed.), *A Sociological Yearbook of Religion in Britain*, 4 (London, 1971), pp.1-20.

Linda Wilson, *Constrained by Zeal: female spirituality amongst Nonconformists 1825-1875* (Carlisle, 2000).

— 'Women and personal devotions in nineteenth-century English Nonconformity', *Christianity and History Newsletter*, no.18 (summer 1999), pp.22-45.

John Wolffe, 'The end of Victorian values? Women, religion, and death of Queen Victoria', in W. J. Sheils and Diana Wood (eds), *SCH*, 27 (Oxford, 1990), pp.481-504.

— 'The Evangelical Alliance in the 1840s: an attempt to institutionalise Christian unity', in W. J. Shiels and Diana Wood (eds), *SCH*, 23 (1986), pp.333-46.

— *The Protestant Crusade in Great Britain 1829-1860* (Oxford, 1991).

Nigel Yates, 'Urban church attendance and the use of statistical evidence', in Derek Baker (ed.), *SCH*, 16 (Oxford, 1979), pp.384-400.

Stephen Yeo, *Religion and Voluntary Organisations in Crises* (London, 1976).

J. Milton Yinger, *The Scientific Study of Religion* (New York, 1970).

Geo Yuille (ed.), *History of the Baptists in Scotland* (Glasgow, 1926).

(iii) Reference works

Nigel M. deS. Cameron *et al.* (eds), *Dictionary of Scottish Church History and Theology* (Edinburgh, 1993).

F. L. Cross and E. A. Livingston, *The Oxford Dictionary of the Christian Church*, 3rd edn (Oxford, 1997).

The Dictionary of New Zealand Biography, 5 vols (Wellington, NZ, 1990-2000).

Joe Fisher, *The Glasgow Encyclopaedia* (Edinburgh, 1994).

Francis H. Groome (ed.), *Ordnance Gazetteer of Scotland: a survey of Scottish topography, statistical, biographical and historical*, new edition, 6 vols (London [1894-5]).

William Knox (ed.), *Scottish Labour Leaders 1918-39: a biographical dictionary* (Edinburgh, 1984).

Donald M. Lewis (ed.), *The Blackwell Dictionary of Evangelical Biography 1730-1860*, 2 vols (Oxford, 1995).

Michael Lynch (ed.), *The Oxford Companion to Scottish History* (Oxford, 2001).

Leslie Stephen and Sydney Lee (eds), *Dictionary of National Biography*, 66 vols (London, 1885-1901).
Parliamentary Debates (Hansard), 5th Series.
The Third Statistical Account of Scotland, 29 vols (1950s-1980s).
Who Was Who 1971-1980, 7, 2nd edn (London, 1989).

Index

References to individual Scottish assemblies are listed under Assemblies; some places where assemblies existed are also listed under the place name when the reference is to the place rather than to the assembly. Where possible, the vital dates of deceased Brethren individuals are given.

87, 260, 261, 263, 264; holiness
157, 268-9, 274, 282-3; reception
163, 169, 172-3, 180-1, 240;
restorationism 10-11; solo singing
154; war 221 n.7, 225; women's
roles 86, 152-3; work 298, 301, 303
Caldwell, Thomas R. (d.1954) 1
Caldwell, William 61
Calvinism 25, 27, 34, 42, 94, 155,
255 n.10, 268
Cambridge 26
Cambuslang 8, 294
Cameron, Dan (d.1977) 203
Camp meetings 30, 74, 362
Campbell, Alexander 28
Campbell, Andrew P. (1908-68) 216,
242 n.178, 359
Campbell, Colin (1841-1928) 101,
108, 113
Campbell, Ivie 50
Campbell, John 339
Campbell, John McLeod 26 n.7
Campbell, Mary 50
Campbell, Mrs Napier 68, 85
Campbell, R. J. 178
Capitalism 301-2
Carlisle 11, 41, 55, 102
Carluke 82, 305
Carnie, Alex 95
Carrick, John (1875-1954) 124 n.249
Carrick, John 337
Castle Douglas 34
Catholic Apostolic Church 50
Cavell, Edith 222
Celtic Church 8
Chalmers, Thomas 25, 42
Change 18, 26, 60, 114, 133, 196,
216, 227, 231, 232, 243, 287, 304-
5, 350, 371-3; see also Open
Brethren: changes
Chapelton 69, 123
Chapman, Robert (1872-1946) 144,
151
Chapman, Robert C. (1803-1902) 35
Charismatic Movement 354-5, 359,
361
Chartism 38
Cheltenham 40
Chicago 103, 336
Children 133, 134, 135, 152, 198,
202-3, 204, 229, 244, 276-7, 278,
280, 296, 300-1, 336, 338, 340,
341, 345, 351, 356; children's

meetings 135-6, 208, 276-7, 301,
376
China 117, 151, 246
Christadelphinianism 105, 156
Christian Brethren (Unitarian) 41
Christian Graphic, The 246
*Christian Magazine and Herald of
Union* 37, 51
Christian Mission 31-3
Christian Union 100-1, 106, 237
Christian Worker, The 241, 248
Christian Youth Centres (CYC) 203,
206
Christmas 212, 276, 277, 349
Church of England: see Anglicans
Church of Scotland 48, 67, 68, 92,
106, 136, 190, 202, 216, 231, 332,
341
Church order 143; church government
150, 174, 175, 183, 318; church
truth 165, 181, 216, 234, 262, 370;
see also Open Brethren: ecclesiology
Church planting: see Assembly:
formation
Churches of Christ 28, 41-2, 54, 308
n.95
Churches of God 10, 12, 91, 109
n.147, 118-20, 128, 143, 148 n.41,
168-171, 180, 182, 185, 224 n.34,
233, 251, 282, 298, 322 n.206, 368-
9, 372, 375
Churches Together in Scotland 354
Churchill, Sir Winston 323
Cinema 132, 201, 219, 220 n.4, 312,
342
Cities 188, 198, 200, 205-6, 210, 331,
340, 371
Clackmannanshire assemblies 124
n.249
Clannahan, William 103
Clarke, Andrew 323
Clergy 6, 27, 41, 57, 71-2, 90, 93, 96,
160, 241, 256
Clifford, Jamie (1872-1936) 133, 284,
321, 322
Close Brethren: see Exclusive Brethren
Clunas, John 335
Coad, F. Roy 12, 302, 357
Cochrane, Thomas (1829-1911) 158
Coggan, Donald 134 n.316
Colvilles Ltd 299, 302 (and n.34)
Common Sense philosophy 177, 265,
373

Studies in Evangelical History and Thought

John Brencher
Martyn Lloyd-Jones (1899–1981) and
Twentieth-Century Evangelicalism
This study critically demonstrates the significance of the life and
ministry of Martyn Lloyd-Jones for post-war British evangelicalism
and demonstrates that his preaching was his greatest influence on
twentieth-century Christianity. The factors which shaped his view
of the church are examined, as is the way his reformed evangelicalism led to a separatist ecclesiology which divided evangelicals.
2002 / 1-84227-051-6 /

Neil T.R. Dickson
Brethren in Scotland 1838–2000
A Social Study of an Evangelical Movement
The Brethren were remarkably pervasive throughout Scottish
society. This study of the Open Brethren in Scotland places them in
their social context and examines their growth, development and
relationship to society.
2002 / 1-84227-113-X /

David Hilborn
The Words of our Lips
Language-Use in Free Church Worship
Studies of liturgical language have tended to focus on the written
canons of Roman Catholic and Anglican communities. By contrast,
David Hilborn analyses the more extemporary approach of English
Nonconformity. Drawing on recent developments in linguistic
pragmatics, he explores similarities and differences between 'fixed'
and 'free' worship, and argues for the interdependence of each.
2003 / 0-85364-977-4 /

Mark Hopkins
Baptists, Congregationalists, and Theological Change
Some Late Nineteenth-Century Leaders and Controversies
2003 / 1-84227-150-4 /

Kenneth S. Jeffrey
When the Lord Walked the Land
The 1858–1862 Revival in the North East of Scotland
Previous studies of revivals have tended to approach religious movements from either a broad, national or a strictly local level. This study of the multifaceted nature of the 1859 revival as it appeared in three distinct social contexts within a single region reveals the heterogeneous nature of simultaneous religious movements in the same vicinity.
2002 / 1-84227-057-5 /

R.T. Kendall
Calvin and English Calvinism to 1649
The author's thesis is that those who formed the Westminster Confession of Faith, which is regarded as Calvinism, in fact departed from John Calvin on two points: (1) the extent of the atonement and (2) the ground of assurance of salvation.
1997 / 0-85364-827-1 / xii + 263pp

John Kenneth Lander
Tent Methodism: 1814–1832
2003 / 1-84227-151-2 /

Herbert McGonigle
'Sufficient Saving Grace'
John Wesley's Evangelical Arminianism
A thorough investigation of the theological roots of John Wesley's evangelical Arminianism and how these convictions were hammered out in controversies on predestination, limited atonement and the perseverance of the saints.
2001 / 1-84227-045-1 / xvi + 350pp

James I. Packer
Richard Baxter
2002 / 1-84227-147-4 /

Ian M Randall
Evangelical Experiences
A Study in the Spirituality of English Evangelicalism 1918–1939
This book makes a detailed historical examination of evangelical
spirituality between the First and Second World Wars. It shows
how patterns of devotion led to tensions and divisions. In a wide-
ranging study, Anglican, Wesleyan, Reformed and Pentecostal-
charismatic spiritualities are analysed.
1999 / 0-85364-919-7 / xii + 309pp

Geoffrey Robson
Dark Satanic Mills?
Religion and Irreligion in Birmingham and the Black Country
This book analyses and interprets the nature and extent of popular
Christian belief and practice in Birmingham and the Black Country
during the first half of the nineteenth century, with particular reference to the impact of cholera epidemics and evangelism on church
extension programmes.
2002 / 1-84227-102-4 /

James H.S. Steven
Worship in the Spirit
*A Sociological Analysis and Theological Appraisal of Charismatic
Worship in the Church of England*
This book explores the nature and function of worship in six
Church of England churches influenced by the Charismatic
Movement, focusing on congregational singing and public prayer
ministry. The theological adequacy of such ritual is discussed in
relation to pneumatological and christological understandings in
Christian worship.
2002 / 1-84227-103-2 /

Martin Sutherland
Peace, Toleration and Decay
The Ecclesiology of Later Stuart Dissent
2003 / 1-84227-152-0

Martin Wellings
Evangelicals Embattled
Responses of Evangelicals in the Church of England to Ritualism,
Darwinism and Theological Liberalism 1890–1930.
In the closing years of the nineteenth century and the first decades
of the twentieth century Anglican Evangelicals faced a series of
challenges. In responding to Anglo-Catholicism, liberal theology,
Darwinism and biblical criticism, the unity and identity of the
Evangelical school were severely tested.
2002 / 1-84227-049-4 /

James Whisenant
A Fragile Unity
Anti-Ritualism and the Division of the Evangelicalism
in the Nineteenth Century.
This book deals with the ritualist controversy (approximately
1850–1900) from the perspective of its evangelical participants and
considers the divisive effects it had on the party.
2002 / 1-84227-105-9 /

Linda Wilson
Constrained by Zeal
Female Spirituality amongst Nonconformists 1825–1875
Constrained by Zeal investigates the neglected area of Nonconformist female spirituality. Against the background of separate
spheres, it analyses the experience of women from four denominations, and argues that the churches provided a 'third sphere' in
which they could find opportunities for participation.
2000 / 0-85364-972-3 / xvi + 293pp

The Paternoster Press
P.O. Box 300
Carlisle, Cumbria,
CA3 0QS
United Kingdom

Web: www.paternoster-publishing.com